Object-Oriented Programming in C++,
Fourth Edition

Robert Lafore

Revised & Updated
Fourth Edition
2004

Original ISBN 0-672-32308-7

Copyrights © 2004 by Sams Publishing

Composed in AGramond and MCP digital by Macmillan Computer Publishing.

Overview

Contents

Preface

The major changes to this Fourth Edition include an earlier introduction to UML, a new section on inter-file communication in Chapter 13, and a revised approach to software development in Chapter 16.

Introducing the UML at the beginning allows the use of UML diagrams where they fit naturally with topics in the text, so there are many new UML diagrams throughout the book. The section on inter-file communication gathers together many concepts that were previously scattered throughout the book. The industry's approach to object-oriented analysis and design has evolved since the last edition, and accordingly we've modified the chapter on this topic to reflect recent developments.

C++ itself has changed very little since the last edition. However, besides the revisions just mentioned, we've made many smaller changes to clarify existing topics and correct typos and inaccuracies in the text.

About the Author

Robert Lafore has been writing books about computer programming since 1982. His best-selling titles include *Assembly Language Programming for the IBM PC*, *C Programming Using Turbo C++*, *C++ Interactive Course*, and *Data Structures and Algorithms in Java*. Mr. Lafore holds degrees in mathematics and electrical engineering, and has been active in programming since the days of the PDP-5, when 4K of main memory was considered luxurious. His interests include hiking, windsurfing, and recreational mathematics.

Dedication

This book is dedicated to GGL and her indomitable spirit.

Acknowledgments to the Fourth Edition

My thanks to many readers who e-mailed comments and corrections. I am also indebted to the following professors of computer science who offered their suggestions and corrections: Bill Blomberg of Regis University in Denver; Richard Daehler-Wilking of the College of Charleston in South Carolina; Frank Hoffmann of the Royal Institute of Technology in Sweden, and David Blockus of San Jose State University in California. My special thanks to David Topham of Ohlone College in Fremont, California, for his many detailed ideas and his sharp eye for problems.

At Sams Publishing, Michael Stephens provided an expert and friendly liaison with the details of publishing. Reviewer Robin Rowe and Technical Editor Mark Cashman attempted with great care to save me from myself; any lack of success is entirely my fault. Project Manager Christina Smith made sure that everything came together in an amazingly short time, Angela Boley helped keep everything moving smoothly, and Matt Wynalda provided expert proofreading. I'm grateful to you all.

Acknowledgments to the Third Edition

I'd like to thank the entire team at MacMillan Computer Publishing. In particular, Tracy Dunkelberger ably spearheaded the entire project and exhibited great patience with what turned out to be a lengthy schedule. Jeff Durham handled the myriad details involved in interfacing between me and the editors with skill and good humor. Andrei Kossorouko lent his expertise in C++ to ensure that I didn't make this edition worse instead of better.

Acknowledgments to the Second Edition

My thanks to the following professors—users of this book as a text at their respective colleges and universities—for their help in planning the second edition: Dave Bridges, Frank Cioch, Jack Davidson, Terrence Fries, Jimmie Hattemer, Jack Van Luik, Kieran Mathieson, Bill McCarty, Anita Millspaugh, Ian Moraes, Jorge Prendes, Steve Silva, and Edward Wright.

I would like to thank the many readers of the first edition who wrote in with corrections and suggestions, many of which were invaluable.

At Waite Group Press, Joanne Miller has ably ridden herd on my errant scheduling and filled in as academic liaison, and Scott Calamar, as always, has made sure that everyone knew what they were doing. Deirdre Greene provided an uncannily sharp eye as copy editor.

Thanks, too, to Mike Radtke and Harry Henderson for their expert technical reviews.

Special thanks to Edward Wright, of Western Oregon State College, for reviewing and experimenting with the new exercises.

Acknowledgments to the First Edition

My primary thanks go to Mitch Waite, who poured over every inch of the manuscript with painstaking attention to detail and made a semi-infinite number of helpful suggestions.

Bill McCarty of Azusa Pacific University reviewed the content of the manuscript and its suitability for classroom use, suggested many excellent improvements, and attempted to correct my dyslexic spelling.

George Leach ran all the programs, and, to our horror, found several that didn't perform correctly in certain circumstances. I trust these problems have all been fixed; if not, the fault is entirely mine.

Scott Calamar of the Waite Group dealt with the myriad organizational aspects of writing and producing this book. His competence and unfailing good humor were an important ingredient in its completion.

I would also like to thank Nan Borreson of Borland for supplying the latest releases of the software (among other useful tidbits), Harry Henderson for reviewing the exercises, Louise Orlando of the Waite Group for ably shepherding the book through production, Merrill Peterson of Matrix Productions for coordinating the most trouble-free production run I've ever been involved with, Juan Vargas for the innovative design, and Frances Hasegawa for her uncanny ability to decipher my sketches and produce beautiful and effective art.

Introduction

This book teaches you how to write programs in a the C++ programming language. However, it does more than that. In the past few years, several major innovations in software development have appeared on the scene. This book teaches C++ in the context of these new developments. Let's see what they are.

Programming Innovations

In the old days, 20 or so years ago, programmers starting a project would sit down almost immediately and start writing code. However, as programming projects became large and more complicated, it was found that this approach did not work very well. The problem was complexity.

Large programs are probably the most complicated entities ever created by humans. Because of this complexity, programs are prone to error, and software errors can be expensive and even life threatening (in air traffic control, for example). Three major innovations in programming have been devised to cope with the problem of complexity. They are

- Object-oriented programming (OOP)
- The Unified Modeling Language (UML)
- Improved software development processes

This book teaches the C++ language with these developments in mind. You will not only learn a computer language, but new ways of conceptualizing software development.

Object-Oriented Programming

Why has object-oriented programming become the preferred approach for most software projects? OOP offers a new and powerful way to cope with complexity. Instead of viewing a program as a series of steps to be carried out, it views it as a group of objects that have certain properties and can take certain actions. This may sound obscure until you learn more about it, but it results in programs that are clearer, more reliable, and more easily maintained.

A major goal of this book is to teach object-oriented programming. We introduce it as early as possible, and cover all its major features. The majority of our example programs are object-oriented.

The Unified Modeling Language

The Unified Modeling Language (UML) is a graphical language consisting of many kinds of diagrams. It helps program analysts figure out what a program should do, and helps programmers design and understand how a program works. The UML is a powerful tool that can make programming easier and more effective.

We give an overview of the UML in Chapter 1, and then discuss specific features of the UML throughout the book. We introduce each UML feature where it will help to clarify the OOP topic being discussed. In this way you learn the UML painlessly at the same time the UML helps you to learn C++.

Languages and Development Platforms

Of the object-oriented programming languages, C++ is by far the most widely used. Java, a recent addition to the field of OO languages, lacks certain features—such as pointers, templates, and multiple inheritance—that make it less powerful and versatile than C++. (If you ever do want to learn Java, its syntax is very similar to that of C++, so learning C++ gives you a head start in Java.)

Several other OO languages have been introduced recently, such as C#, but they have not yet attained the wide acceptance of C++.

Until recently the standards for C++ were in a constant state of evolution. This meant that each compiler vendor handled certain details differently. However, in November 1997, the ANSI/ISO C++ standards committee approved the final draft of what is now known as Standard C++. (ANSI stands for American National Standards Institute, and ISO stands for International Standards Institute.) Standard C++ adds many new features to the language, such as the Standard Template Library (STL). In this book we follow Standard C++ (in all but a few places, which we'll note as we go along).

The most popular development environments for C++ are manufactured by Microsoft and Borland (Inprise) and run on the various flavors of Microsoft Windows. In this book we've attempted to ensure that all sample programs run on the current versions of both Borland and Microsoft compilers. (See Appendix C, "Microsoft Visual C++," and Appendix D, "Borland C++Builder," for more on these compilers.)

What This Book Does

This book teaches object-oriented programming with the C++ programming language, using either Microsoft or Borland compilers. It also introduces the UML and software development processes. It is suitable for professional programmers, students, and kitchen-table enthusiasts.

New Concepts

OOP involves concepts that are new to programmers of traditional languages such as Pascal, Basic, and C. These ideas, such as classes, inheritance, and polymorphism, lie at the heart of object-oriented programming. But it's easy to lose sight of these concepts when discussing the specifics of an object-oriented language. Many books overwhelm the reader with the details of language features, while ignoring the reason these features exist. This book attempts to keep an eye on the big picture and relate the details to the larger concepts.

The Gradual Approach

We take a gradual approach in this book, starting with very simple programming examples and working up to full-fledged object-oriented applications. We introduce new concepts slowly so that you will have time to digest one idea before going on to the next. We use illustrations whenever possible to help clarify new ideas. There are questions and programming exercises at the end of most chapters to enhance the book's usefulness in the classroom. Answers to the questions and to the first few (starred) exercises can be found in Appendix G. The exercises vary in difficulty to pose a variety of challenges for the student.

What You Need to Know to Use This Book

You can use this book even if you have no previous programming experience. However, such experience, in Visual Basic for example, certainly won't hurt.

You do not need to know the C language to use this book. Many books on C++ assume that you already know C, but this one does not. It teaches C++ from the ground up. If you do know C, it won't hurt, but you may be surprised at how little overlap there is between C and C++.

You should be familiar with the basic operations of Microsoft Windows, such as starting applications and copying files.

Software and Hardware

You will need a C++ compiler. The programs in this book have been tested with Microsoft Visual C++ and Borland C++Builder. Both compilers come in low-priced "Learning Editions" suitable for students.

Appendix C provides detailed information on operating the Microsoft compiler, while Appendix D does the same for the Inprise (Borland) product. Other compilers, if they adhere to Standard C++, will probably handle most of the programs in this book as written.

Your computer should have enough processor speed, memory, and hard disk space to run the compiler you've chosen. You can check the manufacturer's specifications to determine these requirements.

Console-Mode Programs

There are numerous example programs throughout the book. They are console-mode programs, which run in a character-mode window within the compiler environment, or directly within an MS-DOS box. This avoids the complexity of full-scale graphics-oriented Windows programs.

Example Program Source Code

You can obtain the source code for the example programs from the Sams Publishing Web site at

http://www.samspublishing.com

Type the ISBN (found at the front of the book) or the book's title and click Search to find the data on this book. Then click Source Code to download the program examples.

Console Graphics Lite

A few example programs draw pictures using a graphics library we call Console Graphics Lite. The graphics rely on console characters, so they are not very sophisticated, but they allow some interesting programs. The files for this library are provided on the publisher's Web site, along with the source files for the example programs.

To compile and run these graphics examples, you'll need to include a header file in your program, either MSOFTCON.H or BORLACON.H, depending on your compiler. You'll also need to add either MSOFTCON.CPP or BORLACON.CPP to the project for the graphics example. Appendix E, "Console Graphics Lite," provides listings of these files and tells how to use them. Appendixes C and D explain how to work with files and projects in a specific compiler's environment.

Programming Exercises

Each chapter contains roughly 12 exercises, each requiring the creation of a complete C++ program. Solutions for the first three or four exercises in each chapter are provided in Appendix G. For the remainder of the exercises, readers are on their own. (However, if you are teaching a C++ course, see the "Note to Teachers" at the end of this Introduction.)

Easier Than You Think

You may have heard that C++ is difficult to learn, but it's really quite similar to other languages, with two or three "grand ideas" thrown in. These new ideas are fascinating in themselves, and we think you'll have fun learning about them. They are also becoming part of the programming culture; they're something everyone should know a little bit about, like evolution and psychoanalysis. We hope this book will help you enjoy learning about these new ideas, at the same time that it teaches you the details of programming in C++.

A Note to Teachers

Teachers, and others who already know something about C++ or C, may be interested in some details of the approach we use in this book and how it's organized.

Standard C++

All the programs in this book are compatible with Standard C++, with a few minor exceptions that are needed to accommodate compiler quirks. We devote a chapter to the STL (Standard Template Library), which is included in Standard C++.

The Unified Modeling Language (UML)

In the previous edition, we introduced the UML in the final chapter. In this edition we have integrated the UML into the body of the book, introducing UML topics in appropriate places. For example, UML class diagrams are introduced where we first show different classes communicating, and generalization is covered in the chapter on inheritance.

Chapter 1, "The Big Picture," includes a list showing where the various UML topics are introduced.

Software Development Processes

Formal software development processes are becoming an increasingly important aspect of programming. Also, students are frequently mystified by the process of designing an object-oriented program. For these reasons we include a chapter on software development processes, with an emphasis on object-oriented programming. In the last edition we focused on CRC cards, but the emphasis in software development has shifted more in the direction of use case analysis, so we use that to analyze our programming projects.

C++ Is Not the Same as C

A few institutions still want their students to learn C before learning C++. In our view this is a mistake. C and C++ are entirely separate languages. It's true that their syntax is similar, and C is actually a subset of C++. But the similarity is largely a historical accident. In fact, the basic approach in a C++ program is radically different from that in a C program.

C++ has overtaken C as the preferred language for serious software development. Thus we don't believe it is necessary or advantageous to teach C before teaching C++. Students who don't know C are saved the time and trouble of learning C and then learning C++, an inefficient approach. Students who already know C may be able to skim parts of some chapters, but they will find that a remarkable percentage of the material is new.

Optimize Organization for OOP

We could have begun the book by teaching the procedural concepts common to C and C++, and moved on to the new OOP concepts once the procedural approach had been digested. That seemed counterproductive, however, because one of our goals is to begin true object-oriented programming as quickly as possible. Accordingly, we provide a minimum of procedural groundwork before getting to classes in Chapter 6. Even the initial chapters are heavily steeped in C++, as opposed to C, usage.

We introduce some concepts earlier than is traditional in books on C. For example, structures are a key feature for understanding C++ because classes are syntactically an extension of structures. For this reason, we introduce structures in Chapter 5 so that they will be familiar when we discuss classes.

Some concepts, such as pointers, are introduced later than in traditional C books. It's not necessary to understand pointers to follow the essentials of OOP, and pointers are usually a stumbling block for C and C++ students. Therefore, we defer a discussion of pointers until the main concepts of OOP have been thoroughly digested.

Substitute Superior C++ Features

Some features of C have been superseded by new approaches in C++. For instance, the printf() and scanf() functions, input/output workhorses in C, are seldom used in C++ because cout and cin do a better job. Consequently, we leave out descriptions of these functions. Similarly, #define constants and macros in C have been largely superseded by the const qualifier and inline functions in C++, and need be mentioned only briefly.

Minimize Irrelevant Capabilities

Because the focus in this book is on object-oriented programming, we can leave out some features of C that are seldom used and are not particularly relevant to OOP. For instance, it isn't necessary to understand the C bit-wise operators (used to operate on individual bits) to learn object-oriented programming. These and a few other features can be dropped from our discussion, or mentioned only briefly, with no loss in understanding of the major features of C++.

The result is a book that focuses on the fundamentals of OOP, moving the reader gently but briskly toward an understanding of new concepts and their application to real programming problems.

Programming Exercises

No answers to the unstarred exercises are provided in this book. However, qualified instructors can obtain suggested solutions from the Sams Publishing Web site. Type the ISBN or title and click Search to move to this book's page, then click Downloads.

The exercises vary considerably in their degree of difficulty. In each chapter the early exercises are fairly easy, while later ones are more challenging. Instructors will probably want to assign only those exercises suited to the level of a particular class.

The Big Picture

IN THIS CHAPTER

This book teaches you how to program in C++, a computer language that supports *object-oriented programming* (*OOP*). Why do we need OOP? What does it do that traditional languages such as C, Pascal, and BASIC don't? What are the principles behind OOP? Two key concepts in OOP are *objects* and *classes*. What do these terms mean? What is the relationship between C++ and the older C language?

This chapter explores these questions and provides an overview of the features to be discussed in the balance of the book. What we say here will necessarily be rather general (although mercifully brief). If you find the discussion somewhat abstract, don't worry. The concepts we mention here will come into focus as we demonstrate them in detail in subsequent chapters.

Why Do We Need Object-Oriented Programming?

Object-oriented programming was developed because limitations were discovered in earlier approaches to programming. To appreciate what OOP does, we need to understand what these limitations are and how they arose from traditional programming languages.

Procedural Languages

C, Pascal, FORTRAN, and similar languages are *procedural languages*. That is, each statement in the language tells the computer to do something: Get some input, add these numbers, divide by six, display that output. A program in a procedural language is a list of instructions.

For very small programs, no other organizing principle (often called a *paradigm*) is needed. The programmer creates the list of instructions, and the computer carries them out.

Division into Functions

When programs become larger, a single list of instructions becomes unwieldy. Few programmers can comprehend a program of more than a few hundred statements unless it is broken down into smaller units. For this reason the *function* was adopted as a way to make programs more comprehensible to their human creators. (The term function is used in C++ and C. In other languages the same concept may be referred to as a subroutine, a subprogram, or a procedure.) A procedural program is divided into functions, and (ideally, at least) each function has a clearly defined purpose and a clearly defined interface to the other functions in the program.

The idea of breaking a program into functions can be further extended by grouping a number of functions together into a larger entity called a *module* (which is often a file), but the principle is similar: a grouping of components that execute lists of instructions.

Dividing a program into functions and modules is one of the cornerstones of *structured programming*, the somewhat loosely defined discipline that influenced programming organization for several decades before the advent of object-oriented programming.

Problems with Structured Programming

As programs grow ever larger and more complex, even the structured programming approach begins to show signs of strain. You may have heard about, or been involved in, horror stories of program development. The project is too complex, the schedule slips, more programmers are added, complexity increases, costs skyrocket, the schedule slips further, and disaster ensues. (See *The Mythical Man-Month* by Frederick P. Brooks, Jr. [Addison Wesley, 1982] for a vivid description of this process.)

Analyzing the reasons for these failures reveals that there are weaknesses in the procedural paradigm itself. No matter how well the structured programming approach is implemented, large programs become excessively complex.

What are the reasons for these problems with procedural languages? There are two related problems. First, functions have unrestricted access to global data. Second, unrelated functions and data, the basis of the procedural paradigm, provide a poor model of the real world.

Let's examine these problems in the context of an inventory program. One important global data item in such a program is the collection of items in the inventory. Various functions access this data to input a new item, display an item, modify an item, and so on.

Unrestricted Access

In a procedural program, one written in C for example, there are two kinds of data. *Local data* is hidden inside a function, and is used exclusively by the function. In the inventory program a display function might use local data to remember which item it was displaying. Local data is closely related to its function and is safe from modification by other functions.

However, when two or more functions must access the same data—and this is true of the most important data in a program—then the data must be made *global*, as our collection of inventory items is. Global data can be accessed by *any* function in the program. (We ignore the issue of grouping functions into modules, which doesn't materially affect our argument.) The arrangement of local and global variables in a procedural program is shown in Figure 1.1.

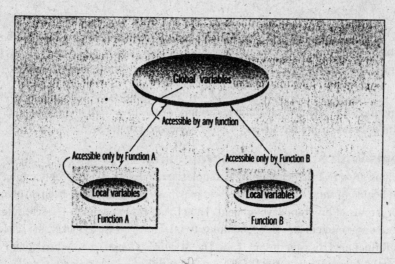

FIGURE 1.1
Global and local variables.

In a large program, there are many functions and many global data items. The problem with the procedural paradigm is that this leads to an even larger number of potential connections between functions and data, as shown in Figure 1.2.

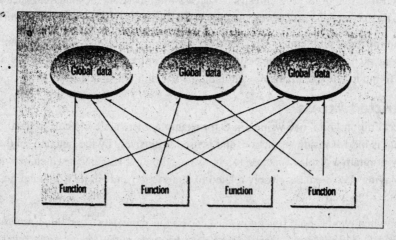

FIGURE 1.2
The procedural paradigm.

This large number of connections causes problems in several ways. First, it makes a program's structure difficult to conceptualize. Second, it makes the program difficult to modify. A change made in a global data item may necessitate rewriting all the functions that access that item.

For example, in our inventory program, someone may decide that the product codes for the inventory items should be changed from 5 digits to 12 digits. This may necessitate a change from a short to a long data type.

Now all the functions that operate on the data must be modified to deal with a long instead of a short. It's similar to what happens when your local supermarket moves the bread from aisle 4 to aisle 7. Everyone who patronizes the supermarket must then figure out where the bread has gone, and adjust their shopping habits accordingly.

When data items are modified in a large program it may not be easy to tell which functions access the data, and even when you figure this out, modifications to the functions may cause them to work incorrectly with other global data items. Everything is related to everything else, so a modification anywhere has far-reaching, and often unintended, consequences.

Real-World Modeling

The second—and more important—problem with the procedural paradigm is that its arrangement of separate data and functions does a poor job of modeling things in the real world. In the physical world we deal with objects such as people and cars. Such objects aren't like data and they aren't like functions. Complex real-world objects have both *attributes* and *behavior*.

Attributes

Examples of attributes (sometimes called *characteristics*) are, for people, eye color and job title; and, for cars, horsepower and number of doors. As it turns out, attributes in the real world are equivalent to data in a program: they have a certain specific values, such as blue (for eye color) or four (for the number of doors).

Behavior

Behavior is something a real-world object does in response to some stimulus. If you ask your boss for a raise, she will generally say yes or no. If you apply the brakes in a car, it will generally stop. Saying something and stopping are examples of behavior. Behavior is like a function: you call a function to do something (display the inventory, for example) and it does it.

So neither data nor functions, by themselves, model real-world objects effectively.

The Object-Oriented Approach

The fundamental idea behind object-oriented languages is to combine into a single unit both *data* and the *functions that operate on that data*. Such a unit is called an *object*.

An object's functions, called *member functions* in C++, typically provide the only way to access its data. If you want to read a data item in an object, you call a member function in the object. It will access the data and return the value to you. You can't access the data directly. The data is *hidden*, so it is safe from accidental alteration. Data and its functions are said to be *encapsulated* into a single entity. *Data encapsulation* and *data hiding* are key terms in the description of object-oriented languages.

If you want to modify the data in an object, you know exactly what functions interact with it: the member functions in the object. No other functions can access the data. This simplifies writing, debugging, and maintaining the program.

A C++ program typically consists of a number of objects, which communicate with each other by calling one another's member functions. The organization of a C++ program is shown in Figure 1.3.

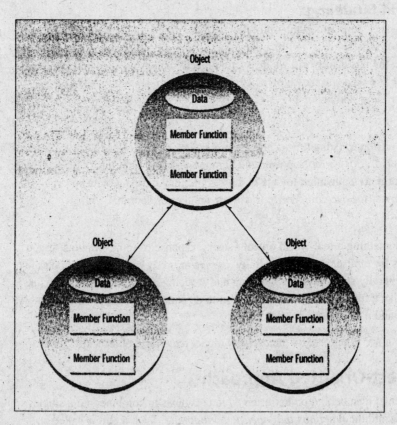

FIGURE 1.3
The object-oriented paradigm.

We should mention that what are called member functions in C++ are called *methods* in some other object-oriented (OO) languages (such as Smalltalk, one of the first OO languages). Also, data items are referred to as *attributes* or *instance variables*. Calling an object's member function is referred to as *sending a message* to the object. These terms are not official C++ terminology, but they are used with increasing frequency, especially in object-oriented design.

An Analogy

You might want to think of objects as departments—such as sales, accounting, personnel, and so on—in a company. Departments provide an important approach to corporate organization. In most companies (except very small ones), people don't work on personnel problems one day, the payroll the next, and then go out in the field as salespeople the week after. Each department has its own personnel, with clearly assigned duties. It also has its own data: the accounting department has payroll figures, the sales department has sales figures, the personnel department keeps records of each employee, and so on.

The people in each department control and operate on that department's data. Dividing the company into departments makes it easier to comprehend and control the company's activities, and helps maintain the integrity of the information used by the company. The accounting department, for instance, is responsible for the payroll data. If you're a sales manager, and you need to know the total of all the salaries paid in the southern region in July, you don't just walk into the accounting department and start rummaging through file cabinets. You send a memo to the appropriate person in the department, then wait for that person to access the data and send you a reply with the information you want. This ensures that the data is accessed accurately and that it is not corrupted by inept outsiders. This view of corporate organization is shown in Figure 1.4. In the same way, objects provide an approach to program organization while helping to maintain the integrity of the program's data.

OOP: An Approach to Organization

Keep in mind that object-oriented programming is not primarily concerned with the details of program operation. Instead, it deals with the overall organization of the program. Most individual program statements in C++ are similar to statements in procedural languages, and many are identical to statements in C. Indeed, an entire member function in a C++ program may be very similar to a procedural function in C. It is only when you look at the larger context that you can determine whether a statement or a function is part of a procedural C program or an object-oriented C++ program.

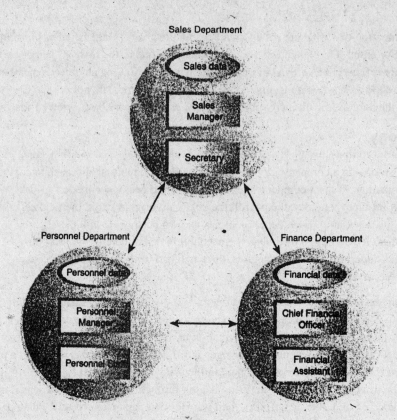

FIGURE 1.4
The corporate paradigm.

Characteristics of Object-Oriented Languages

Let's briefly examine a few of the major elements of object-oriented languages in general, and C++ in particular.

Objects

When you approach a programming problem in an object-oriented language, you no longer ask how the problem will be divided into functions, but how it will be divided into objects. Thinking in terms of objects, rather than functions, has a surprisingly helpful effect on how easily programs can be designed. This results from the close match between objects in the programming sense and objects in the real world. This process is described in detail in Chapter 16, "Object-Oriented Software Development."

What kinds of things become objects in object-oriented programs? The answer to this is limited only by your imagination, but here are some typical categories to start you thinking:

- **Physical objects**

  Automobiles in a traffic-flow simulation

  Electrical components in a circuit-design program

  Countries in an economics model

  Aircraft in an air traffic control system

- **Elements of the computer-user environment**

  Windows

  Menus

  Graphics objects (lines, rectangles, circles)

  The mouse, keyboard, disk drives, printer

- **Data-storage constructs**

  Customized arrays

  Stacks

  Linked lists

  Binary trees

- **Human entities**

  Employees

  Students

  Customers

  Salespeople

- **Collections of data**

  An inventory

  A personnel file

  A dictionary

  A table of the latitudes and longitudes of world cities

- **User-defined data types**

  Time

  Angles

  Complex numbers

  Points on the plane

- Components in **computer games**

  Cars in an auto race

  Positions in a board game (chess, checkers)

  Animals in an ecological simulation

  Opponents and friends in adventure games

The match between programming objects and real-world objects is the happy result of combining data and functions: The resulting objects offer a revolution in program design. No such close match between programming constructs and the items being modeled exists in a procedural language.

Classes

In OOP we say that objects are members of *classes*. What does this mean? Let's look at an analogy. Almost all computer languages have built-in data types. For instance, a data type int, meaning integer, is predefined in C++ (as we'll see in Chapter 3, "Loops and Decisions"). You can declare as many variables of type int as you need in your program:

```
int day;
int count;
int divisor;
int answer;
```

In a similar way, you can define many objects of the same class, as shown in Figure 1.5. A class serves as a plan, or blueprint. It specifies what data and what functions will be included in objects of that class. Defining the class doesn't create any objects, just as the mere existence of data type int doesn't create any variables.

A class is thus a description of a number of similar objects. This fits our non-technical understanding of the word *class*. Prince, Sting, and Madonna are members of the rock musician class. There is no one person called "rock musician," but specific people with specific names are members of this class if they possess certain characteristics. An object is often called an "instance" of a class.

Inheritance

The idea of classes leads to the idea of *inheritance*. In our daily lives, we use the concept of classes divided into subclasses. We know that the animal class is divided into mammals, amphibians, insects, birds, and so on. The vehicle class is divided into cars, trucks, buses, motorcycles, and so on.

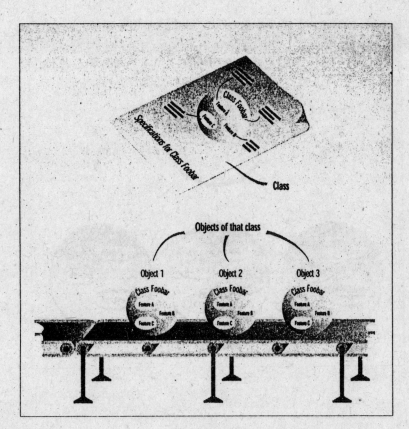

FIGURE 1.5
A class and its objects.

The principle in this sort of division is that each subclass shares common characteristics with the class from which it's derived. Cars, trucks, buses, and motorcycles all have wheels and a motor; these are the defining characteristics of vehicles. In addition to the characteristics shared with other members of the class, each subclass also has its own particular characteristics: Buses, for instance, have seats for many people, while trucks have space for hauling heavy loads.

This idea is shown in Figure 1.6. Notice in the figure that features A and B, which are part of the base class, are common to all the derived classes, but that each derived class also has features of its own.

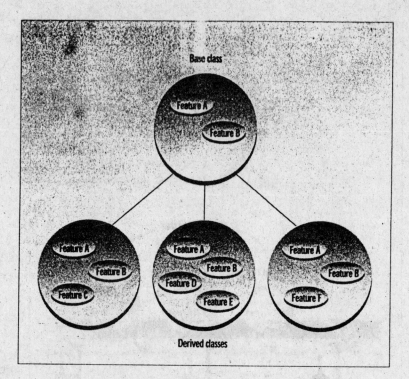

FIGURE 1.6
Inheritance.

In a similar way, an OOP class can become a parent of several subclasses. In C++ the original class is called the *base class*; other classes can be defined that share its characteristics, but add their own as well. These are called *derived classes*.

Don't confuse the relation of objects to classes, on the one hand, with the relation of a base class to derived classes, on the other. Objects, which exist in the computer's memory, each embody the exact characteristics of their class, which serves as a template. Derived classes inherit some characteristics from their base class, but add new ones of their own.

Inheritance is somewhat analogous to using functions to simplify a traditional procedural program. If we find that three different sections of a procedural program do almost exactly the same thing, we recognize an opportunity to extract the common elements of these three sections and put them into a single function. The three sections of the program can call the function to execute the common actions, and they can perform their own individual processing as well. Similarly, a base class contains elements common to a group of derived classes. As functions do in a procedural program, inheritance shortens an object-oriented program and clarifies the relationship among program elements.

1

Reusability

Once a class has been written, created, and debugged, it can be distributed to other programmers for use in their own programs. This is called *reusability*. It is similar to the way a library of functions in a procedural language can be incorporated into different programs.

However, in OOP, the concept of inheritance provides an important extension to the idea of reusability. A programmer can take an existing class and, without modifying it, add additional features and capabilities to it. This is done by deriving a new class from the existing one. The new class will inherit the capabilities of the old one, but is free to add new features of its own.

For example, you might have written (or purchased from someone else) a class that creates a menu system, such as that used in Windows or other Graphic User Interfaces (GUIs). This class works fine, and you don't want to change it, but you want to add the capability to make some menu entries flash on and off. To do this, you simply create a new class that inherits all the capabilities of the existing one but adds flashing menu entries.

The ease with which existing software can be reused is an important benefit of OOP. Many companies find that being able to reuse classes on a second project provides an increased return on their original programming investment. We'll have more to say about this in later chapters.

Creating New Data Types

One of the benefits of objects is that they give the programmer a convenient way to construct new data types. Suppose you work with two-dimensional positions (such as x and y coordinates; or latitude and longitude) in your program. You would like to express operations on these positional values with normal arithmetic operations, such as

```
position1 = position2 + origin
```

where the variables position1, position2, and origin each represent a pair of independent numerical quantities. By creating a class that incorporates these two values, and declaring position1, position2, and origin to be objects of this class, we can, in effect, create a new data type. Many features of C++ are intended to facilitate the creation of new data types in this manner.

Polymorphism and Overloading

Note that the = (equal) and + (plus) operators, used in the position arithmetic shown above, don't act the same way they do in operations on built-in types such as int. The objects position1 and so on are not predefined in C++, but are programmer-defined

objects of class Position. How do the = and + operators know how to operate on
objects? The answer is that we can define new behaviors for these operators. These
operations will be member functions of the Position class.

Using operators or functions in different ways, depending on what they are operating on, is
called *polymorphism* (one thing with several distinct forms). When an existing operator, such
as + or =, is given the capability to operate on a new data type, it is said to be *overloaded*.
Overloading is a kind of polymorphism; it is also an important feature of OOP.

C++ and C

C++ is derived from the C language. Strictly speaking, it is a superset of C: Almost
every correct statement in C is also a correct statement in C++, although the reverse is
not true. The most important elements added to C to create C++ concern classes,
objects, and object-oriented programming. (C++ was originally called "C with
classes.") However, C++ has many other new features as well, including an improved
approach to input/output (I/O) and a new way to write comments. Figure 1.7 shows
the relationship of C and C++.

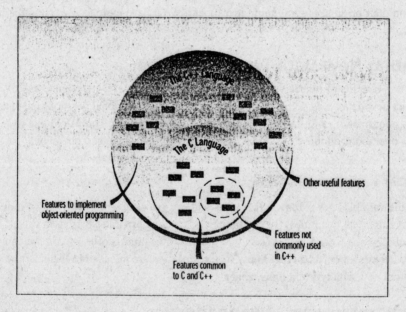

FIGURE 1.7
The relationship between C and C++.

In fact, the practical differences between C and C++ are larger than you might think. Although you can write a program in C++ that looks like a program in C, hardly anyone does. C++ programmers not only make use of the new features of C++, they also emphasize the traditional C features in different proportions than do C programmers.

If you already know C, you will have a head start in learning C++ (although you may also have some bad habits to unlearn), but much of the material will be new.

Laying the Groundwork

Our goal is to help you begin writing OOP programs as soon as possible. However, as we noted, much of C++ is inherited from C, so while the overall structure of a C++ program may be OOP, down in the trenches you need to know some old-fashioned procedural fundamentals. Chapters 2–5 therefore deal with the "traditional" aspects of C++, many of which are also found in C. You will learn about variables and I/O, about control structures such as loops and decisions, and about functions themselves. You will also learn about structures, since the same syntax that's used for structures is used for classes.

If you already know C, you might be tempted to skip these chapters. However, you will find that there are many differences, some obvious and some rather subtle, between C and C++. Our advice is to read these chapters, skimming what you know, and concentrating on the ways C++ differs from C.

The specific discussion of OOP starts in Chapter 6, "Objects and Classes." From then on the examples will be object oriented.

The Unified Modeling Language (UML)

The UML is a graphical "language" for modeling computer programs. "Modeling" means to create a simplified representation of something, as a blueprint models a house. The UML provides a way to visualize the higher-level organization of programs without getting mired down in the details of actual code.

The UML began as three separate modeling languages, one created by Grady Booch at Rational Software, one by James Rumbaugh at General Electric, and one by Ivar Jacobson at Ericson. Eventually Rumbaugh and Jacobson joined Booch at Rational, where they became known as the three amigos. During the late 1990s they unified (hence the name) their modeling languages into the Unified Modeling Language. The result was adopted by the Object Management Group (OMG), a consortium of companies devoted to industry standards.

Why do we need the UML? One reason is that in a large computer program it's often hard to understand, simply by looking at the code, how the parts of the program relate to each other. As we've seen, object-oriented programming is a vast improvement over procedural programs. Nevertheless, figuring out what a program is supposed to do requires, at best, considerable study of the program listings.

The trouble with code is that it's very detailed. It would be nice if there were a way to see a bigger picture, one that depicts the major parts of the program and how they work together. The UML answers this need.

The most important part of the UML is a set of different kinds of diagrams. Class diagrams show the relationships among classes, object diagrams show how specific objects relate, sequence diagrams show the communication among objects over time, use case diagrams show how a program's users interact with the program, and so on. These diagrams provide a variety of ways to look at a program and its operation.

The UML plays many roles besides helping us to understand how a program works. As we'll see in Chapter 16, it can help in the initial design of a program. In fact, the UML is useful throughout all phases of software development, from initial specification to documentation, testing, and maintenance.

The UML is not a software development process. Many such processes exist for specifying the stages of the development process. The UML is simply a way to look at the software being developed. Although it can be applied to any kind of programming language, the UML is especially attuned to OOP.

As we noted in the Introduction, we introduce specific features of the UML in stages throughout the book.

- Chapter 1: (this section) introduction to the UML
- Chapter 8: class diagrams, associations, and navigability
- Chapter 9: generalization, aggregation, and composition
- Chapter 10: state diagrams and multiplicity
- Chapter 11: object diagrams
- Chapter 13: more complex state diagrams
- Chapter 14: templates, dependencies, and stereotypes
- Chapter 16: use cases, use case diagrams, activity diagrams, and sequence diagrams

Summary

OOP is a way of organizing programs. The emphasis is on the way programs are designed, not on coding details. In particular, OOP programs are organized around objects, which contain both data and functions that act on that data. A class is a template for a number of objects.

Inheritance allows a class to be derived from an existing class without modifying it. The derived class has all the data and functions of the parent class, but adds new ones of its own. Inheritance makes possible reusability, or using a class over and over in different programs.

C++ is a superset of C. It adds to the C language the capability to implement OOP. It also adds a variety of other features. In addition, the emphasis is changed in C++ so that some features common to C, although still available in C++, are seldom used, while others are used far more frequently. The result is a surprisingly different language.

The Unified Modeling Language (UML) is a standardized way to visualize a program's structure and operation using diagrams.

The general concepts discussed in this chapter will become more concrete as you learn more about the details of C++. You may want to refer back to this chapter as you progress further into this book.

Questions

Answers to these questions can be found in Appendix G. Note that throughout this book, multiple-choice questions can have more than one correct answer.

1. Pascal, BASIC, and C are p_____ languages, while C++ is an o_____ language.

2. A widget is to the blueprint for a widget as an object is to

   a. a member function.

   b. a class.

   c. an operator.

   d. a data item.

3. The two major components of an object are _____ and functions that _____.

4. In C++, a function contained within a class is called

   a. a member function.

   b. an operator.

   c. a class function.

   d. a method.

5. Protecting data from access by unauthorized functions is called _____.

6. Which of the following are good reasons to use an object-oriented language?

   a. You can define your own data types.

   b. Program statements are simpler than in procedural languages.

   c. An OO program can be taught to correct its own errors.

   d. It's easier to conceptualize an OO program.

7. _____ model entities in the real world more closely than do functions.

8. True or false: A C++ program is similar to a C program except for the details of coding.

9. Bundling data and functions together is called _____.

10. When a language has the capability to produce new data types, it is said to be

    a. reprehensible.

    b. encapsulated.

    c. overloaded.

    d. extensible.

11. True or false: You can easily tell, from any two lines of code, whether a program is written in C or C++.

12. The ability of a function or operator to act in different ways on different data types is called _____.

13. A normal C++ operator that acts in special ways on newly defined data types is said to be

    a. glorified.

    b. encapsulated.

    c. classified.

    d. overloaded.

14. Memorizing the new terms used in C++ is

    a. critically important.

    b. something you can return to later.

    c. the key to wealth and success.

    d. completely irrelevant.

15. The Unified Modeling Language is

   a. a program that builds physical models.

   b. a way to look at the organization of a program.

   c. the combination of C++ and FORTRAN.

   d. helpful in developing software systems.

C++ Programming Basics

IN THIS CHAPTER

In any language there are some fundamentals you need to know before you can write even the most elementary programs. This chapter introduces three such fundamentals: basic program construction, variables, and input/output (I/O). It also touches on a variety of other language features, including comments, arithmetic operators, the increment operator, data conversion, and library functions.

These topics are not conceptually difficult, but you may find that the style in C++ is a little austere compared with, say, BASIC or Pascal. Before you learn what it's all about, a C++ program may remind you more of a mathematics formula than a computer program. Don't worry about this. You'll find that as you gain familiarity with C++, it starts to look less forbidding, while other languages begin to seem unnecessarily fancy and verbose.

Getting Started

As we noted in the Introduction, you can use either a Microsoft or a Borland compiler with this book. Appendixes C and D provide details about their operation. (Other compilers may work as well.) Compilers take source code and transform it into executable files, which your computer can run as it does other programs. Source files are text files (extension .CPP) that correspond with the listings printed in this book. Executable files have the .EXE extension, and can be executed either from within your compiler, or, if you're familiar with MS-DOS, directly from a DOS window.

The programs run without modification on the Microsoft compiler or in an MS-DOS window. If you're using the Borland compiler, you'll need to modify the programs slightly before running them; otherwise the output won't remain on the screen long enough to see. Make sure to read Appendix D, "Borland C++Builder," to see how this is done.

Basic Program Construction

Let's look at a very simple C++ program. This program is called FIRST, so its source file is FIRST.CPP. It simply prints a sentence on the screen. Here it is:

```
#include <iostream>
using namespace std;

int main()
   {
   cout << "Every age has a language of its own\n";
   return 0;
   }
```

Despite its small size, this program demonstrates a great deal about the construction of C++ programs. Let's examine it in detail.

Functions

Functions are one of the fundamental building blocks of C++. The FIRST program consists almost entirely of a single function called main(). The only parts of this program that are not part of the function are the first two lines—the ones that start with #include and using. (We'll see what these lines do in a moment.)

We noted in Chapter 1, "The Big Picture," that a function can be part of a class, in which case it is called a *member function*. However, functions can also exist independently of classes. We are not yet ready to talk about classes, so we will show functions that are separate standalone entities, as main() is here.

Function Name

The parentheses following the word main are the distinguishing feature of a function. Without the parentheses the compiler would think that main refers to a variable or to some other program element. When we discuss functions in the text, we'll follow the same convention that C++ uses: We'll put parentheses following the function name. Later on we'll see that the parentheses aren't always empty. They're used to hold function *arguments*: values passed from the calling program to the function.

The word int preceding the function name indicates that this particular function has a return value of type int. Don't worry about this now; we'll learn about data types later in this chapter and return values in Chapter 5, "Functions."

Braces and the Function Body

The *body* of a function is surrounded by *braces* (sometimes called *curly brackets*). These braces play the same role as the BEGIN and END keywords in some other languages: They surround or *delimit* a block of program statements. Every function must use this pair of braces around the function body. In this example there are only two statements in the function body: the line starting with cout, and the line starting with return. However, a function body can consist of many statements.

Always Start with main()

When you run a C++ program, the first statement executed will be at the beginning of a function called main(). (At least that's true of the console mode programs in this book.) The program may consist of many functions, classes, and other program elements, but on startup, control always goes to main(). If there is no function called main() in your program, an error will be reported when you run the program.

In most C++ programs, as we'll see later, main() calls member functions in various objects to carry out the program's real work. The main() function may also contain calls to other standalone functions. This is shown in Figure 2.1.

2
C++
PROGRAMMING
BASICS

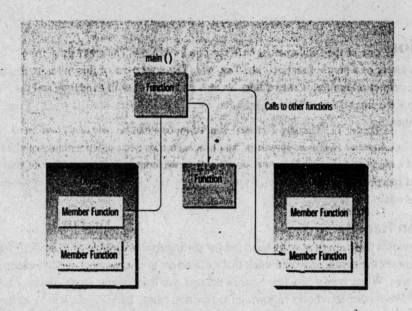

FIGURE 2.1
Objects, functions, and `main()`.

Program Statements

The program *statement* is the fundamental unit of C++ programming. There are two statements in the FIRST program: the line

```
cout << "Every age has a language of its own\n";
```

and the return statement

```
return 0;
```

The first statement tells the computer to display the quoted phrase. Most statements tell the computer to do something. In this respect, statements in C++ are similar to statements in other languages. In fact, as we've noted, the majority of statements in C++ are identical to statements in C.

A semicolon signals the end of the statement. This is a crucial part of the syntax but easy to forget. In some languages (like BASIC), the end of a statement is signaled by the end of the line, but that's not true in C++. If you leave out the semicolon, the compiler will often (although not always) signal an error.

The last statement in the function body is return 0;. This tells main() to return the value 0 to whoever called it, in this case the operating system or compiler. In older versions of C++ you could give main() the return type of void and dispense with the return statement, but this is not considered correct in Standard C++. We'll learn more about return in Chapter 5.

Whitespace

We mentioned that the end of a line isn't important to a C++ compiler. Actually, the compiler ignores whitespace almost completely. *Whitespace* is defined as spaces, carriage returns, line-feeds, tabs, vertical tabs, and formfeeds. These characters are invisible to the compiler. You can put several statements on one line, separated by any number of spaces or tabs, or you can run a statement over two or more lines. It's all the same to the compiler. Thus the FIRST program could be written this way:

```
#include <iostream>
using
namespace std;

int main () { cout
<<
"Every age has a language of its own\n"
; return
0;}
```

We don't recommend this syntax—it's nonstandard and hard to read—but it does compile correctly.

There are several exceptions to the rule that whitespace is invisible to the compiler. The first line of the program, starting with #include, is a preprocessor directive, which must be written on one line. Also, string constants, such as "Every age has a language of its own", cannot be broken into separate lines. (If you need a long string constant, you can insert a back-slash (\) at the line break or divide the string into two separate strings, each surrounded by quotes.)

Output Using cout

As you have seen, the statement

```
cout << "Every age has a language of its own\n";
```

causes the phrase in quotation marks to be displayed on the screen. How does this work? A complete description of this statement requires an understanding of objects, operator overloading, and other topics we won't discuss until later in the book, but here's a brief preview.

The identifier ῀῀῀ (pronounced "C out") is actually an *object*. It is predefined in C++ to correspond to the *standard output stream*. A *stream* is an abstraction that refers to a flow of data. The standard output stream normally flows to the screen display—although it can be redirected to other output devices. We'll discuss streams (and redirection) in Chapter 12, "Streams and Files."

The operator << is called the *insertion* ᴏʀ *put to* operator. It directs the contents of the variable on its right to the object on its left. In FIᴋᴢᴛ it directs the string constant "Every age has a language of its own\n" to cout, which sends it to the display.

(If you know C, you'll recognize << as the *left-shift* bit-wise operator and wonder how it can also be used to direct output. In C++, operators can be overloaded. That is, they can perform different activities, depending on the context. We'll learn about overloading in Chapter 8, "Operator Overloading.")

Although the concepts behind the use of cout and << may be obscure at this point, using them is easy. They'll appear in almost every example program. Figure 2.2 shows the result of using cout and the insertion operator <<.

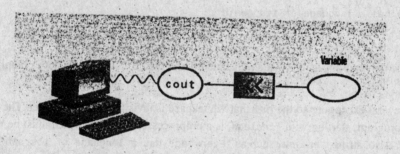

FIGURE 2.2
Output with cout.

String Constants

The phrase in quotation marks, "Every age has a language of its own\n", is an example of a *string constant*. As you probably know, a constant, unlike a variable, cannot be given a new value as the program runs. Its value is set when the program is written, and it retains this value throughout the program's existence.

As we'll see later, the situation regarding strings is rather complicated in C++. Two ways of handling strings are commonly used. A string can be represented by an array of characters, or it can be represented as an object of a class. We'll learn more about both kinds of strings in Chapter 7, "Arrays and Strings."

The '\n' character at the end of the string constant is an example of an *escape sequence*. It causes the next text output to be displayed on a new line. We use it here so that the phrases such as "Press any key to continue," inserted by some compilers for display after the program terminates, will appear on a new line. We'll discuss escape sequences later in this chapter.

Directives

The two lines that begin the FIRST program are *directives*. The first is a *preprocessor directive*, and the second is a using *directive*. They occupy a sort of gray area: They're not part of the basic C++ language, but they're necessary anyway

Preprocessor Directives

The first line of the FIRST program

```
#include <iostream>
```

might look like a program statement, but it's not. It isn't part of a function body and doesn't end with a semicolon, as program statements must. Instead, it starts with a number sign (#). It's called a *preprocessor directive*. Recall that program statements are instructions to the *computer* to do something, such as adding two numbers or printing a sentence. A preprocessor directive, on the other hand, is an instruction to the *compiler*. A part of the compiler called the *preprocessor* deals with these directives before it begins the real compilation process.

The preprocessor directive #include tells the compiler to insert another file into your source file. In effect, the #include directive is replaced by the contents of the file indicated. Using an #include directive to insert another file into your source file is similar to pasting a block of text into a document with your word processor.

#include is only one of many preprocessor directives, all of which can be identified by the initial # sign. The use of preprocessor directives is not as common in C++ as it is in C, but we'll look at a few additional examples as we go along. The type file usually included by #include is called a *header file*.

Header Files

In the FIRST example, the preprocessor directive #include tells the compiler to add the source file IOSTREAM to the FIRST.CPP source file before compiling. Why do this? IOSTREAM is an example of a *header file* (sometimes called an *include file*). It's concerned with basic input/output operations, and contains declarations that are needed by the cout identifier and the << operator. Without these declarations, the compiler won't recognize cout and will think << is being used incorrectly. There are many such include files. The newer Standard C++ header files don't hav a file extension, but some older header files, left over from the days of the C language, have the extension .H.

If you want to see what's in IOSTREAM, you can find the include directory for your compiler and display it as a source file in the Edit window. (See the appropriate appendix for hints on how to do this.) Or you can look at it with the WordPad or Notepad utilities. The contents won't make much sense at this point, but you will at least prove to yourself that IOSTREAM is a source file, written in normal ASCII characters.

We'll return to the topic of header files at the end of this chapter, when we introduce library functions.

The using Directive

A C++ program can be divided into different *namespaces*. A namespace is a part of the program in which certain names are recognized; outside of the namespace they're unknown. The directive

```
using namespace std;
```

says that all the program statements that follow are within the std namespace. Various program components such as cout are declared within this namespace. If we didn't use the using directive, we would need to add the std name to many program elements. For example, in the FIRST program we'd need to say

```
std::cout << "Every age has a language of its own.";
```

To avoid adding std:: dozens of times in programs we use the using directive instead. We'll discuss namespaces further in Chapter 13, "Multifile Programs."

Comments

Comments are an important part of any program. They help the person writing a program, and anyone else who must read the source file, understand what's going on. The compiler ignores comments, so they do not add to the file size or execution time of the executable program.

Comment Syntax

Let's rewrite our FIRST program, incorporating comments into our source file. We'll call the new program COMMENTS:

```
// comments.cpp
// demonstrates comments
#include <iostream>          //preprocessor directive
using namespace std;         //"using" directive
```

```
int main()                       //function name "main"
  {                              //start function body
  cout << "Every age has a language of its own\n";  //statement
  return 0;                      //statement
  }                              //end function body
```

Comments start with a double slash symbol (//) and terminate at the end of the line. (This is one of the exceptions to the rule that the compiler ignores whitespace.) A comment can start at the beginning of the line or on the same line following a program statement. Both possibilities are shown in the COMMENTS example.

When to Use Comments

Comments are almost always a good thing. Most programmers don't use enough of them. If you're tempted to leave out comments, remember that not everyone is as smart as you; they may need more explanation than you do about what your program is doing. Also, you may not be as smart next month, when you've forgotten key details of your program's operation, as you are today.

Use comments to explain to the person looking at the listing what you're trying to do. The details are in the program statements themselves, so the comments should concentrate on the big picture, clarifying your reasons for using a certain statement or group of statements.

Alternative Comment Syntax

There's a second comment style available in C++:

```
/* this is an old-style comment */
```

This type of comment (the only comment originally available in C) begins with the /* character pair and ends with */ (not with the end of the line). These symbols are harder to type (since / is lowercase while * is uppercase) and take up more space on the line, so this style is not generally used in C++. However, it has advantages in special situations. You can write a multi-line comment with only two comment symbols:

```
/* this
is a
potentially
very long
multiline
comment
*/
```

This is a good approach to making a comment out of a large text passage, since it saves inserting the // symbol on every line.

You can also insert a /* */ comment anywhere within the text of a program line:

```
func1()
   {  /* empty function body */  }
```

If you attempt to use the // style comment in this case, the closing brace won't be visible to the compiler—since a // style comment runs to the end of the line—and the code won't compile correctly.

Integer Variables

Variables are the most fundamental part of any language. A variable has a symbolic name and can be given a variety of values. Variables are located in particular places in the computer's memory. When a variable is given a value, that value is actually placed in the memory space assigned to the variable. Most popular languages use the same general variable types, such as integers, floating-point numbers, and characters, so you are probably already familiar with the ideas behind them.

Integer variables represent integer numbers like 1, 30,000, and –27. Such numbers are used for counting discrete numbers of objects, like 11 pencils or 99 bottles of beer. Unlike floating-point numbers, integers have no fractional part; you can express the idea of *four* using integers, but not *four and one-half*.

Defining Integer Variables

Integer variables exist in several sizes, but the most commonly used is type int. The amount of memory occupied by the integer types is system dependent. On a 32-bit system such as Windows, an int occupies 4 bytes (which is 32 bits) of memory. This allows an int to hold numbers in the range from –2,147,483,648 to 2,147,483,647. Figure 2.3 shows an integer variable in memory.

While type int occupies 4 bytes on current Windows computers, it occupied only 2 bytes in MS-DOS and earlier versions of Windows. The ranges occupied by the various types are listed in the header file LIMITS; you can also look them up using your compiler's help system.

Here's a program that defines and uses several variables of type int:

```
// intvars.cpp
// demonstrates integer variables
#include <iostream>
using namespace std;

int main()
   {
   int var1;              //define var1
   int var2;              //define var2
```

```
var1 = 20;              //assign value to var1
var2 = var1 + 10;       //assign value to var2
cout << "var1+10 is ";  //output text
cout << var2 << endl;   //output value of var2
return 0;
}
```

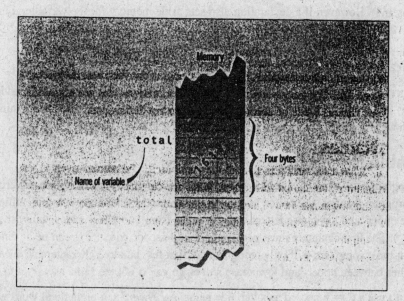

FIGURE 2.3
Variable of type int *in memory.*

Type this program into your compiler's edit screen (or load it from the Web site), compile and link it, and then run it. Examine the output window. The statements

```
int var1;
int var2;
```

define two integer variables, var1 and var2. The keyword int signals the type of variable. These statements, which are called *declarations*, must terminate with a semicolon, like other program statements.

You must declare a variable before using it. However, you can place variable declarations anywhere in a program. It's not necessary to declare variables before the first executable statement (as was necessary in C). However, it's probably more readable if commonly-used variables are located at the beginning of the program.

Declarations and Definitions

Let's digress for a moment to note a subtle distinction between the terms *definition* and *declaration* as applied to variables.

A *declaration* introduces a variable's name (such as var1) into a program and specifies its type (such as int). However, if a declaration also sets aside memory for the variable, it is also called a *definition*. The statements

```
int var1;
int var2;
```

in the INTVARS program are definitions, as well as declarations, because they set aside memory for var1 and var2. We'll be concerned mostly with declarations that are also definitions, but later on we'll see various kinds of declarations that are not definitions.

Variable Names

The program INTVARS uses variables named var1 and var2. The names given to variables (and other program features) are called *identifiers*. What are the rules for writing identifiers? You can use upper- and lowercase letters, and the digits from 1 to 9. Y can also use the underscore (_). The first character must be a letter or underscore. Identifiers can be as long as you like, but most compilers will only recognize the first few hundred characters. The compiler distinguishes between upper- and lowercase letters, so Var is not the same as var or VAR.

You can't use a C++ keyword as a variable name. A *keyword* is a predefined word with a special meaning. int, class, if, and while are examples of keywords. A complete list of keywords can be found in Appendix B, "C++ Precedence Table and Keywords," and in your compiler's documentation.

Many C++ programmers follow the convention of using all lowercase letters for variable names. Other programmers use a mixture of upper- and lowercase, as in IntVar or dataCount. Still others make liberal use of underscores. Whichever approach you use, it's good to be consistent throughout a program. Names in all uppercase are sometimes reserved for constants (see the discussion of const that follows). These same conventions apply to naming other program elements such as classes and functions.

A variable's name should make clear to anyone reading the listing the variable's purpose and how it is used. Thus boilerTemperature is better than something cryptic like bT or t.

Assignment Statements

The statements

```
var1 = 20;
var2 = var1 + 10;
```

assign values to the two variables. The equal sign (=), as you might guess, causes the value on the right to be assigned to the variable on the left. The = in C++ is equivalent to the := in Pascal or the = in BASIC. In the first line shown here, var1, which previously had no value, is given the value 20.

Integer Constants

The number 20 is an *integer constant*. Constants don't change during the course of the program. An integer constant consists of numerical digits. There must be no decimal point in an integer constant, and it must lie within the range of integers.

In the second program line shown here, the plus sign (+) adds the value of var1 and 10, in which 10 is another constant. The result of this addition is then assigned to var2.

Output Variations

The statement

```
cout << "var1+10 is ";
```

displays a string constant, as we've seen before. The next statement

```
cout << var2 << endl;
```

displays the value of the variable var2. As you can see in your console output window, the output of the program is

```
var1+10 is 30
```

Note that cout and the << operator know how to treat an integer and a string differently. If we send them a string, they print it as text. If we send them an integer, they print it as a number. This may seem obvious, but it is another example of operator overloading, a key feature of C++. (C programmers will remember that such functions as printf() need to be told not only the variable to be displayed, but the type of the variable as well, which makes the syntax far less intuitive.)

As you can see, the output of the two cout statements appears on the same line on the output screen. No linefeed is inserted automatically. If you want to start on a new line, you must insert a linefeed yourself. We've seen how to do this with the '\n' escape sequence. Now we'll see another way: using something called a *manipulator*.

The endl Manipulator

The last cout statement in the INTVARS program ends with an unfamiliar word: endl. This causes a linefeed to be inserted into the stream, so that subsequent text is displayed on the next line. It has the same effect as sending the '\n' character, but is somewhat clearer. It's an example of a *manipulator*. Manipulators are instructions to the output stream that modify the output in various ways; we'll see more of them as we go along. Strictly speaking, endl (unlike '\n') also causes the output buffer to be flushed, but this happens invisibly so for most purposes the two are equivalent.

Other Integer Types

There are several numerical integer types besides type int. The two most common types are long and short. (Strictly speaking type char is an integer type as well, but we'll cover it separately.) We noted that the size of type int is system dependent. In contrast, types long and short have fixed sizes no matter what system is used.

Type long always occupies four bytes, which is the same as type int on 32-bit Windows systems. Thus it has the same range, from –2,147,483,648 to 2,147,483,647. It can also be written as long int; this means the same as long. There's little point in using type long on 32-bit systems, since it's the same as int. However, if your program may need to run on a 16-bit system such as MS-DOS, or on older versions of Windows, specifying type long will guarantee a four-bit integer type. In 16-bit systems, type int has the same range as type short.

On all systems type short occupies two bytes, giving it a range of –32,768 to 32,767. There's probably not much point using type short on modern Windows systems unless it's important to save memory. Type int, although twice as large, is accessed faster than type short.

If you want to create a constant of type long, use the letter L following the numerical value, as in

```
longvar = 7678L; // assigns long constant 7678 to longvar
```

Many compilers offer integer types that explicitly specify the number of bits used. (Remember there are 8 bits to a byte.) These type names are preceded by two underscores. They are __int8, __int16, __int32, and __int64. The __int8 type corresponds to char, and (at least in 32-bit systems) the type name __int16 corresponds to short and __int32 corresponds to both int and long. The __int64 type holds huge integers with up to 19 decimal digits. Using these type names has the advantage that the number of bytes used for a variable is not implementation dependent. However, this is not usually an issue, and these types are seldom used.

Character Variables

Type char stores integers that range in value from –128 to 127. Variables of this type occupy only 1 byte (eight bits) of memory. Character variables are sometimes used to store numbers that confine themselves to this limited range, but they are much more commonly used to store ASCII characters.

As you may already know, the ASCII character set is a way of representing characters such as 'a', 'B', '$', '3', and so on, as numbers. These numbers range from 0 to 127. Most Windows systems extend this range to 255 to accommodate various foreign-language and graphics characters. Appendix A, "ASCII Table," shows the ASCII character set.

Complexities arise when foreign languages are used, and even when programs are transferred between computer systems in the same language. This is because the characters in the range 128 to 255 aren't standardized and because the one-byte size of type char is too small to accommodate the number of characters in many languages, such as Japanese. Standard C++ provides a larger character type called wchar_t to handle foreign languages. This is important if you're writing programs for international distribution. However, in this book we'll ignore type wchar_t and assume that we're dealing with the ASCII character set found in current versions of Windows.

Character Constants

Character constants use single quotation marks around a character, like 'a' and 'b'. (Note that this differs from *string* constants, which use double quotation marks.) When the C++ compiler encounters such a character constant, it translates it into the corresponding ASCII code. The constant 'a' appearing in a program, for example, will be translated into 97, as shown in Figure 2.4.

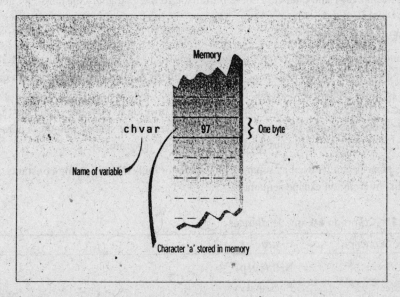

FIGURE 2.4
Variable of type char *in memory.*

Character variables can be assigned character constants as values. The following program shows some examples of character constants and variables.

```
// charvars.cpp
// demonstrates character variables
#include <iostream>        //for cout, etc.
using namespace std;

int main()
    {
    char charvar1 = 'A';     //define char variable as character
    char charvar2 = '\t';    //define char variable as tab

    cout << charvar1;        //display character
    cout << charvar2;        //display character
    charvar1 = 'B';          //set char variable to char constant
    cout << charvar1;        //display character
    cout << '\n';            //display newline character
    return 0;
    }
```

Initialization

Variables can be initialized at the same time they are defined. In this program two variables of type char—charvar1 and charvar2—are initialized to the character constants 'A' and '\t'.

Escape Sequences

This second character constant, '\t', is an odd one. Like '\n', which we encountered earlier, it's an example of an *escape sequence*. The name reflects the fact that the backslash causes an "escape" from the normal way characters are interpreted. In this case the t is interpreted not as the character 't' but as the tab character. A tab causes printing to continue at the next tab stop. In console-mode programs, tab stops are positioned every eight spaces. Another character constant, '\n', is sent directly to cout in the last line of the program.

Escape sequences can be used as separate characters or embedded in string constants. Table 2.1 shows a list of common escape sequences.

TABLE 2.1 Common Escape Sequences

Escape Sequence	Character
\ a	Bell (beep)
\ b	Backspace
\ f	Formfeed

TABLE 2.1   Continued

Escape Sequence	Character
\ n	Newline
\ r	Return
\ t	Tab
\ \	Backslash
\ '	Single quotation mark
\ "	Double quotation marks
\ xdd	Hexadecimal notation

Since the backslash, the single quotation marks, and the double quotation marks all have specialized meanings when used in constants, they must be represented by escape sequences when we want to display them as characters. Here's an example of a quoted phrase in a string constant:

```
cout << "\"Run, Spot, run,\" she said.";
```

This translates to

```
"Run, Spot, run," she said.
```

Sometimes you need to represent a character constant that doesn't appear on the keyboard, such as the graphics characters above ASCII code 127. To do this, you can use the '\xdd' representation, where each d stands for a hexadecimal digit. If you want to print a solid rectangle, for example, you'll find such a character listed as decimal number 178, which is hexadecimal number B2 in the ASCII table. This character would be represented by the character constant '\xB2'. We'll see some examples of this later.

The CHARVARS program prints the value of charvar1 ('A') and the value of charvar2 (a tab). It then sets charvar1 to a new value ('B'), prints that, and finally prints the newline. The output looks like this:

```
A       B
```

Input with cin

Now that we've seen some variable types in use, let's see how a program accomplishes input. The next example program asks the user for a temperature in degrees Fahrenheit, converts it to Celsius, and displays the result. It uses integer variables.

```
// fahren.cpp
// demonstrates cin, newline
#include <iostream>
using namespace std;

int main()
   {
   int ftemp;   //for temperature in fahrenheit

   cout << "Enter temperature in fahrenheit: ";
   cin >> ftemp;
   int ctemp = (ftemp-32) * 5 / 9;
   cout << "Equivalent in Celsius is: " << ctemp << '\n';
   return 0;
   }
```

The statement

```
cin >> ftemp;
```

causes the program to wait for the user to type in a number. The resulting number is placed in the variable ftemp. The keyword cin (pronounced "C in") is an object, predefined in C++ to correspond to the standard input stream. This stream represents data coming from the keyboard (unless it has been redirected). The >> is the *extraction* or *get from* operator. It takes the value from the stream object on its left and places it in the variable on its right.

Here's some sample interaction with the program:

```
Enter temperature in fahrenheit: 212
Equivalent in Celsius is: 100
```

Figure 2.5 shows input using cin and the extraction operator >>.

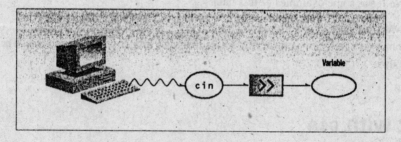

FIGURE 2.5
Input with cin.

Variables Defined at Point of Use

The FAHREN program has several new wrinkles besides its input capability. Look closely at the listing. Where is the variable ctemp defined? Not at the beginning of the program, but in the next-to-the-last line, where it's used to store the result of the arithmetic operation. As we noted earlier, you can define variables throughout a program, not just at the beginning. (Many languages, including C, require all variables to be defined before the first executable statement.)

Defining variables where they are used can make the listing easier to understand, since you don't need to refer repeatedly to the start of the listing to find the variable definitions. However, the practice should be used with discretion. Variables that are used in many places in a function are better defined at the start of the function.

Cascading <<

The insertion operator << is used repeatedly in the second cout statement in FAHREN. This is perfectly legal. The program first sends the phrase *Equivalent in Celsius is:* to cout, then it sends the value of ctemp, and finally the newline character '\n'.

The extraction operator >> can be cascaded with cin in the same way, allowing the user to enter a series of values. However, this capability is not used so often, since it eliminates the opportunity to prompt the user between inputs.

Expressions

Any arrangement of variables, constants, and operators that specifies a computation is called an *expression*. Thus, alpha+12 and (alpha-37)*beta/2 are expressions. When the computations specified in the expression are performed, the result is usually a value. Thus if alpha is 7, the first expression shown has the value 19.

Parts of expressions may also be expressions. In the second example, alpha-37 and beta/2 are expressions. Even single variables and constants, like alpha and 37, are considered to be expressions.

Note that expressions aren't the same as statements. Statements tell the compiler to do something and terminate with a semicolon, while expressions specify a computation. There can be several expressions in a statement.

Precedence

Note the parentheses in the expression

```
(ftemp-32) * 5 / 9
```

Without the parentheses, the multiplication would be carried out first, since * has higher priority than -. With the parentheses, the subtraction is done first, then the multiplication, since all operations inside parentheses are carried out first. What about the precedence of the * and / signs? When two arithmetic operators have the same precedence, the one on the left is executed first, so in this case the multiplication will be carried out next, then the division. Precedence and parentheses are normally applied this same way in algebra and in other computer languages, so their use probably seems quite natural. However, precedence is an important topic in C++. We'll return to it later when we introduce different kinds of operators.

Floating Point Types

We've talked about type int and type char, both of which represent numbers as integers—that is, numbers without a fractional part. Now let's examine a different way of storing numbers— as floating-point variables.

Floating-point variables represent numbers with a decimal place—like 3.1415927, 0.0000625, and −10.2. They have both an integer part, to the left of the decimal point, and a fractional part, to the right. Floating-point variables represent what mathematicians call *real numbers*, which are used for measurable quantities such as distance, area, and temperature. They typically have a fractional part.

There are three kinds of floating-point variables in C++: type float, type double, and type long double. Let's start with the smallest of these, type float.

Type float

Type float stores numbers in the range of about 3.4×10^{-38} to 3.4×10^{38}, with a precision of seven digits. It occupies 4 bytes (32 bits) in memory, as shown in Figure 2.6.

The following example program prompts the user to type in a floating-point number representing the radius of a circle. It then calculates and displays the circle's area.

```
// circarea.cpp
// demonstrates floating point variables
#include <iostream>                    //for cout, etc.
using namespace std;

int main()
   {
   float rad;                          //variable of type float
   const float PI = 3.14159F;          //type const float

   cout << "Enter radius of circle: "; //prompt
   cin >> rad;                         //get radius
```

```
float area = PI * rad * rad;        //find area
cout << "Area is " << area << endl; //display answer
return 0;
}
```

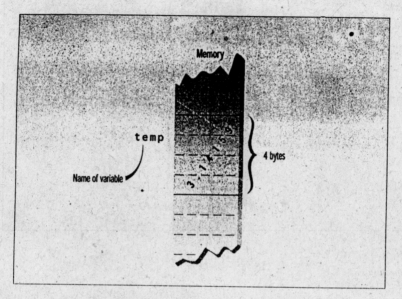

FIGURE 2.6
Variable of type float *in memory.*

Here's a sample interaction with the program:

```
Enter radius of circle: 0.5
Area is 0.785398
```

This is the area in square feet of a 12-inch LP record (which has a radius of 0.5 feet). At one time this was an important quantity for manufacturers of vinyl.

Type double and long double

The larger floating point types, double and long double, are similar to float except that they require more memory space and provide a wider range of values and more precision. Type double requires 8 bytes of storage and handles numbers in the range from 1.7×10^{-308} to 1.7×10^{308} with a precision of 15 digits. Type long double is compiler-dependent but is often the same as double. Type double is shown in Figure 2.7.

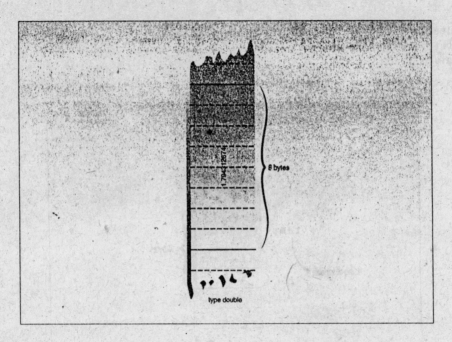

8 bytes

type double

FIGURE 2.7
Variable of type double.

Floating-Point Constants

The number 3.14159F in CIRCAREA is an example of a *floating-point constant*. The decimal point signals that it is a floating-point constant, and not an integer, and the F specifies that it's type float, rather than double or long double. The number is written in normal decimal notation. You don't need a suffix letter with constants of type double; it's the default. With type long double, use the letter L.

You can also write floating-point constants using *exponential notation*. Exponential notation is a way of writing large numbers without having to write out a lot of zeros. For example, 1,000,000,000 can be written as 1.0E9 in exponential notation. Similarly, 1234.56 would be written 1.23456E3. (This is the same as 1.23456 times 10^3.) The number following the E is called the *exponent*. It indicates how many places the decimal point must be moved to change the number to ordinary decimal notation.

The exponent can be positive or negative. The exponential number 6.35239E–5 is equivalent to 0.0000635239 in decimal notation. This is the same as 6.35239 times 10^{-5}.

The const Qualifier

Besides demonstrating variables of type float, the CIRCAREA example also introduces the qualifier const. It's used in the statement

```
const float PI = 3.14159F;  //type const float
```

The keyword const (for constant) precedes the data type of a variable. It specifies that the value of a variable will not change throughout the program. Any attempt to alter the value of a variable defined with this qualifier will elicit an error message from the compiler.

The qualifier const ensures that your program does not inadvertently alter a variable that you intended to be a constant, such as the value of PI in CIRCAREA. It also reminds anyone reading the listing that the variable is not intended to change. The const modifier can apply to other entities besides simple variables. We'll learn more about this as we go along.

The #define Directive

Although the construction is not recommended in C++, constants can also be specified using the preprocessor directive #define. This directive sets up an equivalence between an identifier and a text phrase. For example, the line

```
#define PI 3.14159
```

appearing at the beginning of your program specifies that the identifier PI will be replaced by the text 3.14159 throughout the program. This construction has long been popular in C. However, you can't specify the data type of the constant using #define, which can lead to program bugs; so even in C #define has been superseded by const used with normal variables. However, you may encounter this construction in older programs.

Type bool

For completeness we should mention type bool here, although it won't be important until we discuss relational operators in the next chapter.

We've seen that variables of type int can have billions of possible values, and those of type char can have 256. Variables of type bool can have only two possible values: true and false. In theory a bool type requires only one bit (not byte) of storage, but in practice compilers often store them as bytes because a byte can be quickly accessed, while an individual bit must be extracted from a byte, which requires additional time.

As we'll see, type bool is most commonly used to hold the results of comparisons. Is alpha less than beta? If so, a bool value is given the value true; if not, it's given the value false.

Type bool gets its name from George Boole, a 19th century English mathematician who invented the concept of using logical operators with true-or-false values. Thus such true/false values are often called *Boolean* values.

The setw Manipulator

We've mentioned that manipulators are operators used with the insertion operator (<<) to modify—or manipulate—the way data is displayed. We've already seen the endl manipulator; now we'll look at another one: setw, which changes the field width of output.

You can think of each value displayed by cout as occupying a field: an imaginary box with a certain width. The default field is just wide enough to hold the value. That is, the integer 567 will occupy a field three characters wide, and the string "pajamas" will occupy a field seven characters wide. However, in certain situations this may not lead to optimal results. Here's an example. The WIDTH1 program prints the names of three cities in one column, and their populations in another.

```
// width1.cpp
// demonstrates need for setw manipulator
#include <iostream>
using namespace std;

int main()
   {
   long pop1=2425785, pop2=47, pop3=9761;

   cout << "LOCATION " << "POP." << endl
        << "Portcity " << pop1 << endl
        << "Hightown " << pop2 << endl
        << "Lowville " << pop3 << endl;
   return 0;
   }
```

Here's the output from this program:

```
LOCATION POP.
Portcity 2425785
Hightown 47
Lowville 9761
```

Unfortunately, this format makes it hard to compare the numbers; it would be better if they lined up to the right. Also, we had to insert spaces into the names of the cities to separate them from the numbers. This is an inconvenience.

Here's a variation of this program, WIDTH2, that uses the setw manipulator to eliminate these problems by specifying field widths for the names and the numbers:

```cpp
// width2.cpp
// demonstrates setw manipulator
#include <iostream>
#include <iomanip>        // for setw
using namespace std;

int main()
   {
   long pop1=2425785, pop2=47, pop3=9761;

   cout << setw(8) << "LOCATION" << setw(12)
        << "POPULATION" << endl
        << setw(8) << "Portcity" << setw(12) << pop1 << endl
        << setw(8) << "Hightown" << setw(12) << pop2 << endl
        << setw(8) << "Lowville" << setw(12) << pop3 << endl;
   return 0;
   }
```

The setw manipulator causes the number (or string) that follows it in the stream to be printed within a field n characters wide, where n is the argument to setw(n). The value is right-justified within the field. Figure 2.8 shows how this looks. Type long is used for the population figures, which prevents a potential overflow problem on systems that use 2-byte integer types, in which the largest integer value is 32,767.

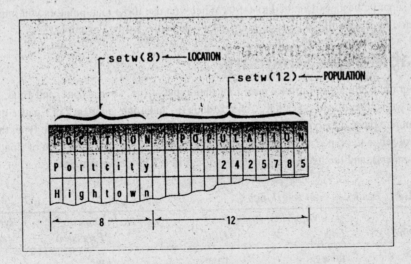

FIGURE 2.8
Field widths and setw.

Here's the output of WIDTH2:

```
LOCATION  POPULATION
Portcity    2425785
Hightown         47
Lowville       9761
```

Cascading the Insertion Operator

Note that there's only one cout statement in WIDTH1 and WIDTH2, although it's written on multiple lines. In doing this, we take advantage of the fact that the compiler ignores whitespace, and that the insertion operator can be cascaded. The effect is the same as using four separate statements, each beginning with cout.

Multiple Definitions

We initialized the variables pop1, pop2, and pop3 to specific values at the same time we defined them. This is similar to the way we initialized char variables in the CHARVARS example. Here, however, we've defined and initialized all three variables on one line, using the same long keyword and separating the variable names with commas. This saves space where a number of variables are all the same type.

The IOMANIP Header File

The declarations for the manipulators (except endl) are not in the usual IOSTREAM header file, but in a separate header file called IOMANIP. When you use these manipulators you must #include this header file in your program, as we do in the WIDTH2 example.

Variable Type Summary

Our program examples so far have used four data types—int, char, float, and long. In addition we've mentioned types bool, short, double, and long double. Let's pause now to summarize these data types. Table 2.2 shows the keyword used to define the type, the numerical range the type can accommodate, the digits of precision (in the case of floating-point numbers), and the bytes of memory occupied in a 32-bit environment.

TABLE 2.2   Basic C++ Variable Types

| Keyword | Numerical Range | | Digits of Precision | Bytes of Memory |
	Low	High		
bool	false	true	n/a	1
char	−128	127	n/a	1
short	−32,768	32,767	n/a	2

TABLE 2.2 Continued

| Keyword | Numerical Range | | Digits of Precision | Bytes of Memory |
	Low	High		
int	−2,147,483,648	2,147,483,647	n/a	4
long	−2,147,483,648	2,147,483,647	n/a	4
float	3.4×10^{-38}	3.4×10^{38}	7	4
double	1.7×10^{-308}	1.7×10^{308}	15	8

unsigned Data Types

By eliminating the sign of the character and integer types, you can change their range to start at 0 and include only positive numbers. This allows them to represent numbers twice as big as the signed type. Table 2.3 shows the unsigned versions.

TABLE 2.3 Unsigned Integer Types

| Keyword | Numerical Range | | Bytes of Memory |
	Low	High	
unsigned char	0	255	1
unsigned short	0	65,535	2
unsigned int	0	4,294,967,295	4
unsigned long	0	4,294,967,295	4

The unsigned types are used when the quantities represented are always positive—such as when representing a count of something—or when the positive range of the signed types is not quite large enough.

To change an integer type to an unsigned type, precede the data type keyword with the keyword unsigned. For example, an unsigned variable of type char would be defined as

```
unsigned char ucharvar;
```

Exceeding the range of signed types can lead to obscure program bugs. In certain (probably rare) situations such bugs can be eliminated by using unsigned types. For example, the following program stores the constant 1,500,000,000 (1.5 billion) both as an int in signedVar and as an unsigned int in unsignVar.

```
// signtest.cpp
// tests signed and unsigned integers
#include <iostream>
```

```
using namespace std;

int main()
    {
    int signedVar = 1500000000;              //signed
    unsigned int unsignVar = 1500000000;    //unsigned

    signedVar = (signedVar * 2) / 3;   //calculation exceeds range
    unsignVar = (unsignVar * 2) / 3;   //calculation within range

    cout << "signedVar = " << signedVar << endl;   //wrong
    cout << "unsignVar = " << unsignVar << endl;   //OK
    return 0;
    }
```

The program multiplies both variables by 2, then divides them by 3. Although the result is smaller than the original number, the intermediate calculation is larger than the original number. This is a common situation, but it can lead to trouble. In SIGNTEST we expect that two-thirds the original value, or 1,000,000,000, will be restored to both variables. Unfortunately, in signedVar the multiplication created a result—3,000,000,000—that exceeded the range of the int variable (–2,147,483,648 to 2,147,483,647). Here's the output:

```
signedVar = -431,655,765
unsignVar = 1,000,000,000
```

The signed variable now displays an incorrect answer, while the unsigned variable, which is large enough to hold the intermediate result of the multiplication, records the result correctly. The moral is this: Be careful that all values generated in your program are within the range of the variables that hold them. (The results will be different on 16-bit or 64-bit computers, which use different numbers of bytes for type int.)

Type Conversion

C++, like C, is more forgiving than some languages in the way it treats expressions involving several different data types. As an example, consider the MIXED program:

```
// mixed.cpp
// shows mixed expressions
#include <iostream>
using namespace std;

int main()
    {
    int count = 7;
    float avgWeight = 155.5F;
```

```
double totalWeight = count * avgWeight;
cout << "totalWeight=" << totalWeight << endl;
return 0;
}
```

Here a variable of type int is multiplied by a variable of type float to yield a result of type double. This program compiles without error; the compiler considers it normal that you want to multiply (or perform any other arithmetic operation on) numbers of different types.

Not all languages are this relaxed. Some don't permit mixed expressions, and would flag the line that performs the arithmetic in MIXED as an error. Such languages assume that when you mix types you're making a mistake, and they try to save you from yourself. C++ and C, however, assume that you must have a good reason for doing what you're doing, and they help carry out your intentions. This is one reason for the popularity of C++ and C. They give you more freedom. Of course, with more freedom, there's also more opportunity for you to make a mistake.

Automatic Conversions

Let's consider what happens when the compiler confronts such mixed-type expressions as the one in MIXED. Types are considered "higher" or "lower," based roughly on the order shown in Table 2.4.

TABLE 2.4   Order of Data Types

Data Type	Order
long double	Highest
double	
float	
long	
int	
short	
char	Lowest

The arithmetic operators such as + and * like to operate on two operands of the same type. When two operands of different types are encountered in the same expression, the lower-type variable is converted to the type of the higher-type variable. Thus in MIXED, the int value of count is converted to type float and stored in a temporary variable before being multiplied by the float variable avgWeight. The result (still of type float) is then converted to double so that it can be assigned to the double variable totalWeight. This process is shown in Figure 2.9.

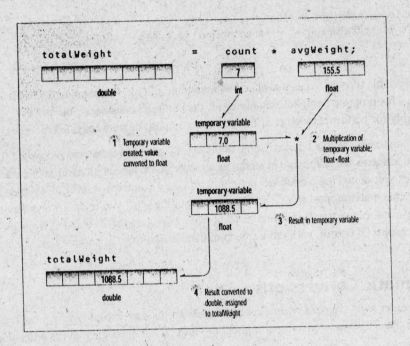

FIGURE 2.9
Data conversion.

These conversions take place invisibly, and ordinarily you don't need to think too much about them; C++ automatically does what you want. However, sometimes the compiler isn't so happy about conversions, as we'll see in a moment. Also, when we start to use objects, we will in effect be defining our own data types. We may want to use these new data types in mixed expressions, just as we use normal variables in mixed expressions. When this is the case, we must be careful to create our own conversion routines to change objects of one type into objects of another. The compiler won't do it for us, as it does here with the built-in data types.

Casts

Casts sounds like something to do with social classes in India, but in C++ the term applies to data conversions specified by the programmer, as opposed to the automatic data conversions we just described. Casts are also called *type casts*. What are casts for? Sometimes a programmer needs to convert a value from one type to another in a situation where the compiler will not do it automatically or without complaining.

There are several kinds of casts in Standard C++: static casts, dynamic casts, reinterpret casts, and const casts. Here we'll be concerned only with static casts; we'll learn about the others, which are used in more specialized situations, in later chapters.

C++ casts have a rather forbidding appearance. Here's a statement that uses a C++ cast to change a variable of type int into a variable of type char:

```
aCharVar = static_cast<char>(anIntVar);
```

Here the variable to be cast (anIntVar) is placed in parentheses and the type it's to be changed to (char) is placed in angle brackets. The result is that anIntVar is changed to type char before it's assigned to aCharVar. In this case the assignment statement would have carried out the cast itself, but there are situations where the cast is essential.

Recall that in the SIGNTEST example an intermediate result exceeded the capacity of the variable type, resulting in an erroneous result. We fixed the problem by using unsigned int instead of int. This worked because the intermediate result—3,000,000,000—would fit in the range of the unsigned variable.

But suppose an intermediate result won't fit the unsigned type either. In such a case we might be able to solve the problem by using a cast. Here's an example:

```
// cast.cpp
// tests signed and unsigned integers
#include <iostream>
using namespace std;

int main()
   {
   int intVar = 1500000000;                        //1,500,000,000
   intVar = (intVar * 10) / 10;                    //result too large
   cout << "intVar = " << intVar << endl;          //wrong answer

   intVar = 1500000000;                            //cast to double
   intVar = (static_cast<double>(intVar) * 10) / 10;
   cout << "intVar = " << intVar << endl;          //right answer
   return 0;
   }
```

When we multiply the variable intVar by 10, the result—15,000,000,000—is far too large to fit in a variable of type int or unsigned int. This leads to the wrong answer, as shown by the output of the first part of the program.

We could redefine the data type of the variables to be double; this provides plenty of room, since this type holds numbers with up to 15 digits. But suppose that for some reason, such as keeping the program small, we don't want to change the variables to type double. In this case there's another solution: We can cast intVar to type double before multiplying. This is sometimes called *coercion*; the data is coerced into becoming another type. The expression

```
static_cast<double>(intVar)
```

casts `intVar` to type `double`. It generates a temporary variable of type `double` with the same value as `intVar`. It is this temporary variable that is multiplied by 10. Since it is type `double`, the result fits. This result is then divided by 10 and assigned to the normal `int` variable `intVar`. Here's the program's output:

```
intVar = 211509811
intVar = 1500000000
```

The first answer, without the cast, is wrong; but in the second answer, the cast produces the correct result.

Before Standard C++, casts were handled using quite a different format. Instead of

```
aCharVar = static_cast<char>(anIntVar);
```

you could say

```
aCharVar = (char)anIntVar;
```

or alternatively

```
aCharVar = char(anIntVar);
```

One problem with these approaches is that they are hard to see; the syntax blends into the rest of the listing. They are also hard to search for using a Find operation with your source code editor. The new format solves this problem: `static_cast` is easy to see and easy to search for. These old casts still work, but their use is discouraged (or *deprecated*, to use the technical term).

Casts should be used only when absolutely necessary. They are a controlled way of evading *type safety* (which means making sure that variables don't change types by mistake) and can lead to trouble because they make it impossible for the compiler to spot potential problems. However, sometimes casts can't be avoided. We'll see some examples of situations where casts are necessary as we go along.

Arithmetic Operators

As you have probably gathered by this time, C++ uses the four normal arithmetic operators +, -, *, and / for addition, subtraction, multiplication, and division. These operators work on all the data types, both integer and floating-point. They are used in much the same way that they are used in other languages, and are closely analogous to their use in algebra. However, there are some other arithmetic operators whose use is not so obvious.

The Remainder Operator

There is a fifth arithmetic operator that works only with integer variables (types char, short, int, and long). It's called the *remainder operator*, and is represented by the percent symbol (%). This operator (also called the *modulus operator*) finds the remainder when one number is divided by another. The REMAIND program demonstrates the effect.

```
// remaind.cpp
// demonstrates remainder operator
#include <iostream>
using namespace std;

int main()
   {
   cout <<  6 % 8 << endl      // 6
        <<  7 % 8 << endl      // 7
        <<  8 % 8 << endl      // 0
        <<  9 % 8 << endl      // 1
        << 10 % 8 << endl;     // 2
   return 0;
   }
```

Here the numbers 6–10 are divided by 8, using the remainder operator. The answers are 6, 7, 0, 1, and 2—the remainders of these divisions. The remainder operator is used in a wide variety of situations. We'll show examples as we go along.

A note about precedence: In the expression

```
cout << 6 % 8
```

the remainder operator is evaluated first because it has higher precedence than the << operator. If it did not, we would need to put parentheses around 6 % 8 to ensure it was evaluated before being acted on by <<.

Arithmetic Assignment Operators

C++ offers several ways to shorten and clarify your code. One of these is the *arithmetic assignment operator*. This operator helps to give C++ listings their distinctive appearance.

The following kind of statement is common in most languages.

```
total = total + item;  // adds "item" to "total"
```

In this situation you add something to an existing value (or you perform some other arithmetic operation on it). But the syntax of this statement offends those for whom brevity is important, because the name total appears twice. So C++ offers a condensed approach: the arithmetic assignment operator, which combines an arithmetic operator and an assignment operator and eliminates the repeated operand. Here's a statement that has exactly the same effect as the preceding one.

```
total += item;    // adds "item" to "total"
```

Figure 2.10 emphasizes the equivalence of the two forms.

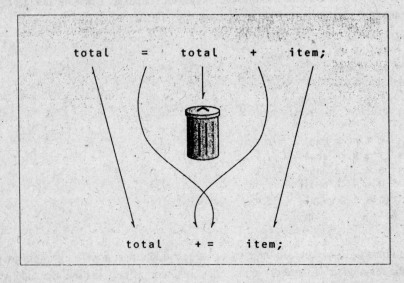

FIGURE 2.10
Arithmetic assignment operator.

There are arithmetic assignment operators corresponding to all the arithmetic operations: +=, -=, *=, /=, and %= (and some other operators as well). The following example shows the arithmetic assignment operators in use:

```cpp
// assign.cpp
// demonstrates arithmetic assignment operators
#include <iostream>
using namespace std;

int main()
   {
   int ans = 27;

   ans += 10;              //same as: ans = ans + 10;
   cout << ans << ", ";
   ans -= 7;               //same as: ans = ans - 7;
   cout << ans << ", ";
   ans *= 2;               //same as: ans = ans * 2;
   cout << ans << ", ";
```

```
  ans /= 3;                 //same as: ans = ans / 3;
  cout << ans << ", ";
  ans %= 3;                 //same as: ans = ans % 3;
  cout << ans << endl;
  return 0;
  }
```

Here's the output from this program:

```
37, 30, 60, 20, 2
```

You don't need to use arithmetic assignment operators in your code, but they are a common feature of the language; they'll appear in numerous examples in this book.

Increment Operators

Here's an even more specialized operator. You often need to add 1 to the value of an existing variable. You can do this the "normal" way:

```
count = count + 1;   // adds 1 to "count"
```

Or you can use an arithmetic assignment operator:

```
count += 1;   // adds 1 to "count"
```

But there's an even more condensed approach:

```
++count;   // adds 1 to "count"
```

The ++ operator increments (adds 1 to) its argument.

Prefix and Postfix

As if this weren't weird enough, the increment operator can be used in two ways: as a *prefix*, meaning that the operator precedes the variable; and as a *postfix*, meaning that the operator follows the variable. What's the difference? Often a variable is incremented within a statement that performs some other operation on it. For example

```
totalWeight = avgWeight * ++count;
```

The question here is this: Is the multiplication performed before or after count is incremented? In this case count is incremented first. How do we know that? Because prefix notation is used: ++count. If we had used postfix notation, count++, the multiplication would have been performed first, then count would have been incremented. This is shown in Figure 2.11.

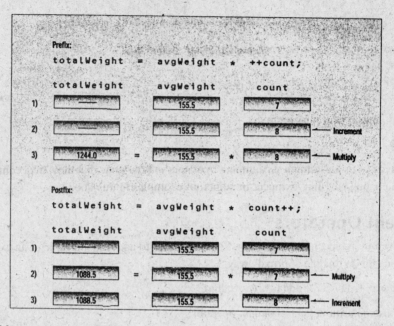

FIGURE 2.11
The increment operator.

Here's an example that shows both the prefix and postfix versions of the increment operator:

```
// increm.cpp
// demonstrates the increment operator
#include <iostream>
using namespace std;

int main()
   {
   int count = 10;

   cout << "count=" << count << endl;     //displays 10
   cout << "count=" << ++count << endl;   //displays 11 (prefix)
   cout << "count=" << count << endl;     //displays 11
   cout << "count=" << count++ << endl;   //displays 11 (postfix)
   cout << "count=" << count << endl;     //displays 12
   return 0;
   }
```

Here's the program's output:

```
count=10
count=11
```

```
count=11
count=11
count=12
```

The first time count is incremented, the prefix ++ operator is used. This causes the increment to happen at the beginning of the statement evaluation, before the output operation has been carried out. When the value of the expression ++count is displayed, it has already been incremented, and << sees the value 11. The second time count is incremented, the postfix ++ operator is used. When the expression count++ is displayed, it retains its unincremented value of 11. Following the completion of this statement, the increment takes effect, so that in the last statement of the program we see that count has acquired the value 12.

The Decrement (--) Operator

The decrement operator, --, behaves very much like the increment operator, except that it subtracts 1 from its operand. It too can be used in both prefix and postfix forms.

Library Functions

Many activities in C++ are carried out by *library functions*. These functions perform file access, mathematical computations, and data conversion, among other things. We don't want to dig too deeply into library functions before we explain how functions work (see Chapter 5), but you can use simple library functions without a thorough understanding of their operation.

The next example, SQRT, uses the library function sqrt() to calculate the square root of a number entered by the user.

```cpp
// sqrt.cpp
// demonstrates sqrt() library function
#include <iostream>            //for cout, etc.
#include <cmath>               //for sqrt()
using namespace std;

int main()
   {
   double number, answer;      //sqrt() requires type double

   cout << "Enter a number: ";
   cin >> number;              //get the number
   answer = sqrt(number);      //find square root
   cout << "Square root is "
     << answer << endl;        //display it
   return 0;
   }
```

The program first obtains a number from the user. This number is then used as an argument to the sqrt() function, in the statement

```
answer = sqrt(number);
```

An *argument* is the input to the function; it is placed inside the parentheses following the function name. The function then processes the argument and returns a value; this is the output from the function. In this case the return value is the square root of the original number. Returning a value means that the function expression takes on this value, which can then be assigned to another variable—in this case answer. The program then displays this value. Here's some output from the program:

```
Enter a number: 1000
Square root is 31.622777
```

Multiplying 31.622777 by itself on your pocket calculator will verify that this answer is pretty close.

The arguments to a function, and their return values, must be the correct data type. You can find what these data types are by looking at the description of the library function in your compiler's help file, which describes each of the hundreds of library functions. For sqrt(), the description specifies both an argument and a return value of type double, so we use variables of this type in the program.

Header Files

As with cout and other such objects, you must #include a header file that contains the declaration of any library functions you use. In the documentation for the sqrt() function, you'll see that the specified header file is CMATH. In SQRT the preprocessor directive

```
#include <cmath>
```

takes care of incorporating this header file into our source file.

If you don't include the appropriate header file when you use a library function, you'll get an error message like this from the compiler: *'sqrt' unidentified identifier*.

Library Files

We mentioned earlier that various files containing library functions and objects will be linked to your program to create an executable file. These files contain the actual machine-executable code for the functions. Such library files often have the extension .LIB. The sqrt() function is found in such a file. It is automatically extracted from the file by the linker, and the proper connections are made so that it can be called (that is, invoked or accessed) from the SQRT program. Your compiler takes care of all these details for you, so ordinarily you don't need to worry about the process. However, you should understand what these files are for.

Header Files and Library Files

The relationship between library files and header files can be confusing, so let's review it. To use a library function like sqrt(), you must link the library file that contains it to your program. The appropriate functions from the library file are then connected to your program by the linker.

However, that's not the end of the story. The functions in your source file need to know the names and types of the functions and other elements in the library file. They are given this information in a header file. Each header file contains information for a particular group of functions. The functions themselves are grouped together in a library file, but the information about them is scattered throughout a number of header files. The IOSTREAM header file contains information for various I/O functions and objects, including cout, while the CMATH header file contains information for mathematics functions such as sqrt(). If you were using string functions such as strcpy(), you would include STRING.H, and so on.

Figure 2.12 shows the relationship of header files and library files to the other files used in program development.

The use of header files is common in C++. Whenever you use a library function or a predefined object or operator, you will need to use a header file that contains appropriate declarations.

Two Ways to Use #include

You can use #include in two ways. The angle brackets < and > surrounding the filenames IOSTREAM and CMATH in the SQRT example indicate that the compiler should begin searching for these files in the standard INCLUDE directory. This directory, which is traditionally called INCLUDE, holds the header files supplied by the compiler manufacturer for the system.

Instead of angle brackets around the filename, you can also use quotation marks, as in

```
#include "myheader.h"
```

Quotation marks instruct the compiler to begin its search for the header file in the current directory; this is usually the directory that contains the source file. You normally use quotation marks for header files you write yourself (a situation we'll explore in Chapter 13, "Multifile Programs"). Quotation marks or angle brackets work in any case, but making the appropriate choice speeds up the compilation process slightly by giving the compiler a hint about where to find the file.

Appendix C, "Microsoft Visual C++," and Appendix D, "Borland C++Builder," explain how to handle header files with specific compilers.

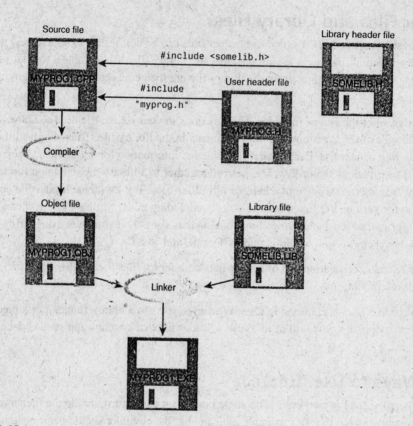

FIGURE 2.12
Header and library files.

Summary

In this chapter we've learned that a major building block of C++ programs is the *function*. A function named main() is always the first one executed when a program is executed.

A function is composed of *statements*, which tell the computer to do something. Each statement ends with a semicolon. A statement may contain one or more *expressions*, which are sequences of variables and operators that usually evaluate to a specific value.

Output is most commonly handled in C++ with the cout object and << insertion operator, which together cause variables or constants to be sent to the standard output device—usually the screen. Input is handled with cin and the extraction operator >>, which cause values to be received from the standard input device—usually the keyboard.

Various data types are built into C++: char, int, long, and short are the integer types and float, double, and long double are the floating-point types. All of these types are signed. Unsigned versions of the integer types, signaled by the keyword unsigned, don't hold negative numbers but hold positive ones twice as large. Type bool is used for Boolean variables and can hold only the constants true or false.

The const keyword stipulates that a variable's value will not change in the course of a program. Strictly speaking, the variable is no longer a variable but a constant.

A variable is automatically converted from one type to another in mixed expressions (those involving different data types) and by casting, which allows the programmer to specify a conversion.

C++ employs the usual arithmetic operators +, -, *, and /. In addition, the remainder operator, %, returns the remainder of integer division.

The arithmetic assignment operators +=, +-, and so on perform an arithmetic operation and an assignment simultaneously. The increment and decrement operators ++ and -- increase or decrease a variable by 1.

Preprocessor directives consist of instructions to the compiler, rather than to the computer. The #include directive tells the compiler to insert another file into the present source file, and the #define directive tells it to substitute one thing for another. The using directive tells the compiler to recognize names that are in a certain namespace.

If you use a library function in your program, the code for the function is in a library file, which is automatically linked to your program. A header file containing the function's declaration must be inserted into your source file with an #include statement.

Questions

Answers to these questions can be found in Appendix G.

1. Dividing a program into functions

    a. is the key to object-oriented programming.

    b. makes the program easier to conceptualize.

    c. may reduce the size of the program.

    d. makes the program run faster.

2. A function name must be followed by _____.

3. A function body is delimited by _____.

4. Why is the main() function special?

5. A C++ instruction that tells the computer to do something is called a _____.

6. Write an example of a normal C++ comment and an example of an old-fashioned /* comment.

7. An expression

   a. usually evaluates to a numerical value.

   b. indicates the emotional state of the program.

   c. always occurs outside a function.

   d. may be part of a statement.

8. Specify how many bytes are occupied by the following data types in a 32-bit system:

   a. Type `int`

   b. Type `long double`

   c. Type `float`

   d. Type `long`

9. True or false: A variable of type `char` can hold the value 301.

10. What kind of program elements are the following?

    a. 12

    b. 'a'

    c. 4.28915

    d. `JungleJim`

    e. `JungleJim()`

11. Write statements that display on the screen

    a. the character 'x'

    b. the name *Jim*

    c. the number 509

12. True or false: In an assignment statement, the value on the left of the equal sign is always equal to the value on the right.

13. Write a statement that displays the variable `george` in a field 10 characters wide.

14. What header file must you #include with your source file to use `cout` and `cin`?

15. Write a statement that gets a numerical value from the keyboard and places it in the variable `temp`.

16. What header file must you #include with your program to use `setw`?

17. Two exceptions to the rule that the compiler ignores whitespace are _____ and _____.

18. True or false: It's perfectly all right to use variables of different data types in the same arithmetic expression.

19. The expression 11%3 evaluates to _____.

20. An arithmetic assignment operator combines the effect of what two operators?

21. Write a statement that uses an arithmetic assignment operator to increase the value of the variable temp by 23. Write the same statement without the arithmetic assignment operator.

22. The increment operator increases the value of a variable by how much?

23. Assuming var1 starts with the value 20, what will the following code fragment print out?
```
cout << var1--;
cout << ++var1;
```

24. In the examples we've seen so far, header files have been used for what purpose?

25. The actual code for library functions is contained in a _____ file.

Exercises

Answers to the starred exercises can be found in Appendix G.

*1. Assuming there are 7.481 gallons in a cubic foot, write a program that asks the user to enter a number of gallons, and then displays the equivalent in cubic feet.

*2. Write a program that generates the following table:
```
1990      135
1991     7290
1992    11300
1993    16200
```
Use a single cout statement for all output.

*3. Write a program that generates the following output:
```
10
20
19
```
Use an integer constant for the 10, an arithmetic assignment operator to generate the 20, and a decrement operator to generate the 19.

4. Write a program that displays your favorite poem. Use an appropriate escape sequence for the line breaks. If you don't have a favorite poem, you can borrow this one by Ogden Nash:
```
Candy is dandy,
But liquor is quicker.
```

5. A library function, `islower()`, takes a single character (a letter) as an argument and returns a nonzero integer if the letter is lowercase, or zero if it is uppercase. This function requires the header file CTYPE.H. Write a program that allows the user to enter a letter, and then displays either zero or nonzero, depending on whether a lowercase or uppercase letter was entered. (See the SQRT program for clues.)

6. On a certain day the British pound was equivalent to $1.487 U.S., the French franc was $0.172, the German deutschemark was $0.584, and the Japanese yen was $0.00955. Write a program that allows the user to enter an amount in dollars, and then displays this value converted to these four other monetary units.

7. You can convert temperature from degrees Celsius to degrees Fahrenheit by multiplying by 9/5 and adding 32. Write a program that allows the user to enter a floating-point number representing degrees Celsius, and then displays the corresponding degrees Fahrenheit.

8. When a value is smaller than a field specified with `setw()`, the unused locations are, by default, filled in with spaces. The manipulator `setfill()` takes a single character as an argument and causes this character to be substituted for spaces in the empty parts of a field. Rewrite the WIDTH program so that the characters on each line between the location name and the population number are filled in with periods instead of spaces, as in

```
Portcity.....2425785
```

9. If you have two fractions, a/b and c/d, their sum can be obtained from the formula

```
 a     c     a*d + b*c
 --- + -.- = -----------
 b     d        b*d
```

For example, 1/4 plus 2/3 is

```
 1     2     1*3 + 4*2      3 + 8      11
 --- + -.- = ----------- = ------- = ----
 4     3        4*3          12       12
```

Write a program that encourages the user to enter two fractions, and then displays their sum in fractional form. (You don't need to reduce it to lowest terms.) The interaction with the user might look like this:

```
Enter first fraction: 1/2
   Enter second fraction: 2/5
   Sum = 9/10
```

You can take advantage of the fact that the extraction operator (>>) can be chained to read in more than one quantity at once:

```
cin >> a >> dummychar >> b;
```

10. In the heyday of the British empire, Great Britain used a monetary system based on pounds, shillings, and pence. There were 20 shillings to a pound, and 12 pence to a shilling. The notation for this old system used the pound sign, £, and two decimal points, so that, for example, £5.2.8 meant 5 pounds, 2 shillings, and 8 pence. (*Pence* is the plural of *penny*.) The new monetary system, introduced in the 1950s, consists of only pounds and pence, with 100 pence to a pound (like U.S. dollars and cents). We'll call this new system *decimal pounds*. Thus £5.2.8 in the old notation is £5.13 in decimal pounds (actually £5.1333333). Write a program to convert the old pounds-shillings-pence format to decimal pounds. An example of the user's interaction with the program would be

```
Enter pounds: 7
Enter shillings: 17
Enter pence: 9
Decimal pounds = £7.89
```

In most compilers you can use the decimal number 156 (hex character constant '\x9c') to represent the pound sign (£). In some compilers, you can put the pound sign into your program directly by pasting it from the Windows Character Map accessory.

11. By default, output is right-justified in its field. You can left-justify text output using the manipulator `setiosflags(ios::left)`. (For now, don't worry about what this new notation means.) Use this manipulator, along with `setw()`, to help generate the following output:

```
Last name   First name   Street address      Town        State
...............................................................
Jones       Bernard      109 Pine Lane       Littletown  MI
O'Brian     Coleen       42 E. 99th Ave.     Bigcity     NY
Wong        Harry        121-A Alabama St.   Lakeville   IL
```

12. Write the inverse of Exercise 10, so that the user enters an amount in Great Britain's new decimal-pounds notation (pounds and pence), and the program converts it to the old pounds-shillings-pence notation. An example of interaction with the program might be

```
Enter decimal pounds: 3.51
Equivalent in old notation = £3.10.2.
```

Make use of the fact that if you assign a floating-point value (say 12.34) to an integer variable, the decimal fraction (0.34) is lost; the integer value is simply 12. Use a cast to avoid a compiler warning. You can use statements like

```
float decpounds;     // input from user (new-style pounds)
int pounds;          // old-style (integer) pounds
float decfrac;       // decimal fraction (smaller than 1.0)
```

```
pounds = static_cast<int>(decpounds); // remove decimal fraction
decfrac = decpounds - pounds;  // regain decimal fraction
```

You can then multiply `decfrac` by 20 to find shillings. A similar operation obtains pence.

Loops and Decisions

IN THIS CHAPTER

Not many programs execute all their statements in strict order from beginning to end. Most programs (like many humans) decide what to do in response to changing circumstances. The flow of control jumps from one part of the program to another, depending on calculations performed in the program. Program statements that cause such jumps are called *control statements*. There are two major categories: loops and decisions.

How many times a loop is executed, or whether a decision results in the execution of a section of code, depends on whether certain expressions are true or false. These expressions typically involve a kind of operator called a *relational operator*, which compares two values. Since the operation of loops and decisions is so closely involved with these operators, we'll examine them first.

Relational Operators

A relational operator compares two values. The values can be any built-in C++ data type, such as char, int, and float, or—as we'll see later—they can be user-defined classes. The comparison involves such relationships as equal to, less than, and greater than. The result of the comparison is true or false; for example, either two values are equal (true), or they're not (false).

Our first program, RELAT, demonstrates relational operators in a comparison of integer variables and constants.

```
// relat.cpp
// demonstrates relational operators
#include <iostream>
using namespace std;

int main()
   {
   int numb;

   cout << "Enter a number: ";
   cin >> numb;
   cout << "numb<10  is " << (numb < 10)  << endl;
   cout << "numb>10  is " << (numb > 10)  << endl;
   cout << "numb==10 is " << (numb == 10) << endl;
   return 0;
   }
```

This program performs three kinds of comparisons between 10 and a number entered by the user. Here's the output when the user enters 20:

```
Enter a number: 20
numb<10  is 0
numb>10  is 1
numb==10 is 0
```

The first expression is true if numb is less than 10. The second expression is true if numb is greater than 10, and the third is true if numb is equal to 10. As you can see from the output, the C++ compiler considers that a true expression has the value 1, while a false expression has the value 0.

As we mentioned in the last chapter, Standard C++ includes a type bool, which can hold one of two constant values, true or false. You might think that results of relational expressions like numb<10 would be of type bool, and that the program would print false instead of 0 and true instead of 1. In fact, C++ is rather schizophrenic on this point. Displaying the results of relational operations, or even the values of type bool variables, with cout<< yields 0 or 1, not false or true. Historically this is because C++ started out with no bool type. Before the advent of Standard C++, the *only* way to express false and true was with 0 and 1. Now false can be represented by either a bool value of false, or by an integer value of 0; and true can be represented by either a bool value of true or an integer value of 1.

In most simple situations the difference isn't apparent because we don't need to *display* true/false values; we just *use* them in loops and decisions to influence what the program will do next.

Here's the complete list of C++ relational operators:

Operator	Meaning
>	Greater than (greater than)
<	Less than
==	Equal to
!=	Not equal to
>=	Greater than or equal to
<=	Less than or equal to

Now let's look at some expressions that use relational operators, and also look at the value of each expression. The first two lines are assignment statements that set the values of the variables harry and jane. You might want to hide the comments with your old Jose Canseco baseball card and see whether you can predict which expressions evaluate to true and which to false.

```
jane = 44;          //assignment statement
harry = 12;         //assignment statement
(jane == harry)     //false
(harry <= 12)       //true
(jane > harry)      //true
(jane >= 44)        //true
(harry != 12)       // false
(7 < harry)         //true
(0)                 //false (by definition)
(44)                //true (since it's not 0)
```

Note that the equal operator, ==, uses two equal signs. A common mistake is to use a single equal sign—the assignment operator—as a relational operator. This is a nasty bug, since the compiler may not notice anything wrong. However, your program won't do what you want (unless you're very lucky).

Although C++ generates a 1 to indicate true, it assumes that any value other than 0 (such as –7 or 44) is true; only 0 is false. Thus, the last expression in the list is true.

Now let's see how these operators are used in typical situations. We'll examine loops first, then decisions.

Loops

Loops cause a section of your program to be repeated a certain number of times. The repetition continues while a condition is true. When the condition becomes false, the loop ends and control passes to the statements following the loop.

There are three kinds of loops in C++: the for loop, the while loop, and the do loop.

The for Loop

The for loop is (for many people, anyway) the easiest C++ loop to understand. All its loop-control elements are gathered in one place, while in the other loop constructions they are scattered about the program, which can make it harder to unravel how these loops work.

The for loop executes a section of code a fixed number of times. It's usually (although not always) used when you know, before entering the loop, how many times you want to execute the code.

Here's an example, FORDEMO, that displays the squares of the numbers from 0 to 14:

```cpp
// fordemo.cpp
// demonstrates simple FOR loop
#include <iostream>
using namespace std;

int main()
   {
   int j;                     //define a loop variable

   for(j=0; j<15; j++)        //loop from 0 to 14,
      cout << j * j << " ";   //displaying the square of j
   cout << endl;
   return 0;
   }
```

Here's the output:

```
0  1  4  9  16  25  36  49  64  81  100  121  144  169  196
```

How does this work? The for statement controls the loop. It consists of the keyword for, followed by parentheses that contain three expressions separated by semicolons:

```
for(j=0; j<15; j++)
```

These three expressions are the *initialization expression*, the *test expression*, and the *increment expression*, as shown in Figure 3.1.

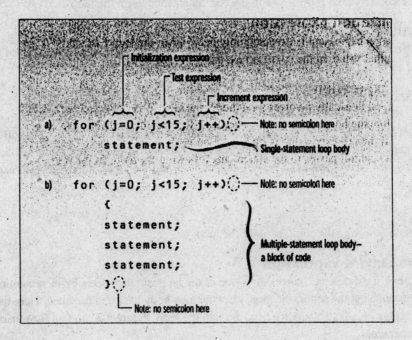

FIGURE 3.1
Syntax of the for loop.

These three expressions usually (but not always) involve the same variable, which we call the *loop variable*. In the FORDEMO example the loop variable is j. It's defined before the statements within the loop body start to execute.

The *body* of the loop is the code to be executed each time through the loop. Repeating this code is the raison d'être for the loop. In this example the loop body consists of a single statement:

```
cout << j * j << "  ";
```

This statement prints out the square of j, followed by two spaces. The square is found by multiplying j by itself. As the loop executes, j goes through the sequence 0, 1, 2, 3, and so on up to 14; so the squares of these numbers are displayed—0, 1, 4, 9, up to 196.

Note that the for statement is not followed by a semicolon. That's because the for statement and the loop body are together considered to be a program statement. This is an important detail. If you put a semicolon after the for statement, the compiler will think there is no loop body, and the program will do things you probably don't expect.

Let's see how the three expressions in the for statement control the loop.

The Initialization Expression

The initialization expression is executed only once, when the loop first starts. It gives the loop variable an initial value. In the FORDEMO example it sets j to 0.

The Test Expression

The test expression usually involves a relational operator. It is evaluated each time through the loop, just before the body of the loop is executed. It determines whether the loop will be executed again. If the test expression is true, the loop is executed one more time. If it's false, the loop ends, and control passes to the statements following the loop. In the FORDEMO example the statement

```
cout << endl;
```

is executed following the completion of the loop.

The Increment Expression

The increment expression changes the value of the loop variable, often by incrementing it. It is always executed at the end of the loop, after the loop body has been executed. Here the increment operator ++ adds 1 to j each time through the loop. Figure 3.2 shows a flowchart of a for loop's operation.

How Many Times?

The loop in the FORDEMO example executes exactly 15 times. The first time, j is 0. This is ensured in the initialization expression. The last time through the loop, j is 14. This is determined by the test expression j<15. When j becomes 15, the loop terminates; the loop body is not executed when j has this value. The arrangement shown is commonly used to do something a fixed number of times: start at 0, use a test expression with the less-than operator and a value equal to the desired number of iterations, and increment the loop variable after each iteration.

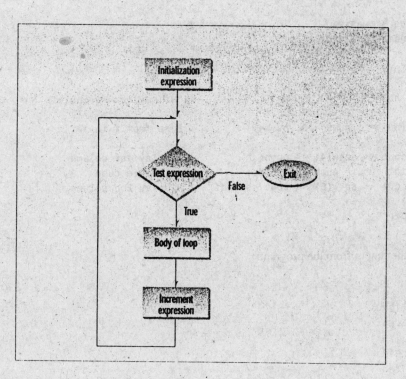

FIGURE 3.2
Operation of the for *loop.*

Here's another for loop example:

```
for(count=0; count<100; count++)
   // loop body
```

How many times will the loop body be repeated here? Exactly 100 times, with count going
from 0 to 99.

Multiple Statements in the Loop Body

Of course you may want to execute more than one statement in the loop body. Multiple statements are delimited by braces, just as functions are. Note that there is no semicolon following
the final brace of the loop body, although there are semicolons following the individual statements in the loop body.

The next example, CUBELIST, uses three statements in the loop body. It prints out the cubes of
the numbers from 1 to 10, using a two-column format.

```
// cubelist.cpp
// lists cubes from 1 to 10
#include <iostream>
```

```
#include <iomanip>                        //for setw
using namespace std;

int main()
   {
   int numb;                              //define loop variable .

   for(numb=1; numb<=10; numb++)          //loop from 1 to 10
      {
      cout << setw(4) << numb;            //display 1st column
      int cube = numb*numb*numb;          //calculate cube
      cout << setw(6) << cube << endl;    //display 2nd column
      }
   return 0;
   }
```

Here's the output from the program:

```
 1     1
 2     8
 3    27
 4    64
 5   125
 6   216
 7   343
 8   512
 9   729
10  1000
```

We've made another change in the program to show there's nothing immutable about the format used in the last example. The loop variable is initialized to 1, not to 0, and it ends at 10, not at 9, by virtue of <=, the less-than-or-equal-to operator. The effect is that the loop body is executed 10 times, with the loop variable running from 1 to 10 (not from 0 to 9).

We should note that you : .: .lso put braces around the single statement loop body shown previously. They're not n.: .ssary, but many programmers feel it improves clarity to use them whether the loop body consists of a single statement or not.

Blocks and Variable Visibility

The loop body, which consists of braces delimiting several statements, is called a *block* of code. One important aspect of a block is that a variable defined inside the block is not visible outside it. *Visible* means that program statements can access or "see" the variable. (We'll discuss visibility further in Chapter 5, "Functions.") In CUBELIST we define the variable cube inside the block, in the statement

```
int cube = numb*numb*numb;
```

You can't access this variable outside the block; it's only visible within the braces. Thus if you placed the statement

```
cube = 10;
```

after the loop body, the compiler would signal an error because the variable cube would be undefined outside the loop.

One advantage of restricting the visibility of variables is that the same variable name can be used within different blocks in the same program. (Defining variables inside a block, as we did in CUBELIST, is common in C++ but is not popular in C.)

Indentation and Loop Style

Good programming style dictates that the loop body be indented—that is, shifted right, relative to the loop statement (and to the rest of the program). In the FORDEMO example one line is indented, and in CUBELIST the entire block, including the braces, is indented. This indentation is an important visual aid to the programmer: It makes it easy to see where the loop body begins and ends. The compiler doesn't care whether you indent or not (at least there's no way to tell if it cares).

There is a common variation on the style we use for loops in this book. We show the braces aligned vertically, but some programmers prefer to place the opening brace just after the loop statement, like this:

```
for(numb=1; numb<=10; numb++)  {
   cout << setw(4) << numb;
   int cube = numb*numb*numb;
   cout << setw(6) << cube << endl;
   }
```

This saves a line in the listing but makes it more difficult to read, since the opening brace is harder to see and harder to match with the corresponding closing brace. Another style is to indent the body but not the braces:

```
for(numb=1; numb<=10; numb++)
{
   cout << setw(4) << numb;
   int cube = numb*numb*numb;
   cout << setw(6) << cube << endl;
}
```

This is a common approach, but at least for some people it makes it harder for the eye to connect the braces to the loop body. However, you can get used to almost anything. Whatever style you choose, use it consistently.

Debugging Animation

You can use the debugging features built into your compiler to create a dramatic animated display of loop operation. The key feature is *single-stepping*. Your compiler makes this easy. Start by opening a project for the program to be debugged, and a window containing the source file. The exact instructions necessary to launch the debugger vary with different compilers, so consult Appendix C, "Microsoft Visual C++," or Appendix D, "Borland C++Builder," as appropriate. By pressing a certain function key you can cause one line of your program to be executed at a time. This will show you the sequence of statements executed as the program proceeds. In a loop you'll see the statements within the loop executed; then control will jump back to the start of the loop and the cycle will be repeated.

You can also use the debugger to watch what happens to the values of different variables as you single-step through the program. This is a powerful tool when you're debugging your program. You can experiment with this technique with the CUBELIST program by putting the numb and cube variables in a *Watch window* in your debugger and seeing how they change as the program proceeds. Again, consult the appropriate appendix for instructions on how to use Watch windows.

Single-stepping and the Watch window are powerful debugging tools. If your program doesn't behave as you think it should, you can use these features to monitor the values of key variables as you step through the program. Usually the source of the problem will become clear.

for Loop Variations

The increment expression doesn't need to increment the loop variable; it can perform any operation it likes. In the next example it *decrements* the loop variable. This program, FACTOR, asks the user to type in a number, and then calculates the factorial of this number. (The factorial is calculated by multiplying the original number by all the positive integers smaller than itself. Thus the factorial of 5 is 5*4*3*2*1, or 120.)

```cpp
// factor.cpp
// calculates factorials, demonstrates FOR loop
#include <iostream>
using namespace std;

int main()
   {
   unsigned int numb;
   unsigned long fact=1;               //long for larger numbers

   cout << "Enter a number: ";
   cin >> numb;                        //get number
```

```
for(int j=numb; j>0; j--)          //multiply 1 by
    fact *= j;                     //numb, numb-1, ..., 2, 1
cout << "Factorial is " << fact << endl;
return 0;
}
```

In this example the initialization expression sets j to the value entered by the user. The test expression causes the loop to execute as long as j is greater than 0. The increment expression decrements j after each iteration.

We've used type unsigned long for the factorial, since the factorials of even small numbers are very large. On 32-bit systems such as Windows int is the same as long, but long gives added capacity on 16-bit systems. The following output shows how large factorials can be, even for small input numbers:

```
Enter a number: 10
Factorial is 3628800
```

The largest number you can use for input is 12. You won't get an error message for larger inputs, but the results will be wrong, as the capacity of type long will be exceeded.

Variables Defined in for Statements

There's another wrinkle in this program: The loop variable j is defined inside the for statement:

```
for(int j=numb; j>0; j--)
```

This is a common construction in C++, and in most cases it's the best approach to loop variables. It defines the variable as closely as possible to its point of use in the listing. Variables defined in the loop statement this way are visible in the loop body only. (The Microsoft compiler makes them visible from the point of definition onward to the end of the file, but this is not Standard C++.)

Multiple Initialization and Test Expressions

You can put more than one expression in the initialization part of the for statement, separating the different expressions by commas. You can also have more than one increment expression. You can have only one test expression. Here's an example:

```
for( j=0, alpha=100; j<50; j++, beta-- )
    {
    // body of loop
    }
```

This example has a normal loop variable j, but it also initializes another variable, alpha, and decrements a third, beta. The variables alpha and beta don't need to have anything to do with each other, or with j. Multiple initialization expressions and multiple increment expressions are separated by commas.

Actually, you can leave out some or all of the expressions if you want to. The expression

```
for(;;)
```

is the same as a while loop with a test expression of true. We'll look at while loops next.

We'll avoid using such multiple or missing expressions. While these approaches can make the listing more concise, they also tend to decrease its readability. It's always possible to use stand-alone statements or a different form of loop to achieve the same effect.

The while Loop

The for loop does something a fixed number of times. What happens if you don't know how many times you want to do something before you start the loop? In this case a different kind of loop may be used: the while loop.

The next example, ENDON0, asks the user to enter a series of numbers. When the number entered is 0, the loop terminates. Notice that there's no way for the program to know in advance how many numbers will be typed before the 0 appears; that's up to the user.

```
// endon0.cpp
// demonstrates WHILE loop
#include <iostream>
using namespace std;

int main()
   {
   int n = 99;        // make sure n isn't initialized to 0

   while( n != 0 )    // loop until n is 0
      cin >> n;       // read a number into n
   cout << endl;
   return 0;
   }
```

Here's some sample output. The user enters numbers, and the loop continues until 0 is entered, at which point the loop and the program terminate.

```
1
27
33
144
9
0
```

The while loop looks like a simplified version of the for loop. It contains a test expression but no initialization or increment expressions. Figure 3.3 shows the syntax of the while loop.

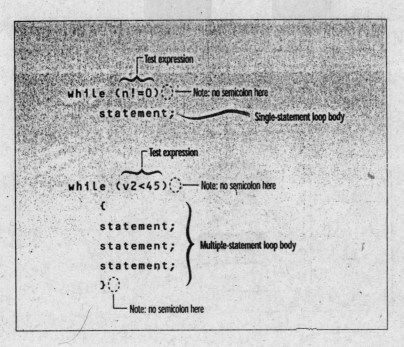

FIGURE 3.3
Syntax of the while *loop.*

As long as the test expression is true, the loop continues to be executed. In ENDON0, the text expression

n != 0

(n not equal to 0) is true until the user enters 0.

Figure 3.4 shows the operation of a while loop. The simplicity of the while loop is a bit illusory. Although there is no initialization expression, the loop variable (n in ENDON0) must be initialized before the loop begins. The loop body must also contain some statement that changes the value of the loop variable; otherwise the loop would never end. In ENDON0 it's cin>>n;.

Multiple Statements in a while Loop

The next example, WHILE4, uses multiple statements in a while loop. It's a variation of the CUBELIST program shown earlier with a for loop, but it calculates the fourth power, instead of the cube, of a series of integers. Let's assume that in this program it's important to put the results in a column four digits wide. To ensure that the results fit this column width, we must stop the loop before the results become larger than 9999. Without prior calculation we don't know what number will generate a result of this size, so we let the program figure it out. The test expression in the while statement terminates the program before the powers become too large.

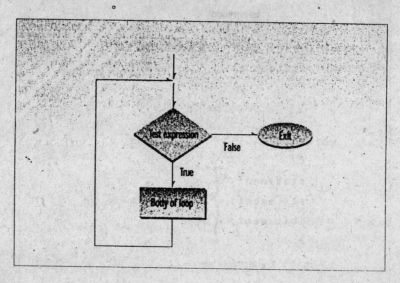

FIGURE 3.4
Operation of the while loop.

```cpp
// while4.cpp
// prints numbers raised to fourth power
#include <iostream>
#include <iomanip>                    //for setw
using namespace std;

int main()
    {
    int pow=1;                        //power initially 1
    int numb=1;                       //numb goes from 1 to ???

    while( pow<10000 )                //loop while power <= 4 digits
        {
        cout << setw(2) << numb;      //display number
        cout << setw(5) << pow << endl; //display fourth power
        ++numb;                       //get ready for next power
        pow = numb*numb*numb*numb;    //calculate fourth power
        }
    cout << endl;
    return 0;
    }
```

To find the fourth power of numb, we simply multiply it by itself four times. Each time through the loop we increment numb. But we don't use numb in the test expression in while; instead, the resulting value of pow determines when to terminate the loop. Here's the output:

```
1    1
2   16
3   81
4  256
5  625
6 1296
7 2401
8 4096
9 6561
```

The next number would be 10,000—too wide for our four-digit column; but by this time the loop has terminated.

Precedence: Arithmetic and Relational Operators

The next program touches on the question of operator precedence. It generates the famous sequence of numbers called the *Fibonacci series*. Here are the first few terms of the series:

```
1  1  2  3  5  8  13  21  34  55
```

Each term is found by adding the two previous ones: 1+1 is 2, 1+2 is 3, 2+3 is 5, 3+5 is 8, and so on. The Fibonacci series has applications in amazingly diverse fields, from sorting methods in computer science to the number of spirals in sunflowers.

One of the most interesting aspects of the Fibonacci series is its relation to the golden ratio. The golden ratio is supposed to be the ideal proportion in architecture and art, and was used in the design of ancient Greek temples. As the Fibonacci series is carried out further and further, the ratio of the last two terms approaches closer and closer to the golden ratio. Here's the listing for FIBO.CPP:

```cpp
// fibo.cpp
// demonstrates WHILE loops using fibonacci series
#include <iostream>
using namespace std;

int main()
   {                               //largest unsigned long
   const unsigned long limit = 4294967295;
   unsigned long next=0;           //next-to-last term
   unsigned long last=1;           //last term
```

```
    while( next < limit / 2 )    //don't let results get too big
       {
       cout << last << " ";      //display last term
       long sum = next + last;   //add last two terms
       next = last;              //variables move forward
       last = sum;               //    in the series
       }
    cout << endl;
    return 0;
    }
```

Here's the output:

```
1  1  2  3  5  8  13  21  34  55  89  144  233  377  610  987
1597  2584  4181  6765  10946  17711  28657  46368  75025  121393
196418  317811  514229  832040  1346269  2178309  3524578
5702887  9227465  14930352  24157817  39088169  63245986
102334155  165580141  267914296  433494437  701408733  1134903170
1836311903  2971215073
```

For you temple builders, the ratio of the last two terms gives an approximation of the golden ratio as 0.618033988—close enough for government work.

The FIBO program uses type unsigned long, the type that holds the largest positive integers. The test expression in the while statement terminates the loop before the numbers exceed the limit of this type. We define this limit as a const type, since it doesn't change. We must stop when next becomes larger than half the limit; otherwise, sum would exceed the limit.

The test expression uses two operators:

```
(next < limit / 2)
```

Our intention is to compare next with the result of limit/2. That is, we want the division to be performed before the comparison. We could put parentheses around the division, to ensure that it's performed first.

```
(next < (limit/2) )
```

But we don't need the parentheses. Why not? Because arithmetic operators have a higher precedence than relational operators. This guarantees that limit/2 will be evaluated before the comparison is made, even without the parentheses. We'll summarize the precedence situation later in this chapter, when we look at logical operators.

The do Loop

In a while loop, the test expression is evaluated at the *beginning* of the loop. If the test expression is false when the loop is entered, the loop body won't be executed at all. In some situations this is what you want. But sometimes you want to guarantee that the loop body is executed at least once, no matter what the initial state of the test expression. When this is the case you should use the do loop, which places the test expression at the *end* of the loop.

Our example, DIVDO, invites the user to enter two numbers: a dividend (the top number in a division) and a divisor (the bottom number). It then calculates the quotient (the answer) and the remainder, using the / and % operators, and prints out the result.

```
// divdo.cpp
// demonstrates DO loop
#include <iostream>
using namespace std;

int main()
   {
   long dividend, divisor;
   char ch;

   do                                       //start of do loop
      {                                      //do some processing
      cout << "Enter dividend: "; cin >> dividend;
      cout << "Enter divisor: ";  cin >> divisor;
      cout << "Quotient is " << dividend / divisor;
      cout << ", remainder is " << dividend % divisor;

      cout << "\nDo another? (y/n): ";  //do it again?
      cin >> ch;
      }
   while( ch != 'n' );                       //loop condition
   return 0;
   }
```

Most of this program resides within the do loop. First, the keyword do marks the beginning of the loop. Then, as with the other loops, braces delimit the body of the loop. Finally, a while statement provides the test expression and terminates the loop. This while statement looks much like the one in a while loop, except for its position at the end of the loop and the fact that it ends with a semicolon (which is easy to forget!). The syntax of the do loop is shown in Figure 3.5.

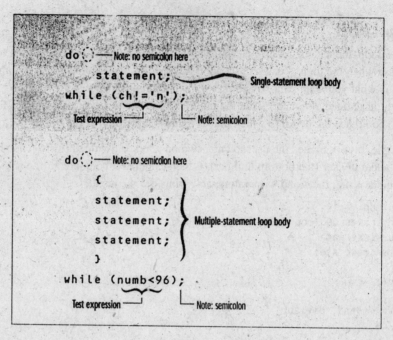

FIGURE 3.5
Syntax of the do loop.

Following each computation, DIVDO asks if the user wants to do another. If so, the user enters a 'y' character, and the test expression

```
ch != 'n'
```

remains true. If the user enters 'n', the test expression becomes false and the loop terminates. Figure 3.6 charts the operation of the do loop. Here's an example of DIVDO's output:

```
Enter dividend: 11
Enter divisor: 3
Quotient is 3, remainder is 2
Do another? (y/n): y
Enter dividend: 222
Enter divisor: 17
Quotient is 13, remainder is 1
Do another? (y/n): n
```

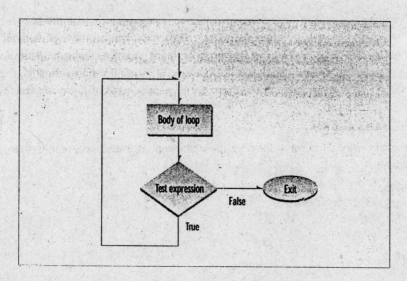

FIGURE 3.6
Operation of the do loop.

When to Use Which Loop

We've made some general statements about how loops are used. The for loop is appropriate when you know in advance how many times the loop will be executed. The while and do loops are used when you don't know in advance when the loop will terminate (the while loop when you may not want to execute the loop body even once, and the do loop when you're sure you want to execute the loop body at least once).

These criteria are somewhat arbitrary. Which loop type to use is more a matter of style than of hard-and-fast rules. You can actually make any of the loop types work in almost any situation. You should choose the type that makes your program the clearest and easiest to follow.

Decisions

The decisions in a loop always relate to the same question: Should we do this (the loop body) again? As humans we would find it boring to be so limited in our decision-making processes. We need to decide not only whether to go to work again today (continuing the loop), but also whether to buy a red shirt or a green one (or no shirt at all), whether to take a vacation, and if so, in the mountains or by the sea.

Programs also need to make these one-time decisions. In a program a decision causes a one-time jump to a different part of the program, depending on the value of an expression.

Decisions can be made in C++ in several ways. The most important is with the `if...else` statement, which chooses between two alternatives. This statement can be used without the `else`, as a simple `if` statement. Another decision statement, `switch`, creates branches for multiple alternative sections of code, depending on the value of a single variable. Finally, the conditional operator is used in specialized situations. We'll examine each of these constructions.

The `if` Statement

The `if` statement is the simplest of the decision statements. Our next program, IFDEMO, provides an example.

```
// ifdemo.cpp
// demonstrates IF statement
#include <iostream>
using namespace std;

int main()
   {
   int x;

   cout << "Enter a number: ";
   cin >> x;
   if( x > 100 )
      cout << "That number is greater than 100\n";
   return 0;
   }
```

The `if` keyword is followed by a test expression in parentheses. The syntax of the `if` statement is shown in Figure 3.7. As you can see, the syntax of `if` is very much like that of `while`. The difference is that the statements following the `if` are executed only once if the test expression is true; the statements following `while` are executed repeatedly until the test expression becomes false. Figure 3.8 shows the operation of the `if` statement.

Here's an example of the IFDEMO program's output when the number entered by the user is greater than 100:

```
Enter a number: 2000
That number is greater than 100
```

If the number entered is not greater than 100, the program will terminate without printing the second line.

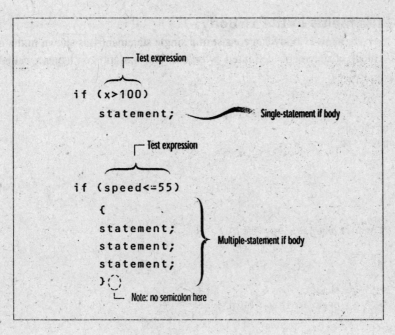

FIGURE 3.7

Syntax of the if statement.

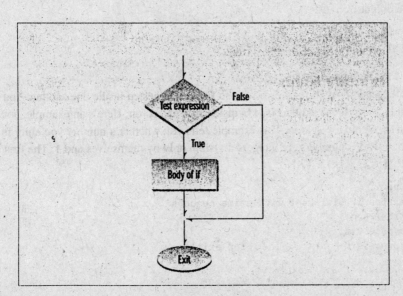

FIGURE 3.8

Operation of the if statement.

Multiple Statements in the `if` Body

As in loops, the code in an `if` body can consist of a single statement—as shown in the IFDEMO example—or a block of statements delimited by braces. This variation on IFDEMO, called IF2, shows how that looks.

```cpp
// if2.cpp
// demonstrates IF with multiline body
#include <iostream>
using namespace std;

int main()
   {
   int x;

   cout << "Enter a number: ";
   cin >> x;
   if( x > 100 )
      {
      cout << "The number " << x;
      cout << " is greater than 100\n";
      }
   return 0;
   }
```

Here's some output from IF2:

```
Enter a number: 12345
The number 12345 is greater than 100
```

Nesting `if`s Inside Loops

The loop and decision structures we've seen so far can be nested inside one another. You can nest `if`s inside loops, loops inside `if`s, `if`s inside `if`s, and so on. Here's an example, PRIME, that nests an `if` within a `for` loop. This example tells you whether a number you enter is a prime number. (Prime numbers are integers divisible only by themselves and 1. The first few primes are 2, 3, 5, 7, 11, 13, 17.)

```cpp
// prime.cpp
// demonstrates IF statement with prime numbers
#include <iostream>
using namespace std;
#include <process.h>                //for exit()

int main()
   {
   unsigned long n, j;
```

```
    cout << "Enter a number: ";
    cin >> n;                        //get number to test
    for(j=2; j <= n/2; j++)          //divide by .every integer from
       if(n%j == 0)                  //2 on up;.if remainder is 0,
          {                          //it's divisible by j
          cout << "It's not prime; divisible by " << j << endl;
          exit(0);                   //exit from the program
          }
    cout << "It's prime\n";
    return 0;
    }
```

In this example the user enters a number that is assigned to n. The program then uses a for loop to divide n by all the numbers from 2 up to n/2. The divisor is j, the loop variable. If any value of j divides evenly into n, then n is not prime. When a number divides evenly into another, the remainder is 0; we use the remainder operator % in the if statement to test for this condition with each value of j. If the number is not prime, we tell the user and we exit from the program.

Here's output from three separate invocations of the program:

```
Enter a number: 13
It's prime
Enter a number: 22229
It's prime
Enter a number: 22231
It's not prime; divisible by 11
```

Notice that there are no braces around the loop body. This is because the if statement, and the statements in its body, are considered to be a single statement. If you like you can insert braces for readability, even though the compiler doesn't need them.

Library Function exit()

When PRIME discovers that a number is not prime, it exits immediately, since there's no use proving more than once that a number isn't prime. This is accomplished with the library function exit(). This function causes the program to terminate, no matter where it is in the listing. It has no return value. Its single argument, 0 in our example, is returned to the operating system when the program exits. (This value is useful in batch files, where you can use the ERRORLEVEL value to query the return value provided by exit(). The value 0 is normally used for a successful termination; other numbers indicate errors.)

The `if...else` Statement

The `if` statement lets you do something if a condition is true. If it isn't true, nothing happens. But suppose we want to do one thing if a condition is true, and do something else if it's false. That's where the `if...else` statement comes in. It consists of an `if` statement, followed by a statement or block of statements, followed by the keyword `else`, followed by *another* statement or block of statements. The syntax is shown in Figure 3.9.

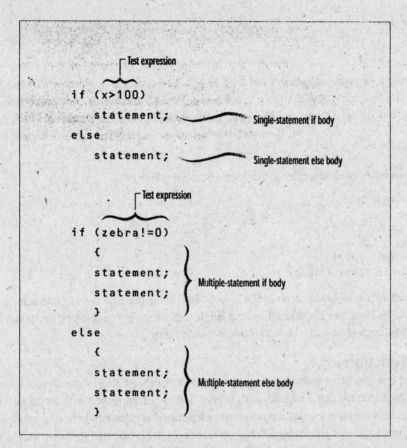

FIGURE 3.9
Syntax of the `if...else` statement.

Here's a variation of our IF example, with an `else` added to the `if`:

```
// ifelse.cpp
// demonstrates IF...ELSE statememt
#include <iostream>
using namespace std;
```

```cpp
int main()
   {
   int x;

   cout << "\nEnter a number: ";
   cin >> x;
   if( x > 100 )
      cout << "That number is greater than 100\n";
   else
      cout << "That number is not greater than 100\n";
   return 0;
   }
```

If the test expression in the if statement is true, the program prints one message; if it isn't, it prints the other.

Here's output from two different invocations of the program:

```
Enter a number: 300
That number is greater than 100
Enter a number: 3
That number is not greater than 100
```

The operation of the if...else statement is shown in Figure 3.10.

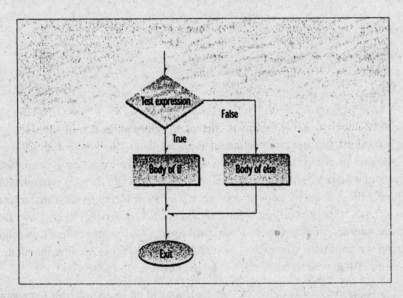

FIGURE 3.10
Operation of the if...else *statement.*

The `getche()` Library Function

Our next example shows an `if...else` statement embedded in a `while` loop. It also introduces a new library function: `getche()`. This program, CHCOUNT, counts the number of words and the number of characters in a phrase typed in by the user.

```
// chcount..cpp
// counts characters and words typed in
#include <iostream>
using namespace std;
#include <conio.h>              //for getche()

int main()
   {
   int chcount=0;              //counts non-space characters
   int wdcount=1;              //counts spaces between words
   char ch = 'a';             //ensure it isn't '\r'

   cout << "Enter a phrase: ";
   while( ch != '\r' )         //loop until Enter typed
      {
      ch = getche();          //read one character
      if( ch==' ' )           //if it's a space
      wdcount++;              //count a word
      else                    //otherwise,
      chcount++;             //count a character
      }                       //display results
   cout << "\nWords=" << wdcount << endl
        << "Letters=" << (chcount-1) << endl;
   return 0;
   }
```

So far we've used only `cin` and `>>` for input. That approach requires that the user always press the Enter key to inform the program that the input is complete. This is true even for single characters: The user must type the character, then press Enter. However, as in the present example, a program often needs to process each character typed by the user without waiting for an Enter. The `getche()` library function performs this service. It returns each character as soon as it's typed. It takes no arguments, and requires the CONIO.H header file. In CHCOUNT the value of the character returned from `getche()` is assigned to `ch`. (The `getche()` function echoes the character to the screen. That's why there's an e at the end of `getche`. Another function, `getch()`, is similar to `getche()` but doesn't echo the character to the screen.)

The `if...else` statement causes the word count `wdcount` to be incremented if the character is a space, and the character count `chcount` to be incremented if the character is anything *but* a space. Thus anything that isn't a space is assumed to count as a character. (Note that this program is fairly naïve; it will be fooled by multiple spaces between words.)

Here's some sample interaction with CHCOUNT:

```
For while and do
Words=4
Letters≈13
```

The test expression in the while statement checks to see if ch is the '\r' character, which is the character received from the keyboard when the Enter key is pressed. If so, the loop and the program terminate.

Assignment Expressions

The CHCOUNT program can be rewritten to save a line of code and demonstrate some important points about assignment expressions and precedence. The result is a construction that looks rather peculiar but is commonly used in C++ (and in C).

Here's the rewritten version, called CHCNT2:

```
// chcnt2.cpp
// counts characters and words typed in
#include <iostream>
using namespace std;
#include <conio.h>                // for getche()

int main()
   {
   int chcount=0;
   int wdcount=1;                 // space between two words
   char ch;

   while( (ch=getche()) != '\r' )  // loop until Enter typed
      {
      if( ch==' ' )               // if it's a space
         wdcount++;               // count a word
      else                        // otherwise,
         chcount++;               // count a character
      }                           // display results
   cout << "\nWords=" << wdcount << endl
        << "Letters=" << chcount << endl;
   return 0;
   }
```

The value returned by getche() is assigned to ch as before, but this entire assignment expression has been moved inside the test expression for while. The assignment expression is compared with '\r' to see whether the loop should terminate. This works because the entire assignment expression takes on the value used in the assignment. That is, if getche() returns 'a', then not only does ch take on the value 'a', but the expression

```
(ch=getche())
```

also takes on the value 'a'. This is then compared with '\r'.

The fact that assignment expressions have a value is also used in statements such as

```
x = y = z = 0;
```

This is perfectly legal in C++. First, z takes on the value 0, then z = 0 takes on the value 0, which is assigned to y. Then the expression y = z = 0 likewise takes on the value 0, which is assigned to x.

The parentheses around the assignment expression in

```
(ch=getche())
```

are necessary because the assignment operator = has a lower precedence than the relational operator !=. Without the parentheses the expression would be evaluated as

```
while( ch = (getche() != '\r') )    // not what we want
```

which would assign a true or false value to ch (not what we want).

The while statement in CHCNT2 provides a lot of power in a small space. It is not only a test expression (checking ch to see whether it's '\r'); it also gets a character from the keyboard and assigns it to ch. It's also not easy to unravel the first time you see it.

Nested if...else Statements

You're probably too young to remember adventure games on early character-mode MS-DOS systems, but let's resurrect the concept here. You moved your "character" around an imaginary landscape and discovered castles, sorcerers, treasure, and so on, using text—not pictures—for input and output. The next program, ADIFELSE, models a small part of such an adventure game.

```cpp
// adifelse.cpp
// demonstrates IF...ELSE with adventure program
#include <iostream>
using namespace std;
#include <conio.h>                  //for getche()

int main()
   {
   char dir='a';
   int x=10, y=10;

   cout << "Type Enter to quit\n";
   while( dir != '\r' )             //until Enter is typed
      {
      cout << "\nYour location is " << x << ", " << y;
      cout << "\nPress direction key (n, s, e, w): ";
```

```
       dir = getche();            //get character
       if( dir=='n')              //go north
          y--;
       else
          if( dir=='s' )          //go south
             y++;
          else
             if( dir=='e' )       //go east
                x++;
             else
                if( dir=='w' )    //go west
                   x--;
    }  //end while
  return 0;
  }  //end main
```

When the game starts, you find yourself on a barren moor. You can go one "unit" north, south, east, or west, while the program keeps track of where you are and reports your position, which starts at coordinates 10,10. Unfortunately, nothing exciting happens to your character, no matter where you go; the moor stretches almost limitlessly in all directions, as shown in Figure 3.11. We'll try to provide a little more excitement to this game later on.

Here's some sample interaction with ADIFELSE:

```
Your location is 10, 10
Press direction key (n, s, e, w): n
Your location is 10, 9
Press direction key (n, s, e, w): e
Your location is 11, 9
Press direction key (n, s, e, w):
```

You can press the Enter key to exit the program.

This program may not cause a sensation in the video arcades, but it does demonstrate one way to handle multiple branches. It uses an if statement nested inside an if...else statement, which is nested inside another if...else statement, which is nested inside yet another if...else statement. If the first test condition is false, the second one is examined, and so on until all four have been checked. If any one proves true, the appropriate action is taken—changing the x or y coordinate—and the program exits from all the nested decisions. Such a nested group of if...else statements is called a *decision tree*.

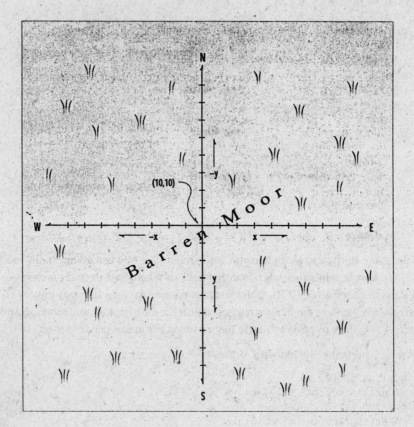

FIGURE 3.11
The barren moor.

Matching the `else`

There's a potential problem in nested `if...else` statements: You can inadvertently match an `else` with the wrong `if`. BADELSE provides an example:

```
// badelse.cpp
// demonstrates ELSE matched with wrong IF
#include <iostream>
using namespace std;

int main()
   {
   int a, b, c;
   cout << "Enter three numbers, a, b, and c:\n";
   cin >> a >> b >> c;
```

```
if( a==b )
    if( b==c )
        cout << "a, b, and c are the same\n";
else
    cout << "a and b are different\n";
return 0;
}
```

We've used multiple values with a single cin. Press Enter following each value you type in; the three values will be assigned to a, b, and c.

What happens if you enter 2, then 3, and then 3? Variable a is 2, and b is 3. They're different, so the first test expression is false, and you would expect the else to be invoked, printing *a and b are different*. But in fact nothing is printed. Why not? Because the else is matched with the wrong if. The indentation would lead you to believe that the else is matched with the first if, but in fact it goes with the second if. Here's the rule: An else is matched with the last if that doesn't have its own else.

Here's a corrected version:

```
if(a==b)
    if(b==c)
        cout << "a, b, and c are the same\n";
    else
        cout << "b and c are different\n";
```

We changed the indentation and also the phrase printed by the else body. Now if you enter 2, 3, 3, nothing will be printed. But entering 2, 2, 3 will cause the output

```
b and c are different
```

If you really want to pair an else with an earlier if, you can use braces around the inner if:

```
if(a==b)
    {
    if(b==c)
        cout << "a, b, and c are the same";
    }
else
    cout << "a and b are different";
```

Here the else is paired with the first if, as the indentation indicates. The braces make the if within them invisible to the following else.

The else...if Construction

The nested if...else statements in the ADIFELSE program look clumsy and can be hard—for humans—to interpret, especially if they are nested more deeply than shown. However, there's another approach to writing the same statements. We need only reformat the program, obtaining the next example, ADELSEIF.

```
// adelseif.cpp
// demonstrates ELSE...IF with adventure program
#include <iostream>
using namespace std;
#include <conio.h>              //for getche()

int main()
   {
   char dir='a';
   int x=10, y=10;

   cout << "Type Enter to quit\n";
   while( dir != '\r' )         //until Enter is typed
      {
      cout << "\nYour location is " << x << ", " << y;
      cout << "\nPress direction key (n, s, e, w): ";
      dir = getche();           //get character
      if( dir=='n')             //go north
         y--;
      else if( dir=='s' )       //go south
         y++;
      else if( dir=='e' )       //go east
         x++;
      else if( dir=='w' )       //go west
         x--;
      } //end while
   return 0;
   } //end main
```

The compiler sees this as identical to ADIFELSE, but we've rearranged the ifs so they directly follow the elses. The result looks almost like a new keyword: else if. The program goes down the ladder of else ifs until one of the test expressions is true. It then executes the following statement and exits from the ladder. This format is clearer and easier to follow than the if...else approach.

The `switch` Statement

If you have a large decision tree, and all the decisions depend on the value of the same variable, you will probably want to consider a `switch` statement instead of a ladder of `if...else` or `else if` constructions. Here's a simple example called PLATTERS that will appeal to nostalgia buffs:

```
// platters.cpp
// demonstrates SWITCH statement
#include <iostream>
using namespace std;

int main()
    {
    int speed;                       //turntable speed

    cout << "\nEnter 33, 45, or 78: ";
    cin >> speed;                    //user enters speed
    switch(speed)                    //selection based on speed
        {
        case 33:                     //user entered 33
            cout << "LP album\n";
            break;
        case 45:                     //user entered 45
            cout << "Single selection\n";
            break;
        case 78:                     //user entered 78
            cout << "Obsolete format\n";
            break;
        }
    return 0;
    }
```

This program prints one of three possible messages, depending on whether the user inputs the number 33, 45, or 78. As old-timers may recall, long-playing records (LPs) contained many songs and turned at 33 rpm, the smaller 45's held only a single song, and 78s were the format that preceded LPs and 45s.

The keyword `switch` is followed by a switch variable in parentheses.

```
switch(speed)
```

Braces then delimit a number of case statements. Each `case` keyword is followed by a constant, which is not in parentheses but is followed by a colon.

```
case 33:
```

The data type of the case constants should match that of the switch variable. Figure 3.12 shows the syntax of the `switch` statement.

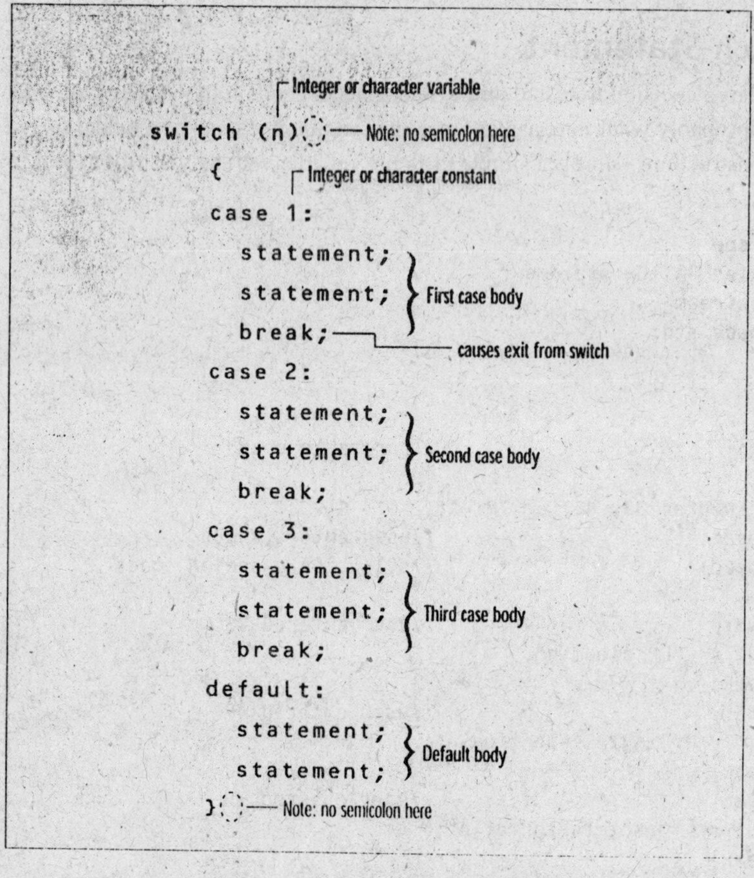

```
                    ┌─ Integer or character variable
         switch (n) ⟨⟩ ── Note: no semicolon here
            {        ┌─ Integer or character constant
            case 1:
               statement;  ⎫
               statement;  ⎬ First case body
               break; ────┘────── causes exit from switch
            case 2:
               statement;  ⎫
               statement;  ⎬ Second case body
               break;      ⎭
            case 3:
               statement;  ⎫
               statement;  ⎬ Third case body
               break;      ⎭
            default:
               statement;  ⎫
               statement;  ⎬ Default body
            } ⟨⟩ ── Note: no semicolon here
```

FIGURE 3.12
Syntax of the switch *statement.*

Before entering the switch, the program should assign a value to the switch variable. This value will usually match a constant in one of the case statements. When this is the case (pun intended!), the statements immediately following the keyword case will be executed, until a break is reached.

Here's an example of PLATTER's output:

```
Enter 33, 45, or 78: 45
Single selection
```

The break Statement

PLATTERS has a break statement at the end of each case section. The break keyword causes the entire switch statement to exit. Control goes to the first statement following the end of the switch construction, which in PLATTERS is the end of the program. Don't forget the break; without it, control passes down (or "falls through") to the statements for the next case, which is usually not what you want (although sometimes it's useful).

If the value of the switch variable doesn't match any of the case constants, control passes to the end of the switch without doing anything. The operation of the switch statement is shown in Figure 3.13. The break keyword is also used to escape from loops; we'll discuss this soon.

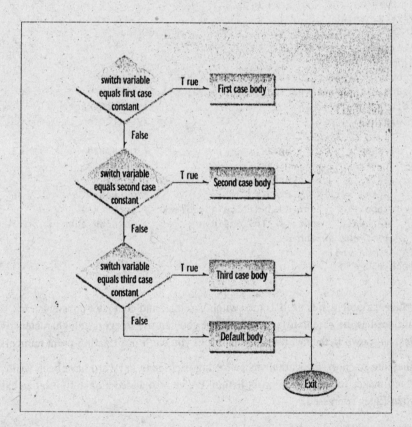

FIGURE 3.13

Operation of the switch *statement.*

switch Statement with Character Variables

The PLATTERS example shows a switch statement based on a variable of type int. You can also use type char. Here's our ADELSEIF program rewritten as ADSWITCH:

```cpp
// adswitch.cpp
// demonstrates SWITCH with adventure program
#include <iostream>
using namespace std;
#include <conio.h>                              //for getche()

int main()
   {
   char dir='a';
   int x=10, y=10;

   while( dir != '\r' )
      {
      cout << "\nYour location is " << x << ", " << y;
      cout << "\nEnter direction (n, s, e, w): ";
      dir = getche();                           //get character
      switch(dir)                               //switch on it
         {
         case 'n':  y--; break;                 //go north
         case 's':  y++; break;                 //go south
         case 'e':  x++; break;                 //go east
         case 'w':  x--; break;                 //go west
         case '\r': cout << "Exiting\n"; break; //Enter key
         default:   cout << "Try again\n";      //unknown char
         } //end switch
      } //end while
   return 0;
   } //end main
```

A character variable dir is used as the switch variable, and character constants 'n', 's', and so on are used as the case constants. (Note that you can use integers and characters as switch variables, as shown in the last two examples, but you can't use floating-point numbers.)

Since they are so short, the statements following each case keyword have been written on one line, which makes for a more compact listing. We've also added a case to print an exit message when Enter is pressed.

The default Keyword

In the ADSWITCH program, where you expect to see the last case at the bottom of the switch construction, you instead see the keyword default. This keyword gives the switch construction a way to take an action if the value of the loop variable doesn't match any of the case constants. Here we use it to print Try again if the user types an unknown character. No break is necessary after default, since we're at the end of the switch anyway.

A `switch` statement is a common approach to analyzing input entered by the user. Each of the possible characters is represented by a `case`.

It's a good idea to use a `default` statement in all `switch` statements, even if you don't think you need it. A construction such as

```
default:
    cout << "Error: incorrect input to switch"; break;
```

alerts the programmer (or the user) that something has gone wrong in the operation of the program. In the interest of brevity we don't always include such a `default` statement, but you should, especially in serious programs.

switch Versus if...else

When do you use a series of `if...else` (or `else if`) statements, and when do you use a `switch` statement? In an `else if` construction you can use a series of expressions that involve unrelated variables and are as complex as you like. For example:

```
if( SteamPressure*Factor > 56 )
    // statements
else if( VoltageIn + VoltageOut < 23000)
    // statements
else if( day==Thursday )
    // statements
else
    // statements
```

In a `switch` statement, however, all the branches are selected by the same variable; the only thing distinguishing one branch from another is the value of this variable. You can't say

```
case a<3:
    // do something
    break;
```

The case constant must be an integer or character constant, like 3 or `'a'`, or an expression that evaluates to a constant, like `'a'+32`.

When these conditions are met, the `switch` statement is very clean—easy to write and to understand. It should be used whenever possible, especially when the decision tree has more than a few possibilities.

The Conditional Operator

Here's a strange sort of decision operator. It exists because of a common programming situation: A variable is given one value if something is true and another value if it's false. For example, here's an `if...else` statement that gives the variable min the value of alpha or the value of beta, depending on which is smaller:

```
if( alpha < beta )
   min = alpha;
else
   min = beta;
```

This sort of construction is so common that the designers of C++ (actually the designers of C, long ago) invented a compressed way to express it: the *conditional operator*. This operator consists of two symbols, which operate on three operands. It's the only such operator in C++; other operators operate on one or two operands. Here's the equivalent of the same program fragment, using a conditional operator:

```
min = (alpha<beta) ? alpha : beta;
```

The part of this statement to the right of the equal sign is called the *conditional expression*:

```
(alpha<beta) ? alpha : beta    // conditional expression
```

The question mark and the colon make up the conditional operator. The expression before the question mark

```
(alpha<beta)
```

is the test expression. It and `alpha` and `beta` are the three operands.

If the test expression is true, the entire conditional expression takes on the value of the operand following the question mark: `alpha` in this example. If the test expression is false, the conditional expression takes on the value of the operand following the colon: `beta`. The parentheses around the test expression aren't needed for the compiler, but they're customary; they make the statement easier to read (and it needs all the help it can get). Figure 3.14 shows the syntax of the conditional statement, and Figure 3.15 shows its operation.

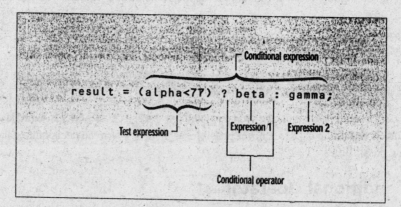

FIGURE 3.14
Syntax of the conditional operator.

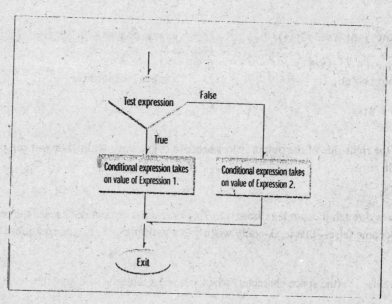

FIGURE 3.15
Operation of the conditional operator.

The conditional expression can be assigned to another variable or used anywhere a value can be used. In this example it's assigned to the variable min.

Here's another example: a statement that uses a conditional operator to find the absolute value of a variable n. (The absolute value of a number is the number with any negative sign removed, so it's always positive.)

```
absvalue = n<0 ? -n : n;
```

If n is less than 0, the expression becomes -n, a positive number. If n is not less than 0, the expression remains n. The result is the absolute value of n, which is assigned to absvalue.

Here's a program, CONDI.CPP, that uses the conditional operator to print an x every eight spaces in a line of text. You might use this to see where the tab stops are on your screen.

```
// condi.cpp
// prints 'x' every 8 columns
// demonstrates conditional operator
#include <iostream>
using namespace std;

int main()
   {
```

```
for(int j=0; j<80; j++)        //for every column,
    {                          //ch is 'x' if column is
    char ch = (j%8) ? ' ' : 'x';  //multiple of 8, and
    cout << ch;                //' ' (space) otherwise
    }
return 0;
}
```

Some of the right side of the output is lost because of the page width, but you can probably imagine it:

x   x   x   x   x   x   x   x   x

As j cycles through the numbers from 0 to 79, the remainder operator causes the expression (j % 8) to become false—that is, 0—only when j is a multiple of 8. So the conditional expression

```
(j%8) ? ' ' : 'x'
```

has the value ' ' (the space character) when j is not a multiple of 8, and the value 'x' when it is.

You may think this is terse, but we could have combined the two statements in the loop body into one, eliminating the ch variable:

```
cout << ( (j%8) ? ' ' : 'x' );
```

Hotshot C++ (and C) programmers love this sort of thing—getting a lot of bang from very little code. But you don't need to strive for concise code if you don't want to. Sometimes it becomes so obscure it's not worth the effort. Even using the conditional operator is optional: An if...else statement and a few extra program lines will accomplish the same thing.

Logical Operators

So far we've seen two families of operators (besides the oddball conditional operator). First are the arithmetic operators +, -, *, /, and %. Second are the relational operators <, >, <=, >=, ==, and !=.

Let's examine a third family of operators, called *logical operators*. These operators allow you to logically combine Boolean variables (that is, variables of type bool, with true or false values). For example, *today is a weekday* has a Boolean value, since it's either true or false. Another Boolean expression is *Maria took the car*. We can connect these expressions logically: If today is a weekday, and Maria took the car, then I'll have to take the bus. The logical connection here is the word *and*, which provides a true or false value to the combination of the two phrases. Only if they are *both* true will I have to take the bus.

Logical AND Operator

Let's see how logical operators combine Boolean expressions in C++. Here's an example, ADVENAND, that uses a logical operator to spruce up the adventure game from the ADSWITCH example. We'll bury some treasure at coordinates (7,11) and see whether the player can find it.

```cpp
// advenand.cpp
// demonstrates AND logical operator
#include <iostream>
using namespace std;
#include <process.h>          //for exit()
#include <conio.h>            //for getche()

int main()
   {
   char dir='a';
   int x=10, y=10;

   while( dir != '\r' )
      {
      cout << "\nYour location is " << x << ", " << y;
      cout << "\nEnter direction (n, s, e, w): ";
      dir = getche();              //get direction
      switch(dir)
         {
         case 'n': y--; break;   //update coordinates
         case 's': y++; break;
         case 'e': x++; break;
         case 'w': x--; break;
         }
      if( x==7 && y==11 )         //if x is 7 and y is 11
         {
         cout << "\nYou found the treasure!\n";
         exit(0);                 //exit from program
         }
      } //end switch
   return 0;
   } //end main
```

The key to this program is the `if` statement

```cpp
if( x==7 && y==11 )
```

The test expression will be true only if x is 7 *and* y is 11. The logical AND operator `&&` joins the two relational expressions to achieve this result. (A *relational expression* is one that uses a relational operator.)

Notice that parentheses are not necessary around the relational expressions.

```
( (x==7) && (y==11) )   // inner parentheses not necessary
```

This is because the relational operators have higher precedence than the logical operators.

Here's some interaction as the user arrives at these coordinates:

```
Your location is 7, 10
Enter direction (n, s, e, w): s
You found the treasure!
```

There are three logical operators in C++:

Operator	Effect
&&	Logical AND
||	Logical OR
!	Logical NOT

There is no logical XOR (exclusive OR) operator in C++.

Let's look at examples of the || and ! operators.

Logical OR Operator

Suppose in the adventure game you decide there will be dragons if the user goes too far east or too far west. Here's an example, ADVENOR, that uses the logical OR operator to implement this frightening impediment to free adventuring. It's a variation on the ADVENAND program.

```
// advenor.cpp
// demonstrates OR logical operator
#include <iostream>
using namespace std;
#include <process.h>          //for exit()
#include <conio.h>            //for getche()

int main()
   {
   char dir='a';
   int x=10, y=10;

   while( dir != '\r' )           //quit on Enter key
      {
      cout << "\n\nYour location is " << x << ", " << y;

      if( x<5 || x>15 )           //if x west of 5 OR east of 15
         cout << "\nBeware: dragons lurk here";
```

```
    cout << "\nEnter direction (n, s, e, w): ";
    dir = getche();                //get direction
    switch(dir)
      {
      case 'n': y--; break;    //update coordinates
      case 's': y++; break;
      case 'e': x++; break;
      case 'w': x--; break;
      } //end switch
    } //end while
  return 0;
  } //end main()
```

The expression

```
x<5 || x>15
```

is true whenever either x is less than 5 (the player is too far west), or x is greater than 15 (the player is too far east). Again, the || operator has lower precedence than the relational operators < and >, so no parentheses are needed in this expression.

Logical NOT Operator

The logical NOT operator ! is a *unary* operator—that is, it takes only one operand. (Almost all the operators we've seen thus far are *binary* operators; they take two operands. The conditional operator is the only *ternary* operator in C++.) The effect of the ! is that the logical value of its operand is reversed: If something is true, ! makes it false; if it is false, ! makes it true. (It would be nice if life were so easily manipulated.)

For example, (x==7) is true if x is equal to 7, but !(x==7) is true if x is not equal to 7. (In this situation you could use the relational *not equals* operator, x != 7, to achieve the same effect.)

A True/False Value for Every Integer Variable

We may have given you the impression that for an expression to have a true/false value, it must involve a relational operator. But in fact, every integer expression has a true/false value, even if it is only a single variable. The expression x is true whenever x is not 0, and false when x is 0. Applying the ! operator to this situation, we can see that the !x is true whenever x is 0, since it reverses the truth value of x.

Let's put these ideas to work. Imagine in your adventure game that you want to place a mushroom on all the locations where both x and y are a multiple of 7. (As you probably know, mushrooms, when consumed by the player, confer magical powers.) The remainder when x is divided by 7, which can be calculated by x%7, is 0 only when x is a multiple of 7. So to specify the mushroom locations, we can write

```
if( x%7==0 && y%7==0 )
  cout << "There's a mushroom here.\n";
```

However, remembering that expressions are true or false even if they don't involve relational operators, you can use the ! operator to provide a more concise format.

```
if( !(x%7) && !(y%7) )    // if not x%7 and not y%7
```

This has exactly the same effect.

We've said that the logical operators && and || have lower precedence than the relational operators. Why then do we need parentheses around x%7 and y%7? Because, even though it is a logical operator, ! is a unary operator, which has higher precedence than relational operators.

Precedence Summary

Let's summarize the precedence situation for the operators we've seen so far. The operators higher on the list have higher precedence than those lower down. Operators with higher precedence are evaluated before those with lower precedence. Operators on the same row have equal precedence. You can force an expression to be evaluated first by placing parentheses around it.

You can find a more complete precedence table in Appendix B, "C++ Precedence Table and Keywords."

Operator type	Operators	Precedence
Unary	!, ++, --, +, -	Highest
Arithmetic	Multiplicative *, /, %	
	Additive +, -	
Relational	Inequality <, >, <=, >=	
	Equality ==, !=	
Logical	And &&	
	Or ||	
Conditional	?:	
Assignment	=, +=, -=, *=, /=, %=	Lowest

We should note that if there is any possibility of confusion in a relational expression that involves multiple operators, you should use parentheses whether they are needed or not. They don't do any harm, and they guarantee the expression does what you want, even if you've made a mistake with precedence. Also, they make it clear to anyone reading the listing what you intended.

Other Control Statements

There are several other control statements in C++. We've already seen one, break, used in switch statements, but it can be used other places as well. Another statement, continue, is used only in loops, and a third, goto, should be avoided. Let's look at these statements in turn.

The break Statement

The break statement causes an exit from a loop, just as it does from a switch statement. The next statement after the break is executed is the statement following the loop. Figure 3.16 shows the operation of the break statement.

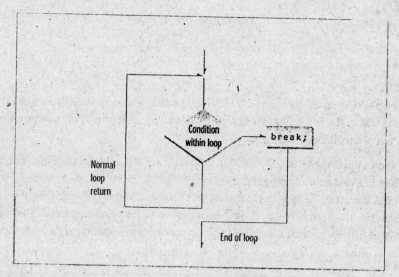

FIGURE 3.16
Operation of the break statement.

To demonstrate break, here's a program, SHOWPRIM, that displays the distribution of prime numbers in graphical form:

```
// showprim.cpp
// displays prime number distribution
#include <iostream>
using namespace std;
#include <conio.h>                    //for getche()

int main()
   {
   const unsigned char WHITE = 219;  //solid color (primes)
   const unsigned char GRAY  = 176;  //gray (non primes)
   unsigned char ch;
                                     //for each screen position
   for(int count=0; count<80*25-1; count++)
      {
      ch = WHITE;                    //assume it's prime
```

3

LOOPS AND
DECISIONS

```
        for(int j=2; j<count; j++) //divide by every integer from
           if(count%j == 0)          //2 on up; if remainder is 0,
              {
              ch = GRAY;              //it's not prime
              break;                  //break out of inner loop
              }
           cout << ch;               //display the character
           }
        getch();                     //freeze screen until keypress
        return 0;
        }
```

In effect every position on an 80-column by 25-line console screen is numbered, from 0 to 1999 (which is 80*25–1). If the number at a particular position is prime, the position is colored white; if it's not prime, it's colored gray.

Figure 3.17 shows the display. Strictly speaking, 0 and 1 are not considered prime, but they are shown as white to avoid complicating the program. Think of the columns across the top as being numbered from 0 to 79. Notice that no primes (except 2) appear in even-numbered columns, since they're all divisible by 2. Is there a pattern to the other numbers? The world of mathematics will be very excited if you find a pattern that allows you to predict whether any given number is prime.

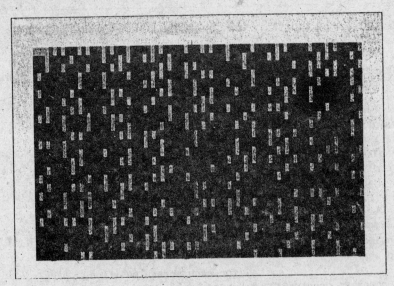

FIGURE 3.17
Output of SHOWPRIM program.

When the inner for loop determines that a number is not prime, it sets the character ch to GRAY, and then executes break to escape from the inner loop. (We don't want to exit from the entire program, as in the PRIME example, since we have a whole series of numbers to work on.)

Notice that break only takes you out of the innermost loop. This is true no matter what constructions are nested inside each other: break only takes you out of the construction in which it's embedded. If there were a switch within a loop, a break in the switch would only take you out of the switch, not out of the loop.

The last cout statement prints the graphics character, and then the loop continues, testing the next number for primeness.

ASCII Extended Character Set

This program uses two characters from the *extended ASCII character set*, the characters represented by the numbers from 128 to 255, as shown in Appendix A, "ASCII Table." The value 219 represents a solid-colored block (white on a black-and-white monitor), while 176 represents a gray block.

The SHOWPRIM example uses getch() in the last line to keep the DOS prompt from scrolling the screen up when the program terminates. It freezes the screen until you press a key.

We use type unsigned char for the character variables in SHOWPRIM, since it goes up to 255. Type char only goes up to 127.

The continue Statement

The break statement takes you out of the bottom of a loop. Sometimes, however, you want to go back to the top of the loop when something unexpected happens. Executing continue has this effect. (Strictly speaking, the continue takes you to the closing brace of the loop body, from which you may jump back to the top.) Figure 3.18 shows the operation of continue

Here's a variation on the DIVDO example. This program, which we saw earlier in this chapter, does division, but it has a fatal flaw: If the user inputs 0 as the divisor, the program undergoes catastrophic failure and terminates with the runtime error message *Divide Error*. The revised version of the program, DIVDO2, deals with this situation more gracefully.

```
// divdo2.cpp
// demonstrates CONTINUE statement
#include <iostream>
using namespace std;

int main()
    {
    long dividend, divisor;
    char ch;
```

```
do {
   cout << "Enter dividend: "; cin >> dividend;
   cout << "Enter divisor: ";  cin >> divisor;
   if( divisor == 0 )                 //if attempt to
      {                               //divide by 0,
      cout << "Illegal divisor\n";    //display message
      continue;                       //go to top of loop
      }
   cout << "Quotient is " << dividend / divisor;
   cout << ", remainder is " << dividend % divisor;

   cout << "\nDo another? (y/n): ";
   cin >> ch;
   } while( ch != 'n' );
return 0;
}
```

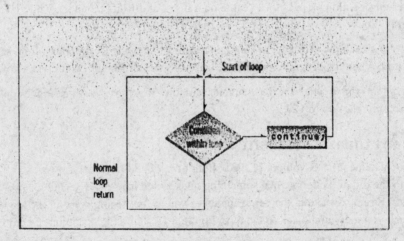

FIGURE 3.18
Operation of the continue *statement.*

If the user inputs 0 for the divisor, the program prints an error message and, using continue, returns to the top of the loop to issue the prompts again. Here's some sample output:

```
Enter dividend: 10
Enter divisor: 0
Illegal divisor
Enter dividend:
```

A break statement in this situation would cause an exit from the do loop and the program, an unnecessarily harsh response.

Notice that we've made the format of the do loop a little more compact. The do is on the same line as the opening brace, and the while is on the same line as the closing brace.

The goto Statement

We'll mention the goto statement here for the sake of completeness—not because it's a good idea to use it. If you've had any exposure to structured programming principles, you know that gotos can quickly lead to "spaghetti" code that is difficult to understand and debug. There is almost never any need to use goto, as is demonstrated by its absence from the program examples in this book.

With that lecture out of the way, here's the syntax. You insert a label in your code at the desired destination for the goto. The label is always terminated by a colon. The keyword goto, followed by this label name, then takes you to the label. The following code fragment demonstrates this approach.

```
goto SystemCrash;
// other statements
SystemCrash:
// control will begin here following goto
```

Summary

Relational operators compare two values to see whether they're equal, whether one is larger than the other, and so on. The result is a logical or Boolean (type bool) value, which is true or false. False is indicated by 0, and true by 1 or any other non-zero number.

There are three kinds of loops in C++. The for loop is most often used when you know in advance how many times you want to execute the loop. The while loop and do loops are used when the condition causing the loop to terminate arises within the loop, with the while loop not necessarily executing at all, and the do loop always executing at least once.

A loop body can be a single statement or a block of multiple statements delimited by braces. A variable defined within a block is visible only within that block.

There are four kinds of decision-making statements. The if statement does something if a test expression is true. The if...else statement does one thing if the test expression is true, and another thing if it isn't. The else if construction is a way of rewriting a ladder of nested if...else statements to make it more readable. The switch statement branches to multiple sections of code, depending on the value of a single variable. The conditional operator simplifies returning one value if a test expression is true, and another if it's false.

The logical AND and OR operators combine two Boolean expressions to yield another one, and the logical NOT operator changes a Boolean value from true to false, or from false to true.

3

LOOPS AND
DECISIONS

The break statement sends control to the end of the innermost loop or switch in which it occurs. The continue statement sends control to the top of the loop in which it occurs. The goto statement sends control to a label.

Precedence specifies which kinds of operations will be carried out first. The order is unary, arithmetic, relational, logical, conditional, assignment.

Questions

Answers to these questions can be found in Appendix G.

1. A relational operator

   a. assigns one operand to another.

   b. yields a Boolean result.

   c. compares two operands.

   d. logically combines two operands.

2. Write an expression that uses a relational operator to return true if the variable george is not equal to sally.

3. Is –1 true or false?

4. Name and describe the usual purpose of three expressions in a for statement.

5. In a for loop with a multistatement loop body, semicolons should appear following

   a. the for statement itself.

   b. the closing brace in a multistatement loop body.

   c. each statement within the loop body.

   d. the test expression.

6. True or false: The increment expression in a for loop can decrement the loop variable.

7. Write a for loop that displays the numbers from 100 to 110.

8. A block of code is delimited by _____.

9. A variable defined within a block is visible

   a. from the point of definition onward in the program.

   b. from the point of definition onward in the function.

   c. from the point of definition onward in the block.

   d. throughout the function.

10. Write a while loop that displays the numbers from 100 to 110.

11. True or false: Relational operators have a higher precedence than arithmetic operators.

12. How many times is the loop body executed in a do loop?

13. Write a do loop that displays the numbers from 100 to 110.

14. Write an if statement that prints Yes if a variable age is greater than 21.

15. The library function exit() causes an exit from

    a. the loop in which it occurs.

    b. the block in which it occurs.

    c. the function in which it occurs.

    d. the program in which it occurs.

16. Write an if...else statement that displays Yes if a variable age is greater than 21, and displays No otherwise.

17. The getche() library function

    a. returns a character when any key is pressed.

    b. returns a character when Enter is pressed.

    c. displays a character on the screen when any key is pressed.

    d. does not display a character on the screen.

18. What is the character obtained from cin when the user presses the Enter key?

19. An else always matches the _____ if, unless the if is _____.

20. The else...if construction is obtained from a nested if...else by _____.

21. Write a switch statement that prints Yes if a variable ch is 'y', prints No if ch is 'n', and prints Unknown response otherwise.

22. Write a statement that uses a conditional operator to set ticket to 1 if speed is greater than 55, and to 0 otherwise.

23. The && and || operators

    a. compare two numeric values.

    b. combine two numeric values.

    c. compare two Boolean values.

    d. combine two Boolean values.

24. Write an expression involving a logical operator that is true if limit is 55 and speed is greater than 55.

25. Arrange in order of precedence (highest first) the following kinds of operators: logical, unary, arithmetic, assignment, relational, conditional.

26. The break statement causes an exit

    a. only from the innermost loop.

    b. only from the innermost switch.

    c. from all loops and switches.

    d. from the innermost loop or switch.

27. Executing the continue operator from within a loop causes control to go to _____.

28. The goto statement causes control to go to

    a. an operator.

    b. a label.

    c. a variable.

    d. a function.

Exercises

Answers to the starred exercises can be found in Appendix G.

*1. Assume that you want to generate a table of multiples of any given number. Write a program that allows the user to enter the number and then generates the table, formatting it into 10 columns and 20 lines. Interaction with the program should look like this (only the first three lines are shown):

```
Enter a number: 7
    7   14   21   28   35   42   49   56   63   70
   77   84   91   98  105  112  119  126  133  140
  147  154  161  168  175  182  189  196  203  210
```

*2. Write a temperature-conversion program that gives the user the option of converting Fahrenheit to Celsius or Celsius to Fahrenheit. Then carry out the conversion. Use floating-point numbers. Interaction with the program might look like this:

```
Type 1 to convert Fahrenheit to Celsius,
     2 to convert Celsius to Fahrenheit: 1
Enter temperature in Fahrenheit: 70
In Celsius that's 21.111111
```

*3. Operators such as >>, which read input from the keyboard, must be able to convert a series of digits into a number. Write a program that does the same thing. It should allow the user to type up to six digits, and then display the resulting number as a type long integer. The digits should be read individually, as characters, using getche(). Constructing the number involves multiplying the existing value by 10 and then adding the new digit. (Hint: Subtract 48 or '0' to go from ASCII to a numerical digit.)

Here's some sample interaction:

```
Enter a number: 123456
Number is: 123456
```

*4. Create the equivalent of a four-function calculator. The program should ask the user to enter a number, an operator, and another number. (Use floating point.) It should then carry out the specified arithmetical operation: adding, subtracting, multiplying, or dividing the two numbers. Use a `switch` statement to select the operation. Finally, display the result.

When it finishes the calculation, the program should ask whether the user wants to do another calculation. The response can be `'y'` or `'n'`. Some sample interaction with the program might look like this:

```
Enter first number, operator, second number: 10 / 3
Answer = 3.333333
Do another (y/n)? y
Enter first number, operator, second number: 12 + 100
Answer = 112
Do another (y/n)? n
```

5. Use for loops to construct a program that displays a pyramid of Xs on the screen. The pyramid should look like this

```
    X
   XXX
  XXXXX
 XXXXXXX
XXXXXXXXX
```

except that it should be 20 lines high, instead of the 5 lines shown here. One way to do this is to nest two inner loops, one to print spaces and one to print Xs, inside an outer loop that steps down the screen from line to line.

6. Modify the FACTOR program in this chapter so that it repeatedly asks for a number and calculates its factorial, until the user enters 0, at which point it terminates. You can enclose the relevant statements in FACTOR in a while loop or a do loop to achieve this effect.

7. Write a program that calculates how much money you'll end up with if you invest an amount of money at a fixed interest rate, compounded yearly. Have the user furnish the initial amount, the number of years, and the yearly interest rate in percent. Some interaction with the program might look like this:

```
Enter initial amount: 3000
Enter number of years: 10
Enter interest rate (percent per year): 5.5
At the end of 10 years, you will have 5124.43 dollars.
```

At the end of the first year you have 3000 + (3000 * 0.055), which is 3165. At the end of the second year you have 3165 + (3165 * 0.055), which is 3339.08. Do this as many times as there are years. A `for` loop makes the calculation easy.

8. Write a program that repeatedly asks the user to enter two money amounts expressed in old-style British currency: pounds, shillings, and pence. (See Exercises 10 and 12 in Chapter 2, "C++ Programming Basics.") The program should then add the two amounts and display the answer, again in pounds, shillings, and pence. Use a do loop that asks the user whether the program should be terminated. Typical interaction might be

```
Enter first amount: £5.10.6
Enter second amount: £3.2.6
Total is £8.13.0
Do you wish to continue (y/n)?
```

To add the two amounts, you'll need to carry 1 shilling when the pence value is greater than 11, and carry 1 pound when there are more than 19 shillings.

9. Suppose you give a dinner party for six guests, but your table seats only four. In how many ways can four of the six guests arrange themselves at the table? Any of the six guests can sit in the first chair. Any of the remaining five can sit in the second chair. Any of the remaining four can sit in the third chair, and any of the remaining three can sit in the fourth chair. (The last two will have to stand.) So the number of possible arrangements of six guests in four chairs is 6*5*4*3, which is 360. Write a program that calculates the number of possible arrangements for any number of guests and any number of chairs. (Assume there will never be fewer guests than chairs.) Don't let this get too complicated. A simple `for` loop should do it.

10. Write another version of the program from Exercise 7 so that, instead of finding the final amount of your investment, you tell the program the final amount and it figures out how many years it will take, at a fixed rate of interest compounded yearly, to reach this amount. What sort of loop is appropriate for this problem? (Don't worry about fractional years; use an integer value for the year.)

11. Create a three-function calculator for old-style English currency, where money amounts are specified in pounds, shillings, and pence. (See Exercises 10 and 12 in Chapter 2.) The calculator should allow the user to add or subtract two money amounts, or to multiply a money amount by a floating-point number. (It doesn't make sense to multiply two money amounts; there is no such thing as square money. We'll ignore division. Use the general style of the ordinary four-function calculator in Exercise 4 in this chapter.)

12. Create a four-function calculator for fractions. (See Exercise 9 in Chapter 2, and Exercise 4 in this chapter.) Here are the formulas for the four arithmetic operations applied to fractions:

Addition: `a/b + c/d = (a*d + b*c) / (b*d)`

Subtraction: `a/b - c/d = (a*d - b*c) / (b*d)`

Multiplication: `a/b * c/d = (a*c) / (b*d)`

Division: `a/b / c/d = (a*d) / (b*c)`

The user should type the first fraction, an operator, and a second fraction. The program should then display the result and ask whether the user wants to continue.

Structures

IN THIS CHAPTER

We've seen variables of simple data types, such as float, char, and int. Variables of such types represent one item of information: a height, an amount, a count, and so on. But just as groceries are organized into bags, employees into departments, and words into sentences, it's often convenient to organize simple variables into more complex entities. The C++ construction called the *structure* is one way to do this.

The first part of this chapter is devoted to structures. In the second part we'll look at a related topic: enumerations.

Structures

A structure is a collection of simple variables. The variables in a structure can be of different types: Some can be int, some can be float, and so on. (This is unlike the array, which we'll meet later, in which all the variables must be the same type.) The data items in a structure are called the *members* of the structure.

In books on C programming, structures are often considered an advanced feature and are introduced toward the end of the book. However, for C++ programmers, structures are one of the two important building blocks in the understanding of objects and classes. In fact, the syntax of a structure is almost identical to that of a class. A structure (as typically used) is a collection of data, while a class is a collection of both data and functions. So by learning about structures we'll be paving the way for an understanding of classes and objects. Structures in C++ (and C) serve a similar purpose to *records* in some other languages such as Pascal.

A Simple Structure

Let's start off with a structure that contains three variables: two integers and a floating-point number. This structure represents an item in a widget company's parts inventory. The structure is a kind of blueprint specifying what information is necessary for a single part. The company makes several kinds of widgets, so the widget model number is the first member of the structure. The number of the part itself is the next member, and the final member is the part's cost. (Those of you who consider part numbers unexciting need to open your eyes to the romance of commerce.)

The program PARTS defines the structure part, defines a structure variable of that type called part1, assigns values to its members, and then displays these values.

```
// parts.cpp
// uses parts inventory to demonstrate structures
#include <iostream>
using namespace std;
```

```
//////////////////////////////////////////////////////////////
struct part                    //declare a structure
   {
   int modelnumber;            //ID number of widget
   int partnumber;             //ID number of widget part
   float cost;                 //cost of part
   };
//////////////////////////////////////////////////////////////
int main()
   {
   part part1;                 //define a structure variable

   part1.modelnumber = 6244;   //give values to structure members
   part1.partnumber = 373;
   part1.cost = 217.55F;
                               //display structure members
   cout << "Model "    << part1.modelnumber;
   cout << ", part "   << part1.partnumber;
   cout << ", costs $" << part1.cost << endl;
   return 0;
   }
```

The program's output looks like this:

```
Model 6244, part 373, costs $217.55
```

The PARTS program has three main aspects: defining the structure, defining a structure variable, and accessing the members of the structure. Let's look at each of these.

Defining the Structure

The structure definition tells how the structure is organized: It specifies what members the structure will have. Here it is:

```
struct part
   {
   int modelnumber;
   int partnumber;
   float cost;
   };
```

Syntax of the Structure Definition

The keyword struct introduces the structure definition. Next comes the *structure name* or *tag*, which is part. The declarations of the structure members—modelnumber, partnumber, and cost—are enclosed in braces. A semicolon follows the closing brace, terminating the entire

4

STRUCTURES

structure. Note that this use of the semicolon for structures is unlike the usage for a block of code. As we've seen, blocks of code, which are used in loops, decisions, and functions, are also delimited by braces. However, they don't use a semicolon following the final brace. Figure 4.1 shows the syntax of the structure declaration.

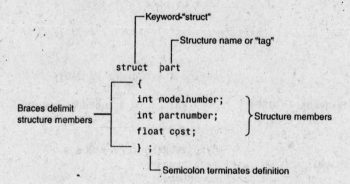

FIGURE 4.1
Syntax of the structure definition.

Use of the Structure Definition

The structure definitiondefinition serves only as a blueprint for the creation of variables of type part. It does not itself create any structure variables; that is, it does not set aside any space in memory or even name any variables. This is unlike the definition of a simple variable, which does set aside memory. A structure definition is merely a specification for how structure variables will look when they are defined. This is shown in Figure 4.2.

It's not accidental that this description sounds like the distinction we noted between classes and objects in Chapter 1, "The Big Picture." As we'll see, an object has the same relationship to its class that a variable of a structure type has to the structure definition.

Defining a Structure Variable

The first statement in main()

```
part part1;
```

defines a variable, called part1, of type structure part. This definition reserves space in memory for part1. How much space? Enough to hold all the members of part1—namely modelnumber, partnumber, and cost. In this case there will be 4 bytes for each of the two ints (assuming a 32-bit system), and 4 bytes for the float. Figure 4.3 shows how part1 looks in memory. (The figure shows 2-byte integers.)

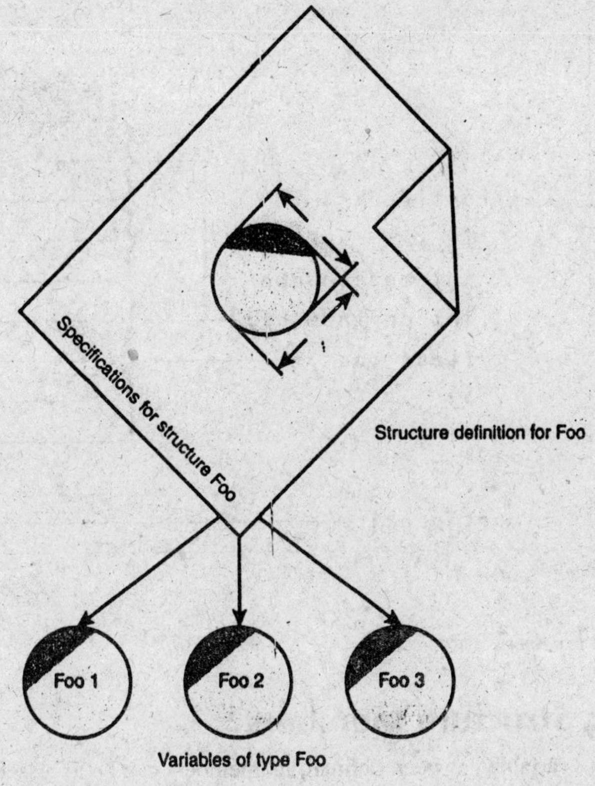

FIGURE 4.2
Structures and structure variables.

In some ways we can think of the part structure as the specification for a new data type. This will become more clear as we go along, but notice that the format for defining a structure variable is the same as that for defining a basic built-in data type such as int:

```
part part1;
int var1;
```

This similarity is not accidental. One of the aims of C++ is to make the syntax and the operation of user-defined data types as similar as possible to that of built-in data types. (In C you need to include the keyword struct in structure definitions, as in struct part part1;. In C++ the keyword is not necessary.)

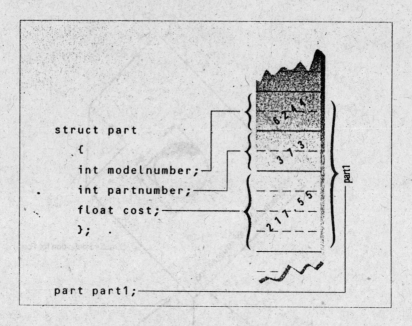

FIGURE 4.3
Structure members in memory.

Accessing Structure Members

Once a structure variable has been defined, its members can be accessed using something called the *dot operator*. Here's how the first member is given a value:

```
part1.modelnumber = 6244;
```

The structure member is written in three parts: the name of the structure variable (part1); the dot operator, which consists of a period (.); and the member name (modelnumber). This means "the modelnumber member of part1." The real name of the dot operator is *member access operator*, but of course no one wants to use such a lengthy term.

Remember that the first component of an expression involving the dot operator is the name of the specific structure variable (part1 in this case), not the name of the structure definition (part). The variable name must be used to distinguish one variable from another, such as part1, part2, and so on, as shown in Figure 4.4.

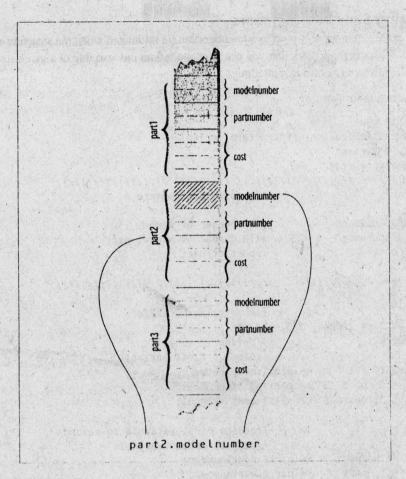

part2.modelnumber

FIGURE 4.4
The dot operator.

Structure members are treated just like other variables. In the statement `part1.modelnumber = 6244;`, the member is given the value 6244 using a normal assignment operator. The program also shows members used in `cout` statements such as

```
cout << "\nModel " << part1.modelnumber;
```

These statements output the values of the structure members.

Other Structure Features

Structures are surprisingly versatile. Let's look at some additional features of structure syntax and usage.

4

Initializing Structure Members

The next example shows how structure members can be initialized when the structure variable is defined. It also demonstrates that you can have more than one variable of a given structure type (we hope you suspected this all along).

Here's the listing for PARTINIT:

```
// partinit.cpp
// shows initialization of structure variables
#include <iostream>
using namespace std;
/////////////////////////////////////////////////////////////////
struct part                     //specify a structure
   {
   int modelnumber;             //ID number of widget
   int partnumber;              //ID number of widget part
   float cost;                  //cost of part
   };
/////////////////////////////////////////////////////////////////
int main()
   {                            //initialize variable
   part part1 = { 6244, 373, 217.55F };
   part part2;                  //define variable
                                //display first variable
   cout << "Model "    << part1.modelnumber;
   cout << ", part "   << part1.partnumber;
   cout << ", costs $" << part1.cost << endl;

   part2 = part1;               //assign first variable to second
                                //display second variable
   cout << "Model "    << part2.modelnumber;
   cout << ", part "   << part2.partnumber;
   cout << ", costs $" << part2.cost << endl;
   return 0;
   }
```

This program defines two variables of type part: part1 and part2. It initializes part1, prints out the values of its members, assigns part1 to part2, and prints out its members.

Here's the output:

```
Model 6244, part 373, costs $217.55
Model 6244, part 373, costs $217.55
```

Not surprisingly, the same output is repeated since one variable is made equal to the other.

The part1 structure variable's members are initialized when the variable is defined:

```
part part1 = { 6244, 373, 217.55 };
```

The values to be assigned to the structure members are surrounded by braces and separated by commas. The first value in the list is assigned to the first member, the second to the second member, and so on.

Structure Variables in Assignment Statements

As can be seen in PARTINIT, one structure variable can be assigned to another:

```
part2 = part1;
```

The value of each member of part1 is assigned to the corresponding member of part2. Since a large structure can have dozens of members, such an assignment statement can require the computer to do a considerable amount of work.

Note that one structure variable can be assigned to another only when they are of the same structure type. If you try to assign a variable of one structure type to a variable of another type, the compiler will complain.

A Measurement Example

Let's see how a structure can be used to group a different kind of information. If you've ever looked at an architectural drawing, you know that (at least in the United States) distances are measured in feet and inches. (As you probably know, there are 12 inches in a foot.) The length of a living room, for example, might be given as 15'–8", meaning 15 feet plus 8 inches. The hyphen isn't a negative sign; it merely separates the feet from the inches. This is part of the English system of measurement. (We'll make no judgment here on the merits of English versus metric.) Figure 4.5 shows typical length measurements in the English system.

Suppose you want to create a drawing or architectural program that uses the English system. It will be convenient to store distances as two numbers, representing feet and inches. The next example, ENGLSTRC, gives an idea of how this could be done using a structure. This program will show how two measurements of type Distance can be added together.

4

STRUCTURES

```
// englstrc.cpp
// demonstrates structures using English measurements
#include <iostream>
using namespace std;
/////////////////////////////////////////////////////////////////
struct Distance                    //English distance
   {
   int feet;
   float inches;
   };
/////////////////////////////////////////////////////////////////
```

```
int main()
    {
    Distance d1, d3;              //define two lengths
    Distance d2 = { 11, 6.25 };  //define & initialize one length

                                 //get length d1 from user
    cout << "\nEnter feet: ";  cin >> d1.feet;
    cout << "Enter inches: ";  cin >> d1.inches;

                                 //add lengths d1 and d2 to get d3
    d3.inches = d1.inches + d2.inches;  //add the inches
    d3.feet = 0;                 //(for possible carry)
    if(d3.inches >= 12.0)        //if total exceeds 12.0,
        {                        //then decrease inches by 12.0
        d3.inches -= 12.0;       //and
        d3.feet++;               //increase feet by 1
        }
    d3.feet += d1.feet + d2.feet;  //add the feet

                                 //display all lengths
    cout << d1.feet << "\'-" << d1.inches << "\" + ";
    cout << d2.feet << "\'-" << d2.inches << "\" = ";
    cout << d3.feet << "\'-" << d3.inches << "\"\n";
    return 0;
    }
```

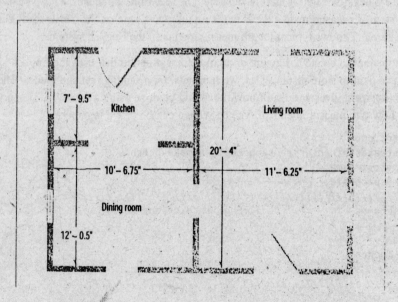

FIGURE 4.5
Measurements in the English system.

Here the structure `Distance` has two members: `feet` and `inches`. The `inches` variable may have a fractional part, so we'll use type `float` for it. Feet are always integers, so we'll use type `int` for them.

We define two such distances, `d1` and `d3`, without initializing them, while we initialize another, `d2`, to 11'–6.25". The program asks the user to enter a distance in feet and inches, and assigns this distance to `d1`. (The inches value should be smaller than 12.0.) It then adds the distance `d1` to `d2`, obtaining the total distance `d3`. Finally the program displays the two initial distances and the newly calculated total distance. Here's some output:

```
Enter feet: 10
Enter inches: 6.75
10'-6.75" + 11'-6.25" = 22'-1"
```

Notice that we can't add the two distances with a program statement like

```
d3 = d1 + d2;   // can't do this in ENGLSTRC
```

Why not? Because there is no routine built into C++ that knows how to add variables of type `Distance`. The + operator works with built-in types like `float`, but not with types we define ourselves, like `Distance`. (However, one of the benefits of using classes, as we'll see in Chapter 8, "Operator Overloading," is the ability to add and perform other operations on user-defined data types.)

Structures Within Structures

You can nest structures within other structures. Here's a variation on the ENGLSTRC program that shows how this looks. In this program we want to create a data structure that stores the dimensions of a typical room: its length and width. Since we're working with English distances, we'll use two variables of type `Distance` as the length and width variables.

```
struct Room
    {
    Distance length;
    Distance width;
    }
```

Here's a program, ENGLAREA, that uses the Room structure to represent a room.

```
// englarea.cpp
// demonstrates nested structures
#include <iostream>
using namespace std;
/////////////////////////////////////////////////////////////////
struct Distance                      //English distance
    {
    int feet;
```

4

```
      float inches;
      };
///////////////////////////////////////////////////////////////////
struct Room                          //rectangular area
      {
      Distance length;              //length of rectangle
      Distance width;               //width of rectangle
      };
///////////////////////////////////////////////////////////////////
int main()
      {
      Room dining;                  //define a room

      dining.length.feet = 13;      //assign values to room
      dining.length.inches = 6.5;
      dining.width.feet = 10;
      dining.width.inches = 0.0;
                                    //convert length & width
      float l = dining.length.feet + dining.length.inches/12;
      float w = dining.width.feet  + dining.width.inches/12;
                                    //find area and display it
      cout << "Dining room area is " << l * w
           << " square feet\n" ;
      return 0;
      }
```

This program defines a single variable—dining—of type Room, in the line

```
Room dining;   // variable dining of type Room
```

It then assigns values to the various members of this structure.

Accessing Nested Structure Members

Because one structure is nested inside another, we must apply the dot operator twice to access
the structure members.

```
dining.length.feet = 13;
```

In this statement, dining is the name of the structure variable, as before; length is the name of
a member in the outer structure (Room); and feet is the name of a member of the inner structure (Distance). The statement means "take the feet member of the length member of the
variable dining and assign it the value 13." Figure 4.6 shows how this works.

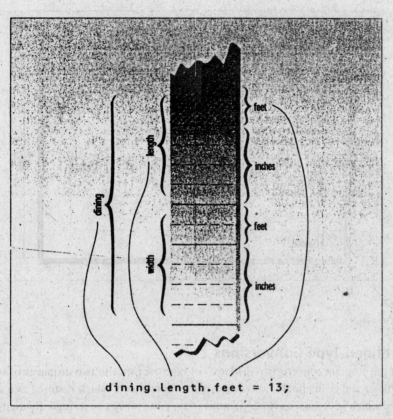

dining.length.feet = 13;

FIGURE 4.6
Dot operator and nested structures.

Once values have been assigned to members of dining, the program calculates the floor area of the room, as shown in Figure 4.7.

To find the area, the program converts the length and width from variables of type Distance to variables of type float, l, and w, representing distances in feet. The values of l and w are found by adding the feet member of Distance to the inches member divided by 12. The feet member is converted to type float automatically before the addition is performed, and the result is type float. The l and w variables are then multiplied together to obtain the area.

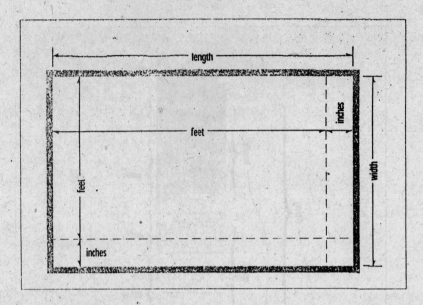

FIGURE 4.7
Area in feet and inches.

User-Defined Type Conversions

Note that the program converts two distances of type Distance to two distances of type float: the variables 1 and w. In effect it also converts the room's area, which is stored as a structure of type Room (which is defined as two structures of type Distance), to a single floating-point number representing the area in square feet. Here's the output:

```
Dining room area is 135.416672 square feet
```

Converting a value of one type to a value of another is an important aspect of programs that employ user-defined data types.

Initializing Nested Structures

How do you initialize a structure variable that itself contains structures? The following statement initializes the variable dining to the same values it is given in the ENGLAREA program:

```
Room dining = { {13, 6.5}, {10, 0.0} };
```

Each structure of type Distance, which is embedded in Room, is initialized separately. Remember that this involves surrounding the values with braces and separating them with commas. The first Distance is initialized to

```
{13, 6.5}
```

and the second to

```
{10, 0.0}
```

These two Distance values are then used to initialize the Room variable; again, they are surrounded with braces and separated by commas.

Depth of Nesting

In theory, structures can be nested to any depth. In a program that designs apartment buildings, you might find yourself with statements like this one:

```
apartment1.laundry_room.washing_machine.width.feet
```

A Card Game Example

Let's examine a different kind of example. This one uses a structure to model a playing card. The program imitates a game played by cardsharps (professional gamblers) at carnivals. The cardsharp shows you three cards, then places them face down on the table and interchanges their positions several times. If you can guess correctly where a particular card is, you win. Everything is in plain sight, yet the cardsharp switches the cards so rapidly and confusingly that the player (the *mark*) almost always loses track of the card and loses the game, which is, of course, played for money.

Here's the structure the program uses to represent a playing card:

```
struct card
    {
    int number;
    int suit;
    };
```

This structure uses separate members to hold the number of the card and the suit. The number runs from 2 to 14, where 11, 12, 13, and 14 represent the jack, queen, king, and ace, respectively (this is the order used in poker). The suit runs from 0 to 3, where these four numbers represent clubs, diamonds, hearts, and spades.

Here's the listing for CARDS:

```
// cards.cpp
// demonstrates structures using playing cards
#include <iostream>
using namespace std;

const int clubs = 0;                          //suits
const int diamonds = 1;
const int hearts = 2;
const int spades = 3;
```

4

```
const int jack = 11;                          //face cards
const int queen = 12;
const int king = 13;
const int ace = 14;
//////////////////////////////////////////////////////////////////
struct card
    {
    int number;    //  o 10, jack, queen, king, ace
    int suit;          s, diamonds, hearts, spades
    };
////////////////  ////////////////////////  ////////////////////////////
int main()
    {
    card temp, chosen, prize;                 //define cards
    int position;

    card card1 = { 7, clubs };                //initialize card1
    cout << "Card 1 is the 7 of clubs\n";

    card card2 = { jack, hearts };            //initialize card2
    cout << "Card 2 is the jack of hearts\n";

    card card3 = { ace, spades };             //initialize card3
    cout << "Card 3 is the ace of spades\n";

    prize = card3;                //copy this card, to remember it

    cout << "I'm swapping card 1 and card 3\n";
    temp = card3; card3 = card1; card1 = temp;

    cout << "I'm swapping card 2 and card 3\n";
    temp = card3; card3 = card2; card2 = temp;

    cout << "I'm swapping card 1 and card 2\n";
    temp = card2; card2 = card1; card1 = temp;

    cout << "Now, where (1, 2, or 3) is the ace of spades? ";
    cin >> position;

    switch (position)
        {
        case 1: chosen = card1; break;
        case 2: chosen = card2; break;
        case 3: chosen = card3; break;
        }
```

```
    if(chosen.number == prize.number &&          // compare cards
       chosen.suit == prize.suit)
       cout << "That's right!  You win!\n";
    else
       cout << "Sorry. You lose.\n";
    return 0;
    }
```

Here's some sample interaction with the program:

```
Card 1 is the 7 of clubs
Card 2 is the jack of hearts
Card 3 is the ace of spades
I'm swapping card 1 and card 3
I'm swapping card 2 and card 3
I'm swapping card 1 and card 2
Now, where (1, 2, or 3) is the ace of spades? 3
Sorry. You lose.
```

In this case the hapless mark chose the wrong card (the right answer is 2).

The program begins by defining a number of variables of type const int for the face card and suit values. (Not all these variables are used in the program; they're included for completeness.) Next the card structure is specified. The program then defines three uninitialized variables of type card: temp, chosen, and prize. It also defines three cards—card1, card2, and card3—which it initializes to three arbitrary card values. It prints out the values of these cards for the user's information. It then sets a card variable, prize, to one of these card values as a way of remembering it. This card is the one whose location the player will be asked to guess at the end of the game.

Next the program rearranges the cards. It swaps the first and third cards, the second and third cards, and the first and second cards. Each time it tells the user what it's doing. (If you find the program too easy, you can add more such statements to further shuffle the cards. Flashing the statements on the screen for a limited time would also increase the challenge.)

Finally the program asks the player what position a particular card is in. It sets a card variable, chosen, to the card in this position, and then compares chosen with the prize card. If they match, it's a win for the player; if not, it's a loss.

Notice how easy swapping cards is.

```
temp = card3;   card3 = card1;   card1 = temp;
```

Although the cards represent structures, they can be moved around very naturally, thanks to the ability of the assignment operator (=) to work with structures.

4

Unfortunately, just as structures can't be added, they also can't be compared. You can't say

```
if( chosen == prize )                    //not legal yet
```

because there's no routine built into the == operator that knows about the card structure. But, as with addition, this problem can be solved with operator overloading, as we'll see later.

Structures and Classes

We must confess to having misled you slightly on the capabilities of structures. It's true that structures are usually used to hold data only, and classes are used to hold both data and functions. However, in C++, structures can in fact hold both data and functions. (In C they can hold only data.) The syntactical distinction between structures and classes in C++ is minimal, so they can in theory be used almost interchangeably. But most C++ programmers use structures as we have in this chapter, exclusively for data. Classes are usually used to hold both data and functions, as we'll see in Chapter 6, "Objects and Classes."

Enumerations

As we've seen, structures can be looked at as a way to provide user-defined data types. A different approach to defining your own data type is the *enumeration*. This feature of C++ is less crucial than structures. You can write perfectly good object-oriented programs in C++ without knowing anything about enumerations. However, they are very much in the spirit of C++, in that, by allowing you to define your own data types, they can simplify and clarify your programming.

Days of the Week

Enumerated types work when you know in advance a finite (usually short) list of values that a data type can take on. Here's an example program, DAYENUM, that uses an enumeration for the days of the week:

```
// dayenum.cpp
// demonstrates enum types
#include <iostream>
using namespace std;
                              //specify enum type
enum days_of_week { Sun, Mon, Tue, Wed, Thu, Fri, Sat };

int main()
    {
    days_of_week day1, day2;    //define variables
                                //of type days_of_week
```

```
day1 = Mon;                  //give values to
day2 = Thu;                  //variables

int diff = day2 - day1;      //can do integer arithmetic
cout << "Days between = " << diff << endl;

if(day1 < day2)              //can do comparisons
    cout << "day1 comes before day2\n";
return 0;
}
```

An enum declaration defines the set of all names that will be permissible values of the type. These permissible values are called *enumerators*. The enum type days_of_week has seven enumerators: Sun, Mon, Tue, and so on, up to Sat. Figure 4.8 shows the syntax of an enum declaration.

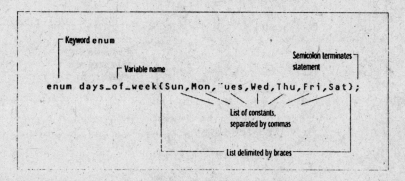

FIGURE 4.8
Syntax of enum specifier.

An *enumeration* is a list of all possible values. This is unlike the specification of an int, for example, which is given in terms of a range of values. In an enum you must give a specific name to every possible value. Figure 4.9 shows the difference between an int and an enum.

Once you've declared the enum type days_of_week as shown, you can define variables of this type. DAYENUM has two such variables, day1 and day2, defined in the statement

days_of_week day1, day2;

(In C you must use the keyword enum before the type name, as in

enum days_of_week day1, day2;

In C++ this isn't necessary.)

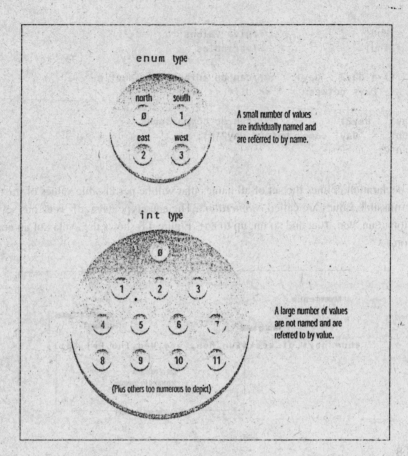

FIGURE 4.9
Usage of ints and enums.

Variables of an enumerated type, like day1 and day2, can be given any of the values listed in the enum declaration. In the example we give them the values Mon and Thu. You can't use values that weren't listed in the declaration. Such statements as

```
day1 = halloween;
```

are illegal.

You can use the standard arithmetic operators on enum types. In the program we subtract two values. You can also use the comparison operators, as we show. Here's the program's output:

```
Days between = 3
day1 comes before day2
```

The use of arithmetic and relational operators doesn't make much sense with some enum types. For example, if you have the declaration

```
enum pets { cat, dog, hamster, canary, ocelot };
```

then it may not be clear what expressions like dog + canary or (cat < hamster) mean.

Enumerations are treated internally as integers. This explains why you can perform arithmetic and relational operations on them. Ordinarily the first name in the list is given the value 0, the next name is given the value 1, and so on. In the DAYENUM example, the values Sun through Sat are stored as the integer values 0–6.

Arithmetic operations on enum types take place on the integer values. However, although the compiler knows that your enum variables are really integers, you must be careful of trying to take advantage of this fact. If you say

```
day1 = 5;
```

the compiler will issue a warning (although it will compile). It's better to forget—whenever possible—that enums are really integers.

One Thing or Another

Our next example counts the words in a phrase typed in by the user. Unlike the earlier CHCOUNT example, however, it doesn't simply count spaces to determine the number of words. Instead it counts the places where a string of nonspace characters changes to a space, as shown in Figure 4.10.

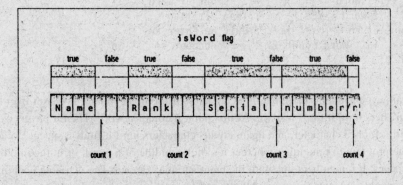

FIGURE 4.10

Operation of the WDCOUNT program.

This way you don't get a false count if you type multiple spaces between words. (It still doesn't handle tabs and other whitespace characters.) Here's the listing for WDCOUNT: This example shows an enumeration with only two enumerators.

```
// wdcount.cpp
// demonstrates enums, counts words in phrase
#include <iostream>
using namespace std;
#include <conio.h>                //for getche()

enum itsaWord { NO, YES };        //NO=0, YES=1

int main()
   {
   itsaWord isWord = NO;          //YES when in a word,
                                  //NO when in whitespace
   char ch = 'a';                 //character read from keyboard
   int wordcount = 0;             //number of words read

   cout << "Enter a phrase:\n";
   do {
      ch = getche();              //get character
      if(ch==' ' || ch=='\r')     //if white space,
         {
         if( isWord == YES ).     //and doing a word,
            {                     //then it's end of word
            wordcount++;          //count the word
            isWord = NO;          //reset flag
            }
         }                        //otherwise, it's
      else                        //normal character
         if( isWord == NO )       //if start of word,
            isWord = YES;         //then set flag
      } while( ch != '\r' );      //quit on Enter key
   cout << "\n---Word count is " << wordcount << "---\n";
   return 0;
   }
```

The program cycles in a do loop, reading characters from the keyboard. It passes over (non-space) characters until it finds a space. At this point it counts a word. Then it passes over spaces until it finds a character, and again counts characters until it finds a space. Doing this requires the program to remember whether it's in the middle of a word, or in the middle of a string of spaces. It remembers this with the enum variable isWord. This variable is defined to be of type itsaWord. This type is specified in the statement

```
enum itsaWord { NO, YES };
```

Variables of type itsaWord have only two possible values: NO and YES. Notice that the list starts with NO, so this value will be given the value 0—the value that indicates false. (We could also use a variable of type bool for this purpose.)

The `isWord` variable is set to `NO` when the program starts. When the program encounters the first nonspace character, it sets `isWord` to `YES` to indicate that it's in the middle of a word. It keeps this value until the next space is found, at which point it's set back to `NO`. Behind the scenes, `NO` has the value 0 and `YES` has the value 1, but we avoid making use of this fact. We could have used `if(isWord)` instead of `if(isWord == YES)`, and `if(!isWord)` instead of `if(isWord == NO)`, but this is not good style.

Note also that we need an extra set of braces around the second `if` statement in the program, so that the `else` will match the first `if`.

Another approach to a yes/no situation such as that in WDCOUNT is to use a variable of type `bool`. This may be a little more straightforward, depending on the situation.

Organizing the Cards

Here's our final example of enum types. Remember that in the CARDS program earlier in this chapter we defined a group of constants of type `const int` to represent a card's suits.

```
const int clubs = 0;
const int diamonds = 1;
const int hearts = 2;
const int spades = 3;
```

This sort of list is somewhat clumsy. Let's revise the CARDS program to use enumerations instead. Here's the listing for CARDENUM:

```
// cardenum.cpp
// demonstrates enumerations
#include <iostream>
using namespace std;

const int jack = 11;          //2 through 10 are unnamed integers
const int queen = 12;
const int king = 13;
const int ace = 14;

enum Suit { clubs, diamonds, hearts, spades };
/////////////////////////////////////////////////////////////////
struct card
    {
    int number;               //2 to 10, jack, queen, king, ace
    Suit suit;                //clubs, diamonds, hearts, spades
    };
/////////////////////////////////////////////////////////////////
int main()
    {
```

```
      card temp, chosen, prize;                    //define cards
      int position;

      card card1 = { 7, clubs };                    //initialize card1
      cout << "Card 1 is the seven of clubs\n";

      card card2 = { jack, hearts };                //initialize card2
      cout << "Card 2 is the jack of hearts\n";

      card card3 = { ace, spades };                 //initialize card3
      cout << "Card 3 is the ace of spades\n";

      prize = card3;                        //copy this card, to remember it

      cout << "I'm swapping card 1 and card 3\n";
      temp = card3; card3 = card1; card1 = temp;

      cout << "I'm swapping card 2 and card 3\n";
      temp = card3; card3 = card2; card2 = temp;

      cout << "I'm swapping card 1 and card 2\n";
      temp = card2; card2 = card1; card1 = temp;

      cout << "Now, where (1, 2, or 3) is the ace of spades? ";
      cin >> position;

      switch (position)
         {
         case 1: chosen = card1; break;
         case 2: chosen = card2; break;
         case 3: chosen = card3; break;
         }
      if(chosen.number == prize.number &&           //compare cards
              chosen.suit == prize.suit)
         cout << "That's right!  You win!\n";
      else
         cout << "Sorry. You lose.\n";
      return 0;
      }
```

Here the set of definitions for suits used in the CARDS program has been replaced by an enum declaration:

```
enum Suit { clubs, diamonds, hearts, spades };
```

This is a cleaner approach than using `const` variables. We know exactly what the possible values of the `suit` are; attempts to use other values, as in

```
card1.suit = 5;
```

result in warnings from the compiler.

Specifying Integer Values

We said that in an `enum` declaration the first enumerator was given the integer value 0, the second the value 1, and so on. This ordering can be altered by using an equal sign to specify a starting point other than 0. For example, if you want the suits to start with 1 instead of 0, you can say

```
enum Suit { clubs=1, diamonds, hearts, spades };
```

Subsequent names are given values starting at this point, so `diamonds` is 2, `hearts` is 3, and `spades` is 4. Actually you can use an equal sign to give a specified value to any enumerator.

Not Perfect

One annoying aspect of `enum` types is that they are not recognized by C++ input/output (I/O) statements. As an example, what do you think the following code fragment will cause to be displayed?

```
enum direction { north, south, east, west };
direction dir1 = south;
cout << dir1;
```

Did you guess the output would be `south`? That would be nice, but C++ I/O treats variables of `enum` types as integers, so the output would be 1.

Other Examples

Here are some other examples of enumerated data declarations, to give you a feeling for possible uses of this feature:

```
enum months { Jan, Feb, Mar, Apr, May, Jun,
              Jul, Aug, Sep, Oct, Nov, Dec };

enum switch { off, on };

enum meridian { am, pm };

enum chess { pawn, knight, bishop, rook, queen, king };

enum coins { penny, nickel, dime, quarter, half-dollar, dollar };
```

We'll see other examples in future programs.

4

STRUCTURES

Summary

We've covered two topics in this chapter: structures and enumerations. *Structures* are an important component of C++, since their syntax is the same as that of classes. In fact, classes are (syntactically, at least) nothing more than structures that include functions. Structures are typically used to group several data items together to form a single entity. A structure definition lists the variables that make up the structure. Other definitions then set aside memory for structure variables. Structure variables are treated as indivisible units in some situations (such as setting one structure variable equal to another), but in other situations their members are accessed individually (often using the dot operator).

An *enumeration* is a programmer-defined type that is limited to a fixed list of values. A declaration gives the type a name and specifies the permissible values, which are called *enumerators*. Definitions can then create variables of this type. Internally the compiler treats enumeration variables as integers.

Structures should not be confused with enumerations. Structures are a powerful and flexible way of grouping a diverse collection of data into a single entity. An enumeration allows the definition of variables that can take on a fixed set of values that are listed (enumerated) in the type's declaration.

Questions

Answers to these questions can be found in Appendix G.

1. A structure brings together a group of

   a. items of the same data type.

   b. related data items.

   c. integers with user-defined names.

   d. variables.

2. True or false: A structure and a class use similar syntax.

3. The closing brace of a structure is followed by a _____.

4. Write a structure specification that includes three variables—all of type `int`—called `hrs`, `mins`, and `secs`. Call this structure `time`.

5. True or false: A structure definition creates space in memory for a variable.

6. When accessing a structure member, the identifier to the left of the dot operator is the name of
   a. a structure member.
   b. a structure tag.
   c. a structure variable.
   d. the keyword `struct`.

7. Write a statement that sets the `hrs` member of the `time2` structure variable equal to 11.

8. If you have three variables defined to be of type `struct time`, and this structure contains three `int` members, how many bytes of memory do the variables use together?

9. Write a definition that initializes the members of `time1`—which is a variable of type `struct time`, as defined in Question 4—to `hrs` = 11, `mins` = 10, `secs` = 59.

10. True or false: You can assign one structure variable to another, provided they are of the same type.

11. Write a statement that sets the variable `temp` equal to the `paw` member of the `dogs` member of the `fido` variable.

12. An enumeration brings together a group of
    a. items of different data types.
    b. related data variables.
    c. integers with user-defined names.
    d. constant values.

13. Write a statement that declares an enumeration called `players` with the values B1, B2, SS, B3, RF, CF, LF, P, and C.

14. Assuming the enum type `players` as declared in Question 13, define two variables `joe` and `tom`, and assign them the values LF and P, respectively.

15. Assuming the statements of Questions 13 and 14, state whether each of the following statements is legal.
    a. `joe = QB;`
    b. `tom = SS;`
    c. `LF = tom;`
    d. `difference = joe - tom;`

16. The first three enumerators of an `enum` type are normally represented by the values
    _____, _____, and _____.

17. Write a statement that declares an enumeration called `speeds` with the enumerators `obsolete`, `single`, and `album`. Give these three names the integer values 78, 45, and 33.

18. State the reason that

```
enum isWord{ NO, YES };
```

is better than

```
enum isWord{ YES, NO };
```

Exercises

Answers to the starred exercises can be found in Appendix G.

*1. A phone number, such as (212) 767-8900, can be thought of as having three parts: the area code (212), the exchange (767), and the number (8900). Write a program that uses a structure to store these three parts of a phone number separately. Call the structure phone. Create two structure variables of type phone. Initialize one, and have the user input a number for the other one. Then display both numbers. The interchange might look like this:

```
Enter your area code, exchange, and number: 415 555 1212
My number is (212) 767-8900
Your number is (415) 555-1212
```

*2. A point on the two-dimensional plane can be represented by two numbers: an x coordinate and a y coordinate. For example, (4,5) represents a point 4 units to the right of the vertical axis, and 5 units up from the horizontal axis. The sum of two points can be defined as a new point whose x coordinate is the sum of the x coordinates of the two points, and whose y coordinate is the sum of the y coordinates.

Write a program that uses a structure called point to model a point. Define three points, and have the user input values to two of them. Then set the third point equal to the sum of the other two, and display the value of the new point. Interaction with the program might look like this:

```
Enter coordinates for p1: 3 4
Enter coordinates for p2: 5 7
Coordinates of p1+p2 are: 8, 11
```

*3. Create a structure called Volume that uses three variables of type Distance (from the ENGLSTRC example) to model the volume of a room. Initialize a variable of type Volume to specific dimensions, then calculate the volume it represents, and print out the result. To calculate the volume, convert each dimension from a Distance variable to a variable of type float representing feet and fractions of a foot, and then multiply the resulting three numbers.

4. Create a structure called employee that contains two members: an employee number (type int) and the employee's compensation (in dollars; type float). Ask the user to fill in this data for three employees, store it in three variables of type struct employee, and then display the information for each employee.

5. Create a structure of type date that contains three members: the month, the day of the month, and the year, all of type int. (Or use day-month-year order if you prefer.) Have the user enter a date in the format 12/31/2001, store it in a variable of type struct date, then retrieve the values from the variable and print them out in the same format.

6. We said earlier that C++ I/O statements don't automatically understand the data types of enumerations. Instead, the (>>) and (<<) operators think of such variables simply as integers. You can overcome this limitation by using switch statements to translate between the user's way of expressing an enumerated variable and the actual values of the enumerated variable. For example, imagine an enumerated type with values that indicate an employee type within an organization:

```
enum etype { laborer, secretary, manager, accountant, executive,
researcher };
```

Write a program that first allows the user to specify a type by entering its first letter ('l', 's', 'm', and so on), then stores the type chosen as a value of a variable of type enum etype, and finally displays the complete word for this type.

```
Enter employee type (first letter only)
    laborer, secretary, manager,
    accountant, executive, researcher): a
Employee type is accountant.
```

You'll probably need two switch statements: one for input and one for output.

7. Add a variable of type enum etype (see Exercise 6), and another variable of type struct date (see Exercise 5) to the employee class of Exercise 4. Organize the resulting program so that the user enters four items of information for each of three employees: an employee number, the employee's compensation, the employee type, and the date of first employment. The program should store this information in three variables of type employee, and then display their contents.

8. Start with the fraction-adding program of Exercise 9 in Chapter 2, "C++ Programming Basics." This program stores the numerator and denominator of two fractions before adding them, and may also store the answer, which is also a fraction. Modify the program so that all fractions are stored in variables of type struct fraction, whose two members are the fraction's numerator and denominator (both type int). All fraction-related data should be stored in structures of this type.

9. Create a structure called time. Its three members, all type int, should be called hours, minutes, and seconds. Write a program that prompts the user to enter a time value in hours, minutes, and seconds. This can be in 12:59:59 format, or each number can be entered at a separate prompt ("Enter hours:", and so forth). The program should then store the time in a variable of type struct time, and finally print out the total number of seconds represented by this time value:

```
long totalsecs = t1.hours 3600 + t1.minutes*60 + t1.seconds
```

10. Create a structure called `sterling` that stores money amounts in the old-style British system discussed in Exercises 8 and 11 in Chapter 3, "Loops and Decisions." The members could be called `pounds`, `shillings`, and `pence`, all of type `int`. The program should ask the user to enter a money amount in new-style decimal pounds (type `double`), convert it to the old-style system, store it in a variable of type `struct sterling`, and then display this amount in pounds-shillings-pence format.

11. Use the `time` structure from Exercise 9, and write a program that obtains two `time` values from the user in 12:59:59 format, stores them in `struct time` variables, converts each one to seconds (type `int`), adds these quantities, converts the result back to hours-minutes-seconds, stores the result in a `time` structure, and finally displays the result in 12:59:59 format.

12. Revise the four-function fraction calculator program of Exercise 12 in Chapter 3 so that each fraction is stored internally as a variable of type `struct fraction`, as discussed in Exercise 8 in this chapter.

Functions

IN THIS CHAPTER

A function groups a number of program statements into a unit and gives it a name. This unit can then be invoked from other parts of the program.

The most important reason to use functions is to aid in the conceptual organization of a program. Dividing a program into functions is, as we discussed in Chapter 1, "The Big Picture," one of the major principles of structured programming. (However, object-oriented programming provides additional, more powerful ways to organize programs.)

Another reason to use functions (and the reason they were invented, long ago) is to reduce program size. Any sequence of instructions that appears in a program more than once is a candidate for being made into a function. The function's code is stored in only one place in memory, even though the function is executed many times in the course of the program. Figure 5.1 shows how a function is invoked from different sections of a program.

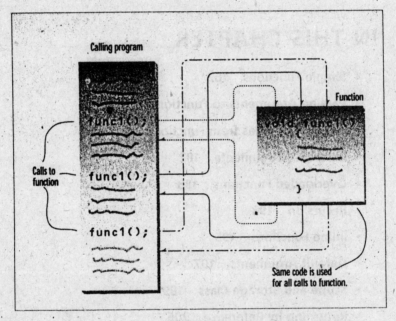

FIGURE 5.1
Flow of control to a function.

Functions in C++ (and C) are similar to subroutines and procedures in various other languages.

Simple Functions

Our first example demonstrates a simple function whose purpose is to print a line of 45 asterisks. The example program generates a table, and lines of asterisks are used to make the table more readable. Here's the listing for TABLE:

```
// table.cpp
// demonstrates simple function
#include <iostream>
using namespace std;

void starline();                          //function declaration
                                          //   (prototype)

int main()
   {
   starline();                            //call to function
   cout << "Data type    Range" << endl;
   starline();                            //call to function
   cout << "char         -128 to 127" << endl
        << "short        -32,768 to 32,767" << endl
        << "int          System dependent" << endl
        << "long         -2,147,483,648 to 2,147,483,647" << endl;
   starline();                            //call to function
   return 0;
   }
//--------------------------------------------------------------
// starline()
// function definition
void starline()                           //function declarator
   {
   for(int j=0; j<45; j++)                //function body
      cout << '*';
   cout << endl;
   }
```

The output from the program looks like this:

```
*********************************************
Data type    Range
*********************************************
char         -128 to 127
short        -32,768 to 32,767
int          System dependent
long     -2,147,483,648 to 2,147,483,647
*********************************************
```

The program consists of two functions: main() and starline(). You've already seen many programs that use main() alone. What other components are necessary to add a function to the program? There are three: the function *declaration*, the *calls* to the function, and the function *definition*.

5

FUNCTIONS

The Function Declaration

Just as you can't use a variable without first telling the compiler what it is, you also can't use a function without telling the compiler about it. There are two ways to do this. The approach we show here is to *declare* the function before it is called. (The other approach is to *define* it before it's called; we'll examine that next.) In the TABLE program, the function starline() is declared in the line

```
void starline();
```

The declaration tells the compiler that at some later point we plan to present a function called *starline*. The keyword void specifies that the function has no return value, and the empty parentheses indicate that it takes no arguments. (You can also use the keyword void in parentheses to indicate that the function takes no arguments, as is often done in C, but leaving them empty is the more common practice in C++.) We'll have more to say about arguments and return values soon.

Notice that the function declaration is terminated with a semicolon. It is a complete statement in itself.

Function declarations are also called *prototypes*, since they provide a model or blueprint for the function. They tell the compiler, "a function that looks like this is coming up later in the program, so it's all right if you see references to it before you see the function itself." The information in the declaration (the return type and the number and types of any arguments) is also sometimes referred to as the function *signature*.

Calling the Function

The function is *called* (or *invoked*, or *executed*) three times from main(). Each of the three calls looks like this:

```
starline();
```

This is all we need to call the function: the function name, followed by parentheses. The syntax of the call is very similar to that of the declaration, except that the return type is not used. The call is terminated by a semicolon. Executing the call statement causes the function to execute; that is, control is transferred to the function, the statements in the function definition (which we'll examine in a moment) are executed, and then control returns to the statement following the function call.

The Function Definition

Finally we come to the function itself, which is referred to as the function *definition*. The definition contains the actual code for the function. Here's the definition for starline():

```
void starline()                //declarator
  {
  for(int j=0; j<45; j++)
      cout << '*';             //function body
  cout << endl;
  }
```

The definition consists of a line called the *declarator*, followed by the function *body*. The function body is composed of the statements that make up the function, delimited by braces.

The declarator must agree with the declaration; It must use the same function name, have the same argument types in the same order (if there are arguments), and have the same return type.

Notice that the declarator is *not* terminated by a semicolon. Figure 5.2 shows the syntax of the function declaration, function call, and function definition.

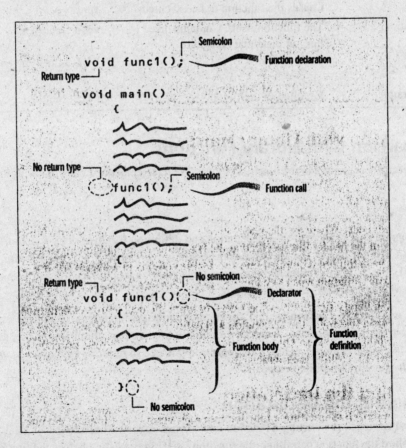

FIGURE 5.2
Function syntax.

When the function is called, control is transferred to the first statement in the function body. The other statements in the function body are then executed, and when the closing brace is encountered, control returns to the calling program.

Table 5.1 summarizes the different function components.

TABLE 5.1 Function Components

Component	Purpose	Example
Declaration (prototype)	Specifies function name, argument types, and return value. Alerts compiler (and programmer) that a function is coming up later.	`void func();`
Call	Causes the function to be executed.	`func();`

Definition	The function itself. Contains the lines of code that constitute the function.	`void func()`
		 `{`
		 `// lines of code`
		 `}`

Declarator	First line of definition.	`void func()`

Comparison with Library Functions

We've already seen some library functions in use. We have embedded calls to library functions, such as

```
ch = getche();
```

in our program code. Where are the declaration and definition for this library function? The declaration is in the header file specified at the beginning of the program (CONIO.H, for getche()). The definition (compiled into executable code) is in a library file that's linked automatically to your program when you build it.

When we use a library function we don't need to write the declaration or definition. But when we write our own functions, the declaration and definition are part of our source file, as we've shown in the TABLE example. (Things get more complicated in multifile programs, as we'll discuss in Chapter 13, "Multifile Programs.")

Eliminating the Declaration

The second approach to inserting a function into a program is to eliminate the function declaration and place the function definition (the function itself) in the listing before the first call to the function. For example, we could rewrite TABLE to produce TABLE2, in which the definition for starline() appears first.

```
// table2.cpp
// demonstrates function definition preceding function calls
#include <iostream>
using namespace std;                    //no function declaration
//-------------------------------------------------------------
// starline()                           //function definition
void starline()
   {
   for(int j=0; j<45; j++)
      cout << '*';
   cout << endl;
   }
//-------------------------------------------------------------
int main()                              //main() follows function
   {
   starline();                          //call to function
   cout << "Data type    Range" << endl;
   starline();                          //call to function
   cout << "char         -128 to 127" << endl
        << "short        -32,768 to 32,767" << endl
        << "int          System dependent" << endl
        << "long         -2,147,483,648 to 2,147,483,647" << endl;
   starline();                          //call to function
   return 0;
   }
```

This approach is simpler for short programs, in that it removes the declaration, but it is less flexible. To use this technique when there are more than a few functions, the programmer must give considerable thought to arranging the functions so that each one appears before it is called by any other. Sometimes this is impossible. Also, many programmers prefer to place main() first in the listing, since it is where execution begins. In general we'll stick with the first approach, using declarations and starting the listing with main().

Passing Arguments to Functions

An *argument* is a piece of data (an int value, for example) passed from a program to the function. Arguments allow a function to operate with different values, or even to do different things, depending on the requirements of the program calling it.

Passing Constants

As an example, let's suppose we decide that the starline() function in the last example is too rigid. Instead of a function that always prints 45 asterisks, we want a function that will print any character any number of times.

Here's a program, TABLEARG, that incorporates just such a function. We use arguments to pass the character to be printed and the number of times to print it.

```cpp
// tablearg.cpp
// demonstrates function arguments
#include <iostream>
using namespace std;
void repchar(char, int);                    //function declaration

int main()
   {
   repchar('-', 43);                        //call to function
   cout << "Data type    Range" << endl;
   repchar('=', 23);                        //call to function
   cout << "char         -128 to 127" << endl
        << "short        -32,768 to 32,767" << endl
        << "int          System dependent" << endl
        << "double       -2,147,483,648 to 2,147,483,647" << endl;
   repchar('-', 43);                        //call to function
   return 0;
   }
//--------------------------------------------------------------
// repchar()
// function definition
void repchar(char ch, int n)                //function declarator
   {
   for(int j=0; j<n; j++)                    //function body
      cout << ch;
   cout << endl;
   }
```

The new function is called repchar(). Its declaration looks like this:

```cpp
void repchar(char, int);   // declaration specifies data types
```

The items in the parentheses are the data types of the arguments that will be sent to repchar(): char and int.

In a function call, specific values—constants in this case—are inserted in the appropriate place in the parentheses:

```cpp
repchar('-', 43);   // function call specifies actual values
```

This statement instructs repchar() to print a line of 43 dashes. The values supplied in the call must be of the types specified in the declaration: the first argument, the - character, must be of type char; and the second argument, the number 43, must be of type int. The types in the declaration and the definition must also agree.

The next call to repchar()

```
repchar('=', 23);
```

tells it to print a line of 23 equal signs. The third call again prints 43 dashes. Here's the output from TABLEARG:

```
. . . . . . . . . . . . . . . . . . . . . . . . . . . . . . . . . . . . . . . . . .
Data type    Range
=========================
char         -128 to 127
short        -32,768 to 32,767
int          System dependent
long         -2,147,483,648 to 2,147,483,647
. . . . . . . . . . . . . .-. . . . . . . . . . . . . . . . . . . . . . . .
```

The calling program supplies *arguments*, such as '-' and 43, to the function. The variables used within the function to hold the argument values are called *parameters*; in repchar() they are ch and n. (We should note that many programmers use the terms argument and parameter somewhat interchangeably.) The declarator in the function definition specifies both the data types and the names of the parameters:

```
void repchar(char ch, int n)   //declarator specifies parameter
                               //names and data types
```

These parameter names, ch and n, are used in the function as if they were normal variables. Placing them in the declarator is equivalent to defining them with statements like

```
char ch;
int n;
```

When the function is called, its parameters are automatically initialized to the values passed by the calling program.

Passing Variables

In the TABLEARG example the arguments were constants: '-', 43, and so on. Let's look at an example where variables, instead of constants, are passed as arguments. This program, VARARG, incorporates the same repchar() function as did TABLEARG, but lets the user specify the character and the number of times it should be repeated.

```
// vararg.cpp
// demonstrates variable arguments
#include <iostream>
using namespace std;
void repchar(char, int);                    //function declaration
```

```
int main()
   {
   char chin;
   int nin;

   cout << "Enter a character: ";
   cin >> chin;
   cout << "Enter number of times to repeat it: ";
   cin >> nin;
   repchar(chin, nin);
   return 0;
   }
//·····················································································
// repchar()
// function definition
void repchar(char ch, int n)                    //function declarator
   {
   for(int j=0; j<n; j++)                       //function body
     cout << ch;
   cout << endl;
   }
```

Here's some sample interaction with VARARG:

```
Enter a character: +
Enter number of times to repeat it: 20
++++++++++++++++++++
```

Here chin and nin in main() are used as arguments to repchar():

```
repchar(chin, nin);    // function call
```

The data types of variables used as arguments must match those specified in the function declaration and definition, just as they must for constants. That is, chin must be a char, and nin must be an int.

Passing by Value

In VARARG the particular values possessed by chin and nin when the function call is executed will be passed to the function. As it did when constants were passed to it, the function creates new variables to hold the values of these variable arguments. The function gives these new variables the names and data types of the parameters specified in the declarator: ch of type char and n of type int. It initializes these parameters to the values passed. They are then accessed like other variables by statements in the function body.

Passing arguments in this way, where the function creates copies of the arguments passed to it, is called *passing by value*. We'll explore another approach, *passing by reference*, later in this chapter. Figure 5.3 shows how new variables are created in the function when arguments are passed by value.

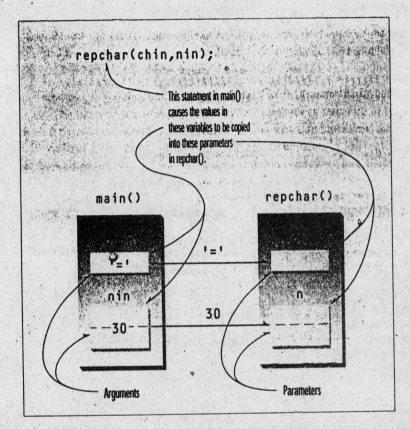

```
repchar(chin,nin);
```

This statement in main()
causes the values in
these variables to be copied
into these parameters
in repchar().

main()   repchar()

'='

nin   n

30   30

Arguments   Parameters

FIGURE 5.3
Passing by value.

Structures as Arguments

Entire structures can be passed as arguments to functions. We'll show two examples, one with the Distance structure, and one with a structure representing a graphics shape.

Passing a Distance Structure

This example features a function that uses an argument of type Distance, the same structure type we saw in several programs in Chapter 4, "Structures." Here's the listing for ENGLDISP:

```
// engldisp.cpp
// demonstrates passing structure as argument
#include <iostream>
using namespace std;
///////////////////////////////////////////////////////////
struct Distance                    //English distance
    {
    int feet;
    float inches;
    };
///////////////////////////////////////////////////////////
void engldisp( Distance );         //declaration

int main()
    {
    Distance d1, d2;                    //define two lengths

                                        //get length d1 from user
    cout << "Enter feet: ";   cin >> d1.feet;
    cout << "Enter inches: "; cin >> d1.inches;


                                        //get length d2 from user
    cout << "\nEnter feet: ";  cin >> d2.feet;
    cout << "Enter inches: "; cin >> d2.inches;

    cout << "\nd1 = ";
    engldisp(d1);                  //display length 1
    cout << "\nd2 = ";
    engldisp(d2);                  //display length 2
    cout << endl;
    return 0;
    }
//------------------------------------------------------------
// engldisp()
// display structure of type Distance in feet and inches
void engldisp( Distance dd )    //parameter dd of type Distance
    {
    cout << dd.feet << "\'-" << dd.inches << "\"";
    }
```

The main() part of this program accepts two distances in feet-and-inches format from the user, and places these values in two structures, d1 and d2. It then calls a function, engldisp(), that takes a Distance structure variable as an argument. The purpose of the function is to display the distance passed to it in the standard format, such as 10'–2.25". Here's some sample interaction with the program:

```
Enter feet: 6
Enter inches: 4
```

```
Enter feet: 5
Enter inches: 4.25

d1 = 6'-4"
d2 = 5'-4.25"
```

The function declaration and the function calls in main(), and the declarator in the function body, treat the structure variables just as they would any other variable used as an argument; this one just happens to be type Distance, rather than a basic type like char or int.

In main() there are two calls to the function engldisp(). The first passes the structure d1; the second passes d2. The function engldisp() uses a parameter that is a structure of type Distance, which it names dd. As with simple variables, this structure variable is automatically initialized to the value of the structure passed from main(). Statements in engldisp() can then access the members of dd in the usual way, with the expressions dd.feet and dd.inches. Figure 5.4 shows a structure being passed as an argument to a function.

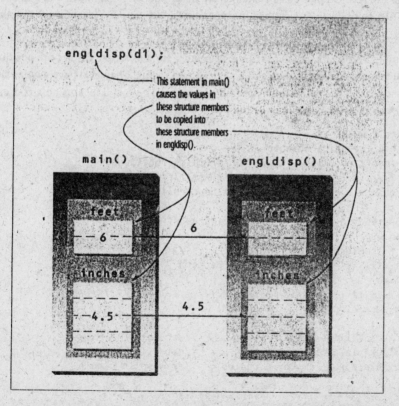

FIGURE 5.4
Structure passed as an argument.

As with simple variables, the structure parameter dd in engldisp() is not the same as the arguments passed to it (d1 and d2). Thus, engldisp() could (although it doesn't do so here) modify dd without affecting d1 and d2. That is, if engldisp() contained statements like

```
dd.feet = 2;
dd.inches = 3.25;
```

this would have no effect on d1 or d2 in main().

Passing a circle Structure

The next example of passing a structure to a function makes use of the Console Graphics Lite functions. The source and header files for these functions are shown in Appendix E, "Console Graphics Lite," and can be downloaded from the publisher's Web site as described in the Introduction. You'll need to include the appropriate header file (MSOFTCON.H or BORLACON.H, depending on your compiler), and add the source file (MSOFTCON.CPP or BORLACON.CPP) to your project. The Console Graphics Lite functions are described in Appendix E, and the procedure for adding files to projects is described in Appendix C, "Microsoft Visual C++," and Appendix D, "Borland C++Builder."

In this example a structure called circle represents a circular shape. Circles are positioned at a certain place on the console screen, and have a certain radius. They also have a color and a fill pattern. Possible values for the colors and fill patterns can be found in Appendix E. Here's the listing for CIRCSTRC:

```
// circstrc.cpp
// circles as graphics objects
#include "msoftcon.h"           // for graphics functions
///////////////////////////////////////////////////////////////////
struct circle                   //graphics circle
   {
   int xCo, yCo;                //coordinates of center
   int radius;
   color fillcolor;             //color
   fstyle fillstyle;            //fill pattern
   };
///////////////////////////////////////////////////////////////////
void circ_draw(circle c)
   {
   set_color(c.fillcolor);               //set color
   set_fill_style(c.fillstyle);          //set fill pattern
   draw_circle(c.xCo, c.yCo, c.radius);  //draw solid circle
   }
//-------------------------------------------------------------------
int main()
   {
   init_graphics();             //initialize graphics system
                                //create circles
```

```
circle  1 = { 15, 7, 5, cBLUE, X_FILL };
circle c2 = { 41, 12, 7, cRED, O_FILL };
circle c3 = { 65, 18, 4, cGREEN, MEDIUM_FILL };

circ_draw(c1);            //draw circles
circ_draw(c2);
circ_draw(c3);
set_cursor_pos(1, 25);    //cursor to lower left corner
return 0;
}
```

The variables of type circle, which are c1, c2, and c3, are initialized to different sets of values. Here's how that looks for c1:

```
circle c1 = { 15, 7, 5, cBLUE, X_FILL };
```

We assume that your console screen has 80 columns and 25 rows. The first value in this definition, 15, is the *column number* (the x coordinate) and the 7 is the *row number* (the y coordinate, starting at the top of the screen) where the center of the circle will be located. The 5 is the radius of the circle, the cBLUE is its color, and the X_FILL constant means it will be filled with the letter X. The two other circles are initialized similarly.

Once all the circles are created and initialized, we draw them by calling the circ_draw() function three times, once for each circle. Figure 5.5 shows the output of the CIRCSTRC program. Admittedly the circles are a bit ragged; a result of the limited number of pixels in console-mode graphics.

FIGURE 5.5
Output of the CIRCSTRC program.

Notice how the structure holds the characteristics of the circles, while the `circ_draw()` function causes them to actually do something (draw themselves). As we'll see in Chapter 6, "Objects and Classes," objects are formed by combining structures and functions to create entities that both possess characteristics and perform actions.

Names in the Declaration

Here's a way to increase the clarity of your function declarations. The idea is to insert meaningful names in the declaration, along with the data types. For example, suppose you were using a function that displayed a point on the screen. You could use a declaration with only data types

```
void display_point(int, int);  //declaration
```

but a better approach is

```
void display_point(int horiz, int vert);  //declaration
```

These two declarations mean exactly the same thing to the compiler. However, the first approach, with (`int`, `int`), doesn't contain any hint about which argument is for the vertical coordinate and which is for the horizontal coordinate. The advantage of the second approach is clarity for the programmer: Anyone seeing this declaration is more likely to use the correct arguments when calling the function.

Note that the names in the declaration have no effect on the names you use when calling the function. You are perfectly free to use any argument names you want:

```
display_point(x, y);  // function call
```

We'll use this name-plus-datatype approach when it seems to make the listing clearer.

Returning Values from Functions

When a function completes its execution, it can return a single value to the calling program. Usually this return value consists of an answer to the problem the function has solved. The next example demonstrates a function that returns a weight in kilograms after being given a weight in pounds. Here's the listing for CONVERT:

```
// convert.cpp
// demonstrates return values, converts pounds to kg
#include <iostream>
using namespace std;
float lbstokg(float);    //declaration

int main()
    {
    float lbs, kgs;
```

```
    cout << "\nEnter your weight in pounds: ";
    cin >> lbs;
    kgs = lbstokg(lbs);
    cout << "Your weight in kilograms is " << kgs << endl;
    return 0;
    }
//-------------------------------------------------------------
// lbstokg()
// converts pounds to kilograms
float lbstokg(float pounds)
    {
    float kilograms =  0.453592 * pounds;
    return kilograms;
    }
```

Here's some sample interaction with this program:

```
Enter your weight in pounds: 182
Your weight in kilograms is 82.553741
```

When a function returns a value, the data type of this value must be specified. The function declaration does this by placing the data type, float in this case, before the function name in the declaration and the definition. Functions in earlier program examples returned no value, so the return type was void. In the CONVERT program, the function lbstokg() (*pounds to kilograms*, where lbs means pounds) returns type float, so the declaration is

```
float lbstokg(float);
```

The first float specifies the return type. The float in parentheses specifies that an argument to be passed to lbstokg() is also of type float.

When a function returns a value, the call to the function

```
lbstokg(lbs)
```

is considered to be an expression that takes on the value returned by the function. We can treat this expression like any other variable; in this case we use it in an assignment statement:

```
kgs = lbstokg(lbs);
```

This causes the variable kgs to be assigned the value returned by lbstokg().

The return Statement

The function lbstokg() is passed an argument representing a weight in pounds, which it stores in the parameter pounds. It calculates the corresponding weight in kilograms by multiplying this pounds value by a constant; the result is stored in the variable kilograms. The value of this variable is then returned to the calling program using a return statement:

```
return kilograms;
```

Notice that both `main()` and `lbstokg()` have a place to store the kilogram variable: `kgs` in `main()`, and `kilograms` in `lbstokg()`. When the function returns, the value in `kilograms` is *copied into* `kgs`. The calling program does not access the `kilograms` variable in the function; only the value is returned. This process is shown in Figure 5.6.

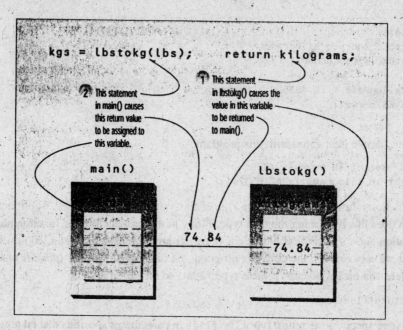

FIGURE 5.6
Returning a value.

While many arguments may be sent to a function, only one argument may be returned from it. This is a limitation when you need to return more information. However, there are other approaches to returning multiple variables from functions. One is to pass arguments by reference, which we'll look at later in this chapter. Another is to return a structure with the multiple values as members, as we'll see soon.

You should always include a function's return type in the function declaration. If the function doesn't return anything, use the keyword `void` to indicate this fact. If you don't use a return type in the declaration, the compiler will assume that the function returns an `int` value. For example, the declaration

```
somefunc();    // declaration -- assumes return type is int
```

tells the compiler that `somefunc()` has a return type of `int`.

The reason for this is historical, based on usage in early versions of C. In practice, you shouldn't take advantage of this default type. Always specify the return type explicitly, even if it actually is int. This keeps the listing consistent and readable.

Eliminating Unnecessary Variables

The CONVERT program contains several variables that are used in the interest of clarity but are not really necessary. A variation of this program, CONVERT2, shows how expressions containing functions can often be used in place of variables.

```cpp
// convert2.cpp
// eliminates unnecessary variables
#include <iostream>
using namespace std;
float lbstokg(float);    //declaration

int main()
    {
    float lbs;

    cout << "\nEnter your weight in pounds: ";
    cin >> lbs;
    cout << "Your weight in kilograms is " << lbstokg(lbs)
        << endl;
    return 0;
    }
//------------------------------------------------------
// lbstokg()
// converts pounds to kilograms
float lbstokg(float pounds)
    {
    return 0.453592 * pounds;
    }
```

In main() the variable kgs from the CONVERT program has been eliminated. Instead the function lbstokg(lbs) is inserted directly into the cout statement:

```cpp
cout << "Your weight in kilograms is " << lbstokg(lbs) << endl;
```

Also in the lbstokg() function, the variable kilograms is no longer used. The expression 0.453592*pounds is inserted directly into the return statement:

```cpp
return 0.453592 * pounds;
```

The calculation is carried out and the resulting value is returned to the calling program, just as the value of a variable would be.

5

FUNCTIONS

For clarity, programmers often put parentheses around the expression used in a return statement:

```
return (0.453592 * pounds);
```

Even when not required by the compiler, extra parentheses in an expression don't do any harm, and they may help make the listing easier for us poor humans to read.

Experienced C++ (and C) programmers will probably prefer the concise form of CONVERT2 to the more verbose CONVERT. However, CONVERT2 is not so easy to understand, especially for the non-expert. The brevity-versus-clarity issue is a question of style, depending on your personal preference and on the expectations of those who will be reading your code.

Returning Structure Variables

We've seen that structures can be used as arguments to functions. You can also use them as return values. Here's a program, RETSTRC, that incorporates a function that adds variables of type Distance and returns a value of this same type:

```
// retstrc.cpp
// demonstrates returning a structure
#include <iostream>
using namespace std;
/////////////////////////////////////////////////////////////
struct Distance                            //English distance
   {
   int feet;
   float inches;
   };
/////////////////////////////////////////////////////////////
Distance addengl(Distance, Distance);  //declarations
void engldisp(Distance);

int main()
   {
   Distance d1, d2, d3;                    //define three lengths
                                           //get length d1 from user
   cout << "\nEnter feet: ";  cin >> d1.feet;
   cout << "Enter inches: ";  cin >> d1.inches;
                                           //get length d2 from user
   cout << "\nEnter feet: ";  cin >> d2.feet;
   cout << "Enter inches: ";  cin >> d2.inches;

   d3 = addengl(d1, d2);                   //d3 is sum of d1 and d2
   cout << endl;
   engldisp(d1); cout << " + ";            //display all lengths
```

```
    engldisp(d2); cout << " = ";
    engldisp(d3); cout << endl;
    return 0;
    }
//--------------------------------------------------
// addengl()
// adds two structures of type Distance, returns sum
Distance addengl( Distance dd1, Distance dd2 )
    {
    Distance dd3;                    //define a new structure for sum

    dd3.inches = dd1.inches + dd2.inches;  //add the inches
    dd3.feet = 0;                          //(for possible carry)
    if(dd3.inches >= 12.0)                 //if inches >= 12.0,
        {                                  //then decrease inches
        dd3.inches -= 12.0;                //by 12.0 and
        dd3.feet++;                        //increase feet
        }                                  //by 1
    dd3.feet += dd1.feet + dd2.feet;       //add the feet
    return dd3;                            //return structure
    }
//--------------------------------------------------
// engldisp()
// display structure of type Distance in feet and inches
void engldisp( Distance dd )
    {
    cout << dd.feet << "\'-" << dd.inches << "\"";
    }
```

The program asks the user for two lengths, in feet-and-inches format, adds them together by calling the function addengl(), and displays the results using the engldisp() function introduced in the ENGLDISP program. Here's some output from the program:

```
Enter feet: 4
Enter inches: 5.5

Enter feet: 5
Enter inches: 6.5

4'-5.5" + 5'-6.5" = 10'-0"
```

The main() part of the program adds the two lengths, each represented by a structure of type Distance, by calling the function addengl():

```
d3 = addengl(d1, d2);
```

This function returns the sum of d1 and d2, in the form of a structure of type Distance. In main() the result is assigned to the structure d3.

5

Besides showing how structures are used as return values, this program also shows two functions (three if you count main()) used in the same program. You can arrange the functions in any order. The only rule is that the function declarations must appear in the listing before any calls are made to the functions.

Reference Arguments

A *reference* provides an *alias*—a different name—for a variable. One of the most important uses for references is in passing arguments to functions.

We've seen examples of function arguments passed by value. When arguments are passed by value, the called function creates a new variable of the same type as the argument and copies the argument's value into it. As we noted, the function cannot access the original variable in the calling program, only the copy it created. Passing arguments by value is useful when the function does not need to modify the original variable in the calling program. In fact, it offers insurance that the function cannot harm the original variable.

Passing arguments by reference uses a different mechanism. Instead of a value being passed to the function, a *reference to* the original variable, in the calling program, is passed. (It's actually the *memory address* of the variable that is passed, although you don't need to know this.)

An important advantage of passing by reference is that the function can access the actual variables in the calling program. Among other benefits, this provides a mechanism for passing more than one value from the function back to the calling program.

Passing Simple Data Types by Reference

The next example, REF, shows a simple variable passed by reference.

```
// ref.cpp
// demonstrates passing by reference
#include <iostream>
using namespace std;

int main()
   {
   void intfrac(float, float&, float&);        //declaration
   float number, intpart, fracpart;            //float variables

   do {
      cout << "\nEnter a real number: ";       //number from user
      cin >> number;
      intfrac(number, intpart, fracpart);      //find int and frac
      cout << "Integer part is " << intpart    //print them
           << ", fraction part is " << fracpart << endl;
```

```
    } while( number != 0.0 );                      //exit loop on 0.0
  return 0;
  }
//------------------------------------------------------------
// intfrac()
// finds integer and fractional parts of real number
void intfrac(float n, float& intp, float& fracp)
  {
  long temp = static_cast<long>(n);      //convert to long,
  intp = static_cast<float>(temp);       //back to float
  fracp = n - intp;                      //subtract integer part
  }
```

The main() part of this program asks the user to enter a number of type float. The program will separate this number into an integer and a fractional part. That is, if the user's number is 12.456, the program should report that the integer part is 12.0 and the fractional part is 0.456. To find these two values, main() calls the function intfrac(). Here's some sample interaction:

```
Enter a real number: 99.44
Integer part is 99, fractional part is 0.44
```

Some compilers may generate spurious digits in the fractional part, such as 0.440002. This is an error in the compiler's conversion routine and can be ignored. Refer to Figure 5.7 in the following discussion.

The intfrac() function finds the integer part by converting the number (which was passed to the parameter n) into a variable of type long with a cast, using the expression

```
long temp = static_cast<long>(n);
```

This effectively chops off the fractional part of the number, since integer types (of course) store only the integer part. The result is then converted back to type float with another cast:

```
intp = static_cast<float>(temp);
```

The fractional part is simply the original number less the integer part. (We should note that a library function, fmod(), performs a similar task for type double.)

The intfrac() function can find the integer and fractional parts, but how does it pass them back to main()? It could use a return statement to return one value, but not both. The problem is solved using reference arguments. Here's the declarator for the function:

```
void intfrac(float n, float& intp, float& fracp)
```

5

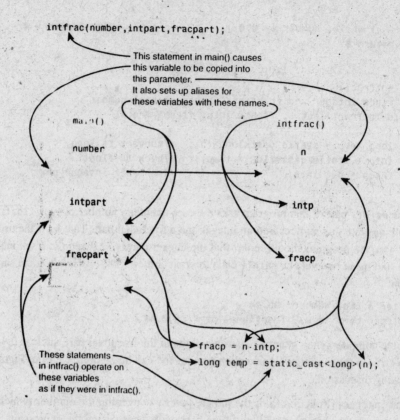

FIGURE 5.7
Passing by reference in the REF program.

Reference arguments are indicated by the ampersand (&) following the data type:

```
float& intp
```

The & indicates that intp is an *alias*—another name—for whatever variable is passed as an argument. In other words, when you use the name intp in the intfrac() function, you are really referring to intpart in main(). The & can be taken to mean *reference to*, so

```
float& intp
```

means intp is a reference to the float variable passed to it. Similarly, fracp is an alias for—or a reference to—fracpart.

The function declaration echoes the usage of the ampersand in the definition:

```
void intfrac(float, float&, float&);   // ampersands
```

As in the definition, the ampersand follows those arguments that are passed by reference.

The ampersand is not used in the function call:

```
intfrac(number, intpart, fracpart);    // no ampersands
```

From the function call alone, there's no way to tell whether an argument will be passed by reference or by value.

While intpart and fracpart are passed by reference, the variable number is passed by value. intp and intpart are different names for the same place in memory, as are fracp and fracpart. On the other hand, since it is passed by value, the parameter n in intfrac() is a separate variable into which the value of number is copied. It can be passed by value because the intfrac() function doesn't need to modify number.

(C programmers should not confuse the ampersand that is used to mean reference to with the same symbol used to mean address of. These are different usages. We'll discuss the *address of* meaning of & in Chapter 10, "Pointers.")

A More Complex Pass by Reference

Here's a somewhat more complex example of passing simple arguments by reference. Suppose you have pairs of numbers in your program and you want to be sure that the smaller one always precedes the larger one. To do this you call a function, order(), which checks two numbers passed to it by reference and swaps the originals if the first is larger than the second. Here's the listing for REFORDER:

```
// reforder.cpp
// orders two arguments passed by reference
#include <iostream>
using namespace std;

int main()
   {
   void order(int&, int&);          //prototype

   int n1=99, n2=11;                //this pair not ordered
   int n3=22, n4=88;                //this pair ordered

   order(n1, n2);                   //order each pair of numbers
   order(n3, n4);

   cout << "n1=" << n1 << endl;     //print out all numbers
   cout << "n2=" << n2 << endl;
   cout << "n3=" << n3 << endl;
   cout << "n4=" << n4 << endl;
   return 0;
   }
```

```
//------------------    ----------------------    ----------------------
void order(int& numb , int& numb2)    //order  two numbers
    {
    if(numb1 > numb2)                  //if 1st larger than 2nd,
        {
        int temp = numb1;              //swap them
        numb1 = numb2;
        numb2 = temp;
        }
    }
```

In main() there are two pairs of numbers—the first pair is not ordered and the second pair is ordered. The order() function is called once for each pair, and then all the numbers are printed out. The output reveals that the first pair has been swapped while the second pair hasn't. Here it is:

```
n1=11
n2=99
n3=22
n4=88
```

In the order() function the first variable is called numb1 and the second is numb2. If numb1 is greater than numb2 the function stores numb1 in temp, puts numb2 in numb1, and finally puts temp back in numb2. Remember that numb1 and numb2 are simply different names for whatever arguments were passed; in this case, n1 and n2 on the first call to the function, and n2 and n3 on the second call. The effect is to check the ordering of the original arguments in the calling program and swap them if necessary.

Using reference arguments in this way is a sort of remote-control operation. The calling program tells the function what variables in the calling program to operate on, and the function modifies these variables without ever knowing their real names. It's as if you called the house painters and, although they never left their office, you sat back and watched as your dining room walls mysteriously changed color.

Passing Structures by Reference

You can pass structures by reference just as you can simple data types. Here's a program, REFERST, that performs scale conversions on values of type Distance. A scale conversion involves multiplying a group of distances by a factor. If a distance is 6'–8", and a scale factor is 0.5, the new distance is 3'–4". Such a conversion might be applied to all the dimensions of a building to make the building shrink but remain in proportion.

```
// referst.cpp
// demonstrates passing structure by reference
#include <iostream>
```

```
using namespace std;
//////////////////////////////////////////////////////////////////
struct Distance                         //English distance
   {
   int feet;
   float inches;
   };
//////////////////////////////////////////////////////////////////
void scale( Distance&, float );         //function
void engldisp( Distance );              //declarations

int main()
   {
   Distance d1 = { 12, 6.5 };           //initialize d1 and d2
   Distance d2 = { 10, 5.5 };

   cout << "d1 = "; engldisp(d1);       //display old d1 and d2
   cout << "\nd2 = "; engldisp(d2);

   scale(d1, 0.5);                      //scale d1 and d2
   scale(d2, 0.25);

   cout << "\nd1 = "; engldisp(d1);     //display new d1 and d2
   cout << "\nd2 = "; engldisp(d2);
   cout << endl;
   return 0;
   }
//------------------------------------------------------------------
// scale()
// scales value of type Distance by factor
void scale( Distance& dd, float factor)
   {
   float inches = (dd.feet*12 + dd.inches) * factor;
   dd.feet = static_cast<int>(inches / 12);
   dd.inches = inches - dd.feet * 12;
   }
//------------------------------------------------------------------
// engldisp()
// display structure of type Distance in feet and inches
void engldisp( Distance dd )   //parameter dd of type Distance
   {
   cout << dd.feet << "\'-" << dd.inches << "\"";
   }
```

REFERST initialize: two Distance variables—d1 and d2—to specific values, and displays them. Then it calls the scale() function to multiply d1 by 0.5 and d2 by 0.25. Finally, it displays the resulting values of the distances. Here's the program's output:

```
d1 = 12'-6.5"
d2 = 10'-5.5"
d1 = 6'-3.25"
d2 = 2'-7.375"
```

Here are the two calls to the function scale():

```
scale(d1, 0.5);
scale(d2, 0.25);
```

The first call causes d1 to be multiplied by 0.5 and the second causes d2 to be multiplied by 0.25. Notice that these changes take place directly to d1 and d2. The function doesn't return anything; the operation is performed directly on the Distance argument, which is passed by reference to scale(). (Since only one value is changed in the calling program, you could rewrite the function to pass the argument by value and return the scaled value. Calling such a function would look like this:

```
d1 = scale(d1, 0.5);
```

However, this is unnecessarily verbose.)

Notes on Passing by Reference

References don't exist in C, where pointers serve a somewhat similar purpose, although often less conveniently. Reference arguments were introduced into C++ to provide flexibility in a variety of situations involving objects as well as simple variables.

The third way to pass arguments to functions, besides by value and by reference, is to use pointers. We'll explore this in Chapter 10.

Overloaded Functions

An overloaded function appears to perform different activities depending on the kind of data sent to it. Overloading is like the joke about the famous scientist who insisted that the thermos bottle was the greatest invention of all time. Why? "It's a miracle device," he said. "It keeps hot things hot, but cold things it keeps cold. How does it know?"

It may seem equally mysterious how an overloaded function knows what to do. It performs one operation on one kind of data but another operation on a different kind. Let's clarify matters with some examples.

Different Numbers of Arguments

Recall the starline() function in the TABLE example and the repchar() function from the TABLEARG example, both shown earlier in this chapter. The starline() function printed a line using 45 asterisks, while repchar() used a character and a line length that were both specified when the function was called. We might imagine a third function, charline(), that always prints 45 characters but that allows the calling program to specify the character to be printed. These three functions—starline(), repchar(), and charline()—perform similar activities but have different names. For programmers using these functions, that means three names to remember and three places to look them up if they are listed alphabetically in an application's *Function Reference* documentation.

It would be far more convenient to use the same name for all three functions, even though they each have different arguments. Here's a program, OVERLOAD, that makes this possible:

```
// overload.cpp
// demonstrates function overloading
#include <iostream>
using namespace std;

void repchar();                    //declarations
void repchar(char);
void repchar(char, int);

int main()
   {
   repchar();
   repchar('=');
   repchar('+', 30);
   return 0;
   }
//--------------------------------------------------------------
// repchar()
// displays 45 asterisks
void repchar()
   {
   for(int j=0; j<45; j++)  // always loops 45 times
      cout << '*';          // always prints asterisk
   cout << endl;
   }
//--------------------------------------------------------------
// repchar()
// displays 45 copies of specified character
void repchar(char ch)
   {
   for(int j=0; j<45; j++)  // always loops 45 times
      cout << ch;           // prints specified character
```

```
    cout << endl;
    }
//------------------      ----------------------------------
// repchar()
// displays specified number of copies of specified character
void repchar(char ch, int n)
    {
    for(int j=0; j<n; j++)    // loop n times
        cout << ch;           // print specified character
    cout << endl;
    }
```

This program prints out three lines of characters. Here's the output:

```
*********************************************
=============================================
++++++++++++++++++++++++++++++
```

The first two lines are 45 characters long, and the third is 30.

The program contains three functions with the same name. There are three declarations, three function calls, and three function definitions. What keeps the compiler from becoming hopelessly confused? It uses the function signature—the number of arguments, and their data types—to distinguish one function from another. In other words, the declaration

```
void repchar();
```

which takes no arguments, describes an entirely different function than the declaration

```
void repchar(char);
```

which takes one argument of type char, or the declaration

```
void repchar(char, int);
```

which takes one argument of type char and another of type int.

The compiler, seeing several functions with the same name but different numbers of arguments, could decide the programmer had made a mistake (which is what it would do in C). Instead, it very tolerantly sets up a separate function for every such definition. Which one of these functions will be called depends on the number of arguments supplied in the call. Figure 5.8 shows this process.

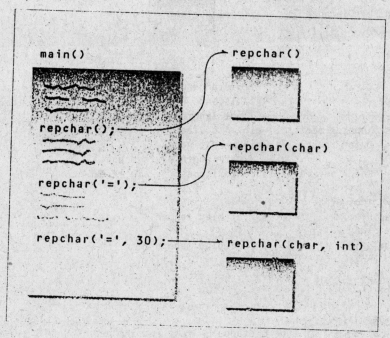

Figure 5.8
Overloaded functions.

Different Kinds of Arguments

In the OVERLOAD example we created several functions with the same name but different numbers of arguments. The compiler can also distinguish between overloaded functions with the same number of arguments, provided their type is different. Here's a program, OVERENGL, that uses an overloaded function to display a quantity in feet-and-inches format. The single argument to the function can be either a structure of type Distance (as used in the ENGLDISP example) or a simple variable of type float. Different functions are used depending on the type of argument.

```cpp
// overengl.cpp
// demonstrates overloaded functions
#include <iostream>
using namespace std;
//////////////////////////////////////////////////////////////////
struct Distance                     //English distance
   {
   int feet;
   float inches;
   };
//////////////////////////////////////////////////////////////////
```

```
void  ngldisp( Distance );        //declarations
void  ngldisp( float );

int main()
   {
   Distan  d1;                    //distance of type Distance
   float d2;                      //distance of type float
                                  //get length d1 from user
   cout << "\nEnter feet: ";  cin >> d1.feet;
   cout << "Enter inches: ";  cin >> d1.inches;
                                  //get length d2 from user
   cout << "Enter entire distance in inches: "; cin >> d2;

   cout << "\nd1 = ";
   engldisp(d1);                  //display length 1
   cout << "\nd2 = ";
   engldisp(d2);                  //display length 2
   cout << endl;
   return 0;
   }
//------------------------------------------------------------
// engldisp()
// display structure of type Distance in feet and inches
void engldisp( Distance dd )    //parameter dd of type Distance
   {
   cout << dd.feet << "\'-" << dd.inches << "\"";
   }
//------------------------------------------------------------
// engldisp()
// display variable of type float in feet and inches
void engldisp( float dd )         //parameter dd of type float
   {
   int feet = static_cast<int>(dd / 12);
   float inches = dd - feet*12;
   cout << feet << "\'-" << inches << "\"";
   }
```

The user is invited to enter two distances, the first with separate feet and inches inputs, the second with a single large number for inches (109.5 inches, for example, instead of 9'-1.5"). The program calls the overloaded function engldisp() to display a value of type Distance for the first distance and of type float for the second. Here's some sample interaction with the program:

```
Enter feet: 5
Enter inches: 10.5
Enter entire distance in inches: 76.5
d1 = 5'-10.5"
d2 = 6'-4.5"
```

Notice that, while the different versions of `engldisp()` do similar things, the code is quite different. The version that accepts the all-inches input has to convert to feet and inches before displaying the result.

Overloaded functions can simplify the programmer's life by reducing the number of function names to be remembered. As an example of the complexity that arises when overloading is not used, consider the C++ library routines for finding the absolute value of a number. Because these routines must work with C (which does not allow overloading) as well as with C++, there must be separate versions of the absolute value routine for each data type. There are four of them: `abs()` for type `int`, `cabs()` for complex numbers, `fabs()` for type `double`, and `labs()` for type `long`. In C++, a single name, `abs()`, would suffice for all these data types.

As we'll see later, overloaded functions are also useful for handling different types of objects.

Recursion

The existence of functions makes possible a programming technique called *recursion*. Recursion involves a function calling itself. This sounds rather improbable, and indeed a function calling itself is often a bug. However, when used correctly this technique can be surprisingly powerful.

Recursion is much easier to understand with an example than with lengthy explanations, so let's apply it to a program we've seen before: the FACTOR program of Chapter 3, "Loops and Decisions." That program used a `for` loop to calculate the factorial of a number. (See that example for an explanation of factorials.) Our new program, FACTOR2, uses recursion instead of a loop.

```
//factor2.cpp
//calculates factorials using recursion
#include <iostream>
using namespace std;

unsigned long factfunc(unsigned long);   //declaration

int main()
   {
   int n;                    //number entered by user
   unsigned long fact;       //factorial

   cout << "Enter an integer: ";
   cin >> n;
   fact = factfunc(n);
   cout << "Factorial of " << n << " is " << fact << endl;
   return 0;
   }
```

```
//--------------------------------------------------------
// factfunc()
// calls itself to calculate factorials
unsigned long factfunc(unsigned long n)
   {
   if(n > 1)
      return n * factfunc(n-1);   //self call
   else
      return 1;
   }
```

The output of this program is the same as the FACTOR program in Chapter 3.

The main() part of FACTOR2 looks reasonable: it calls a function. factfunc(), with an argument that is a number entered by the user. This function then returns the factorial of that number to main().

The function factfunc() is another story. What's it doing? If n is greater than 1, the function calls itself. Notice that when it does this it uses an argument one less than the argument it was called with. Suppose it was called from main() with an argument of 5. It will call a second version of itself with an argument of 4. Then this function will call a third version with an argument of 3, and so on.

Notice that each version of the function stores its own value of n while it's busy calling another version of itself.

After factfunc() calls itself four times, the fifth version of the function is called with an argument of 1. It discovers this with the if statement, and instead of calling itself, as previous versions have, it returns 1 to the fourth version. The fourth version has stored a value of 2, so it multiplies the stored 2 by the returned 1, and returns 2 to the third version. The third version has stored 3, so it multiplies 3 by the returned 2, and returns 6 to the second version. The second version has stored 4, so it multiplies this by the returned 6 and returns 24 to the first version. The first version has stored 5, so it multiplies this by the returned 24 and returns 120 to main().

Thus in this example we have five function calls followed by five function returns. Here's a summary of this process:

Version	Action	Argument or Return Value
1	Call	-
2	Call	4
3	Call	3
4	Call	2

Version	Action	Argument or Return Value
5	Call	1
5	Return	1
4	Return	2
3	Return	6
2	Return	24
1	Return	120

Every recursive function must be provided with a way to end the recursion. Otherwise it will call itself forever and crash the program. The if statement in factfunc() plays this role, terminating the recursion when n is 1.

Is it true that many versions of a recursive function are stored in memory while it's calling itself? Not really. Each version's variables are stored, but there's only one copy of the function's code. Even so, a deeply-nested recursion can create a great many stored variables, which can pose a problem to the system if it doesn't have enough space for them.

Inline Functions

We mentioned that functions save memory space because all the calls to the function cause the same code to be executed; the function body need not be duplicated in memory. When the compiler sees a function call, it normally generates a jump to the function. At the end of the function it jumps back to the instruction following the call, as shown in Figure 5.1 earlier in this chapter.

While this sequence of events may save memory space, it takes some extra time. There must be an instruction for the jump to the function (actually the assembly-language instruction CALL or something similar), instructions for saving registers, instructions for pushing arguments onto the stack in the calling program and removing them from the stack in the function (if there are arguments), instructions for restoring registers, and an instruction to return to the calling program. The return value (if any) must also be dealt with. All these instructions slow down the program.

To save execution time in short functions, you may elect to put the code in the function body directly inline with the code in the calling program. That is, each time there's a function call in the source file, the actual code from the function is inserted, instead of a jump to the function. The difference between a function and inline code is shown in Figure 5.9.

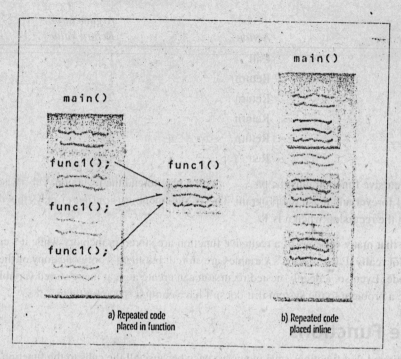

FIGURE 5.9
Functions versus inline code.

Long sections of repeated code are generally better off as normal functions: The savings in memory space is worth the comparatively small sacrifice in execution speed. But making a short section of code into an ordinary function may result in little savings in memory space, while imposing just as much time penalty as a larger function. In fact, if a function is very short, the instructions necessary to call it may take up as much space as the instructions within the function body, so that there is not only a time penalty but a space penalty as well.

In such cases you could simply repeat the necessary code in your program, inserting the same group of statements wherever it was needed. The trouble with repeatedly inserting the same code is that you lose the benefits of program organization and clarity that come with using functions. The program may run faster and take less space, but the listing is longer and more complex.

The solution to this quandary is the *inline function*. This kind of function is written like a normal function in the source file but compiles into inline code instead of into a function. The source file remains well organized and easy to read, since the function is shown as a separate entity. However, when the program is compiled, the function body is actually inserted into the program wherever a function call occurs.

Functions that are very short, say one or two statements, are candidates to be inlined. Here's INLINE, a variation on the CONVERT2 program. It inlines the lbstokg() function.

```
// inliner.cpp
// demonstrates inline functions
#include <iostream>
using namespace std;

// lbstokg()
// converts pounds to kilograms
inline float lbstokg(float pounds)
   {
   return 0.453592 * pounds;
   }
//--------------------------------------------------------------
int main()
   {
   float lbs;

   cout << "\nEnter your weight in pounds: ";
   cin >> lbs;
   cout << "Your weight in kilograms is " << lbstokg(lbs)
        << endl;
   return 0;
   }
```

It's easy to make a function inline: All you need is the keyword inline in the function definition:

```
inline float lbstokg(float pounds)
```

You should be aware that the inline keyword is actually just a *request* to the compiler. Sometimes the compiler will ignore the request and compile the function as a normal function. It might decide the function is too long to be inline, for instance.

(C programmers should note that inline functions largely take the place of #define macros in C. They serve the same purpose but provide better type checking and do not need special care with parentheses, as macros do.)

Default Arguments

Surprisingly, a function can be called without specifying all its arguments. This won't work on just any function: The function declaration must provide default values for those arguments that are not specified.

Here's an example, a variation on the OVERLOAD program that demonstrates this effect. In OVERLOAD we used three different functions with the same name to handle different numbers of arguments. The present example, MISSARG, achieves the same effect in a different way.

```
// missarg.cpp
// demonstrates missing and default arguments
#include <iostream>
using namespace std;

void repchar(char='*', int=45);      //declaration with
                                     //default arguments
int main()
    {
    repchar();                       //prints 45 asterisks
    repchar('=');                    //prints 45 equal signs
    repchar('+', 30);                //prints 30 plus signs
    return 0;
    }
//--------------------------------------------------------------
// repchar()
// displays line of characters
void repchar(char ch, int n)         //defaults supplied
    {                                //    if necessary
    for(int j=0; j<n; j++)           //loops n times
        cout << ch;                  //prints ch
    cout << endl;
    }
```

In this program the function repchar() takes two arguments. It's called three times from main(). The first time it's called with no arguments, the second time with one, and the third time with two. Why do the first two calls work? Because the called function provides default arguments, which will be used if the calling program doesn't supply them. The default arguments are specified in the declaration for repchar():

```
void repchar(char='*', int=45);  //declaration
```

The default argument follows an equal sign, which is placed directly after the type name. You can also use variable names, as in

```
void repchar(char reptChar='*', int numberReps=45);
```

If one argument is missing when the function is called, it is assumed to be the last argument. The repchar() function assigns the value of the single argument to the ch parameter and uses the default value 45 for the n parameter.

If both arguments are missing, the function assigns the default value '*' to ch and the default value 45 to n. Thus the three calls to the function all work, even though each has a different number of arguments.

Remember that missing arguments must be the trailing arguments—those at the end of the argument list. You can leave out the last three arguments, but you can't leave out the next-to-last and then put in the last. This is reasonable; how would the compiler know which arguments you meant if you left out some in the middle? (Missing arguments could have been indicated with commas, but commas are notoriously subject to misprints, so the designers of C++ ignored this possibility.) Not surprisingly, the compiler will flag an error if you leave out arguments for which the function does not provide default values.

Default arguments are useful if you don't want to go to the trouble of writing arguments that, for example, almost always have the same value. They are also useful in cases where, after a program is written, the programmer decides to increase the capability of a function by adding another argument. Using default arguments means that the existing function calls can continue to use the old number of arguments, while new function calls can use more.

Scope and Storage Class

Now that we know about functions, we can explore two features of C++ that are related to the interaction of variables and functions: *scope* and *storage class*. The scope of a variable determines which parts of the program can access it, and its storage class determines how long it stays in existence. We'll summarize this briefly and then look at the situation in more detail.

Two different kinds of scope are important here: local and file. (We'll see another one, class scope, later.)

- Variables with *local* scope are visible only within a block.
- Variables with *file* scope are visible throughout a file.

A block is basically the code between an opening brace and a closing brace. Thus a function body is a block.

There are two storage classes: automatic and static.

- Variables with storage class *automatic* exist during the lifetime of the function in which they're defined.
- Variables with storage class *static* exist for the lifetime of the program.

Now let's see what all this means.

Local Variables

So far almost all the variables we've used in example programs have been defined inside the function in which they are used. That is, the definition occurs inside the braces that delimit the function body:

```
void somefunc()
  {
  int somevar;          //variables defined within
  float othervar;       //the function body
  // other statements
  }
```

Variables may be defined inside main() or inside other functions; the effect is the same, since main() is a function. Variables defined within a function body are called *local variables* because they have local scope. However, they are also sometimes called automatic variables, because they have the automatic storage class.

Let's look at these two important characteristics of variables that are defined within functions.

Storage Class

A local variable is not created until the function in which it is defined is called. (More accurately, we can say that variables defined within *any* block of code are not created until the block is executed. Thus variables defined within a loop body only exist while the loop is executing.) In the program fragment just given, the variables somevar and othervar don't exist until the somefunc() function is called. That is, there is no place in memory where their values can be stored; they are undefined. When control is transferred to somefunc(), the variables are created and memory space is set aside for them. Later, when somefunc() returns and control is passed back to the calling program, the variables are destroyed and their values are lost. The name *automatic* is used because the variables are automatically created when a function is called and automatically destroyed when it returns.

The time period between the creation and destruction of a variable is called its *lifetime* (or sometimes its *duration*). The lifetime of a local variable coincides with the time when the function in which it is defined is executing.

The idea behind limiting the lifetime of variables is to save memory space. If a function is not executing, the variables it uses during execution are presumably not needed. Removing them frees up memory that can then be used by other functions.

Scope

A variable's *scope*, also called *visibility*, describes the locations within a program from which it can be accessed. It can be referred to in statements in some parts of the program; but in others, attempts to access it lead to an *unknown variable* error message. The scope of a variable is that part of the program where the variable is visible.

Variables defined within a function are only visible, meaning they can only be accessed, from within the function in which they are defined. Suppose you have two functions in a program:

```
void somefunc()
   {
   int somevar;      //local variables
   float othervar;

   somevar = 10;     //OK
   othervar = 11;    //OK
   nextvar = 12;     //illegal: not visible in somefunc()
   }

void otherfunc()
   {
   int nextvar;      //local variable

   somevar = 20;     //illegal: not visible in otherfunc()
   othervar = 21;    //illegal: not visible in otherfunc()
   nextvar = 22;     //OK
   }
```

The variable nextvar is invisible in function somefunc(), and the variables somevar and othervar are invisible in otherfunc().

Limiting the visibility of variables helps organize and modularize the program. You can be confident that the variables in one function are safe from accidental alteration by other functions because the other functions can't see them. This is an important part of *structured programming*, the methodology for organizing old-fashioned procedural programs. Limiting visibility is also an important part of object-oriented programming.

In the case of variables declared within a function, storage class and scope coincide: These variables exist only while the function in which they are defined is executing, and are only visible within that function. For some kinds of variables, however, lifetime and visibility are not the same.

Initialization

When a local variable is created, the compiler does not try to initialize it. Thus it will start off with an arbitrary value, which may be 0 but probably will be something else. If you want it initialized, you must initialize it explicitly, as in

```
int n = 33;
```

Then it will start off with this value.

5

FUNCTIONS

Global Variables

The next kind of variable is *global*. While local variables are defined within functions, global variables are defined outside of any function. (They're also defined outside of any class, as we'll see later.) A global variable is visible to all the functions in a file (and potentially in other files). More precisely, it is visible to all those functions that follow the variable's definition in the listing. Usually you want global variables to be visible to all functions, so you put their declarations at the beginning of the listing. Global variables are also sometimes called *external variables*, since they are defined external to any function.

Here's a program, EXTERN, in which three functions all access a global variable.

```
// extern.cpp
// demonstrates global variables
#include <iostream>
using namespace std;
#include <conio.h>          //for getch()

char ch = 'a';              //global variable ch

void getachar();            //function declarations
void putachar();

int main()
   {
   while( ch != '\r' )    //main() accesses ch
      {
      getachar();
      putachar();
      }
   cout << endl;
   return 0;
   }
//-------------------------------------------------------------
void getachar()             //getachar() accesses ch
   {
   ch = getch();
   }
//-------------------------------------------------------------
void putachar()             //putachar() accesses ch
   {
   cout << ch;
   }
```

One function in EXTERN, getachar(), reads characters from the keyboard. It uses the library function getch(), which is like getche() except that it doesn't echo the character typed to the screen (hence the absence of the final e in the name). A second EXTERN function, putachar(), displays each character on the screen. The effect is that what you type is displayed in the normal way:

```
I'm typing in this line of text
```

The significant thing about this program is that the variable ch is not defined in any of the functions. Instead it is defined at the beginning of the file, before the first function. It is a global (external) variable. Any function that follows the definition of ch in the listing can access it—in this case all the functions in EXTERN: main(), getachar(), and putachar(). Thus the visibility of ch is the entire source file.

Role of Global Variables

A global variable is used when it must be accessible to more than one function in a program. Global variables are often the most important variables in procedural programs. However, as we noted in Chapter 1, global variables create organizational problems because they can be accessed by any function. The wrong functions may access them, or functions may access them incorrectly. In an object-oriented program, there is much less necessity for global variables.

Initialization

If a global variable is initialized, as in

```
int exvar = 199;
```

this initialization takes place when the program is first loaded. If a global variable is not initialized explicitly by the program—for example, if it is defined as

```
int exvar;
```

then it is initialized automatically to 0 when it is created. (This is unlike local variables, which are not initialized and probably contain random or *garbage* values when they are created.)

Lifetime and Visibility

Global variables have storage class static, which means they exist for the life of the program. Memory space is set aside for them when the program begins, and continues to exist until the program ends. You don't need to use the keyword static when declaring global variables; they are given this storage class automatically.

As we noted, global variables are visible in the file in which they are defined, starting at the point where they are defined. If ch were defined following main() but before getachar(), it would be visible in getachar() and putachar(), but not in main().

5

FUNCTIONS

Static Local Variables

Let's look at another kind of variable: the *static local variable*. There are static global variables, but they are meaningful only in multifile programs, which we don't examine until Chapter 13.

A static local variable has the visibility of an automatic local variable (that is, inside the function containing it). However, its lifetime is the same as that of a global variable, except that it doesn't come into existence until the first call to the function containing it. Thereafter it remains in existence for the life of the program.

Static local variables are used when it's necessary for a function to remember a value when it is not being executed; that is, between calls to the function. In the next example, a function, getavg(), calculates a running average. It remembers the total of the numbers it has averaged before, and how many there were. Each time it receives a new number, sent as an argument from the calling program, it adds this number to the total, adds 1 to a count, and returns the new average by dividing the total by the count. Here's the listing for STATIC:

```cpp
// static.cpp
// demonstrates static variables
#include <iostream>
using namespace std;
float getavg(float);        //declaration

int main()
   {
   float data=1, avg;

   while( data != 0 )
      {
      cout << "Enter a number: ";
      cin >> data;
      avg = getavg(data);
      cout << "New average is " << avg << endl;
      }
   return 0;
   }
//----------------------------------------------------------
// getavg()
// finds average of old plus new data
float getavg(float newdata)
   {
   static float total = 0;  //static variables are initialized
   static int count = 0;    //   only once per program
```

```
count++;              //increment count
total += newdata;     //add new data to total
return total / count; //return the new average
}
```

Here's some sample interaction:

```
Enter a number: 10
New average is 10     ←──────── total is 10, count is 1
Enter a number: 20
New average is 15     ←──────── total is 30, count is 2
Enter a number: 30
New average is 20     ←──────── total is 60, count is 3
```

The static variables total and count in getavg() retain their values after getavg() returns, so they're available the next time it's called.

Initialization

When static variables are initialized, as total and count are in getavg(), the initialization takes place only once—the first time their function is called. They are not reinitialized on subsequent calls to the function, as ordinary local variables are.

Storage

If you're familiar with operating system architecture, you might be interested to know that local variables and function arguments are stored on the stack, while global and static variables are stored on the heap.

Table 5.2 summarizes the lifetime, visibility, and some other aspects of local, static local, and global variables.

TABLE 5.2   Storage Types

	Local	Static Local	Global
Visibility	function	function	file
Lifetime	function	program	program
Initialized value	not initialized	0	0
Storage	stack	heap	heap
Purpose	Variables used by a single function	Same as local, but retains value when function terminates	Variables used by several functions

5

Returning by Reference

Now that we know about global variables, we can examine a rather odd-looking C++ feature. Besides passing values by reference, you can also return a value by reference. Why you would want to do this may seem obscure. One reason is to avoid copying a large object, as we'll see in Chapter 11, "Virtual Functions." Another reason is to allow you to use a function call on the left side of the equal sign. This is a somewhat bizarre concept, so let's look at an example. The RETREF program shows the mechanism.

```
// retref.cpp
// returning reference values
#include <iostream>
using namespace std;
int x;                      // global variable
int& setx();                // function declaration

int main()
   {                        // set x to a value, using
   setx() = 92;             // function call on left side
   cout << "x=" << x << endl;  // display new value in x
   return 0;
   }
//------------------------------------------------------------
int& setx()
   {
   return x;                // returns the value to be modified
   }
```

In this program the function setx() is declared with a reference type, int&, as the return type:

```
int& setx();
```

This function contains the statement

```
return x;
```

where x has been defined as a global variable. Now—and this is what looks so strange—you can put a call to this function on the left side of the equal sign:

```
setx() = 92;
```

The result is that the variable returned by the function is assigned the value on the right side of the equal sign. That is, x is given the value 92. The output from the program

```
x=92
```

verifies that this assignment has taken place.

Function Calls on the Left of the Equal Sign

Does this still sound obscure? Remember that an ordinary function—one that returns a value—can be used as if it were a value:

```
y=squareroot(x);
```

Here, whatever value `squareroot(x)` has (for instance, 27.2) is assigned to y. The function is treated as if it were a value. A function that returns a reference, on the other hand, is treated as if it were a variable. It returns an *alias* to a variable, namely the variable in the function's return statement. In RETREF.C the function `setx()` returns a reference to the variable x. When this function is called, it's treated as if it were the variable x. Thus it can be used on the left side of an equal sign.

There are two corollaries to this. One is that you can't return a constant from a function that returns by reference. In `setx()`, you can't say

```
int& setx()
   {
   return 3;
   }
```

If you try this the compiler will complain that you need an *lvalue*, that is, something that can go on the left side of the equal sign: a variable and not a constant.

More subtly, you can't return a reference to a local variable:

```
int& setx()
   {
   int x = 3;
   return x;      // error
   }
```

What's wrong with this? The problem is that a function's local variables are probably destroyed when the function returns, and it doesn't make sense to return a reference to something that no longer exists.

Don't Worry Yet

Of course, the question remains why one would ever want to use a function call on the left of an equal sign. In procedural programming there probably isn't too much use for this technique. As in the above example, there are easier ways to achieve the same result. However, in Chapter 8, "Operator Overloading," we'll find that returning by reference is an indispensable technique. Until then, keep it in the back of your mind.

5

const Function Arguments

We've seen that passing an argument by reference can be used to allow a function to modify a variable in the calling program. However, there are other reasons to pass by reference. One is efficiency. Some variables used for function arguments can be very large; a large structure would be an example. If an argument is large, passing by reference is more efficient because, behind the scenes, only an address is really passed, not the entire variable.

Suppose you want to pass an argument by reference for efficiency, but not only do you want the function not to modify it, you want a guarantee that the function *cannot* modify it.

To obtain such a guarantee, you can apply the const modifier to the variable in the function declaration. The CONSTARG program shows how this looks.

```
//constarg.cpp
//demonstrates constant function arguments

void aFunc(int& a, const int& b);   //declaration

int main()
    {
    int alpha = 7;
    int beta = 11;
    aFunc(alpha, beta);
    return 0;
    }
//------------------------------------------------------------
void aFunc(int& a, const int& b)    //definition
    {
    a = 107;    //OK
    b = 111;    //error: can't modify constant argument
    }
```

Here we want to be sure that aFunc() can't modify the variable beta. (We don't care if it modifies alpha.) So we use the const modifier with beta in the function declaration (and definition):

```
void aFunc(int& alpha, const int& beta);
```

Now the attempt to modify the beta in aFunc() is flagged as an error by the compiler. One of the design philosophies in C++ is that it's better for the compiler to find errors than to wait for them to surface at runtime. The use of const function arguments is an example of this approach in action.

If you want to pass a const variable to a function as a reference argument, you don't have a choice: It *must* be declared const in the function declaration. (There's no problem passing a const argument by value, because the function can't modify the original variable anyway.)

Many library functions use constant arguments in a similar way. We'll see examples as we go along.

Summary

Functions provide a way to help organize programs, and to reduce program size, by giving a block of code a name and allowing it to be executed from other parts of the program. Function *declarations* (prototypes) specify what the function looks like, function *calls* transfer control to the function, and function *definitions* contain the statements that make up the function. The function *declarator* is the first line of the definition.

Arguments can be sent to functions either *by value*, where the function works with a copy of the argument, or *by reference*, where the function works with the original argument in the calling program.

Functions can return only one value. Functions ordinarily return by value, but they can also return by reference, which allows the function call to be used on the left side of an assignment statement. Arguments and return values can be either simple data types or structures.

An *overloaded* function is actually a group of functions with the same name. Which of them is executed when the function is called depends on the type and number of arguments supplied in the call.

An *inline* function looks like a normal function in the source file but inserts the function's code directly into the calling program. Inline functions execute faster but may require more memory than normal functions unless they are very small.

If a function uses default arguments, calls to it need not include all the arguments shown in the declaration. Default values supplied by the function are used for the missing arguments.

Variables possess a characteristic called the *storage class*. The most common storage class is *automatic*. Local variables have the automatic storage class: they exist only while the function in which they are defined is executing. They are also visible only within that function. *Global* variables have static storage class: they exist for the life of a program. They are also visible throughout an entire file. *Static* local variables exist for the life of a program but are visible only in their own function.

A function cannot modify any of its arguments that are given the const modifier. A variable already defined as const in the calling program must be passed as a const argument.

In Chapter 4 we examined one of the two major parts of objects: structures, which are collections of data. In this chapter we explored the second part: functions. Now we're ready to put these two components together to create objects, the subject of Chapter 6.

Questions

Answers to these questions can be found in Appendix G.

1. A function's single most important role is to
   a. give a name to a block of code.
   b. reduce program size.
   c. accept arguments and provide a return value.
   d. help organize a program into conceptual units.

2. A function itself is called the function d_____.

3. Write a function called foo() that displays the word foo.

4. A one-statement description of a function is referred to as a function d_____ or a
   p_____.

5. The statements that carry out the work of the function constitute the function _____.

6. A program statement that invokes a function is a function _____.

7. The first line of a function definition is referred to as the _____.

8. A function argument is
   a. a variable in the function that receives a value from the calling program.
   b. a way that functions resist accepting the calling program's values.
   c. a value sent to the function by the calling program.
   d. a value returned by the function to the calling program.

9. True or false: When arguments are passed by value, the function works with the original arguments in the calling program.

10. What is the purpose of using argument names in a function declaration?

11. Which of the following can legitimately be passed to a function?
    a. A constant
    b. A variable
    c. A structure
    d. A header file

12. What is the significance of empty parentheses in a function declaration?

13. How many values can be returned from a function?

14. True or false: When a function returns a value, the entire function call can appear on the right side of the equal sign and be assigned to another variable.

15. Where is a function's return type specified?

16. A function that doesn't return anything has return type _____ .

17. Here's a function:

```
int times2(int a)
    {
    return (a*2);
    }
```

Write a main() program that includes everything necessary to call this function.

18. When an argument is passed by reference

    a. a variable is created in the function to hold the argument's value.

    b. the function cannot access the argument's value.

    c. a temporary variable is created in the calling program to hold the argument's value.

    d. the function accesses the argument's original value in the calling program.

19. What is a principal reason for passing arguments by reference?

20. Overloaded functions

    a. are a group of functions with the same name.

    b. all have the same number and types of arguments.

    c. make life simpler for programmers.

    d. may fail unexpectedly due to stress.

21. Write declarations for two overloaded functions named bar(). They both return type int. The first takes one argument of type char, and the second takes two arguments of type char. If this is impossible, say why.

22. In general, an inline function executes _____ than a normal function, but requires _____ memory.

23. Write the declarator for an inline function named foobar() that takes one argument of type float and returns type float.

24. A default argument has a value that

    a. may be supplied by the calling program.

    b. may be supplied by the function.

    c. must have a constant value.

    d. must have a variable value.

25. Write a declaration for a function called blyth() that takes two arguments and returns type char. The first argument is type int, and the second is type float with a default value of 3.14159.

26. Scope and storage class are concerned with the _____ and _____ of a variable.

5

FUNCTIONS

27. What functions can access a global variable that appears in the same file with them?

28. What functions can access a local variable?

29. A static local variable is used to

    a. make a variable visible to several functions.

    b. make a variable visible to only one function.

    c. conserve memory when a function is not executing.

    d. retain a value when a function is not executing.

30. In what unusual place can you use a function call when a function returns a value by reference?

Exercises

Answers to the starred exercises can be found in Appendix G.

*1. Refer to the CIRCAREA program in Chapter 2, "C++ Programming Basics." Write a function called circarea() that finds the area of a circle in a similar way. It should take an argument of type float and return an argument of the same type. Write a main() function that gets a radius value from the user, calls circarea(), and displays the result.

*2. Raising a number n to a power p is the same as multiplying n by itself p times. Write a function called power() that takes a double value for n and an int value for p, and returns the result as a double value. Use a default argument of 2 for p, so that if this argument is omitted, the number n will be squared. Write a main() function that gets values from the user to test this function.

*3. Write a function called zeroSmaller() that is passed two int arguments by reference and then sets the smaller of the two numbers to 0. Write a main() program to exercise this function.

*4. Write a function that takes two Distance values as arguments and returns the larger one. Include a main() program that accepts two Distance values from the user, compares them, and displays the larger. (See the RETSTRC program for hints.)

5. Write a function called hms_to_secs() that takes three int values—for hours, minutes, and seconds—as arguments, and returns the equivalent time in seconds (type long). Create a program that exercises this function by repeatedly obtaining a time value in hours, minutes, and seconds from the user (format 12:59:59), calling the function, and displaying the value of seconds it returns.

6. Start with the program from Exercise 11 in Chapter 4, "Structures," which adds two struct time values. Keep the same functionality, but modify the program so that it uses two functions. The first, time_to_secs(), takes as its only argument a structure of type

time, and returns the equivalent in seconds (type long). The second function, secs_to_time(), takes as its only argument a time in seconds (type long), and returns a structure of type time.

7. Start with the power() function of Exercise 2, which works only with type double. Create a series of overloaded functions with the same name that, in addition to double, also work with types char, int, long, and float. Write a main() program that exercises these overloaded functions with all argument types.

8. Write a function called swap() that interchanges two int values passed to it by the calling program. (Note that this function swaps the values of the variables in the calling program, not those in the function.) You'll need to decide how to pass the arguments. Create a main() program to exercise the function.

9. Repeat Exercise 8, but instead of two int variables, have the swap() function interchange two struct time values (see Exercise 6).

10. Write a function that, when you call it, displays a message telling how many times it has been called: "I have been called 3 times", for instance. Write a main() program that calls this function at least 10 times. Try implementing this function in two different ways. First, use a global variable to store the count. Second, use a local static variable. Which is more appropriate? Why can't you use a local variable?

11. Write a program, based on the sterling structure of Exercise 10 in Chapter 4, that obtains from the user two money amounts in old-style British format (£9:19:11), adds them, and displays the result, again in old-style format. Use three functions. The first should obtain a pounds-shillings-pence value from the user and return the value as a structure of type sterling. The second should take two arguments of type sterling and return a value of the same type, which is the sum of the arguments. The third should take a sterling structure as its argument and display its value.

12. Revise the four-function fraction calculator from Exercise 12, Chapter 4, so that it uses functions for each of the four arithmetic operations. They can be called fadd(), fsub(), fmul(), and fdiv(). Each of these functions should take two arguments of type struct fraction, and return an argument of the same type.

Objects and Classes

CHAPTER

6

IN THIS CHAPTER

And now, the topics you've all been waiting for: objects and classes. The preliminaries are out of the way. We've learned about structures, which provide a way to group data elements. We've examined functions, which organize program actions into named entities. In this chapter we'll put these ideas together to create classes. We'll introduce several classes, starting with simple ones and working toward more complicated examples. We'll focus first on the details of classes and objects. At the end of the chapter we'll take a wider view, discussing what is to be gained by using the OOP approach.

As you read this chapter you may want to refer back to the concepts introduced in Chapter 1, "The Big Picture."

A Simple Class

Our first program contains a class and two objects of that class. Although it's simple, the program demonstrates the syntax and general features of classes in C++. Here's the listing for the SMALLOBJ program:

```cpp
// smallobj.cpp
// demonstrates a small, simple object
#include <iostream>
using namespace std;
////////////////////////////////////////////////////////////
class smallobj                    //define a class
   {
   private:
      int somedata;               //class data
   public:
      void setdata(int d)         //member function to set data
         { somedata = d; }
      void showdata()             //member function to display data
         { cout << "Data is " << somedata << endl; }
   };
////////////////////////////////////////////////////////////
int main()
   {
   smallobj s1, s2;     //define two objects of class smallobj

   s1.setdata(1066);    //call member function to set data
   s2.setdata(1776);

   s1.showdata();       //call member function to display data
   s2.showdata();
   return 0;
   }
```

The class smallobj defined in this program contains one data item and two member functions. The two member functions provide the only access to the data item from outside the class. The first member function sets the data item to a value, and the second displays the value. (This may sound like Greek, but we'll see what these terms mean as we go along.)

Placing data and functions together into a single entity is a central idea in object-oriented programming. This is shown in Figure 6.1.

FIGURE 6.1
Classes contain data and functions.

Classes and Objects

Recall from Chapter 1 that an object has the same relationship to a class that a variable has to a data type. An object is said to be an *instance of* a class, in the same way my 1954 Chevrolet is an instance of a vehicle. In SMALLOBJ, the class—whose name is smallobj—is defined in the first part of the program. Later, in main(), we define two objects—s1 and s2—that are instances of that class.

Each of the two objects is given a value, and each displays its value. Here's the output of the program:

```
Data is 1066      ←——— object s1 displayed this
Data is 1776      ←——— object s2 displayed this
```

We'll begin by looking in detail at the first part of the program—the definition of the class smallobj. Later we'll focus on what main() does with objects of this class.

Defining the Class

Here's the definition (sometimes called a *specifier*) for the class smallobj, copied from the SMALLOBJ listing:

```
class smallobj              //define a class
   {
   private:
      int somedata;         //class data
   public:
      void setdata(int d)   //member function to set data
         { somedata = d; }
      void showdata()       //member function to display data
         { cout << "\nData is " << somedata; }
   };
```

The definition starts with the keyword class, followed by the class name—smallobj in this example. Like a structure, the body of the class is delimited by braces and terminated by a semicolon. (Don't forget the semicolon. Remember, data constructs such as structures and classes end with a semicolon, while control constructs such as functions and loops do not.)

private and public

The body of the class contains two unfamiliar keywords: private and public. What is their purpose?

A key feature of object-oriented programming is *data hiding*. This term does not refer to the activities of particularly paranoid programmers; rather it means that data is concealed within a class so that it cannot be accessed mistakenly by functions outside the class. The primary mechanism for hiding data is to put it in a class and make it private. Private data or functions can only be accessed from within the class. Public data or functions, on the other hand, are accessible from outside the class. This is shown in Figure 6.2.

Hidden from Whom?

Don't confuse data hiding with the security techniques used to protect computer databases. To provide a security measure you might, for example, require a user to supply a password before granting access to a database. The password is meant to keep unauthorized or malevolent users from altering (or often even reading) the data.

Data hiding, on the other hand, means hiding data from parts of the program that don't need to access it. More specifically, one class's data is hidden from other classes. Data hiding is designed to protect well-intentioned programmers from honest mistakes. Programmers who really want to can figure out a way to access private data, but they will find it hard to do so by accident.

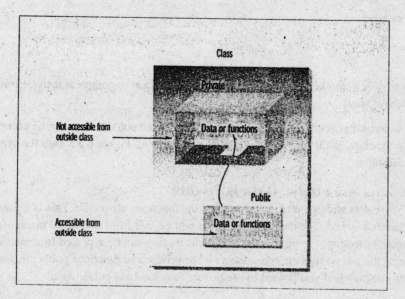

FIGURE 6.2
Private and public.

Class Data

The `smallobj` class contains one data item: `somedata`, which is of type `int`. The data items within a class are called *data members* (or sometimes *member data*). There can be any number of data members in a class, just as there can be any number of data items in a structure. The data member `somedata` follows the keyword `private`, so it can be accessed from within the class, but not from outside.

Member Functions

Member functions are functions that are included within a class. (In some object-oriented languages, such as Smalltalk, member functions are called *methods*; some writers use this term in C++ as well.) There are two member functions in `smallobj`: `setdata()` and `showdata()`. The function bodies of these functions have been written on the same line as the braces that delimit them. You could also use the more traditional format for these function definitions:

```
void setdata(int d)
   {
   somedata = d;
   }
```

and

```
void showdata()
  {
  cout << "\nData is " << somedata;
  }
```

However, when member functions are small, it is common to compress their definitions this way to save space.

Because setdata() and showdata() follow the keyword public, they can be accessed from outside the class. We'll see how th' is done in a moment. Figure 6.3 shows the syntax of a class definition.

Functions Are Public, Data Is Private

e data within a class is private and the functions are public. This is a result of the way classes a used The data is hidden so it will be safe from accidental manipulation, while the functions that op te on the data are public so they can be accessed from outside the class. However, there is no rule tha says data must be private and functions public; in some circumstances you may find you'll need to use private functions and public data.

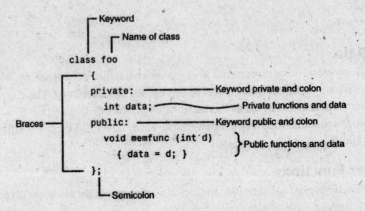

FIGURE 6.3
Syntax of a class definition.

Member Functions Within Class Definition

The member functions in the smallobj class perform operations that are quite common in classes: setting and retrieving the data stored in the class. The setdata() function accepts a value as a parameter and sets the somedata variable to this value. The showdata() function displays the value stored in somedata.

Note that the member functions setdata() and showdata() are *definitions* in that the actual code for the function is contained within the class definition. (The functions are not definitions in the sense that memory is set aside for the function code; this doesn't happen until an object of the class is created.) Member functions defined inside a class this way are created as inline functions by default. (Inline functions were discussed in Chapter 5, "Functions.") We'll see later that it is also possible to *declare* a function within a class but to *define* it elsewhere. Functions defined outside the class are not normally inline.

Using the Class

Now that the class is defined, let's see how main() makes use of it. We'll see how objects are defined, and, once defined, how their member functions are accessed.

Defining Objects

The first statement in main()

```
smallobj s1, s2;
```

defines two objects, s1 and s2, of class smallobj. Remember that the definition of the class smallobj does not create any objects. It only describes how they will look when they are created, just as a structure definition describes how a structure will look but doesn't create any structure variables. It is objects that participate in program operations. Defining an object is similar to defining a variable of any data type: Space is set aside for it in memory.

Defining objects in this way means *creating* them. This is also called *instantiating* them. The term *instantiating* arises because an *instance* of the class is created. An object is an instance (that is, a specific example) of a class. Objects are sometimes called *instance variables*.

Calling Member Functions

The next two statements in main() call the member function setdata():

```
s1.setdata(1066);
s2.setdata(1776);
```

These statements don't look like normal function calls. Why are the object names s1 and s2 connected to the function names with a period? This strange syntax is used to call a member function that is *associated with a specific object*. Because setdata() is a member function of the smallobj class, it must always be called in connection with an object of this class. It doesn't make sense to say

```
setdata(1066);
```

by itself, because a member function is always called to act on a specific object, not on the class in general. Attempting to access the class this way would be like trying to drive the blueprint of a car. Not only does this statement not make sense, but the compiler will issue an error message if you attempt it. Member functions of a class can be accessed only by an object of that class.

To use a member function, the dot operator (the period) connects the object name and the member function. The syntax is similar to the way we refer to structure members, but the parentheses signal that we're executing a member function rather than referring to a data item. (The dot operator is also called the *class member access* operator.)

The first call to setdata()

```
s1.setdata(1066);
```

executes the setdata() member function of the s1 object. This function sets the variable somedata in object s1 to the value 1066. The second call

```
s2.setdata(1776);
```

causes the variable somedata in s2 to be set to 1776. Now we have two objects whose somedata variables have different values, as shown in Figure 6.4.

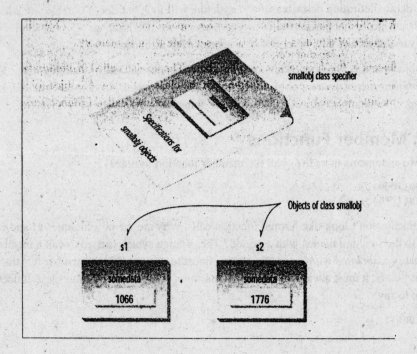

FIGURE 6.4
Two objects of class smallobj.

Similarly, the following two calls to the showdata() function will cause the two objects to display their values:

```
s1.showdata();
s2.showdata();
```

Messages

Some object-oriented languages refer to calls to member functions as *messages*. Thus the call

```
s1.showdata();
```

can be thought of as *sending a message* to s1 telling it to show its data. The term *message* is not a formal term in C++, but it is a useful idea to keep in mind as we discuss member functions. Talking about messages emphasizes that objects are discrete entities and that we communicate with them by calling their member functions. Referring to the analogy with company organization in Chapter 1, it's like sending a message to the secretary in the sales department asking for a list of products sold in the southwest distribution area.

C++ Objects as Physical Objects

In many programming situations, objects in programs represent physical objects: things that can be felt or seen. These situations provide vivid examples of the correspondence between the program and the real world. We'll look at two such situations: widget parts and graphics circles.

Widget Parts as Objects

The smallobj class in the last example had only one data item. Let's look at an example of a somewhat more ambitious class. (These are not the same ambitious classes discussed in political science courses.) We'll create a class based on the structure for the widget parts inventory, last seen in such examples as PARTS in Chapter 4, "Structures." Here's the listing for OBJPART:

```
// objpart.cpp
// widget part as an object
#include <iostream>
using namespace std;
/////////////////////////////////////////////////////////////
class part                  //define class
   {
   private:
      int modelnumber;       //ID number of widget
      int partnumber;        //ID number of widget part
      float cost;            //cost of part
   public:
      void setpart(int mn, int pn, float c)  //set data
         {
```

```
        modelnumber = mn;
        partnumber = pn;
        cost = c;
        }
    void showpart()                          //display data
        {
        cout << "Model "    << modelnumber;
        cout << ", part "   << partnumber;
        cout << ", costs $" << cost << endl;
        }
    };
/////////////////////////////////////////////////////////////////
int main()
    {
    part part1;                          //define object
                                         //  of class part
    part1.setpart(6244, 373, 217.55F);   //call member function
    part1.showpart();                    //call member function
    return 0;
    }
```

This program features the class part. Instead of one data item, as SMALLOBJ had, this class has three: modelnumber, partnumber, and cost. A single member function, setpart(), supplies values to all three data items at once. Another function, showpart(), displays the values stored in all three items.

In this example only one object of type part is created: part1. The member function setpart() sets the three data items in this part to the values 6244, 373, and 217.55. The member function showpart() then displays these values. Here's the output:

```
Model 6244, part 373, costs $217.55
```

This is a somewhat more realistic example than SMALLOBJ. If you were designing an inventory program you might actually want to create a class something like part. It's an example of a C++ object representing a physical object in the real world—a widget part.

Circles as Objects

In our next example we'll examine an object used to represent a circle: the kind of circle displayed on your computer screen. An image isn't quite as tangible an object as a widget part, which you can presumably hold in your hand, but you can certainly see such a circle when your program runs.

Our example is an object-oriented version of the CIRCSTRC program from Chapter 5. (As in that program, you'll need to add the appropriate Console Graphics Lite files to your project. These files can be downloaded from the publisher's Web site as described in the Introduction. Appendix E, "Console Graphics Lite," describes these files. See also the appendix for your particular compiler.) The program creates three circles with various characteristics and displays them. Here's the listing for CIRCLES:

```cpp
// circles.cpp
// circles as graphics objects
#include "msoftcon.h"          // for graphics functions
//////////////////////////////////////////////////////////////
class circle                   //graphics circle
   {
   protected:
      int xCo, yCo;            //coordinates of center
      int radius;
      color fillcolor;         //color
      fstyle fillstyle;        //fill pattern
   public:                     //sets circle attributes
      void set(int x, int y, int r, color fc, fstyle fs)
        {
        xCo = x;
        yCo = y;
        radius = r;
        fillcolor = fc;
        fillstyle = fs;
        }
      void draw()              //draws the circle
        {
        set_color(fillcolor);                //set color
        set_fill_style(fillstyle);           //set fill
        draw_circle(xCo, yCo, radius);       //draw solid circle
        }
   };
//////////////////////////////////////////////////////////////
int main()
   {
   init_graphics();            //initialize graphics system

   circle c1;                  //create circles
   circle c2;
   circle c3;
                               //set circle attributes
   c1.set(15, 7, 5, cBLUE, X_FILL);
   c2.set(41, 12, 7, cRED, O_FILL);
   c3.set(65, 18, 4, cGREEN, MEDIUM_FILL);
```

```
   c1.draw();                      //draw circles
   c2.draw();
   c3.draw();
   set_cursor_pos(1, 25);        //lower left corner
   return 0;
   }
```

The output of this program is the same as that of the CIRCSTRC program in Chapter 5, shown in Figure 5.5 in that chapter. You may find it interesting to compare the two programs. In CIRCLES, each circle is represented as a C++ object rather than as a combination of a structure variable and an unrelated circ_draw() function, as it was in CIRCSTRC. Notice in CIRCLES how everything connected with a circle—attributes and functions—is brought together in the class definition.

In CIRCLES, besides the draw() function, the circle class also requires the five-argument set() function to set its attributes. We'll see later that it's advantageous to dispense with this function and use a constructor instead.

C++ Objects as Data Types

Here's another kind of entity C++ objects can represent: variables of a user-defined data type. We'll use objects to represent distances measured in the English system, as discussed in Chapter 4. Here's the listing for ENGLOBJ:

```
// englobj.cpp
// objects using English measurements
#include <iostream>
using namespace std;
//////////////////////////////////////////////////////////////////
class Distance                       //English Distance class
   {
   private:
      int feet;
      float inches;
   public:
      void setdist(int ft, float in)  //set Distance to args
         { feet = ft; inches = in; }

      void getdist()                  //get length from user
         {
         cout << "\nEnter feet: ";  cin >> feet;
         cout << "Enter inches: ";  cin >> inches;
         }

      void showdist()                //display distance
         { cout << feet << "\'-" << inches << '\"'; }
```

```
};
/////////////////////////////////////////////////////////////////
int main()
   {
   Distance dist1, dist2;            //define two lengths

   dist1.setdist(11, 6.25);          //set dist1
   dist2.getdist();                  //get dist2 from user

                                     //display lengths
   cout << "\ndist1 = ";  dist1.showdist();
   cout << "\ndist2 = ";  dist2.showdist();
   cout << endl;
   return 0;
   }
```

In this program, the class Distance contains two data items, feet and inches. This is similar to the Distance structure seen in examples in Chapter 4, but here the class Distance also has three member functions: setdist(), which uses arguments to set feet and inches; getdist(), which gets values for feet and inches from the user at the keyboard; and showdist(), which displays the distance in feet-and-inches format.

The value of an object of class Distance can thus be set in either of two ways. In main(), we define two objects of class Distance: dist1 and dist2. The first is given a value using the setdist() member function with the arguments 11 and 6.25, and the second is given a value that is supplied by the user. Here's a sample interaction with the program:

```
Enter feet: 10
Enter inches: 4.75

dist1 = 11'-6.25"        ←————    provided by arguments
dist2 = 10'-4.75"        ←————    input by the user
```

Constructors

The ENGLOBJ example shows two ways that member functions can be used to give values to the data items in an object. Sometimes, however, it's convenient if an object can initialize itself when it's first created, without requiring a separate call to a member function. Automatic initialization is carried out using a special member function called a *constructor*. A constructor is a member function that is executed automatically whenever an object is created. (The term *constructor* is sometimes abbreviated *ctor*, especially in comments in program listings.)

A Counter Example

As an example, we'll create a class of objects that might be useful as a general-purpose programming element. A *counter* is a variable that counts things. Maybe it counts file accesses, or the number of times the user presses the Enter key, or the number of customers entering a bank. Each time such an event takes place, the counter is incremented (1 is added to it). The counter can also be accessed to find the current count.

Let's assume that this counter is important in the program and must be accessed by many different functions. In procedural languages such as C, a counter would probably be implemented as a global variable. However, as we noted in Chapter 1, global variables complicate the program's design and may be modified accidentally. This example, COUNTER, provides a counter variable that can be modified only through its member functions.

```cpp
// counter.cpp
// object represents a counter variable
#include <iostream>
using namespace std;
////////////////////////////////////////////////////////////////
class Counter
   {
   private:
      unsigned int count;                    //count
   public:
      Counter() : count(0)                   //constructor
         { /*empty body*/ }
      void inc_count()                       //increment count
         { count++; }
      int get_count()                        //return count
         { return count; }
   };
////////////////////////////////////////////////////////////////
int main()
   {
   Counter c1, c2;                           //define and initialize

   cout << "\nc1=" << c1.get_count();        //display
   cout << "\nc2=" << c2.get_count();

   c1.inc_count();                           //increment c1
   c2.inc_count();                           //increment c2
   c2.inc_count();                           //increment c2

   cout << "\nc1=" << c1.get_count();        //display again
   cout << "\nc2=" << c2.get_count();
```

```
    cout << endl;
    return 0;
    }
```

The Counter class has one data member: count, of type unsigned int (since the count is always positive). It has three member functions: the constructor Counter(), which we'll look at in a moment; inc_count(), which adds 1 to count; and get_count(), which returns the current value of count.

Automatic Initialization

When an object of type Counter is first created, we want its count to be initialized to 0. After all, most counts start at 0. We could provide a set_count() function to do this and call it with an argument of 0, or we could provide a zero_count() function, which would always set count to 0. However, such functions would need to be executed every time we created a Counter object.

```
Counter c1;          //every time we do this,
c1.zero_count();     //we must do this too
```

This is mistake prone, because the programmer may forget to initialize the object after creating it. It's more reliable and convenient, especially when there are a great many objects of a given class, to cause each object to initialize itself when it's created. In the Counter class, the constructor Counter() does this. This function is called automatically whenever a new object of type Counter is created. Thus in main() the statement

```
Counter c1, c2;
```

creates two objects of type Counter. As each is created, its constructor, Counter(), is executed. This function sets the count variable to 0. So the effect of this single statement is to not only create two objects, but also to initialize their count variables to 0.

Same Name as the Class

There are some unusual aspects of constructor functions. First, it is no accident that they have exactly the same name (Counter in this example) as the class of which they are members. This is one way the compiler knows they are constructors.

Second, no return type is used for constructors. Why not? Since the constructor is called automatically by the system, there's no program for it to return anything to; a return value wouldn't make sense. This is the second way the compiler knows they are constructors.

Initializer List

One of the most common tasks a constructor carries out is initializing data members. In the Counter class the constructor must initialize the count member to 0. You might think that this would be done in the constructor's function body, like this:

```
count()
   { count = 0; }
```

However, this is not the preferred approach (although it does work). Here's how you should initialize a data member:

```
count() : count(0)
   { }
```

The initialization takes place following the member function declarator but before the function body. It's preceded by a colon. The value is placed in parentheses following the member data.

If multiple members must be initialized, they're separated by commas. The result is the *initializer list* (sometimes called by other names, such as the *member-initialization list*).

```
someClass() : m1(7), m2(33), m2(4)  ←————    initializer list
   { }
```

Why not initialize members in the body of the constructor? The reasons are complex, but have to do with the fact that members initialized in the initializer list are given a value before the constructor even starts to execute. This is important in some situations. For example, the initializer list is the only way to initialize const member data and references.

Actions more complicated than simple initialization must be carried out in the constructor body, as with ordinary functions.

Counter Output

The main() part of this program exercises the Counter class by creating two counters, c1 and c2. It causes the counters to display their initial values, which—as arranged by the constructor—are 0. It then increments c1 once and c2 twice, and again causes the counters to display themselves (non-criminal behavior in this context). Here's the output:

```
c1=0
c2=0
c1=1
c2=2
```

If this isn't enough proof that the constructor is operating as advertised, we can rewrite the constructor to print a message when it executes.

```
Counter() : count(0)

   { cout << "I'm the constructor\n";
```

Now the program's output looks like this:

```
I'm the constructor
I'm the constructor
```

```
c1=0
c2=0
c1=1
c2=2
```

As you can see, the constructor is executed twice—once for c1 and once for c2—when the statement

```
Counter c1, c2;
```

is executed in main().

Do-It-Yourself Data

Constructors are pretty amazing when you think about it. Whoever writes language compilers (for C or VB or even C++) must execute the equivalent of a constructor when the user defines a variable. If you define an int, for example, somewhere there's a constructor allocating four bytes of memory for it. If we can write our own constructors, we can start to take over some of the tasks of a compiler writer. This is one step on the path to creating our own data types, as we'll see later.

A Graphics Example

Let's rewrite our earlier CIRCLES example to use a constructor instead of a set() function. To handle the initialization of the five attributes of circles, this constructor will have five arguments and five items in its initialization list. Here's the listing for CIRCTOR:

```
// circtor.cpp
// circles use constructor for initialization
#include "msoftcon.h"          // for graphics functions
//////////////////////////////////////////////////////////////////
class circle                    //graphics circle
   {
   protected:
      int xCo, yCo;             //coordinates of center
      int radius;
      color fillcolor;          //color
      fstyle fillstyle;         //fill pattern
   public:
                                //constructor
      circle(int x, int y, int r, color fc, fstyle fs) :
         xCo(x), yCo(y), radius(r), fillcolor(fc), fillstyle(fs)
         { }

      void draw()               //draws the circle
         {
         set_color(fillcolor);             //set color
```

```
                set_fill_style(fillstyle);        //set fill
                draw_circle(xCo, yCo, radius);     //draw solid circle
                }
        };
/////////////////////////////////////////////////////////////////
int main()
    {
    init_graphics();                //initialize graphics system
                                    //create circles
    circle c1(15, 7, 5, cBLUE, X_FILL);
    circle c2(41, 12, 7, cRED, O_FILL);
    circle c3(65, 18, 4, cGREEN, MEDIUM_FILL);

    c1.draw();                      //draw circles
    c2.draw();
    c3.draw();
    set_cursor_pos(1, 25);          //lower left corner
    return 0;
    }
```

This program is similar to CIRCLES, except that set() has been replaced by the constructor.
Note how this simplifies main(). Instead of two separate statements for each object, one to
create it and one to set its attributes, now one statement both creates the object and sets its
attributes at the same time.

Destructors

We've seen that a special member function—the constructor—is called automatically when
an object is first created. You might guess that another function is called automatically when an
object is destroyed. This is indeed the case. Such a function is called a *destructor*. A destructor
has the same name as the constructor (which is the same as the class name) but is preceded by
a tilde:

```
class Foo
    {
    private:
        int data;
    public:
        Foo() : data(0)       //constructor (same name as class)
            { }
        ~Foo()                //destructor (same name with tilde)
            { }
    };
```

Like constructors, destructors do not have a return value. They also take no arguments (the assumption being that there's only one way to destroy an object).

The most common use of destructors is to deallocate memory that was allocated for the object by the constructor. We'll investigate these activities in Chapter 10, "Pointers." Until then we won't have much use for destructors.

Objects as Function Arguments

Our next program adds some embellishments to the ENGLOBJ example. It also demonstrates some new aspects of classes: constructor overloading, defining member functions outside the class, and—perhaps most importantly—objects as function arguments. Here's the listing for ENGLCON:

```cpp
// englcon.cpp
// constructors, adds objects using member function
#include <iostream>
using namespace std;
/////////////////////////////////////////////////////////////////
class Distance                     //English Distance class
   {
   private:
      int feet;
      float inches;
   public:                         //constructor (no args)
      Distance() : feet(0), inches(0.0)
         {  }
                                   //constructor (two args)
      Distance(int ft, float in)  : feet(ft), inches(in)
         {  }

      void getdist()               //get length from user
         {
         cout << "\nEnter feet: ";  cin >> feet;
         cout << "Enter inches: ";  cin >> inches;
         }

      void showdist()              //display distance
         { cout << feet << "\'-" << inches << '\"'; }

      void add_dist( Distance, Distance );     //declaration
   };
//------------------------------------------------------------
                                   //add  engths d2 and d3
void Distance::add_dist(Distance d2, Dis nce d3)
```

```
      {
   inches = d2.inches + d3.inches;  //add the inches
   feet = 0;                        //(for possible carry)
   if(inches >= 12.0)               //if total exceeds 12.0,
      {                             //then decrease inches
      inches -= 12.0;               //by 12.0 and
      feet++;                       //increase feet
      }                             //by 1
   feet += d2.feet + d3.feet;       //add the feet
   }
/////////////////////////////////////////////////////////////////
int main()
   {
   Distance dist1, dist3;           //define two lengths
   Distance dist2(11, 6.25);        //define and initialize dist2

   dist1.getdist();                 //get dist1 from user
   dist3.add_dist(dist1, dist2);    //dist3 = dist1 + dist2

                                    //display all lengths
   cout << "\ndist1 = ";  dist1.showdist();
   cout << "\ndist2 = ";  dist2.showdist();
   cout << "\ndist3 = ";  dist3.showdist();
   cout << endl;
   return 0;
   }
```

This program starts with a distance dist2 set to an initial value and adds to it a distance dist1, whose value is supplied by the user, to obtain the sum of the distances. It then displays all three distances:

```
Enter feet: 17
Enter inches: 5.75

dist1 = 17'-5.75"
dist2 = 11'-6.25"
dist3 = 29'-0"
```

Let's see how the new features in this program are implemented.

Overloaded Constructors

It's convenient to be able to give variables of type Distance a value when they are first created. That is, we would like to use definitions like

```
Distance width(5, 6.25);
```

which defines an object, width, and simultaneously initializes it to a value of 5 for feet and 6.25 for inches.

To do this we write a constructor like this:

```
Distance(int ft, float in) : feet(ft), inches(in)
   { }
```

This sets the member data feet and inches to whatever values are passed as arguments to the constructor. So far so good.

However, we also want to define variables of type Distance without initializing them, as we did in ENGLOBJ.

```
Distance dist1, dist2;
```

In that program there was no constructor, but our definitions worked just fine. How could they work without a constructor? Because an implicit no-argument constructor is built into the program automatically by the compiler, and it's this constructor that created the objects, even though we didn't define it in the class. This no-argument constructor is called the *default constructor*. If it weren't created automatically by the constructor, you wouldn't be able to create objects of a class for which no constructor was defined.

Often we want to initialize data members in the default (no-argument) constructor as well. If we let the default constructor do it, we don't really know what values the data members may be given. If we care what values they may be given, we need to explicitly define the constructor. In ENGLECON we show how this looks:

```
Distance() : feet(0), inches(0.0)     //default constructor
     { }          //no function body, doesn't do anything
```

The data members are initialized to constant values, in this case the integer value 0 and the float value 0.0, for feet and inches respectively. Now we can use objects initialized with the no-argument constructor and be confident that they represent no distance (0 feet plus 0.0 inches) rather than some arbitrary value.

Since there are now two explicit constructors with the same name, Distance(), we say the constructor is *overloaded*. Which of the two constructors is executed when an object is created depends on how many arguments are used in the definition:

```
Distance length;           // calls first constructor
Distance width(11, 6.0);   // calls second constructor
```

Member Functions Defined Outside the Class

So far we've seen member functions that were defined inside the class definition. This need not always be the case. ENGLCON shows a member function, add_dist(), that is not defined within the Distance class definition. It is only *declared* inside the class, with the statement

```
void add_dist( Distance, Distance );
```

This tells the compiler that this function is a member of the class but that it will be defined outside the class declaration, someplace else in the listing.

In ENGLCON the add_dist() function is defined following the class definition. It is adapted from the ENGLSTRC program in Chapter 4:

```
                                         //add lengths d2 and d3
void Distance::add_dist(Distance d2, Distance d3)
   {
   inches = d2.inches + d3.inches;  //add the inches
   feet = 0;                        //(for possible carry)
   if(inches >= 12.0)               //if total exceeds 12.0,
      {                             //then decrease inches
      inches -= 12.0,               //by 12.0 and
      feet++;                       //increase feet
      }                             //by 1
   feet += d2.feet + d3.feet;       //add the feet
   }
```

The declarator in this definition contains some unfamiliar syntax. The function name, add_dist(), is preceded by the class name, Distance, and a new symbol—the double colon (::). This symbol is called the *scope resolution operator*. It is a way of specifying what class something is associated with. In this situation, Distance::add_dist() means "the add_dist() member function of the Distance class." Figure 6.5 shows its usage.

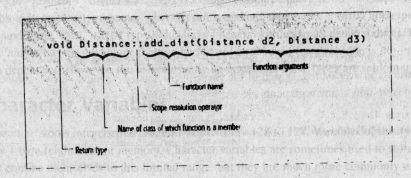

FIGURE 6.5
The scope resolution operator.

Objects as Arguments

Now we can see how ENGLCON works. The distances dist1 and dist3 are created using the default constructor (the one that takes no arguments). The distance dist2 is created with the constructor that takes two arguments, and is initialized to the values passed in these arguments. A value is obtained for dist1 by calling the member function getdist(), which obtains values from the user.

Now we want to add dist1 and dist2 to obtain dist3. The function call in main()

```
dist3.add_dist(dist1, dist2);
```

does this. The two distances to be added, dist1 and dist2, are supplied as arguments to add_dist(). The syntax for arguments that are objects is the same as that for arguments that are simple data types such as int: The object name is supplied as the argument. Since add_dist() is a member function of the Distance class, it can access the private data in any object of class Distance supplied to it as an argument, using names like dist1.inches and dist2.feet.

Close examination of add_dist() emphasizes some important truths about member functions. A member function is always given access to the object for which it was called: the object connected to it with the dot operator. But it may be able to access other objects. In the following statement in ENGLCON, what objects can add_dist() access?

```
dist3.add_dist(dist1, dist2);
```

Besides dist3, the object for which it was called, it can also access dist1 and dist2, because they are supplied as arguments. You might think of dist3 as a sort of phantom argument; the member function always has access to it, even though it is not supplied as an argument. That's what this statement means: "Execute the add_dist() member function of dist3." When the variables feet and inches are referred to within this function, they refer to dist3.feet and dist3.inches.

Notice that the result is not returned by the function. The return type of add_dist() is void. The result is stored automatically in the dist3 object. Figure 6.6 shows the two distances dist1 and dist2 being added together, with the result stored in dist3.

To summarize, every call to a member function is associated with a particular object (unless it's a static function; we'll get to that later). Using the member names alone (feet and inches), the function has direct access to all the members, whether private or public, of that object. It also has indirect access, using the object name and the member name, connected with the dot operator (dist1.inches or dist2.feet) to other objects of the same class that are passed as arguments.

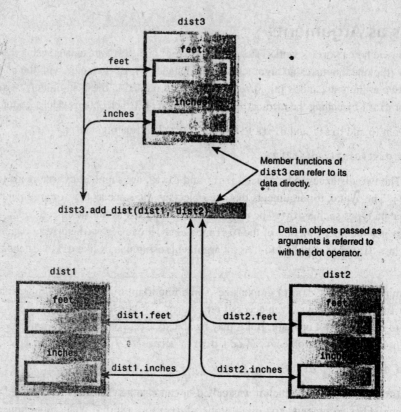

dist3.add_dist(dist1, dist2)

Member functions of
dist3 can refer to its
data directly.

Data in objects passed as
arguments is referred to
with the dot operator.

FIGURE 6.6
Result in this object.

The Default Copy Constructor

We've seen two ways to initialize objects. A no-argument constructor can initialize data members to constant values, and a multi-argument constructor can initialize data members to values passed as arguments. Let's mention another way to initialize an object: you can initialize it with *another object of the same type*. Surprisingly, you don't need to create a special constructor for this; one is already built into all classes. It's called the *default copy constructor*. It's a one-argument constructor whose argument is an object of the same class as the constructor. The ECOPYCON program shows how this constructor is used.

```
// ecopycon.cpp
// initialize objects using default copy constructor
#include <iostream>
using namespace std;
//////////////////////////////////////////////////////////////////
```

```cpp
class Distance                      //English Distance class
   {
   private:
      int feet;
      float inches;
   public:
                                    //constructor (no args)
      Distance() : feet(0), inches(0.0)
         {  }
      //Note: no one-arg constructor
                                    //constructor (two args)
      Distance(int ft, float in)  : feet(ft), inches(in)
         {  }

      void getdist()                //get length from user
         {
         cout << "\nEnter feet: ";  cin >> feet;
         cout << "Enter inches: ";  cin >> inches;
         }
      void showdist()               //display distance
         { cout << feet << "\'-" << inches << '\"'; }
   };
/////////////////////////////////////////////////////////////////
int main()
   {
   Distance dist1(11, 6.25);       //two-arg constructor
   Distance dist2(dist1);          //one-arg constructor
   Distance dist3 = dist1;         //also one-arg constructor

                                   //display all lengths
   cout << "\ndist1 = ";  dist1.showdist();
   cout << "\ndist2 = ";  dist2.showdist();
   cout << "\ndist3 = ";  dist3.showdist();
   cout << endl;
   return 0;
   }
```

We initialize dist1 to the value of 11'-6.25" using the two-argument constructor. Then we define two more objects of type Distance, dist2 and dist3, initializing both to the value of dist1. You might think this would require us to define a one-argument constructor, but initializing an object with another object of the same type is a special case. These definitions both use the default copy constructor. The object dist2 is initialized in the statement

```cpp
Distance dist2(dist1);
```

This causes the default copy constructor for the Distance class to perform a member-by-member copy of dist1 into dist2. Surprisingly, a different format has exactly the same effect, causing dist1 to be copied member-by-member into dist3:

```
Distance dist3 = dist1;
```

Although this looks like an assignment statement, it is not. Both formats invoke the default copy constructor, and can be used interchangeably. Here's the output from the program:

```
dist1 = 11'-6.25"
dist2 = 11'-6.25"
dist3 = 11'-6.25"
```

This shows that the dist2 and dist3 objects have been initialized to the same value as dist1. In Chapter 11, "Virtual Functions," we discuss how to create your own custom copy constructor by overloading the default.

Returning Objects from Functions

In the ENGLCON example, we saw objects being passed as arguments to functions. Now we'll see an example of a function that returns an object. We'll modify the ENGLCON program to produce ENGLRET:

```cpp
// englret.cpp
// function returns value of type Distance
#include <iostream>
using namespace std;
//////////////////////////////////////////////////////////////////
class Distance                       //English Distance class
   {
   private:
     int feet;
     float inches;
   public:                           //constructor (no args)
     Distance() : feet(0), inches(0.0)
       { }                           //constructor (two args)
     Distance(int ft, float in) : feet(ft), inches(in)
       { }

     void getdist()                  //get length from user
       {
       cout << "\nEnter feet: ";  cin >> feet;
       cout << "Enter inches: ";  cin >> inches;
       }
     void showdist()                 //display distance
       { cout << feet << "\'-" << inches << '\"'; }
```

```
        Distance add_dist(Distance);      //add
    };
//----------------------------------------------------------------
//add this distance to d2, return the sum
Distance Distance::add_dist(Distance d2)
    {
    Distance temp;                        //temporary variable
    temp.inches = inches + d2.inches;     //add the inches
    if(temp.inches >= 12.0)               //if total exceeds 12.0,
        {                                 //then decrease inches
        temp.inches -= 12.0;              //by 12.0 and
        temp.feet = 1;                    //increase feet
        }                                 //by 1
    temp.feet += feet + d2.feet;          //add the feet
    return temp;
    }
////////////////////////////////////////////////////////////////
int main()
    {
    Distance dist1, dist3;                //define two lengths
    Distance dist2(11, 6.25);             //define, initialize dist2

    dist1.getdist();                      //get dist1 from user
    dist3 = dist1.add_dist(dist2);        //dist3 = dist1 + dist2

                                          //display all lengths
    cout << "\ndist1 = ";  dist1.showdist();
    cout << "\ndist2 = ";  dist2.showdist();
    cout << "\ndist3 = ";  dist3.showdist();
    cout << endl;
    return 0;
    }
```

The ENGLRET program is very similar to ENGLCON, but the differences reveal important aspects of how functions work with objects.

Arguments and Objects

In ENGLCON, two distances were passed to add_dist() as arguments, and the result was stored in the object of which add_dist() was a member, namely dist3. In ENGLRET, one distance, dist2, is passed to add_dist() as an argument. It is added to the object, dist1, of which add_dist() is a member, and the result is returned from the function. In main(), the result is assigned to dist3 in the statement

```
dist3 = dist1.add_dist(dist2);
```

The effect is the same as the corresponding statement in ENGLCON, but it is somewhat more natural looking, since the assignment operator, =, is used in a natural way. In Chapter 8, "Operator Overloading," we'll see how to use the arithmetic + operator to achieve the even more natural expression

```
dist3 = dist1 + dist2;
```

Here's the add_dist() function from ENGLRET:

```
//add this distance to d2, return the sum
Distance Distance::add_dist(Distance d2)
    {
    Distance temp;                         //temporary variable
    temp.inches = inches + d2.inches;      //add the inches
    if(temp.inches >= 12.0)                //if total exceeds 12.0,
        {                                  //then decrease inches
        temp.inches -= 12.0;               //by 12.0 and
        temp.feet = 1;                     //increase feet
        }                                  //by 1
    temp.feet += feet + d2.feet;           //add the feet
    return temp;
    }
```

Compare this with the same function in ENGLCON. As you can see, there are some subtle differences. In the ENGLRET version, a temporary object of class Distance is created. This object holds the sum until it can be returned to the calling program. The sum is calculated by adding two distances. The first is the object of which add_dist() is a member, dist1. Its member data is accessed in the function as feet and inches. The second is the object passed as an argument, dist2. Its member data is accessed as d2.feet and d2.inches. The result is stored in temp and accessed as temp.feet and temp.inches. The temp object is then returned by the function using the statement

```
return temp;
```

and the statement in main() assigns it to dist3. Notice that dist1 is not modified; it simply supplies data to add_dist(). Figure 6.7 shows how this looks.

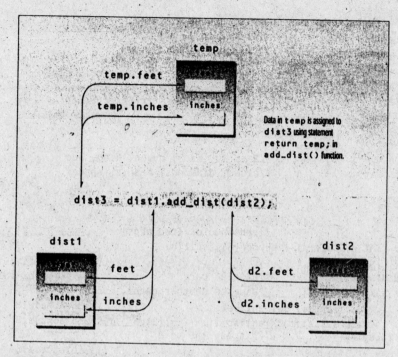

FIGURE. 6.7
Result returned from the temporary object.

A Card-Game Example

As a larger example of objects modeling the real world, let's look at a variation of the CARDS
program from Chapter 4. This program, CARDOBJ, has been rewritten to use objects. It does not
introduce any new concepts, but it does use almost all the programming ideas we've discussed
up to this point.

As the CARDS example did, CARDOBJ creates three cards with fixed values and switches them
around in an attempt to confuse the user about their location. But in CARDOBJ each card is an
object of class card. Here's the listing:

```
// cardobj.cpp
// cards as objects
#include <iostream>
using namespace std;
```

```
enum Suit { clubs, diamonds, hearts, spades };
const int jack = 11;          //from 2 to 10 are
const int queen = 12;         //integers without names
const int king = 13;
const int ace = 14;
//////////////////////////////////////////////////////////////////
class card
    {
    private:
        int number;            //2 to 10, jack, queen, king, ace
        Suit suit;             //clubs, diamonds, hearts, spades
    public:
        card ()                //constructor (no args)
           { }
                               //constructor (two args)
        card (int n, Suit s) : number(n), suit(s)
           { }
        void display();        //display card
        bool isEqual(card);    //same as another card?
    };
//------------------------------------------------------------------
void card::display()          //display the card
    {
    if( number >= 2 && number <= 10 )
        cout << number << " of ";
    else
        switch(number)
           {
           case jack:  cout << "jack of ";  break;
           case queen: cout << "queen of "; break;
           case king:  cout << "king of ";  break;
           case ace:   cout << "ace of ";   break;
           }
    switch(suit)
        {
        case clubs:    cout << "clubs"; break;
        case diamonds: cout << "diamonds"; break;
        case hearts:   cout << "hearts"; break;
        case spades:   cout << "spades"; break;
        }
    }
//------------------------------------------------------------------
bool card::isEqual(card c2)          //return true if cards equal
    {
    return ( number==c2.number && suit==c2.suit ) ? true : false;
    }
```

```
///////////////////////////////////////////////////////////
int main()
    {
    card temp, chosen, prize;        //define various cards
    int position;

    card card1( 7, clubs );          //define & initialize card1
    cout << "\nCard 1 is the ";
    card1.display();                 //display card1

    card card2( jack, hearts );      //define & initialize card2
    cout << "\nCard 2 is the ";
    card2.display();                 //display card2

    card card3( ace, spades );       //define & initialize card3
    cout << "\nCard 3 is the ";
    card3.display();                 //display card3

    prize = card3;                   //prize is the card to guess

    cout << "\nI'm swapping card 1 and card 3";
    temp = card3; card3 = card1; card1 = temp;

    cout << "\nI'm swapping card 2 and card 3";
    temp = card3; card3 = card2; card2 = temp;

    cout << "\nI'm swapping card 1 and card 2";
    temp = card2; card2 = card1; card1 = temp;

    cout << "\nNow, where (1, 2, or 3) is the ";
    prize.display();                 //display prize card
    cout << "? ";
    cin >> position;                 //get user's guess of position

    switch (position)
        {                            //set chosen to user's choice
        case 1: chosen = card1; break;
        case 2: chosen = card2; break;
        case 3: chosen = card3; break;
        }
    if( chosen.isEqual(prize) )      //is chosen card the prize?
        cout << "That's right!  You win!";
    else
        cout << "Sorry.  You lose.";
    cout << " You chose the ";
    chosen.display();                //display chosen card
```

```
    cout << endl;
    return 0;
    }
```

There are two constructors in class card. The first, which takes no arguments, is used in main() to create the cards temp, chosen, and prize, which are not initialized. The second constructor, which takes two arguments, is used to create card1, card2, and card3 and to initialize them to specific values. Besides the constructors, card has two other member functions, both defined outside the class.

The display() function takes no arguments; it simply displays the card object of which it is a member, using the number and suit data items in the card. The statement in main()

```
chosen.display();
```

displays the card chosen by the user.

The isEqual() function checks whether the card is equal to a card supplied as an argument. It uses the conditional operator to compare the card of which it is a member with a card supplied as an argument. This function could also have been written with an if...else statement

```
if( number==c2.number && suit==c2.suit )
    return true;
else
    return false;
```

but the conditional operator is more compact.

In isEqual() the argument is called c2 as a reminder that there are two cards in the comparison: The first card is the object of which isEqual() is a member. The expression

```
if( chosen.isEqual(prize) )
```

in main() compares the card chosen with the card prize.

Here's the output when the user guesses an incorrect card:

```
Card 1 is the 7 of clubs
Card 2 is the jack of hearts
Card 3 is the ace of spades
I'm swapping card 1 and card 3
I'm swapping card 2 and card 3
I'm swapping card 1 and card 2
Now, where (1, 2, or 3) is the ace of spades? 1
Sorry, you lose. You chose the 7 of clubs
```

Structures and Classes

The examples so far in this book have portrayed structures as a way to group data and classes as a way to group both data and functions. In fact, you can use structures in almost exactly the same way that you use classes. The only formal difference between class and struct is that in a class the members are private by default, while in a structure they are public by default.

Here's the format we've been using for classes:

```
class foo
   {
   private:
      int data1;
   public:
      void func();
   };
```

Because private is the default in classes, this keyword is unnecessary. You can just as well write

```
class foo
   {
      int data1;
   public:
      void func();
   };
```

and the data1 will still be private. Many programmers prefer this style. We like to include the private keyword because it offers an increase in clarity.

If you want to use a structure to accomplish the same thing as this class, you can dispense with the keyword public, provided you put the public members before the private ones

```
struct foo
   {
      void func();
   private:
      int data1;
   };
```

since public is the default. However, in most situations programmers don't use a struct this way. They use structures to group only data, and classes to group both data and functions.

Classes, Objects, and Memory

We've probably given you the impression that each object created from a class contains separate copies of that class's data and member functions. This is a good first approximation, since it emphasizes that objects are complete, self-contained entities, designed using the class definition. The mental image here is of cars (objects) rolling off an assembly line, each one made according to a blueprint (the class definitions).

Actually, things are not quite so simple. It's true that each object has its own separate data items. On the other hand, contrary to what you may have been led to believe, all the objects in a given class use the same member functions. The member functions are created and placed in memory only once—when they are defined in the class definition. This makes sense; there's really no point in duplicating all the member functions in a class every time you create another object of that class, since the functions for each object are identical. The data items, however, will hold different values, so there must be a separate instance of each data item for each object. Data is therefore placed in memory when each object is defined, so there is a separate set of data for each object. Figure 6.8 shows how this looks.

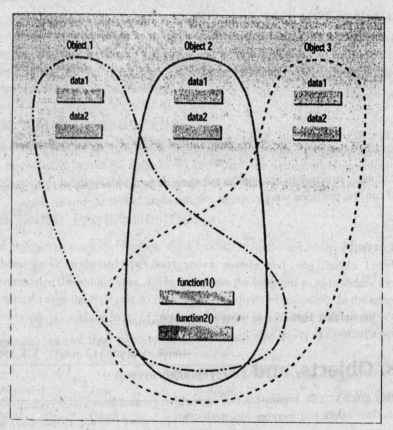

FIGURE 6.8
Objects, data, functions, and memory.

In the SMALLOBJ example at the beginning of this chapter there are two objects of type smallobj, so there are two instances of somedata in memory. However, there is only one instance of the functions setdata() and showdata(). These functions are shared by all the objects of the class. There is no conflict because (at least in a single-threaded system) only one function is executed at a time.

In most situations you don't need to know that there is only one member function for an entire class. It's simpler to visualize each object as containing both its own data and its own member functions. But in some situations, such as in estimating the size of an executing program, it's helpful to know what's happening behind the scenes.

Static Class Data

Having said that each object contains its own separate data, we must now amend that slightly. If a data item in a class is declared as static, only one such item is created for the entire class, no matter how many objects there are. A static data item is useful when all objects of the same class must share a common item of information. A member variable defined as static has characteristics similar to a normal static variable: It is visible only within the class, but its lifetime is the entire program. It continues to exist even if there are no objects of the class. (See Chapter 5 for a discussion of static variables.) However, while a normal static variable is used to retain information between calls to a function, static class member data is used to share information among the objects of a class.

Uses of Static Class Data

Why would you want to use static member data? As an example, suppose an object needed to know how many other objects of its class were in the program. In a road-racing game, for example, a race car might want to know how many other cars are still in the race. In this case a static variable count could be included as a member of the class. All the objects would have access to this variable. It would be the same variable for all of them; they would all see the same count.

An Example of Static Class Data

Here's an example, STATDATA, that demonstrates a simple static data member:

```
// statdata.cpp
// static class data
#include <iostream>
using namespace std;
/////////////////////////////////////////////////////////////////
class foo
    {
```

```
    private:
        static int count;     //only one data item for all objects
                              //note: "declaration" only!
    public:
        foo()                 //increments count when object created
            { count++; }
        int getcount()        //returns count
            { return count; }
    };
//--------------------------------------------------------------
int foo::count = 0;         //*definition* of count
/////////////////////////////////////////////////////////////////
int main()
    {
    foo f1, f2, f3;          //create three objects

    cout << "count is " << f1.getcount() << endl;  //each object
    cout << "count is " << f2.getcount() << endl;  //sees the
    cout << "count is " << f3.getcount() << endl;  //same value
    return 0;
    }
```

The class foo in this example has one data item, count, which is type static int. The constructor for this class causes count to be incremented. In main() we define three objects of class foo. Since the constructor is called three times, count is incremented three times. Another member function, getcount(), returns the value in count. We call this function from all three objects, and—as we expected—each prints the same value. Here's the output:

```
count is 3      ←——————   static data
count is 3
count is 3
```

If we had used an ordinary automatic variable—as opposed to a static variable—for count, each constructor would have incremented its own private copy of count once, and the output would have been

```
count is 1      ←——————   automatic data
count is 1
count is 1
```

Static class variables are not used as often as ordinary non-static variables, but they are important in many situations. Figure 6.9 shows how static variables compare with automatic variables.

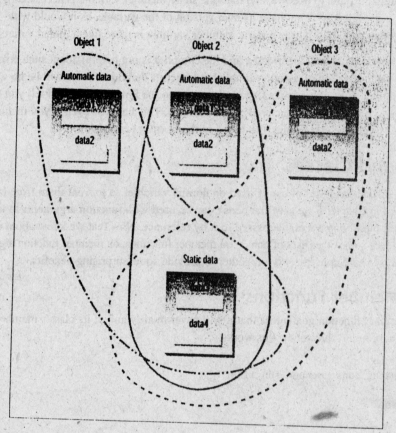

FIGURE 6.9

Static versus automatic member variables.

Separate Declaration and Definition

Static member data requires an unusual format. Ordinary variables are usually declared (the compiler is told about their name and type) and defined (the compiler sets aside memory to hold the variable) in the same statement. Static member data, on the other hand, requires two separate statements. The variable's declaration appears in the class definition, but the variable is actually defined outside the class, in much the same way as a global variable.

Why is this two-part approach used? If static member data were defined inside the class (as it actually was in early versions of C++), it would violate the idea that a class definition is only a blueprint and does not set aside any memory. Putting the definition of static member data outside the class also serves to emphasize that the memory space for such data is allocated only once, before the program starts to execute, and that one static member variable is accessed by an entire class; each object does not have its own version of the variable, as it would with ordinary member data. In this way a static member variable is more like a global variable.

It's easy to handle static data incorrectly, and the compiler is not helpful about such errors. If you include the declaration of a static variable but forget its definition, there will be no warning from the compiler. Everything looks fine until you get to the linker, which will tell you that you're trying to reference an undeclared global variable. This happens even if you include the definition but forget the class name (the foo:: in the STATDATA example).

const and Classes

We've seen several examples of const used on normal variables to prevent them from being modified, and in Chapter 5 we saw that const can be used with function arguments to keep a function from modifying a variable passed to it by reference. Now that we know about classes, we can introduce some other uses of const: on member functions, on member function arguments, and on objects. These concepts work together to provide some surprising benefits.

const Member Functions

A const member function guarantees that it will never modify any of its class's member data. The CONSTFU program shows how this works.

```
//constfu.cpp
//demonstrates const member functions
/
class aClass
   {
   private:
      int alpha;
   public:
      void nonFunc()          //non-const member function
         { alpha = 99; }      //OK

      void conFunc() const    //const member function
         { alpha = 99; }      //ERROR: can't modify a member
   };
```

The non-const function nonFunc() can modify member data alpha, but the constant function conFunc() can't. If it tries to, a compiler error results.

A function is made into a constant function by placing the keyword const after the declarator but before the function body. If there is a separate function declaration, const must be used in both declaration and definition. Member functions that do nothing but acquire data from an object are obvious candidates for being made const, because they don't need to modify any data.

Making a function const helps the compiler flag errors, and tells anyone looking at the listing that you intended the function not to modify anything in its object. It also makes possible the creation and use of const objects, which we'll discuss soon.

A Distance Example

To avoid raising too many subjects at once we have, up to now, avoided using const member functions in the example programs. However, there are many places where const member functions should be used. For example, in the Distance class, shown in several programs, the showdist() member function could be made const because it doesn't (or certainly shouldn't!) modify any of the data in the object for which it was called. It should simply display the data.

Also, in ENGLRET, the add_dist() function should not modify any of the data in the object for which it was called. This object should simply be added to the object passed as an argument, and the resulting sum should be returned. We've modified the ENGLRET program to show how these two constant functions look. Note that const is used in both the declaration and the definition of add_dist(). Here's the listing for ENGCONST:

```cpp
// engConst.cpp
// const member functions and const arguments to member functions
#include <iostream>
using namespace std;
/////////////////////////////////////////////////////////////////////
class Distance                          //English Distance class
    {
    private:
        int feet;
        float inches;
    public:                             //constructor (no args)
        Distance() : feet(0), inches(0.0)
            { }                         //constructor (two args)
        Distance(int ft, float in) : feet(ft), inches(in)
            { }

        void getdist()                  //get length from user
            {
            cout << "\nEnter feet: ";  cin >> feet;
            cout << "Enter inches: ";  cin >> inches;
            }
        void showdist() const           //display distance
            { cout << feet << "\'-" << inches << '\"'; }

        Distance add_dist(const Distance&) const;      //add
    };
//---------------------------------------------------------------
//add this distance to d2, return the sum
```

```
Distance Distance::add_dist(const Distance& d2) const
   {
   Distance temp;                       //temporary variable

// feet = 0;                            //ERROR: can't modify this
// d2.feet = 0;                         //ERROR: can't modify d2
   temp.inches = inches + d2.inches;    //add the inches
   if(temp.inches >= 12.0)              //if total exceeds 12.0,
      {                                 //then decrease inches
      temp.inches -= 12.0;              //by 12.0 and
      temp.feet = 1;                    //increase feet
      }                                 //by 1
   temp.feet += feet + d2.feet;         //add the feet
   return temp;
   }
/////////////////////////////////////////////////////////////////
int main()
   {
   Distance dist1, dist3;               //define two lengths
   Distance dist2(11, 6.25);            //define, initialize dist2

   dist1.getdist();                     //get dist1 from user
   dist3 = dist1.add_dist(dist2);       //dist3 = dist1 + dist2


                                        //display all lengths
   cout << "\ndist1 = ";  dist1.showdist();
   cout << "\ndist2 = ";  dist2.showdist();
   cout << "\ndist3 = ";  dist3.showdist();
   cout << endl;
   return 0;
   }
```

Here, showdist() and add_dist() are both constant member functions. In add_dist() we show in the first commented statement, feet = 0, that a compiler error is generated if you attempt to modify any of the data in the object for which this constant function was called.

const Member Function Arguments

We mentioned in Chapter 5 that if an argument is passed to an ordinary function by reference, and you don't want the function to modify it, the argument should be made const in the function declaration (and definition). This is true of member functions as well. In ENGCONST the argument to add_dist() is passed by reference, and we want to make sure that ENGCONST won't modify this variable, which is dist2 in main(). Therefore we make the argument d2 to add_dist() const in both declaration and definition. The second commented statement shows that the compiler will flag as an error any attempt by add_dist() to modify any member data of its argument dist2.

const Objects

In several example programs, we've seen that we can apply const to variables of basic types such as int to keep them from being modified. In a similar way, we can apply const to objects of classes. When an object is declared as const, you can't modify it. It follows that you can use only const member functions with it, because they're the only ones that guarantee not to modify it. The CONSTOBJ program shows an example.

```
// constObj.cpp
// constant Distance objects
#include <iostream>
using namespace std;
/////////////////////////////////////////////////////////////////
class Distance                      //English Distance class
   {
   private:
      int feet;
      float inches;
   public:                          //2-arg constructor
      Distance(int ft, float in) : feet(ft), inches(in)
         { }
      void getdist()                //user input; non-const func
         {
         cout << "\nEnter feet: ";  cin >> feet;
         cout << "Enter inches: ";  cin >> inches;
         }
      void showdist() const         //display distance; const func
         { cout << feet << "\'-" << inches << '\"'; }
   };
/////////////////////////////////////////////////////////////////
int main()
   {
   const Distance football(300, 0);

// football.getdist();             //ERROR: getdist() not const
   cout << "football = ";
   football.showdist();            //OK
   cout << endl;
   return 0;
   }
```

A football field (for American-style football) is exactly 300 feet long. If we were to use the length of a football field in a program, it would make sense to make it const, because changing it would represent the end of the world for football fans. The CONSTOBJ program makes football a const variable. Now only const functions, such as showdist(), can be called for this object. Non-const functions, such as getdist(), which gives the object a new value obtained from the user, are illegal. In this way the compiler enforces the const value of football.

When you're designing classes it's a good idea to make const any function that does not modify any of the data in its object. This allows the user of the class to create const objects. These objects can use any const function, but cannot use any non-const function. Remember, using const helps the compiler to help you.

What Does It All Mean?

Now that you've been introduced to classes and objects, you may wonder what benefit they really offer. After all, as you can see by comparing several of the programs in this chapter with those in Chapter 4, it's possible to do the same sorts of things with a procedural approach as it is with objects.

One benefit of OOP that you may have glimpsed already is the close correspondence between the real-world things being modeled *by* the program and the C++ objects *in* the program. A widget part object in a program represents a widget part in the real world, a card object represents a card, a circle object represents a graphics circle, and so on. In C++, everything about a widget part is included in its class description—the part number and other data items, and the functions necessary to access and operate on this data. This makes it easy to conceptualize a programming problem. You figure out what parts of the problem can be most usefully represented as objects, and then put all the data and functions connected with that object into the class. If you're using a C++ class to represent a playing card, you put into this class the data items that represent the value of the card, and also the functions to set value, retrieve it, display it, compare it, and so on.

In a procedural program, by contrast, the global variables and functions connected with a real-world object are distributed all over the listing; they don't form a single, easily grasped unit.

In some situations it may not be obvious what parts of a real-life situation should be made into objects. If you're writing a program that plays chess, for instance, what are the objects? The chessmen, the squares on the board, or possibly entire board positions?

In small programs, such as many of the ones in this book, you can often proceed by trial and error. You break a problem into objects in one way and write trial class definitions for these objects. If the classes seem to match reality in a useful way, you continue. If they don't, you may need to start over, selecting different entities to be classes. The more experience you have with OOP, the easier it will be to break a programming problem into classes.

Larger programs may prove too complex for this trial-and-error approach. A new field, object-oriented design (OOD) is increasingly applied to analyzing a programming problem and figuring out what classes and objects should be used to represent the real-world situation (which is often called the *problem domain*). We'll discuss this methodology in detail in Chapter 16, "Object-Oriented Software Development."

Some of the benefits of object-oriented programming are probably not apparent at this point. Remember that OOP was devised to cope with the complexity of large programs. Smaller programs, such as the examples in this chapter, have less need for the organizational power that OOP provides. The larger the program, the greater the benefit. But even for small programs, once you start thinking in object-oriented terms, the OO design approach becomes natural and surprisingly helpful. One advantage is that in an OO program the compiler can find many more conceptual errors than in a procedural program.

Summary

A class is a specification or blueprint for a number of objects. Objects consist of both data and functions that operate on that data. In a class definition, the members—whether data or functions—can be private, meaning they can be accessed only by member functions of that class, or public, meaning they can be accessed by any function in the program.

A member function is a function that is a member of a class. Member functions have access to an object's private data, while non-member functions do not.

A constructor is a member function, with the same name as its class, that is executed every time an object of the class is created. A constructor has no return type but can take arguments. It is often used to give initial values to object data members. Constructors can be overloaded, so an object can be initialized in different ways.

A destructor is a member function with the same name as its class but preceded by a tilde (~). It is called when an object is destroyed. A destructor takes no arguments and has no return value.

In the computer's memory there is a separate copy of the data members for each object that is created from a class, but there is only one copy of a class's member functions. You can restrict a data item to a single instance for all objects of a class by making it static.

One reason to use OOP is the close correspondence between real-world objects and OOP classes. Deciding what objects and classes to use in a program can be complicated. For small programs, trial and error may be sufficient. For large programs, a more systematic approach is usually needed.

Questions

Answers to these questions can be found in Appendix G.

1. What is the purpose of a class definition?

2. A _____ has the same relation to an _____ that a basic data type has to a variable of that type.

3. In a class definition, data or functions designated private are accessible

    a. to any function in the program.

    b. only if you know the password.

    c. to member functions of that class.

    d. only to public members of the class.

4. Write a class definition that creates a class called leverage with one private data member, crowbar, of type int and one public function whose declaration is void pry().

5. True or false: Data items in a class must be private.

6. Write a statement that defines an object called lever1 of the leverage class described in Question 4.

7. The dot operator (or class member access operator) connects the following two entities (reading from left to right):

    a. A class member and a class object

    b. A class object and a class

    c. A class and a member of that class

    d. A class object and a member of that class

8. Write a statement that executes the pry() function in the lever1 object, as described in Questions 4 and 6.

9. Member functions defined inside a class definition are _____ by default.

10. Write a member function called getcrow() for the leverage class described in Question 4. This function should return the value of the crowbar data. Assume the function is defined within the class definition.

11. A constructor is executed automatically when an object is _____.

12. A constructor's name is the same as _____.

13. Write a constructor that initializes to 0 the crowbar data, a member of the leverage class described in Question 4. Assume that the constructor is defined within the class definition.

14. True or false: In a class you can have more than one constructor with the same name.

15. A member function can always access the data

    a. in the object of which it is a member.

    b. in the class of which it is a member.

    c. in any object of the class of which it is a member.

    d. in the public part of its class.

16. Assume that the member function getcrow() described in Question 10 is defined outside the class definition. Write the declaration that goes inside the class definition.

17. Write a revised version of the `getcrow()` member function from Question 10 that is defined outside the class definition.

18. The only technical difference between structures and classes in C++ is that _____.

19. If three objects of a class are defined, how many copies of that class's data items are stored in memory? How many copies of its member functions?

20. Sending a message to an object is the same as _____.

21. Classes are useful because they

    a. are removed from memory when not in use.

    b. permit data to be hidden from other classes.

    c. bring together all aspects of an entity in one place.

    d. can closely model objects in the real world.

22. True or false: There is a simple but precise methodology for dividing a real-world programming problem into classes.

23. For the object for which it was called, a `const` member function.

    a. can modify both `const` and non-`const` member data.

    b. can modify only `const` member data.

    c. can modify only non-`const` member data.

    d. can modify neither `const` nor non-`const` member data.

24. True or false: If you declare a `const` object, it can only be used with `const` member functions.

25. Write a declaration (not a definition) for a `const void` function called `aFunc()` that takes one `const` argument called `jerry` of type `float`.

Exercises

Answers to the starred exercises can be found in Appendix G.

*1. Create a class that imitates part of the functionality of the basic data type `int`. Call the class `Int` (note different capitalization). The only data in this class is an `int` variable. Include member functions to initialize an `Int` to 0, to initialize it to an `int` value, to display it (it looks just like an `int`), and to add two `Int` values.

Write a program that exercises this class by creating one uninitialized and two initialized `Int` values, adding the two initialized values and placing the response in the uninitialized value, and then displaying this result.

*2. Imagine a tollbooth at a bridge. Cars passing by the booth are expected to pay a 50 cent toll. Mostly they do, but sometimes a car goes by without paying. The tollbooth keeps track of the number of cars that have gone by, and of the total amount of money collected.

Model this tollbooth with a class called tollBooth. The two data items are a type unsigned int to hold the total number of cars, and a type double to hold the total amount of money collected. A constructor initializes both of these to 0. A member function called payingCar() increments the car total and adds 0.50 to the cash total. Another function, called nopayCar(), increments the car total but adds nothing to the cash total. Finally, a member function called display() displays the two totals. Make appropriate member functions const.

Include a program to test this class. This program should allow the user to push one key to count a paying car, and another to count a nonpaying car. Pushing the Esc key should cause the program to print out the total cars and total cash and then exit.

*3. Create a class called time that has separate int member data for hours, minutes, and seconds. One constructor should initialize this data to 0, and another should initialize it to fixed values. Another member function should display it, in 11:59:59 format. The final member function should add two objects of type time passed as arguments.

A main() program should create two initialized time objects (should they be const?) and one that isn't initialized. Then it should add the two initialized values together, leaving the result in the third time variable. Finally it should display the value of this third variable. Make appropriate member functions const.

4. Create an employee class, basing it on Exercise 4 of Chapter 4. The member data should comprise an int for storing the employee number and a float for storing the employee's compensation. Member functions should allow the user to enter this data and display it. Write a main() that allows the user to enter data for three employees and display it.

5. Start with the date structure in Exercise 5 in Chapter 4 and transform it into a date class. Its member data should consist of three ints: month, day, and year. It should also have two member functions: getdate(), which allows the user to enter a date in 12/31/02 format, and showdate(), which displays the date.

6. Extend the employee class of Exercise 4 to include a date class (see Exercise 5) and an etype enum (see Exercise 6 in Chapter 4). An object of the date class should be used to hold the date of first employment; that is, the date when the employee was hired. The etype variable should hold the employee's type: laborer, secretary, manager, and so on. These two items will be private member data in the employee definition, just like the employee number and salary. You'll need to extend the getemploy() and putemploy() functions to obtain this new information from the user and display it. These functions will probably need switch statements to handle the etype variable. Write a main() program that allows the user to enter data for three employee variables and then displays this data.

7. In ocean navigation, locations are measured in degrees and minutes of latitude and longitude. Thus if you're lying off the mouth of Papeete Harbor in Tahiti, your location is 149 degrees 34.8 minutes west longitude, and 17 degrees 31.5 minutes south latitude. This is

written as 149°34.8' W, 17°31.5' S. There are 60 minutes in a degree. (An older system also divided a minute into 60 seconds, but the modern approach is to use decimal minutes instead.) Longitude is measured from 0 to 180 degrees, east or west from Greenwich, England, to the international dateline in the Pacific. Latitude is measured from 0 to 90 degrees, north or south from the equator to the poles.

Create a class angle that includes three member variables: an int for degrees, a float for minutes, and a char for the direction letter (N, S, E, or W). This class can hold either a latitude variable or a longitude variable. Write one member function to obtain an angle value (in degrees and minutes) and a direction from the user, and a second to display the angle value in 179°59.9' E format. Also write a three-argument constructor. Write a main() program that displays an angle initialized with the constructor, and then, within a loop, allows the user to input any angle value, and then displays the value. You can use the hex character constant '\xF8', which usually prints a degree (°) symbol.

8. Create a class that includes a data member that holds a "serial number" for each object created from the class. That is, the first object created will be numbered 1, the second 2, and so on.

    To do this, you'll need another data member that records a count of how many objects have been created so far. (This member should apply to the class as a whole; not to individual objects. What keyword specifies this?) Then, as each object is created, its constructor can examine this count member variable to determine the appropriate serial number for the new object.

    Add a member function that permits an object to report its own serial number. Then write a main() program that creates three objects and queries each one about its serial number. They should respond I am object number 2, and so on.

9. Transform the fraction structure from Exercise 8 in Chapter 4 into a fraction class. Member data is the fraction's numerator and denominator. Member functions should accept input from the user in the form 3/5, and output the fraction's value in the same format. Another member function should add two fraction values. Write a main() program that allows the user to repeatedly input two fractions and then displays their sum. After each operation, ask whether the user wants to continue.

10. Create a class called ship that incorporates a ship's number and location. Use the approach of Exercise 8 to number each ship object as it is created. Use two variables of the angle class from Exercise 7 to represent the ship's latitude and longitude. A member function of the ship class should get a position from the user and store it in the object; another should report the serial number and position. Write a main() program that creates three ships, asks the user to input the position of each, and then displays each ship's number and position.

11. Modify the four-function fraction calculator of Exercise 12 in Chapter 5 to use a `fraction` class rather than a structure. There should be member functions for input and output, as well as for the four arithmetical operations. While you're at it, you might as well install the capability to reduce fractions to lowest terms. Here's a member function that will reduce the `fraction` object of which it is a member to lowest terms. It finds the greatest common divisor (gcd) of the fraction's numerator and denominator, and uses this gcd to divide both numbers.

```
void fraction::lowterms()          // change ourself to lowest terms
   {
   long tnum, tden, temp, gcd;

   tnum = labs(num);               // use non-negative copies.
   tden = labs(den);               //     (needs cmath)
   if(tden==0 )     // check for n/0
      { cout << "Illegal fraction: division by 0"; exit(1); }
   else if( tnum==0 )              // check for 0/n
      { num=0; den = 1; return; }

   // this 'while' loop finds the gcd of tnum and tden
   while(tnum != 0)
      {
      if(tnum < tden)              // ensure numerator larger
         { temp=tnum; tnum=tden; tden=temp; }  // swap them
      tnum = tnum - tden;          // subtract them
      }
   gcd = tden;                     // this is greatest common divisor
   num = num / gcd;                // divide both num and den by gcd
   den = den / gcd;                // to reduce frac to lowest terms
   }
```

You can call this function at the end of each arithmetic function, or just before you perform output. You'll also need the usual member functions: four arithmetic operations, input, and display. You may find a two-argument constructor useful.

12. Note that one advantage of the OOP approach is that an entire class can be used, without modification, in a different program. Use the `fraction` class from Exercise 11 in a program that generates a multiplication table for fractions. Let the user input a denominator, and then generate all combinations of two such fractions that are between 0 and 1, and multiply them together. Here's an example of the output if the denominator is 6:

	1/6	1/3	1/2	2/3	5/6
1/6	1/36	1/18	1/12	1/9	5/36
1/3	1/18	1/9	1/6	2/9	5/18
1/2	1/12	1/6	1/4	1/3	5/12
2/3	1/9	2/9	1/3	4/9	5/9
5/6	5/36	5/18	5/12	5/9	25/36

Arrays and Strings

IN THIS CHAPTER

In everyday life we commonly group similar objects into units. We buy peas by the can and eggs by the carton. In computer languages we also need to group together data items of the same type. The most basic mechanism that accomplishes this in C++ is the *array*. Arrays can hold a few data items or tens of thousands. The data items grouped in an array can be simple types such as int or float, or they can be user-defined types such as structures and objects.

Arrays are like structures in that they both group a number of items into a larger unit. But while a structure usually groups items of different types, an array groups items of the same type. More importantly, the items in a structure are accessed by name, while those in an array are accessed by an index number. Using an index number to specify an item allows easy access to a large number of items.

Arrays exist in almost every computer language. Arrays in C++ are similar to those in other languages, and identical to those in C.

In this chapter we'll look first at arrays of basic data types such as int and char. Then we'll examine arrays used as data members in classes, and arrays used to hold objects. Thus this chapter is intended not only to introduce arrays, but to increase your understanding of object-oriented programming.

In Standard C++ the array is not the only way to group elements of the same type. A *vector*, which is part of the Standard Template library, is another approach. We'll look at vectors in Chapter 15, "The Standard Template Library."

In this chapter we'll also look at two different approaches to strings, which are used to store and manipulate text. The first kind of string is an array of type char, and the second is a member of the Standard C++ string class.

Array Fundamentals

A simple example program will serve to introduce arrays. This program, REPLAY, creates an array of four integers representing the ages of four people. It then asks the user to enter four values, which it places in the array. Finally, it displays all four values.

```
// replay.cpp
// gets four ages from user, displays them
#include <iostream>
using namespace std;

int main()
   {
   int age[4];                        //array 'age' of 4 ints
```

```
for(int j=0; j<4; j++)              //get 4 ages
   {
   cout << "Enter an age: ";
   cin >> age[j];                   //access array element
   }
for(j=0; j<4; j++)                  //display 4 ages
   cout << "You entered " << age[j] << endl;
return 0;
}
```

Here's a sample interaction with the program:

```
Enter an age: 44
Enter an age: 16
Enter an age: 23
Enter an age: 68

You entered 44
You entered 16
You entered 23
You entered 68
```

The first for loop gets the ages from the user and places them in the array, while the second reads them from the array and displays them.

Defining Arrays

Like other variables in C++, an array must be defined before it can be used to store information. And, like other definitions, an array definition specifies a variable type and a name. But it includes another feature: a size. The size specifies how many data items the array will contain. It immediately follows the name, and is surrounded by square brackets. Figure 7.1 shows the syntax of an array definition.

In the REPLAY example, the array is type int. The name of the array comes next, followed immediately by an opening bracket, the array size, and a closing bracket. The number in brackets must be a constant or an expression that evaluates to a constant, and should also be an integer. In the example we use the value 4.

Array Elements

The items in an array are called *elements* (in contrast to the items in a structure, which are called *members*). As we noted, all the elements in an array are of the same type; only the values vary. Figure 7.2 shows the elements of the array age.

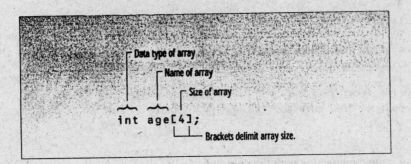

FIGURE 7.1
Syntax of array definition.

Memory

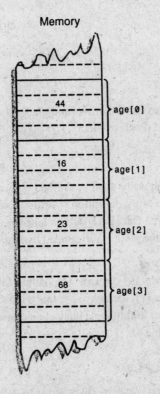

FIGURE 7.2
Array elements.

Following the conventional (although in some ways backward) approach, memory grows downward in the figure. That is, the first array elements are on the top of the page; later elements extend downward. As specified in the definition, the array has exactly four elements.

Notice that the first array element is numbered 0. Thus, since there are four elements, the last one is number 3. This is a potentially confusing situation; you might think the last element in a four-element array would be number 4, but it's not.

Accessing Array Elements

In the REPLAY example we access each array element twice. The first time, we insert a value into the array, with the line

```
cin >> age[j];
```

The second time, we read it out with the line

```
cout << "\nYou entered " << age[j];
```

In both cases the expression for the array element is

```
age[j]
```

This consists of the name of the array, followed by brackets delimiting a variable j. Which of the four array elements is specified by this expression depends on the value of j; age[0] refers to the first element, age[1] to the second, age[2] to the third, and age[3] to the fourth. The variable (or constant) in the brackets is called the *array index*.

Since j is the loop variable in both for loops, it starts at 0 and is incremented until it reaches 3, thereby accessing each of the array elements in turn.

Averaging Array Elements

Here's another example of an array at work. This one, SALES, invites the user to enter a series of six values representing widget sales for each day of the week (excluding Sunday), and then calculates the average of these values. We use an array of type double so that monetary values can be entered.

```
// sales.cpp
// averages a weeks's widget sales (6 days)
#include <iostream>
using namespace std;

int main()
   {
   const int SIZE = 6;              //size of array
   double sales[SIZE];              //array of 6 variables

   cout << "Enter widget sales for 6 days\n";
   for(int j=0; j<SIZE; j++)        //put figures in array
      cin >> sales[j];
```

```
double total = 0;
for(j=0; j<SIZE; j++)          //read figures from array
    total += sales[j];         //to find total
double average = total / SIZE; // find average
cout << "Average = " << average << endl;
return 0;
}
```

Here's some sample interaction with SALES:

```
Enter widget sales for 6 days
352.64
867.70
781.32
867.35
746.21
189.45
Average = 634.11
```

A new detail in this program is the use of a const variable for the array size and loop limits. This variable is defined at the start of the listing:

```
const int SIZE = 6;
```

Using a variable (instead of a number, such as the 4 used in the last example) makes it easier to change the array size: Only one program line needs to be changed to change the array size, loop limits, and anywhere else the array size appears. The all-uppercase name reminds us that the variable cannot be modified in the program.

Initializing Arrays

You can give values to each array element when the array is first defined. Here's an example, DAYS, that sets 12 array elements in the array days_per_month to the number of days in each month.

```
// days.cpp
// shows days from start of year to date specified
#include <iostream>
using namespace std;

int main()
    {
    int month, day, total_days;
    int days_per_month[12] = { 31, 28, 31, 30, 31, 30,
                               31, 31, 30, 31, 30, 31 };

    cout << "\nEnter month (1 to 12): ";  //get date
    cin >> month;
    cout << "Enter day (1 to 31): ";
```

```
cin >> day;
total_days = day;                      //separate days
for(int j=0; j<month-1; j++)           //add days each month
   total_days += days_per_month[j];
cout << "Total days from start of year is: " << total_days
     << endl;
return 0;
}
```

The program calculates the number of days from the beginning of the year to a date specified by the user. (Beware: It doesn't work for leap years.) Here's some sample interaction:

```
Enter month (1 to 12): 3
Enter day (1 to 31): 11
Total days from start of year is: 70
```

Once it gets the month and day values, the program first assigns the day value to the `total_days` variable. Then it cycles through a loop, where it adds values from the `days_per_month` array to `total_days`. The number of such values to add is one less than the number of months. For instance, if the user enters month 5, the values of the first four array elements (31, 28, 31, and 30) are added to the total.

The values to which `days_per_month` is initialized are surrounded by braces and separated by commas. They are connected to the array expression by an equal sign. Figure 7.3 shows the syntax.

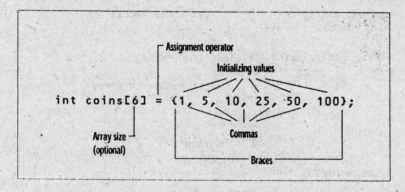

FIGURE 7.3
Syntax of array initialization.

Actually, we don't need to use the array size when we initialize all the array elements, since the compiler can figure it out by counting the initializing variables. Thus we can write

```
int days_per_month[] = { 31, 28, 31, 30, 31, 30,
                         31, 31, 30, 31, 30, 31 };
```

What happens if you do use an explicit array size, but it doesn't agree with the number of initializers? If there are too few initializers, the missing elements will be set to 0. If there are too many, an error is signaled.

Multidimensional Arrays

So far we've looked at arrays of one dimension: A single variable specifies each array element. But arrays can have higher dimensions. Here's a program, SALEMON, that uses a two-dimensional array to store sales figures for several districts and several months:

```
// salemon.cpp
// displays sales chart using 2-d array
#include <iostream>
#include <iomanip>                     //for setprecision, etc.
using namespace std;

const int DISTRICTS = 4;               //array dimensions
const int MONTHS = 3;

int main()
   {
   int d, m;
   double sales[DISTRICTS][MONTHS];    //two-dimensional array
                                       //definition

   cout << endl;
   for(d=0; d<DISTRICTS; d++)          //get array values
      for(m=0; m<MONTHS; m++)
         {
         cout << "Enter sales for district " << d+1;
         cout << ", month " << m+1 << ": ";
         cin >> sales[d][m];           //put number in array
         }

   cout << "\n\n";
   cout << "                    Month\n";
   cout << "                1         2         3";
   for(d=0; d<DISTRICTS; d++)
      {
      cout <<"\nDistrict " << d+1;
      for(m=0; m<MONTHS; m++)          //display array values
         cout << setiosflags(ios::fixed)      //not exponential
              << setiosflags(ios::showpoint)  //always use point
              << setprecision(2)              //digits to right
              << setw(10)                      //field width
              << sales[d][m];          //get number from array
      } //end for(d)
```

```
    cout << endl;
    return 0;
    }  //end main
```

This program accepts the sales figures from the user and then displays them in a table.

```
Enter sales for district 1, month 1: 3964.23
Enter sales for district 1, month 2: 4135.87
Enter sales for district 1, month 3: 4397.98
Enter sales for district 2, month 1: 867.75
Enter sales for district 2, month 2: 923.59
Enter sales for district 2, month 3: 1037.01
Enter sales for district 3, month 1: 12.77
Enter sales for district 3, month 2: 378.32
Enter sales for district 3, month 3: 798.22
Enter sales for district 4, month 1: 2983.53
Enter sales for district 4, month 2: 3983.73
Enter sales for district 4, month 3: 9494.98
```

```
                    Month
            1          2          3
District 1  3964.23    4135.87    4397.98
District 2   867.75     923.59    1037.01
District 3    12.77     378.32     798.22
District 4  2983.53    3983.73    9494.98
```

Defining Multidimensional Arrays

The array is defined with two size specifiers, each enclosed in brackets:

```
double sales[DISTRICTS][MONTHS];
```

You can think about sales as a two-dimensional array, laid out like a checkerboard. Another way to think about it is that sales is an array of arrays. It is an array of DISTRICTS elements, each of which is an array of MONTHS elements. Figure 7.4 shows how this looks.

Of course there can be arrays of more than two dimensions. A three-dimensional array is an array of arrays of arrays. It is accessed with three indexes:

```
elem = dimen3[x][y][z];
```

This is entirely analogous to one- and two-dimensional arrays.

Accessing Multidimensional Array Elements

Array elements in two-dimensional arrays require two indexes:

```
sales[d][m]
```

Notice that each index has its own set of brackets. Commas are not used. Don't write sales[d,m]; this works in some languages, but not in C++.

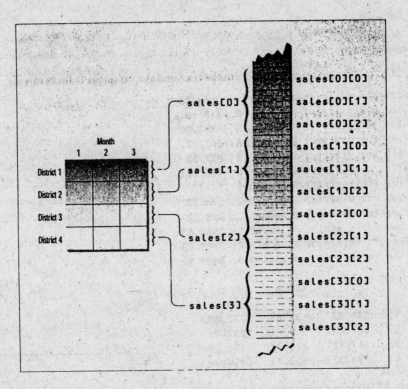

FIGURE 7.4
Two-dimensional array.

Formatting Numbers

The SALEMON program displays a table of dollar values. It's important that such values be formatted properly, so let's digress to see how this is done in C++. With dollar values you normally want to have exactly two digits to the right of the decimal point, and you want the decimal points of all the numbers in a column to line up. It's also nice if trailing zeros are displayed; you want 79.50, not 79.5.

Convincing the C++ I/O streams to do all this requires a little work. You've already seen the manipulator setw(), used to set the output field width. Formatting decimal numbers requires several additional manipulators.

Here's a statement that prints a floating-point number called fpn in a field 10 characters wide, with two digits to the right of the decimal point:

```
cout << setiosflags(ios::fixed)        //fixed (not exponential)
     << setiosflags(ios::showpoint)    //always show decimal point
```

```
<< setprecision(2)          //two decimal places
<< setw(10)                 //field width 10
<< fpn;                     //finally, the number
```

A group of one-bit formatting flags in a long int in the ios class determines how formatting will be carried out. At this point we don't need to know what the ios class is, or the reasons for the exact syntax used with this class, to make the manipulators work.

We're concerned with two of the ios flags: fixed and showpoint. To set the flags, use the manipulator setiosflags, with the name of the flag as an argument. The name must be preceded by the class name, ios, and the scope resolution operator (::).

The first two lines of the cout statement set the ios flags. (If you need to unset—that is, clear—the flags at some later point in your program, you can use the resetiosflags manipulator.) The fixed flag prevents numbers from being printed in exponential format, such as 3.45e3. The showpoint flag specifies that there will always be a decimal point, even if the number has no fractional part: 123.00 instead of 123.

To set the precision to two digits to the right of the decimal place, use the setprecision manipulator, with the number of digits as an argument. We've already seen how to set the field width by using the setw manipulator. Once all these manipulators have been sent to cout, you can send the number itself; it will be displayed in the desired format.

We'll talk more about the ios formatting flags in Chapter 12, "Streams and Files."

Initializing Multidimensional Arrays

As you might expect, you can initialize multidimensional arrays. The only prerequisite is a willingness to type a lot of braces and commas. Here's a variation of the SALEMON program that uses an initialized array instead of asking for input from the user. This program is called SALEINIT.

```cpp
// saleinit.cpp
// displays sales chart, initializes 2-d array
#include <iostream>
#include <iomanip>                //for setprecision, etc.
using namespace std;
const int DISTRICTS = 4;          //array dimensions
const int MONTHS = 3;

int main()
   {
   int d, m;
                                  //initialize array elements
   double sales[DISTRICTS][MONTHS]
```

```
           = {  {  1432.07,    234.50,    654.01 },
                {   322.00, 13838.32, 17589.88 },
                {  9328.34,    934.00,   4492.30 },
                { 12838.29,   2332.63,     32.93 }  };
      cout << "\n\n";
      cout << "                        Month\n";
      cout << "             1         2         3";
      for(d=0; d<DISTRICTS; d++)
         {
         cout <<"\nDistrict " << d+1;
         for(m=0; m<MONTHS; m++)
            cout << setw(10) << setiosflags(ios::fixed)
                 << setiosflags(ios::showpoint) << setprecision(2)
                 << sales[d][m];   //access array element
         }
      cout << endl;
      return 0;
      }
```

Remember that a two-dimensional array is really an array of arrays. The format for initializing such an array is based on this fact. The initializing values for each subarray are enclosed in braces and separated by commas

```
{ 1432.07, 234.50, 654.01 }
```

and then all four of these subarrays, each of which is an element in the main array, is likewise enclosed by braces and separated by commas, as can be seen in the listing.

Passing Arrays to Functions

Arrays can be used as arguments to functions. Here's an example, a variation of the SALEINIT program, that passes the array of sales figures to a function whose purpose is to display the data as a table. Here's the listing for SALEFUNC:

```
// salefunc.cpp
// passes array as argument
#include <iostream>
#include <iomanip>              //for setprecision, etc.
using namespace std;
const int DISTRICTS = 4;      //array dimensions
const int MONTHS = 3;
void display( double[DISTRICTS][MONTHS] );  //declaration
//----------------------------------------------------------
int main()
   {                           //initialize two-dimensional array
   double sales[DISTRICTS][MONTHS]
```

```
        = { {  1432.07,    234.50,    654.01 },
            {   322.00, 13838.32, 17589.88 },
            {  9328.34,    934.00,   4492.30 },
            { 12838.29,  2332.63,     32.93 } };

   display(sales);          //call function; array as argument
   cout << endl;
   return 0;
   } //end main
//------------------------------------------------------------
//display()
//function to display 2-d array passed as argument
void display( double funsales[DISTRICTS][MONTHS] )
   {
   int d, m;

   cout << "\n\n";
   cout << "                      Month\n";
   cout << "              1        2        3";

   for(d=0; d<DISTRICTS; d++)
      {
      cout <<"\nDistrict " << d+1;
      for(m=0; m<MONTHS; m++)
         cout << setiosflags(ios::fixed) << setw(10)
              << setiosflags(ios::showpoint) << setprecision(2)
              << funsales[d][m];    //array element
      } //end for(d)
} //end display
```

Function Declaration with Array Arguments

In a function declaration, array arguments are represented by the data type and size of the array. Here's the declaration of the display() function:

```
void display( float[DISTRICTS][MONTHS] );  // declaration
```

Actually, there is one unnecessary piece of information here. The following statement works just as well:

```
void display( float[][MONTHS] );  // declaration
```

Why doesn't the function need the size of the first dimension? Again, remember that a two-dimensional array is an array of arrays. The function first thinks of the argument as an array of districts. It doesn't need to know how many districts there are, but it does need to know how big each district element is, so it can calculate where a particular element is (by multiplying the bytes per element times the index). So we must tell it the size of each element, which is MONTHS, but not how many there are, which is DISTRICTS.

It follows that if we were declaring a function that used a one-dimensional array as an argument, we would not need to use the array size:

```
void somefunc( int elem[] );    // declaration
```

Function Call with Array Arguments

When the function is called, only the name of the array is used as an argument.

```
display(sales);    // function call
```

This name (`sales` in this case) actually represents the memory address of the array. We aren't going to explore addresses in detail until Chapter 10, "Pointers," but here are a few preliminary points about them.

Using an address for an array argument is similar to using a reference argument, in that the values of the array elements are not duplicated (copied) into the function. (See the discussion of reference arguments in Chapter 5, "Functions.") Instead, the function works with the original array, although it refers to it by a different name. This system is used for arrays because they can be very large; duplicating an entire array in every function that called it would be both time-consuming and wasteful of memory.

However, an address is not the same as a reference. No ampersand (`&`) is used with the array name in the function declaration. Until we discuss pointers, take it on faith that arrays are passed using their name alone, and that the function accesses the original array, not a duplicate.

Function Definition with Array Arguments

In the function definition the declarator looks like this:

```
void display( double funsales[DISTRICTS][MONTHS] )
```

The array argument uses the data type, a name, and the sizes of the array dimensions. The array name used by the function (`funsales` in this example) can be different from the name that defines the array (`sales`), but they both refer to the same array. All the array dimensions must be specified (except in some cases the first one); the function needs them to access the array elements properly.

References to array elements in the function use the function's name for the array:

```
funsales[d][m]
```

But in all other ways the function can access array elements as if the array had been defined in the function.

Arrays of Structures

Arrays can contain structures as well as simple data types. Here's an example based on the part structure from Chapter 4, "Structures."

```cpp
// partaray.cpp
// structure variables as array elements
#include <iostream>
using namespace std;
const int SIZE = 4;                 //number of parts in array
/////////////////////////////////////////////////////////////
struct part                         //specify a structure
   {
   int modelnumber;                 //ID number of widget
   int partnumber;                  //ID number of widget part
   float cost;                      //cost of part
   };
/////////////////////////////////////////////////////////////
int main()
   {
   int n;
   part apart[SIZE];                //define array of structures

   for(n=0; n<SIZE; n++)            //get values for all members
      {
      cout << endl;
      cout << "Enter model number: ";
      cin >> apart[n].modelnumber;     //get model number
      cout << "Enter part number: ";
      cin >> apart[n].partnumber;      //get part number
      cout << "Enter cost: ";
      cin >> apart[n].cost;            //get cost
      }
   cout << endl;
   for(n=0; n<SIZE; n++)            //show values for all members
      {
      cout << "Model " << apart[n].modelnumber;
      cout << "  Part " << apart[n].partnumber;
      cout << "  Cost " << apart[n].cost << endl;
      }
   return 0;
   }
```

The user types in the model number, part number, and cost of a part. The program records this data in a structure. However, this structure is only one element in an array of structures. The program asks for the data for four different parts, and stores it in the four elements of the apart array. It then displays the information. Here's some sample input:

```
Enter model number: 44
Enter part number: 4954
Enter cost: 133.45

Enter model number: 44
Enter part number: 8431
Enter cost: 97.59

Enter model number: 77
Enter part number: 9343
Enter cost: 109.99

Enter model number: 77
Enter part number: 4297
Enter cost: 3456.55

Model 44   Part 4954   Cost 133.45
Model 44   Part 8431   Cost 97.59
Model 77   Part 9343   Cost 109.99
Model 77   Part 4297   Cost 3456.55
```

The array of structures is defined in the statement

```
part apart[SIZE];
```

This has the same syntax as that of arrays of simple data types. Only the type name, part, shows that this is an array of a more complex type.

Accessing a data item that is a member of a structure that is itself an element of an array involves a new syntax. For example

```
apart[n].modelnumber
```

refers to the modelnumber member of the structure that is element n of the apart array. Figure 7.5 shows how this looks.

Arrays of structures are a useful data type in a variety of situations. We've shown an array of car parts, but we could also store an array of personnel data (name, age, salary), an array of geographical data about cities (name, population, elevation), and many other types of data.

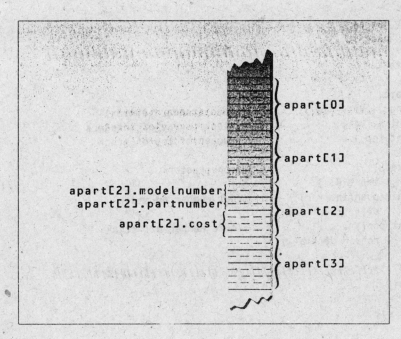

FIGURE 7.5
Array of structures.

Arrays as Class Member Data

Arrays can be used as data items in classes. Let's look at an example that models a common computer data structure: the stack.

A stack works like the spring-loaded devices that hold trays in cafeterias. When you put a tray on top, the stack sinks down a little; when you take a tray off, it pops up. The last tray placed on the stack is always the first tray removed.

Stacks are one of the cornerstones of the architecture of the microprocessors used in most modern computers. As we mentioned earlier, functions pass their arguments and store their return address on the stack. This kind of stack is implemented partly in hardware and is most conveniently accessed in assembly language. However, stacks can also be created completely in software. Software stacks offer a useful storage device in certain programming situations, such as in parsing (analyzing) algebraic expressions.

Our example program, STAKARAY, creates a simple stack class.

```
// stakaray.cpp
// a stack as a class
```

```
#include <iostream>
using namespace std;
/////////////////////////////////////////////////////////////////
class Stack
    {
    private:
        enum { MAX = 10 };          //(non-standard syntax)
        int st[MAX];                //stack: array of integers
        int top;                    //number of top of stack
    public:
        Stack()                     //constructor
            { top = 0; }
        void push(int var)          //put number on stack
            { st[++top] = var; }
        int pop()                   //take number off stack
            { return st[top--]; }
    };
/////////////////////////////////////////////////////////////////
int main()
    {
    Stack s1;

    s1.push(11);
    s1.push(22);
    cout << "1: " << s1.pop() << endl;   //22
    cout << "2: " << s1.pop() << endl;   //11
    s1.push(33);
    s1.push(44);
    s1.push(55);
    s1.push(66);
    cout << "3: " << s1.pop() << endl;   //66
    cout << "4: " << s1.pop() << endl;   //55
    cout << "5: " << s1.pop() << endl;   //44
    cout << "6: " << s1.pop() << endl;   //33
    return 0;
    }
```

The important member of the stack is the array st. An int variable, top, indicates the index of the last item placed on the stack; the location of this item is the *top* of the stack.

The size of the array used for the stack is specified by MAX, in the statement

```
enum { MAX = 10 };
```

This definition of MAX is unusual. In keeping with the philosophy of encapsulation, it's preferable to define constants that will be used entirely within a class, as MAX is here, within the class. Thus the use of global const variables for this purpose is nonoptimal. Standard C++ mandates that we should be able to declare MAX within the class as

```
static const int MAX = 10;
```

This means that MAX is constant and applies to all objects in the class. Unfortunately, some compilers, including the current version of Microsoft Visual C++, do not allow this newly-approved construction.

As a workaround we can define such constants to be enumerators (described in Chapter 4). We don't need to name the enumeration, and we need only the one enumerator:

```
enum { MAX = 10 };
```

This defines MAX as an integer with the value 10, and the definition is contained entirely within the class. This approach works, but it's awkward. If your compiler supports the static const approach, you should use it instead to define constants within the class.

Figure 7.6 shows a stack. Since memory grows downward in the figure, the top of the stack is at the bottom in the figure. When an item is added to the stack, the index in top is incremented to point to the new top of the stack. When an item is removed, the index in top is decremented. (We don't need to erase the old value left in memory when an item is removed; it just becomes irrelevant.)

To place an item on the stack—a process called *pushing* the item—you call the push() member function with the value to be stored as an argument. To retrieve (or *pop*) an item from the stack, you use the pop() member function, which returns the value of the item.

The main() program in STAKARAY exercises the stack class by creating an object, s1, of the class. It pushes two items onto the stack, and pops them off and displays them. Then it pushes four more items onto the stack, and pops them off and displays them. Here's the output:

```
1: 22
2: 11
3: 66
4: 55
5: 44
6: 33
```

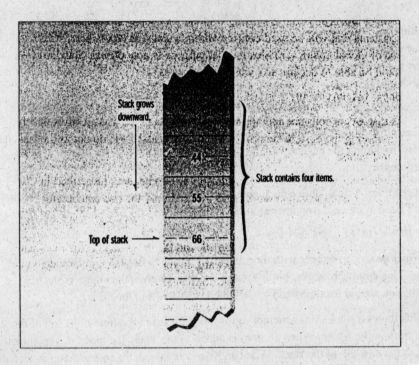

FIGURE 7.6
A stack.

As you can see, items are popped off the stack in reverse order; the last thing pushed is the first thing popped.

Notice the subtle use of prefix and postfix notation in the increment and decrement operators. The statement

```
st[++top] = var;
```

in the push() member function first increments top so that it points to the next available array element—one past the last element. It then assigns var to this element, which becomes the new top of the stack. The statement

```
return st[top--];
```

first returns the value it finds at the top of the stack, then decrements top so that it points to the preceding element.

The stack class is an example of an important feature of object-oriented programming: using a class to implement a *container* or data-storage mechanism. In Chapter 15 we'll see that a stack is only one of a number of ways to store data. There are also queues, sets, linked lists, and so on. A data-storage scheme is chosen that matches the specific requirements of the program. Using a preexisting class to provide data storage means that the programmer does not need to waste time duplicating the details of the data-storage mechanism.

Arrays of Objects

We've seen how an object can contain an array. We can also reverse that situation and create an array of objects. We'll look at two situations: an array of English distances and a deck of cards.

Arrays of English Distances

In Chapter 6, "Objects and Classes," we showed several examples of an English Distance class that incorporated feet and inches into an object representing a new data type. The next program, ENGLARAY, demonstrates an array of such objects.

```
// englaray.cpp
// objects using English measurements
#include <iostream>
using namespace std;
/////////////////////////////////////////////////////////////////
class Distance                      //English Distance class
   {
   private:
      int feet;
      float inches;
   public:
      void getdist()                //get length from user
         {
         cout << "\n   Enter feet: ";  cin >> feet;
         cout << "   Enter inches: ";  cin >> inches;
         }
      void showdist() const         //display distance
         { cout << feet << "\'-" << inches << '\"'; }
   };
/////////////////////////////////////////////////////////////////
int main()
   {
   Distance dist[100];              //array of distances
   int n=0;                         //count the entries
   char ans;                        //user response ('y' or 'n')
```

```
    cout << endl;

    do {                              //get distances from user
        cout << "Enter distance number " << n+1;
        dist[n++].getdist();          //store distance in array
        cout << "Enter another (y/n)?: ";
        cin >> ans;
        } while( ans != 'n' );         //quit if user types 'n'

    for(int j=0; j<n; j++)            //display all distances
        {
        cout << "\nDistance number " << j+1 << " is ";
        dist[j].showdist();
        }
    cout << endl;
    return 0;
    }
```

In this program the user types in as many distances as desired. After each distance is entered, the program asks if the user desires to enter another. If not, it terminates, and displays all the distances entered so far. Here's a sample interaction when the user enters three distances:

```
Enter distance number 1
    Enter feet: 5
    Enter inches: 4
Enter another (y/n)? y
Enter distance number
    Enter feet: 6
    Enter inches: 2.5
Enter another (y/n)? y
Enter distance number 3
    Enter feet: 5
    Enter inches: 10.75
Enter another (y/n)? n

Distance number 1 is 5'-4"
Distance number 2 is 6'-2.5"
Distance number 3 is 5'-10.75"
```

Of course, instead of simply displaying the distances already entered, the program could have averaged them, written them to disk, or operated on them in other ways.

Array Bounds

This program uses a do loop to get input from the user. This way the user can input data for as many structures of type part as seems desirable, up to MAX, the size of the array (which is set to 100).

Although it's hard to imagine anyone having the patience, what would happen if the user entered more than 100 distances? The answer is, something unpredictable but almost certainly bad. There is no bounds-checking in C++ arrays. If the program inserts something beyond the end of the array, neither the compiler nor the runtime system will object. However, the renegade data will probably be written on top of other data or the program code itself. This may cause bizarre effects or crash the system completely.

The moral is that it is up to the programmer to deal with the array bounds-checking. If it seems possible that the user will insert too much data for an array to hold, the array should be made larger or some means of warning the user should be devised. For example, you could insert the following code at the beginning of the do loop in ENGLARAY:

```
if( n >= MAX )
    {
    cout << "\nThe array is full!!!";
    break;
    }
```

This causes a break out of the loop and prevents the array from overflowing.

Accessing Objects in an Array

The declaration of the Distance class in this program is similar to that used in previous programs. However, in the main() program we define an array of such objects:

```
Distance dist[MAX];
```

Here the data type of the dist array is Distance, and it has MAX elements. Figure 7.7 shows what this looks like.

A class member function that is an array element is accessed similarly to a structure member that is an array element, as in the PARTARAY example. Here's how the showdist() member function of the jth element of the array dist is invoked:

```
dist[j].showdist();
```

As you can see, a member function of an object that is an array element is accessed using the dot operator: The array name followed by the index in brackets is joined, using the dot operator, to the member function name followed by parentheses. This is similar to accessing a structure (or class) data member, except that the function name and parentheses are used instead of the data name.

Notice that when we call the getdist() member function to put a distance into the array, we take the opportunity to increment the array index n:

```
dist[n++].getdist();
```

7

ARRAYS AND
STRINGS

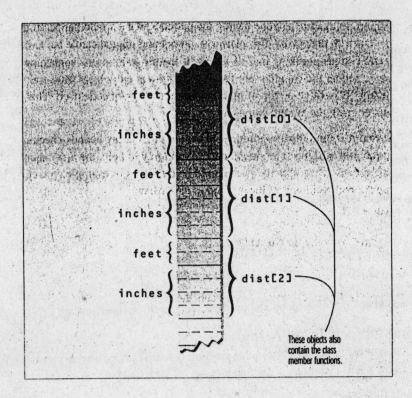

feet
inches

dist[0]

feet

dist[1]

inches

feet

dist[2]

inches

These objects also
contain the class
member functions.

FIGURE 7.7
Array of objects.

This way the next group of data obtained from the user will be placed in the structure in the next array element in dist. The n variable must be incremented manually like this because we use a do loop instead of a for loop. In the for loop, the loop variable—which is incremented automatically—can serve as the array index.

Arrays of Cards

Here's another, somewhat longer, example of an array of objects. You will no doubt remember the CARDOBJ example from Chapter 6. We'll borrow the card class from that example, and group an array of 52 such objects together in an array, thus creating a deck of cards. Here's the listing for CARDARAY:

```
// cardaray.cpp
// cards as objects
#include <iostream>
```

```cpp
#include <cstdlib>              //for srand(), rand()
#include <ctime>               //for time for srand()
using namespace std;


enum Suit { clubs, diamonds, hearts, spades };
//from 2 to 10 are integers without names
const int jack = 11;
const int queen = 12;
const int king = 13;
const int ace = 14;
////////////////////////////////////////////////////////////////
class card
   {
   private:
      int number;           //2 to 10, jack, queen, king, ace
      Suit suit;            //clubs, diamonds, hearts, spades
   public:
      card()                        //constructor
         { }
      void set(int n, Suit s)      //set card
         { suit = s; number = n; }
      void display();              //display card
   };
//-------------------------------------------------------------
void card::display()               //display the card
   {
   if( number >= 2 && number <= 10 )
      cout << number;
   else
      switch(number)
         {
         case jack:  cout << "J"; break;
         case queen: cout << "Q"; break;
         case king:  cout << "K"; break;
         case ace:   cout << "A"; break;
         }
   switch(suit)
      {
      case clubs:    cout << static_cast<char>(5); break;
      case diamonds: cout << static_cast<char>(4); break;
      case hearts:   cout << static_cast<char>(3); break;
      case spades:   cout << static_cast<char>(6); break;
      }
   }
////////////////////////////////////////////////////////////////
```

```
int main()
   {
   card deck[52];
   int j;

   cout << endl;
   for(j=0; j<52; j++)            //make an ordered deck
      {
      int num = (j % 13) + 2;    //cycles through 2 to 14, 4 times
      Suit su = Suit(j / 13);    //cycles through 0 to 3, 13 times
      deck[j].set(num, su);      //set card
      }
   cout << "\nOrdered deck:\n";
   for(j=0; j<52; j++)            //display ordered deck
      {
      deck[j].display();
      cout << "   ";
      if( !( (j+1) % 13) )       //newline every 13 cards
         cout << endl;
      }
   srand( time(NULL) );           //seed random numbers with time
   for(j=0; j<52; j++)            //for each card in the deck,
      {
      int k = rand() % 52;       //pick another card at random
      card temp = deck[j];       //and swap them
      deck[j] = deck[k];
      deck[k] = temp;
      }
   cout << "\nShuffled deck:\n";
   for(j=0; j<52; j++)            //display shuffled deck
      {
      deck[j].display();
      cout << ", ";
      if( !( (j+1) % 13) )       //newline every 13 cards
         cout << endl;
      }
   return 0;
   }  //end main
```

Once we've created a deck, it's hard to resist the temptation to shuffle it. We display the cards in the deck, shuffle it, and then display it again. To conserve space we use graphics characters for the club, diamond, heart, and spade. Figure 7.8 shows the output from the program. This program incorporates several new ideas, so let's look at them in turn.

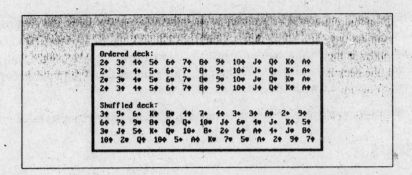

```
Ordered deck:
2♦  3♦  4♦  5♦  6♦  7♦  8♦  9♦  10♦  J♦  Q♦  K♦  A♦
2♣  3♣  4♣  5♣  6♣  7♣  8♣  9♣  10♣  J♣  Q♣  K♣  A♣
2♥  3♥  4♥  5♥  6♥  7♥  8♥  9♥  10♥  J♥  Q♥  K♥  A♥
2♠  3♠  4♠  5♠  6♠  7♠  8♠  9♠  10♠  J♠  Q♠  K♠  A♠

Shuffled deck:
3♠  9♦  6♦  K♥  8♦  4♥  7♠  4♣  3♦  3♠  A♥  2♦  9♣
6♦  7♠  9♥  8♠  Q♠  Q♣  10♣  J♠  6♥  4♥  J♦  K♦  5♦
3♥  J♦  5♦  K♠  Q♥  10♠  8♦  2♠  6♦  A♠  4♦  J♥  8♦
10♦  2♦  Q♣  10♦  5♦  A♥  K♥  7♦  5♥  A♠  2♦  9♣  7♥
```

FIGURE 7.8
Output of the CARDARAY *program.*

Graphics Characters

There are several special graphics characters in the range below ASCII code 32. (See Appendix A, "ASCII Table," for a list of ASCII codes.) In the display() member function of card we use codes 5, 4, 3, and 6 to access the characters for a club, a diamond, a heart, and a spade, respectively. Casting these numbers to type char, as in

```
static_cast<char>(5)
```

causes the << operator to print them as characters rather than as numbers.

The Card Deck

The array of structures that constitutes the deck of cards is defined in the statement

```
card deck[52];
```

which creates an array called deck, consisting of 52 objects of type card. To display the jth card in the deck, we call the display() member function:

```
deck[j].display();
```

Random Numbers

It's always fun and sometimes even useful to generate random numbers. In this program we use them to shuffle the deck. Two steps are necessary to obtain random numbers. First the random-number generator must be *seeded*, or initialized. To do this we call the srand() library function. This function uses the system time as the seed, so it requires two header files, CSTDLIB and CTIME.

To actually generate a random number we call the rand() library function. This function returns a random integer. To get a number in the range from 0 to 51, we apply the remainder operator and 52 to the result of rand().

```
int k = rand() % 52;
```

The resulting random number k is then used as an index to swap two cards. We go through the `for` loop, swapping one card, whose index points to each card in 0-to-51 order, with another card, whose index is the random number. When all 52 cards have been exchanged with a random card, the deck is considered to be shuffled. This program could form the basis for a card-playing program, but we'll leave these details for you.

Arrays of objects are widely used in C++ programming. We'll see other examples as we go along.

C-Strings

We noted at the beginning of this chapter that two kinds of strings are commonly used in C++: C-strings and strings that are objects of the `string` class. In this section we'll describe the first kind, which fits the theme of the chapter in that C-strings are arrays of type `char`. We call these strings *C-strings*, or *C-style strings*, because they were the only kind of strings available in the C language (and in the early days of C++, for that matter). They may also be called `char*` strings, because they can be represented as pointers to type char. (The * indicates a pointer, as we'll learn in Chapter 10.)

Although strings created with the `string` class, which we'll examine in the next section, have superseded C-strings in many situations, C-strings are still important for a variety of reasons. First, they are used in many C library functions. Second, they will continue to appear in legacy code for years to come. And third, for students of C++, C-strings are more primitive and therefore easier to understand on a fundamental level.

C-String Variables

As with other data types, strings can be variables or constants. We'll look at these two entities before going on to examine more complex string operations. Here's an example that defines a single string variable. (In this section we'll assume the word *string* refers to a C-string.) It asks the user to enter a string, and places this string in the string variable. Then it displays the string. Here's the listing for STRINGIN:

```
// stringin.cpp
// simple string variable
#include <iostream>
using namespace std;

int main()
   {
   const int MAX = 80;         //max characters in string
   char str[MAX];              //string variable str
```

```
cout << "Enter a string: ";
cin >> str;                          //put string in str
                                     //display string from str
cout << "You entered: " << str << endl;
return 0;
}
```

The definition of the string variable str looks like (and is) the definition of an array of type char:

```
char str[MAX];
```

We use the extraction operator >> to read a string from the keyboard and place it in the string variable str. This operator knows how to deal with strings; it understands that they are arrays of characters. If the user enters the string "Amanuensis" (one employed to copy manuscripts) in this program, the array str will look something like Figure 7.9.

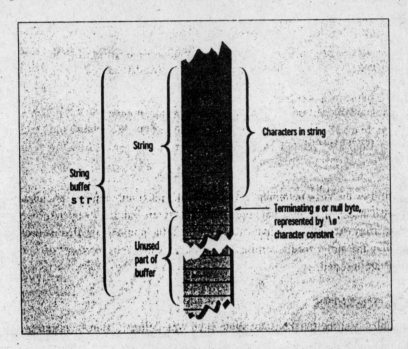

FIGURE 7.9
String stored in string variable.

Each character occupies 1 byte of memory. An important aspect of C-strings is that they must terminate with a byte containing 0. This is often represented by the character constant ' \0', which is a character with an ASCII value of 0. This terminating zero is called the *null character*. When the << operator displays the string, it displays characters until it encounters the null character.

Avoiding Buffer Overflow

The STRINGIN program invites the user to type in a string. What happens if the user enters a string that is longer than the array used to hold it? As we mentioned earlier, there is no built-in mechanism in C++ to keep a program from inserting array elements outside an array. So an overly enthusiastic typist could end up crashing the system.

However, it is possible to tell the >> operator to limit the number of characters it places in an array. The SAFETYIN program demonstrates this approach.

```cpp
// safetyin.cpp
// avoids buffer overflow with cin.width
#include <iostream>
#include <iomanip>                      //for setw
using namespace std;

int main()
   {
   const int MAX = 20;                  //max characters in string
   char str[MAX];                       //string variable str

   cout << "\nEnter a string: ";
   cin >> setw(MAX) >> str;             //put string in str,
                                        // no more than MAX chars
   cout << "You entered: " << str << endl;
   return 0;
   }
```

This program uses the setw manipulator to specify the maximum number of characters the input buffer can accept. The user may type more characters, but the >> operator won't insert them into the array. Actually, one character fewer than the number specified is inserted, so there is room in the buffer for the terminating null character. Thus, in SAFETYIN, a maximum of 19 characters are inserted.

String Constants

You can initialize a string to a constant value when you define it. Here's an example, STRINIT, that does just that (with the first line of a Shakespearean sonnet):

```cpp
// strinit.cpp
// initialized string
#include <iostream>
using namespace std;

int main()
   {
   char str[] = "Farewell! thou art too dear for my possessing.";
```

```
   cout << str << endl;
   return 0;
   }
```

Here the string constant is written as a normal English phrase, delimited by quotes. This may seem surprising, since a string is an array of type char. In past examples you've seen arrays initialized to a series of values delimited by braces and separated by commas. Why isn't str initialized the same way? In fact you could use such a sequence of character constants:

```
char str[] = { 'F', 'a', 'r', 'e', 'w', 'e', 'l', 'l', 'l',' ', 't', 'h',
```

and so on. Fortunately, the designers of C++ (and C) took pity on us and provided the shortcut approach shown in STRINIT. The effect is the same: The characters are placed one after the other in the array. As with all C-strings, the last character is a null (zero).

Reading Embedded Blanks

If you tried the STRINGIN program with strings that contained more than one word, you may have had an unpleasant surprise. Here's an example:

```
Enter a string: Law is a bottomless pit.
You entered: Law
```

Where did the rest of the phrase (a quotation from the Scottish writer John Arbuthnot, 1667–1735) go? It turns out that the extraction operator >> considers a space to be a terminating character. Thus it will read strings consisting of a single word, but anything typed after a space is thrown away.

To read text containing blanks we use another function, cin.get(). This syntax means a member function get() of the stream class of which cin is an object. The following example, BLANKSIN, shows how it's used.

```
// blanksin.cpp
// reads string with embedded blanks
#include <iostream>
using namespace std;

int main()
   {
   const int MAX = 80;              //max characters in string
   char str[MAX];                   //string variable str

   cout << "\nEnter a string: ";
   cin.get(str, MAX);               //put string in str
   cout << "You entered: " << str << endl;
   return 0;
   }
```

The first argument to cin::get() is the array address where the string being input will be placed. The second argument specifies the maximum size of the array, thus automatically avoiding buffer overrun.

Using this function the input string is now stored in its entirety.

```
Enter a string: Law is a bottomless pit.
You entered: Law is a bottomless pit.
```

There's a potential problem when you mix cin.get() with cin and the extraction operator (>>). We'll discuss the use of the ignore() member function of cin to solve this problem in Chapter 12, "Streams and Files."

Reading Multiple Lines

We may have solved the problem of reading strings with embedded blanks, but what about strings with multiple lines? It turns out that the cin::get() function can take a third argument to help out in this situation. This argument specifies the character that tells the function to stop reading. The default value for this argument is the newline ('\n') character, but if you call the function with some other character for this argument, the default will be overridden by the specified character.

In the next example, LINESIN, we call the function with a dollar sign ('$') as the third argument:

```cpp
// linesin.cpp
// reads multiple lines, terminates on '$' character
#include <iostream>
using namespace std;

const int MAX = 2000;                //max characters in string
char str[MAX];                       //string variable str

int main()
   {
   cout << "\nEnter a string:\n";
   cin.get(str, MAX, '$');           //terminate with $
   cout << "You entered:\n" << str << endl;
   return 0;
   }
```

Now you can type as many lines of input as you want. The function will continue to accept characters until you enter the terminating character (or until you exceed the size of the array). Remember, you must still press Enter after typing the '$' character. Here's a sample interaction with a poem from Thomas Carew (1595–1639):

```
Enter a string:
Ask me no more where Jove bestows
When June is past, the fading rose;
For in your beauty's orient deep
These flowers, as in their causes, sleep.
$
You entered:
Ask me no more where Jove bestows
When June is past, the fading rose;
For in your beauty's orient deep
These flowers, as in their causes, sleep.
```

We terminate each line with Enter, but the program continues to accept input until we enter '$'.

Copying a String the Hard Way

The best way to understand the true nature of strings is to deal with them character by character. The following program does this.

```
// strcopy1.cpp
// copies a string using a for loop
#include <iostream>
#include <cstring>                      //for strlen()
using namespace std;

int main()
    {                                   //initialized string
    char str1[] = "Oh, Captain, my Captain! "
        "our fearful trip is done.";

    const int MAX = 80;                 //size of str2 buffer
    char str2[MAX];                     //empty string

    for(int j=0; j<strlen(str1); j++)   //copy strlen characters
        str2[j] = str1[j];              //    from str1 to str2
    str2[j] = '\0';                     //insert NULL at end
    cout << str2 << endl;               //display str2
    return 0;
    }
```

This program creates a string constant, str1, and a string variable, str2. It then uses a for loop to copy the string constant to the string variable. The copying is done one character at a time, in the statement

```
str2[j] = str1[j];
```

Recall that the compiler concatenates two adjacent string constants into a single one, which allows us to write the quotation on two lines.

This program also introduces C-string library functions. Because there are no string operators built into C++, C-strings must usually be manipulated using library functions. Fortunately there are many such functions. The one we use in this program, `strlen()`, finds the length of a C-string (that is, how many characters are in it). We use this length as the limit in the `for` loop so that the right number of characters will be copied. When string functions are used, the header file CSTRING (or STRING.H) must be included (with #include) in the program.

The copied version of the string must be terminated with a null. However, the string length returned by `strlen()` does not include the null. We could copy one additional character, but it's safer to insert the null explicitly. We do this with the line

```
str2[j] = '\0';
```

If you don't insert this character, you'll find that the string printed by the program includes all sorts of weird characters following the string you want. The << just keeps on printing characters, whatever they are, until by chance it encounters a '\0'.

Copying a String the Easy Way

Of course, you don't need to use a `for` loop to copy a string. As you might have guessed, a library function will do it for you. Here's a revised version of the program, STRCOPY2, that uses the `strcpy()` function.

```cpp
// strcopy2.cpp
// copies a string using strcpy() function
#include <iostream>
#include <cstring>                        //for strcpy()
using namespace std;

int main()
  {
  char str1[] = "Tiger, tiger, burning bright\n"
                "In the forests of the night";
  const int MAX = 80;             //size of str2 buffer
  char str2[MAX];                 //empty string

  strcpy(str2, str1);             //copy str1 to str2
  cout << str2 << endl;           //display str2
  return 0;
  }
```

Note that you call this function with the destination first:

```
strcpy(destination, source)
```

The right-to-left order is reminiscent of the format of normal assignment statements: The variable on the right is copied to the variable on the left.

Arrays of Strings

If there are arrays of arrays, of course there can be arrays of strings. This is actually quite a useful construction. Here's an example, STRARAY, that puts the names of the days of the week in an array:

```
// straray.cpp
// array of strings
#include <iostream>
using namespace std;

int main()
   {
   const int DAYS = 7;              //number of strings in array
   const int MAX = 10;              //maximum size of each string
                                    //array of strings
   char star[DAYS][MAX] = { "Sunday", "Monday", "Tuesday",
                            "Wednesday", "Thursday",
                            "Friday", "Saturday" };
   for(int j=0; j<DAYS; j++)        //display every string
      cout << star[j] << endl;
   return 0;
   }
```

The program prints out each string from the array:

```
Sunday
Monday
Tuesday
Wednesday
Thursday
Friday
Saturday
```

Since a string is an array, it must be true that star—an array of strings—is really a two-dimensional array. The first dimension of this array, DAYS, tells how many strings are in the array. The second dimension, MAX, specifies the maximum length of the strings (9 characters for "Wednesday" plus the terminating null makes 10). Figure 7.10 shows how this looks.

Notice that some bytes are wasted following strings that are less than the maximum length. We'll learn how to remove this inefficiency when we talk about pointers.

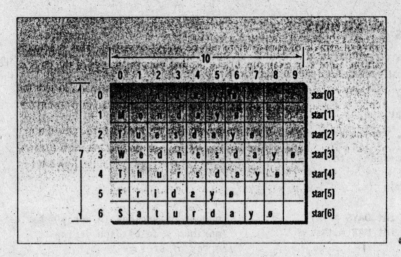

FIGURE 7.10
Array of strings.

The syntax for accessing a particular string may look surprising:

```
star[j];
```

If we're dealing with a two-dimensional array, where's the second index? Since a two-dimensional array is an array of arrays, we can access elements of the "outer" array, each of which is an array (in this case a string), individually. To do this we don't need the second index. So star[j] is string number j in the array of strings.

Strings as Class Members

Strings frequently appear as members of classes. The next example, a variation of the OBJPART program in Chapter 6, uses a C-string to hold the name of the widget part.

```cpp
// strpart.cpp
// string used in widget part object
#include <iostream>
#include <cstring>              //for strcpy()
using namespace std;
//////////////////////////////////////////////////////////////////
class part
   {
   private:
      char partname[30];   //name of widget part
      int partnumber;      //ID number of widget part
      double cost;         //cost of part
```

```
   public:
      void setpart(char pname[], int pn, double c)
         {
         strcpy(partname, pname);
         partnumber = pn;
         cost = c;
         }
      void showpart()       //display data
         {
         cout << "\nName="   << partname;
         cout << ", number=" << partnumber;
         cout << ", cost=$"  << cost;
         }
   };
//////////////////////////////////////////////////////////////////
int main()
   {
   part part1, part2;

   part1.setpart("handle bolt", 4473, 217.55);    //set parts
   part2.setpart("start lever", 9924, 419.25);
   cout << "\nFirst part: ";  part1.showpart();    //show parts
   cout << "\nSecond part: "; part2.showpart();
   cout << endl;
   return 0;
   }
```

This program defines two objects of class part and gives them values with the setpart()
member function. Then it displays them with the showpart() member function. Here's the
output:

```
First part:
Name=handle bolt, number=4473, cost=$217.55
Second part:
Name=start lever, number=9924, cost=$419.25
```

To reduce the size of the program we've dropped the model number from the class members.

In the setpart() member function, we use the strcpy() string library function to copy the
string from the argument pname to the class data member partname. Thus this function serves
the same purpose with string variables that an assignment statement does with simple variables. (A similar function, strncpy(), takes a third argument, which is the maximum number
of characters it will copy. This can help prevent overrunning the array.)

Besides those we've seen, there are library functions to add a string to another, compare
strings, search for specific characters in strings, and perform many other actions. Descriptions
of these functions can be found in your compiler's documentation.

A User-Defined String Type

There are some problems with C-strings as they are normally used in C++. For one thing, you can't use the perfectly reasonable expression

```
strDest = strSrc;
```

to set one string equal to another. (In some languages, like BASIC, this is perfectly all right.) The Standard C++ string class we'll examine in the next section will take care of this problem, but for the moment let's see if we can use object-oriented technology to solve the problem ourselves. Creating our own string class will give us an insight into representing strings as objects of a class, which will illuminate the operation of the Standard C++ string class.

If we define our own string type, using a C++ class, we can use assignment statements. (Many other C-string operations, such as concatenation, ca be simplified this way as well, but we'll have to wait until Chapter 8, "Operator Overloading," to see how this is done.)

The STROBJ program creates a class called String. (Don't confuse this homemade class String with the Standard C++ built-in class string, which has a lowercase 's'.) Here's the listing:

```cpp
// strobj.cpp
// a string as a class
#include <iostream>
#include <cstring>          // for strcpy(), strcat()
using namespace std;
////////////////////////////////////////////////////////////////////
class String
    {
    private:
        enum { SZ = 80; };                  //max size of Strings
        char str[SZ];                       //array
    public:
        String()                            //constructor, no args
            { str[0] = '\0'; }
        String( char s[] )                  //constructor, one arg
            { strcpy(str, s); }
        void display()                      //display string
            { cout << str; }
        void concat(String s2)              //add arg string to
            {                               //this string
            if( strlen(str)+strlen(s2.str) < SZ )
                strcat(str, s2.str);
            else
                cout << "\nString too long";
            }
    };
```

```
/////////////////////////////////////////////////////////////////
int main()
   {
   String s1("Merry Christmas!  ");     //uses constructor 2
   String s2 = "Season's Greetings!";   //alternate form of 2
   String s3;                           //uses constructor 1

   cout << "\ns1="; s1.display();       //display them all
   cout << "\ns2="; s2.display();
   cout << "\ns3="; s3.display();

   s3 = s1;                             //assignment
   cout << "\ns3="; s3.display();       //display s3

   s3.concat(s2);                       //concatenation
   cout << "\ns3="; s3.display();       //display s3
   cout << endl;
   return 0;
   }
```

The String class contains an array of type char. It may seem that our newly defined class is just the same as the original definition of a string: an array of type char. But, by wrapping the array in a class, we have achieved some interesting benefits. Since an object can be assigned the value of another object of the same class using the = operator, we can use statements like

```
s3 = s1;
```

as we do in main(), to set one String object equal to another. We can also define our own member functions to deal with Strings (objects of class String).

In the STROBJ program, all Strings have the same length: SZ characters (which we set to 80). There are two constructors. The first sets the first character in str to the null character, '\0', so the string has a length of 0. This constructor is called with statements like

```
String s3;
```

The second constructor sets the String object to a "normal" (that is, a C-string) string constant. It uses the strcpy() library function to copy the string constant into the object's data. It's called with statements like

```
String s1("Merry Christmas! ");
```

The alternative format for calling this constructor, which works with any one-argument constructor, is

```
String s1 = "Merry Christmas! ";
```

Whichever format is used, this constructor effectively converts a C-string to a String—that is, a normal string constant to an object of class String. A member function, display(), displays the String.

Another member function of our String class, concat(), *concatenates* (adds) one String to another. The original String is the object of which concat() is a member. To this String will be added the String passed as an argument. Thus the statement in main()

```
s3.concat(s2);
```

causes s2 to be added to the existing s3. Since s2 has been initialized to "Season's Greetings!" and s3 has been assigned the value of s1, which was "Merry Christmas!" the resulting value of s3 is "Merry Christmas! Season's Greetings!"

The concat() function uses the strcat() C library function to do the concatenation. This library function adds the string specified in the second argument to the string specified in the first argument. The output from the program is

```
s1=Merry Christmas!
s2=Season's Greetings!
s3=          ←——— nothing here yet
s3=Merry Christmas!     ←——— set equal to s1
s3=Merry Christmas! Season's Greetings!      ←——— s2 concatenated
```

If the two Strings given to the concat() function together exceed the maximum String length, then the concatenation is not carried out, and a message is sent to the user.

We've just examined a simple string class. Now we'll see a far more sophisticated version of the same approach.

The Standard C++ string Class

Standard C++ includes a new class called string. This class improves on the traditional C-string in many ways. For one thing, you no longer need to worry about creating an array of the right size to hold string variables. The string class assumes all the responsibility for memory management. Also, the string class allows the use of overloaded operators, so you can concatenate string objects with the + operator:

```
s3 = s1 + s2
```

There are other benefits as well. This new class is more efficient and safer to use than C-strings were. In most situations it is the preferred approach. (However, as we noted earlier, there are still many situations in which C-strings must be used.) In this section we'll examine the string class and its various member functions and operators.

Defining and Assigning string Objects

You can define a string object in several ways. You can use a constructor with no arguments, creating an empty string. You can also use a one-argument constructor, where the argument is a

C-string constant; that is, characters delimited by double quotes. As in our homemade `String` class, objects of class `string` can be assigned to one another with a simple assignment operator. The SSTRASS example shows how this looks.

```
//sstrass.cpp
//defining and assigning string objects
#include <iostream>
#include <string>
using namespace std;

int main()
    {
    string s1("Man");                    //initialize
    string s2 = "Beast";                 //initialize
    string s3;

    s3 = s1;                             //assign
    cout << "s3 = " << s3 << endl;

    s3 = "Neither " + s1 + " nor ";  //concatenate
    s3 += s2;                            //concatenate
    cout << "s3 = " << s3 << endl;

    s1.swap(s2);                         //swap s1 and s2
    cout << s1 << " nor " << s2 << endl;
    return 0;
    }
```

Here, the first three lines of code show three ways to define `string` objects. The first two initialize `string`s, and the second creates an empty `string` variable. The next line shows simple assignment with the = operator.

The `string` class uses a number of overloaded operators. We won't learn about the inner workings of operator overloading until the next chapter, but you can use these operators without knowing how they're constructed.

The overloaded + operator concatenates one string object with another. The statement

```
s3 = "Neither " + s1 + " nor ";
```

places the string `"Neither Man nor "` in the variable s3.

You can also use the += operator to append a string to the end of an existing string. The statement

```
s3 += s2;
```

appends s2, which is `"Beast"`, to the end of s3, producing the string `"Neither Man nor Beast"` and assigning it to s3.

This example also introduces our first string class member function: swap(), which exchanges the values of two string objects. It's called for one object with the other as an argument. We apply it to s1 ("Man") and s2 ("Beast"), and then display their values to show that s1 is now "Beast" and s2 is now "Man".

Here's the output of SSTRASS:

```
s3 = Man
s3 = Neither Man nor Beast
Beast nor Man
```

Input/Output with string Objects

Input and output are handled in a similar way to that of C-strings. The << and >> operators are overloaded to handle string objects, and a function getline() handles input that contains embedded blanks or multiple lines. The SSTRIO example shows how this looks.

```cpp
// sstrio.cpp
// string class input/output
#include <iostream>
#include <string>                    //for string class
using namespace std;

int main()
    {                                //objects of string class
    string full_name, nickname, address;
    string greeting("Hello, ");

    cout << "Enter your full name: ";
    getline(cin, full_name);         //reads embedded blanks
    cout << "Your full name is: " << full_name << endl;

    cout << "Enter your nickname: ";
    cin >> nickname;                 //input to string object

    greeting += nickname;            //append name to greeting
    cout << greeting << endl;        //output: "Hello, Jim"

    cout << "Enter your address on separate lines\n";
    cout << "Terminate with '$'\n";
    getline(cin, address, '$');      //reads multiple lines
    cout << "Your address is: " << address << endl;
    return 0;
    }
```

The program reads the user's name, which presumably contains embedded blanks, using `getline()`. This function is similar to the `get()` function used with C-strings, but is not a member function. Instead, its first argument is the stream object from which the input will come (here it's `cin`), and the second is the `string` object where the text will be placed, `full_name`. This variable is then displayed using the `cout` and `<<`.

The program then reads the user's nickname, which is assumed to be one word, using `cin` and the `>>` operator. Finally the program uses a variation of `getline()`, with three arguments, to read the user's address, which may require multiple lines. The third argument specifies the character to be used to terminate the input. In the program we use the `'$'` character, which the user must input as the last character before pressing the Enter key. If no third argument is supplied to `getline()`, the delimiter is assumed to be `'\n'`, which represents the Enter key. Here's some interaction with SSTRIO:

```
Enter your full name: F. Scott Fitzgerald
Your full name is: F. Scott Fitzgerald
Enter your nickname: Scotty
Hello, Scotty
Enter your address on separate lines:
Terminate with '$'
1922 Zelda Lane
East Egg, New York$
Your address is:
1922 Zelda Lane
East Egg, New York
```

Finding `string` Objects

The `string` class includes a variety of member functions for finding strings and substrings in `string` objects. The SSTRFIND example shows some of them.

```cpp
//sstrfind.cpp
//finding substrings in string objects
#include <iostream>
#include <string>
using namespace std;

int main()
   {
   string s1 =
      "In Xanadu did Kubla Kahn a stately pleasure dome decree";
   int n;

   n = s1.find("Kubla");
   cout << "Found Kubla at " << n << endl;
```

```
n = s1.find_first_of("spde");
cout << "First of spde at " << n << endl;

n = s1.find_first_not_of("aeiouAEIOU");
cout << "First consonant at " << n << endl;
return 0;
}
```

The find() function looks for the string used as its argument in the string for which it was called. Here it finds "Kubla" in s1, which holds the first line of the poem *Kubla Kahn* by Samuel Taylor Coleridge. It finds it at position 14. As with C-strings, the leftmost character position is numbered 0.

The find_first_of() function looks for any of a group of characters, and returns the position of the first one it finds. Here it looks for any of the group 's', 'p', 'd', or 'e'. The first of these it finds is the 'd' in Xanadu, at position 7.

A similar function find_first_not_of() finds the first character in its string that is *not* one of a specified group. Here the group consists of all the vowels, both upper- and lowercase, so the function finds the first consonant, which is the second letter. The output of SSTRFIND is

```
Found Kubla at 14
First of spde at 7
First consonent at 1
```

There are variations on many of these functions that we don't demonstrate here, such as rfind(), which scans its string backward; find_last_of(), which finds the last character matching one of a group of characters, and find_last_not_of(). All these functions return −1 if the target is not found.

Modifying string Objects

There are various ways to modify string objects. Our next example shows the member functions erase(), replace(), and insert() at work.

```
//sstrchng.cpp
//changing parts of string objects
#include <iostream>
#include <string>
using namespace std;

int main()
   {
   string s1("Quick! Send for Count Graystone.");
   string s2("Lord");
   string s3("Don't ");
```

```
      s1.erase(0, 7);              //remove "Quick! "
      s1.replace(9, 5, s2);        //replace "Count" with "Lord"
      s1.replace(0, 1, "s");       //replace 'S' with 's'
      s1.insert(0, s3);            //insert "Don't " at beginning
      s1.erase(s1.size()-1, 1);    //remove '.'
      s1.append(3, '!');           //append "!!!"

      int x = s1.find(' ');        //find a space
      while( x < s1.size() )       //loop while spaces remain
         {
         s1.replace(x, 1, "/");    //replace with slash
         x = s1.find(' ');         //find next space
         }
      cout << "s1: " << s1 << endl;
      return 0;
      }
```

The erase() function removes a substring from a string. Its first argument is the position of the first character in the substring, and the second is the length of the substring. In the example it removes "Quick " from the beginning of the string. The replace() function replaces part of the string with another string. The first argument is the position where the replacement should begin, the second is the number of characters in the original string to be replaced, and the third is the replacement string. Here "Count" is replaced by "Lord".

The insert() function inserts the string specified by its second argument at the location specified by its first argument. Here it inserts "Don't " at the beginning of s1. The second use of erase() employs the size() member function, which returns the number of characters in the string object. The expression size()-1 is the position of the last character, the period, which is erased. The append() function installs three exclamation points at the end of the sentence. In this version of the function the first argument is the number of characters to append, and the second is the character to be appended.

At the end of the program we show an idiom you can use to replace multiple instances of a substring with another string. Here, in a while loop, we look for the space character ' ' using find(), and replace each one with a slash using replace().

We start with s1 containing the string "Quick! Send for Count Graystone." After these changes, the output of SSTRCHNG is

```
s1: Don't/send/for/Lord/Graystone!!!
```

Comparing string Objects

You can use overloaded operators or the compare() function to compare string objects. These discover whether strings are the same, or whether they precede or follow one another alphabetically. The SSTRCOM program shows some of the possibilities.

```cpp
//sstrcom.cpp
//comparing string objects
#include <iostream>
#include <string>
using namespace std;

int main()
   {
   string aName = "George";
   string userName;

   cout << "Enter your first name: ";
   cin >> userName;
   if(userName==aName)                       //operator ==
      cout << "Greetings, George\n";
   else if(userName < aName)                 //operator <
      cout << "You come before George\n";
   else
      cout << "You come after George\n";
                                             //compare() function
   int n = userName.compare(0, 2, aName, 0, 2);
   cout << "The first two letters of your name ";
   if(n==0)
      cout << "match ";
   else if(n < 0)
      cout << "come before ";
   else
      cout << "come after ";
   cout << aName.substr(0, 2) << endl;
   return 0;
   }
```

In the first part of the program the == and < operators are used to determine whether a name typed by the user is equal to, or precedes or follows alphabetically, the name George. In the second part of the program the compare() function compares only the first two letters of "George" with the first two letters of the name typed by the user (userName). The arguments to this version of compare() are the starting position in userName and the number of characters to compare, the string used for comparison (aName), and the starting position and number of characters in aName. Here's some interaction with SSTRCOM:

```
Enter your first name: Alfred
You come before George
The first two letters of your name come before Ge
```

The first two letters of "George" are obtained using the substr() member function. It returns a substring of the string for which it was called. Its first argument is the position of the substring, and the second is the number of characters.

Accessing Characters in string Objects

You can access individual characters within a string object in several ways. In our next example we'll show access using the at() member function. You can also use the overloaded [] operator, which makes the string object look like an array. However, the [] operator doesn't warn you if you attempt to access a character that's out of bounds (beyond the end of the string, for example). The [] operator behaves this way with real arrays, and it's more efficient. However, it can lead to hard-to-diagnose program bugs. It's safer to use the at() function, which causes the program to stop if you use an out-of-bounds index. (It actually throws an exception; we'll discuss exceptions in Chapter 14, "Templates and Exceptions.")

```
//sstrchar.cpp
//accessing characters in string objects
#include <iostream>
#include <string>
using namespace std;

int main()
   {
   char charray[80];
   string word;

   cout << "Enter a word: ";
   cin >> word;
   int wlen = word.length();       //length of string object

   cout << "One character at a time: ";
   for(int j=0; j<wlen; j++)
      cout << word.at(j);          //exception if out-of-bounds
//    cout << word[j];             //no warning if out-of-bounds

   word.copy(charray, wlen, 0);    //copy string object to array
   charray[wlen] = 0;              //terminate with '\0'
   cout << "\nArray contains: " << charray << endl;
   return 0;
   }
```

In this program we use at() to display all the characters in a string object, character by character. The argument to at() is the location of the character in the string.

We then show how you can use the copy() member function to copy a string object into a array of type char, effectively transforming it into a C-string. Following the copy, a null character ('\0') must be inserted after the last character in the array to complete the transformation to a

C-string. The `length()` member function of `string` returns the same number as `size()`.
Here's the output of sstrchar:

```
Enter a word: symbiosis
One character at a time: symbiosis
Array contains: symbiosis
```

(You can also convert `string` objects to C-strings using the `c_str()` or `data()` member
functions. However, to use these functions you need to know about pointers, which we'll
examine in Chapter 10.)

Other `string` Functions

We've seen that `size()` and `length()` both return the number of characters currently in a
`string` object. The amount of memory occupied by a string is usually somewhat larger than
that actually needed for the characters. (Although if it hasn't been initialized it uses 0 bytes for
characters.) The `capacity()` member function returns the actual memory occupied. You can
add characters to the string without causing it to expand its memory until this limit is reached.
The `max_size()` member function returns the maximum possible size of a string object.
This amount corresponds to the size of `int` variables on your system, less 3 bytes. In 32-bit
Windows systems this is 4,294,967,293 bytes, but the size of your memory will probably
restrict this amount.

Most of the `string` member functions we've discussed have numerous variations in the numbers
and types of arguments they take. Consult your compiler's documentation for details.

You should be aware that `string` objects are not terminated with a null or zero as C-strings
are. Instead, the length of the string is a member of the class. So if you're stepping along the
string, don't rely on finding a null to tell you when you've reached the end.

The `string` class is actually only one of many possible string-like classes, all derived from the
template class `basic_string`. The `string` class is based on type `char`, but a common variant is
to use type `wchar_t` instead. This allows `basic_string` to be used for foreign languages with
many more characters than English. Your compiler's help file may list the `string` member
functions under `basic_string`.

Summary

Arrays contain a number of data items of the same type. This type can be a simple data type, a
structure, or a class. The items in an array are called *elements*. Elements are accessed by number;
this number is called an *index*. Elements can be initialized to specific values when the array
is defined. Arrays can have multiple dimensions. A two-dimensional array is an array of arrays.
The address of an array can be used as an argument to a function; the array itself is not copied.

Arrays can be used as member data in classes. Care must be taken to prevent data from being placed in memory outside an array.

C-strings are arrays of type char. The last character in a C-string must be the null character, '\0'. C-string constants take a special form so that they can be written conveniently: the text is surrounded by double quotes. A variety of library functions are used to manipulate C-strings. An array of C-strings is an array of arrays of type char. The creator of a C-string variable must ensure that the array is large enough to hold any text placed in it. C-strings are used as arguments to C-style library functions and will be found in older programs. They are not normally recommended for general use in new programs.

The preferred approach to strings is to use objects of the string class. These strings can be manipulated with numerous overloaded operators and member functions. The user need not worry about memory management with string objects.

Questions

Answers to these questions can be found in Appendix G.

1. An array element is accessed using

   a. a first-in-first-out approach.

   b. the dot operator.

   c. a member name.

   d. an index number.

2. All the elements in an array must be the _____ data type.

3. Write a statement that defines a one-dimensional array called doubleArray of type double that holds 100 elements.

4. The elements of a 10-element array are numbered from _____ to _____.

5. Write a statement that takes element j of array doubleArray and writes it to cout with the insertion operator.

6. Element doubleArray[7] is which element of the array?

   a. The sixth

   b. The seventh

   c. The eighth

   d. Impossible to tell

7

7. Write a statement that defines an array coins of type int and initializes it to the values of the penny, nickel, dime, quarter, half-dollar, and dollar.

8. When a multidimensional array is accessed, each array index is

   a. separated by commas.

   b. surrounded by brackets and separated by commas.

   c. separated by commas and surrounded by brackets.

   d. surrounded by brackets.

9. Write an expression that accesses element 4 in subarray 2 in a two-dimensional array called twoD.

10. True or false: In C++ there can be an array of four dimensions.

11. For a two-dimensional array of type float, called flarr, write a statement that declares the array and initializes the first subarray to 52, 27, 83; the second to 94, 73, 49; and the third to 3, 6, 1.

12. An array name, used in the source file, represents the _____ of the array.

13. When an array name is passed to a function, the function

   a. accesses exactly the same array as the calling program.

   b. accesses a copy of the array passed by the program.

   c. refers to the array using the same name as that used by the calling program.

   d. refers to the array using a different name than that used by the calling program.

14. Tell what this statement defines:

```
employee emplist[1000];
```

15. Write an expression that accesses a structure member called salary in a structure variable that is the 17th element in an array called emplist.

16. In a stack, the data item placed on the stack first is

   a. not given an index number.

   b. given the index number 0.

   c. the first data item to be removed.

   d. the last data item to be removed.

17. Write a statement that defines an array called manybirds that holds 50 objects of type bird.

18. True or false: The compiler will complain if you try to access array element 14 in a 10-element array.

19. Write a statement that executes the member function cheep() in an object of class bird that is the 27th element in the array manybirds.

20. A string in C++ is an _____ of type _____.

21. Write a statement that defines a string variable called city that can hold a string of up to 20 characters (this is slightly tricky).

22. Write a statement that defines a string constant, called dextrose, that has the value "C6H12O6-H2O".

23. True or false: The extraction operator (>>) stops reading a string when it encounters a space.

24. You can read input that consists of multiple lines of text using

a. the normal cout << combination.

b. the cin.get() function with one argument.

c. the cin.get() function with two arguments.

d. the cin.get() function with three arguments.

25. Write a statement that uses a string library function to copy the string name to the string blank.

26. Write the declaration for a class called dog that contains two data members: a string called breed and an int called age. (Don't include any member functions.)

27. True or false: You should prefer C-strings to the Standard C++ string class in new programs.

28. Objects of the string class

a. are zero-terminated.

b. can be copied with the assignment operator.

c. do not require memory management.

d. have no member functions.

29. Write a statement that finds where the string "cat" occurs in the string s1.

30. Write a statement that inserts the string "cat" into string s1 at position 12.

Exercises

Answers to the starred exercises can be found in Appendix G.

*1. Write a function called reversit() that reverses a C-string (an array of char). Use a for loop that swaps the first and last characters, then the second and next-to-last characters, and so on. The string should be passed to reversit() as an argument.

Write a program to exercise reversit(). The program should get a string from the user, call reversit(), and print out the result. Use an input method that allows embedded blanks. Test the program with Napoleon's famous phrase, "Able was I ere I saw Elba."

*2. Create a class called `employee` that contains a name (an object of class `string`) and an employee number (type `long`). Include a member function called `getdata()` to get data from the user for insertion into the object, and another function called `putdata()` to display the data. Assume the name has no embedded blanks.

Write a `main()` program to exercise this class. It should create an array of type `employee`, and then invite the user to input data for up to 100 employees. Finally, it should print out the data for all the employees.

*3. Write a program that calculates the average of up to 100 English distances input by the user. Create an array of objects of the `Distance` class, as in the ENGLARAY example in this chapter. To calculate the average, you can borrow the `add_dist()` member function from the ENGLCON example in Chapter 6. You'll also need a member function that divides a `Distance` value by an integer. Here's one possibility:

```
void Distance::div_dist(Distance d2, int divisor)
   {
   float fltfeet = d2.feet + d2.inches/12.0;
   fltfeet /= divisor;
   feet = int(fltfeet);
   inches = (fltfeet-feet) * 12.0;
   }
```

4. Start with a program that allows the user to input a number of integers, and then stores them in an `int` array. Write a function called `maxint()` that goes through the array, element by element, looking for the largest one. The function should take as arguments the address of the array and the number of elements in it, and return the index number of the largest element. The program should call this function and then display the largest element and its index number. (See the SALES program in this chapter.)

5. Start with the `fraction` class from Exercises 11 and 12 in Chapter 6. Write a `main()` program that obtains an arbitrary number of fractions from the user, stores them in an array of type `fraction`, averages them, and displays the result.

6. In the game of contract bridge, each of four players is dealt 13 cards, thus exhausting the entire deck. Modify the CARDARAY program in this chapter so that, after shuffling the deck, it deals four hands of 13 cards each. Each of the four players' hands should then be displayed.

7. One of the weaknesses of C++ for writing business programs is that it does not contain a built-in type for monetary values such as $173,698,001.32. Such a money type should be able to store a number with a fixed decimal point and about 17 digits of precision, which is enough to handle the national debt in dollars and cents. Fortunately, the built-in C++ type `long double` has 19 digits of precision, so we can use it as the basis of a money class, even though it uses a floating decimal. However, we'll need to add the capability to input and output money amounts preceded by a dollar sign and divided by commas into

groups of three digits; this makes it much easier to read large numbers. As a first step toward developing such a class, write a function called mstold() that takes a *money string*, a string representing a money amount like

"$1,234,567,890,123.99"

as an argument, and returns the equivalent long double.

You'll need to treat the money string as an array of characters, and go through it character by character, copying only digits (1–9) and the decimal point into another string. Ignore everything else, including the dollar sign and the commas. You can then use the _atold() library function (note the initial underscore—header file STDLIB.H or MATH.H) to convert the resulting pure string to a long double. Assume that money values will never be negative. Write a main() program to test mstold() by repeatedly obtaining a money string from the user and displaying the corresponding long double.

8. Another weakness of C++ is that it does not automatically check array indexes to see whether they are in bounds. (This makes array operations faster but less safe.) We can use a class to create a safe array that checks the index of all array accesses.

Write a class called safearay that uses an int array of fixed size (call it LIMIT) as its only data member. There will be two member functions. The first, putel(), takes an index number and an int value as arguments and inserts the int value into the array at the index. The second, getel(), takes an index number as an argument and returns the int value of the element with that index.

```
safearay sa1;          // define a safearay object
int temp = 12345;      // define an int value
sa1.putel(7, temp);    // insert value of temp into array at index 7
temp = sa1.getel(7);   // obtain value from array at index 7
```

Both functions should check the index argument to make sure it is not less than 0 or greater than LIMIT-1. You can use this array without fear of writing over other parts of memory.

Using functions to access array elements doesn't look as eloquent as using the [ ] operator. In Chapter 8 we'll see how to overload this operator to make our safearay class work more like built-in arrays.

9. A queue is a data storage device much like a stack. The difference is that in a stack the last data item stored is the first one retrieved, while in a queue the first data item stored is the first one retrieved. That is, a stack uses a last-in-first-out (LIFO) approach, while a queue uses first-in-first-out (FIFO). A queue is like a line of customers in a bank: The first one to join the queue is the first one served.

Rewrite the STAKARAY program from this chapter to incorporate a class called queue instead of a class called stack. Besides a constructor, it should have two functions: one called put() to put a data item on the queue, and one called get() to get data from the queue. These are equivalent to push() and pop() in the stack class.

Both a queue and a stack use an array to hold the data. However, instead of a single `int` variable called `top`, as the stack has, you'll need two variables for a queue: one called head to point to the head of the queue, and one called `tail` to point to the tail. Items are placed on the queue at the tail (like the last customer getting in line at the bank) and removed from the queue at the head. The tail will follow the head along the array as items are added and removed from the queue. This results in an added complexity: When either the tail or the head gets to the end of the array, it must wrap around to the beginning. Thus you'll need a statement like

```
if(tail == MAX-1)
    tail = -1;
```

to wrap the tail, and a similar one for the head. The array used in the queue is sometimes called a circular buffer, because the head and tail circle around it, with the data between them.

10. A matrix is a two-dimensional array. Create a class `matrix` that provides the same safety feature as the array class in Exercise 7; that is, it checks to be sure no array index is out of bounds. Make the member data in the `matrix` class a 10-by-10 array. A constructor should allow the programmer to specify the actual dimensions of the matrix (provided they're less than 10 by 10). The member functions that access data in the matrix will now need two index numbers: one for each dimension of the array. Here's what a fragment of a `main()` program that operates on such a class might look like:

```
matrix m1(3, 4);          // define a matrix object
int temp = 12345;         // define an int value
m1.putel(7, 4, temp);     // insert value of temp into matrix at 7,4
temp = m1.getel(7, 4);    // obtain value from matrix at 7,4
```

11. Refer back to the discussion of money strings in Exercise 6. Write a function called `ldtoms()` to convert a number represented as type `long double` to the same value represented as a money string. First you should check that the value of the original long double is not too large. We suggest that you don't try to convert any number greater than 9,999,999,999,999,990.00. Then convert the `long double` to a pure string (no dollar sign or commas) stored in memory, using an `ostrstream` object, as discussed earlier in this chapter. The resulting formatted string can go in a buffer called `ustring`.

You'll then need to start another string with a dollar sign; copy one digit from `ustring` at a time, starting from the left, and inserting a comma into the new string every three digits. Also, you'll need to suppress leading zeros. You want to display $3,124.95, for example, not $0,000,000,000,003,124.95. Don't forget to terminate the string with a `'\0'` character.

Write a `main()` program to exercise this function by having the user repeatedly input numbers in type `long double` format, and printing out the result as a money string.

12. Create a class called bMoney. It should store money amounts as long doubles. Use the function mstold() to convert a money string entered as input into a long double, and the function ldtoms() to convert the long double to a money string for display. (See Exercises 6 and 10.) You can call the input and output member functions getmoney() and putmoney(). Write another member function that adds two bMoney amounts; you can call it madd(). Adding bMoney objects is easy: Just add the long double member data amounts in two bMoney objects. Write a main() program that repeatedly asks the user to enter two money strings, and then displays the sum as a money string. Here's how the class specifier might look:

```
class bMoney
    {
    private:
        long double money;
    public:
        bMoney();
        bMoney(char s[]);
        void madd(bMoney m1, bMoney m2);
        void getmoney();
        void putmoney();
    };
```

Operator Overloading

IN THIS CHAPTER

Operator overloading is one of the most exciting features of object-oriented programming. It can transform complex, obscure program listings into intuitively obvious ones. For example, statements like

```
d3.addobjects(d1, d2);
```

or the similar but equally obscure

```
d3 = d1.addobjects(d2);
```

can be changed to the much more readable

```
d3 = d1 + d2;
```

The rather forbidding term *operator overloading* refers to giving the normal C++ operators, such as +, *, <=, and +=, additional meanings when they are applied to user-defined data types. Normally

```
a = b + c;
```

works only with basic types such as int and float, and attempting to apply it when a, b, and c are objects of a user-defined class will cause complaints from the compiler. However, using overloading, you can make this statement legal even when a, b, and c are user-defined types.

In effect, operator overloading gives you the opportunity to redefine the C++ language. If you find yourself limited by the way the C++ operators work, you can change them to do whatever you want. By using classes to create new kinds of variables, and operator overloading to create new definitions for operators, you can extend C++ to be, in many ways, a new language of your own design.

Another kind of operation, *data type conversion*, is closely connected with operator overloading. C++ handles the conversion of simple types, such as int and float, automatically; but conversions involving user-defined types require some work on the programmer's part. We'll look at data conversions in the second part of this chapter.

Overloaded operators are not all beer and skittles. We'll discuss some of the dangers of their use at the end of the chapter.

Overloading Unary Operators

Let's start off by overloading a *unary operator*. As you may recall from Chapter 2, unary operators act on only one operand. (An operand is simply a variable acted on by an operator.) Examples of unary operators are the increment and decrement operators ++ and --, and the unary minus, as in -33.

In the COUNTER example in Chapter 6, "Objects and Classes," we created a class Counter to keep track of a count. Objects of that class were incremented by calling a member function:

```
c1.inc_count();
```

That did the job, but the listing would have been more readable if we could have used the increment operator ++ instead:

```
++c1;
```

All dyed-in-the-wool C++ (and C) programmers would guess immediately that this expression increments c1.

Let's rewrite COUNTER to make this possible. Here's the listing for COUNTPP1:

```
// countpp1.cpp
// increment counter variable with ++ operator
#include <iostream>
using namespace std;
/////////////////////////////////////////////////////////////////
class Counter
   {
   private:
      unsigned int count;                     //count
   public:
      Counter() : count(0)                    //constructor
         { }
      unsigned int get_count()                //return count
         { return count; }
      void operator ++ ()                     //increment (prefix)
         {
         ++count;
         }
   };
/////////////////////////////////////////////////////////////////
int main()
   {
   Counter c1, c2;                            //define and initialize

   cout << "\nc1=" << c1.get_count();  //display
   cout << "\nc2=" << c2.get_count();

   ++c1;                      //increment c1
   ++c2;                      //increment c2
   ++c2;                      //increment c2
```

```
    cout << "\nc1=" << c1.get_count();  //display again
    cout << "\nc2=" << c2.get_count() << endl;
    return 0;
    }
```

In this program we create two objects of class Counter: c1 and c2. The counts in the objects are displayed; they are initially 0. Then, using the overloaded ++ operator, we increment c1 once and c2 twice, and display the resulting values. Here's the program's output:

```
c1=0    ←——— counts are initially 0
c2=0
c1=1    ←——— incremented once
c2=2    ←——— incremented twice
```

The statements responsible for these operations are

```
++c1;
++c2;
++c2;
```

The ++ operator is applied once to c1 and twice to c2. We use prefix notation in this example; we'll explore postfix later.

The operator Keyword

How do we teach a normal C++ operator to act on a user-defined operand? The keyword operator is used to overload the ++ operator in this declarator:

```
void operator ++ ()
```

The return type (void in this case) comes first, followed by the keyword operator, followed by the operator itself (++), and finally the argument list enclosed in parentheses (which are empty here). This declarator syntax tells the compiler to call this member function whenever the ++ operator is encountered, provided the operand (the variable operated on by the ++) is of type Counter.

We saw in Chapter 5, "Functions," that the only way the compiler can distinguish between overloaded functions is by looking at the data types and the number of their arguments. In the same way, the only way it can distinguish between overloaded operators is by looking at the data type of their operands. If the operand is a basic type such as an int, as in

```
++intvar;
```

then the compiler will use its built-in routine to increment an int. But if the operand is a Counter variable, the compiler will know to use our user-written operator++() instead.

Operator Arguments

In main() the ++ operator is applied to a specific object, as in the expression ++c1. Yet operator++() takes no arguments. What does this operator increment? It increments the count data in the object of which it is a member. Since member functions can always access the particular object for which they've been invoked, this operator requires no arguments. This is shown in Figure 8.1.

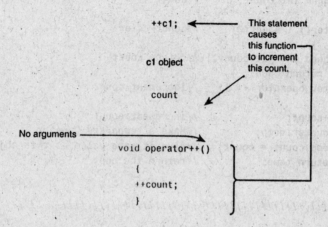

FIGURE 8.1
Overloaded unary operator: no arguments.

Operator Return Values

The operator++() function in the COUNTPP1 program has a subtle defect. You will discover it if you use a statement like this in main():

```
c1 = ++c2;
```

The compiler will complain. Why? Because we have defined the ++ operator to have a return type of void in the operator++() function, while in the assignment statement it is being asked to return a variable of type Counter. That is, the compiler is being asked to return whatever value c2 has after being operated on by the ++ operator, and assign this value to c1. So as defined in COUNTPP1, we can't use ++ to increment Counter objects in assignments; it must always stand alone with its operand. Of course the normal ++ operator, applied to basic data types such as int, would not have this problem.

To make it possible to use our homemade operator++() in assignment expressions, we must provide a way for it to return a value. The next program, COUNTPP2, does just that.

```
// countpp2.cpp
// increment counter variable with ++ operator, return value
#include <iostream>
using namespace std;
//////////////////////////////////////////////////////////////////
class Counter
    {
    private:
       unsigned int count;          //count
    public:
       Counter() : count(0)         //constructor
          { }
       unsigned int get_count()     //return count
          { return count; }
       Counter operator ++ ()       //increment count
          {
          ++count;                  //increment count
          Counter temp;             //make a temporary Counter
          temp.count = count;       //give it same value as this obj
          return temp;              //return the copy
          }
    };
//////////////////////////////////////////////////////////////////
int main()
    {
    Counter c1, c2;                          //c1=0, c2=0

    cout << "\nc1=" << c1.get_count();       //display
    cout << "\nc2=" << c2.get_count();

    ++c1;                                    //c1=1
    c2 = ++c1;                               //c1=2, c2=2

    cout << "\nc1=" << c1.get_count();       //display again
    cout << "\nc2=" << c2.get_count() << endl;
    return 0;
    }
```

Here the operator++() function creates a new object of type Counter, called temp, to use as a
return value. It increments the count data in its own object as before, then creates the new
temp object and assigns count in the new object the same value as in its own object. Finally, it
returns the temp object. This has the desired effect. Expressions like

++c1

now return a value, so they can be used in other expressions, such as

```
c2 = ++c1;
```

as shown in main(), where the value returned from c1++ is assigned to c2. The output from
this program is

```
c1=0
c2=0
c1=2
c2=2
```

Nameless Temporary Objects

In COUNTPP2 we created a temporary object of type Counter, named temp, whose sole purpose
was to provide a return value for the ++ operator. This required three statements.

```
Counter temp;            // make a temporary Counter object
temp.count = count;      // give it same value as this object
return temp;             // return it
```

There are more convenient ways to return temporary objects from functions and overloaded
operators. Let's examine another approach, as shown in the program COUNTPP3:

```
// countpp3.cpp
// increment counter variable with ++ operator
// uses unnamed temporary object
#include <iostream>
using namespace std;
//////////////////////////////////////////////////////////////
class Counter
   {
   private:
     unsigned int count;         //count
   public:
     Counter() : count(0)        //constructor  no args
        { }
     Counter(int c) : count(c)   //constructor, one arg
        { }
     unsigned int get_count()    //return count
        { return count; }
     Counter operator ++ ()      //increment count
        {
        ++count;                 // increment count, then return
        return Counter(count);   // an unnamed temporary object
        }                        // initialized to this count
   };
//////////////////////////////////////////////////////////////
```

```
int main()
   {
   Counter c1, c2;                           //c1=0, c2=0

   cout << "\nc1=" << c1.net_count();    //display
   cout << "\nc2=" << c2.get_count();

   ++c1;                                     //c1=1
   c2 = ++c1;                                //c1=2, c2=2

   cout << "\nc1=" << c1.get_count();    //display again
   cout << "\nc2=" << c2.get_count() << endl;
   return 0;
   }
```

In this program a single statement

```
return Counter(count);
```

does what all three statements did in COUNTPP2. This statement creates an object of type Counter. This object has no name; it won't be around long enough to need one. This unnamed object is initialized to the value provided by the argument count.

But wait: Doesn't this require a constructor that takes one argument? It does, and to make this statement work we sneakily inserted just such a constructor into the member function list in COUNTPP3.

```
Counter(int c) : count(c)     //constructor, one arg
   { }
```

Once the unnamed object is initialized to the value of count, it can then be returned. The output of this program is the same as that of COUNTPP2.

The approaches in both COUNTPP2 and COUNTPP3 involve making a copy of the original object (the object of which the function is a member), and returning the copy. (Another approach, as we'll see in Chapter 11, "Virtual Functions," is to return the value of the original object using the this pointer.)

Postfix Notation

So far we've shown the increment operator used only in its prefix form.

```
++c1
```

What about postfix, where the variable is incremented after its value is used in the expression?

```
c1++
```

To make both versions of the increment operator work, we define two overloaded ++ operators, as shown in the POSTFIX program:

```
// postfix.cpp
// overloaded ++ operator in both prefix and postfix
#include <iostream>
using namespace std;
//////////////////////////////////////////////////////////////
class Counter
   {
   private:
      unsigned int count;            //count
   public:
      Counter() : count(0)           //constructor  no args
         { }
      Counter(int c) : count(c)      //constructor, one arg
         { }
      unsigned int get_count() const //return count
         { return count; }

      Counter operator ++ ()         //increment count (prefix)
         {                           //increment count, then return
         return Counter(++count);    //an unnamed temporary object
         }                           //initialized to this count

      Counter operator ++ (int)      //increment count (postfix)
         {                           //return an unnamed temporary
         return Counter(count++);    //object initialized to this
         }                           //count, then increment count
   };
//////////////////////////////////////////////////////////////
int main()
   {
   Counter c1, c2;                              //c1=0, c2=0

   cout << "\nc1=" << c1.get_count();           //display
   cout << "\nc2=" << c2.get_count();

   ++c1;                                        //c1=1
   c2 = ++c1;                                   //c1=2, c2=2 (prefix)

   cout << "\nc1=" << c1.get_count();           //display
   cout << "\nc2=" << c2.get_count();

   c2 = c1++;                                   //c1=3, c2=2 (postfix)
```

```
cout << "\nc1=" << c1.get_count();     //display again
cout << "\nc2=" << c2.get_count() << endl;
return 0;
}
```

Now there are two different declarators for overloading the ++ operator. The one we've seen before, for prefix notation, is

```
Counter operator ++ ()
```

The new one, for postfix notation, is

```
Counter operator ++ (int)
```

The only difference is the int in the parentheses. This int isn't really an argument, and it doesn't mean integer. It's simply a signal to the compiler to create the postfix version of the operator. The designers of C++ are fond of recycling existing operators and keywords to play multiple roles, and int is the one they chose to indicate postfix. (Well, can you think of a better syntax?) Here's the output from the program:

```
c1=0
c2=0
c1=2
c2=2
c1=3
c2=2
```

We saw the first four of these output lines in COUNTPP2 and COUNTPP3. But in the last two lines we see the results of the statement

```
c2=c1++;
```

Here, c1 is incremented to 3, but c2 is assigned the value of c1 before it is incremented, so c2 retains the value 2.

Of course, you can use this same approach with the decrement operator (--).

Overloading Binary Operators

Binary operators can be overloaded just as easily as unary operators. We'll look at examples that overload arithmetic operators, comparison operators, and arithmetic assignment operators.

Arithmetic Operators

In the ENGLCON program in Chapter 6 we showed how two English Distance objects could be added using a member function add_dist():

```
    dist3.add_dist(dist1, dist2);
```

By overloading the + operator we can reduce this dense-looking expression to

```
    dist3 = dist1 + dist2;
```

Here's the listing for ENGLPLUS, which does just that:

```
// englplus.cpp
// overloaded '+' operator adds two Distances
#include <iostream>
using namespace std;
/////////////////////////////////////////////////////////////////
class Distance                       //English Distance class
   {
   private:
      int feet;
      float inches;
   public:                           //constructor (no args)
      Distance() : feet(0), inches(0.0)
         { }                         //constructor (two args)
      Distance(int ft, float in) : feet(ft), inches(in)
         { }
      void getdist()                 //get length from user
         {
         cout << "\nEnter feet: ";  cin >> feet;
         cout << "Enter inches: ";  cin >> inches;
         }
      void showdist() const         //display distance
         { cout << feet << "\'-" << inches << '\"'; }

      Distance operator + ( Distance ) const;  //add 2 distances
   };
//--------------------------------------------------------------
                                     //add this distance to d2
Distance Distance::operator + (Distance d2) const  //return sum
   {
   int f = feet + d2.feet;           //add the feet
   float i = inches + d2.inches;     //add the inches
   if(i >= 12.0)                     //if total exceeds 12.0,
      {                              //then decrease inches
      i -= 12.0;                     //by 12.0 and
      f++;                           //increase feet by 1
      }                              //return a temporary Distance
   return Distance(f,i);             //initialized to sum
   }
/////////////////////////////////////////////////////////////////
```

```
int main()
   {
   Distance dist1, dist3, dist4;    //define distances
   dist1.getdist();                 //get dist1 from user

   Distance dist2(11, 6.25);        //define, initialize dist2

   dist3 = dist1 + dist2;           //single '+' operator

   dist4 = dist1 + dist2 + dist3;   //multiple '+' operators
                                    //display all lengths
   cout << "dist1 = ";  dist1.showdist(); cout << endl;
   cout << "dist2 = ";  dist2.showdist(); cout << endl;
   cout << "dist3 = ";  dist3.showdist(); cout << endl;
   cout << "dist4 = ";  dist4.showdist(); cout << endl;
   return 0;
   }
```

To show that the result of an addition can be used in another addition as well as in an assignment, another addition is performed in main(). We add dist1, dist2, and dist3 to obtain dist4 (which should be double the value of dist3), in the statement

```
dist4 = dist1 + dist2 + dist3;
```

Here's the output from the program:

```
Enter feet: 10
Enter inches: 6.5

dist1 = 10'-6.5"       ←——— from user
dist2 = 11'-6.25"      ←——— initialized in program
dist3 = 22'-0.75"      ←——— dist1+dist2.
dist4 = 44'-1.5"       ←——— dist1+dist2+dist3
```

In class Distance the declaration for the operator+() function looks like this:

```
Distance operator + ( Distance );
```

This function has a return type of Distance, and takes one argument of type Distance.

In expressions like

```
dist3 = dist1 + dist2;
```

it's important to understand how the return value and arguments of the operator relate to the objects. When the compiler sees this expression it looks at the argument types, and finding only type Distance, it realizes it must use the Distance member function operator+(). But what does this function use as its argument—dist1 or dist2? And doesn't it need two arguments, since there are two numbers to be added?

Here's the key: The argument on the *left side* of the operator (dist1 in this case) is the object of which the operator is a member. The object on the *right side* of the operator (dist2) must be furnished as an argument to the operator. The operator returns a value, which can be assigned or used in other ways; in this case it is assigned to dist3. Figure 8.2 shows how this looks.

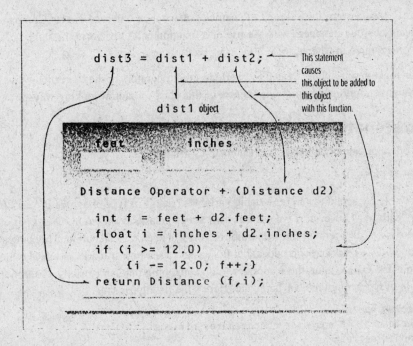

```
dist3 = dist1 + dist2;        This statement
                              causes
                              this object to be added to
                              this object
            dist1 object      with this function.


     feet         inches



    Distance Operator + (Distance d2)

        int f = feet + d2.feet;
        float i = inches + d2.inches;
        if (i >= 12.0)
            {i -= 12.0;  f++;}
        return Distance (f,i);
```

FIGURE 8.2
Overloaded binary operator: one argument.

In the operator+() function, the left operand is accessed directly—since this is the object of which the operator is a member—using feet and inches. The right operand is accessed as the function's argument, as d2.feet and d2.inches.

We can generalize and say that an overloaded operator always requires one less argument than its number of operands, since one operand is the object of which the operator is a member. That's why unary operators require no arguments. (This rule does not apply to friend functions and operators, C++ features we'll discuss in Chapter 11.)

To calculate the return value of operator+() in ENGLPLUS, we first add the feet and inches from the two operands (adjusting for a carry if necessary). The resulting values, f and i, are then used to initialize a nameless Distance object, which is returned in the statement

```
return Distance(f, i);
```

This is similar to the arrangement used in COUNTPP3, except that the constructor takes two arguments instead of one. The statement

```
dist3 = dist1 + dist2;
```

in main() then assigns the value of the nameless Distance object to dist3. Compare this intuitively obvious statement with the use of a function call to perform the same task, as in the ENGLCON example in Chapter 6.

Similar functions could be created to overload other operators in the Distance class, so you could subtract, multiply, and divide objects of this class in natural-looking ways.

Concatenating Strings

The + operator cannot be used to concatenate C-strings. That is, you can't say

```
str3 = str1 + str2;
```

where str1, str2, and str3 are C-string variables (arrays of type char), as in "cat" plus "bird" equals "catbird." However, if we use our own String class, as shown in the STROBJ program in Chapter 6, we can overload the + operator to perform such concatenation. This is what the Standard C++ string class does, but it's easier to see how it works in our less ambitious String class. Overloading the + operator to do something that isn't strictly addition is another example of redefining the C++ language. Here's the listing for STRPLUS:

```
// strplus.cpp
// overloaded '+' operator concatenates strings
#include <iostream>
using namespace std;
#include <string.h>        //for strcpy(), strcat()
#include <stdlib.h>        //for exit()
////////////////////////////////////////////////////////////
class String                //user-defined string type
   {
   private:
      enum { SZ=80 };                  //size of String objects
      char str[SZ];                    //holds a string
   public:
      String()                         //constructor, no args
         { strcpy(str, ""); }
      String( char s[] )               //constructor, one arg
         { strcpy(str, s); }
      void display() const             //display the String
         { cout << str; }
      String operator + (String ss) const   //add Strings
```

```
      {
      String temp;                    //make a temporary String
      if( strlen(str) + strlen(ss.str) < SZ )
        {
        strcpy(temp.str, str);   //copy this string to temp
        strcat(temp.str, ss.str); //add the argument string
        }
      else
        { cout << "\nString overflow"; exit(1); }
      return temp;                    //return temp String
      }
  };
/////////////////////////////////////////////////////////////
int main()
  {
  String s1 = "\nMerry Christmas!  ";   //uses constructor 2
  String s2 = "Happy new year!";        //uses constructor 2
  String s3;                            //uses constructor 1

  s1.display();                         //display strings
  s2.display();
  s3.display();

  s3 = s1 + s2;                         //add s2 to s1,
                                        //assign to s3
  s3.display();                         //display s3
  cout << endl;
  return 0;
  }
```

The program first displays three strings separately. (The third is empty at this point, so nothing is printed when it displays itself.) Then the first two strings are concatenated and placed in the third, and the third string is displayed again. Here's the output:

```
Merry Christmas!  Happy new year!    ←──── s1, s2, and s3 (empty)
Merry Christmas!  Happy new year!    ←──── s3 after concatenation
```

By now the basics of overloading the + operator should be somewhat familiar. The declarator

```
String operator + (String ss)
```

shows that the + operator takes one argument of type String and returns an object of the same type. The concatenation process in operator+() involves creating a temporary object of type String, copying the string from our own String object into it, concatenating the argument string using the library function strcat(), and returning the resulting temporary string. Note that we can't use the

```
return String(string);
```

approach, where a nameless temporary String is created, because we need access to the temporary String not only to initialize it, but to concatenate the argument string to it.

We must be careful that we don't overflow the fixed-length strings used in the String class. To prevent such accidents in the operator+() function, we check that the combined length of the two strings to be concatenated will not exceed the maximum string length. If they do, we print an error message instead of carrying out the concatenation operation. (We could handle errors in other ways, like returning 0 if an error occurred, or better yet, throwing an exception, as discussed in Chapter 14, "Templates and Exceptions.")

Remember that using an enum to set the constant value SZ is a temporary fix. When all compilers comply with Standard C++ you can change it to

```
static const int SZ = 80;
```

Multiple Overloading

We've seen different uses of the + operator: to add English distances and to concatenate strings. You could put both these classes together in the same program, and C++ would still know how to interpret the + operator: It selects the correct function to carry out the "addition" based on the type of operand.

Comparison Operators

Let's see how to overload a different kind of C++ operator: comparison operators.

Comparing Distances

In our first example we'll overload the *less than* operator (<) in the Distance class so that we can compare two distances. Here's the listing for ENGLESS:

```
// engless.cpp
// overloaded '<' operator compares two Distances
#include <iostream>
using namespace std;
/////////////////////////////////////////////////////////////////
class Distance                      //English Distance class
    {
    private:
        int feet;
        float inches;
    public:                         //constructor (no args)
        Distance() : feet(0), inches(0.0)
            { }                     //constructor (two args)
```

```
        Distance(int ft, float in) : feet(ft), inches(in)
           { }
        void getdist()                //get length from user
           {
           cout << "\nEnter feet: ";  cin >> feet;
           cout << "Enter inches: ";  cin >> inches;
           }
        void showdist() const         //display distance
           { cout << feet << "\'-" << inches << '\"'; }
        bool operator < (Distance) const;  //compare distances
     };
//········································································
                               //compare this distance with d2
bool Distance::operator < (Distance d2) const  //return the sum
     {
     float bf1 = feet + inches/12;
     float bf2 = d2.feet + d2.inches/12;
     return (bf1 < bf2) ? true : false;
     }
//////////////////////////////////////////////////////////////////////
int main()
     {
     Distance dist1;                //define Distance dist1
     dist1.getdist();               //get dist1 from user

     Distance dist2(6, 2.5);  .     //define and initialize dist2
                                    //display distances
     cout << "\ndist1 = ";  dist1.showdist();
     cout << "\ndist2 = ";  dist2.showdist();

     if( dist1 < dist2 )            //overloaded '<' operator
        cout << "\ndist1 is less than dist2";
     else
        cout << "\ndist1 is greater than (or equal to) dist2";
     cout << endl;
     return 0;
     }
```

This program compares a distance entered by the user with a distance, 6'–2.5", initialized by the program. Depending on the result, it then prints one of two possible sentences. Here's some typical output:

```
Enter feet: 5
Enter inches: 11.5
dist1 = 5'-11.5"
dist2 = 6'-2.5"
dist1 is less than dist2
```

The approach used in the operator<() function in ENGLESS is similar to overloading the + operator in the ENGLPLUS program, except that here the operator<() function has a return type of bool. The return value is false or true, depending on the comparison of the two distances. The comparison is made by converting both distances to floating-point feet, and comparing them using the normal < operator. Remember that the use of the conditional operator

```
return (bf1 < bf2) ? true : false;
```

is the same as

```
if(bf1 < bf2)
   return true;
else
   return false;
```

Comparing Strings

Here's another example of overloading an operator, this time the *equal to* (==) operator. We'll use it to compare two of our homemade String objects, returning true if they're the same and false if they're different. Here's the listing for STREQUAL:

```
//strequal.cpp
//overloaded '==' operator compares strings
#include <iostream>
using namespace std;
#include <string.h>      //for strcmp()
/////////////////////////////////////////////////////////////////////
class String               //user-defined string type
   {
   private:
      enum { SZ = 80 };                //size of String objects
      char str[SZ];                    //holds a string
   public:
      String()                         //constructor, no args
         { strcpy(str, ""); }
      String( char s[] )               //constructor, one arg
         { strcpy(str, s); }
      void display() const             //display a String
         { cout << str; }
      void getstr()                    //read a string
         { cin.get(str, SZ); }
      bool operator == (String ss) const  //check for equality
         {
         return ( strcmp(str, ss.str)==0 ) ? true : false;
         }
   };
/////////////////////////////////////////////////////////////////////
```

```
int main()
   {
   String s1 = "yes";
   String s2 = "no";
   String s3;

   cout << "\nEnter 'yes' or 'no': ";
   s3.getstr();                        //get String from user

   if(s3==s1)                          //compare with "yes"
      cout << "You typed yes\n";
   else if(s3==s2)                     //compare with "no"
      cout << "You typed no\n";
   else
      cout << "You didn't follow instructions\n";
   return 0;
   }
```

The main() part of this program uses the == operator twice, once to see if a string input by the user is "yes" and once to see if it's "no." Here's the output when the user types "yes":

```
Enter 'yes' or 'no': yes
You typed yes
```

The operator==() function uses the library function strcmp() to compare the two C-strings. This function returns 0 if the strings are equal, a negative number if the first is less than the second, and a positive number if the first is greater than the second. Here *less than* and *greater than* are used in their lexicographical sense to indicate whether the first string appears before or after the second in an alphabetized listing.

Other comparison operators, such as < and >, could also be used to compare the lexicographical value of strings. Or, alternatively, these comparison operators could be redefined to compare string lengths. Since you're the one defining how the operators are used, you can use any definition that seems appropriate to your situation.

Arithmetic Assignment Operators

Let's finish up our exploration of overloaded binary operators with an arithmetic assignment operator: the += operator. Recall that this operator combines assignment and addition into one step. We'll use this operator to add one English distance to a second, leaving the result in the first. This is similar to the ENGLPLUS example shown earlier, but there is a subtle difference. Here's the listing for ENGLPLEQ:

```
// englpleq.cpp
// overloaded '+=' assignment operator
```

```cpp
#include <iostream>
using namespace std;
////////////////////////////////////////////////////////////////
class Distance                      //English Distance class
   {
   private:
      int feet;
      float inches;
   public:                          //constructor (no args)
      Distance() : feet(0), inches(0.0)
         { }                        //constructor (two args)
      Distance(int ft, float in) : feet(ft), inches(in)
         { }
      void getdist()                //get length from user
         {
         cout << "\nEnter feet: ";  cin >> feet;
         cout << "Enter inches: ";  cin >> inches;
         }
      void showdist() const         //display distance
         { cout << feet << "\'-" << inches << '\"'; }
      void operator += ( Distance );
   };
//--------------------------------------------------------------
                                    //add distance to this one
void Distance::operator += (Distance d2)
   {
   feet += d2.feet;                 //add the feet
   inches += d2.inches;             //add the inches
   if(inches >= 12.0)               //if total exceeds 12.0,
      {                             //then decrease inches
      inches -= 12.0;               //by 12.0 and
      feet++;                       //increase feet
      }                             //by 1
   }
////////////////////////////////////////////////////////////////
int main()
   {
   Distance dist1;                  //define dist1
   dist1.getdist();                 //get dist1 from user
   cout << "\ndist1 = ";  dist1.showdist();

   Distance dist2(11, 6.25);        //define, initialize dist2
   cout << "\ndist2 = ";  dist2.showdist();

   dist1 += dist2;                  //dist1 = dist1 + dist2
   cout << "\nAfter addition,";
```

```
cout << "\ndist1 = ";  dist1.showdist();
cout << endl;
return 0;
}
```

In this program we obtain a distance from the user and add to it a second distance, initialized to 11'–6.25" by the program. Here's a sample of interaction with the program:

```
Enter feet: 3
Enter inches: 5.75
dist1 = 3'-5.75"
dist2 = 11'-6.25"
After addition,
dist1 = 15'-0"
```

In this program the addition is carried out in main() with the statement

```
dist1 += dist2;
```

This causes the sum of dist1 and dist2 to be placed in dist1.

Notice the difference between the function used here, operator+=(), and that used in ENGLPLUS, operator+(). In the earlier operator+() function, a new object of type Distance had to be created and returned by the function so it could be assigned to a third Distance object, as in

```
dist3 = dist1 + dist2;
```

In the operator+=() function in ENGLPLEQ, the object that takes on the value of the sum is the object of which the function is a member. Thus it is feet and inches that are given values, not temporary variables used only to return an object. The operator+=() function has no return value; it returns type void. A return value is not necessary with arithmetic assignment operators such as +=, because the result of the assignment operator is not assigned to anything. The operator is used alone, in expressions like the one in the program.

```
dist1 += dist2;
```

If you wanted to use this operator in more complex expressions, like

```
dist3 = dist1 += dist2;
```

then you would need to provide a return value. You can do this by ending the operator+=() function with a statement like

```
return Distance(feet, inches);
```

in which a nameless object is initialized to the same values as this object and returned.

8
OPERATOR
OVERLOADING

The Subscript Operator ([ ])

The subscript operator, [ ], which is normally used to access array elements, can be overloaded. This is useful if you want to modify the way arrays work in C++. For example, you might want to make a "safe" array: One that automatically checks the index numbers you use to access the array, to ensure that they are not out of bounds. (You can also use the vector class, described in Chapter 15, "The Standard Template Library.")

To demonstrate the overloaded subscript operator, we must return to another topic, first mentioned in Chapter 5: returning values from functions by reference. To be useful, the overloaded subscript operator must return by reference. To see why this is true, we'll show three example programs that implement a safe array, each one using a different approach to inserting and reading the array elements:

- Separate put() and get() functions
- A single access() function using return by reference
- The overloaded [ ] operator using return by reference

All three programs create a class called safearay, whose only member data is an array of 100 int values, and all three check to ensure that all array accesses are within bounds. The main() program in each program tests the class by filling the safe array with values (each one equal to 10 times its array index) and then displaying them all to assure the user that everything is working as it should.

Separate get() and put() Functions

The first program provides two functions to access the array elements: putel() to insert a value into the array, and getel() to find the value of an array element. Both functions check the value of the index number supplied to ensure it's not out of bounds; that is, less than 0 or larger than the array size (minus 1). Here's the listing for ARROVER1:

```
// arrover1.cpp
// creates safe array (index values are checked before access)
// uses separate put and get functions
#include <iostream>
using namespace std;
#include <process.h>                    // for exit()
const int LIMIT = 100;
//////////////////////////////////////////////////////////////////
class safearay
    {
    private:
        int arr[LIMIT];
    public:
```

```
        void putel(int n, int elvalue)   //set value of element
           {
        if( n< 0 || n>=LIMIT )
            { cout << "\nIndex out of bounds"; exit(1); }
        arr[n] = elvalue;
        }
     int getel(int n) const              //get value of element
        {
        if( n< 0 || n>=LIMIT )
            { cout << "\nIndex out of bounds"; exit(1); }
        return arr[n];
        }
   };
///////////////////////////////////////////////////////////////////
int main()
   {
   safearay sa1;

   for(int j=0; j<LIMIT; j++)   // insert elements
     sa1.putel(j, j*10);

   for(j=0; j<LIMIT; j++)        // display elements
      {
      int temp = sa1.getel(j);
      cout << "Element " << j << " is " << temp << endl;
      }
   return 0;
   }
```

The data is inserted into the safe array with the putel() member function, and then displayed with getel(). This implements a safe array; you'll receive an error message if you attempt to use an out-of-bounds index. However, the format is a bit crude.

Single access() Function Returning by Reference

As it turns out, we can use the same member function both to insert data into the safe array and to read it out. The secret is to return the value from the function by reference. This means we can place the function on the left side of the equal sign, and the value on the right side will be assigned to the variable returned by the function, as explained in Chapter 5. Here's the listing for ARROVER2:

```
// arrover2.cpp
// creates safe array (index values are checked before access)
// uses one access() function for both put and get
#include <iostream>
using namespace std;
```

```
#include <process.h>              //for exit()
const int LIMIT = 100;            //array size
/////////////////////////////////////////////////////////////////
class safearay
    {
    private:
        int arr[LIMIT];
    public:
        int& access(int n)        //note: return by reference
            {
            if( n< 0 || n>=LIMIT )
                { cout << "\nIndex out of bounds"; exit(1); }
            return arr[n];
            }
    };
/////////////////////////////////////////////////////////////////
int main()
    {
    safearay sa1;

    for(int j=0; j<LIMIT; j++)    //insert elements
        sa1.access(j) = j*10;     //*left* side of equal sign

    for(j=0; j<LIMIT; j++)        //display elements
        {
        int temp = sa1.access(j); //*right* side of equal sign
        cout << "Element " << j << " is " << temp << endl;
        }
    return 0;
    }
```

The statement

```
sa1.access(j) = j*10;      // *left* side of equal sign
```

causes the value j*10 to be placed in arr[j], the return value of the function.

It's perhaps slightly more convenient to use the same function for input and output of the safe array than it is to use separate functions; there's one less name to remember. But there's an even better way, with no names to remember at all.

Overloaded [] Operator Returning by Reference

To access the safe array using the same subscript ([ ]) operator that's used for normal C++ arrays, we overload the subscript operator in the safearay class. However, since this operator is commonly used on the left side of the equal sign, this overloaded function must return by reference, as we showed in the previous program. Here's the listing for ARROVER3:

```
// arrover3.cpp
// creates safe array (index values are checked before access)
// uses overloaded [] operator for both put and get

#include <iostream>
using namespace std;
#include <process.h>             //for exit()
const int LIMIT = 100;           //array size
/////////////////////////////////////////////////////////////
class safearay
   {
   private:
      int arr[LIMIT];
   public:
      int& operator [](int n)   //note: return by reference
         {
         if( n< 0 || n>=LIMIT )
            { cout << "\nIndex out of bounds"; exit(1); }
         return arr[n];
         }
   };
/////////////////////////////////////////////////////////////
int main()
   {
   safearay sa1;

   for(int j=0; j<LIMIT; j++)   //insert elements
      sa1[j] = j*10;            //*left* side of equal sign

   for(j=0; j<LIMIT; j++)       //display elements
      {
      int temp = sa1[j];        //*right* side of equal sign
      cout << "Element " << j << " is " << temp << endl;
      }
   return 0;
   }
```

In this program we can use the natural subscript expressions

```
sa1[j] = j*10;
```

and

```
temp = sa1[j];
```

for input and output to the safe array.

Data Conversion

You already know that the = operator will assign a value from one variable to another, in statements like

```
intvar1 = intvar2;
```

where `intvar1` and `intvar2` are integer variables. You may also have noticed that = assigns the value of one user-defined object to another, provided they are of the same type, in statements like

```
dist3 = dist1 + dist2;
```

where the result of the addition, which is type `Distance`, is assigned to another object of type `Distance`, `dist3`. Normally, when the value of one object is assigned to another of the same type, the values of all the member data items are simply copied into the new object. The compiler doesn't need any special instructions to use = for the assignment of user-defined objects such as `Distance` objects.

Thus, assignments between types, whether they are basic types or user-defined types, are handled by the compiler with no effort on our part, provided that the same data type is used on both sides of the equal sign. But what happens when the variables on different sides of the = are of different types? This is a more thorny question, to which we will devote the balance of this chapter. We'll first review how the compiler handles the conversion of basic types, which it does automatically. Then we'll explore several situations where the compiler doesn't handle things automatically and we need to tell it what to do. These include conversions between basic types and user-defined types, and conversions between different user-defined types.

You might think it represents poor programming practice to convert routinely from one type to another. After all, languages such as Pascal go to considerable trouble to keep you from doing such conversions. However, the philosophy in C++ (and C) is that the flexibility provided by allowing conversions outweighs the dangers. This is a controversial issue; we'll return to it at the end of this chapter.

Conversions Between Basic Types

When we write a statement like

```
intvar = floatvar;
```

where `intvar` is of type `int` and `floatvar` is of type `float`, we are assuming that the compiler will call a special routine to convert the value of `floatvar`, which is expressed in floating-point format, to an integer format so that it can be assigned to `intvar`. There are of course many such conversions: from `float` to `double`, `char` to `float`, and so on. Each such conversion has its own routine, built into the compiler and called up when the data types on different sides of the equal sign so dictate. We say such conversions are *implicit* because they aren't apparent in the listing.

Sometimes we want to force the compiler to convert one type to another. To do this we use the cast operator. For instance, to convert `float` to `int`, we can say

```
intvar = static_cast<int>(floatvar);
```

Casting provides *explicit* conversion: It's obvious in the listing that `static_cast<int>()` is intended to convert from `float` to `int`. However, such explicit conversions use the same built-in routines as implicit conversions.

Conversions Between Objects and Basic Types

When we want to convert between user-defined data types and basic types, we can't rely on built-in conversion routines, since the compiler doesn't know anything about user-defined types besides what we tell it. Instead, we must write these routines ourselves.

Our next example shows how to convert between a basic type and a user-defined type. In this example the user-defined type is (surprise!) the English `Distance` class from previous examples, and the basic type is `float`, which we use to represent meters, a unit of length in the metric measurement system.

The example shows conversion both from `Distance` to `float`, and from `float` to `Distance`. Here's the listing for ENGLCONV:

```
// englconv.cpp
// conversions: Distance to meters, meters to Distance
#include <iostream>
using namespace std;
/////////////////////////////////////////////////////////////////
class Distance                      //English Distance class
   {
   private:
     const float MTF;               //meters to feet
     int feet;
     float inches;
   public:                          //constructor (no args)
     Distance() : feet(0), inches(0.0), MTF(3.280833F)
        { }                         //constructor (one arg)
     Distance(float meters) : MTF(3.280833F)
        {                           //convert meters to Distance
        float fltfeet = MTF * meters;  //convert to float feet
        feet = int(fltfeet);        //feet is integer part
        inches = 12*(fltfeet-feet); //inches is what's left
        }                           //constructor (two args)
```

```
        Distance(int ft, float in) : feet(ft),
                                inches(in), MTF(3.280833F)
        { }
    void getdist()                //get length from user
        {
        cout << "\nEnter feet: ";  cin >> feet;
        cout << "Enter inches: ";  cin >> inches;
        }
    void showdist() const         //display distance
        { cout << feet << "\'-" << inches << '\"'; }

    operator float() const        //conversion operator
        {                         //converts Distance to meters
        float fracfeet = inches/12;      //convert the inches
        fracfeet += static_cast<float>(feet); //add the feet
        return fracfeet/MTF;             //convert to meters
        }
    };
//////////////////////////////////////////////////////////////
int main()
    {
    float mtrs;
    Distance dist1 = 2.35F;           //uses 1-arg constructor to
                                      //convert meters to Distance
    cout << "\ndist1 = "; dist1.showdist();

    mtrs = static_cast<float>(dist1); //uses conversion operator
                                      //for Distance to meters
    cout << "\ndist1 = " << mtrs << " meters\n";

    Distance dist2(5, 10.25);         //uses 2-arg constructor

    mtrs = dist2;                     //also uses conversion op
    cout << "\ndist2 = " << mtrs << " meters\n";

//  dist2 = mtrs;                     //error, = won't convert
    return 0;
    }
```

In main() the program first converts a fixed float quantity—2.35, representing meters—to feet and inches, using the one-argument constructor:

Distance dist1 = 2.35F;

Going in the other direction, it converts a Distance to meters in the statements

mtrs = static_cast<float>(dist2);

and

```
mtrs = dist2;
```

Here's the output:

```
dist1 = 7'-8.51949"        ←——— this is 2.35 meters
dist1 = 2.35 meters        ←——— this is 7'-8.51949"
dist2 = 1.78435 meters     ←——— this is 5'-10.25"
```

We've seen how conversions are performed using simple assignment statements in main().
Now let's see what goes on behind the scenes, in the Distance member functions. Converting
a user-defined type to a basic type requires a different approach than converting a basic type to
a user-defined type. We'll see how both types of conversions are carried out in ENGLCONV.

From Basic to User-Defined

To go from a basic type—float in this case—to a user-defined type such as Distance, we use
a constructor with one argument. These are sometimes called *conversion constructors*. Here's
how this constructor looks in ENGLCONV:

```
Distance(float meters)
   {
   float fltfeet = MTF * meters;
   feet = int(fltfeet);
   inches = 12 * (fltfeet-feet);
   }
```

This function is called when an object of type Distance is created with a single argument. The
function assumes that this argument represents meters. It converts the argument to feet and
inches, and assigns the resulting values to the object. Thus the conversion from meters to
Distance is carried out along with the creation of an object in the statement

```
Distance dist1 = 2.35;
```

From User-Defined to Basic

What about going the other way, from a user-defined type to a basic type? The trick here is to
create something called a *conversion operator*. Here's where we do that in ENGLCONV:

```
operator float()
   {
   float fracfeet = inches/12;
   fracfeet += float(feet);
   return fracfeet/MTF;
   }
```

This operator takes the value of the Distance object of which it is a member, converts it to a
float value representing meters, and returns this value.

8

OPERATOR
OVERLOADING

This operator can be called with an explicit cast

```
mtrs = static_cast<float>(dist1);
```

or with a simple assignment

```
mtrs = dist2;
```

Both forms convert the Distance object to its equivalent float value in meters.

Conversion Between C-Strings and String Objects

Here's another example that uses a one-argument constructor and a conversion operator. It
operates on the String class that we saw in the STRPLUS example earlier in this chapter.

```
// strconv.cpp
// convert between ordinary strings and class String
#include <iostream>
using namespace std;
#include <string.h>                //for strcpy(), etc.
/////////////////////////////////////////////////////////////////
class String                       //user-defined string type
   {
   private:
      enum { SZ = 80 };            //size of all String objects
      char str[SZ];                //holds a C-string
   public:
      String()                     //no-arg constructor
         { str[0] = '\0'; }
      String( char s[] )           //1-arg constructor
         { strcpy(str, s); }       //   convert C-string to String
      void display() const         //display the String
         { cout << str; }
      operator char*()             //conversion operator
         { return str; }           //convert String to C-string
   };
/////////////////////////////////////////////////////////////////
int main()
   {
   String s1;                       //use no-arg constructor
                                    //create and initialize C-string
   char xstr[] = "Joyeux Noel! ";

   s1 = xstr;                       //use 1-arg constructor
                                    //   to convert C-string to String
   s1.display();                    //display String
```

```
  String s2 = "Bonne Annee!";   //uses 1-arg constructor
                                 //to initialize String
  cout << static_cast<char*>(s2); //use conversion operator
  cout << endl;                  //to convert String to C-string
  return 0;                      //before sending to << op
  }
```

The one-argument constructor converts a normal string (an array of char) to an object of class String:

```
String(char s[])
  { strcpy(str, s); }
```

The C-string s is passed as an argument, and copied into the str data member in a newly created String object, using the strcpy() library function.

This conversion will be applied when a String is created, as in

```
String s2 = "Bonne Annee!";
```

or it will be applied in assignment statements, as in

```
s1 = xstr;
```

where s1 is type String and xstr is a C-string.

A conversion operator is used to convert from a String type to a C-string:

```
operator char*()
  { return str; }
```

The asterisk in this expression means *pointer to*. We won't explore pointers until Chapter 10, but its use here is not hard to figure out. It means *pointer to* char, which is very similar to *array of type* char. Thus char* is similar to char[]. It's another way of specifying a C-string data type.

The conversion operator is used by the compiler in the statement

```
cout << static_cast<char*>(s2);
```

Here the s2 variable is an argument supplied to the overloaded operator <<. Since the << operator doesn't know anything about our user-defined String type, the compiler looks for a way to convert s2 to a type that << does know about. We specify the type we want to convert it to with the char* cast, so it looks for a conversion from String to C-string, finds our operator char*() function, and uses it to generate a C-string, which is then sent on to << to be displayed. (The effect is similar to calling the String::display() function, but given the ease and intuitive clarity of displaying with <<, the display() function is redundant and could be removed.)

Here's the output from STRCONV:

```
Joyeux Noel! Bonne Annee!
```

The STRCONV example demonstrates that conversions take place automatically not only in assignment statements but in other appropriate places, such as in arguments sent to operators (such as <<) or functions. If you supply an operator or a function with arguments of the wrong type, they will be converted to arguments of an acceptable type, provided you have defined such a conversion.

Note that you can't use an explicit assignment statement to convert a String to a C-string:

```
xstr = s2;
```

The C-string xstr is an array, and you can't normally assign to arrays (although as we'll see in Chapter 11, when you overload the assignment operator, all sorts of things are possible).

Conversions Between Objects of Different Classes

What about converting between objects of different user-defined classes? The same two methods just shown for conversions between basic types and user-defined types also apply to conversions between two user-defined types. That is, you can use a one-argument constructor or you can use a conversion operator. The choice depends on whether you want to put the conversion routine in the class declaration of the source object or of the destination object. For example, suppose you say

```
objecta = objectb;
```

where objecta is a member of class A and objectb is a member of class B. Is the conversion routine located in class A (the destination class, since objecta receives the value) or class B (the source class)? We'll look at both cases.

Two Kinds of Time

Our example programs will convert between two ways of measuring time: 12-hour time and 24-hour time. These methods of telling time are sometimes called *civilian time* and *military time*. Our time12 class will represent civilian time, as used in digital clocks and airport flight departure displays. We'll assume that in this context there is no need for seconds, so time12 uses only hours (from 1 to 12), minutes, and an "a.m." or "p.m." designation. Our time24 class, which is for more exacting applications such as air navigation, uses hours (from 00 to 23), minutes, and seconds. Table 8.1 shows the differences.

TABLE 8.1   12-Hour and 24-Hour Time

12-Hour Time	24-Hour Time
12:00 a.m. (midnight)	00:00
12:01 a.m.	00:01
1:00 a.m.	01:00
6:00 a.m.	06:00
11:59 a.m	11:59
12:00 p.m. (noon)	12:00
12:01 p.m.	12:01
6:00 p.m.	18:00
11:59 p.m.	23:59

Note that 12 a.m. (midnight) in civilian time is 00 hours in military time. There is no 0 hour in civilian time.

Routine in Source Object

The first example program shows a conversion routine located in the source class. When the conversion routine is in the source class, it is commonly implemented as a conversion operator. Here's the listing for TIMES1:

```
//times1.cpp
//converts from time24 to time12 using operator in time24
#include <iostream>
#include <string>
using namespace std;
/////////////////////////////////////////////////////////////////
class time12
    {
    private:
        bool pm;                       //true = pm, false = am
        int hrs;                       //1 to 12
        int mins;                      //0 to 59
    public:                            //no-arg constructor
        time12() : pm(true), hrs(0), mins(0)
            {  }
                                       //3-arg constructor
        time12(bool ap, int h, int m) : pm(ap), hrs(h), mins(m)
            {  }
        void display() const           //format: 11:59 p.m.
            {
            cout << hrs << ':';
```

```
                 if(mins < 10)
                    cout << '0';                //extra zero for "01"
                 cout << mins << ' ';
                 string am_pm = pm ? "p.m." : "a.m.";
                 cout << am_pm;
                 }
         };
/////////////////////////////////////////////////////////////////////
class time24
      {
      private:
         int hours;                    //0 to 23
         int minutes;                  //0 to 59
         int seconds;                  //0 to 59
      public:                          //no-arg constructor
         time24() : hours(0), minutes(0), seconds(0)
            { }
         time24(int h, int m, int s) :  //3-arg constructor
               hours(h), minutes(m), seconds(s)
            { }
         void display() const           //format: 23:15:01
            {
            if(hours < 10)    cout << '0';
            cout << hours << ':';
            if(minutes < 10)  cout << '0';
            cout << minutes << ':';
            if(seconds < 10)  cout << '0';
            cout << seconds;
            }
         operator time12() const;       //conversion operator
      };
//------------------------------------------------------------
time24::operator time12() const               //conversion operator
      {
      int hrs24 = hours;
      bool pm = hours < 12 ? false : true;   //find am/pm
                                             //round secs
      int roundMins = seconds < 30 ? minutes : minutes+1;
      if(roundMins == 60)                    //carry mins?
         {
         roundMins=0;
         ++hrs24;
         if(hrs24 == 12 || hrs24 == 24)      //carry hrs?
            pm = (pm==true) ? false : true;  //toggle am/pm
         }
      int hrs12 = (hrs24 < 13) ? hrs24 : hrs24-12;
```

```
    if(hrs12==0)                          //00 is 12 a.m.
        { hrs12=12; pm=false; }
    return time12(pm, hrs12, roundMins);
    }
//////////////////////////////////////////////////////////////////
int main()
    {
    int h, m, s;

    while(true)
        {                                 //get 24-hr time from user
        cout << "Enter 24-hour time: \n";
        cout << "  Hours (0 to 23): "; cin >> h;
        if(h > 23)                        //quit if hours > 23
            return(1);
        cout << "  Minutes: ";  cin >> m;
        cout << "  Seconds: ";  cin >> s;

        time24 t24(h, m, s);             //make a time24
        cout << "You entered: ";         //display the time24
        t24.display();

        time12 t12 = t24;                //convert time24 to time12

        cout << "\n12-hour time: ";      //display equivalent time12
        t12.display();
        cout << "\n\n";
        }
    return 0;
    }
```

In the main() part of TIMES1 we define an object of type time24, called t24, and give it values for hours, minutes, and seconds obtained from the user. We also define an object of type time12, called t12, and initialize it to t24 in the statement

```
time12 t12 = t24;
```

Since these objects are from different classes, the assignment involves a conversion, and—as we specified—in this program the conversion operator is a member of the time24 class. Here's its declarator:

```
time24::operator time12() const          //conversion operator
}
```

This function transforms the object of which it is a member to a time12 object, and returns this object, which main() then assigns to t12. Here's some interaction with TIMES1:

```
Enter 24-hour time:
    Hours (0 to 23): 17
    Minutes: 59
    Seconds: 45
You entered: 17:59:45
12-hour time: 6:00 p.m.
```

The seconds value is rounded up, pushing the 12-hour time from 5:59 p.m. to 6:00 p.m.
Entering an hours value greater than 23 causes the program to exit.

Routine in Destination Object

Let's see how the same conversion is carried out when the conversion routine is in the destination
class. In this situation it's common to use a one-argument constructor. However, things are
complicated by the fact that the constructor in the destination class must be able to access the
data in the source class to perform the conversion. The data in time24—hours, minutes and
seconds—is private, so we must provide special member functions in time24 to allow direct
access to it. These are called getHrs(), getMins(), and getSecs().

Here's the listing for TIMES2:

```cpp
//times2.cpp
//converts from time24 to time12 using constructor in time12
#include <iostream>
#include <string>
using namespace std;
//////////////////////////////////////////////////////////////////
class time24
    {
    private:
        int hours;                     //0 to 23
        int minutes;                   //0 to 59
        int seconds;                   //0 to 59
    public:                            //no-arg constructor
        time24() : hours(0), minutes(0), seconds(0)
            { }
        time24(int h, int m, int s) :  //3-arg constructor
                hours(h), minutes(m), seconds(s)
            { }
        void display() const           //format 23:15:01
            {
            if(hours < 10)    cout << '0';
            cout << hours << ':';
            if(minutes < 10)  cout << '0';
            cout << minutes << ':';
            if(seconds < 10)  cout << '0';
            cout << seconds;
            }
```

```
      int getHrs() const    { return hours; }
      int getMins() const   { return minutes; }
      int getSecs() const   { return seconds; }
   };
/////////////////////////////////////////////////////////////
class time12
   {
   private:
      bool pm;                         //true = pm, false = am
      int hrs;                         //1 to 12
      int mins;                        //0 to 59
   public:                             //no-arg constructor
      time12() : pm(true), hrs(0), mins(0)
         { }
      time12(time24);                  //1-arg constructor
                                       //3-arg constructor
      time12(bool ap, int h, int m) : pm(ap), hrs(h), mins(m)
         { }
      void display() const
         {
         cout << hrs << ':';
         if(mins < 10)  cout << '0';  //extra zero for "01"
         cout << mins << ' ';
         string am_pm = pm ? "p.m." : "a.m.";
         cout << am_pm;
         }
   };
//..........................................................
time12::time12( time24 t24 )          //1-arg constructor
   {                                  //converts time24 to time12
   int hrs24 = t24.getHrs();          //get hours
                                      //find am/pm
   pm = t24.getHrs() < 12 ? false : true;

   mins = (t24.getSecs() < 30) ?      //round secs
                     t24.getMins() : t24.getMins()+1;
   if(mins == 60)                     //carry mins?
      {
      mins=0;
      ++hrs24;
      if(hrs24 == 12 || hrs24 == 24)  //carry hrs?
         pm = (pm==true) ? false : true;  //toggle am/pm
      }
   hrs = (hrs24 < 13) ? hrs24 : hrs24-12; //convert hrs
   if(hrs==0)                         //00 is 12 a.m.
```

```
         { hrs=12; pm=false; }
      }
///////////////////////////////////////////////////////////////////
int main()
   {
   int h, m, s;

   while(true)
      {                               //get 24-hour time from user
      cout << "Enter 24-hour time: \n";
      cout << "   Hours (0 to 23): "; cin >> h;
      if(h > 23)                      //quit if hours > 23
         return(1);
      cout << "   Minutes: ";  cin >> m;
      cout << "   Seconds: ";  cin >> s;

      time24 t24(h, m, s);            //make a time24
      cout << "You entered: ";        //display the time24
      t24.display();

      time12 t12 = t24;               //convert time24 to time12

      cout << "\n12-hour time: ";     //display equivalent time12
      t12.display();
      cout << "\n\n";
      }
   return 0;
   }
```

The conversion routine is the one-argument constructor from the time12 class. This function sets the object of which it is a member to values that correspond to the time24 values of the object received as an argument. It works in much the same way as the conversion operator in TIMES1, except that it must work a little harder to access the data in the time24 object, using getHrs() and similar functions.

The main() part of TIMES2 is the same as that in TIMES1. The one-argument constructor again allows the time24-to-time12 conversion to take place in the statement

```
time12 t12 = t24;
```

The output is similar as well. The difference is behind the scenes, where the conversion is handled by a constructor in the destination object rather than a conversion operator in the source object.

Conversions: When to Use What

When should you use the one-argument constructor in the destination class, as opposed to the conversion operator in the source class? Mostly you can take your pick. However, sometimes the choice is made for you. If you have purchased a library of classes, you may not have access to their source code. If you use an object of such a class as the source in a conversion, you'll have access only to the destination class, and you'll need to use a one-argument constructor. If the library class object is the destination, you must use a conversion operator in the source.

UML Class Diagrams

We introduced the UML in Chapter 1, "The Big Picture." Now that you know something about classes, let's take a look at our first UML feature: the *class diagram*. This diagram offers a new way of looking at object-oriented programs, and may throw some additional light on the workings of the TIMES1 and TIMES2 programs.

Looking at the listing for TIMES1 we can see that there are two classes: time12 and time24. In a UML class diagram, classes are represented by rectangles, as shown in Figure 8.3.

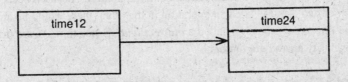

FIGURE 8.3
UML class diagram of the TIMES1 program.

Each class rectangle is divided into sections by horizontal lines. The class name goes in the top section. We don't show them here, but you can include sections for member data (called *attributes* in the UML) and member functions (called *operations*).

Associations

Classes may have various kinds of relationships with each other. The classes in TIMES1 are related by *association*. We indicate this with a line connecting their rectangles. (We'll see what another kind of class relationship, generalization, looks like in Chapter 9, "Inheritance.")

What constitutes an association? Conceptually, the real-world entities that are represented by classes in the program have some kind of obvious relationship. Drivers are related to cars, books are related to libraries, race horses are related to race tracks. If such entities were classes in a program, they would be related by association.

In the TIMES2.CPP program, we can see that class time12 is associatd with class time24 because we are converting objects of one class into objects of the other.

A class association actually implies that objects of the classes, rather than the classes themselves, have some kind of relationship. Typically, two classes are associated if an object of one class calls a member function (an *operation*) of an object of the other class. An association might also exist if an attribute of one class is an object of the other class.

In the TIMES1 program, an object of the time12 class, called t12, calls the conversion routine operator time12() in the object t24 of the time24 class. This happens in main() in the statement

```
time12 t12 = t24;                //convert time24 to time12
```

Such a call is represented by an association line between the two classes.

Navigability

We can add an open arrowhead to indicate the direction or *navigability* of the association. (As we'll see later, closed arrowheads have a different meaning.) Because time12 calls time24, the arrow points from time12 to time24. It's called a *unidirectional* association because it only goes one way. If each of two classes called an operation in the other, there would be arrowheads on both ends of the line and it would be called a *bidirectional* association. As are many things in the UML, navigability arrows are optional.

Pitfalls of Operator Overloading and Conversion

Operator overloading and type conversions give you the opportunity to create what amounts to an entirely new language. When a, b, and c are objects from user-defined classes, and + is overloaded, the statement

```
a = b + c;
```

can mean something quite different than it does when a, b, and c are variables of basic data types. The ability to redefine the building blocks of the language can be a blessing in that it can make your listing more intuitive and readable. It can also have the opposite effect, making your listing more obscure and hard to understand. Here are some guidelines.

Use Similar Meanings

Use overloaded operators to perform operations that are as similar as possible to those performed on basic data types. You could overload the + sign to perform subtraction, for example, but that would hardly make your listings more comprehensible.

Overloading an operator assumes that it makes sense to perform a particular operation on objects of a certain class. If we're going to overload the + operator in class X, the result of adding two objects of class X should have a meaning at least somewhat similar to addition. For example, in this chapter we showed how to overload the + operator for the English Distance class. Adding two distances is clearly meaningful. We also overloaded + for the String class. Here we interpret the addition of two strings to mean placing one string after another to form a third. This also has an intuitively satisfying interpretation. But for many classes it may not be reasonable to talk about "adding" their objects. You probably wouldn't want to add two objects of a class called employee that held personal data, for example.

Use Similar Syntax

Use overloaded operators in the same way you use basic types. For example, if alpha and beta are basic types, the assignment operator in the statement

```
alpha += beta;
```

sets alpha to the sum of alpha and beta. Any overloaded version of this operator should do something analogous. It should probably do the same thing as

```
alpha = alpha + beta;
```

where the + is overloaded.

If you overload one arithmetic operator, you may for consistency want to overload all of them. This will prevent confusion.

Some syntactical characteristics of operators can't be changed. As you may have discovered, you can't overload a binary operator to be a unary operator, or vice versa.

Show Restraint

Remember that if you have overloaded the + operator, anyone unfamiliar with your listing will need to do considerable research to find out what a statement like

```
a = b + c;
```

really means. If the number of overloaded operators grows too large, and if the operators are used in nonintuitive ways, the whole point of using them is lost, and reading the listing becomes harder instead of easier. Use overloaded operators sparingly, and only when the usage is obvious. When in doubt, use a function instead of an overloaded operator, since a function name can state its own purpose. If you write a function to find the left side of a string, for example, you're better off calling it getleft() than trying to overload some operator such as && to do the same thing.

8

OPERATOR
OVERLOADING

Avoid Ambiguity

Suppose you use both a one-argument constructor and a conversion operator to perform the same conversion (time24 to time12, for example). How will the compiler know which conversion to use? It won't. The compiler does not like to be placed in a situation where it doesn't know what to do, and it will signal an error. So avoid doing the same conversion in more than one way.

Not All Operators Can Be Overloaded

The following operators cannot be overloaded: the member access or dot operator (.), the scope resolution operator (::), and the conditional operator (?:). Also, the pointer-to-member operator (->), which we have not yet encountered, cannot be overloaded. In case you wondered, no, you can't create new operators (like *&) and try to overload them; only existing operators can be overloaded.

Keywords explicit and mutable

Let's look at two unusual keywords: explicit and mutable. They have quite different effects, but are grouped together here because they both modify class members. The explicit keyword relates to data conversion, but mutable has a more subtle purpose.

Preventing Conversions with explicit

There may be some specific conversions you have decided are a good thing, and you've taken steps to make them possible by installing appropriate conversion operators and one-argument constructors, as shown in the TIME1 and TIME2 examples. However, there may be other conversions that you don't want to happen. You should actively discourage any conversion that you don't want. This prevents unpleasant surprises.

It's easy to prevent a conversion performed by a conversion operator: just don't define the operator. However, things aren't so easy with constructors. You may want to construct objects using a single value of another type, but you may not want the implicit conversions a one-argument constructor makes possible in other situations. What to do?

Standard C++ includes a keyword, explicit, to solve this problem. It's placed just before the declaration of a one-argument constructor. The EXPLICIT example program (based on the ENGLCON program) shows how this looks.

```
//explicit.cpp
#include <iostream>
using namespace std;
/////////////////////////////////////////////////////////////////
class Distance                        //English Distance class
```

```
   {
   private:
      const float MTF;                //meters to feet
      int feet;
      float inches;
   public:                           //no-args constructor
      Distance() : feet(0), inches(0.0), MTF(3.280833F)
         { }
                                     //EXPLICIT one-arg constructor
      explicit Distance(float meters) : MTF(3.280833F)
         {
         float fltfeet = MTF * meters;
         feet = int(fltfeet);
         inches = 12*(fltfeet-feet);
         }
      void showdist()                //display distance
         { cout << feet << "\'-" << inches << '\"'; }
   };
/////////////////////////////////////////////////////////////////
int main()
   {
   void fancyDist(Distance);        //declaration
   Distance dist1(2.35F);           //uses 1-arg constructor to
                                    //convert meters to Distance

// Distance dist1 = 2.35F;          //ERROR if ctor is explicit
   cout << "\ndist1 = "; dist1.showdist();

   float mtrs = 3.0F;
   cout << "\ndist1 ";
// fancyDist(mtrs);                 //ERROR if ctor is explicit

   return 0;
   }
//...........................................................
void fancyDist(Distance d)
   {
   cout << "(in feet and inches) = ";
   d.showdist();
   cout << endl;
   }
```

This program includes a function (fancyDist()) that embellishes the output of a Distance object by printing the phrase "(in feet and inches)" before the feet and inches figures. The argument to this function is a Distance variable, and you can call fancyDist() with such a variable with no problem.

The tricky part is that, unless you take some action to prevent it, you can also call fancyDist() with a variable of type float as the argument:

```
fancyDist(mtrs);
```

The compiler will realize it's the wrong type and look for a conversion operator. Finding a Distance constructor that takes type float as an argument, it will arrange for this constructor to convert float to Distance and pass the Distance value to the function. This is an *implicit* conversion, one which you may not have intended to make possible.

However, if we make the constructor *explicit*, we prevent implicit conversions. You can check this by removing the comment symbol from the call to fancyDist() in the program: the compiler will tell you it can't perform the conversion. Without the explicit keyword, this call is perfectly legal.

As a side effect of the explicit constructor, note that you can't use the form of object initialization that uses an equal sign

```
Distance dist1 = 2.35F;
```

whereas the form with parentheses

```
Distance dist1(2.35F);
```

works as it always has.

Changing const Object Data Using mutable

Ordinarily, when you create a const object (as described in Chapter 6), you want a guarantee that none of its member data can be changed. However, a situation occasionally arises where you want to create const objects that have some specific member data item that needs to be modified despite the object's constness.

As an example, let's imagine a window (the kind that Windows programs commonly draw on the screen). It may be that some of the features of the window, such as its scrollbars and menus, are *owned* by the window. Ownership is common in various programming situations, and indicates a greater degree of independence than when one object is an attribute of another. In such a situation an object may remain unchanged, except that its owner may change. A scrollbar retains the same size, color, and orientation, but its ownership may be transferred from one window to another. It's like what happens when your bank sells your mortgage to another bank; all the terms of the mortgage are the same, but the owner is different.

Let's say we want to be able to create const scrollbars in which attributes remain unchanged, except for their ownership. That's where the mutable keyword comes in. The MUTABLE program shows how this looks.

```cpp
//mutable.cpp
#include <iostream>
#include <string>
using namespace std;
/////////////////////////////////////////////////////////////////
class scrollbar
   {
   private:
     int size;                       //related to constness
     mutable string owner;           //not relevant to constness
   public:
     scrollbar(int sz, string own) : size(sz), owner(own)
        { }
     void setSize(int sz)            //changes size
        { size = sz; }
     void setOwner(string own) const //changes owner
        { owner = own; }
     int getSize() const             //returns size
        { return size; }
     string getOwner() const         //returns owner
        { return owner; }
   };
/////////////////////////////////////////////////////////////////
int main()
   {
   const scrollbar sbar(60, "Window1");

// sbar.setSize(100);               //can't do this to const obj
   sbar.setOwner("Window2");        //this is OK
                                    //these are OK too
   cout << sbar.getSize() << ", " << sbar.getOwner() << endl;
   return 0;
   }
```

The size attribute represents the scrollbar data that cannot be modified in const objects. The owner attribute, however, can change, even if the object is const. To permit this, it's made mutable. In main() we create a const object sbar. Its size cannot be modified, but its owner can, using the setOwner() function. (In a non-const object, of course, both attributes could be modified.) In this situation, sbar is said to have *logical* const*ness*. That means that in theory it can't be modified, but in practice it can, in a limited way.

Summary

In this chapter we've seen how the normal C++ operators can be given new meanings when applied to user-defined data types. The keyword operator is used to overload an operator, and the resulting operator will adopt the meaning supplied by the programmer.

Closely related to operator overloading is the issue of *type conversion*. Some conversions take place between user-defined types and basic types. Two approaches are used in such conversions: A one-argument constructor changes a basic type to a user-defined type, and a conversion operator converts a user-defined type to a basic type. When one user-defined type is converted to another, either approach can be used.

Table 8.2 summarizes these conversions.

TABLE 8.2   Type Conversions

	Routine in Destination	*Routine in Source*
Basic to basic	(Built-In Conversion Operators)	
Basic to class	Constructor	N/A
Class to basic	N/A	Conversion operator
Class to class	Constructor	Conversion operator

A constructor given the keyword explicit cannot be used in implicit data conversion situations. A data member given the keyword mutable can be changed, even if its object is const.

UML class diagrams show classes and relationships between classes. An association represents a conceptual relationship between the real-world objects that the program's classes represent. Associations can have a direction from one class to another; this is called navigability.

Questions

Answers to these questions can be found in Appendix G.

1. Operator overloading is
   a. making C++ operators work with objects.
   b. giving C++ operators more than they can handle.
   c. giving new meanings to existing C++ operators.
   d. making new C++ operators.

2. Assuming that class X does not use any overloaded operators, write a statement that subtracts an object of class X, x1, from another such object, x2, and places the result in x3.

3. Assuming that class X includes a routine to overload the - operator, write a statement that would perform the same task as that specified in Question 2.

4. True or false: The >= operator can be overloaded.

5. Write a complete definition for an overloaded operator for the Counter class of the COUNTPP1 example that, instead of incrementing the count, decrements it.

6. How many arguments are required in the definition of an overloaded unary operator?

7. Assume a class C with objects obj1, obj2, and obj3. For the statement obj3 = obj1 - obj2 to work correctly, the overloaded - operator must.

    a. take two arguments.

    b. return a value.

    c. create a named temporary object.

    d. use the object of which it is a member as an operand.

8. Write a complete definition for an overloaded ++ operator for the Distance class from the ENGLPLUS example. It should add 1 to the feet member data, and make possible statements like

    dist1++;

9. Repeat Question 8, but allow statements like the following:

    dist2 = dist1++;

10. When used in prefix form, what does the overloaded ++ operator do differently from what it does in postfix form?

11. Here are two declarators that describe ways to add two string objects:

    void add(String s1, String s2)
    String operator + (String s)

    Match the following from the first declarator with the appropriate selection from the second:

    function name (add) matches _____.

    return value (type void) matches _____.

    first argument (s1) matches _____.

    second argument (s2) matches _____.

    object of which function is a member matches _____.

    a. argument (s)

    b. object of which operator is a member

    c. operator (+)

    d. return value (type String)

    e. no match for this item

12. True or false: An overloaded operator always requires one less argument than its number of operands.

13. When you overload an arithmetic assignment operator, the result

    a. goes in the object to the right of the operator.

    b. goes in the object to the left of the operator.

    c. goes in the object of which the operator is a member.

    d. must be returned.

14. Write the complete definition of an overloaded ++ operator that works with the String class from the STRPLUS example and has the effect of changing its operand to uppercase. You can use the library function toupper() (header file CCTYPE), which takes as its only argument the character to be changed and returns the changed character (or the same character if no change is necessary).

15. To convert from a user-defined class to a basic type, you would most likely use

    a. a built-in conversion operator.

    b. a one-argument constructor.

    c. an overloaded = operator.

    d. a conversion operator that's a member of the class.

16. True or false: The statement objA=objB; will cause a compiler error if the objects are of different classes.

17. To convert from a basic type to a user-defined class, you would most likely use

    a. a built-in conversion operator.

    b. a one-argument constructor.

    c. an overloaded = operator.

    d. a conversion operator that's a member of the class.

18. True or false: If you've defined a constructor to handle definitions like aclass obj = intvar; you can also make statements like obj = intvar;.

19. If objA is in class A, and objB is in class B, and you want to say objA = objB;, and you want the conversion routine to go in class A, what type of conversion routine might you use?

20. True or false: The compiler won't object if you overload the * operator to perform division.

21. In a UML class diagram, an association arises whenever

    a. two classes are in the same program.

    b. one class is descended from another.

    c. two classes use the same global variable.

    d. one class calls a member function in the other class.

22. In the UML, member data items are called _____ and member functions are called _____.

23. True or false: rectangles that symbolize classes have rounded corners.

24. Navigability from class A to class B means that

    a. an object of class A can call an operation in an object of class B.

    b. there is a relationship between class A and class B.

    c. objects can go from class A to class B.

    d. messages from class B are received by class A.

Exercises

Answers to starred exercises can be found in Appendix G.

*1. To the Distance class in the ENGLPLUS program in this chapter, add an overloaded - operator that subtracts two distances. It should allow statements like dist3= dist1-dist2;. Assume that the operator will never be used to subtract a larger number from a smaller one (that is, negative distances are not allowed).

*2. Write a program that substitutes an overloaded += operator for the overloaded + operator in the STRPLUS program in this chapter. This operator should allow statements like

    s1 += s2;

    where s2 is added (concatenated) to s1 and the result is left in s1. The operator should also permit the results of the operation to be used in other calculations, as in

    s3 = s1 += s2;

*3. Modify the time class from Exercise 3 in Chapter 6 so that instead of a function add_time() it uses the overloaded + operator to add two times. Write a program to test this class.

*4. Create a class Int based on Exercise 1 in Chapter 6. Overload four integer arithmetic operators (+, -, *, and /) so that they operate on objects of type Int. If the result of any such arithmetic operation exceeds the normal range of ints (in a 32-bit environment)—from 2,147,483,648 to -2,147,483,647—have the operator print a warning and terminate the program. Such a data type might be useful where mistakes caused by arithmetic overflow are unacceptable. Hint: To facilitate checking for overflow, perform the calculations using type long double. Write a program to test this class.

5. Augment the time class referred to in Exercise 3 to include overloaded increment (++) and decrement (--) operators that operate in both prefix and postfix notation and return values. Add statements to main() to test these operators.

6. Add to the time class of Exercise 5 the ability to subtract two time values using the overloaded (-) operator, and to multiply a time value by a number of type float, using the overloaded (*) operator.

7. Modify the fraction class in the four-function fraction calculator from Exercise 11 in Chapter 6 so that it uses overloaded operators for addition, subtraction, multiplication, and division. (Remember the rules for fraction arithmetic in Exercise 12 in Chapter 3, "Loops and Decisions.") Also overload the == and != comparison operators, and use them to exit from the loop if the user enters 0/1, 0/1 for the values of the two input fractions. You may want to modify the lowterms() function so that it returns the value of its argument reduced to lowest terms. This makes it more useful in the arithmetic functions, where it can be applied just before the answer is returned.

8. Modify the bMoney class from Exercise 12 in Chapter 7, "Arrays and Strings," to include the following arithmetic operations, performed with overloaded operators:

```
bMoney = bMoney + bMoney
bMoney = bMoney - bMoney
bMoney = bMoney * long double   (price per widget times number of widgets)
long double = bMoney / bMoney   (total price divided by price per widget)
bMoney = bMoney / long double   (total price divided by number of widgets)
```

Notice that the / operator is overloaded twice. The compiler can distinguish between the two usages because the arguments are different. Remember that it's easy to perform arithmetic operations on bMoney objects by performing the same operation on their long double data.

Make sure the main() program asks the user to enter two money strings and a floating-point number. It should then carry out all five operations and display the results. This should happen in a loop, so the user can enter more numbers if desired.

Some money operations don't make sense: bMoney * bMoney doesn't represent anything real, since there is no such thing as square money; and you can't add bMoney to long double (what's dollars plus widgets?). To make it impossible to compile such illegal operations, don't include conversion operators for bMoney to long double or long double to bMoney. If you do, and you write an expression like

```
bmon2 = bmon1 + widgets;  // doesn't make sense
```

then the compiler will automatically convert widgets to bMoney and carry out the addition. Without them, the compiler will flag such conversions as errors, making it easier to catch conceptual mistakes. Also, make any conversion constructors explicit.

There are some other plausible money operations that we don't yet know how to perform with overloaded operators, since they require an object on the right side of the operator but not the left:

```
long double * bMoney  // can't do this yet: bMoney only on right
long double / bMoney  // can't do this yet: bMoney only on right
```

We'll learn how to handle this situation when we discuss friend functions in Chapter 11.

9. Augment the safearay class in the ARROVER3 program in this chapter so that the user can specify both the upper and lower bound of the array (indexes running from 100 to 200, for example). Have the overloaded subscript operator check the index each time the array is accessed to ensure that it is not out of bounds. You'll need to add a two-argument constructor that specifies the upper and lower bounds. Since we have not yet learned how to allocate memory dynamically, the member data will still be an array that starts at 0 and runs up to 99, but perhaps you can map the indexes for the safearay into different indexes in the real int array. For example, if the client selects a range from 100 to 175, you could map this into the range from arr[0] to arr[75].

10. For math buffs only: Create a class Polar that represents the points on the plain as polar coordinates (radius and angle). Create an overloaded +operator for addition of two Polar quantities. "Adding" two points on the plain can be accomplished by adding their X coordinates and then adding their Y coordinates. This gives the X and Y coordinates of the "answer." Thus you'll need to convert two sets of polar coordinates to rectangular coordinates, add them, then convert the resulting rectangular representation back to polar.

1. Remember the sterling structure? We saw it in Exercise 10 in Chapter 2, "C++ Programming Basics," and in Exercise 11 in Chapter 5, among other places. Turn it into a class, with pounds (type long), shillings (type int), and pence (type int) data items. Create the following member functions:

- no-argument constructor
- one-argument constructor, taking type double (for converting from decimal pounds)
- three-argument constructor, taking pounds, shillings, and pence
- getSterling() to get an amount in pounds, shillings, and pence from the user, format £9.19.11
- putSterling() to display an amount in pounds, shillings, and pence, format £9.19.11
- addition (sterling + sterling) using overloaded + operator
- subtraction (sterling - sterling) using overloaded - operator
- multiplication (sterling * double) using overloaded * operator
- division (sterling / sterling) using overloaded / operator
- division (sterling / double) using overloaded / operator
- operator double (to convert to double)

To perform arithmetic, you could (for example) add each object's data separately: Add the pence, carry, add the shillings, carry, and so on. However, it's easier to use the conversion operator to convert both sterling objects to type double, perform the arithmetic on the doubles, and convert back to sterling. Thus the overloaded + operator looks like this:

8
OPERATOR OVERLOADING

```
sterling sterling::operator + (sterling s2)
   {
   return sterling( double(sterling(pounds, shillings, pence))
                   + double(s2) );
   }
```

This creates two temporary double variables, one derived from the object of which the function is a member, and one derived from the argument s2. These double variables are then added, and the result is converted back to sterling and returned.

Notice that we use a different philosophy with the sterling class than with the bMoney class. With sterling we use conversion operators, thus giving up the ability to catch illegal math operations but gaining simplicity in writing the overloaded math operators.

12. Write a program that incorporates both the bMoney class from Exercise 8 and the sterling class from Exercise 11. Write conversion operators to convert between bMoney and sterling, assuming that one pound (£1.0.0) equals fifty dollars ($50.00). This was the approximate exchange rate in the 19th century when the British Empire was at its height and the pounds-shillings-pence format was in use. Write a main() program that allows the user to enter an amount in either currency and then converts it to the other currency and displays the result. Minimize any modifications to the existing bMoney and sterling classes.

Inheritance

IN THIS CHAPTER

Inheritance is probably the most powerful feature of object-oriented programming, after classes themselves. Inheritance is the process of creating new classes, called *derived classes*, from existing or *base classes*. The derived class inherits all the capabilities of the base class but can add embellishments and refinements of its own. The base class is unchanged by this process. The inheritance relationship is shown in Figure 9.1.

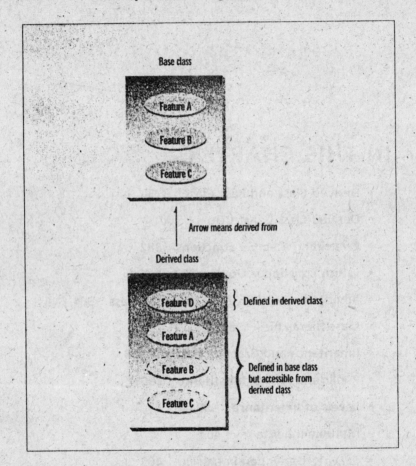

FIGURE 9.1
Inheritance.

The arrow in Figure 9.1 goes in the opposite direction of what you might expect. If it pointed down we would label it *inheritance*. However, the more common approach is to point the arrow up, from the derived class to the base class, and to think of it as a "derived from" arrow.

Inheritance is an essential part of OOP. Its big payoff is that it permits code *reusability*. Once a base class is written and debugged, it need not be touched again, but, using inheritance, can nevertheless be adapted to work in different situations. Reusing existing code saves time and money and increases a program's reliability. Inheritance can also help in the original conceptualization of a programming problem, and in the overall design of the program.

An important result of reusability is the ease of distributing class libraries. A programmer can use a class created by another person or company, and, without modifying it, derive other classes from it that are suited to particular situations.

We'll examine these features of inheritance in more detail after we've seen some specific instances of inheritance at work.

Derived Class and Base Class

Remember the COUNTPP3 example from Chapter 8, "Operator Overloading"? This program used a class Counter as a general-purpose counter variable. A count could be initialized to 0 or to a specified number with constructors, incremented with the ++ operator, and read with the .get_count() operator.

Let's suppose that we have worked long and hard to make the Counter class operate just the way we want, and we're pleased with the results, except for one thing. We really need a way to decrement the count. Perhaps we're counting people entering a bank, and we want to increment the count when they come in and decrement it when they go out, so that the count represents the number of people in the bank at any moment.

We could insert a decrement routine directly into the source code of the Counter class. However, there are several reasons that we might not want to do this. First, the Counter class works very well and has undergone many hours of testing and debugging. (Of course that's an exaggeration in this case, but it would be true in a larger and more complex class.) If we start fooling around with the source code for Counter, the testing process will need to be carried out again, and of course we may foul something up and spend hours debugging code that worked fine before we modified it.

In some situations there might be another reason for not modifying the Counter class: We might not have access to its source code, especially if it was distributed as part of a class library. (We'll discuss this issue further in Chapter 13, "Multifile Programs.")

To avoid these problems we can use inheritance to create a new class based on Counter, without modifying Counter itself. Here's the listing for COUNTEN, which includes a new class, CountDn, that adds a decrement operator to the Counter class:

9

INHERITANCE

```
// counten.cpp
// inheritance with Counter class
#include <iostream>
using namespace std;
////////////////////////////////////////////////////////////////
class Counter                              //base class
    {
    protected:                             //NOTE: not private
        unsigned int count;                //count
    public:
        Counter() : count(0)               //no-arg constructor
            { }
        Counter(int c) : count(c)          //1-arg constructor
            { }
        unsigned int get_count() const     //return count
            { return count; }
        Counter operator ++ ()             //incr count (prefix)
            { return Counter(++count); }
    };
////////////////////////////////////////////////////////////////
class CountDn : public Counter             //derived class
    {
    public:
        Counter operator -- ()             //decr count (prefix)
            { return Counter(--count); }
    };
////////////////////////////////////////////////////////////////
int main()
    {
    CountDn c1;                            //c1 of class CountDn

    cout << "\nc1=" << c1.get_count();     //display c1

    ++c1; ++c1; ++c1;                      //increment c1, 3 times
    cout << "\nc1=" << c1.get_count();     //display it

    --c1; --c1;                            //decrement c1, twice
    cout << "\nc1=" << c1.get_count();     //display it
    cout << endl;
    return 0;
    }
```

The listing starts off with the Counter class, which (with one small exception, which we'll look at later) has not changed since its appearance in COUNTPP3. Notice that, for simplicity, we haven't modeled this program on the POSTFIX program, which incorporated the second overloaded ++ operator to provide postfix notation.

Specifying the Derived Class

Following the Counter class in the listing is the specification for a new class, CountDn. This class incorporates a new function, operator--(), which decrements the count. However—and here's the key point—the new CountDn class inherits all the features of the Counter class. CountDn doesn't need a constructor or the get_count() or operator++() functions, because these already exist in Counter.

The first line of CountDn specifies that it is derived from Counter:

```
class CountDn : public Counter
```

Here we use a single colon (not the double colon used for the scope resolution operator), followed by the keyword public and the name of the base class Counter. This sets up the relationship between the classes. This line says that CountDn *is derived from the base class* Counter. (We'll explore the effect of the keyword public later.)

Generalization in UML Class Diagrams

In the UML, inheritance is called *generalization*, because the parent class is a more general form of the child class. Or to put it another way, the child is more specific version of the parent. (We introduced the UML in Chapter 1, "The Big Picture," and encountered class diagrams in Chapter 8, "Operator Overloading.") The generalization in the COUNTEN program is shown in Figure 9.2.

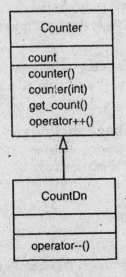

FIGURE 9.2
UML class diagram for COUNTEN.

In UML class diagrams, generalization is indicated by a triangular arrowhead on the line connecting the parent and child classes. Remember that the arrow means *inherited from* or *derived from* or *is a more specific version of*. The direction of the arrow emphasizes that the derived class *refers to* functions and data in the base class, while the base class has no access to the derived class.

Notice that we've added attributes (member data) and operations (member functions) to the classes in the diagram. The top area holds the class title, the middle area holds attributes, and the bottom area is for operations.

Accessing Base Class Members

An important topic in inheritance is knowing when a member function in the base class can be used by objects of the derived class. This is called *accessibility*. Let's see how the compiler handles the accessibility issue in the COUNTEN example.

Substituting Base Class Constructors

In the main() part of COUNTEN we create an object of class CountDn:

```
CountDn c1;
```

This causes c1 to be created as an object of class CountDn and initialized to 0. But wait—how is this possible? There is no constructor in the CountDn class specifier, so what entity carries out the initialization? It turns out that—at least under certain circumstances—if you don't specify a constructor, the derived class will use an appropriate constructor from the base class. In COUNTEN there's no constructor in CountDn, so the compiler uses the no-argument constructor from Count.

This flexibility on the part of the compiler—using one function because another isn't available—appears regularly in inheritance situations. Generally, the substitution is what you want, but sometimes it can be unnerving.

Substituting Base Class Member Functions

The object c1 of the CountDn class also uses the operator++() and get_count() functions from the Counter class. The first is used to increment c1:

```
++c1;
```

The second is used to display the count in c1:

```
cout << "\nc1=" << c1.get_count();
```

Again the compiler, not finding these functions in the class of which c1 is a member, uses member functions from the base class.

Output of COUNTEN

In main() we increment c1 three times, print out the resulting value, decrement c1 twice, and finally print out its value again. Here's the output:

```
c1=0    ←——— after initialization
c1=3    ←——— after ++c1, ++c1, ++c1
c1=1    ←——— after --c1, --c1
```

The ++ operator, the constructors, the get_count() function in the Counter class, and the -- operator in the CountDn class all work with objects of type CountDn.

The protected Access Specifier

We have increased the functionality of a class without modifying it. Well, almost without modifying it. Let's look at the single change we made to the Counter class.

The data in the classes we've looked at so far, including count in the Counter class in the earlier COUNTPP3 program, have used the private access specifier.

In the Counter class in COUNTEN, count is given a new specifier: protected. What does this do?

Let's first review what we know about the access specifiers private and public. A member function of a class can always access class members, whether they are public or private. But an object declared externally can only invoke (using the dot operator, for example) public members of the class. It's not allowed to use private members. For instance, suppose an object objA is an instance of class A, and function funcA() is a member function of A. Then in main() (or any other function that is not a member of A) the statement

```
objA.funcA();
```

will not be legal unless funcA() is public. The object objA cannot invoke private members of class A. Private members are, well, *private*. This is shown in Figure 9.3.

This is all we need to know if we don't use inheritance. With inheritance, however, there is a whole raft of additional possibilities. The question that concerns us at the moment is, can member functions of the derived class access members of the base class? In other words, can operator--() in CountDn access count in Counter? The answer is that member functions can access members of the base class if the members are public, or if they are protected. They can't access private members.

We don't want to make count public, since that would allow it to be accessed by any function anywhere in the program and eliminate the advantages of data hiding. A protected member, on the other hand, can be accessed by member functions in its own class or—and here's the key—in any class derived from its own class. It can't be accessed from functions outside these classes, such as main(). This is just what we want. The situation is shown in Figure 9.4.

9

INHERITANCE

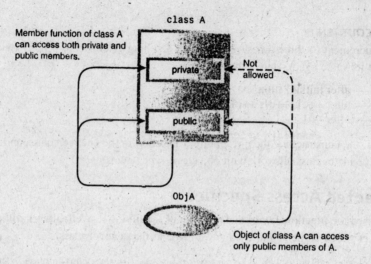

Member function of class A
can access both private and
public members.

class A

private

Not
allowed

public

ObjA

Object of class A can access
only public members of A.

FIGURE 9.3

Access specifiers without inheritance.

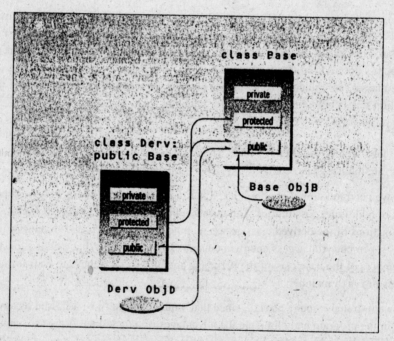

class Pase

private

protected

public

class Derv:
public Base

Base ObjB

private

protected

public

Derv ObjD

FIGURE 9.4

Access specifiers with inheritance.

Table 9.1 summarizes the situation in a different way.

TABLE 9.1 Inheritance and Accessibility

Access Specifier	Accessible from Own Class	Accessible from Derived Class	Accessible from Objects Outside Class
public	yes	yes	yes
protected	yes	yes	no
private	yes	no	no

The moral is that if you are writing a class that you suspect might be used, at any point in the future, as a base class for other classes, then any member data that the derived classes might need to access should be made protected rather than private. This ensures that the class is "inheritance ready."

Dangers of protected

You should know that there's a disadvantage to making class members protected. Say you've written a class library, which you're distributing to the public. Any programmer who buys this library can access protected members of your classes simply by deriving other classes from them. This makes protected members considerably less secure than private members. To avoid corrupted data, it's often safer to force derived classes to access data in the base class using only public functions in the base class, just as ordinary main() programs must do. Using the protected specifier leads to simpler programming, so we rely on it—perhaps a bit too much—in the examples in this book. You'll need to weigh the advantages of protected against its disadvantages in your own programs.

Base Class Unchanged

Remember that, even if other classes have been derived from it, the base class remains unchanged. In the main() part of COUNTEN, we could define objects of type Counter:

```
Counter c2;        ←——— object of base class
```

Such objects would behave just as they would if CountDn didn't exist.

Note also that inheritance doesn't work in reverse. The base class and its objects don't know anything about any classes derived from the base class. In this example that means that objects of class Counter, such as c2, can't use the operator--() function in CountDn. If you want a counter that you can decrement, it must be of class CountDn, not Counter.

Other Terms

In some languages the base class is called the *superclass* and the derived class is called the *subclass*. Some writers also refer to the base class as the *parent* and the derived class as the *child*.

Derived Class Constructors

There's a potential glitch in the COUNTEN program. What happens if we want to initialize a CountDn object to a value? Can the one-argument constructor in Counter be used? The answer is no. As we saw in COUNTEN, the compiler will substitute a no-argument constructor from the base class, but it draws the line at more complex constructors. To make such a definition work we must write a new set of constructors for the derived class. This is shown in the COUNTEN2 program.

```cpp
// counten2.cpp
// constructors in derived class
#include <iostream>
using namespace std;
/////////////////////////////////////////////////////////////////
class Counter
    {
    protected:                                  //NOTE: not private
        unsigned int count;                     //count
    public:
        Counter() : count()                     //constructor, no args
            { }
        Counter(int c) : count(c)               //constructor, one arg
            { }
        unsigned int get_count() const          //return count
            { return count; }
        Counter operator ++ ()                  //incr count (prefix)
            { return Counter(++count); }
    };
/////////////////////////////////////////////////////////////////
class CountDn : public Counter
    {
    public:
        CountDn() : Counter()                   //constructor, no args
            { }
        CountDn(int c) : Counter(c)             //constructor, 1 arg
            { }
        CountDn operator -- ()                  //decr count (prefix)
            { return CountDn(--count); }
    };
/////////////////////////////////////////////////////////////////
int main()
    {
```

```
        CountDn c1;                             //class CountDn
        CountDn c2(100);

        cout << "\nc1=" << c1.get_count();       //display
        cout << "\nc2=" << c2.get_count();       //display

        ++c1; ++c1; ++c1;                        //increment c1
        cout << "\nc1=" << c1.get_count();       //display it

        --c2; --c2;                              //decrement c2
        cout << "\nc2=" << c2.get_count();       //display it

        CountDn c3 = --c2;                       //create c3 from c2
        cout << "\nc3=" << c3.get_count();       //display c3
        cout << endl;
        return 0;
        }
```

This program uses two new constructors in the CountDn class. Here is the no-argument constructor:

```
CountDn() : Counter()
   { }
```

This constructor has an unfamiliar feature: the function name following the colon. This construction causes the CountDn() constructor to call the Counter() constructor in the base class. In main(), when we say

```
CountDn c1;
```

the compiler will create an object of type CountDn and then call the CountDn constructor to initialize it. This constructor will in turn call the Counter constructor, which carries out the work. The CountDn() constructor could add additional statements of its own, but in this case it doesn't need to, so the function body between the braces is empty.

Calling a constructor from the initialization list may seem odd, but it makes sense. You want to initialize any variables, whether they're in the derived class or the base class, before any statements in either the derived or base-class constructors are executed. By calling the base-class constructor before the derived-class constructor starts to execute, we accomplish this.

The statement

```
CountDn c2(100);
```

in main() uses the one-argument constructor in CountDn. This constructor also calls the corresponding one-argument constructor in the base class:

```
CountDn(int c) : Counter(c)        ←——— argument c is passed to Counter
   { }
```

9

INHERITANCE

This construction causes the argument c to be passed from CountDn() to Counter(), where it is used to initialize the object.

In main(), after initializing the c1 and c2 objects, we increment one and decrement the other and then print the results. The one-argument constructor is also used in an assignment statement.

```
CountDn c3 = --c2;
```

Overriding Member Functions

You can use member functions in a derived class that override—that is, have the same name as—those in the base class. You might want to do this so that calls in your program work the same way for objects of both base and derived classes.

Here's an example based on the STAKARAY program from Chapter 7, "Arrays and Strings." That program modeled a stack, a simple data storage device. It allowed you to push integers onto the stack and pop them off. However, STAKARAY had a potential flaw. If you tried to push too many items onto the stack, the program might bomb, since data would be placed in memory beyond the end of the st[] array. Or if you tried to pop too many items, the results would be meaningless, since you would be reading data from memory locations outside the array.

To cure these defects we've created a new class, Stack2, derived from Stack. Objects of Stack2 behave in exactly the same way as those of Stack, except that you will be warned if you attempt to push too many items on the stack or if you try to pop an item from an empty stack. Here's the listing for STAKEN:

```
// staken.cpp
// overloading functions in base and derived classes
#include <iostream>
using namespace std;
#include <process.h>              //for exit()
/////////////////////////////////////////////////////////////////
class Stack
    {
    protected:                    //NOTE: can't be private
        enum { MAX = 3 };         //size of stack array
        int st[MAX];              //stack: array of integers
        int top;                  //index to top of stack
    public:
        Stack()                   //constructor
            { top = -1; }
        void push(int var)        //put number on stack
            { st[++top] = var; }
        int pop()                 //take number off stack
            { return st[top--]; }
```

```
   };
////////////////////////////////////////////////////////////////////
class Stack2 : public Stack
   {
   public:
      void push(int var)              //put number on stack
         {
         if(top >= MAX-1)             //error if stack full
            { cout << "\nError: stack is full"; exit(1); }
         Stack::push(var);            //call push() in Stack class
         }
      int pop()                       //take number off stack
         {
         if(top < 0)                  //error if stack empty
            { cout << "\nError: stack is empty\n"; exit(1); }
         return Stack::pop();         //call pop() in Stack class
         }
   };
////////////////////////////////////////////////////////////////////
int main()
   {
   Stack2 s1;

   s1.push(11);                       //push some values onto stack
   s1.push(22);
   s1.push(33);

   cout << endl << s1.pop();          //pop some values from stack
   cout << endl << s1.pop();
   cout << endl << s1.pop();
   cout << endl << s1.pop();          //oops, popped one too many...
   cout << endl;
   return 0;
   }
```

In this program the Stack class is just the same as it was in the STAKARAY program, except that the data members have been made protected.

Which Function Is Used?

The Stack2 class contains two functions, push() and pop(). These functions have the same names, and the same argument and return types, as the functions in Stack. When we call these functions from main(), in statements like

```
s1.push(11);
```

9

INHERITANCE

how does the compiler know which of the two push() functions to use? Here's the rule: When the same function exists in both the base class and the derived class, the function in the derived class will be executed. (This is true of objects of the derived class. Objects of the base class don't know anything about the derived class and will always use the base class functions.) We say that the derived class function *overrides* the base class function. So in the preceding statement, since s1 is an object of class Stack2, the push() function in Stack2 will be executed, not the one in Stack.

The push() function in Stack2 checks to see whether the stack is full. If it is, it displays an error message and causes the program to exit. If it isn't, it calls the push() function in Stack. Similarly, the pop() function in Stack2 checks to see whether the stack is empty. If it is, it prints an error message and exits; otherwise, it calls the pop() function in Stack.

In main() we push three items onto the stack, but we pop four. The last pop elicits an error message

```
33
22
11
Error: stack is empty
```

and terminates the program.

Scope Resolution with Overridden Functions

How do push() and pop() in Stack2 access push() and pop() in Stack? They use the scope resolution operator, ::, in the statements

```
Stack::push(var);
```

and

```
return Stack::pop();
```

These statements specify that the push() and pop() functions in Stack are to be called. Without the scope resolution operator, the compiler would think the push() and pop() functions in Stack2 were calling themselves, which—in this case—would lead to program failure. Using the scope resolution operator allows you to specify exactly what class the function is a member of.

Inheritance in the English Distance Class

Here's a somewhat more complex example of inheritance. So far in this book the various programs that used the English Distance class assumed that the distances to be represented would always be positive. This is usually the case in architectural drawings. However, if we were measuring, say, the water level of the Pacific Ocean as the tides varied, we might want to be able to represent negative feet-and-inches quantities. (Tide levels below mean-lower-low-water are called *minus tides*; they prompt clam diggers to take advantage of the larger area of exposed beach.)

Let's derive a new class from `Distance`. This class will add a single data item to our feet-and-inches measurements: a sign, which can be positive or negative. When we add the sign, we'll also need to modify the member functions so they can work with signed distances. Here's the listing for ENGLEN:

```cpp
// englen.cpp
// inheritance using English Distances
#include <iostream>
using namespace std;
enum posneg { pos, neg };            //for sign in DistSign
/////////////////////////////////////////////////////////////////
class Distance                       //English Distance class
    {
    protected:                       //NOTE: can't be private
        int feet;
        float inches;
    public:                          //no-arg constructor
        Distance() : feet(0), inches(0.0)
            { }                      //2-arg constructor)
        Distance(int ft, float in) : feet(ft), inches(in)
            { }
        void getdist()               //get length from user
            {
            cout << "\nEnter feet: ";  cin >> feet;
            cout << "Enter inches: ";  cin >> inches;
            }
        void showdist() const        //display distance
            { cout << feet << "\'-" << inches << '\"'; }
    };
/////////////////////////////////////////////////////////////////
class DistSign : public Distance   //adds sign to Distance
    {
    private:
        posneg sign;                 //sign is pos or neg
    public:
                                     //no-arg constructor
                                     //call base constructor
        DistSign() : Distance()      //set the sign to +
            { sign = pos; }
```

```
                                    //2- or 3-arg constructor
    DistSign(int ft, float in, posneg sg=pos) :
            Distance(ft, in)       //call base constructor
        { sign = sg; }             //set the sign

    void getdist()                 //get length from user
        {
        Distance::getdist();       //call base getdist()
        char ch;                   //get sign from user
        cout << "Enter sign (+ or -): ";  cin >> ch;
        sign = (ch=='+') ? pos : neg;
        }
    void showdist() const          //display distance
        {
        cout << ( (sign==pos) ? "(+)" : "(-)" );  //show sign
        Distance::showdist();                     //ft and in
        }
    };
////////////////////////////////////////////////////////////////
int main()
    {
    DistSign alpha;                    //no-arg constructor
    alpha.getdist();                   //get alpha from user

    DistSign beta(11, 6.25);           //2-arg constructor

    DistSign gamma(100, 5.5, neg);     //3-arg constructor

                                       //display all distances
    cout << "\nalpha = ";  alpha.showdist();
    cout << "\nbeta = ";   beta.showdist();
    cout << "\ngamma = ";  gamma.showdist();
    cout << endl;
    return 0;
    }
```

Here the DistSign class adds the functionality to deal with signed numbers. The Distance class in this program is just the same as in previous programs, except that the data is protected. Actually in this case it could be private, because none of the derived-class functions accesses it. However, it's safer to make it protected so that a derived-class function could access it if necessary.

Operation of ENGLEN

The `main()` program declares three different signed distances. It gets a value for `alpha` from the user and initializes `beta` to (+)11'–6.25" and `gamma` to (–)100'–5.5". In the output we use parentheses around the sign to avoid confusion with the hyphen separating feet and inches. Here's some sample output:

```
Enter feet: 6
Enter inches: 2.5
Enter sign (+ or -): -

alpha = (-)6'-2.5"
beta = (+)11'-6.25"
gamma = (-)100'-5.5"
```

The `DistSign` class is derived from `Distance`. It adds a single variable, `sign`, which is of type `posneg`. The `sign` variable will hold the sign of the distance. The `posneg` type is defined in an enum statement to have two possible values: `pos` and `neg`.

Constructors in DistSign

`DistSign` has two constructors, mirroring those in `Distance`. The first takes no arguments, the second takes either two or three arguments. The third, optional, argument in the second constructor is a sign, either `pos` or `neg`. Its default value is `pos`. These constructors allow us to define variables (objects) of type `DistSign` in several ways.

Both constructors in `DistSign` call the corresponding constructors in `Distance` to set the feet-and-inches values. They then set the `sign` variable. The no-argument constructor always sets it to `pos`. The second constructor sets it to `pos` if no third-argument value has been provided, or to a value (`pos` or `neg`) if the argument is specified.

The arguments `ft` and `in`, passed from `main()` to the second constructor in `DistSign`, are simply forwarded to the constructor in `Distance`.

Member Functions in DistSign

Adding a sign to `Distance` has consequences for both of its member functions. The `getdist()` function in the `DistSign` class must ask the user for the sign as well as for feet-and-inches values, and the `showdist()` function must display the sign along with the feet and inches. These functions call the corresponding functions in `Distance`, in the lines

```
Distance::getdist();
```

and

```
Distance::showdist();
```

These calls get and display the feet and inches values. The body of getdist() and showdist() in DistSign then go on to deal with the sign.

Abetting Inheritance

C++ is designed to make it efficient to create a derived class. Where we want to use parts of the base class, it's easy to do so, whether these parts are data, constructors, or member functions. Then we add the functionality we need to create the new improved class. Notice that in ENGLEN we didn't need to duplicate any code; instead we made use of the appropriate functions in the base class.

Class Hierarchies

In the examples so far in this chapter, inheritance has been used to add functionality to an existing class. Now let's look at an example where inheritance is used for a different purpose: as part of the original design of a program.

Our example models a database of employees of a widget company. We've simplified the situation so that only three kinds of employees are represented. Managers manage, scientists perform research to develop better widgets, and laborers operate the dangerous widget-stamping presses.

The database stores a name and an employee identification number for all employees, no matter what their category. However, for managers, it also stores their titles and golf club dues. For scientists, it stores the number of scholarly articles they have published. Laborers need no additional data beyond their names and numbers.

Our example program starts with a base class employee. This class handles the employee's last name and employee number. From this class three other classes are derived: manager, scientist, and laborer. The manager and scientist classes contain additional information about these categories of employee, and member functions to handle this information, as shown in Figure 9.5.

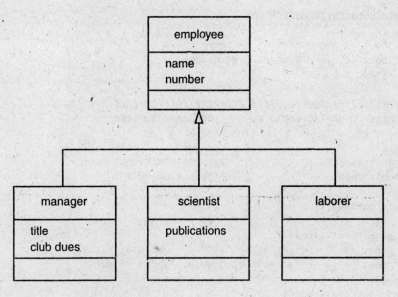

FIGURE 9.5
UML class diagram for EMPLOY.

Here's the listing for EMPLOY:

```
// employ.cpp
// models employee database using inheritance
#include <iostream>
using namespace std;
const int LEN = 80;                  //maximum length of names
//////////////////////////////////////////////////////////////////
class employee                       //employee class
   {
   private:
      char name[LEN];                //employee name
      unsigned long number;          //employee number
   public:
      void getdata()
         {
         cout << "\n   Enter last name: "; cin >> name;
         cout << "   Enter number: ";      cin >> number;
         }
```

```
      void putdata() const
         {
         cout << "\n   Name: " << name;
         cout << "\n   Number: " << number;
         }
   };
/////////////////////////////////////////////////////////////////
class manager : public employee      //management class
   {
   private:
      char title[LEN];                //"vice-president" etc.
      double dues;                    //golf club dues
   public:
      void getdata()
         {
         employee::getdata();
         cout << "   Enter title: ";           cin >> title;
         cout << "   Enter golf club dues: "; cin >> dues;
         }
      void putdata() const
         {
         employee::putdata();
         cout << "\n   Title: " << title;
         cout << "\n   Golf club dues: " << dues;
         }
   };
/////////////////////////////////////////////////////////////////
class scientist : public employee  //scientist class
   {
   private:
      int pubs;                       //number of publications
   public:
      void getdata()
         {
         employee::getdata();
         cout << "   Enter number of pubs: "; cin >> pubs;
         }
      void putdata() const
         {
         employee::putdata();
         cout << "\n   Number of publications: " << pubs;
         }
   };
/////////////////////////////////////////////////////////////////
class laborer : public employee      //laborer class
   {
```

```
    };
    //////////////////////////////////////////////////////////////////
int main()
    {
    manager m1, m2;
    scientist s1;
    laborer l1;

    cout << endl;              //get data for several employees
    cout << "\nEnter data for manager 1";
    m1.getdata();

    cout << "\nEnter data for manager 2";
    m2.getdata();

    cout << "\nEnter data for scientist 1";
    s1.getdata();

    cout << "\nEnter data for laborer 1";
    l1.getdata();
                               //display data for several employees
    cout << "\nData on manager 1";
    m1.putdata();

    cout << "\nData on manager 2";
    m2.putdata();

    cout << "\nData on scientist 1";
    s1.putdata();

    cout << "\nData on laborer 1";
    l1.putdata();
    cout << endl;
    return 0;
    }
```

The main() part of the program declares four objects of different classes: two managers, a scientist, and a laborer. (Of course many more employees of each type could be defined, but the output would become rather large.) It then calls the getdata() member functions to obtain information about each employee, and the putdata() function to display this information. Here's a sample interaction with EMPLOY. First the user supplies the data.

```
Enter data for manager 1
    Enter last name: Wainsworth
    Enter number: 10
    Enter title: President
```

```
      Enter golf club dues: 1000000
Enter data on manager 2
   Enter last name: Bradley
   Enter number: 124
   Enter title: Vice-President
   Enter golf club dues: 500000
Enter data for scientist 1
   Enter last name: Hauptman-Frenglish
   Enter number: 234234
   Enter number of pubs: 999
Enter data for laborer 1
   Enter last name: Jones
   Enter number: 6546544
```

The program then plays it back.

```
Data on manager 1
   Name: Wainsworth
   Number: 10
   Title: President
   Golf club dues: 1000000
Data on manager 2
   Name: Bradley
   Number: 124
   Title: Vice-President
   Golf club dues: 500000
Data on scientist 1
   Name: Hauptman-Frenglish
   Number: 234234
   Number of publications: 999
Data on laborer 1
   Name: Jones
   Number: 6546544
```

A more sophisticated program would use an array or some other container to arrange the data so that a large number of employee objects could be accommodated.

"Abstract" Base Class

Notice that we don't define any objects of the base class employee. We use this as a general class whose sole purpose is to act as a base from which other classes are derived.

The laborer class operates identically to the employee class, since it contains no additional data or functions. It may seem that the laborer class is unnecessary, but by making it a separate class we emphasize that all classes are descended from the same source, employee. Also, if in the future we decided to modify the laborer class, we would not need to change the declaration for employee.

Classes used only for deriving other classes, as employee is in EMPLOY, are sometimes loosely called *abstract classes*, meaning that no actual instances (objects) of this class are created. However, the term *abstract* has a more precise definition that we'll look at in Chapter 11, "Virtual Functions."

Constructors and Member Functions

There are no constructors in either the base or derived classes, so the compiler creates objects of the various classes automatically when it encounters definitions like

```
manager m1, m2;
```

using the default constructor for manager calling the default constructor for employee.

The getdata() and putdata() functions in employee accept a name and number from the user and display a name and number. Functions also called getdata() and putdata() in the manager and scientist classes use the functions in employee, and also do their own work. In manager, the getdata() function asks the user for a title and the amount of golf club dues, and putdata() displays these values. In scientist, these functions handle the number of publications.

Inheritance and Graphics Shapes

In the CIRCLES program in Chapter 6, "Objects and Classes," we saw a program in which a class represented graphics circles that could be displayed on the screen. Of course, there are other kinds of shapes besides circles, such as squares and triangles. The very phrase "kinds of shapes" implies an inheritance relationship between something called a "shape" and specific kinds of shapes like circles and squares. We can use this relationship to make a program that is more robust and easier to understand than a program that treats different shapes as being unrelated.

In particular we'll make a shape class that's a base class (parent) of three derived classes: a circle class, a rect (for rectangle) class, and a tria (for triangle) class. As with other programs that use the Console Graphics Lite functions, you may need to read Appendix E, "Console Graphics Lite," and either Appendix C, "Microsoft Visual C++," or Appendix D, "Borland C++Builder" for your specific compiler to learn how to build the graphics files into your program. Here's the listing for MULTSHAP:

```
// multshap.cpp
// balls, rects, and polygons
#include "msoftcon.h"          //for graphics functions
///////////////////////////////////////////////////////////////
class shape                    //base class
```

```
    {
. protected:
    int xCo, yCo;              //coordinates of shape
    color fillcolor;           //color
    fstyle fillstyle;          //fill pattern
public:                        //no-arg constructor
    shape() : xCo(0), yCo(0), fillcolor(cWHITE),
                                    fillstyle(SOLID_FILL)
        { }                    //4-arg constructor
    shape(int x, int y, color fc, fstyle fs) :
                xCo(x), yCo(y), fillcolor(fc), fillstyle(fs)
        { }
    void draw() const          //set color and fill style
        {
        set_color(fillcolor);
        set_fill_style(fillstyle);
        }
    };
/////////////////////////////////////////////////////////////////
class circle : public shape
    {
    private:
        int radius;            //(xCo, yCo) is center
    public:
        circle() : shape()     //no-arg constr
            { }
                               //5-arg constructor
        circle(int x, int y, int r, color fc, fstyle fs)
                    : shape(x, y, fc, fs), radius(r)
            { }
        void draw() const      //draw the circle
            {
            shape::draw();
            draw_circle(xCo, yCo, radius);
            }
    };
/////////////////////////////////////////////////////////////////
class rect : public shape
    {
    private:
        int width, height;     //(xCo, yCo) is upper-left corner
    public:
        rect() : shape(), height(0), width(0)   //no-arg ctor
            { }                                 //6-arg ctor
        rect(int x, int y, int h, int w, color fc, fstyle fs) .
                    shape(x, y, fc, fs), height(h), width(w)
```

```
            { }
      void draw() const          //draw the rectangle
         {
         shape::draw();
         draw_rectangle(xCo, yCo, xCo+width, yCo+height);
         set_color(cWHITE);     //draw diagonal
         draw_line(xCo, yCo, xCo+width, yCo+height);
         }
   };
////////////////////////////////////////////////////////////////
class tria : public shape
   {
   private:
      int height;              //(xCo, yCo) is tip of pyramid
   public:
      tria() : shape(), height(0) //no-arg constructor
         { }                      //5-arg constructor
      tria(int x, int y, int h, color fc, fstyle fs) :
                           shape(x, y, fc, fs), height(h)
         { }
      void draw() const          //draw the triangle
         {
         shape::draw();
         draw_pyramid(xCo, yCo, height);
         }
   };
/////////////////////////////////////////////////////////////////
int main()
   {
   init_graphics();              //initialize graphics system

   circle cir(40, 12, 5, cBLUE, X_FILL);        //create circle
   rect rec(12, 7, 10, 15, cRED, SOLID_FILL); //create rectangle
   tria tri(60, 7,  11, cGREEN, MEDIUM_FILL); //create triangle

   cir.draw();                   //draw all shapes
   rec.draw();
   tri.draw();
   set_cursor_pos(1, 25);        //lower-left corner
   return 0;
   }
```

When executed, this program produces three different shapes: a blue circle, a red rectangle, and a green triangle. Figure 9.6 shows the output of MULTSHAP.

9

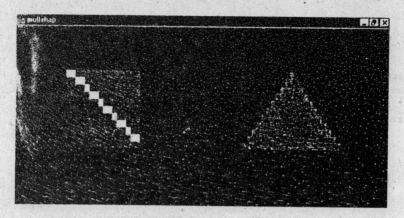

FIGURE 9.6
Output of the MULTSHAP program.

The characteristics that are common to all shapes, such as their location, color, and fill pattern, are placed in the shape class. Individual shapes have more specific attributes. A circle has a radius, for example, while a rectangle has a height and width. A draw() routine in shape handles the tasks specific to all shapes: setting their color and fill pattern. Overloaded draw() functions in the circle, rect, and tria classes take care of drawing their specific shapes once the color and pattern are determined.

As in the last example, the base class shape is an example of an abstract class, in that there is no meaning to instantiating an object of this class. What shape does a shape object display? The question doesn't make sense. Only a specific shape can display itself. The shape class exists only as a repository of attributes and actions that are common to all shapes.

Public and Private Inheritance

C++ provides a wealth of ways to fine-tune access to class members. One such access-control mechanism is the way derived classes are declared. Our examples so far have used publicly derived classes, with declarations like

```
class manager : public employee
```

which appeared in the EMPLOY example.

What is the effect of the public keyword in this statement, and what are the alternatives? Listen up: The keyword public specifies that objects of the derived class are able to access public member functions of the base class. The alternative is the keyword private. When this keyword is used, objects of the derived class cannot access public member functions of the base class. Since objects can never access private or protected members of a class, the result is that no member of the base class is accessible to objects of the derived class.

Access Combinations

There are so many possibilities for access that it's instructive to look at an example program that shows what works and what doesn't. Here's the listing for PUBPRIV:

```cpp
// pubpriv.cpp
// tests publicly- and privately-derived classes
#include <iostream>
using namespace std;
/////////////////////////////////////////////////////////////////
class A                    //base class
   {
   private:
      int privdataA;        //(functions have the same access
   protected:               //rules as the data shown here)
      int protdataA;
   public:
      int pubdataA;
   };
/////////////////////////////////////////////////////////////////
class B : public A         //publicly-derived class
   {
   public:
      void funct()
         {
         int a;
         a = privdataA;   //error: not accessible
         a = protdataA;   //OK
         a = pubdataA;    //OK
         }
   };
/////////////////////////////////////////////////////////////////
class C : private A        //privately-derived class
   {
   public:
      void funct()
         {
         int a;
         a = privdataA;   //error: not accessible
         a = protdataA;   //OK
         a = pubdataA;    //OK
         }
   };
/////////////////////////////////////////////////////////////////
int main()
   {
   int a;
```

```
B objB;
a = objB.privdataA;    //error: not accessible
a = objB.protdataA;    //error: not accessible
a = objB.pubdataA;     //OK (A public to B)

C objC;
a = objC.privdataA;    //error: not accessible
a = objC.protdataA;    //error: not accessible
a = objC.pubdataA;     //error: not accessible (A private to C)
return 0;
}
```

The program specifies a base class, A, with private, protected, and public data items. Two classes, B and C, are derived from A. B is publicly derived and C is privately derived.

As we've seen before, functions in the derived classes can access protected and public data in the base class. Objects of the derived classes cannot access private or protected members of the base class.

What's new is the difference between publicly derived and privately derived classes. Objects of the publicly derived class B can access public members of the base class A, while objects of the privately derived class C cannot; they can only access the public members of their own derived class. This is shown in Figure 9.7.

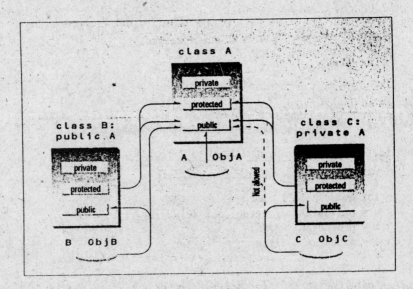

FIGURE 9.7
Public and private derivation.

If you don't supply any access specifier when creating a class, private is assumed.

Access Specifiers: When to Use What

How do you decide when to use private as opposed to public inheritance? In most cases a derived class exists to offer an improved—or a more specialized—version of the base class. We've seen examples of such derived classes (for instance, the CountDn class that adds the decrement operator to the Counter class and the manager class that is a more specialized version of the employee class). In such cases it makes sense for objects of the derived class to access the public functions of the base class if they want to perform a basic operation, and to access functions in the derived class to perform the more specialized operations that the derived class provides. In such cases public derivation is appropriate.

In some situations, however, the derived class is created as a way of completely modifying the operation of the base class, hiding or disguising its original interface. For example, imagine that you have already created a really nice Array class that acts like an array but provides protection against out-of-bounds array indexes. Then suppose you want to use this Array class as the basis for a Stack class, instead of using a basic array. You might derive Stack from Array, but you wouldn't want the users of Stack objects to treat them as if they were arrays, using the [ ] operator to access data items, for example. Objects of Stack should always be treated as if they were stacks, using push() and pop(). That is, you want to disguise the Array class as a Stack class. In this situation, private derivation would allow you to conceal all the Array class functions from objects of the derived Stack class.

Levels of Inheritance

Classes can be derived from classes that are themselves derived. Here's a miniprogram that shows the idea:

```
class A
    { };
class B : public A
    { };
class C : public B
    { };
```

Here B is derived from A, and C is derived from B. The process can be extended to an arbitrary number of levels—D could be derived from C, and so on.

As a more concrete example, suppose that we decided to add a special kind of laborer called a *foreman* to the EMPLOY program. We'll create a new program, EMPLOY2, that incorporates objects of class foreman.

Since a foreman is a kind of laborer, the foreman class is derived from the laborer class, as shown in Figure 9.8.

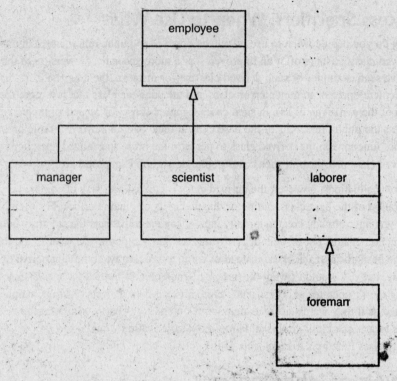

FIGURE 9.8
UML class diagram for EMPLOY2.

Foremen oversee the widget-stamping operation, supervising groups of laborers. They are responsible for the widget production quota for their group. A foreman's ability is measured by the percentage of production quotas successfully met. The quotas data item in the foreman class represents this percentage. Here's the listing for EMPLOY2:

```cpp
// employ2.cpp
// multiple levels of inheritance
#include <iostream>
using namespace std;
const int LEN = 80;                   //maximum length of names
//////////////////////////////////////////////////////////////////
class employee
   {
   private:
      char name[LEN];                 //employee name
      unsigned long number;           //employee number
   public:
      void getdata()
```

```
        {
        cout << "\n   Enter last name: "; cin >> name;
        cout << "   Enter number: ";        cin >> number;
        }
     void putdata() const
        {
        cout << "\n   Name: " << name;
        cout << "\n   Number: " << number;
        }
  };
///////////////////////////////////////////////////////////////////
class manager : public employee     //manager class
  {
  private:
     char title[LEN];               //"vice-president" etc.
     double dues;                   //golf club dues
  public:
     void getdata()
        {
        employee::getdata();
        cout << "   Enter title: ";            cin >> title;
        cout << "   Enter golf club dues: "; cin >> dues;
        }
     void putdata() const
        {
        employee::putdata();
        cout << "\n   Title: " << title;
        cout << "\n   Golf club dues: " << dues;
        }
  };
///////////////////////////////////////////////////////////////////
class scientist : public employee   //scientist class
  {
  private:
     int pubs;                      //number of publications
  public:
     void getdata()
        {
        employee::getdata();
        cout << "   Enter number of pubs: "; cin >> pubs;
        }
     void putdata() const
        {
        employee::putdata();
        cout << "\n   Number of publications: " << pubs;
        }
```

9

INHERITANCE

```cpp
    };
/////////////////////////////////////////////////////////////////
class laborer : public employee      //laborer class
    {
    };
/////////////////////////////////////////////////////////////////
class foreman : public laborer        //foreman class
    {
    private:
        float quotas;  //percent of quotas met successfully
    public:
        void getdata()
            {
            laborer::getdata();
            cout << "   Enter quotas: "; cin >> quotas;
            }
        void putdata() const
            {
            laborer::putdata();
            cout << "\n   Quotas: " << quotas:
            }
    };
/////////////////////////////////////////////////////////////////
int main()
    {
    laborer l1;
    foreman f1;

    cout << endl;
    cout << "\nEnter data for laborer 1";
    l1.getdata();
    cout << "\nEnter data for foreman 1";
    f1.getdata();

    cout << endl;
    cout << "\nData on laborer 1";
    l1.putdata();
    cout << "\nData on foreman 1";
    f1.putdata();
    cout << endl;
    return 0;
    }
```

Notice that a class hierarchy is not the same as an organization chart. An organization chart shows lines of command. A class hierarchy results from generalizing common characteristics. The more general the class, the higher it is on the chart. Thus a laborer is more general than a foreman, who is a specialized kind of laborer, so `laborer` is shown above `foreman` in the class hierarchy, although a foreman is probably paid more than a laborer.

Multiple Inheritance

A class can be derived from more than one base class. This is called *multiple inheritance*. Figure 9.9 shows how this looks when a class C is derived from base classes A and B.

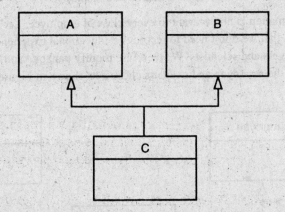

FIGURE 9.9
UML class diagram for multiple inheritance.

The syntax for multiple inheritance is similar to that for single inheritance. In the situation shown in Figure 9.9, the relationship is expressed like this:

```
class A                        // base class A
  {
  };
class B                        // base class B
  {
  };
class C : public A, public B   // C is derived from A and B
  {
  };
```

The base classes from which C is derived are listed following the colon in C's specification; they are separated by commas.

Member Functions in Multiple Inheritance

As an example of multiple inheritance, suppose that we need to record the educational experience of some of the employees in the EMPLOY program. Let's also suppose that, perhaps in a different project, we've already developed a class called student that models students with different educational backgrounds. We decide that instead of modifying the employee class to incorporate educational data, we will add this data by multiple inheritance from the student class.

..tudent class stores the name of the school or university last attended and the highest degree received. Both these data items are stored as strings. Two member functions, getedu() and putedu(), ask the user for this information and display it.

Educational information is not relevant to every class of employee. Let's suppose, somewhat undemocratically, that we don't need to record the educational experience of laborers; it's only relevant for managers and scientists. We therefore modify manager and scientist so that they inherit from both the employee and student classes, as shown in Figure 9.10.

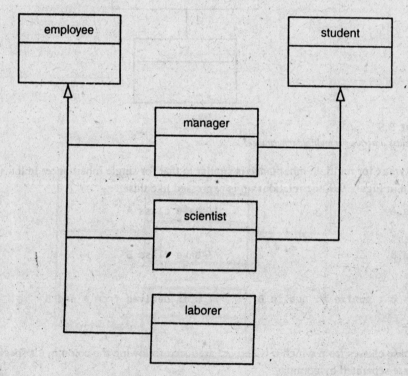

FIGURE 9.10
UML class diagram for EMPMULT.

Here's a miniprogram that shows these relationships (but leaves out everything else):

```cpp
class student
    { };
class employee
    { };
class manager : private employee, private student
    { };
class scientist : private employee, private student
    { };
class laborer : public employee
    { };
```

And here, featuring considerably more detail, is the listing for EMPMULT:

```cpp
//empmult.cpp
//multiple inheritance with employees and degrees
#include <iostream>
using namespace std;
const int LEN = 80;          //maximum length of names
/////////////////////////////////////////////////////////////////
class student                    //educational background
    {
    private:
       char school[LEN];         //name of school or university
       char degree[LEN];         //highest degree earned
    public:
       void getedu()
          {
          cout << "   Enter name of school or university: ";
          cin >> school;
          cout << "   Enter highest degree earned \n";
          cout << "   (Highschool, Bachelor's, Master's, PhD): ";
          cin >> degree;
          }
       void putedu() const
          {
          cout << "\n   School or university: " << school;
          cout << "\n   Highest degree earned: " << degree;
          }
    };
/////////////////////////////////////////////////////////////////
class employee
    {
    private:
       char name[LEN];           //employee name
       unsigned long number;     //employee number
```

9

INHERITANCE

```
    public:
       void getdata()
          {
          cout << "\n    Enter last name: "; cin >> name;
          cout << "    Enter number: ";          cin >> number;
          }
       void putdata() const
          {
          cout << "\n    Name: " << name;
          cout << "\n    Number: " << number;
          }
    };
/////////////////////////////////////////////////////////////////////
class manager : private employee, private student   //management
    {
    private:
       char title[LEN];            //"vice-president" etc.
       double dues;                //golf club dues
    public:
       void getdata()
          {
          employee::getdata();
          cout << "    Enter title: ";            cin >> title;
          cout << "    Enter golf club dues: "; cin >> dues;
          student::getedu();
          }
       void putdata() const
          {
          employee::putdata();
          cout << "\n    Title: " << title;
          cout << "\n    Golf club dues: " << dues;
          student::putedu();
          }
    };
/////////////////////////////////////////////////////////////////////
class scientist : private employee, private student   //scientist
    {
    private:
       int pubs;        //number of publications
    public:
       void getdata()
          {
          employee::getdata();
          cout << "    Enter number of pubs: "; cin >> pubs;
          student::getedu();
          }
```

```
        void putdata() const
            {
            employee::putdata();
            cout << "\n   Number of publications: " << pubs;
            student::putedu();
            }
    };
/////////////////////////////////////////////////////////////////
class laborer : public employee                //laborer
    {
    };
/////////////////////////////////////////////////////////////////
int main()
    {
    manager m1;
    scientist s1, s2;
    laborer l1;

    cout << endl;
    cout << "\nEnter data for manager 1";      //get data for
    m1.getdata();                              //several employees

    cout << "\nEnter data for scientist 1";
    s1.getdata();

    cout << "\nEnter data for scientist 2";
    s2.getdata();

    cout << "\nEnter data for laborer 1";
    l1.getdata();

    cout << "\nData on manager 1";             //display data for
    m1.putdata();                              //several employees

    cout << "\nData on scientist 1";
    s1.putdata();

    cout << "\nData on scientist 2";
    s2.putdata();

    cout << "\nData on laborer 1";
    l1.putdata();
    cout << endl;
    return 0;
    }
```

The getdata() and putdata() functions in the manager and scientist classes incorporate calls to functions in the student class, such as

```
student::getedu();
```

and

```
student::putedu();
```

These routines are accessible in manager and scientist because these classes are descended from student.

Here's some sample interaction with EMPMULT:

```
Enter data for manager 1
    Enter last name: Bradley
    Enter number: 12
    Enter title: Vice-President
    Enter golf club dues: 100000
    Enter name of school or university: Yale
    Enter highest degree earned
    (Highschool, Bachelor's, Master's, PhD): Bachelor's

Enter data for scientist 1
    Enter last name: Twilling
    Enter number: 764
    Enter number of pubs: 99
    Enter name of school or university: MIT
    Enter highest degree earned
    (Highschool, Bachelor's, Master's, PhD): PhD

Enter data for scientist 2
    Enter last name: Yang
    Enter number: 845
    Enter number of pubs: 101
    Enter name of school or university: Stanford
    Enter highest degree earned
    (Highschool, Bachelor's, Master's, PhD): Master's

Enter data for laborer 1
    Enter last name: Jones
    Enter number: 48323
```

As we saw in the EMPLOY and EMPLOY2 examples, the program then displays this information in roughly the same form.

private Derivation in EMPMULT

The manager and scientist classes in EMPMULT are privately derived from the employee and student classes. There is no need to use public derivation because objects of manager and scientist never call routines in the employee and student base classes. However, the laborer class must be publicly derived from employer, since it has no member functions of its own and relies on those in employee.

Constructors in Multiple Inheritance

EMPMULT has no constructors. Let's look at an example that does use constructors, and see how they're handled in multiple inheritance.

Imagine that we're writing a program for building contractors, and that this program models lumber-supply items. It uses a class that represents a quantity of lumber of a certain type: 100 8-foot-long construction grade 2×4s, for example.

The class should store various kinds of data about each such lumber item. We need to know the length (3'–6", for example) and we need to store the number of such pieces of lumber and their unit cost.

We also need to store a description of the lumber we're talking about. This has two parts. The first is the nominal dimensions of the cross-section of the lumber. This is given in inches. For instance, lumber 2 inches by 4 inches (for you metric folks, about 5 cm by 10 cm) is called a *two-by-four*. This is usually written 2×4. We also need to know the grade of lumber—rough-cut, construction grade, surfaced-four-sides, and so on. We find it convenient to create a Type class to hold this data. This class incorporates member data for the nominal dimensions and the grade of the lumber, both expressed as strings, such as 2×6 and *construction*. Member functions get this information from the user and display it.

We'll use the Distance class from previous examples to store the length. Finally we create a Lumber class that inherits both the Type and Distance classes. Here's the listing for ENGLMULT:

```
// englmult.cpp
// multiple inheritance with English Distances
#include <iostream>
#include <string>
using namespace std;
/////////////////////////////////////////////////////////////////
class Type                          //type of lumber
   {
   private:
      string dimensions;
      string grade;
```

```
    public:                            //no-arg constructor
      Type() : dimensions("N/A"), grade("N/A")
         { }
                                       //2-arg constructor
      Type(string di, string gr) : dimensions(di), grade(gr)
         { }
      void gettype()                   //get type from user
         {
         cout << "   Enter nominal dimensions (2x4 etc.): ";
         cin >> dimensions;
         cout << "   Enter grade (rough, const, etc.): ";
         cin >> grade;
         }
      void showtype() const            //display type
         {
         cout << "\n   Dimensions: " << dimensions;
         cout << "\n   Grade: " << grade;
         }
    };
//////////////////////////////////////////////////////////////
class Distance                         //English Distance class
    {
    private:
      int feet;
      float inches;
    public:                            //no-arg constructor
      Distance() : feet(0), inches(0.0)
         { }                           //constructor (two args)
      Distance(int ft, float in) : feet(ft), inches(in)
         { }
      void getdist()                   //get length from user
         {
         cout << "   Enter feet: ";  cin >> feet;
         cout << "   Enter inches: ";  cin >> inches;
         }
      void showdist() const            //display distance
         { cout << feet << "\'-" << inches << '\"'; }
    };
//////////////////////////////////////////////////////////////
class Lumber : public Type, public Distance
    {
    private:
      int quantity;                          //number of pieces
      double price;                          //price of each piece
    public:                                  //constructor (no args)
      Lumber() : Type(), Distance(), quantity(0), price(0.0)
```

```
        { }
                                      //constructor (6 args)
     Lumber( string di, string gr,    //args for Type
             int ft, float in,        //args for Distance
             int qu, float prc ) :    //args for our data
             Type(di, gr),            //call Type ctor
             Distance(ft, in),        //call Distance ctor
             quantity(qu), price(prc) //initialize our data
        { }
     void getlumber()
        {
        Type::gettype();
        Distance::getdist();
        cout << "   Enter quantity: "; cin >> quantity;
        cout << "   Enter price per piece: "; cin >> price;
        }
     void showlumber() const
        {
        Type::showtype();
        cout << "\n   Length: ";
        Distance::showdist();
        cout << "\n   Price for " << quantity
             << " pieces: $" << price * quantity;
        }
   };
/////////////////////////////////////////////////////////////////////
int main()
   {
   Lumber siding;                     //constructor (no args)

   cout << "\nSiding data:\n";
   siding.getlumber();                //get siding from user

                                      //constructor (6 args)
   Lumber studs( "2x4", "const", 8, 0.0, 200, 4.45F );

                                      //display lumber data
   cout << "\nSiding";  siding.showlumber();
   cout << "\nStuds";       studs.showlumber();
   cout << endl;
   return 0;
   }
```

The major new feature in this program is the use of constructors in the derived class Lumber.
These constructors call the appropriate constructors in Type and Distance.

No-Argument Constructor

The no-argument constructor in Type looks like this:

```
Type()
   { strcpy(dimensions, "N/A"); strcpy(grade, "N/A"); }
```

This constructor fills in "N/A" (not available) for the dimensions and grade variables so the user will be made aware if an attempt is made to display data for an uninitialized lumber object.

You're already familiar with the no-argument constructor in the Distance class:

```
Distance() : feet(0), inches(0.0)
   { }
```

The no-argument constructor in Lumber calls both of these constructors.

```
Lumber() : Type(), Distance(), quantity(0), price(0.0)
        { }
```

The names of the base-class constructors follow the colon and are separated by commas. When the Lumber() constructor is invoked, these base-class constructors—Type() and Distance()—will be executed. The quantity and price attributes are also initialized.

Multi-Argument Constructors

Here is the two-argument constructor for Type:

```
Type(string di, string gr) : dimensions(di), grade(gr)
        { }
```

This constructor copies string arguments to the dimensions and grade member data items.

Here's the constructor for Distance, which is again familiar from previous programs:

```
Distance(int ft, float in) : feet(ft), inches(in)
   { }
```

The constructor for Lumber calls both of these constructors, so it must supply values for their arguments. In addition it has two arguments of its own: the quantity of lumber and the unit price. Thus this constructor has six arguments. It makes two calls to the two constructors, each of which takes two arguments, and then initializes its own two data items. Here's what it looks like:

```
Lumber( string di, string gr,      //args for Type
        int ft, float in,          //args for Distance
        int qu, float prc ) :      //args for our data
        Type(di, gr),              //call Type ctor
        Distance(ft, in),          //call Distance ctor
        quantity(qu), price(prc)   //initialize our data
   { }
```

Ambiguity in Multiple Inheritance

Odd sorts of problems may surface in certain situations involving multiple inheritance. Here's a common one. Two base classes have functions with the same name, while a class derived from both base classes has no function with this name. How do objects of the derived class access the correct base class function? The name of the function alone is insufficient, since the compiler can't figure out which of the two functions is meant.

Here's an example, AMBIGU, that demonstrates the situation:

```
// ambigu.cpp
// demonstrates ambiguity in multiple inheritance
#include <iostream>
using namespace std;
///////////////////////////////////////////////////////////////
class A
   {
   public:
      void show()  { cout << "Class A\n"; }
   };
class B
   {
   public:
      void show()  { cout << "Class B\n"; }
   };
class C : public A, public B
   {
   };
///////////////////////////////////////////////////////////////
int main()
   {
   C objC;                 //object of class C
// objC.show();            //ambiguous--will not compile
   objC.A::show();         //OK
   objC.B::show();         //OK
   return 0;
   }
```

The problem is resolved using the scope-resolution operator to specify the class in which the function lies. Thus

```
objC.A::show();
```

refers to the version of show() that's in the A class, while

```
objC.B::show();
```

refs to the function in the B class. Stroustrup (see Appendix H, "Bibliography") calls this *disambiguation*.

Another kind of ambiguity arises if you derive a class from two classes that are each derived from the same class. This creates a diamond-shaped inheritance tree. The DIAMOND program shows how this looks.

```cpp
//diamond.cpp
//investigates diamond-shaped multiple inheritance
#include <iostream>
using namespace std;
/////////////////////////////////////////////////////////////////
class A
   {
   public:
      void func();
   };
class B : public A
   { };
class C : public A
   { };
class D : public B, public C
   { };
/////////////////////////////////////////////////////////////////
int main()
   {
   D objD;
   objD.func();   //ambiguous: won't compile
   return 0;
   }
```

Classes B and C are both derived from class A, and class D is derived by multiple inheritance from both B and C. Trouble starts if you try to access a member function in class A from an object of class D. In this example objD tries to access func(). However, both B and C contain a copy of func(), inherited from A. The compiler can't decide which copy to use, and signals an error.

There are various advanced ways of coping with this problem, but the fact that such ambiguities can arise causes many experts to recommend avoiding multiple inheritance altogether. You should certainly not use it in serious programs unless you have considerable experience.

Aggregation: Classes Within Classes

We'll discuss aggregation here because, while it is not directly related to inheritance, both aggregation and inheritance are class relationships that are more specialized than associations. It is instructive to compare and contrast them.

If a class B is derived by inheritance from a class A, we can say that "B is a *kind of* A." This is because B has all the characteristics of A, and in addition some of its own. It's like saying that a starling is a kind of bird: A starling has the characteristics shared by all birds (wings, feathers, and so on) but has some distinctive characteristics of its own (such as dark iridescent plumage). For this reason inheritance is often called a "kind of" relationship.

Aggregation is called a "has a" relationship. We say a library has a book or an invoice has an item line. Aggregation is also called a "part-whole" relationship: the book is part of the library.

In object-oriented programming, aggregation may occur when one object is an attribute of another. Here's a case where an object of class A is an attribute of class B:

```
class A
    {
    };
class B
    {
    A objA;   // define objA as an object of class A
    };
```

In the UML, aggregation is considered a special kind of association. Sometimes it's hard to tell when an association is also an aggregation. It's always safe to call a relationship an association, but if class A contains objects of class B, and is organizationally superior to class B, it's a good candidate for aggregation. A company might have an aggregation of employees, or a stamp collection might have an aggregation of stamps.

Aggregation is shown in the same way as association in UML class diagrams, except that the "whole" end of the association line has an open diamond-shaped arrowhead. Figure 9.11 shows how this looks.

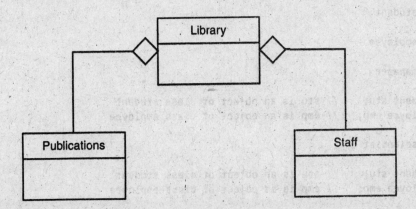

FIGURE 9.11
UML class diagram showing aggregation.

Aggregation in the EMPCONT Program

Let's rearrange the EMPMULT program to use aggregation instead of inheritance. In EMPMULT the manager and scientist classes are derived from the employee and student classes using the inheritance relationship. In our new program, EMPCONT, the manager and scientist classes contain instances of the employee and student classes as attributes. This aggregation relationship is shown in Figure 9.12.

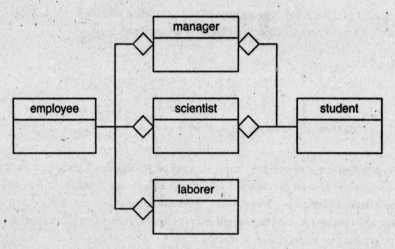

FIGURE 9.12
UML class diagram for EMPCONT.

The following miniprogram shows these relationships in a different way:

```
class student
   {};
class employee
   {};
class manager
   {
   student stu;      // stu is an object of class student
   employee emp;     // emp is an object of class employee
   };
class scientist
   {
   student stu;      // stu is an object of class student
   employee emp;     // emp is an object of class employee
   };
class laborer
   {
   employee emp;     // emp is an object of class employee
   };
```

Here's the full-scale listing for EMPCONT:

```cpp
// empcont.cpp
// containership with employees and degrees
#include <iostream>
#include <string>
using namespace std;
/////////////////////////////////////////////////////////////////
class student                    //educational background
   {
   private:
      string school;             //name of school or university
      string degree;             //highest degree earned
   public:
      void getedu()
         {
         cout << "   Enter name of school or university: ";
         cin >> school;
         cout << "   Enter highest degree earned \n";
         cout << "   (Highschool, Bachelor's, Master's, PhD): ";
         cin >> degree;
         }
      void putedu() const
         {
         cout << "\n   School or university: " << school;
         cout << "\n   Highest degree earned: " << degree;
         }
   };
/////////////////////////////////////////////////////////////////
class employee
   {
   private:
      string name;               //employee name
      unsigned long number;      //employee number
   public:
      void getdata()
         {
         cout << "\n   Enter last name: "; cin >> name;
         cout << "   Enter number: ";      cin >> number;
         }
      void putdata() const
         {
         cout << "\n   Name: " << name;
         cout << "\n   Number: " << number;
         }
   };
/////////////////////////////////////////////////////////////////
class manager                    //management
```

```
        {
    private:
        string title;              //"vice-president" etc.
        double dues;               //golf club dues
        employee emp;              //object of class employee
        student stu;               //object of class student
    public:
        void getdata()
            {
            emp.getdata();
            cout << "   Enter title: ";           cin >> title;
            cout << "   Enter golf club dues: "; cin >> dues;
            stu.getedu();
            }
        void putdata() const
            {
            emp.putdata();
            cout << "\n   Title: " << title;
            cout << "\n   Golf club dues: " << dues;
            stu.putedu();
            }
        };
//////////////////////////////////////////////////////////////////
class scientist                   //scientist
        {
    private:
        int pubs;                  //number of publications
        employee emp;              //object of class employee
        student stu;               //object of class student
    public:
        void getdata()
            {
            emp.getdata();
            cout << "   Enter number of pubs: "; cin >> pubs;
            stu.getedu();
            }
        void putdata() const
            {
            emp.putdata();
            cout << "\n   Number of publications: " << pubs;
            stu.putedu();
            }
        };
//////////////////////////////////////////////////////////////////
class laborer                     //laborer
        {
```

```
   private:
      employee emp;          //object of class employee
   public:
      void getdata()
         { emp.getdata(); }
      void putdata() const
         { emp.putdata(); }
   };
//////////////////////////////////////////////////////////////////
int main()
   {
   manager m1;
   scientist s1, s2;
   laborer l1;

   cout << endl;
   cout << "\nEnter data for manager 1";    //get data for
   m1.getdata();                            //several employees

   cout << "\nEnter data for scientist 1";
   s1.getdata();

   cout << "\nEnter data for scientist 2";
   s2.getdata();

   cout << "\nEnter data for laborer 1";
   l1.getdata();

   cout << "\nData on manager 1";           //display data for
   m1.putdata();                            //several employees

   cout << "\nData on scientist 1";
   s1.putdata();

   cout << "\nData on scientist 2";
   s2.putdata();

   cout << "\nData on laborer 1";
   l1.putdata();
   cout << endl;
   return 0;
   }
```

The student and employee classes are the same in EMPCONT as they were in EMPMULT, but they are related in a different way to the manager and scientist classes.

9

Composition: A Stronger Aggregation

Composition is a stronger form of aggregation. It has all the characteristics of aggregation, plus two more:

- The part may belong to only one whole.
- The lifetime of the part is the same as the lifetime of the whole.

A car is composed of doors (among other things). The doors can't belong to some other car, and they are born and die along with the car. A room is composed of a floor, ceiling, and walls. While aggregation is a "has a" relationship, composition is a "consists of" relationship.

In UML diagrams, composition is shown in the same way as aggregation, except that the diamond-shaped arrowhead is solid instead of open. This is shown in Figure 9.13.

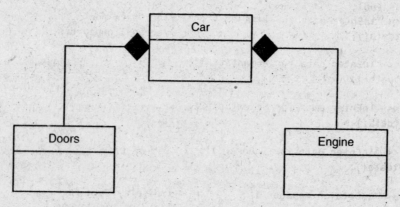

FIGURE 9.13
UML class diagram showing composition.

Even a single object can be related to a class by composition. In a car there is only one engine.

Inheritance and Program Development

The program-development process, as practiced for decades by programmers everywhere, is being fundamentally altered by object-oriented programming. This is due not only to the use of classes in OOP but to inheritance as well. Let's see how this comes about.

Programmer A creates a class. Perhaps it's something like the `Distance` class, with a complete set of member functions for arithmetic operations on a user-defined data type.

Programmer B likes the Distance class but thinks it could be improved by using signed distances. The solution is to create a new class, like DistSign in the ENGLEN example, that is derived from Distance but incorporates the extensions necessary to implement signed distances.

Programmers C and D then write applications that use the DistSign class.

Programmer B may not have access to the source code for the Distance member functions, and programmers C and D may not have access to the source code for DistSign. Yet, because of the software reusability feature of C++, B can modify and extend the work of A, and C and D can make use of the work of B (and A).

Notice that the distinction between software tool developers and application writers is becoming blurred. Programmer A creates a general-purpose programming tool, the Distance class. Programmer B creates a specialized version of this class, the DistSign class. Programmers C and D create applications. A is a tool developer, and C and D are applications developers. B is somewhere in between. In any case OOP is making the programming scene more flexible and at the same time more complex.

In Chapter 13 we'll see how a class can be divided into a client-accessible part and a part that is distributed only in object form, so it can be used by other programmers without the distribution of source code.

Summary

A class, called the *derived class*, can inherit the features of another class, called the *base class*. The derived class can add other features of its own, so it becomes a specialized version of the base class. Inheritance provides a powerful way to extend the capabilities of existing classes, and to design programs using hierarchical relationships.

Accessibility of base class members from derived classes and from objects of derived classes is an important issue. Data or functions in the base class that are prefaced by the keyword *protected* can be accessed from derived classes but not by any other objects, including objects of derived classes. Classes may be publicly or privately derived from base classes. Objects of a publicly derived class can access public members of the base class, while objects of a privately derived class cannot.

A class can be derived from more than one base class. This is called *multiple inheritance*. A class can also be contained within another class.

In the UML, inheritance is called generalization. This relationship is represented in class diagrams by an open triangle pointing to the base (parent) class.

9

INHERITANCE

Aggregation is a "has a" or "part-whole" relationship: one class contains objects of another class. Aggregation is represented in UML class diagrams by an open diamond pointing to the "whole" part of the part-whole pair. Composition is a strong form of aggregation. Its arrowhead is solid rather than open.

Inheritance permits the reusability of software: Derived classes can extend the capabilities of base classes with no need to modify—or even access the source code of—the base class. This leads to new flexibility in the software development process, and to a wider range of roles for software developers.

Questions

Answers to these questions can be found in Appendix G.

1. Inheritance is a way to

    a. make general classes into more specific classes.

    b. pass arguments to objects of classes.

    c. add features to existing classes without rewriting them.

    d. improve data hiding and encapsulation.

2. A "child" class is said to be _____ from a base class.

3. Advantages of inheritance include

    a. providing class growth through natural selection.

    b. facilitating class libraries.

    c. avoiding the rewriting of code.

    d. providing a useful conceptual framework.

4. Write the first line of the specifier for a class Bosworth that is publicly derived from a class Alphonso.

5. True or false: Adding a derived class to a base class requires fundamental changes to the base class.

6. To be accessed from a member function of the derived class, data or functions in the base class must be public or _____.

7. If a base class contains a member function basefunc(), and a derived class does not contain a function with this name, can an object of the derived class access basefunc()?

8. Assume that the classes mentioned in Question 4 and the class Alphonso contain a member function called alfunc(). Write a statement that allows object BosworthObj of class Bosworth to access alfunc().

9. True or false: If no constructors are specified for a derived class, objects of the derived class will use the constructors in the base class.

10. If a base class and a derived class each include a member function with the same name, which member function will be called by an object of the derived class, assuming the scope-resolution operator is not used?

11. Write a declarator for a no-argument constructor of the derived class Bosworth of Question 4 that calls a no-argument constructor in the base class Alphonso.

12. The scope-resolution operator usually

   a. limits the visibility of variables to a certain function.

   b. tells what base class a class is derived from.

   c. specifies a particular class.

   d. resolves ambiguities.

13. True or false: It is sometimes useful to specify a class from which no objects will ever be created.

14. Assume that there is a class Derv that is derived from a base class Base. Write the declarator for a derived-class constructor that takes one argument and passes this argument along to the constructor in the base class.

15. Assume a class Derv that is privately derived from class Base. An object of class Derv located in main() can access

   a. public members of Derv.

   b. protected members of Derv.

   c. private members of Derv.

   d. public members of Base.

   e. protected members of Base.

   f. private members of Base.

16. True or false: A class D can be derived from a class C, which is derived from a class B, which is derived from a class A

17. A class hierarchy

   a. shows the same relationships as an organization chart.

   b. describes "has a" relationships.

   c. describes "is a kind of" relationships.

   d. shows the same relationships as a family tree.

18. Write the first line of a specifier for a class Tire that is derived from class Wheel and from class Rubber.

19. Assume a class `Derv` derived from a base class `Base`. Both classes contain a member function `func()` that takes no arguments. Write a statement to go in a member function of `Derv` that calls `func()` in the base class.

20. True or false: It is illegal to make objects of one class members of another class.

21. In the UML, inheritance is called _____.

22. Aggregation is
    a. a stronger form of instantiation.
    b. a stronger form of generalization.
    c. a stronger form of composition.
    d. a "has a" relationship.

23. True or false: the arrow representing generalization points to the more specific class.

24. Composition is a _____ form of _____.

Exercises

Answers to starred exercises can be found in Appendix G.

*1. Imagine a publishing company that markets both book and audiocassette versions of its works. Create a class `publication` that stores the title (a string) and price (type `float`) of a publication. From this class derive two classes: `book`, which adds a page count (type `int`), and `tape`, which adds a playing time in minutes (type `float`). Each of these three classes should have a `getdata()` function to get its data from the user at the keyboard, and a `putdata()` function to display its data.

Write a `main()` program to test the `book` and `tape` classes by creating instances of them, asking the user to fill in data with `getdata()`, and then displaying the data with `putdata()`.

*2. Recall the STRCONV example from Chapter 8. The `String` class in this example has a flaw: It does not protect itself if its objects are initialized to have too many characters. (The SZ constant has the value 80.) For example, the definition

```
String s = "This string will surely exceed the width of the "
           "screen, which is what the SZ constant represents.";
```

will cause the `str` array in s to overflow, with unpredictable consequences, such as crashing the system.

With `String` as a base class, derive a class `Pstring` (for "protected string") that prevents buffer overflow when too long a string constant is used in a definition. A new constructor in the derived class should copy only SZ-1 characters into `str` if the string constant is longer, but copy the entire constant if it's shorter. Write a `main()` program to test different lengths of strings.

*3. Start with the publication, book, and tape classes of Exercise 1. Add a base class sales that holds an array of three floats so that it can record the dollar sales of a particular publication for the last three months. Include a getdata() function to get three sales amounts from the user, and a putdata() function to display the sales figures. Alter the book and tape classes so they are derived from both publication and sales. An object of class book or tape should input and output sales data along with its other data. Write a main() function to create a book object and a tape object and exercise their input/output capabilities.

4. Assume that the publisher in Exercises 1 and 3 decides to add a third way to distribute books: on computer disk, for those who like to do their reading on their laptop. Add a disk class that, like book and tape, is derived from publication. The disk class should incorporate the same member functions as the other classes. The data item unique to this class is the disk type: either CD or DVD. You can use an enum type to store this item. The user could select the appropriate type by typing c or d.

5. Derive a class called employee2 from the employee class in the EMPLOY program in this chapter. This new class should add a type double data item called compensation, and also an enum type called period to indicate whether the employee is paid hourly, weekly, or monthly. For simplicity you can change the manager, scientist, and laborer classes so they are derived from employee2 instead of employee. However, note that in many circumstances it might be more in the spirit of OOP to create a separate base class called compensation and three new classes manager2, scientist2, and laborer2, and use multiple inheritance to derive these three classes from the original manager, scientist, and laborer classes and from compensation. This way none of the original classes needs to be modified.

6. Start with the ARROVER3 program in Chapter 8. Keep the safearay class the same as in that program, and, using inheritance, derive the capability for the user to specify both the upper and lower bounds of the array in a constructor. This is similar to Exercise 9 in Chapter 8, except that inheritance is used to derive a new class (you can call it safehilo) instead of modifying the original class.

7. Start with the COUNTEN2 program in this chapter. It can increment or decrement a counter, but only using prefix notation. Using inheritance, add the ability to use postfix notation for both incrementing and decrementing. (See Chapter 8 for a description of postfix notation.)

8. Operators in some computer languages, such as Visual Basic, allow you to select parts of an existing string and assign them to other strings. (The Standard C++ string class offers a different approach.) Using inheritance, add this capability to the Pstring class of Exercise 2. In the derived class, Pstring2, incorporate three new functions: left(), mid(), and right().

9

```
s2.left(s1, n)     // s2 is assigned the leftmost n characters
                   //    from s1
s2.mid(s1, s, n)   // s2 is assigned the middle n characters
                   //    from s1, starting at character number s
                   //    (leftmost character is 0)
s2.right(s1, n)    // s2 is assigned the rightmost n characters
                   //    from s1
```

You can use for loops to copy the appropriate parts of s1, character by character, to a temporary Pstring2 object, which is then returned. For extra credit, have these functions return by reference, so they can be used on the left side of the equal sign to change parts of an existing string.

9. Start with the publication, book, and tape classes of Exercise 1. Suppose you want to add the date of publication for both books and tapes. From the publication class, derive a new class called publication2 that includes this member data. Then change book and tape so they are derived from publication2 instead of publication. Make all the necessary changes in member functions so the user can input and output dates along with the other data. For the dates, you can use the date class from Exercise 5 in Chapter 6, which stores a date as three ints, for month, day, and year.

10. There is only one kind of manager in the EMPMULT program in this chapter. Any serious company has executives as well as managers. From the manager class derive a class called executive. (We'll assume an executive is a high-end kind of manager.) The additional data in the executive class will be the size of the employee's yearly bonus and the number of shares of company stock held in his or her stock-option plan. Add the appropriate member functions so these data items can be input and displayed along with the other manager data.

11. Various situations require that pairs of numbers be treated as a unit. For example, each screen coordinate has an x (horizontal) component and a y (vertical) component. Represent such a pair of numbers as a structure called pair that comprises two int member variables.

Now, assume you want to be able to store pair variables on a stack. That is, you want to be able to place a pair (which contains two integers) onto a stack using a single call to a push() function with a structure of type pair as an argument, and retrieve a pair using a single call to a pop() function, which will return a structure of type pair. Start with the Stack2 class in the STAKEN program in this chapter, and from it derive a new class called pairStack. This new class need contain only two members: the overloaded push() and pop() functions. The pairStack::push() function will need to make two calls to Stack2::push() to store the two integers in its pair, and the pairStack::pop() function will need to make two calls to Stack2::pop() (although not necessarily in the same order).

12. Amazing as it may seem, the old British pounds-shillings-pence money notation (£9.19.11—see Exercise 10 in Chapter 4, "Structures") isn't the whole story. A penny was further divided into halfpennies and farthings, with a farthing being worth 1/4 of a penny. There was a halfpenny coin, a farthing coin, and a halffarthing coin. Fortunately all this can be expressed numerically in eighths of a penny:

1/8 penny is a halffarthing

1/4 penny is a farthing

3/8 penny is a farthing and a half

1/2 penny is a halfpenny (pronounced ha'penny)

5/8 penny is a halfpenny plus a halffarthing

3/4 penny is a halfpenny plus a farthing

7/8 penny is a halfpenny plus a farthing and a half

Let's assume we want to add to the sterling class the ability to handle such fractional pennies. The I/O format can be something like £1.1.1-1/4 or £9.19.11-7/8, where the hyphen separates the fraction from the pennies.

Derive a new class called sterfrac from sterling. It should be able to perform the four arithmetic operations on sterling quantities that include eighths of a penny. Its only member data is an int indicating the number of eighths; you can call it eighths. You'll need to overload many of the functions in sterling to handle the eighths. The user should be able to type any fraction in lowest terms, and the display should also show fractions in lowest terms. It's not necessary to use the full-scale fraction class (see Exercise 11 in Chapter 6), but you could try that for extra credit.

9

Pointers

IN THIS CHAPTER

Pointers are the hobgoblin of C++ (and C) programming; seldom has such a simple idea inspired so much perplexity for so many. But fear not. In this chapter we will try to demystify pointers and show practical uses for them in C++ programming.

What are pointers for? Here are some common uses:

- Accessing array elements
- Passing arguments to a function when the function needs to modify the original argument
- Passing arrays and strings to functions
- Obtaining memory from the system
- Creating data structures such as linked lists

Pointers are an important feature of C++ (and C), while many other languages, such as Visual Basic and Java, have no pointers at all. (Java has references, which are sort of watered-down pointers.) Is this emphasis on pointers really necessary? You can do a lot without them, as their absence from the preceding chapters demonstrates. Some operations that use pointers in C++ can be carried out in other ways. For example, array elements can be accessed with array notation rather than pointer notation (we'll see the difference soon), and a function can modify arguments passed by reference, as well as those passed by pointers.

However, in some situations pointers provide an essential tool for increasing the power of C++. A notable example is the creation of data structures such as linked lists and binary trees. In fact, several key features of C++, such as virtual functions, the new operator, and the this pointer (discussed in Chapter 11, "Virtual Functions"), require the use of pointers. So, although you can do a lot of programming in C++ without using pointers, you will find them essential to obtaining the most from the language.

In this chapter we'll introduce pointers gradually, starting with fundamental concepts and working up to complex pointer applications.

If you already know C, you can probably skim over the first half of the chapter. However, you should read the sections in the second half on the new and delete operators, accessing member functions using pointers, arrays of pointers to objects, and linked-list objects.

Addresses and Pointers

The ideas behind pointers are not complicated. Here's the first key concept: Every byte in the computer's memory has an *address*. Addresses are numbers, just as they are for houses on a street. The numbers start at 0 and go up from there—1, 2, 3, and so on. If you have 1MB of memory, the highest address is 1,048,575. (Of course you have much more.)

Your program, when it is loaded into memory, occupies a certain range of these addresses. That means that every variable and every function in your program starts at a particular address. Figure 10.1 shows how this looks.

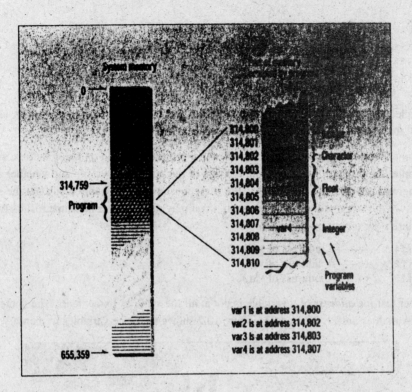

FIGURE 10.1
Memory addresses.

The Address-of Operator &

You can find the address occupied by a variable by using the *address-of* operator &. Here's a
short program, VARADDR, that demonstrates how to do this:

```
// varaddr.cpp
// addresses of variables
#include <iostream>
using namespace std;

int main()
   {
   int var1 = 11;          //define and initialize
   int var2 = 22;          //three variables
   int var3 = 33;
```

10

```
    cout << &var1 << endl      //print the addresses
        << &var2 << endl      //of these variables
        << &var3 << endl;
    return 0;
    }
```

This simple program defines three integer variables and initializes them to the values 11, 22, and 33. It then prints out the addresses of these variables.

The actual addresses occupied by the variables in a program depend on many factors, such as the computer the program is running on, the size of the operating system, and whether any other programs are currently in memory. For these reasons you probably won't get the same addresses we did when you run this program. (You may not even get the same results twice in a row.) Here's the output on our machine:

```
0x8f4ffff4    ←——— address of var1
0x8f4ffff2    ←——— address of var2
0x8f4ffff0    ←——— address of var3
```

Remember that the *address* of a variable is not at all the same as its *contents*. The contents of the three variables are 11, 22, and 33. Figure 10.2 shows the three variables in memory.

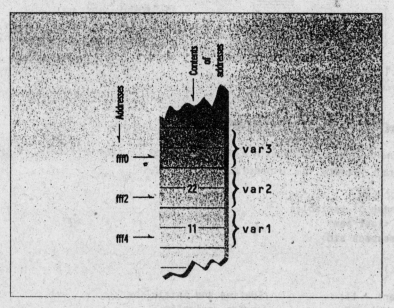

FIGURE 10.2
Addresses and contents of variables.

The << insertion operator interprets the addresses in hexadecimal arithmetic, as indicated by the prefix 0x before each number. This is the usual way to show memory addresses. If you aren't familiar with the hexadecimal number system, don't worry. All you really need to know is that each variable starts at a unique address. However, you might note in the output that each address differs from the next by exactly 2 bytes. That's because integers occupy 2 bytes of memory (on a 16-bit system). If we had used variables of type char, they would have adjacent addresses, since a char occupies 1 byte; and if we had used type double, the addresses would have differed by 8 bytes.

The addresses appear in descending order because local variables are stored on the stack, which grows downward in memory. If we had used global variables, they would have ascending addresses, since global variables are stored on the heap, which grows upward. Again, you don't need to worry too much about these considerations, since the compiler keeps track of the details for you.

Don't confuse the address-of operator &, which precedes a variable name in a variable declaration, with the reference operator &, which follows the type name in a function prototype or definition. (References were discussed in Chapter 5, "Functions.")

Pointer Variables

Addresses by themselves are rather limited. It's nice to know that we can find out where things are in memory, as we did in VARADDR, but printing out address values is not all that useful. The potential for increasing our programming power requires an additional idea: *variables that hold address values*. We've seen variable types that store characters, integers, floating-point numbers, and so on. Addresses are stored similarly. A variable that holds an address value is called a *pointer variable*, or simply a *pointer*.

What is the data type of pointer variables? It's not the same as the variable whose address is being stored; a pointer to int is not type int. You might think a pointer data type would be called something like pointer or ptr. However, things are slightly more complicated. The next program, PTRVAR, shows the syntax for pointer variables.

```
// ptrvar.cpp
// pointers (address variables)
#include <iostream>
using namespace std;

int main()
   {
   int var1 = 11;              //two integer variables
   int var2 = 22;
```

```
    cout << &var1 << endl        //print addresses of variables
         << &var2 << endl << endl;

    int* ptr;                    //pointer to integers

    ptr = &var1;                 //pointer points to var1
    cout << ptr << endl;         //print pointer value

    ptr = &var2;                 //pointer points to var2
    cout << ptr << endl;         //print pointer value
    return 0;
    }
```

This program defines two integer variables, var1 and var2, and initializes them to the values 11 and 22. It then prints out their addresses.

The program next defines a *pointer variable* in the line

```
int* ptr;
```

To the uninitiated this is a rather bizarre syntax. The asterisk means *pointer to*. Thus the statement defines the variable ptr as a *pointer to* int. This is another way of saying that this variable can hold the addresses of integer variables.

What's wrong with the idea of a general-purpose pointer type that holds pointers to any data type? If we called it type pointer we could write declarations like

```
pointer ptr;
```

The problem is that the compiler needs to know *what kind of variable the pointer points to.* (We'll see why when we talk about pointers and arrays.) The syntax used in C++ allows pointers to any type to be declared:

```
char* cptr;          // pointer to char
int* iptr;           // pointer to int
float* fptr;         // pointer to float
Distance* distptr;   // pointer to user-defined Distance class
```

and so on.

Syntax Quibbles

We should note that it is common to write pointer definitions with the asterisk closer to the variable name than to the type.

```
char *charptr;
```

It doesn't matter to the compiler, but placing the asterisk next to the type helps emphasize that the asterisk is part of the variable type (pointer to char), not part of the name itself.

If you define more than one pointer of the same type on one line, you need only insert the type-pointed-to once, but you need to place an asterisk before each variable name.

```
char* ptr1, * ptr2, * ptr3;   // three variables of type char*
```

Or you can use the asterisk-next-to-the-name approach.

```
char *ptr1, *ptr2, *ptr3;   // three variables of type char*
```

Pointers Must Have a Value

An address like 0x8f4ffff4 can be thought of as a *pointer constant*. A pointer like ptr can be thought of as a *pointer variable*. Just as the integer variable var1 can be assigned the constant value 11, so can the pointer variable ptr be assigned the constant value 0x8f4ffff4.

When we first define a variable, it holds no value (unless we initialize it at the same time). It may hold a garbage value, but this has no meaning. In the case of pointers, a garbage value is the address of something in memory, but probably not of something that we want. So before a pointer is used, a specific address must be placed in it. In the PTRVAR program, ptr is first assigned the address of var1 in the line

```
ptr = &var1;        ◄──────  put address of var1 in ptr
```

Following this, the program prints out the value contained in ptr, which should be the same address printed for &var1. The same pointer variable ptr is then assigned the address of var2, and this value is printed out. Figure 10.3 shows the operation of the PTRVAR program. Here's the output of PTRVAR:

```
0x8f51fff4    ◄──────  address of var1
0x8f51fff2    ◄──────  address of var2

0x8f51fff4    ◄──────  ptr set to address of var1
0x8f51fff2    ◄──────  ptr set to address of var2
```

To summarize: A pointer can hold the address of any variable of the correct type; it's a receptacle awaiting an address. However, it must be given some value, or it will point to an address we don't want it to point to, such as into our program code or the operating system. Rogue pointer values can result in system crashes and are difficult to debug, since the compiler gives no warning. The moral: Make sure you give every pointer variable a valid address value before using it.

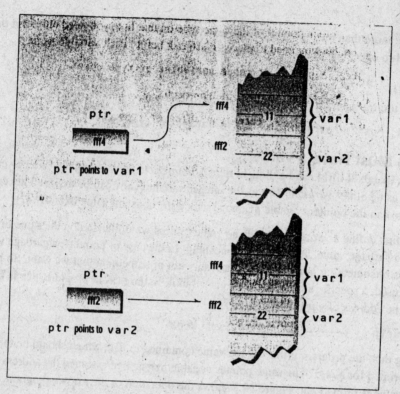

FIGURE 10.3
Changing values in ptr.

Accessing the Variable Pointed To

Suppose that we don't know the name of a variable but we do know its address. Can we access the contents of the variable? (It may seem like mismanagement to lose track of variable names, but we'll soon see that there are many variables whose names we don't know.)

There is a special syntax to access the value of a variable using its address instead of its name. Here's an example program, PTRACC, that shows how it's done:

```
// ptracc.cpp
// accessing the variable pointed to
#include <iostream>
using namespace std;

int main()
   {
   int var1 = 11;
   int var2 = 22;               //two integer variables
```

```
int* ptr;                        //pointer to integers

ptr = &var1;                     //pointer points to var1
cout << *ptr << endl;            //print contents of pointer (11)

ptr = &var2;                     //pointer points to var2
cout << *ptr << endl;            //print contents of pointer (22)
return 0;
}
```

This program is very similar to PTRVAR, except that instead of printing the address values in ptr, we print the integer value stored at the address that's stored in ptr. Here's the output:

11
22

The expression that accesses the variables var1 and var2 is *ptr, which occurs in each of the two cout statements.

When an asterisk is used in front of a variable name, as it is in the *ptr expression, it is called the *dereference operator* (or sometimes the *indirection operator*). It means *the value of the variable pointed to by*. Thus the expression *ptr represents the value of the variable pointed to by ptr. When ptr is set to the address of var1, the expression *ptr has the value 11, since var1 is 11. When ptr is changed to the address of var2, the expression *ptr acquires the value 22, since var2 is 22. Another name for the dereference operator is the *contents of* operator, which is another way to say the same thing. Figure 10.4 shows how this looks.

You can use a pointer not only to display a variable's value, but also to perform any operation you would perform on the variable directly. Here's a program, PTRTO, that uses a pointer to assign a value to a variable, and then to assign that value to another variable:

```
// ptrto.cpp
// other access using pointers
#include <iostream>
using namespace std;

int main()
   {
   int var1, var2;               //two integer variables
   int* ptr;                     //pointer to integers

   ptr = &var1;                  //set pointer to address of var1
   *ptr = 37;                    //same as var1=37
   var2 = *ptr;                  //same as var2=var1

   cout << var2 << endl;         //verify var2 is 37
   return 0;
   }
```

10

POINTERS

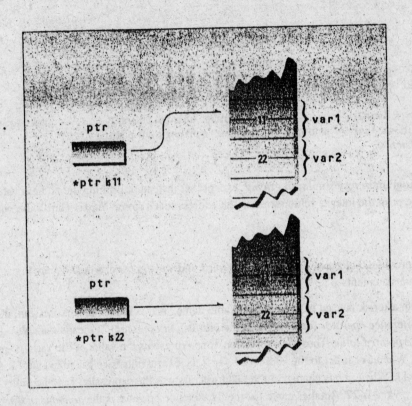

FIGURE 10.4

Access via pointer.

Remember that the asterisk used as the dereference operator has a different meaning than the asterisk used to declare pointer variables. The dereference operator *precedes* the variable and means *value of the variable pointed to by*. The asterisk used in a declaration means *pointer to*.

```
int* ptr;      //declaration: pointer to int
*ptr = 37;     //indirection: value of variable pointed to by ptr
```

Using the dereference operator to access the value stored in an address is called *indirect addressing*, or sometimes *dereferencing*, the pointer.

Here's a capsule summary of what we've learned so far:

```
int v;         //defines variable v of type int
int* p;        //defines p as a pointer to int
p = &v;        //assigns address of variable v to pointer p
v = 3;         //assigns 3 to v
*p = 3;        //also assigns 3 to v
```

The last two statements show the difference between normal or direct addressing, where we refer to a variable by name, and pointer or indirect addressing, where we refer to the same variable using its address.

In the example programs we've shown so far in this chapter, there's really no advantage to using the pointer expression to access variables, since we can access them directly. The value of pointers becomes evident when you can't access a variable directly, as we'll see later.

Pointer to void

Before we go on to see pointers at work, we should note one peculiarity of pointer data types. Ordinarily, the address that you put in a pointer must be the same type as the pointer. You can't assign the address of a float variable to a pointer to int, for example:

```
float flovar = 98.6;
int* ptrint = &flovar;   //ERROR: can't assign float* to int*
```

However, there is an exception to this. There is a sort of general-purpose pointer that can point to any data type. This is called a pointer to void, and is defined like this:

```
void* ptr;    //ptr can point to any data type
```

Such pointers have certain specialized uses, such as passing pointers to functions that operate independently of the data type pointed to.

The next example uses a pointer to void and also shows that, if you don't use void, you must be careful to assign pointers an address of the same type as the pointer. Here's the listing for PTRVOID:

```cpp
// ptrvoid.cpp
// pointers to type void
#include <iostream>
using namespace std;

int main()
   {
   int intvar;              //integer variable
   float flovar;            //float variable

   int* ptrint;             //define pointer to int
   float* ptrflo;           //define pointer to float
   void* ptrvoid;           //define pointer to void

   ptrint = &intvar;        //ok, int* to int*
// ptrint = &flovar;        //error, float* to int*
// ptrflo = &intvar;        //error, int* to float*
   ptrflo = &flovar;        //ok, float* to float*
```

```
    ptrvoid = &intvar;          //ok, int* to void*
    ptrvoid = &flovar;          //ok, float* to void*
    return 0;
    }
```

You can assign the address of intvar to ptrint because they are both type int*, but you can't assign the address of flovar to ptrint because the first is type float* and the second is type int*. However, ptrvoid can be given any pointer value, such as int*, because it is a pointer to void.

If for some unusual reason you really need to assign one kind of pointer type to another, you can use the reinterpret_cast. For the lines commented out in PTRVOID, that would look like this:

```
ptrint = reinterpret_cast<int*>(flovar);
ptrflo = reinterpret_cast<float*>(intvar);
```

The use of reinterpret_cast in this way is not recommended, but occasionally it's the only way out of a difficult situation. Static casts won't work with pointers. Old-style C casts can be used, but are always a bad idea in C++. We'll see examples of reinterpret_cast in Chapter 12, "Streams and Files," where it's used to alter the way a data buffer is interpreted.

Pointers and Arrays

There is a close association between pointers and arrays. We saw in Chapter 7, "Arrays and Strings," how array elements are accessed. The following program, ARRNOTE, provides a review.

```
// arrnote.cpp
// array accessed with array notation
#include <iostream>
using namespace std;

int main()
    {                                           //array
    int intarray[5] = { 31, 54, 77, 52, 93 };

    for(int j=0; j<5; j++)                      //for each element,
        cout << intarray[j] << endl;            //print value
    return 0;
    }
```

The cout statement prints each array element in turn. For instance, when j is 3, the expression intarray[j] takes on the value intarray[3] and accesses the fourth array element, the integer 52. Here's the output of ARRNOTE:

31
54
77
52
93

Surprisingly, array elements can be accessed using pointer notation as well as array notation. The next example, PTRNOTE, is similar to ARRNOTE except that it uses pointer notation.

```
// ptrnote.cpp
// array accessed with pointer notation
#include <iostream>
using namespace std;

int main()
   {                                         //array
   int intarray[5] = { 31, 54, 77, 52, 93 };

   for(int j=0; j<5; j++)                    //for each element,
       cout << *(intarray+j) << endl;        //print value
   return 0;
   }
```

The expression *(intarray+j) in PTRNOTE has exactly the same effect as intarray[j] in ARRNOTE, and the output of the programs is identical. But how do we interpret the expression *(intarray+j)? Suppose j is 3, so the expression is equivalent to *(intarray+3). We want this to represent the contents of the fourth element of the array (52). Remember that the name of an array is its address. The expression intarray+j is thus an address with something added to it. You might expect that intarray+3 would cause 3 bytes to be added to intarray. But that doesn't produce the result we want: intarray is an array of integers, and 3 bytes into this array is the middle of the second element, which is not very useful. We want to obtain the fourth *integer* in the array, not the fourth byte, as shown in Figure 10.5. (This figure assumes 2-byte integers.)

The C++ compiler is smart enough to take the size of the data into account when it performs arithmetic on data addresses. It knows that intarray is an array of type int because it was declared that way. So when it sees the expression intarray+3, it interprets it as the address of the fourth *integer* in intarray, not the fourth byte.

But we want the *value* of this fourth array element, not the *address*. To take the value, we use the dereference operator (*). The resulting expression, when j is 3, is *(intarray+3), which is the content of the fourth array element, or 52.

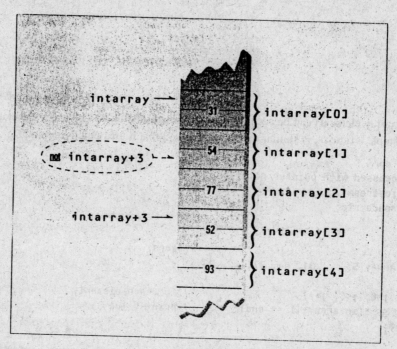

FIGURE 10.5
Counting by integers.

Now we see why a pointer declaration must include the type of the variable pointed to. The compiler needs to know whether a pointer is a pointer to `int` or a pointer to `double` so that it can perform the correct arithmetic to access elements of the array. It multiplies the index value by 2 in the case of type `int`, but by 8 in the case of `double`.

Pointer Constants and Pointer Variables

Suppose that, instead of adding j to `intarray` to step through the array addresses, you wanted to use the increment operator. Could you write `*(intarray++)`?

The answer is no, and the reason is that you can't increment a constant (or indeed change it in any way). The expression `intarray` is the address where the system has chosen to place your array, and it will stay at this address until the program terminates. `intarray` is a pointer constant. You can't say `intarray++` any more than you can say 7++. (In a multitasking system, variable addresses may change during program execution. An active program may be swapped out to disk and then reloaded at a different memory location. However, this process is invisible to your program.)

But while you can't increment an address, you can increment a pointer that holds an address. The next example, PTRINC, shows how:

```
// ptrinc.cpp
// array accessed with pointer
#include <iostream>
using namespace std;

int main()
    {
    int intarray[] = { 31, 54, 77, 52, 93 }; //array
    int* ptrint;                             //pointer to int
    ptrint = intarray;                       //points to intarray

    for(int j=0; j<5; j++)                   //for each element,
        cout << *(ptrint++) << endl;         //print value
    return 0;
    }
```

Here we define a pointer to int—ptrint—and give it the value intarray, the address of the array. Now we can access the contents of the array elements with the expression

```
*(ptrint++)
```

The variable ptrint starts off with the same address value as intarray, thus allowing the first array element, intarray[0], which has the value 31, to be accessed as before. But, because ptrint is a variable and not a constant, it can be incremented. After it is incremented, it points to the second array element, intarray[1]. The expression *(ptrint++) then represents the contents of the second array element, or 54. The loop causes the expression to access each array element in turn. The output of PTRINC is the same as that for PTRNOTE.

Pointers and Functions

In Chapter 5 we noted that there are three ways to pass arguments to a function: by value, by reference, and by pointer. If the function is intended to modify variables in the calling program, these variables cannot be passed by value, since the function obtains only a copy of the variable. However, either a reference argument or a pointer can be used in this situation.

Passing Simple Variables

We'll first review how arguments are passed by reference, and then compare this to passing pointer arguments. The PASSREF program shows passing by reference.

```
// passref.cpp
// arguments passed by reference
#include <iostream>
using namespace std;

int main()
    {
```

```
        void centimize(double&);      //prototype

        double var = 10.0;              //var has value of 10 inches
        cout << "var = " << var << " inches" << endl;

        centimize(var);                 //change var to centimeters
        cout << "var = " << var << " centimeters" << endl;
        return 0;
        }
//---------------------------------------------------------------
void centimize(double& v)
        {
        v *= 2.54;                      //v is the same as var
        }
```

Here we want to convert a variable var in main() from inches to centimeters. We pass the variable by reference to the function centimize(). (Remember that the & following the data type double in the prototype for this function indicates that the argument is passed by reference.) The centimize() function multiplies the original variable by 2.54. Notice how the function refers to the variable. It simply uses the argument name v; v and var are different names for the same thing.

Once it has converted var to centimeters, main() displays the result. Here's the output of PASSREF:

```
var = 10 inches
var = 25.4 centimeters
```

The next example, PASSPTR, shows an equivalent situation when pointers are used:

```
// passptr.cpp
// arguments passed by pointer
#include <iostream>
using namespace std;

int main()
   {
   void centimize(double*);       //prototype

   double var = 10.0;              //var has value of 10 inches
   cout << "var = " << var << " inches" << endl;

   centimize(&var);               //change var to centimeters
   cout << "var = " << var << " centimeters" << endl;
   return 0;
   }
//-------------------------------------------------------------
d centimize(double* ptrd)
```

```
{
*ptrd *= 2.54;                    //*ptrd is the same as var
}
```

The output of PASSPTR is the same as that of PASSREF.

The function centimize() is declared as taking an argument that is a pointer to double:

```
void centimize(double*)    // argument is pointer to double
```

When main() calls the function, it supplies the address of the variable as the argument:

```
centimize(&var);
```

Remember that this is not the variable itself, as it is in passing by reference, but the variable's address.

Because the centimize() function is passed an address, it must use the dereference operator, *ptrd, to access the value stored at this address:

```
*ptrd *= 2.54;  // multiply the contents of ptrd by 2.54
```

Of course this is the same as

```
*ptrd = *ptrd * 2.54;  // multiply the contents of ptrd by 2.54
```

where the standalone asterisk means multiplication. (This operator really gets around.)

Since ptrd contains the address of var, anything done to *ptrd is actually done to var. Figure 10.6 shows how changing *ptrd in the function changes var in the calling program.

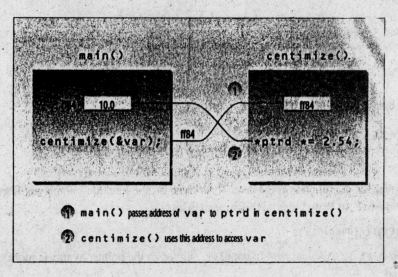

FIGURE 10.6
Pointer passed to function.

Passing a pointer as an argument to a function is in some ways similar to passing a reference. They both permit the variable in the calling program to be modified by the function. However, the mechanism is different. A reference is an alias for the original variable, while a pointer is the address of the variable.

Passing Arrays

We've seen numerous examples, starting in Chapter 7, of arrays passed as arguments to functions, and their elements being accessed by the function. Until this chapter, since we had not yet learned about pointers, this was done using array notation. However, it's more common to use pointer notation instead of array notation when arrays are passed to functions. The PASSARR program shows how this looks:

```
// passarr.cpp
// array passed by pointer
#include <iostream>
using namespace std;
const int MAX = 5;              //number of array elements

int main()
   {
   void centimize(double*);  //prototype

   double varray[MAX] = { 10.0, 43.1, 95.9, 59.7, 87.3 };

   centimize(varray);           //change elements of varray to cm

   for(int j=0; j<MAX; j++)  //display new array values
      cout << "varray[" << j << "]="
           << varray[j] << " centimeters" << endl;
   return 0;
   }
//.............................................................
void centimize(double* ptrd)
   {
   for(int j=0; j<MAX; j++)
      *ptrd++ *= 2.54;          //ptrd points to elements of varray
   }
```

The prototype for the function is the same as in PASSPTR; the function's single argument is a pointer to double. In array notation this is written as

```
void centimize(double[]);
```

That is, double* is equivalent here to double[], although the pointer syntax is more commonly used.

Since the name of an array is the array's address, there is no need for the address operator &
when the function is called:

```
centimize(varray);   // pass array address
```

In `centimize()`, this array address is placed in the variable `ptrd`. To point to each element of
the array in turn, we need only increment `ptrd`:

```
*ptrd++ *= 2.54;
```

Figure 10.7 shows how the array is accessed. Here's the output of PASSARR:

```
varray[0]=25.4 centimeters
varray[1]=109.474 centimeters
varray[2]=243.586 centimeters
varray[3]=151.638 centimeters
varray[4]=221.742 centimeters
```

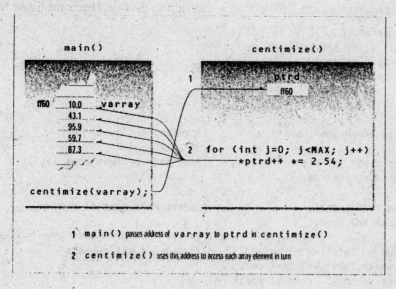

FIGURE 10.7
Accessing an array from a function.

Here's a syntax question: How do we know that the expression `*ptrd++` increments the pointer
and not the pointer contents? In other words, does the compiler interpret it as `*(ptrd++)`,
which is what we want, or as `(*ptrd)++`? It turns out that `*` (when used as the dereference
operator) and `++` have the same precedence. However, operators of the same precedence are
distinguished in a second way: by *associativity*. Associativity is concerned with whether the
compiler performs operations starting with an operator on the right or an operator on the left.

If a group of operators has right associativity, the compiler performs the operation on the right side of the expression first, then works its way to the left. The unary operators such as * and ++ have right associativity, so the expression is interpreted as *(ptrd++), which increments the pointer, not what it points to. That is, the pointer is incremented first and the dereference operator is applied to the resulting address.

Sorting Array Elements

As a further example of using pointers to access array elements, let's see how to sort the contents of an array. We'll use two program examples—the first to lay the groundwork, and the second, an expansion of the first, to demonstrate the sorting process.

Ordering with Pointers

The first program is similar to the REFORDER program in Chapter 6, "Objects and Classes," except that it uses pointers instead of references. It orders two numbers passed to it as arguments, exchanging them if the second is smaller than the first. Here's the listing for PTRORDER:

```
// ptrorder.cpp
// orders two arguments using pointers
#include <iostream>
using namespace std;

int main()
   {
   void order(int*, int*);           //prototype

   int n1=99, n2=11;                 //one pair ordered, one not
   int n3=22, n4=88;

   order(&n1, &n2);                  //order each pair of numbers
   order(&n3, &n4);

   cout << "n1=" << n1 << endl;      //print out all numbers
   cout << "n2=" << n2 << endl;
   cout << "n3=" << n3 << endl;
   cout << "n4=" << n4 << endl;
   return 0;
   }
//------------------------------------------------------------
void order(int* numb1, int* numb2) //orders two numbers
   {
   if(*numb1 > *numb2)               //if 1st larger than 2nd,
      {
      int temp = *numb1;            //swap them
      *numb1 = *numb2;
```

```
         *numb2 = temp;
      }
   }
```

The function order() works the same as it did in REFORDER, except that it is passed the addresses of the numbers to be ordered, and it accesses the numbers using pointers. That is, *numb1 accesses the number in main() passed as the first argument, and *numb2 accesses the second.

Here's the output from PTRORDER:

```
n1=11   ←──────── this and
n2=99   ←──────── this are swapped, since they weren't in order
n3=22   ←──────── this and
n4=88   ←──────── this are not swapped, since they were in order
```

We'll use the order() function from PTRORDER in our next example program, PTRSORT, which sorts an array of integers.

```
// ptrsort.cpp
// sorts an array using pointers
#include <iostream>
using namespace std;

int main()
   {
   void bsort(int*, int);          //prototype
   const int N = 10;               //array size
                                   //test array
   int arr[N] = { 37, 84, 62, 91, 11, 65, 57, 28, 19, 49 };

   bsort(arr, N);                  //sort the array

   for(int j=0; j<N; j++)          //print out sorted array
      cout << arr[j] << " ";
   cout << endl;
   return 0;
   }
//········································································
void bsort(int* ptr, int n)
   {
   void order(int*, int*);         //prototype
   int j, k;                       //indexes to array

   for(j=0; j<n-1; j++)            //outer loop
      for(k=j+1; k<n; k++)         //inner loop starts at outer
         order(ptr+j, ptr+k);      //order the pointer contents
   }
```

10

```
//-----------------------------------------------------------
void order(int* numb1, int* numb2)   //orders two numbers
   {
   if(*numb1 > *numb2)              //if 1st larger than 2nd,
      {
      int temp = *numb1;           //swap them
      *numb1 = *numb2;
      *numb2 = temp;
      }
   }
```

The array arr of integers in main() is initialized to unsorted values. The address of the array, and the number of elements, are passed to the bsort() function. This sorts the array, and the sorted values are then printed. Here's the output of the PTRSORT:

```
11  19  28  37  49  57  62  65  84  91
```

The Bubble Sort

The bsort() function sorts the array using a variation of the bubble sort. This is a simple (although notoriously slow) approach to sorting. Here's how it works, assuming we want to arrange the numbers in the array in ascending order. First the first element of the array (arr[0]) is compared in turn with each of the other elements (starting with the second). If it's greater than any of them, the two are swapped. When this is done we know that at least the first element is in order; it's now the smallest element. Next the second element is compared in turn with all the other elements, starting with the third, and again swapped if it's bigger. When we're done we know that the second element has the second-smallest value. This process is continued for all the elements until the next-to-the-last, at which time the array is assumed to be ordered. Figure 10.8 shows the bubble sort in action (with fewer items than in PTRSORT).

In PTRSORT, the number in the first position, 37, is compared with each element in turn, and swapped with 11. The number in the second position, which starts off as 84, is compared with each element. It's swapped with 62; then 62 (which is now in the second position) is swapped with 37, 37 is swapped with 28, and 28 is swapped with 19. The number in the third position, which is 84 again, is swapped with 62, 62 is swapped with 57, 57 with 37, and 37 with 28. The process continues until the array is sorted.

The bsort() function in PTRSORT consists of two nested loops, each of which controls a pointer. The outer loop uses the loop variable j, and the inner one uses k. The expressions ptr+j and ptr+k point to various elements of the array, as determined by the loop variables. The expression ptr+j moves down the array, starting at the first element (the top) and stepping down integer by integer until one short of the last element (the bottom). For each position taken by ptr+j in the outer loop, the expression ptr+k in the inner loop starts pointing one below ptr+j and moves down to the bottom of the array. Each time through the inner loop, the elements pointed to by `ptr+j` and `ptr+k` are compared, using the `order()` function, and if the first is greater than the second, they're swapped. Figure 10.9 shows this process.

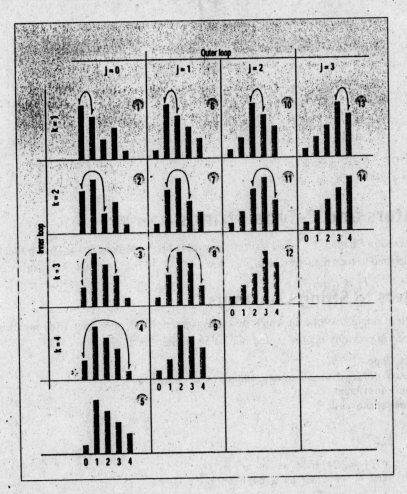

FIGURE 10.8
Operation of the bubble sort.

The PTRSORT example begins to reveal the power of pointers. They provide a consistent and efficient way to operate on array elements and other variable whose names aren't known to a particular function.

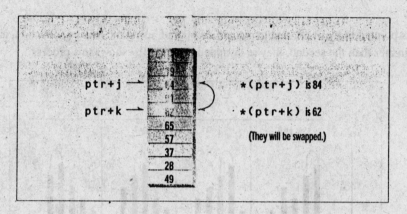

FIGURE 10.9
Operation of PTRSORT.

Pointers and C-Type Strings

As we noted in Chapter 7, C-type strings are simply arrays of type char. Thus pointer notation can be applied to the characters in strings, just as it can to the elements of any array.

Pointers to String Constants

Here's an example, TWOSTR, in which two strings are defined, one using array notation as we've seen in previous examples, and one using pointer notation:

```
// twostr.cpp
// strings defined using array and pointer notation
#include <iostream>
using namespace std;

int main()
   {
   char str1[] = "Defined as an array";
   char* str2 = "Defined as a pointer";

   cout << str1 << endl;      // display both strings
   cout << str2 << endl;

// str1++;                    // can't do this; str1 is a constant
   str2++;                    // this is OK, str2 is a pointer

   cout << str2 << endl;      // now str2 starts "efined..."
   return 0;
   }
```

In many ways these two types of definition are equivalent. You can print out both strings as the example shows, use them as function arguments, and so on. But there is a subtle difference: str1 is an address—that is, a pointer constant—while str2 is a pointer variable. So str2 can be changed, while str1 cannot, as shown in the program. Figure 10.10 shows how these two kinds of strings look in memory.

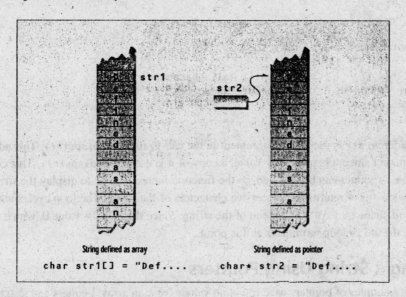

FIGURE 10.10
Strings as arrays and pointers.

We can increment str2, since it is a pointer, but once we do, it no longer points to the first character in the string. Here's the output of TWOSTR:

```
Defined as an array
Defined as a pointer
efined as a pointer      ←——— following str2++ ('D' is gone)
```

A string defined as a pointer is considerably more flexible than one defined as an array. The following examples will make use of this flexibility.

Strings as Function Arguments

Here's an example that shows a string used as a function argument. The function simply prints the string, by accessing each character in turn. Here's the listing for PTRSTR:

```
// ptrstr.cpp
// displays a string with pointer notation
#include <iostream>
using namespace std;
```

```
int main()
   {
   void dispstr(char*);        //prototype
   char str[] = "Idle people have the least leisure.";

   dispstr(str);               //display the string
   return 0;
   }
//----------------------------------------------------------------
void dispstr(char* ps)
   {
   while( *ps )                //until null character,
      cout << *ps++;           //print characters
   cout << endl;
   }
```

The array address str is used as the argument in the call to function dispstr(). This address
is a constant, but since it is passed by value, a copy of it is created in dispstr(). This copy is
a pointer, ps. A pointer can be changed, so the function increments ps to display the string.
The expression *ps++ returns the successive characters of the string. The loop cycles until it
finds the null character ('\0') at the end of the string. Since this has the value 0, which represents *false*, the while loop terminates at this point.

Copying a String Using Pointers

We've seen examples of pointers used to obtain values from an array. Pointers can also be used
to insert values into an array. The next example, COPYSTR, demonstrates a function that copies
one string to another:

```
// copystr.cpp
// copies one string to another with pointers
#include <iostream>
using namespace std;

int main()
   {
   void copystr(char*, const char*);  //prototype
   char* str1 = "Self-conquest is the greatest victory.";
   char str2[80];                  //empty string

   copystr(str2, str1);            //copy str1 to str2
   cout << str2 << endl;           //display str2
   return 0;
   }
```

```
//·······················································
void copystr(char* dest, const char* src)
   {
   while( *src )                    //until null character,
      *dest++ = *src++;             //copy chars from src to dest
   *dest = '\0';                    //terminate dest
   }
```

Here the main() part of the program calls the function copystr() to copy str1 to str2. In this function the expression

```
*dest++ = *src++;
```

takes the value at the address pointed to by src and places it in the address pointed to by dest. Both pointers are then incremented, so the next time through the loop the next character will be transferred. The loop terminates when a null character is found in src; at this point a null is inserted in dest and the function returns. Figure 10.11 shows how the pointers move through the strings.

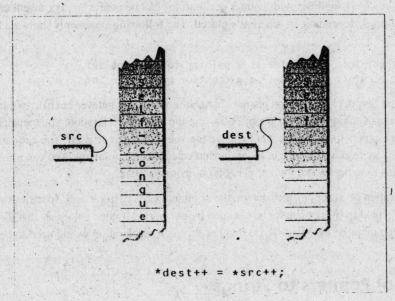

FIGURE 10.11
Operation of COPYSTR.

Library String Functions

Many of the library functions we have already used for strings have string arguments that are specified using pointer notation. As an example you can look at the description of strcpy() in your compiler's documentation (or in the STRING.H header file). This function copies one string to another; we can compare it with our homemade copystr() function in the COPYSTR example. Here's the syntax for the strcpy() library function:

```
char* strcpy(char* dest, const char* src);
```

This function takes two arguments of type char*. (The next section, "The const Modifier and Pointers," explains the meaning of const in this context.) The strcpy() function also returns a pointer to char; this is the address of the dest string. In other respects, this function works very much like our homemade copystr() function.

The const Modifier and Pointers

The use of the const modifier with pointer declarations can be confusing, because it can mean one of two things, depending on where it's placed. The following statements show the two possibilities:

```
const int* cptrInt;   //cptrInt is a pointer to constant int
int* const ptrcInt;   //ptrcInt is a constant pointer to int
```

Following the first declaration, you cannot change the value of whatever cptrInt points to, although you can change cptrInt itself. Following the second declaration, you can change what ptrcInt points to, but you cannot change the value of ptrcInt itself. You can remember the difference by reading from right to left, as indicated in the comments. You can use const in both positions to make the pointer and what it points to constant.

In the declaration of strcpy() just shown, the argument const char* src specifies that the characters pointed to by src cannot be changed by strcpy(). It does not imply that the src pointer itself cannot be modified. To do that the argument declaration would need to be char* const src.

Arrays of Pointers to Strings

Just as there are arrays of variables of type int or type float, there can also be arrays of pointers. A common use for this construction is an array of pointers to strings.

In Chapter 7 the STRARAY program demonstrated an array of char* strings. As we noted, there is a disadvantage to using an array of strings, in that the subarrays that hold the strings must all be the same length, so space is wasted when strings are shorter than the length of the subarrays (see Figure 7.10 in Chapter 7).

Let's see how to use pointers to solve this problem. We will modify STRARAY to create an array of pointers to strings, rather than an array of strings. Here's the listing for PTRTOSTR:

```cpp
// ptrtostr.cpp
// an array of pointers to strings
#include <iostream>
using namespace std;
const int DAYS = 7;                 //number of pointers in array

int main()
   {                                //array of pointers to char
   char* arrptrs[DAYS] = { "Sunday", "Monday", "Tuesday",
             "Wednesday", "Thursday",
             "Friday", "Saturday"  };

   for(int j=0; j<DAYS; j++)    //display every string
      cout << arrptrs[j] << endl;
   return 0;
   }
```

The output of this program is the same as that for STRARAY:

```
Sunday
Monday
Tuesday
Wednesday
Thursday
Friday
Saturday
```

When strings are not part of an array, C++ places them contiguously in memory, so there is no wasted space. However, to find the strings, there must be an array that holds pointers to them. A string is itself an array of type char, so an array of pointers to strings is an array of pointers to char. That is the meaning of the definition of arrptrs in PTRTOSTR. Now recall that a string is always represented by a single address: the address of the first character in the string. It is these addresses that are stored in the array. Figure 10.12 shows how this looks.

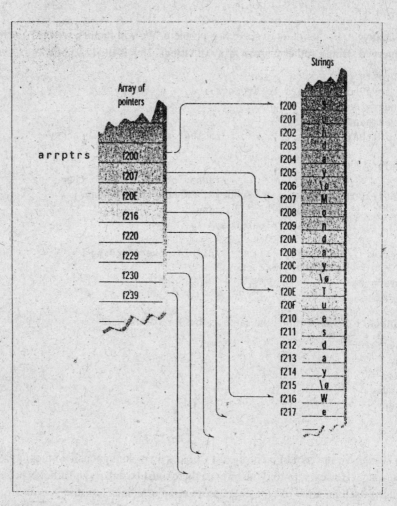

FIGURE 10.12
Array of pointers and strings.

Memory Management: new and delete

We've seen many examples where arrays are used to set aside memory. The statement

```
int arr1[100];
```

reserves memory for 100 integers. Arrays are a useful approach to data storage, but they have a serious drawback: We must know at the time we write the program how big the array will be. We can't wait until the program is running to specify the array size. The following approach won't work:

```
cin >> size;      // get size from user
int arr[size];    // error; array size must be a constant
```

The compiler requires the array size to be a constant.

But in many situations we don't know how much memory we need until runtime. We might want to store a string that was typed in by the user, for example. In this situation we can define an array sized to hold the largest string we expect, but this wastes memory. (As we'll learn in Chapter 15, "The Standard Template Library," you can also use a vector, which is a sort of expandable array.)

The new Operator

C++ provides a different approach to obtaining blocks of memory: the new operator. This versatile operator obtains memory from the operating system and returns a pointer to its starting point. The NEWINTRO example shows how new is used:

```
// newintro.cpp
// introduces operator new
#include <iostream>
#include <cstring>               //for strlen
using namespace std;

int main()
   {
   char* str = "Idle hands are the devil's workshop.";
   int len = strlen(str);       //get length of str

   char* ptr;                   //make a pointer to char
   ptr = new char[len+1];       //set aside memory: string + '\0'

   strcpy(ptr, str);            //copy str to new memory area ptr

   cout << "ptr=" << ptr << endl;  //show that ptr is now in str

   delete[] ptr;                //release ptr's memory
   return 0;
   }
```

The expression

```
ptr = new char[len+1];
```

returns a pointer to a section of memory just large enough to hold the string str, whose length len we found with the strlen() library function, plus an extra byte for the null character '\0' at the end of the string. Figure 10.13 shows the syntax of a statement using the new operator. Remember to use brackets around the size; the compiler won't object if you mistakenly use parentheses, but the results will be incorrect.

10

POINTERS

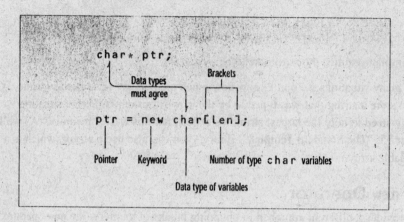

FIGURE 10.13
Syntax of the new *operator.*

Figure 10.14 shows the memory obtained by new and the pointer to it.

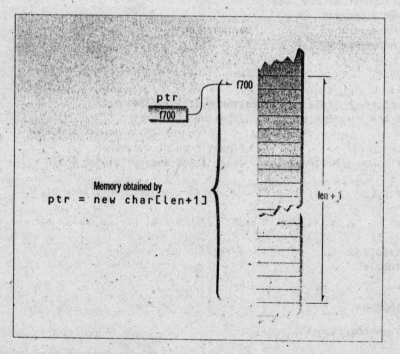

FIGURE 10.14
Memory obtained by the new *operator.*

In NEWINTRO we use strcpy() to copy string str to the newly created memory area pointed to by ptr. Since we made this area equal in size to the length of str, the string fits exactly. The output of NEWINTRO is

```
ptr=Idle hands are the devil's workshop.
```

C programmers will recognize that new plays a role similar to the malloc() family of library functions. The new approach is superior in that it returns a pointer to the appropriate data type, while malloc()'s pointer must be cast to the appropriate type. There are other advantages as well.

C programmers may wonder whether there is a C++ equivalent to realloc() for changing the size of memory that has already been reallocated. Sorry, there's no renew in C++. You'll need to fall back on the ploy of creating a larger (or smaller) space with new, and copying your data from the old area to the new one.

The delete Operator

If your program reserves many chunks of memory using new, eventually all the available memory will be reserved and the system will crash. To ensure safe and efficient use of memory, the new operator is matched by a corresponding delete operator that returns memory to the operating system. In NEWINTRO the statement

```
delete[] ptr;
```

returns to the system whatever memory was pointed to by ptr.

Actually, there is no need for this operator in NEWINTRO, since memory is automatically returned when the program terminates. However, suppose you use new in a function. If the function uses a local variable as a pointer to this memory, the pointer will be destroyed when the function terminates, but the memory will be left as an orphan, taking up space that is inaccessible to the rest of the program. Thus it is always good practice, and often essential, to delete memory when you're through with it.

Deleting the memory doesn't delete the pointer that points to it (str in NEWINTRO), and doesn't change the address value in the pointer. However, this address is no longer valid; the memory it points to may be changed to something entirely different. Be careful that you don't use pointers to memory that has been deleted.

The brackets following delete indicate that we're deleting an array. If you create a single object with new, you don't need the brackets when you delete it.

```
ptr = new SomeClass;   // allocate a single object
. . .
delete ptr;            // no brackets following delete
```

10

POINTERS

However, don't forget the brackets when deleting arrays of objects. Using them ensures that all the members of the array are deleted, and that the destructor is called for each one.

A String Class Using new

The new operator often appears in constructors. As an example, we'll modify the String class, last seen in examples such as STRPLUS in Chapter 8, "Operator Overloading." You may recall that a potential defect of that class was that all String objects occupied the same fixed amount of memory. A string shorter than this fixed length wasted memory, and a longer string—if one were mistakenly generated—could crash the system by extending beyond the end of the array. Our next example uses new to obtain exactly the right amount of memory. Here's the listing for NEWSTR:

```cpp
// newstr.cpp
// using new to get memory for strings
#include <iostream>
#include <cstring>          //for strcpy(), etc
using namespace std;
/////////////////////////////////////////////////////////////////////
class String                    //user-defined string type
   {
   private:
      char* str;                       //pointer to string
   public:
      String(char* s)                  //constructor, one arg
         {
         int length = strlen(s);    //length of string argument
         str = new char[length+1];  //get memory
         strcpy(str, s);            //copy argument to it
         }
      -String()                        //destructor
         {
         cout << "Deleting str.\n";
         delete[] str;                 //release memory
         }
      void display()                   //display the String
         {
         cout << str << endl;
         }
   };
/////////////////////////////////////////////////////////////////////
int main()
   {                                 //uses 1-arg constructor
   String s1 = "Who knows nothing doubts nothing.";
```

```
cout << "s1=";                        //display string
s1.display();
return 0;
}
```

The output from this program is

```
s1=Who knows nothing doubts nothing.
Deleting str.
```

The `String` class has only one data item: a pointer to `char` called `str`. This pointer will point to the string held by the `String` object. There is no array within the object to hold the string. The string is stored elsewhere; only the pointer to it is a member of `String`.

Constructor in NEWSTR

The constructor in this example takes a normal `char*` string as its argument. It obtains space in memory for this string with `new`; `str` points to the newly obtained memory. The constructor then uses `strcpy()` to copy the string into this new space.

Destructor in NEWSTR

We haven't seen many destructors in our examples so far, but now that we're allocating memory with `new`, destructors become important. If we allocate memory when we create an object, it's reasonable to deallocate the memory when the object is no longer needed. As you may recall from Chapter 6, a destructor is a routine that is called automatically when an object is destroyed. The destructor in NEWSTR looks like this:

```
~String()
   {
   cout << "Deleting str.";
   delete[] str;
   }
```

This destructor gives back to the system the memory obtained when the object was created. You can tell from the program's output that the destructor executed at the end of the program. Objects (like other variables) are typically destroyed when the function in which they were defined terminates. This destructor ensures that memory obtained by the `String` object will be returned to the system, and not left in limbo, when the object is destroyed.

We should note a potential glitch in using destructors as shown in NEWSTR. If you copy one `String` object to another, say with a statement like `s2 = s1`, you're really only copying the pointer to the actual (`char*`) string. Both objects now point to the same string in memory. But if you now delete one string, the destructor will delete the `char*` string, leaving the other object with an invalid pointer. This can be subtle, because objects can be deleted in non-obvious ways, such as when a function in which a local object has been created returns. In Chapter 11 we'll see how to make a smarter destructor that counts how many `String` objects are pointing to a string.

Pointers to Objects

Pointers can point to objects as well as to simple data types and arrays. We've seen many examples of objects defined and given a name, in statements like

```
Distance dist;
```

where an object called dist is defined to be of the Distance class.

Sometimes, however, we don't know, at the time that we write the program, how many objects we want to create. When this is the case we can use new to create objects while the program is running. As we've seen, new returns a pointer to an unnamed object. Let's look at a short example program, ENGLPTR, that compares the two approaches to creating objects.

```cpp
// englptr.cpp
// accessing member functions by pointer
#include <iostream>
using namespace std;
//////////////////////////////////////////////////////////////
class Distance               //English Distance class
   {
   private:
      int feet;
      float inches;
   public:
      void getdist()         //get length from user
         {
         cout << "\nEnter feet: ";  cin >> feet;
         cout << "Enter inches: ";  cin >> inches;
         }
      void showdist()        //display distance
         { cout << feet << "\'-" << inches << '\"'; }
   };
//////////////////////////////////////////////////////////////
int main()
   {
   Distance dist;            //define a named Distance object
   dist.getdist();           //access object members
   dist.showdist();          //   with dot operator

   Distance* distptr;        //pointer to Distance
   distptr = new Distance;   //points to new Distance object
   distptr->getdist();       //access object members
   distptr->showdist();      //   with -> operator
   cout << endl;
   return 0;
   }
```

This program uses a variation of the English Distance class seen in previous chapters. The main() function defines dist, uses the Distance member function getdist() to get a distance from the user, and then uses showdist() to display it.

Referring to Members

ENGLPTR then creates another object of type Distance using the new operator, and returns a pointer to it called distptr.

The question is, how do we refer to the member functions in the object pointed to by distptr? You might guess that we would use the dot (.) membership-access operator, as in

```
distptr.getdist();   // won't work; distptr is not a variable
```

but this won't work. The dot operator requires the identifier on its left to be a variable. Since distptr is a pointer to a variable, we need another syntax. One approach is to *dereference* (get the contents of the variable pointed to by) the pointer:

```
(*distptr).getdist(); // ok but inelegant
```

However, this is slightly cumbersome because of the parentheses. (The parentheses are necessary because the dot operator (.) has higher precedence than the dereference operator (*). An equivalent but more concise approach is furnished by the membership-access operator, which consists of a hyphen and a greater-than sign:

```
distptr->getdist();   // better approach
```

As you can see in ENGLPTR, the -> operator works with pointers to objects in just the same way that the . operator works with objects. Here's the output of the program:

```
Enter feet: 10 ←——— this object uses the dot operator
Enter inches: 6.25
10'-6.25"

Enter feet: 6    ←——— this object uses the -> operator
Enter inches: 4.75
6'-4.75"
```

Another Approach to new

You may come across another—less common—approach to using new to obtain memory for objects.

Since new can return a pointer to an area of memory that holds an object, we should be able to refer to the original object by dereferencing the pointer. The ENGLREF example shows how this is done.

```
// englref.cpp
// dereferencing the pointer returned by new
#include <iostream>
using namespace std;
/////////////////////////////////////////////////////////////////
class Distance                       // English Distance class
    {
    private:
        int feet;
        float inches;
    public:
        void getdist()               // get length from user
            {
            cout << "\nEnter feet: ";  cin >> feet;
            cout << "Enter inches: ";  cin >> inches;
            }
        void showdist()              // display distance
            { cout << feet << "\'-" << inches << '\"'; }
    };
/////////////////////////////////////////////////////////////////
int main()
    {
    Distance& dist = *(new Distance);  // create Distance object
                                       // alias is "dist"
    dist.getdist();                    // access object members
    dist.showdist();                   //    with dot operator
    cout << endl;
    return 0;
    }
```

The expression

```
new Distance
```

returns a pointer to a memory area large enough for a `Distance` object, so we can refer to the
original object as

```
*(new Distance)
```

This is the object pointed to by the pointer. Using a reference, we define `dist` to be an object
of type `Distance`, and we set it equal to `*(new Distance)`. Now we can refer to members of
`dist` using the dot membership operator, rather than `->`.

This approach is less common than using pointers to objects obtained with new, or simply
declaring an object, but it works in a similar way.

An Array of Pointers to Objects

A common programming construction is an array of pointers to objects. This arrangement allows easy access to a group of objects, and is more flexible than placing the objects themselves in an array. (For instance, in the PERSORT example in this chapter we'll see how a group of objects can be sorted by sorting an array of pointers to them, rather than sorting the objects themselves.)

Our next example, PTROBJS, creates an array of pointers to the person class. Here's the listing:

```cpp
// ptrobjs.cpp
// array of pointers to objects
#include <iostream>
using namespace std;
/////////////////////////////////////////////////////////////////
class person                    //class of persons
   {
   protected:
      char name[40];            //person's name
   public:
      void setName()            //set the name
         {
         cout << "Enter name: ";
         cin >> name;
         }
      void printName()          //get the name
         {
         cout << "\n   Name is: " << name;
         }
   };
/////////////////////////////////////////////////////////////////
int main()
   {
   person* persPtr[100];    //array of pointers to persons
   int n = 0;               //number of persons in array
   char choice;

   do                                   //put persons in array
      {
      persPtr[n] = new person;          //make new object
      persPtr[n]->setName();            //set person's name
      n++;                              //count new person
      cout << "Enter another (y/n)? "; //enter another
      cin >> choice;                    //person?
      }
   while( choice=='y' );                //quit on 'n'
```

10

POINTERS

```
    for(int j=0; j<n; j++)              //print names of
       {                                //all persons
       cout << "\nPerson number " << j+1;
       persPtr[j]->printName();
       }
    cout << endl;
    return 0;
    } //end main()
```

The class person has a single data item, name, which holds a string representing a person's name. Two member functions, setName() and printName(), allow the name to be set and displayed.

Program Operation

The main() function defines an array, persPtr, of 100 pointers to type person. In a do loop it then asks the user to enter a name. With this name it creates a person object using new, and stores a pointer to this object in the array persPtr. To demonstrate how easy it is to access the objects using the pointers, it then prints out the name data for each person object.

Here's a sample interaction with the program:

```
Enter name: Stroustrup        ←——— user enters names
Enter another (y/n)? y
Enter name: Ritchie
Enter another (y/n)? y
Enter name: Kernighan
Enter another (y/n)? n
Person number 1      ←——— program displays all names stored
   Name is: Stroustrup
Person number 2
   Name is: Ritchie
Person number 3
   Name is: Kernighan
```

Accessing Member Functions

We need to access the member functions setName() and printName() in the person objects pointed to by the pointers in the array persPtr. Each of the elements of the array persPtr is specified in array notation to be persPtr[j] (or equivalently by pointer notation to be *(persPtr+j)). The elements are pointers to objects of type person. To access a member of an object using a pointer, we use the -> operator. Putting this all together, we have the following syntax for getname():

```
persPtr[j]->getName()
```

This executes the getname() function in the person object pointed to by element j of the persPtr array. (It's a good thing we don't have to program using English syntax.)

A Linked List Example

Our next example shows a simple linked list. What is a linked list? It's another way to store
data. You've seen numerous examples of data stored in arrays. Another data structure is an
array of pointers to data members, as in the PTRTOSTRS and PTROBJS examples. Both the array
and the array of pointers suffer from the necessity to declare a fixed-size array before running
the program.

A Chain of Pointers

The linked list provides a more flexible storage system in that it doesn't use arrays at all.
Instead, space for each data item is obtained as needed with new, and each item is connected,
or *linked*, to the next data item using a pointer. The individual items don't need to be located
contiguously in memory the way array elements are; they can be scattered anywhere.

In our example the entire linked list is an object of class linklist. The individual data items,
or links, are represented by structures of type link. Each such structure contains an integer—
representing the object's single data item—and a pointer to the next link. The list itself stores a
pointer to the link at the head of the list. This arrangement is shown in Figure 10.15.

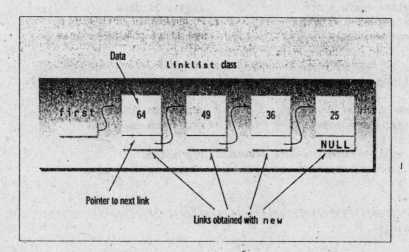

FIGURE 10.15
A linked list.

Here's the listing for LINKLIST:

```
// linklist.cpp
// linked list
#include <iostream>
using namespace std;
```

```
///////////////////////////////////////////////////////////////
struct link                        //one element of list
   {
   int data;                       //data item
   link* next;                     //pointer to next link
   };
///////////////////////////////////////////////////////////////
class linklist                     //a list of links
   {
   private:
      link* first;                 //pointer to first link
   public:
      linklist()                   //no-argument constructor
         { first = NULL; }         //no first link
      void additem(int d);         //add data item (one link)
      void display();              //display all links
   };
//--------------------------------------------------------------
void linklist::additem(int d)      //add data item
   {
   link* newlink = new link;       //make a new link
   newlink->data = d;              //give it data
   newlink->next = first;          //it points to next link
   first = newlink;                //now first points to this
   }
//--------------------------------------------------------------
void linklist::display()           //display all links
   {
   link* current = first;          //set ptr to first link
   while( current != NULL )        //quit on last link
      {
      cout << current->data << endl; //print data
      current = current->next;     //move to next link
      }
   }
///////////////////////////////////////////////////////////////
int main()
   {
   linklist li;         //make linked list

   li.additem(25);      //add four items to list
   li.additem(36);
   li.additem(49);
   li.additem(64);
```

```
    li.display();          //display entire list
    return 0;
    }
```

The linklist class has only one member data item: the pointer to the start of the list. When the list is first created, the constructor initializes this pointer, which is called first, to NULL. The NULL constant is defined to be 0. This value serves as a signal that a pointer does not hold a valid address. In our program a link whose next member has a value of NULL is assumed to be at the end of the list.

Adding an Item to the List

The additem() member function adds an item to the linked list. A new link is inserted at the beginning of the list. (We could write the additem() function to insert items at the end of the list, but that is a little more complex to program.) Let's look at the steps involved in inserting a new link.

First, a new structure of type link is created by the line

```
link* newlink = new link;
```

This creates memory for the new link structure with new and saves the pointer to it in the newlink variable.

Next we want to set the members of the newly created structure to appropriate values. A structure is similar to a class in that, when it is referred to by pointer rather than by name, its members are accessed using the -> member-access operator. The following two lines set the data variable to the value passed as an argument to additem(), and the next pointer to point to whatever address was in first, which holds the pointer to the start of the list.

```
newlink->data = d;
newlink->next = first;
```

Finally, we want the first variable to point to the new link:

```
first = newlink;
```

The effect is to uncouple the connection between first and the old first link, insert the new link, and move the old first link into the second position. Figure 10.16 shows this process.

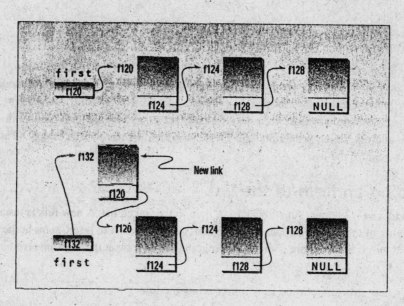

FIGURE 10.16
Adding to a linked list.

Displaying the List Contents

Once the list is created it's easy to step through all the members, displaying them (or performing other operations). All we need to do is follow from one next pointer to another until we find a next that is NULL, signaling the end of the list. In the function display(), the line

```
cout << endl << current->data;
```

prints the value of the data, and

```
current = current->next;
```

moves us along from one link to another, until

```
current != NULL
```

in the while expression becomes false. Here's the output of LINKLIST:

```
64
49
36
25
```

Linked lists are perhaps the most commonly used data storage arrangements after arrays. As we noted, they avoid the wasting of memory space engendered by arrays. The disadvantage is that finding a particular item on a linked list requires following the chain of links from the head of the list until the desired link is reached. This can be time-consuming. An array element, on the other hand, can be accessed quickly, provided its index is known in advance. We'll have more to say about linked lists and other data-storage techniques in Chapter 15, "The Standard Template Library."

Self-Containing Classes

We should note a possible pitfall in the use of self-referential classes and structures. The link structure in LINKLIST contained a pointer to the same kind of structure. You can do the same with classes:

```
class sampleclass
    {
    sampleclass* ptr;  // this is fine
    };
```

However, while a class can contain a pointer to an object of its own type, it cannot contain an *object* of its own type:

```
class sampleclass
    {
    sampleclass obj;  // can't do this
    };
```

This is true of structures as well as classes.

Augmenting LINKLIST

The general organization of LINKLIST can serve for a more complex situation than that shown. There could be more data in each link. Instead of an integer, a link could hold a number of data items or it could hold a pointer to a structure or object.

Additional member functions could perform such activities as adding and removing links from an arbitrary part of the chain. Another important member function is a destructor. As we mentioned, it's important to delete blocks of memory that are no longer in use. A destructor that performs this task would be a highly desirable addition to the linklist class. It could go through the list using delete to free the memory occupied by each link.

10

Pointers to Pointers

Our next example demonstrates an array of pointers to objects, and shows how to sort these pointers based on data in the object. This involves the idea of pointers to pointers, and may help demonstrate why people lose sleep over pointers.

The idea in the next program is to create an array of pointers to objects of the person class. This is similar to the PTROBJS example, but we go further and add variations of the order() and bsort() functions from the PTRSORT example so that we can sort a group of person objects based on the alphabetical order of their names. Here's the listing for PERSORT:

```cpp
// persort.cpp
// sorts person objects using array of pointers
#include <iostream>
#include <string>                    //for string class
using namespace std;
/////////////////////////////////////////////////////////////////
class person                         //class of persons
   {
   protected:
      string name;                   //person's name
   public:
      void setName()                 //set the name
         { cout << "Enter name: "; cin >> name; }
      void printName()               //display the name
         { cout << endl << name; }
      string getName()               //return the name
         { return name; }
   };
/////////////////////////////////////////////////////////////////
int main()
   {
   void bsort(person**, int);        //prototype
   person* persPtr[100];             //array of pointers to persons
   int n = 0;                        //number of persons in array
   char choice;                      //input char

   do {                              //put persons in array
      persPtr[n] = new person;       //make new object
      persPtr[n]->setName();         //set person's name
      n++;                           //count new person
      cout << "Enter another (y/n)? "; //enter another
      cin >> choice;                 //    person?
      }
```

```
    while( choice=='y' );           //quit on 'n'

    cout << "\nUnsorted list:";
    for(int j=0; j<n; j++)          //print unsorted list
        { persPtr[j]->printName(); }

    bsort(persPtr, n);              //sort pointers

    cout << "\nSorted list:";
    for(j=0; j<n; j++)              //print sorted list
        { persPtr[j]->printName(); }
    cout << endl;
    return 0;
    } //end main()
//----------------------------------------------------------------
void bsort(person** pp, int n)      //sort pointers to persons
    {
    void order(person**, person**);  //prototype
    int j, k;                        //indexes to array

    for(j=0; j<n-1; j++)            //outer loop
        for(k=j+1; k<n; k++)        //inner loop starts at outer
            order(pp+j, pp+k);      //order the pointer contents
    }
//----------------------------------------------------------------
void order(person** pp1, person** pp2)  //orders two pointers
    {                               //if 1st larger than 2nd,
    if( (*pp1)->getName() > (*pp2)->getName() )
        {
        person* tempptr = *pp1;     //swap the pointers
        *pp1 = *pp2;
        *pp2 = tempptr;
        }
    }
```

When the program is first executed it asks for a name. When the user gives it one, it creates an object of type person and sets the name data in this object to the name entered by the user. The program also stores a pointer to the object in the persPtr array.

When the user types n to indicate that no more names will be entered, the program calls the bsort() function to sort the person objects based on their name member variables. Here's some sample interaction with the program:

```
Enter name: Washington
Enter another (y/n)? y
Enter name: Adams
```

```
Enter another (y/n)? y
Enter name: Jefferson
Enter another (y/n)? y
Enter name: Madison
Enter another (y/n)? n
Unsorted list:
Washington
Adams
Jefferson
Madison

Sorted list:
Adams
Jefferson
Madison
Washington
```

Sorting Pointers

Actually, when we sort person objects, we don't move the objects themselves; we move the pointers to the objects. This eliminates the need to shuffle the objects around in memory, which can be very time-consuming if the objects are large. It could also, if we wanted, allow us to keep multiple sorts—one by name and another by phone number, for example—in memory at the same time without storing the objects multiple times. The process is shown in Figure 10.17.

To facilitate the sorting activity, we've added a getName() member function to the person class so we can access the names from order() to decide when to swap pointers.

The person** Data Type

You will notice that the first argument to the bsort() function, and both arguments to order(), have the type person**. What do the two asterisks mean? These arguments are used to pass the address of the array persPtr, or—in the case of order()—the addresses of elements of the array. If this were an array of type person, the address of the array would be type person*. However, the array is of type *pointers* to person, or person*, so its address is type person**. The address of a pointer is a pointer to a pointer. Figure 10.18 shows how this looks.

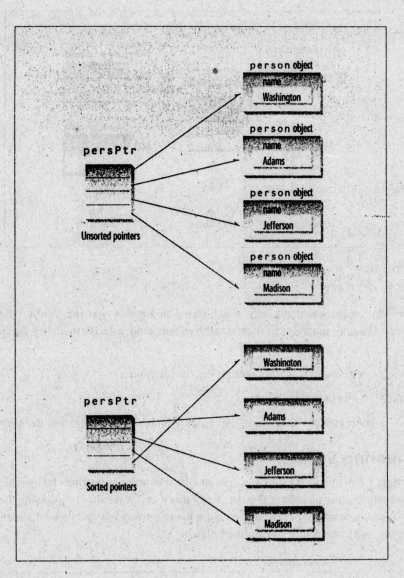

FIGURE 10.17
Sorting an array of pointers.

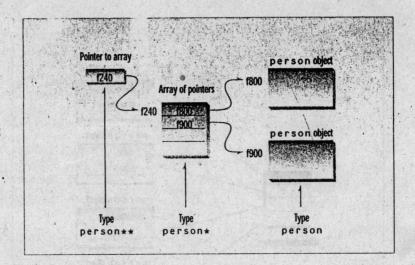

FIGURE 10.18
Pointer to an array of pointers.

Compare this program with PTRSORT, which sorted an array of type int. You'll find that the data types passed to functions in PERSORT all have one more asterisk than they did in PTRSORT, because the array is an array of pointers.

Since the persPtr array contains pointers, the construction

```
persPtr[j]->printName()
```

executes the printName() function in the object pointed to by element j of persPtr.

Comparing Strings

The order() function in PERSORT has been modified to order two strings lexigraphically—that is, by putting them in alphabetical order. To do this it compares the strings using the C++ library function strcmp(). This function takes the two strings s1 and s2 as arguments, as in strcmp(s1, s2), and returns one of the following values.

Value	Condition
<0	s1 comes before s2
0	s1 is the same as s2
>0	s1 comes after s2

The strings are accessed using the syntax

```
(*pp1)->getname()
```

The argument pp1 is a pointer to a pointer, and we want the name pointed to by the pointer it points to. The member-access operator -> dereferences one level, but we need to dereference another level, hence the asterisk preceding pp1.

Just as there can be pointers to pointers, there can be pointers to pointers to pointers, and so on. Fortunately such complexities are seldom encountered.

A Parsing Example

Programmers are frequently faced with the problem of unravelling or *parsing* a string of symbols. Examples are commands typed by a user at the keyboard, sentences in natural languages (such as English), statements in a programming language, and algebraic expressions. Now that we've learned about pointers and strings, we can handle this sort of problem.

Our next (somewhat longer) example will show how to parse arithmetic expressions like

6/3+2*3-1

The user enters the expression, the program works its way through it, character by character, figures out what it means in arithmetic terms, and displays the resulting value (7 in the example). Our expressions will use the four arithmetic operators: +, -, *, and /. We'll simplify the numbers we use to make the programming easier by restricting them to a single digit. Also, we won't allow parentheses.

This program makes use of our old friend the Stack class (see the STAKARAY program in Chapter 7). We've modified this class so that it stores data of type char. We use the stack to store both numbers and operators (both as characters). The stack is a useful storage mechanism because, when parsing expressions, we frequently need to access the last item stored, and a stack is a last-in-first-out (LIFO) container.

Besides the Stack class, we'll use a class called express (short for *expression*), representing an entire arithmetic expression. Member functions for this class allow us to initialize an object with an expression in the form of a string (entered by the user), parse the expression, and return the resulting arithmetic value.

Parsing Arithmetic Expressions

Here's how we parse an arithmetic expression. We start at the left, and look at each character in turn. It can be either a *number* (always a single digit—a character between 0 and 9), or an *operator* (the characters +, -, *, and /).

If the character is a number, we always push it onto the stack. We also push the first operator we encounter. The trick is how we handle subsequent operators. Note that we can't execute the current operator, because we haven't yet read the number that follows it. Finding an operator is

10

merely the signal that we can execute the previous operator, which is stored on the stack. That is, if the sequence 2+3 is on the stack, we wait until we find another operator before carrying out the addition.

Thus whenever we find that the current character is an operator (except the first), we pop the previous number (3 in the preceding example) and the previous operator (+) off the stack, placing them in the variables lastval and lastop. Finally we pop the first number (2) and carry out the arithmetic operation on the two numbers (obtaining 5). Can we always execute the previous operator? No. Remember that * and / have a higher precedence than + and -. In the expression 3+4/2, we can't execute the + until we've done the division. So when we get to the / in this expression, we must put the 2 and the + back on the stack until we've carried out the division.

On the other hand, if the current operator is a + or -, we know we can always execute the previous operator. That is, when we see the + in the expression 4-5+6, we know it's all right to execute the -, and when we see the - in 6/2-3 , we know it's okay to do the division. Table 10.1 shows the four possibilities.

TABLE 10.1 Operators and Parsing Actions

Previous Operator	Current Operator	Example	Action
+ or -	* or /	3+4/	Push previous operator and previous number (+, 4)
* or /	* or /	9/3*	Execute previous operator, push result (3)
+ or -	+ or -	6+3+	Execute previous operator, push result (9)
* or /	+ or -	8/2-	Execute previous operator, push result (4)

The parse() member function carries out this process of going through the input expression and performing those operations it can. However, there is more work to do. The stack still contains either a single number or several sequences of number-operator-number. Working down through the stack, we can execute these sequences. Finally, a single number is left on the stack; this is the value of the original expression. The solve() member function carries out this task, working its way down through the stack until only a single number is left. In general, parse() puts things on the stack, and solve() takes them off.

The PARSE Program

Some typical interaction with PARSE might look like this:

```
Enter an arithmetic expression
of the form 2+3*4/3-2.
No number may have more than one digit.
Don't use any spaces or parentheses.
Expression: 9+6/3

The numerical value is: 11
Do another (Enter y or n)?
```

Note that it's all right if the *results* of arithmetic operations contain more than one digit. They are limited only by the numerical size of type char, from ~128 to +127. Only the input string is limited to numbers from 0 to 9.

Here's the listing for the program:

```cpp
// parse.cpp
// evaluates arithmetic expressions composed of 1-digit numbers
#include <iostream>
#include <cstring>                     //for strlen(), etc
using namespace std;
const int LEN = 80;      //length of expressions, in characters
const int MAX = 40;      //size of stack
//////////////////////////////////////////////////////////////
class Stack
   {
   private:
      char st[MAX];                 //stack: array of chars
      int top;                      //number of top of stack
   public:
      Stack()                       //constructor
         { top = 0; }
      void push(char var)           //put char on stack
         { st[++top] = var; }
      char pop()                    //take char off stack
         { return st[top--]; }
      int gettop()                  //get top of stack
         { return top; }
   };
//////////////////////////////////////////////////////////////
class express                       //expression class
   {
   private:
      Stack s;                      //stack for analysi
      char* pStr;                   //pointer to input string
      int len;                      //length of input string
```

```
    public:
       express(char* ptr)              //constructor
          {
          pStr = ptr;                  //set pointer to string
          len = strlen(pStr);          //set length
          }
       void parse();                   //parse the input string
       int solve();                    //evaluate the stack
    };
//-----------------------------------------------------------
void express::parse()                  //add items to stack
    {
    char ch;                           //char from input string
    char lastval;                      //last value
    char lastop;                       //last operator

    for(int j=0; j<len; j++)           //for each input character
       {
       ch = pStr[j];                   //get next character

       if(ch>='0' && ch<='9')          //if it's a digit,
          s.push(ch-'0');              //save numerical value
                                       //if it's operator
       else if(ch=='+' || ch=='-' || ch=='*' || ch=='/')
          {
          if(s.gettop()==1)            //if it's first operator
             s.push(ch);               //put on stack
          else                         //not first operator
             {
             lastval = s.pop();        //get previous digit
             lastop = s.pop();         //get previous operator
             //if this is * or / AND last operator was + or -
             if( (ch=='*' || ch=='/') &&
                 (lastop=='+' || lastop=='-') )
                {
                s.push(lastop);        //restore last two pops
                s.push(lastval);
                }
             else                      //in all other cases
                {
                switch(lastop)         //do last operation
                   {                   //push result on stack
                   case '+': s.push(s.pop() + lastval); break;
                   case '-': s.push(s.pop() - lastval); break;
                   case '*': s.push(s.pop() * lastval); break;
                   case '/': s.push(s.pop() / lastval); break;
                   default:  cout << "\nUnknown oper"; exit(1);
```

```
                    }  //end switch
               }   //end else, in all other cases
          s.push(ch);                    //put current op on stack
        }  //end else, not first operator
      }  //end else if, it's an operator
    else                               //not a known character
      { cout << "\nUnknown input character"; exit(1); }
    }  //end for
  }  //end parse()
//-------------------------------------------------------------
int express::solve()                   //remove items from stack
  {
  char lastval;                        //previous value

  while(s.gettop() > 1)
    {
    lastval = s.pop();                 //get previous value
    switch( s.pop() )                  //get previous operator
      {                                //do operation, push answer
      case '+': s.push(s.pop() + lastval); break;
      case '-': s.push(s.pop() - lastval); break;
      case '*': s.push(s.pop() * lastval); break;
      case '/': s.push(s.pop() / lastval); break;
      default:  cout << "\nUnknown operator"; exit(1);
      }  //end switch
    }  //end while
  return int( s.pop() );               //last item on stack is ans
  }  //end solve()
//////////////////////////////////////////////////////////////////
int main()
  {
  char ans;                            //'y' or 'n'
  char string[LEN];                    //input string from user

  cout << "\nEnter an arithmetic expression"
       "\nof the form 2+3*4/3-2."
       "\nNo number may have more than one digit."
       "\nDon't use any spaces or parentheses.";
  do {
    cout << "\nEnter expresssion: ";
    cin >> string;                     //input from user
    express* eptr = new express(string); //make expression
    eptr->parse();                     //parse it
    cout << "\nThe numerical value is: "
         << eptr->solve();             //solve it
    delete eptr;                       //delete expression
```

```
        cout << "\nDo another (Enter y or n)? ";
        cin >> ans;
        } while(ans == 'y');
    return 0;
    }
```

This is a longish program, but it shows how a previously designed class, Stack, can come in handy in a new situation; it demonstrates the use of pointers in a variety of ways; and it shows how useful it can be to treat a string as an array of characters.

Simulation: A Horse Race

As our final example in this chapter we'll show a horse-racing game. In this game a number of horses appear on the screen, and, starting from the left, race to a finish line on the right. This program will demonstrate pointers in a new situation, and also a little bit about object-oriented design.

Each horse's speed is determined randomly, so there is no way to figure out in advance which one will win. The program uses console graphics, so the horses are easily, although somewhat crudely, displayed. You'll need to compile the program with the MSOFTCON.H or BORLACON.H header file (depending on your compiler), and the MSOFTCON.CPP or BORLACON.CPP source file. (See Appendix E, "Console Graphics Lite," for more information.)

When our program, HORSE, is started, it asks the user to supply the race's distance and the number of horses that will run in it. The classic unit of distance for horse racing (at least in English-speaking countries) is the *furlong*, which is 1/8 of a mile. Typical races are 6, 8, 10, or 12 furlongs. You can enter from 1 to 7 horses. The program draws vertical lines corresponding to each furlong, along with start and finish lines. Each horse is represented by a rectangle with a number in the middle. Figure 10.19 shows the screen with a race in progress.

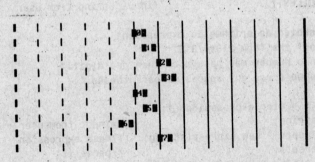

FIGURE 10.19
Output of the HORSE program.

Designing the Horse Race

How do we approach an OOP design for our horse race? Our first question might be, is there a group of similar entities that we're trying to model? The answer is yes, the horses. So it seems reasonable to make each horse an object. There will be a class called horse, which will contain data specific to each horse, such as its number and the distance it has run so far (which is used to display the horse in the correct screen position).

However, there is also data that applies to the entire race track, rather than to individual horses. This includes the track length, the elapsed time in minutes and seconds (0:00 at the start of the race), and the total number of horses. It makes sense then to have a track object, which will be a single member of the track class. You can think of other real-world objects associated with horse racing, such as riders and saddles, but they aren't relevant to this program.

Are there other ways to design the program? For example, what about using inheritance to make the horses descendants of the track? This doesn't make much sense, because the horses aren't a "kind of" race track; they're a completely different thing. Another option is to make the track data into static data of the horse class. However, it's generally better to make each different kind of thing in the problem domain (the real world) a separate class in the program. One advantage of this is that it's easier to use the classes in other contexts, such as using the track to race cars instead of horses.

How will the horse objects and the track object communicate? (Or in UML terms, what will their association consist of?) An array of pointers to horse objects can be a member of the track class, so the track can access the horses through these pointers. The track will create the horses when it's created. As it does so, it will pass a pointer to itself to each horse, so the horse can access the track.

Here's the listing for HORSE:

```
// horse.cpp
// models a horse race
#include "msoftcon.h"          //for console graphics
#include <iostream>            //for I/O
#include <cstdlib>             //for random()
#include <ctime>               //for time()
using namespace std;
const int CPF = 5;             //columns per furlong
const int maxHorses = 7;       //maximum number of horses
class track;                   //for forward references
/////////////////////////////////////////////////////////////////
class horse
    {
    private:
        const track* ptrTrack;     //pointer to track
        const int horse_number;    //this horse's number
```

```
        float finish_time;              //this horse's finish time
        float distance_run;             //distance run so far
    public:                             //create the horse
        horse(const int n, const track* ptrT) :
                horse_number(n), ptrTrack(ptrT),
                distance_run(0.0)       //haven't moved yet
            { }
        ~horse()                        //destroy the horse
            { /*empty*/ }               //display the horse
        void display_horse(const float elapsed_time);
    }; //end class horse
/////////////////////////////////////////////////////////////////
class track
    {
    private:
        horse* hArray[maxHorses];       //array of ptrs-to-horses
        int total_horses;               //total number of horses
        int horse_count;                //horses created so far
        const float track_length;       //track length in furlongs
        float elapsed_time;             //time since start of race

    public:
        track(float lenT, int nH);      //2-arg constructor
        ~track();                       //destructor
        void display_track();           //display track
        void run();                     //run the race
        float get_track_len() const;    //return total track length
    }; //end class track
//------------------------------------------------------------------
void horse::display_horse(float elapsed_time) //for each horse
    {                                   //display horse & number
    set_cursor_pos( 1 + int(distance_run * CPF),
        2 + horse_number*2 );
                                        //horse 0 is blue
    set_color(static_cast<color>(cBLUE+horse_number));
                                        //draw horse
    char horse_char = '0' + static_cast<char>(horse_number);
    putch(' '); putch('\xDB'); putch(horse_char); putch('\xDB');
                                        //until finish,
    if( distance_run < ptrTrack->get_track_len() + 1.0 / CPF )
        {
        if( rand() % 3 )                //skip about 1 of 3 ticks
            distance_run += 0.2F;       //advance 0.2 furlongs
        finish_time = elapsed_time;     //update finish time
        }
```

```
      else
         {                          . //display finish time
         int mins = int(finish_time)/60;
         int secs = int(finish_time) - mins*60;
         cout << " Time=" << mins << ":" << secs;
         }
      }  //end display_horse()
//-------------------------------------------------------------------
track::track(float lenT, int nH) :   //track constructor
                     track_length(lenT), total_horses(nH),
                     horse_count(0), elapsed_time(0.0)
         {
         init_graphics();              //start graphics
         total_horses =                //not more than 7 horses
           (total_horses > maxHorses) ? maxHorses : total_horses;
         for(int j=0; j<total_horses; j++)    //make each horse
            hArray[j] = new horse(horse_count++, this);

         time_t aTime;                 //initialize random numbers
         srand( static_cast<unsigned>(time(&aTime)) );
         display_track();
         }  //end track constructor
//-------------------------------------------------------------------
track::~track()                       //track destructor
    {
    for(int j=0; j<total_horses; j++) //delete each horse
       delete hArray[j];
    }
//-------------------------------------------------------------------
void track::display_track()
    {
    clear_screen();                    //clear screen
                                       //display track
    for(int f=0; f<=track_length; f++)     //for each furlong
       for(int r=1; r<=total_horses*2 + 1; r++) //and screen row
          {                   .
          set_cursor_pos(f*CPF + 5, r);
          if(f==0 || f==track_length)
             cout << '\xDE';        //draw start or finish line
          else
             cout << '\xB3';        //draw furlong marker
          }
    }  //end display_track()
//-------------------------------------------------------------------
void track::run()
```

10

```
      {
    while( !kbhit() )
       {
       elapsed_time += 1.75;          //update time
                                      //update each horse
       for(int j=0; j<total_horses; j++)
          hArray[j]->display_horse(elapsed_time);
       wait(500);
       }
    getch();                          //eat the keystroke
    cout << endl;
    }
//--------------------------------------------------------------
float track::get_track_len() const
   { return track_length; }
///////////////////////////////////////////////////////////////
int main()
   {
   float length;
   int total;
                                      //get data from user
   cout << "\nEnter track length (furlongs; 1 to 12): ";
   cin >> length;
   cout << "\nEnter number of horses (1 to 7): ";
   cin >> total;
   track theTrack(length, total);     //create the track
   theTrack.run();                    //run the race
   return 0;
   }   //end main()
```

Keeping Time

Simulation programs usually involve an activity taking place over a period of time. To model
the passage of time, such programs typically energize themselves at fixed intervals. In the
HORSE program, the main() program calls the track's run() function. This function makes a
series of calls within a while loop, one for each horse, to a function display_horse(). This
function redraws each horse in its new position. The while loop then pauses 500 milliseconds,
using the console graphics wait() function. Then it does the same thing again, until the race is
over or the user presses a key.

Deleting an Array of Pointers to Objects

At the end of the program the destructor for the track must delete the horse objects, which it
obtained with new in its constructor. Notice that we can't just say

```
delete[] hArray;  //deletes pointers, but not horses
```

This deletes the array of pointers, but not what the pointers point to. Instead we must go through the array element by element, and delete each horse individually:

```
for(int j=0; j<total_horses; j++)   //deletes horses
   delete hArray[j];
```

The putch() Function

We want each horse to be a different color, but not all compilers allow cout to generate colors. This is true of the current version of Borland C++Builder. However, some old C functions will generate colors. For this reason we use putch() when displaying the horses, in the line

```
putch(' '); putch('\xDB'); putch(horse_char); putch('\xDB');
```

This function requires the CONIO.H include file (furnished with the compiler). We don't need to include this file explicitly in HORSE.CPP because it is already included in MSOFTCON.H or BORLACON.H.

Multiplicity in the UML

Let's look at a UML class diagram of the HORSE program, shown in Figure 10.20. This diagram will introduce a UML concept called *multiplicity*.

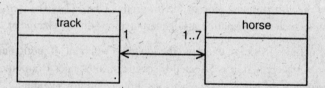

FIGURE 10.20
UML class diagram of the HORSE program.

Sometimes exactly one object of class A relates to exactly one object of class B. In other situations, many objects of a class, or a specific number, may be involved in an association. The number of objects involved in an association is called the *multiplicity* of the association. In class diagrams, numbers or symbols are used at both ends of the association line to indicate multiplicity. Table 10.2 shows the UML multiplicity symbols.

TABLE 10.2   The UML Multiplicity Symbols

Symbol	Meaning
1	One
*	Some (0 to infinity)
0..1	None or one

TABLE 10.2   Continued

Symbol	Meaning
1..*	One or more
2..4	Two, three, or four
7,11	Seven or eleven

If an association line had a 1 at the Class A end and a * at the class B end, that would mean that one object of class A interacted with an unspecified number of class B objects.

In the HORSE program there is one track but there can be up to 7 horses. This is indicated by the 1 at the track end of the association line and the 1..7 at the horse end. We assume that one horse is enough for a race, as might happen in time trials.

UML State Diagrams

In this section we'll introduce a new kind of UML diagram: the *state diagram* (also called the statechart diagram).

The UML class diagrams we examined in earlier chapters show relationships between classes. Class diagrams reflect the organization of the program's code. They are *static* diagrams, in that these relationships (such as association and generalization) do not change as the program runs.

However, it's sometimes useful to examine the *dynamic* behavior of particular class objects over time. An object is created, it is affected by events or messages from other parts of the program, it perhaps makes decisions, it does various things, and it is eventually deleted. That is, its situation changes over time. State diagrams show this graphically.

Everyone is familiar with the concept of *state* when applied to devices in our everyday lives. A radio has an On state and an Off state. A washing machine might have Washing, Rinsing, Spinning, and Stopped states. A television set has a state for each channel it is currently receiving (the Channel 7 Active state, and so on).

Between the states are *transitions*. As a result of a timer having reached (say) the 20-minute point, the washing machine makes a transition from the Rinse state to the Spin state. As a result of a message from the remote-control unit, the TV makes a transition from the Channel 7_Active state to the Channel 2 Active state.

Figure 10.21 shows a state diagram based on the HORSE program seen earlier in this chapter. It shows the different states a horse object can find itself in as the program runs.

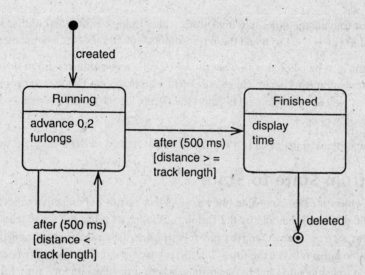

FIGURE 10.21
State diagram of a horse *object.*

States

In UML state diagrams, a state is represented by a rectangle with rounded corners. The state is named at the top of the rectangle. State names usually begin with a capital letter. Below the name are any *activities* the object performs when it enters the state.

State diagrams can include two special states: a black disk represents the *initial state*, and a black disk surrounded by a circle represents the *final state*. These are shown in the figure.

After it is created, a horse object can be in only two major states: before it reaches the finish line it's in the Running state, and afterwards it's in the Finished state.

Unlike classes in a class diagram, there's nothing in a program's code that corresponds exactly to states in a state diagram. To know what states to include, you must have an idea what circumstances an object will find itself in, and what it will do as a result. You then make up appropriate names for the states.

Transitions

Transitions between states are represented by directed arrows from one rectangle to another. If the transition is triggered by an event, it can be labeled with the event name, as are the created and deleted transitions in the figure. Transition names are not capitalized. The names can be closer to English than to C++ usage.

The event that triggers the other two transitions is the timing out of a 500 millisecond timer. The keyword after is used to name these transitions, with the time as a parameter.

Transitions can also be labeled with what the UML calls a *guard*: a condition that must be satisfied if the transition is to occur. Guards are written in brackets. The two after() transitions have guards as well as event names. Because the events are the same, the guards determine which transition will occur.

Note that one of these transitions is a *self transition*: it returns to the same state where it began.

Racing from State to State

Each time it enters the Running state, the horse object carries out an activity that consists of increasing the distance it has run by 0.2 furlongs. As long as it has not yet reached the finish line, the [distance < track length] guard is true and the Running state transitions back to itself. When the horse reaches the finish line, [distance >= track length] becomes true, and the horse transitions to the Finished state, where it displays its total time for the race. It then waits to be deleted.

We've shown enough to give you an idea what state diagrams do. There is of course much more to learn about them. We'll see an example of a more complex state diagram that describes an elevator object in Chapter 13, "Multifile Programs."

Debugging Pointers

Pointers can be the source of mysterious and catastrophic program bugs. The most common problem is that the programmer has failed to place a valid address in a pointer variable. When this happens the pointer can end up pointing anywhere in memory. It could be pointing to the program code, or to the operating system. If the programmer then inserts a value into memory using the pointer, the value will write over the program or operating instructions, and the computer will crash or evince other uncharming behavior.

A particular version of this scenario takes place when the pointer points to address 0, which is called NULL. This happens, for example, if the pointer variable is defined as a *global variable*, since global variables are automatically initialized to 0. Here's a miniprogram that demonstrates the situation:

```
int* intptr;            //global variable, initialized to 0
void main()
    {                   //failure to put valid address in intptr
    *intptr = 37;       //attempts to put 37 in address at 0
    }                   //result is error
```

When `intptr` is defined, it is given the value 0, since it is global. The single program statement will attempt to insert the value 37 into the address at 0.

Fortunately, however, the runtime error-checking unit built into the program by the compiler is waiting for attempts to access address 0, and will display an error message (perhaps an *access violation*, *null pointer assignment*, or *page fault*) and terminate the program. If you see such a message, one possibility is that you have failed to properly initialize a pointer.

Summary

This has been a whirlwind tour through the land of pointers. There is far more to learn, but the topics we've covered here will provide a basis for the examples in the balance of the book and for further study of pointers.

We've learned that everything in the computer's memory has an address, and that addresses are *pointer constants*. We can find the addresses of variables using the address-of operator &.

Pointers are variables that hold address values. Pointers are defined using an asterisk (*) to mean *pointer to*. A data type is always included in pointer definitions (except void*), since the compiler must know what is being pointed to, so that it can perform arithmetic correctly on the pointer. We access the thing pointed to using the asterisk in a different way, as the *dereference operator*, meaning *contents of the variable pointed to by*.

The special type void* means a pointer to *any* type. It's used in certain difficult situations where the same pointer must hold addresses of different types.

Array elements can be accessed using array notation with brackets or pointer notation with an asterisk. Like other addresses, the address of an array is a constant, but it can be assigned to a variable, which can be incremented and changed in other ways.

When the address of a variable is passed to a function, the function can work with the original variable. (This is not true when arguments are passed by value.) In this respect passing by pointer offers the same benefits as passing by reference, although pointer arguments must be *dereferenced* or accessed using the dereference operator. However, pointers offer more flexibility in some cases.

A string constant can be defined as an array or as a pointer. The pointer approach may be more flexible, but there is a danger that the pointer value will be corrupted. Strings, being arrays of type `char`, are commonly passed to functions and accessed using pointers.

The `new` operator obtains a specified amount of memory from the system and returns a pointer to the memory. This operator is used to create variables and data structures during program execution. The `delete` operator releases memory obtained with `new`.

When a pointer points to an object, members of the object's class can be accessed using the access operator ->. The same syntax is used to access structure members.

Classes and structures may contain data members that are pointers to their own type. This permits the creation of complex data structures such as linked lists.

There can be pointers to pointers. These variables are defined using the double asterisk; for example, int** pptr.

Multiplicity in UML class diagrams shows the number of objects involved in an association.

UML state diagrams show how a particular object's situation changes over time. States are represented by rectangles with rounded corners, and transitions between states are represented by directed lines.

Questions

Answers to these questions can be found in Appendix G.

1. Write a statement that displays the address of the variable testvar.

2. The contents of two pointers that point to adjacent variables of type float differ by _____.

3. A pointer is
   a. the address of a variable.
   b. an indication of the variable to be accessed next.
   c. a variable for storing addresses.
   d. the data type of an address variable.

4. Write expressions for the following:
   a. The address of var
   b. The contents of the variable pointed to by var
   c. The variable var used as a reference argument
   d. The data type pointer-to-char

5. An address is a _____, while a pointer is a _____.

6. Write a definition for a variable of type pointer-to-float.

7. Pointers are useful for referring to a memory address that has no _____.

8. If a pointer testptr points to a variable testvar, write a statement that represents the contents of testvar but does not use its name.

9. An asterisk placed after a data type means _____. An asterisk placed in front of a variable name means _____.

10. The expression *test can be said to

    a. be a pointer to test.

    b. refer to the contents of test.

    c. dereference test.

    d. refer to the value of the variable pointed to by test.

11. Is the following code correct?

```
int intvar = 333;
int* intptr;
cout << *intptr;
```

12. A pointer to void can hold pointers to _____.

13. What is the difference between intarr[3] and *(intarr+3)?

14. Write some code that uses pointer notation to display every value in the array intarr, which has 77 elements.

15. If intarr is an array of integers, why is the expression intarr++ not legal?

16. Of the three ways to pass arguments to functions, only passing by _____ and passing by _____ allow the function to modify the argument in the calling program.

17. The type of variable a pointer points to must be part of the pointer's definition so that

    a. data types don't get mixed up when arithmetic is performed on them.

    b. pointers can be added to one another to access structure members.

    c. no one's religious conviction will be attacked.

    d. the compiler can perform arithmetic correctly to access array elements.

18. Using pointer notation, write a prototype (declaration) for a function called func() that returns type void and takes a single argument that is an array of type char.

19. Using pointer notation, write some code that will transfer 80 characters from the string s1 to the string s2.

20. The first element in a string is

    a. the name of the string.

    b. the first character in the string.

    c. the length of the string.

    d. the name of the array holding the string.

21. Using pointer notation, write the prototype for a function called revstr() that returns a string value and takes one argument that represents a string.

10

22. Write a definition for an array numptrs of pointers to the strings One, Two, and Three.

23. The new operator

    a. returns a pointer to a variable.

    b. creates a variable called new.

    c. obtains memory for a new variable.

    d. tells how much memory is available.

24. Using new may result in less _____ memory than using an array.

25. The delete operator returns _____ to the operating system.

26. Given a pointer p that points to an object of type upperclass, write an expression that executes the exclu() member function in this object.

27. Given an object with index number 7 in array objarr, write an expression that executes the exclu() member function in this object.

28. In a linked list

    a. each link contains a pointer to the next link.

    b. an array of pointers points to the links.

    c. each link contains data or a pointer to data.

    d. the links are stored in an array.

29. Write a definition for an array arr of 8 pointers that point to variables of type float.

30. If you wanted to sort many large objects or structures, it would be most efficient to

    a. place them in an array and sort the array.

    b. place pointers to them in an array and sort the array.

    c. place them in a linked list and sort the linked list.

    d. place references to them in an array and sort the array.

31. Express the multiplicities of an association that has fewer than 10 objects at one end and more than 2 objects at the other.

32. The states in a state diagram correspond to

    a. messages between objects.

    b. circumstances in which an object finds itself.

    c. objects in the program.

    d. changes in an object's situation.

33. True or false: a transition between states exists for the duration of the program.

34. A guard in a state diagram is

    a. a constraint on when a transition can occur.

    b. a name for certain kinds of transitions.

    c. a name for certain kinds of states.

    d. a restriction on the creation of certain states.

Exercises

Answers to starred exercises can be found in Appendix G.

*1. Write a program that reads a group of numbers from the user and places them in an array of type float. Once the numbers are stored in the array, the program should average them and print the result. Use pointer notation wherever possible.

*2. Start with the String class from the NEWSTR example in this chapter. Add a member function called upit() that converts the string to all uppercase. You can use the toupper() library function, which takes a single character as an argument and returns a character that has been converted (if necessary) to uppercase. This function uses the CCTYPE header file. Write some code in main() to test upit().

*3. Start with an array of pointers to strings representing the days of the week, as found in the PTRTOSTR program in this chapter. Provide functions to sort the strings into alphabetical order, using variations of the bsort() and order() functions from the PTRSORT program in this chapter. Sort the pointers to the strings, not the actual strings.

*4. Add a destructor to the LINKLIST program. It should delete all the links when a linklist object is destroyed. It can do this by following along the chain, deleting each link as it goes. You can test the destructor by having it display a message each time it deletes a link; it should delete the same number of links that were added to the list. (A destructor is called automatically by the system for any existing objects when the program exits.)

5. Suppose you have a main() with three local arrays, all the same size and type (say float). The first two are already initialized to values. Write a function called addarrays() that accepts the addresses of the three arrays as arguments; adds the contents of the first two arrays together, element by element; and places the results in the third array before returning. A fourth argument to this function can carry the size of the arrays. Use pointer notation throughout: the only place you need brackets is in defining the arrays.

6. Make your own version of the library function strcmp(s1, s2), which compares two strings and returns –1 if s1 comes first alphabetically, 0 if s1 and s2 are the same, and 1 if s2 comes first alphabetically. Call your function compstr(). It should take two char* strings as arguments, compare them character by character, and return an int. Write a main() program to test the function with different combinations of strings. Use pointer notation throughout.

7. Modify the person class in the PERSORT program in this chapter so that it includes not only a name, but also a salary item of type float representing the person's salary. You'll need to change the setName() and printName() member functions to setData() and printData(), and include in them the ability to set and display the salary as well as the name. You'll also need a getSalary() function. Using pointer notation, write a salsort() function that sorts the pointers in the persPtr array by salary rather than by name. Try doing all the sorting in salsort(), rather than calling another function as PERSORT does. If you do this, don't forget that -> takes precedence over *, so you'll need to say

```
if( (*(pp+j))->getSalary() > (*(pp+k))->getSalary() )
   { /* swap the pointers */ }
```

8. Revise the additem() member function from the LINKLIST program so that it adds the item at the end of the list, rather than the beginning. This will cause the first item inserted to be the first item displayed, so the output of the program will be

```
25
36
49
64
```

To add the item, you'll need to follow the chain of pointers to the end of the list, then change the last link to point to the new link.

9. Let's say that you need to store 100 integers so that they're easily accessible. However, let's further assume that there's a problem: The memory in your computer is so fragmented that the largest array that you can use holds only 10 integers. (Such problems actually arise, although usually with larger memory objects.) You can solve this problem by defining 10 separate int arrays of 10 integers each, and an array of 10 pointers to these arrays. The int arrays can have names like a0, a1, a2, and so on. The address of each of these arrays can be stored in the pointer array of type int*, which can have a name like ap (for array of pointers). You can then access individual integers using expressions like ap[j][k], where j steps through the pointers in ap and k steps through individual integers in each array. This looks as if you're accessing a two-dimensional array, but it's really a group of one-dimensional arrays.

Fill such a group of arrays with test data (say the numbers 0, 10, 20, and so on up to 990). Then display the data to make sure it's correct.

10. As presented, Exercise 9 is rather inelegant because each of the 10 int arrays is declared in a different program statement, using a different name. Each of their addresses must also be obtained using a separate statement. You can simplify things by using new, which allows you to allocate the arrays in a loop and assign pointers to them at the same time:

```
for(j=0; j<NUMARRAYS; j++)          // allocate NUMARRAYS arrays
    *(ap+j) = new int[MAXSIZE];     // each MAXSIZE ints long
```

Rewrite the program in Exercise 9 to use this approach. You can access the elements of the individual arrays using the same expression mentioned in Exercise 9, or you can use pointer notation: *(*(ap+j)+k). The two notations are equivalent.

11. Create a class that allows you to treat the 10 separate arrays in Exercise 10 as a single one-dimensional array, using array notation with a single index. That is, statements in main() can access their elements using expressions like a[j], even though the class member functions must access the data using the two-step approach. Overload the subscript operator [ ] (see Chapter 9, "Inheritance") to achieve this result. Fill the arrays with test data and then display it. Although array notation is used in the class interface in main() to access "array" elements, you should use only pointer notation for all the operations in the implementation (within the class member functions).

12. Pointers are complicated, so let's see whether we can make their operation more understandable (or possibly more impenetrable) by simulating their operation with a class.

To clarify the operation of our homemade pointers, we'll model the computer's memory using arrays. This way, since array access is well understood, you can see what's really going on when we access memory with pointers.

We'd like to use a single array of type char to store all types of variables. This is what a computer memory really is: an array of bytes (which are the same size as type char), each of which has an address (or, in array-talk, an index). However, C++ won't ordinarily let us store a float or an int in an array of type char. (We could use unions, but that's another story.) So we'll simulate memory by using a separate array for each data type we want to store. In this exercise we'll confine ourselves to one numerical type, float, so we'll need an array of this type; call it fmemory. However, pointer values (addresses) are also stored in memory, so we'll need another array to store them. Since we're using array indexes to model addresses, and indexes for all but the largest arrays can be stored in type int, we'll create an array of this type (call it pmemory) to hold these "pointers."

An index to fmemory (call it fmem_top) points to the next available place where a float value can be stored. There's a similar index to pmemory (call it pmem_top). Don't worry about running out of "memory." We'll assume these arrays are big enough so that each time we store something we can simply insert it at the next index number in the array. Other than this, we won't worry about memory management.

Create a class called Float. We'll use it to model numbers of type float that are stored in fmemory instead of real memory. The only instance data in Float is its own "address"; that is, the index where its float value is stored in fmemory. Call this instance variable addr. Class Float also needs two member functions. The first is a one-argument constructor to initialize the Float with a float value. This constructor stores the float value in the element of fmemory pointed to by fmem_top, and stores the value of fmem_top in addr. This is similar to how the compiler and linker arrange to store an ordinary variable in real memory. The second member function is the overloaded & operator. It simply returns the pointer (really the index, type int) value in addr.

Create a second class called ptrFloat. The instance data in this class holds the address (index) in pmemory where some other address (index) is stored. A member function initializes this "pointer" with an int index value. The second member function is the overloaded * (dereference, or "contents of") operator. Its operation is a tad more complicated. It obtains the address from pmemory, where its data, which is also an address, is stored. It then uses this new address as an index into fmemory to obtain the float value pointed to by its address data.

```
float& ptrFloat::operator*()
   {
   return fmemory[ pmemory[addr] ];
   }
```

In this way it models the operation of the dereference operator (*). Notice that you need to return by reference from this function so that you can use * on the left side of the equal sign.

The two classes Float and ptrFloat are similar, but Float stores floats in an array representing memory, and ptrFloat stores ints (representing memory pointers, but really array index values) in a different array that also represents memory.

Here's a typical use of these classes, from a sample main():

```
Float var1 = 1.234;          // define and initialize two Floats
Float var2 = 5.678;

ptrFloat ptr1 = &var1;       // define two pointers-to-Floats,
ptrFloat ptr2 = &var2;       // initialize to addresses of Floats

cout << " *ptr1=" << *ptr1;  // get values of Floats indirectly
cout << " *ptr2=" << *ptr2;  // and display them

*ptr1 = 7.123;               // assign new values to variables
*ptr2 = 8.456;               // pointed to by ptr1 and ptr2
```

```
cout << " *ptr1=" << *ptr1;   // get new values indirectly
cout << " *ptr2=" << *ptr2;   // and display them
```

Notice that, aside from the different names for the variable types, this looks just the same as operations on real variables. Here's the output from the program:

```
*ptr1=1.234
*ptr2=2.678

*ptr1=7.123
*ptr2=8.456
```

This may seem like a roundabout way to implement pointers, but by revealing the inner workings of the pointer and address operator, we have provided a different perspective on their true nature.

Virtual Functions

IN THIS CHAPTER

Now that we understand something about pointers, we can delve into more advanced C++ topics. This chapter covers a rather loosely related collection of such subjects: virtual functions, friend functions, static functions, the overloaded = operator, the overloaded copy constructor, and the this pointer. These are advanced features; they are not necessary for every C++ program, especially very short ones. However, they are widely used, and are essential for most full-size programs. Virtual functions in particular are essential for polymorphism, one of the cornerstones of object-oriented programming.

Virtual Functions

Virtual means *existing in appearance but not in reality*. When virtual functions are used, a program that appears to be calling a function of one class may in reality be calling a function of a different class. Why are virtual functions needed? Suppose you have a number of objects of different classes but you want to put them all in an array and perform a particular operation on them using the same function call. For example, suppose a graphics program includes several different shapes: a triangle, a ball, a square, and so on, as in the MULTSHAP program in Chapter 9, "Inheritance." Each of these classes has a member function draw() that causes the object to be drawn on the screen.

Now suppose you plan to make a picture by grouping a number of these elements together, and you want to draw the picture in a convenient way. One approach is to create an array that holds pointers to all the different objects in the picture. The array might be defined like this:

```
shape* ptrarr[100];   // array of 100 pointers to shapes
```

If you insert pointers to all the shapes into this array, you can then draw an entire picture using a simple loop:

```
for(int j=0; j<N; j++)
   ptrarr[j]->draw();
```

This is an amazing capability: Completely different functions are executed by the same function call. If the pointer in ptrarr points to a ball, the function that draws a ball is called; if it points to a triangle, the triangle-drawing function is called. This is called *polymorphism*, which means *different forms*. The functions have the same appearance, the draw() expression, but different actual functions are called, depending on the contents of ptrarr[j]. Polymorphism is one of the key features of object-oriented programming, after classes and inheritance.

For the polymorphic approach to work, several conditions must be met. First, all the different classes of shapes, such as balls and triangles, must be descended from a single base class (called shape in MULTSHAP). Second, the draw() function must be declared to be virtual in the base class.

This is all rather abstract, so let's start with some short programs that show parts of the situation, and put everything together later.

Normal Member Functions Accessed with Pointers

Our first example shows what happens when a base class and derived classes all have functions with the same name, and you access these functions using pointers but without using virtual functions. Here's the listing for NOTVIRT:

```cpp
// notvirt.cpp
// normal functions accessed from pointer
#include <iostream>
using namespace std;
/////////////////////////////////////////////////////////////////
class Base                          //base class
   {
   public:
      void show()                   //normal function
         { cout << "Base\n"; }
   };
/////////////////////////////////////////////////////////////////
class Derv1 : public Base           //derived class 1
   {
   public:
      void show()
         { cout << "Derv1\n"; }
   };
/////////////////////////////////////////////////////////////////
class Derv2 : public Base           //derived class 2
   {
   public:
      void show()
         { cout << "Derv2\n"; }
   };
/////////////////////////////////////////////////////////////////
int main()
   {
   Derv1 dv1;           //object of derived class 1
   Derv2 dv2;           //object of derived class 2
   Base* ptr;           //pointer to base class

   ptr = &dv1;          //put address of dv1 in pointer
   ptr->show();         //execute show()
```

```
    ptr = &dv2;            //put address of dv2 in pointer
    ptr->show();           //execute show()
    return 0;
    }
```

The `Derv1` and `Derv2` classes are derived from class `Base`. Each of these three classes has a member function `show()`. In `main()` we create objects of class `Derv1` and `Derv2`, and a pointer to class `Base`. Then we put the address of a derived class object in the base class pointer in the line

```
ptr = &dv1;  // derived class address in base class pointer
```

But wait—how can we get away with this? Doesn't the compiler complain that we're assigning an address of one type (`Derv1`) to a pointer of another (`Base`)? On the contrary, the compiler is perfectly happy, because type checking has been relaxed in this situation, for reasons that will become apparent soon. The rule is that pointers to objects of a derived class are type-compatible with pointers to objects of the base class.

Now the question is, when you execute the line

```
ptr->show();
```

what function is called? Is it `Base::show()` or `Derv1::show()`? Again, in the last two lines of NOTVIRT we put the address of an object of class `Derv2` in the pointer, and again execute

```
ptr->show();
```

Which of the `show()` functions is called here? The output from the program answers these questions:

```
Base
Base
```

As you can see, the function in the base class is always executed. The compiler ignores the *contents* of the pointer `ptr` and chooses the member function that matches the *type* of the pointer, as shown in Figure 11.1.

Sometimes this is what we want, but it doesn't solve the problem posed at the beginning of this section: accessing objects of different classes using the same statement.

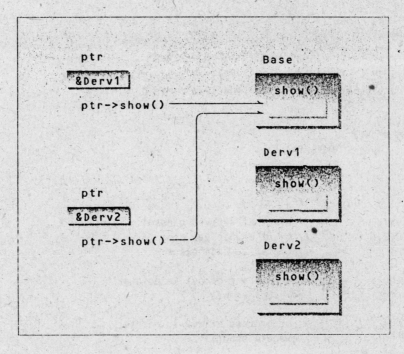

FIGURE 11.1
Nonvirtual pointer access.

Virtual Member Functions Accessed with Pointers

Let's make a single change in our program: We'll place the keyword *virtual* in front of the declarator for the show() function in the base class. Here's the listing for the resulting program, VIRT:

```
// virt.cpp
// virtual functions accessed from pointer
#include <iostream>
using namespace std;
/////////////////////////////////////////////////////////////////
class Base                          //base class
   {
   public:
      virtual void show()           //virtual function
         { cout << "Base\n"; }
   };
/////////////////////////////////////////////////////////////////
class Derv1 : public Base           //derived class 1
   {
```

```
    public:
       void show()
          { cout << "Derv1\n"; }
    };
//////////////////////////////////////////////////////////////////
class Derv2 : public Base        //derived class 2
    {
    public:
       void show()
          { cout << "Derv2\n"; }
    };
//////////////////////////////////////////////////////////////////
int main()
    {
    Derv1 dv1;               //object of derived class 1
    Derv2 dv2;               //object of derived class 2
    Base* ptr;               //pointer to base class

    ptr = &dv1;              //put address of dv1 in pointer
    ptr->show();             //execute show()

    ptr = &dv2;              //put address of dv2 in pointer
    ptr->show();             //execute show()
    return 0;
    }
```

The output of this program is

```
Derv1
Derv2
```

Now, as you can see, the member functions of the derived classes, not the base class, are executed. We change the contents of ptr from the address of Derv1 to that of Derv2, and the particular instance of show() that is executed also changes. So the same function call

```
ptr->show();
```

executes different functions, depending on the contents of ptr. The rule is that the compiler selects the function based on the *contents* of the pointer ptr, not on the *type* of the pointer, as in NOTVIRT. This is shown in Figure 11.2.

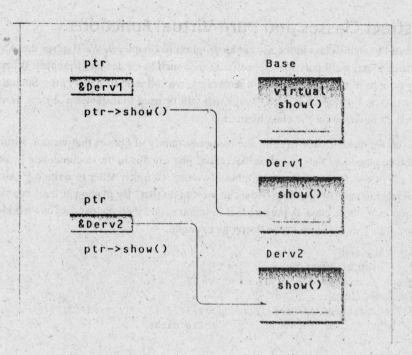

FIGURE 11.2
Virtual pointer access.

Late Binding

The astute reader may wonder how the compiler knows what function to compile. In NOTVIRT the compiler has no problem with the expression

```
ptr->show();
```

It always compiles a call to the show() function in the base class. But in VIRT the compiler doesn't know what class the contents of ptr may contain. It could be the address of an object of the Derv1 class or of the Derv2 class. Which version of draw() does the compiler call? In fact the compiler doesn't know what to do, so it arranges for the decision to be deferred until the program is running. At runtime, when it is known what class is pointed to by ptr, the appropriate version of draw will be called. This is called *late binding* or *dynamic binding*. (Choosing functions in the normal way, during compilation, is called *early binding* or *static binding*.) Late binding requires some overhead but provides increased power and flexibility.

We'll put these ideas to use in a moment, but first let's consider a refinement to the idea of virtual functions.

Abstract Classes and Pure Virtual Functions

Think of the shape class in the multshap program in Chapter 9. We'll never make an object of the shape class; we'll only make specific shapes such as circles and triangles. When we will never want to instantiate objects of a base class, we call it an *abstract class*. Such a class exists only to act as a parent of derived classes that will be used to instantiate objects. It may also provide an interface for the class hierarchy.

How can we make it clear to someone using our family of classes that we don't want anyone to instantiate objects of the base class? We could just say this in the documentation, and count on the users of the class to remember it, but of course it's much better to write our classes so that such instantiation is impossible. How can we can do that? By placing at least one *pure virtual function* in the base class. A pure virtual function is one with the expression =0 added to the declaration. This is shown in the VIRTPURE example.

```cpp
// virtpure.cpp
// pure virtual function
#include <iostream>
using namespace std;
/////////////////////////////////////////////////////////////////
class Base                        //base class
   {
   public:
      virtual void show() = 0;     //pure virtual function
   };
/////////////////////////////////////////////////////////////////
class Derv1 : public Base         //derived class 1
   {
   public:
      void show()
         { cout << "Derv1\n"; }
   };
/////////////////////////////////////////////////////////////////
class Derv2 : public Base         //derived class 2
   {
   public:
      void show()
         { cout << "Derv2\n"; }
   };
/////////////////////////////////////////////////////////////////
int main()
   {
// Base bad;                      //can't make object from abstract class
   Base* arr[2];                  //array of pointers to base class
   Derv1 dv1;                     //object of derived class 1
```

```
Derv2 dv2;              //object of derived class 2

arr[0] = &dv1;          //put address of dv1 in array
arr[1] = &dv2;          //put address of dv2 in array

arr[0]->show();         //execute show() in both objects
arr[1]->show();
return 0;
}
```

Here the virtual function show() is declared as

```
virtual void show() = 0;  // pure virtual function
```

The equal sign here has nothing to do with assignment; the value 0 is not assigned to anything. The =0 syntax is simply how we tell the compiler that a virtual function will be pure. Now if in main() you attempt to create objects of class Base, the compiler will complain that you're trying to instantiate an object of an abstract class. It will also tell you the name of the pure virtual function that makes it an abstract class. Notice that, although this is only a declaration, you never need to write a definition of the base class show(), although you can if you need to.

Once you've placed a pure virtual function in the base class, you must override it in all the derived classes from which you want to instantiate objects. If a class doesn't override the pure virtual function, it becomes an abstract class itself, and you can't instantiate objects from it (although you might from classes derived from it). For consistency, you may want to make all the virtual functions in the base class pure.

As you can see, we've made another, unrelated, change in VIRTPURE: The addresses of the member functions are stored in an array of pointers and accessed using array elements. This works in just the same way as using a single pointer. The output of VIRTPURE is the same as VIRT:

```
Derv1
Derv2
```

Virtual Functions and the person Class

Now that we understand some of the mechanics of virtual functions, let's look at a situation where it makes sense to use them. Our example is an extension of the PTROBJ and PERSORT examples from Chapter 10, "Pointers." It uses the same person class, but adds two derived classes, student and professor. These derived classes each contain a function called isOutstanding(). This function makes it easy for the school administrators to create a list of outstanding students and professors for the venerable Awards Day ceremony. Here's the listing for VIRTPERS:

```
// virtpers.cpp
// virtual functions with person class
#include <iostream>
using namespace std;
//////////////////////////////////////////////////////////////
class person                           //person class
   {
   protected:
      char name[40];
   public:
      void getName()
         { cout << "   Enter name: "; cin >> name; }
      void putName()
         { cout << "Name is: " << name << endl; }
      virtual void getData() = 0;         //pure virtual func
      virtual bool isOutstanding() = 0;  //pure virtual func
   };
//////////////////////////////////////////////////////////////
class student : public person          //student class
   {
   private:
      float gpa;                   //grade point average
   public:
      void getData()               //get student data from user
         {
         person::getName();
         cout << "   Enter student's GPA: "; cin >> gpa;
         }
      bool isOutstanding()
         { return (gpa > 3.5) ? true : false; }
   };
//////////////////////////////////////////////////////////////
class professor : public person        //professor class
   {
   private:
      int numPubs;                 //number of papers published
   public:
      void getData()               //get professor data from user
         {
         person::getName();
         cout << "   Enter number of professor's publications: ";
         cin >> numPubs;
         }
      bool isOutstanding()
         { return (numPubs > 100) ? true : false; }
   };
```

```
//////////////////////////////////////////////////////////////
int main()
   {
   person* persPtr[100];      //array of pointers to persons
   int n = 0;                 //number of persons on list.
   char choice;

   do {
      cout << "Enter student or professor (s/p): ";
      cin >> choice;
      if(choice=='s')              //put new student
         persPtr[n] = new student;  //   in array
      else                          //put new professor
         persPtr[n] = new professor; //   in array
      persPtr[n++]->getData();      //get data for person
      cout << "  Enter another (y/n)? ";  //do another person?
      cin >> choice;
      } while( choice=='y' );       //cycle until not 'y'

   for(int j=0; j<n; j++)           //print names of all
      {                             //persons, and
      persPtr[j]->putName();        //say if outstanding
      if( persPtr[j]->isOutstanding() )
         cout << "   This person is outstanding\n";
      }
   return 0;
   }  //end main()
```

The Classes

The person class is an abstract class because it contains the pure virtual functions getData()
and isOutstanding(). No person objects can ever be created. This class exists only to be the
base class for the student and professor classes. The student and professor classes add
new data items to the base class. The student class contains a variable gpa of type float,
which represents the student's grade point average (GPA). The professor class contains a
variable numPubs, of type int, which represents the number of scholarly publications the professor has published. Students with a GPA of over 3.5 and professors who have published
more than 100 papers are considered outstanding. (We'll refrain from comment on the desirability of these criteria for judging educational excellence.)

The isOutstanding() Function

The isOutstanding() function is declared as a pure virtual function in person. In the student
class this function returns a bool true if the student's GPA is greater than 3.5 and false otherwise. In professor it returns true if the professor's numPubs variable is greater than 100.

The getData() function asks the user for the GPA for a student, but for the number of publications for a professor.

The main() Program

In main() we first let the user enter a number of student and teacher names. For students, the program also asks for the GPA, and for professors it asks for the number of publications. When the user is finished, the program prints out the names of all the students and professors, noting those who are outstanding. Here's some sample interaction:

```
Enter student or professor (s/p): s
    Enter name: Timmy
    Enter student's GPA: 1.2
    Enter another (y/n)? y
Enter student or professor (s/p): s
    Enter name: Brenda
    Enter student's GPA: 3.9
    Enter another (y/n)? y
Enter student or professor (s/p): s
    Enter name: Sandy
    Enter student's GPA: 2.4
    Enter another (y/n)? y
Enter student or professor (s/p): p
    Enter name: Shipley
    Enter number of professor's publications: 714
    Enter another (y/n)? y
Enter student or professor (s/p): p
    Enter name: Wainright
    Enter number of professor's publications: 13
    Enter another (y/n)? n

Name is: Timmy
Name is: Brenda
    This person is outstanding
Name is: Sandy
Name is: Shipley
    This person is outstanding
Name is: Wainright
```

Virtual Functions in a Graphics Example

Let's try another example of virtual functions. This one is a graphics example derived from the MULTSHAP program in Chapter 9, "Inheritance." As we noted at the beginning of this section, you may want to draw a number of shapes using the same statement. The VIRTSHAP program does this. Remember that you must build this program with the appropriate console graphics file, as described in Appendix E, "Console Graphics Lite."

```cpp
// virtshap.cpp
// virtual functions with shapes
#include <iostream>
using namespace std;
#include "msoftcon.h"          //for graphics functions
//////////////////////////////////////////////////////////////
class shape                    //base class
    {
    protected:
        int xCo, yCo;          //coordinates of center
        color fillcolor;       //color
        fstyle fillstyle;      //fill pattern
    public:                    //no-arg constructor
        shape() : xCo(0), yCo(0), fillcolor(cWHITE),
                                      fillstyle(SOLID_FILL)
            { }                //4-arg constructor
        shape(int x, int y, color fc, fstyle fs) :
                    xCo(x), yCo(y), fillcolor(fc), fillstyle(fs)
            { }
        virtual void draw()=0   //pure virtual draw function
            {
            set_color(fillcolor);
            set_fill_style(fillstyle);
            }
    };
//////////////////////////////////////////////////////////////
class ball : public shape
    {
    private:
        int radius;            //(xCo, yCo) is center
    public:
        ball() : shape()       //no-arg constr
            { }
                               //5-arg constructor
        ball(int x, int y, int r, color fc, fstyle fs)
                    : shape(x, y, fc, fs), radius(r)
            { }
        void draw()            //draw the ball
            {
            shape::draw();
            draw_circle(xCo, yCo, radius);
            }
    };
//////////////////////////////////////////////////////////////
class rect : public shape
    {
```

```
        private:
            int width, height;        //(xCo, yCo) is upper left corner
        public:
            rect() : shape(), height(0), width(0)     //no-arg ctor
                { }                                  //6-arg ctor
            rect(int x, int y, int h, int w, color fc, fstyle fs) :
                        shape(x, y, fc, fs), height(h), width(w)
                { }
            void draw()               //draw the rectangle
                {
                shape::draw();
                draw_rectangle(xCo, yCo, xCo+width, yCo+height);
                set_color(cWHITE);    //draw diagonal
                draw_line(xCo, yCo, xCo+width, yCo+height);
                }
        };
/////////////////////////////////////////////////////////////////
class tria : public shape
    {
    private:
        int height;               //(xCo, yCo) is tip of pyramid
    public:
        tria() : shape(), height(0) //no-arg constructor
            { }                     //5-arg constructor
        tria(int x, int y, int h, color fc, fstyle fs) :
                             shape(x, y, fc, fs), height(h)
            { }
        void draw()               //draw the triangle
            {
            shape::draw();
            draw_pyramid(xCo, yCo, height);
            }
    };
/////////////////////////////////////////////////////////////////
int main()
    {
    int j;
    init_graphics();                //initialize graphics system

    shape* pShapes[3];              //array of pointers to shapes
                                    //define three shapes
    pShapes[0] = new ball(40, 12, 5, cBLUE, X_FILL);
    pShapes[1] = new rect(12, 7, 10, 15, cRED, SOLID_FILL);
    pShapes[2] = new tria(60, 7, 11, cGREEN, MEDIUM_FILL);
```

```
for(j=0; j<3; j++)              //draw all shapes
    pShapes[j]->draw();

for(j=0; j<3; j++)              //delete all shapes
    delete pShapes[j];
set_cursor_pos(1, 25);
return 0;
}
```

The class specifiers in VIRTSHAP are similar to those in MULTSHAP, except that the draw() function in the shape class has been made into a pure virtual function.

In main(), we set up an array, ptrarr, of pointers to shapes. Next we create three objects, one of each class, and place their addresses in an array. Now it's easy to draw all three shapes. The statement

```
ptrarr[j]->draw();
```

does this as the loop variable j changes.

This is a powerful approach to combining graphics elements, especially when a large number of objects need to be grouped together and drawn as a unit.

Virtual Destructors

Base class destructors should always be virtual. Suppose you use delete with a base class pointer to a derived class object to destroy the derived-class object. If the base class destructor is not virtual then delete, like a normal member function, calls the destructor for the base class, not the destructor for the derived class. This will cause only the base part of the object to be destroyed. The VIRTDEST program shows how this looks.

```
//vertdest.cpp
//tests non-virtual and virtual destructors
#include <iostream>
using namespace std;
/////////////////////////////////////////////////////////////////
class Base
   {
   public:
      ~Base()                           //non-virtual destructor
//    virtual ~Base()                   //virtual destructor
         { cout << "Base destroyed\n"; }
   };
/////////////////////////////////////////////////////////////////
class Derv : public Base
   {
```

```
public:
    ~Derv()
        { cout << "Derv destroyed\n"; }
};
/////////////////////////////////////////////////////////////////
int main()
    {
    Base* pBase = new Derv;
    delete pBase;
    return 0;
    }
```

The output for this program as written is

```
Base destroyed
```

This shows that the destructor for the Derv part of the object isn't called. In the listing the base class destructor is not virtual, but you can make it so by commenting out the first definition for the destructor and substituting the second. Now the output is

```
Derv destroyed
Base destroyed
```

Now both parts of the derived class object are destroyed properly. Of course, if none of the destructors has anything important to do (like deleting memory obtained with new) then virtual destructors aren't important. But in general, to ensure that derived-class objects are destroyed properly, you should make destructors in all base classes virtual.

Most class libraries have a base class that includes a virtual destructor, which ensures that all derived classes have virtual destructors.

Virtual Base Classes

Before leaving the subject of virtual programming elements, we should mention *virtual base classes* as they relate to multiple inheritance.

Consider the situation shown in Figure 11.3, with a base class, Parent; two derived classes, Child1 and Child2; and a fourth class, Grandchild, derived from both Child1 and Child2.

In this arrangement a problem can arise if a member function in the Grandchild class wants to access data or functions in the Parent class. The NORMBASE program shows what happens.

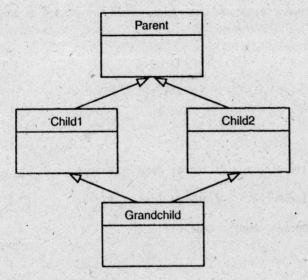

FIGURE 11.3
Virtual base classes.

```
// normbase.cpp
// ambiguous reference to base class

class Parent
    {
    protected:
        int basedata;
    };
class Child1 : public Parent
    { };
class Child2 : public Parent
    { };
class Grandchild : public Child1, public Child2
    {
    public:
        int getdata()
            { return basedata; }    // ERROR: ambiguous
    };
```

A compiler error occurs when the getdata() member function in Grandchild attempts to access basedata in Parent. Why? When the Child1 and Child2 classes are derived from Parent, each inherits a copy of Parent; this copy is called a *subobject*. Each of the two subobjects contains its own copy of Parent's data, including basedata. Now, when Grandchild refers to basedata, which of the two copies will it access? The situation is ambiguous, and that's what the compiler reports.

To eliminate the ambiguity, we make Child1 and Child2 into virtual base classes, as shown by the example VIRTBASE.

```
// virtbase.cpp
// virtual base classes

class Parent
   {
   protected:
      int basedata;
   };
class Child1 : virtual public Parent   // shares copy of Parent
   { };
class Child2 : virtual public Parent   // shares copy of Parent
   { };
class Grandchild : public Child1, public Child2
   {
   public:
      int getdata()
         { return basedata; }    // OK: only one copy of Parent
   };
```

The use of the keyword virtual in these two classes causes them to share a single common subobject of their base class Parent. Since there is only one copy of basedata, there is no ambiguity when it is referred to in Grandchild.

The need for virtual base classes may indicate a conceptual problem with your use of multiple inheritance, so they should be used with caution.

Friend Functions

The concepts of encapsulation and data hiding dictate that nonmember functions should not be able to access an object's private or protected data. The policy is, if you're not a member, you can't get in. However, there are situations where such rigid discrimination leads to considerable inconvenience.

Friends as Bridges

Imagine that you want a function to operate on objects of two different classes. Perhaps the function will take objects of the two classes as arguments, and operate on their private data. In this situation there's nothing like a friend function. Here's a simple example, FRIEND, that shows how friend functions can act as a bridge between two classes:

```
// friend.cpp
// friend functions
```

```
#include <iostream>
using namespace std;
///////////////////////////////////////////////////////////
class beta;                    //needed for frifunc declaration

class alpha
   {
   private:
      int data;
   public:
      alpha() : data(3) {  }            //no-arg constructor
      friend int frifunc(alpha, beta);  //friend function
   };
///////////////////////////////////////////////////////////
class beta
   {
   private:
      int data;
   public:
      beta() : data(7) {  }             //no-arg constructor
      friend int frifunc(alpha, beta);  //friend function
   };
///////////////////////////////////////////////////////////
int frifunc(alpha a, beta b)            //function definition
   {
   return( a.data + b.data );
   }
//------------------------------------------------------------
int main()
   {
   alpha aa;
   beta bb;

   cout << frifunc(aa, bb) << endl;     //call the function
   return 0;
   }
```

In this program, the two classes are `alpha` and `beta`. The constructors in these classes initialize their single data items to fixed values (3 in `alpha` and 7 in `beta`).

We want the function `frifunc()` to have access to both of these private data members, so we make it a `friend` function. It's declared with the `friend` keyword in both classes:

```
friend int frifunc(alpha, beta);
```

This declaration can be placed anywhere in the class; it doesn't matter whether it goes in the `public` or the `private` section.

An object of each class is passed as an argument to the function `frifunc()`, and it accesses the private data member of both classes through these arguments. The function doesn't do much: It adds the data items and returns the sum. The `main()` program calls this function and prints the result.

A minor point: Remember that a class can't be referred to until it has been declared. Class `beta` is referred to in the declaration of the function `frifunc()` in class `alpha`, so `beta` must be declared before `alpha`. Hence the declaration

```
class beta;
```

at the beginning of the program.

Breaching the Walls

We should note that `friend` functions are controversial. During the development of C++, arguments raged over the desirability of including this feature. On the one hand, it adds flexibility to the language; on the other, it is not in keeping with *data hiding*, the philosophy that only member functions can access a class's private data.

How serious is the breach of data integrity when `friend` functions are used? A `friend` function must be declared as such within the class whose data it will access. Thus a programmer who does not have access to the source code for the class cannot make a function into a `friend`. In this respect, the integrity of the class is still protected. Even so, `friend` functions are conceptually messy, and potentially lead to a spaghetti-code situation if numerous `friends` muddy the clear boundaries between classes. For this reason `friend` functions should be used sparingly. If you find yourself using many `friends`, you may need to rethink the design of the program.

English Distance Example

However, sometimes `friend` functions are too convenient to avoid. Perhaps the most common example is when `friends` are used to increase the versatility of overloaded operators. The following program shows a limitation in the use of such operators when friends are not used. This example is a variation on the ENGLPLUS and ENGLCONV programs in Chapter 8, "Operator Overloading." It's called NOFRI.

```
// nofri.cpp
// limitation to overloaded + operator
#include <iostream>
using namespace std;
/////////////////////////////////////////////////////////////////////
class Distance                          //English Distance class
    {
    private:
        int feet;
        float inches;
```

```
public:
    Distance() : feet(0), inches(0.0)   //constructor (no args)
        { }                             //constructor (one arg)
    Distance(float fltfeet)     //convert float to Distance
        {                       //feet is integer part
        feet = static_cast<int>(fltfeet);
        inches = 12*(fltfeet-feet); //inches is what's left
        }
    Distance(int ft, float in)  //constructor (two args)
        { feet = ft; inches = in; }
    void showdist()             //display distance
        { cout << feet << "\'-" << inches << '\"'; }
    Distance operator + (Distance);
    };
//--------------------------------------------------------------
                                //add this distance to d2
Distance Distance::operator + (Distance d2)    //return the sum
    {
    int f = feet + d2.feet;         //add the feet
    float i = inches + d2.inches;   //add the inches
    if(i >= 12.0)                   //if total exceeds 12.0,
        { i -= 12.0; f++; }         //less 12 inches, plus 1 foot
    return Distance(f,i);           //return new Distance with sum
    }
////////////////////////////////////////////////////////////////
int main()
    {
    Distance d1 = 2.5;          //constructor converts
    Distance d2 = 1.25;         //float feet to Distance
    Distance d3;
    cout << "\nd1 = "; d1.showdist();
    cout << "\nd2 = "; d2.showdist();

    d3 = d1 + 10.0;             //distance + float: OK
    cout << "\nd3 = "; d3.showdist();
// d3 = 10.0 + d1;             //float + Distance: ERROR
// cout << "\nd3 = "; d3.showdist();
    cout << endl;
    return 0;
    }
```

In this program, the + operator is overloaded to add two objects of type Distance. Also, there
is a one-argument constructor that converts a value of type float, representing feet and decimal fractions of feet, into a Distance value. (That is, it converts 10.25' into 10'–3".)

When such a constructor exists, you can make statements like this in main():

```
d3 = d1 + 10.0;
```

The overloaded + is looking for objects of type Distance both on its left and on its right, but if the argument on the right is type float, the compiler will use the one-argument constructor to convert this float to a Distance value, and then carry out the addition.

Here is what appears to be a subtle variation on this statement:

```
d3 = 10.0 + d1;
```

Does this work? No, because the object of which the overloaded + operator is a member must be the variable to the left of the operator. When we place a variable of a different type there, or a constant, then the compiler uses the + operator that adds that type (float in this case), not the one that adds Distance objects. Unfortunately, this operator does not know how to convert float to Distance, so it can't handle this situation. Here's the output from NOFRI:

```
d1 = 2'-6"
d2 = 1'-3"
d3 = 12'-6"
```

The second addition won't compile, so these statements are commented out. We could get around this problem by creating a new object of type Distance:

```
d3    Distance(10, 0) + d1;
```

but this is nonintuitive and inelegant. How can we write natural-looking statements that have nonmember data types to the left of the operator? As you may have guessed, a friend can help you out of this dilemma. The FRENGL program shows how.

```
// frengl.cpp
// friend overloaded + operator
#include <iostream>
using namespace std;
/////////////////////////////////////////////////////////////////
class Distance                      //English Distance class
   {
   private:
      int feet;
      float inches;
   public:
      Distance()                    //constructor (no args)
         { feet = 0; inches = 0.0; }
      Distance( float fltfeet )     //constructor (one arg)
         {                          //convert float to Distance
         feet = int(fltfeet);           //feet is integer part
         inches = 12*(fltfeet-feet);    //inches is what's left
         }
```

```
     Distance(int ft, float in)   //constructor (two args)
        { feet = ft; inches = in; }
     void showdist()              //display distance
        { cout << feet << "\'." << inches << '\"'; }
     friend Distance operator + (Distance, Distance); //friend
  };
//
Distance operator + (Distance d1, Distance d2) //add d1 to d2
   {
   int f = d1.feet + d2.feet;        //add the feet
   float i = d1.inches + d2.inches;  //add the inches
   if(i >= 12.0)                     //if inches exceeds 12.0,
      { i -= 12.0; f++; }            //less 12 inches, plus 1 foot
   return Distance(f,i);             //return new Distance with sum
   }
//------------------------------------------------------------
int main()
   {
   Distance d1 = 2.5;               //constructor converts
   Distance d2 = 1.25;              //float-feet to Distance
   Distance d3;
   cout << "\nd1 = "; d1.showdist();
   cout << "\nd2 = "; d2.showdist();

   d3 = d1 + 10.0;                  //distance + float: OK
   cout << "\nd3 = "; d3.showdist();
   d3 = 10.0 + d1;                  //float + Distance: OK
   cout << "\nd3 = "; d3.showdist();
   cout << endl;
   return 0;
   }
```

The overloaded + operator is made into a friend:

```
friend Distance operator + (Distance, Distance);
```

Notice that, while the overloaded + operator took one argument as a member function, it takes two as a friend function. In a member function, one of the objects on which the + operates is the object of which it was a member, and the second is an argument. In a friend, both objects must be arguments.

The only change to the body of the overloaded + function is that the var bles feet and inches, used in NOFRI for direct access to the object's data have en laced in FRENGL by d1.feet and d1.inches, since this object is supplied as an gume t.

Remember that, to make a function a friend, only the function declaration within the class is preceded by the keyword friend. The class definition is written normally, as are calls to the function.

friends for Functional Notation

Sometimes a friend allows a more obvious syntax for calling a function than does a member function. For example, suppose we want a function that will square (multiply by itself) an object of the English Distance class and return the result in square feet, as a type float. The MISQ example shows how this might be done with a member function.

```
// misq.cpp
// member square() function for Distance
#include <iostream>
using namespace std;
///////////////////////////////////////////////////////////////
class Distance                    //English Distance class
   {
   private:
      int feet;
      float inches;
   public:                         //constructor (no args)
      Distance() : feet(0), inches(0.0)
         { }                        //constructor (two args)
      Distance(int ft, float in) : feet(ft), inches(in)
         { }
      void showdist()              //display distance
         { cout << feet << "\'-" << inches << '\"'; }
      float square();              //member function
   };
//........................................................
float Distance::square()          //return square of
   {                              //this Distance
   float fltfeet = feet + inches/12;   //convert to float
   float feetsqrd = fltfeet * fltfeet;  //find the square
   return feetsqrd;               //return square feet
   }
///////////////////////////////////////////////////////////////
int main()
   {
   Distance dist(3, 6.0);         //two-arg constructor (3'-6")
   float sqft;

   sqft = dist.square();          //return square of dist
                                  //display distance and square
```

```
   cout << "\nDistance = "; dist.showdist();
   cout << "\nSquare = " << sqft << " square feet\n";
   return 0;
   }
```

The main() part of the program creates a Distance value, squares it, and prints out the result.
The output shows the original distance and the square:

```
Distance = 3'·6"
Square = 12.25 square feet
```

In main() we use the statement

```
sqft = dist.square();
```

to find the square of dist and assign it to sqft. This works all right, but if we want to work
with Distance objects using the same syntax that we use with ordinary numbers, we would
probably prefer a functional notation:

```
sqft = square(dist);
```

We can achieve this effect by making square() a friend of the Distance class, as shown in
FRISQ:

```
// frisq.cpp
// friend square() function for Distance
#include <iostream>
using namespace std;
/////////////////////////////////////////////////////////////////
class Distance                        //English Distance class
   {
   private:
      int feet;
      float inches;
   public:
      Distance() : feet(0), inches(0.0) //constructor (no args)
         { }
                                        //constructor (two args)
      Distance(int ft, float in) : feet(ft), inches(in)
         { }
      void showdist()                   //display distance
         { cout << feet << "\'." << inches << '\"'; }
      friend float square(Distance);    //friend function
   };
//·······················································
float square(Distance d)              //return square of
   {                                  //this Distance
```

```
    float fltfeet = d.feet + d.inches/12;   //convert to float
    float feetsqrd = fltfeet * fltfeet;     //find the square
    return feetsqrd;                        //return square feet
    }
///////////////////////////////////////////////////////////////
int main()
    {
    Distance dist(3, 6.0);              //two-arg constructor (3'-6")
    float sqft;

    sqft = square(dist);                //return square of dist
                                        //display distance and square
    cout << "\nDistance = "; dist.showdist();
    cout << "\nSquare = " << sqft << " square feet\n";
    return 0;
    }
```

Whereas square() takes no arguments as a member function in MISQ, it takes one as a friend in FRISQ. In general, the friend version of a function requires one more argument than when the function is a member. The square() function in FRISQ is similar to that in MISQ, but it refers to the data in the source Distance object as d.feet and d.inches, instead of as feet and inches.

friend Classes

The member functions of a class can all be made friends at the same time when you make the entire class a friend. The program FRICLASS shows how this looks.

```
// friclass.cpp
// friend classes
#include <iostream>
using namespace std;
///////////////////////////////////////////////////////////////
class alpha
    {
    private:
        int data1;
    public:
        alpha() : data1(99) { }     //constructor
        friend class beta;          //beta is a friend class
    };
///////////////////////////////////////////////////////////////
class beta
    {                               //all member functions can
```

```
public:                        //access private alpha data
   void func1(alpha a)  { cout << "\ndata1=" << a.data1; }
   void func2(alpha a)  { cout << "\ndata1=" << a.data1; }
 };
/////////////////////////////////////////////////////////////
int main()
   {
   alpha a;
   beta b;

   b.func1(a);
   b.func2(a);
   cout << endl;
   return 0;
   }
```

In class alpha the entire class beta is proclaimed a friend. Now all the member functions of beta can access the private data of alpha (in this program, the single data item data1).

Note that in the friend declaration we specify that beta is a class using the class keyword:

```
friend class beta;
```

We could have also declared beta to be a class before the alpha class specifier, as in previous examples

```
class beta;
```

and then, within alpha, referred to beta without the class keyword:

```
friend beta;
```

Static Functions

In the STATIC example in Chapter 6, "Objects and Classes," we introduced static data members. As you may recall, a static data member is not duplicated for each object; rather a single data item is shared by all objects of a class. The STATIC example showed a class that kept track of how many objects of itself there were. Let's extend this concept by showing how functions as well as data may be static. Besides showing static functions, our example will model a class that provides an ID number for each of its objects. This allows you to query an object to find out which object it is—a capability that is sometimes useful in debugging a program, among other situations. The program also casts some light on the operation of destructors. Here's the listing for STATFUNC:

```
// statfunc.cpp
// static functions and ID numbers for objects
#include <iostream>
using namespace std;
```

```
///////////////////////////////////////////////////////////////
class gamma
   {
   private:
      static int total;        //total objects of this class
                               //    (declaration only)
      int id;                  //ID number of this object
   public:
      gamma()                  //no-argument constructor
         {
         total++;              //add another object
         id = total;           //id equals current total
         }
      ~gamma()                 //destructor
         {
         total--;
         cout << "Destroying ID number " << id  << endl;
         }
      static void showtotal()  //static function
         {
         cout << "Total is " << total << endl;
         }
      void showid()            //non-static function
         {
         cout << "ID number is " << id << endl;
         }
   };
//------------------------------------------------------------
int gamma::total = 0;          //definition of total
///////////////////////////////////////////////////////////////
int main()
   {
   gamma g1;
   gamma::showtotal();

   gamma g2, g3;
   gamma::showtotal();

   g1.showid();
   g2.showid();
   g3.showid();
   cout << "----------end of program----------\n";
   return 0;
   }
```

Accessing static Functions

In this program there is a static data member, total, in the class gamma. This data keeps track of how many objects of the class there are. It is incremented by the constructor and decremented by the destructor.

Suppose we want to access total from outside the class. We construct a function, showtotal(), that prints the total's value. But how do we access this function?

When a data member is declared static, there is only one such data value for the entire class, no matter how many objects of the class are created. In fact, there may be no such objects at all, but we still want to be able to learn this fact. We could create a dummy object to use in calling a member function, as in

```
gamma dummyObj;            // make an object so we can call function
dummyObj.showtotal();   // call function
```

But this is rather inelegant. We shouldn't need to refer to a specific object when we're doing something that relates to the entire class. It's more reasonable to use the name of the class itself with the scope-resolution operator.

```
gamma::showtotal();    // more reasonable
```

However, this won't work if showtotal() is a normal member function; an object and the dot member-access operator are required in such cases. To access showtotal() using only the class name, we must declare it to be a static member function. This is what we do in STATFUNC, in the declarator

```
static void showtotal()
```

Now the function can be accessed using only the class name. Here's the output:

```
Total is 1
Total is 3
ID number is 1
ID number is 2
ID number is 3
·········end of program·········
Destroying ID number 3
Destroying ID number 2
Destroying ID number 1
```

We define one object, g1, and then print out the value of total, which is 1. Then we define two more objects, g2 and g3, and again print out the total, which is now 3.

Numbering the Objects

We've placed another function in gamma() to print out the ID number of individual members. This ID number is set equal to total when an object is created, so each object has a unique number. The showid() function prints out the ID of its object. We call it three times in main(), in the statements

```
g1.showid();
g2.showid();
g3.showid();
```

As the output shows, each object has a unique number. The g1 object is numbered 1, g2 is 2, and g3 is 3.

Investigating Destructors

Now that we know how to number objects, we can investigate an interesting fact about destructors. STATFUNC prints an *end of program* message in its last statement, but it's not done yet, as the output shows. The three objects created in the program must be destroyed before the program terminates, so that memory is not left in an inaccessible state. The compiler takes care of this by invoking the destructor.

We can see that this happens by inserting a statement in the destructor that prints a message. Once we've numbered the objects, we can also find out the order in which the objects are destroyed. As the output shows, the last object created, g3, is destroyed first. One can infer from this last-in-first-out approach that local objects are stored on the stack.

Assignment and Copy Initialization

The C++ compiler is always busy on your behalf, doing things you can't be bothered to do. If you take charge, it will defer to your judgment; otherwise it will do things its own way. Two important examples of this process are the assignment operator and the copy constructor.

You've used the assignment operator many times, probably without thinking too much about it. Suppose a1 and a2 are objects. Unless you tell the compiler otherwise, the statement

```
a2 = a1;        // set a2 to the value of a1
```

will cause the compiler to copy the data from a1, member by member, into a2. This is the default action of the assignment operator, =.

You're also familiar with initializing variables. Initializing an object with another object, as in

```
alpha a2(a1);   // initialize a2 to the value of a1
```

causes a similar action. The compiler creates a new object, a2, and copies the data from a1, member by member, into a2. This is the default action of the copy constructor.

Both of these default activities are provided, free of charge, by the compiler. If member-by-member copying is what you want, you need take no further action. However, if you want assignment or initialization to do something more complex, you can override the default functions. We'll discuss the techniques for overloading the assignment operator and the copy constructor separately, and then put them together in an example that gives a String class a more efficient way to manage memory. We'll also introduce a new UML feature: the object diagram.

Overloading the Assignment Operator

Let's look at a short example that demonstrates the technique of overloading the assignment operator. Here's the listing for ASSIGN:

```cpp
// assign.cpp
// overloads assignment operator (=)
#include <iostream>
using namespace std;
/////////////////////////////////////////////////////////////////
class alpha
   {
   private:
      int data;
   public:
      alpha()                            //no-arg constructor
         { }
      alpha(int d)                       //one-arg constructor
         { data = d; }
      void display()                     //display data
         { cout << data; }
      alpha operator = (alpha& a)   //overloaded = operator
         {
         data = a.data;                  //not done automatically
         cout << "\nAssignment operator invoked";
         return alpha(data);        //return copy of this alpha
         }
   };
/////////////////////////////////////////////////////////////////
int main()
   {
   alpha a1(37);
   alpha a2;
```

```
    a2 = a1;                        //invoke overloaded =
    cout << "\na2="; a2.display();  //display a2

    alpha a3 = a2;                  //does NOT invoke =
    cout << "\na3="; a3.display();  //display a3
    cout << endl;
    return 0;
    }
```

The alpha class is very simple; it contains only one data member. Constructors initialize the data, and a member function can print out its value. The new aspect of ASSIGN is the function operator=(), which overloads the = operator.

In main(), we define a1 and give it the value 37, and define a2 but give it no value. Then we use the assignment operator to set a2 to the value of a1:

```
a2 = a1;   // assignment statement
```

This causes our overloaded operator=() function to be invoked. Here's the output from ASSIGN:

```
Assignment operator invoked
a2=37
a3=37
```

Initialization Is Not Assignment
In the last two lines of ASSIGN, we initialize the object a3 to the value a2 and display it. Don't be confused by the syntax here. The equal sign in

```
alpha a3 = a2;   // copy initialization, not an assignment
```

is not an assignment but an initialization, with the same effect as

```
alpha a3(a2);   // alternative form of copy initialization
```

This is why the assignment operator is executed only once, as shown by the single invocation of the line

```
Assignment operator invoked
```

in the output of ASSIGN.

Taking Responsibility
When you overload the = operator you assume responsibility for doing whatever the default assignment operator did. Often this involves copying data members from one object to another. The alpha class in ASSIGN has only one data item, data, so the operator=() function copies its value with the statement

```
data = a.data;
```

The function also prints the Assignment operator invoked message so that we can tell when it executes.

Passing by Reference

Notice that the argument to operator=() is passed by reference. It is not absolutely necessary to do this, but it's usually a good idea. Why? As you know, an argument passed by value generates a copy of itself in the function to which it is passed. The argument passed to the operator=() function is no exception. If such objects are large, the copies can waste a lot of memory. Values passed by reference don't generate copies, and thus help to conserve memory.

Also, there are certain situations in which you want to keep track of the number of objects (as in the STATFUNC example, where we assigned numbers to the objects). If the compiler is generating extra objects every time you use the assignment operator, you may wind up with more objects than you expected. Passing by reference helps avoid such spurious object creation.

Returning a Value

As we've seen, a function can return information to the calling program by value or by reference. When an object is returned by value, a new object is created and returned to the calling program. In the calling program, the value of this object can be assigned to a new object or it can be used in other ways. When an object is returned by reference, no new object is created. A reference to the original object in the function is all that's returned to the calling program.

The operator=() function in ASSIGN returns a value by creating a temporary alpha object and initializing it using the one-argument constructor in the statement

```
return alpha(data);
```

The value returned is a copy of, but not the same object as, the object of which the overloaded = operator is a member. Returning a value makes it possible to chain = operators:

```
a3 = a2 = a1;
```

However, returning by value has the same disadvantages as passing an argument by value: It creates an extra copy that wastes memory and can cause confusion. Can we return this value with a reference, using the declarator shown here for the overloaded = operator?

```
alpha& operator = (alpha& a)  // bad idea in this case
```

Unfortunately, we can't use reference returns on variables that are local to a function. Remember that local (automatic) variables—that is, those created within a function (and not designated static)—are destroyed when the function returns. A return by reference returns only the address of the data being returned, and, for local data, this address points to data within the function. When the function is terminated and this data is destroyed, the pointer is left with a meaningless value. Your compiler may flag this usage with a warning. (We'll see one way to solve this problem in the section "The this Pointer" later in this chapter.)

Not Inherited

The assignment operator is unique among operators in that it is not inherited. If you overload the assignment operator in a base class, you can't use this same function in any derived classes.

The Copy Constructor

As we discussed, you can define and at the same time initialize an object to the value of another object with two kinds of statements:

```
alpha a3(a2);     // copy initialization
alpha a3 = a2;    // copy initialization, alternate syntax
```

Both styles of definition invoke a copy constructor: a constructor that creates a new object and copies its argument into it. The default copy constructor, which is provided automatically by the compiler for every object, performs a member-by-member copy. This is similar to what the assignment operator does; the difference is that the copy constructor also creates a new object.

Like the assignment operator, the copy constructor can be overloaded by the user. The XOFXREF example shows how it's done.

```
// xofxref.cpp
// copy constructor: X(X&)
#include <iostream>
using namespace std;
//////////////////////////////////////////////////////////////
class alpha
   {
   private:
     int data;
   public:
     alpha()                    //no-arg constructor
        { }
     alpha(int d)               //one-arg constructor
        { data = d; }
     alpha(alpha& a)            //copy constructor
        {
        data = a.data;
        cout << "\nCopy constructor invoked";
        }
     void display()             //display
        { cout << data; }
     void operator = (alpha& a) //overloaded = operator
        {
        data = a.data;
        cout << "\nAssignment operator invoked";
        }
   };
```

```
//////////////////////////////////////////////////////////////////
int main()
   {
   alpha a1(37);
   alpha a2;

   a2 = a1;                          //invoke overloaded =
   cout << "\na2="; a2.display();    //display a2

   alpha a3(a1);                     //invoke copy constructor
// alpha a3 = a1;                    //equivalent definition of a3
   cout << "\na3="; a3.display();    //display a3
   cout << endl;
   return 0;
   }
```

This program overloads both the assignment operator and the copy constructor. The overloaded assignment operator is similar to that in the ASSIGN example. The copy constructor takes one argument: an object of type alpha, passed by reference. Here's its declarator:

```
alpha(alpha&)
```

This declarator has the form X(X&) (pronounced "X of X ref"). Here's the output of XOFXREF:

```
Assignment operator invoked
a2=37
Copy constructor invoked
a3=37
```

The statement

```
a2 = a1;
```

invokes the assignment operator, while

```
alpha a3(a1);
```

invokes the copy constructor. The equivalent statement

```
alpha a3 = a1;
```

could also be used to invoke the copy constructor.

We've seen that the copy constructor may be invoked when an object is defined. It is also invoked when arguments are passed by value to functions and when values are returned from functions. Let's discuss these situations briefly.

Function Arguments

The copy constructor is invoked when an object is passed by value to a function. It creates the copy that the function operates on. Thus if the function

```
void func(alpha);
```

were declared in XOFXREF, and this function were called by the statement

```
func(a1);
```

then the copy constructor would be invoked to create a copy of the a1 object for use by func(). (Of course, the copy constructor is not invoked if the argument is passed by reference or if a pointer to it is passed. In these cases no copy is created; the function operates on the original variable.)

Function Return Values

The copy constructor also creates a temporary object when a value is returned from a function. Suppose there was a function like this in XOFXREF

```
alpha func();
```

and this function was called by the statement

```
a2 = func();
```

The copy constructor would be invoked to create a copy of the value returned by func(), and this value would be assigned (invoking the assignment operator) to a2.

Why Not an X(X) Constructor?

Do we need to use a reference in the argument to the copy constructor? Could we pass by value instead? No, the compiler complains that it is out of memory if we try to compile

```
alpha(alpha a)
```

Why? Because when an argument is passed by value, a copy of it is constructed. What makes the copy? The copy constructor. But this *is* the copy constructor, so it calls itself. In fact, it calls itself over and over until the compiler runs out of memory. So, in the copy constructor, the argument must be passed by reference, which creates no copies.

Watch Out for Destructors

In the sections "Passing by Reference" and "Returning a Value," we discussed passing arguments to a function by value and returning by value. These situations cause the destructor to be called as well, when the temporary objects created by the function are destroyed when the function returns. This can cause considerable consternation if you're not expecting it. The moral is, when working with objects that require more than member-by-member copying, pass and return by reference—not by value—whenever possible.

Define Both Copy Constructor and Assignment Operator

When you overload the assignment operator, you almost always want to overload the copy constructor as well (and vice versa). You don't want your custom copying routine used in some situations, and the default member-by-member scheme used in others. Even if you don't think you'll use one or the other, you may find the compiler using them in nonobvious situations, such as passing an argument to a function by value, and returning from a function by value.

In fact, if the constructor to a class involves the use of system resources such as memory or disk files, you should almost always overload both the assignment operator and the copy constructor, and make sure they do what you want.

How to Prohibit Copying

We've discussed how to customize the copying of objects using the assignment operator and the copy constructor. Sometimes, however, you may want to prohibit the copying of an object using these operations. For example, it might be essential that each member of a class be created with a unique value for some member, which is provided as an argument to the constructor. If an object is copied, the copy will be given the same value. To avoid copying, overload the assignment operator and the copy constructor as private members.

```
class alpha
   {
   private:
      alpha& operator = (alpha&);   // private assignment operator
      alpha(alpha&);                // private copy constructor
   };
```

As soon as you attempt a copying operation, such as

```
alpha a1, a2;
a1 = a2;          // assignment
alpha a3(a1);     // copy constructor
```

the compiler will tell you that the function is not accessible. You don't need to define the functions, since they will never be called.

UML Object Diagrams

We've seen examples of class diagrams in previous chapters. It will probably not surprise you to know that the UML supports object diagrams as well. Object diagrams depict specific objects (for instance, the Mike_Gonzalez object of the Professor class). Because the relationships among objects change during the course of a program's operation (indeed, objects may even be created and destroyed) an object diagram is like a snapshot, representing objects at a particular moment in time. It's said to be a *static* UML diagram.

You use an object diagram to model a particular thing your program does. You freeze the program at a moment in time and look at the objects that participate in the behavior you're interested in, and the communications among these objects at that point in time.

In object diagrams, objects are represented by rectangles, just as classes are in class diagrams. The object's name, attributes, and operations are shown in a similar way. However, objects are distinguished from classes by having their names underlined. Both the object name and the class name can be used, separated by a colon:

anObj:aClass

If you don't know the name of the object (because it's only known through a pointer, for example) you can use just the class name preceded by the colon:

:aClass

Lines between the objects are called *links*, and represent one object communicating with another. Navigability can be shown. The value of an attribute can be shown using an equal sign:

count = 0

Notice there's no semicolon at the end; this is the UML, not C++.

Another UML feature we'll encounter is the *note*. Notes are shown as rectangles with a dog-eared (turned down) corner. They hold comments or explanations. A dotted line connects a note to the relevent element in the diagram. Unlike associations and links, a note can refer to an element inside a class or object rectangle. Notes can be used in any kind of UML diagram.

We'll see a number of object diagrams in the balance of this chapter.

A Memory-Efficient String Class

The ASSIGN and XOFXREF examples don't really need to have overloaded assignment operators and copy constructors. They use straightforward classes with only one data item, so the default assignment operator and copy constructor would work just as well. Let's look at an example where it is essential for the user to overload these operators.

Defects with the String Class

We've seen various versions of our homemade String class in previous chapters. However, these versions are not very sophisticated. It would be nice to overload the = operator so that we could assign the value of one String object to another with the statement

s2 = s1;

If we overload the = operator, the question arises of how we will handle the actual string (the array of type char), which is the principal data item in the String class.

One possibility is for each String object to have a place to store a string. If we assign one String object to another (from s1 into s2 in the previous statement), we simply copy the string from the source into the destination object. If you're concerned with conserving memory, the problem with this is that the same string now exists in two (or more) places in memory. This is not very efficient, especially if the strings are long. Figure 11.4 shows how this looks.

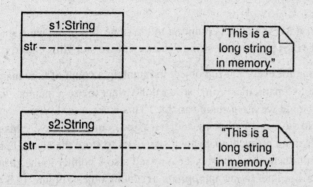

FIGURE 11.4
UML object diagram: replicating strings.

Instead of having each String object contain its own char* string, we could arrange for it to contain only a *pointer* to a string. Now, if we assign one String object to another, we need only copy the pointer from one object to another; both pointers will point to the same string. This is efficient, since only a single copy of the string itself needs to be stored in memory. Figure 11.5 shows how this looks.

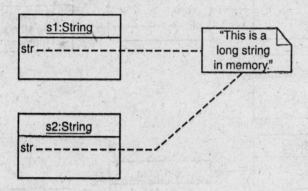

FIGURE 11.5
UML object diagram: replicating pointers to strings.

However, if we use this system we need to be careful when we destroy a String object. If a String's destructor uses delete to free the memory occupied by the string, and if there are several objects with pointers pointing to the string, these other objects will be left with pointers pointing to memory that may no longer hold the string they think it does; they become dangling pointers.

To use pointers to strings in String objects, we need a way to keep track of how many String objects point to a particular string, so that we can avoid using delete on the string until the last String that points to it is itself deleted. Our next example, STRIMEM, does just this.

A String-Counter Class

Suppose we have several String objects pointing to the same string and we want to keep a count of how many strings point to the string. Where will we store this count?

It would be cumbersome for every String object to maintain a count of how many of its fellow Strings were pointing to a particular string, so we don't want to use a member variable in String for the count. Could we use a static variable? This is a possibility; we could create a static array and use it to store a list of string addresses and counts. However, this requires considerable overhead. It's more efficient to create a new class to store the count. Each object of this class, which we call strCount, contains a count and also a pointer to the string itself. Each String object contains a pointer to the appropriate strCount object. Figure 11.6 shows how this looks.

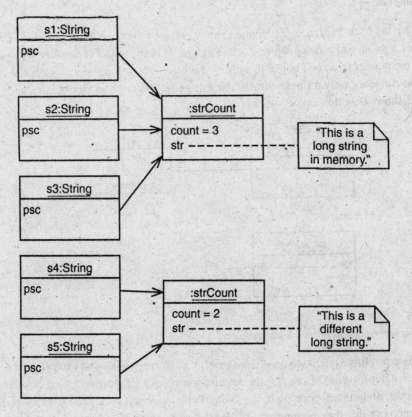

FIGURE 11.6
String *and* strCount *objects.*

To ensure that String objects have access to strCount objects, we make String a friend of strCount. Also, we want to ensure that the strCount class is used only by the String class. To prevent access to any of its functions, we make all member functions of strCount private. Because String is a friend, it can nevertheless access any part of strCount. Here's the listing for STRIMEM:

```cpp
// strimem.cpp
// memory-saving String class
// overloaded assignment and copy constructor
#include <iostream>
#include <cstring>                     //for strcpy(), etc.
using namespace std;
//////////////////////////////////////////////////////////////////
class strCount                         //keep track of number
    {                                  //of unique strings
    private:
      int count;                       //number of instances
      char* str;                       //pointer to string
      friend class String;             //make ourselves available
      //member functions are private
//------------------------------------------------------------------
      strCount(char* s)                //one-arg constructor
        {
        int length = strlen(s);   //length of string argument
        str = new char[length+1];  //get memory for string
        strcpy(str, s);                //copy argument to it
        count=1;                       //start count at 1
        }
//------------------------------------------------------------------
      ~strCount()                      //destructor
        { delete[] str; }              //delete the string
    };
//////////////////////////////////////////////////////////////////
class String                           //String class
    {
    private:
      strCount* psc;                   //pointer to strCount
    public:
      String()                         //no-arg constructor
        { psc = new strCount("NULL"); }
//------------------------------------------------------------------
      String(char* s)                  //1-arg constructor
        { psc = new strCount(s); }
//------------------------------------------------------------------
      String(String& S)                //copy constructor
        {
```

```
            psc = S.psc;
            (psc->count)++;
            }
//------------------------------------------------------------------
      ~String()                    //destructor
         {
         if(psc->count==1)          //if we are its last user,
            delete psc;             //    delete our strCount
         else                       //    otherwise,
            (psc->count)--;         //    decrement its count
         }
//------------------------------------------------------------------
      void display()               //display the String
         {
         cout << psc->str;                //print string
         cout << " (addr=" << psc << ")"; //print address
         }
//------------------------------------------------------------------
      void operator = (String& S) //assign the string
         {
         if(psc->count==1)          //if we are its last user,
            delete psc;             //    delete our strCount
         else                       //    otherwise,
            (psc->count)--;         //    decrement its count
         psc = S.psc;               //use argument's strCount
         (psc->count)++;            //increment its count
         }
   };
////////////////////////////////////////////////////////////////////
int main()
   {
   String s3 = "When the fox preaches, look to your geese.";
   cout << "\ns3="; s3.display();    //display s3

   String s1;                         //define String
   s1 = s3;                           //assign it another String
   cout << "\ns1="; s1.display();     //display it

   String s2(s3);                     //initialize with String
   cout << "\ns2="; s2.display();     //display it
   cout << endl;
   return 0;
   }
```

In the main() part of STRIMEM we define a String object, s3, to contain the proverb "When the fox preaches, look to your geese." We define another String s1 and set it equal to s3; then we define s2 and initialize it to s3. Setting s1 equal to s3 invokes the overloaded assignment operator; initializing s2 to s3 invokes the overloaded copy constructor. We print out all three strings, and also the address of the strCount object pointed to by each object's psc pointer, to show that these objects are all the same. Here's the output from STRIMEM:

```
s3=When the fox preaches, look to your geese. (addr=0x8f510e00)
s1=When the fox preaches, look to your geese. (addr=0x8f510e00)
s2=When the fox preaches, look to your geese. (addr=0x8f510e00)
```

The other duties of the String class are divided between the String and strCount classes. Let's see what they do.

The strCount Class

The strCount class contains the pointer to the actual string and the count of how many String class objects point to this string. Its single constructor takes a pointer to a string as an argument and creates a new memory area for the string. It copies the string into this area and sets the count to 1, since just one String points to it when it is created. The destructor in strCount frees the memory used by the string. (We use delete[] with brackets because a string is an array.)

The String Class

The String class uses three constructors. If a new string is being created, as in the zero-argument and C-string-argument constructors, a new strCount object is created to hold the string, and the psc pointer is set to point to this object. If an existing String object is being copied, as in the copy constructor and the overloaded assignment operator, the pointer psc is set to point to the old strCount object, and the count in this object is incremented.

The overloaded assignment operator, as well as the destructor, must also delete the old strCount object pointed to by psc if the count is 1. (We don't need brackets on delete because we're deleting only a single strCount object.) Why must the assignment operator worry about deletion? Remember that the String object on the left of the equal sign (call it s1) was pointing at some strCount object (call it oldStrCnt) before the assignment. After the assignment s1 will be pointing to the object on the right of the equal sign. If there are now no String objects pointing to oldStrCnt, it should be deleted. If there are other objects pointing to it, its count must be decremented. Figure 11.7 shows the action of the overloaded assignment operator, and Figure 11.8 shows the copy constructor.

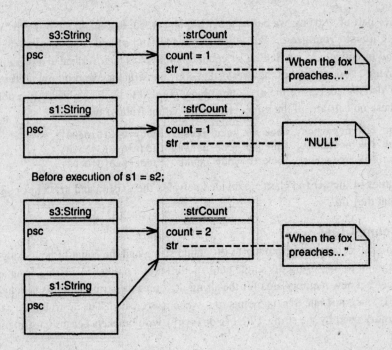

FIGURE 11.7

Assignment operator in STRIMEM.

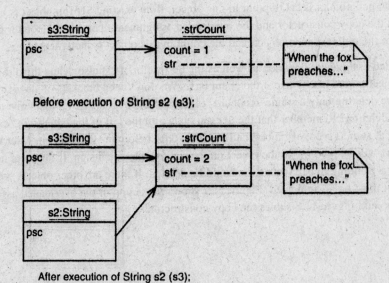

FIGURE 11.8

Copy constructor in STRIMEM.

The this Pointer

The member functions of every object have access to a sort of magic pointer named this, which points to the object itself. Thus any member function can find out the address of the object of which it is a member. Here's a short example, WHERE, that shows the mechanism:

```cpp
// where.cpp
// the this pointer
#include <iostream>
using namespace std;
//////////////////////////////////////////////////////////////////
class where
   {
   private:
      char charray[10];     //occupies 10 bytes
   public:
      void reveal()
         { cout << "\nMy object's address is " << this; }
   };
//////////////////////////////////////////////////////////////////
int main()
   {
   where w1, w2, w3;      //make three objects
   w1.reveal();           //see where they are
   w2.reveal();
   w3.reveal();
   cout << endl;
   return 0;
   }
```

The main() program in this example creates three objects of type where. It then asks each object to print its address, using the reveal() member function. This function prints out the value of the this pointer. Here's the output:

```
My object's address is 0x8f4effec
My object's address is 0x8f4effe2
My object's address is 0x8f4effd8
```

Since the data in each object consists of an array of 10 bytes, the objects are spaced 10 bytes apart in memory. (EC minus E2 is 10 decimal, as is E2 minus D8.) Some compilers may place extra bytes in objects, making them slightly larger than 10 bytes.

Accessing Member Data with this

When you call a member function, it comes into existence with the value of this set to the address of the object for which it was called. The this pointer can be treated like any other pointer to an object, and can thus be used to access the data in the object it points to, as shown in the DOTHIS program:

```
// dothis.cpp
// the this pointer referring to data
#include <iostream>
using namespace std;
/////////////////////////////////////////////////////////////////////
class what
    {
    private:
        int alpha;
    public:
        void tester()
            {
            this->alpha = 11;        //same as alpha = 11;
            cout << this->alpha;     //same as cout << alpha;
            }
    };
/////////////////////////////////////////////////////////////////////
int main()
    {
    what w;
    w.tester();
    cout << endl;
    return 0;
    }
```

This program simply prints out the value 11. Notice that the tester() member function accesses the variable alpha as

this->alpha

This is exactly the same as referring to alpha directly. This syntax works, but there is no reason for it except to show that this does indeed point to the object.

Using this for Returning Values

A more practical use for this is in returning values from member functions and overloaded operators.

Recall that in the ASSIGN program we could not return an object by reference, because the object was local to the function returning it and thus was destroyed when the function returned. We need a more permanent object if we're going to return it by reference. The object of which a function is a member is more permanent than its individual member functions. An object's member functions are created and destroyed every time they're called, but the object itself endures until it is destroyed by some outside agency (for example, when it is deleted). Thus returning by reference the object of which a function is a member is a better bet than returning a temporary object created in a member function. The this pointer makes this easy.

Here's the listing for ASSIGN2, in which the `operator=()` function returns by reference the object that invoked it:

```
//assign2.cpp
// returns contents of the this pointer
#include <iostream>
using namespace std;
////////////////////////////////////////////////////////////////////
class alpha
   {
   private:
      int data;
   public:
      alpha()                           //no-arg constructor
         { }
      alpha(int d)                      //one-arg constructor
         { data = d; }
      void display()                    //display data
         { cout << data; }
      alpha& operator = (alpha& a) //overloaded = operator
         {
         data = a.data;                 //not done automatically
         cout << "\nAssignment operator invoked";
         return *this;                  //return copy of this alpha
         }
   };
////////////////////////////////////////////////////////////////////
int main()
   {
   alpha a1(37);
   alpha a2, a3;

   a3 = a2 = a1;                        //invoke overloaded =, twice
   cout << "\na2="; a2.display();       //display a2
   cout << "\na3="; a3.display();       //display a3
   cout << endl;
   return 0;
   }
```

In this program we can use the declaration

```
alpha& operator = (alpha& a)
```

which returns by reference, instead of

```
alpha operator = (alpha& a)
```

which returns by value. The last statement in this function is

```
return *this;
```

Since this is a pointer to the object of which the function is a member, *this is that object itself, and the statement returns it by reference. Here's the output of ASSIGN2:

```
Assignment operator invoked
Assignment operator invoked
a2=37
a3=37
```

Each time the equal sign is encountered in

```
a3 = a2 = a1;
```

the overloaded operator=() function is called, which prints the messages. The three objects all end up with the same value.

You usually want to return by reference from overloaded assignment operators, using *this, to avoid the creation of extra objects.

Revised STRIMEM Program

Using the this pointer we can revise the operator=() function in STRIMEM to return a value by reference, thus making possible multiple assignment operators for String objects, such as

```
s1 = s2 = s3;
```

At the same time, we can avoid the creation of spurious objects, such as those that are created when objects are returned by value. Here's the listing for STRIMEM2:

```cpp
// strimem2.cpp
// memory-saving String class
// the this pointer in overloaded assignment
#include <iostream>
#include <cstring>                  //for strcpy(), etc
using namespace std;
///////////////////////////////////////////////////////////////
class strCount                      //keep track of number
   {                                //of unique strings
   private:
      int count;                    //number of instances
      char* str;                    //pointer to string
      friend class String;          //make ourselves available
   //member functions are private
      strCount(char* s)             //one-arg constructor
         {
         int length = strlen(s);    //length of string argument
         str = new char[length+1];  //get memory for string
         strcpy(str, s);            //copy argument to it
         count=1;                   //start count at 1
         }
```

```
//-------------------------------------------------------------
      -strCount()                        //destructor
         { delete[] str; }               //delete the string
   };
////////////////////////////////////////////////////////////////
class String                             //String class
   {
   private:
      strCount* psc;                      //pointer to strCount
   public:
      String()                           //no-arg constructor
         { psc = new strCount("NULL"); }
//-------------------------------------------------------------
      String(char* s)                     //1-arg constructor
         { psc = new strCount(s); }
//-------------------------------------------------------------
      String(String& S)                   //copy constructor
         {
         cout << "\nCOPY CONSTRUCTOR";
         psc = S.psc;
            (psc->count)++;
         }
//-------------------------------------------------------------
      ~String()                           //destructor
         {
         if(psc->count==1)                //if we are its last user,
            delete psc;                   //   delete our strCount
         else                             //   otherwise,
            (psc->count)--;               //   decrement its count
         }
//-------------------------------------------------------------
      void display()                      //display the String
         {
         cout << psc->str;                //print string
         cout << " (addr=" << psc << ")"; //print address
         }
//-------------------------------------------------------------
      String& operator = (String& S)      //assign the string
         {
         cout << "\nASSIGNMENT";
         if(psc->count==1)                //if we are its last user,
            delete psc;                   //delete our strCount
         else                             // otherwise,
            (psc->count)--;               // decrement its count
         psc = S.psc;                     //use argument's strCount
         (psc->count)++;                  //increment count
```

```
            return *this;              //return this object
            }
    };

 int main()
    {
    String s3 = "When the fox preaches, look to your geese.";
    cout << "\ns3="; s3.display();   //display s3

    String s1, s2;                     //define Strings
    s1 = s2 = s3;                      //assign them
    cout << "\ns1="; s1.display();     //display it
    cout << "\ns2="; s2.display();     //display it
    cout << endl;                      //wait for keypress
    return 0;
    }
```

Now the declarator for the = operator is

```
String& operator = (String& S)   // return by reference
```

And, as in ASSIGN2, this function returns a pointer to this. Here's the output:

```
s3=When the fox preaches, look to your geese. (addr=0x8f640d3a)
ASSIGNMENT
ASSIGNMENT
s1=When the fox preaches, look to your geese. (addr=0x8f640d3a)
s2=When the fox preaches, look to your geese. (addr=0x8f640d3a)
```

The output shows that, following the assignment statement, all three String objects point to the same strCount object.

We should note that the this pointer is not available in static member functions, since they are not associated with a particular object.

Beware of Self-Assignment

A corollary of Murphy's Law states that whatever is possible, someone will eventually do. This is certainly true in programming, so you can expect that if you have overloaded the = operator, someone will use it to set an object equal to itself:

```
alpha = alpha;
```

Your overloaded assignment operator should be prepared to handle such self-assignment. Otherwise, bad things may happen. For example, in the main() part of the STRIMEM2 program, if you set a String object equal to itself, the program will crash (unless there are other String objects using the same strCount object). The problem is that the code for the assignment operator deletes the strCount object if it thinks the object that called it is the only object using the strCount. Self-assignment will cause it to believe this, even though nothing should be deleted.

To fix this, you should check for self-assignment at the start of any overloaded assignment operator. You can do this in most cases by comparing the address of the object for which the operator was called with the address of its argument. If the addresses are the same, the objects are identical and you should return immediately. (You don't need to assign one to the other; they're already the same.) For example, in STRIMEM2, you can insert the lines

```
if(this == &S)
   return *this;
```

at the start of operator=( ). That should solve the problem.

Dynamic Type Information

It's possible to find out information about an object's class and even change the class of an object at runtime. We'll look briefly at two mechanisms: the dynamic_cast operator, and the typeid operator. These are advanced capabilities, but you may find them useful someday.

These capabilities are usually used in situations where a variety of classes are descended (sometimes in complicated ways) from a base class. For dynamic casts to work, the base class must be polymorphic; that is, it must have at least one virtual function.

For both dynamic_cast and typeid to work, your compiler must enable Run-Time Type Information (RTTI). Borland C++Builder has this capability enabled by default, but in Microsoft Visual C++ you'll need to turn it on overtly. See Appendix C, "Microsoft Visual C++," for details on how this is done. You'll also need to include the header file TYPEINFO.

Checking the Type of a Class with dynamic_cast

Suppose some other program sends your program an object (as the operating system might do with a callback function). It's supposed to be a certain type of object, but you want to check it to be sure. How can you tell if an object is a certain type? The dynamic_cast operator provides a way, assuming that the classes whose objects you want to check are all descended from a common ancestor. The DYNCAST1 program shows how this looks.

```
//dyncast1.cpp
//dynamic cast used to test type of object
//RTTI must be enabled in compiler
#include <iostream>
#include <typeinfo>              //for dynamic_cast
using namespace std;
/////////////////////////////////////////////////////////////
class Base
   {
   virtual void vertFunc()      //needed for dynamic cast
      { }
   };
```

```
class Derv1 : public Base
   { };
class Derv2 : public Base
   { };
///////////////////////////////////////////////////////////////
//checks if pUnknown points to a Derv1
bool isDerv1(Base* pUnknown)  //unknown subclass of Base
   {
   Derv1* pDerv1;
   if( pDerv1 = dynamic_cast<Derv1*>(pUnknown) )
      return true;
   else
      return false;
   }
//----------------------------------------------------------
int main()
   {
   Derv1* d1 = new Derv1;
   Derv2* d2 = new Derv2;

   if( isDerv1(d1) )
      cout << "d1 is a member of the Derv1 class\n";
   else
      cout << "d1 is not a member of the Derv1 class\n";

   if( isDerv1(d2) )
      cout << "d2 is a member of the Derv1 class\n";
   else
      cout << "d2 is not a member of the Derv1 class\n";
   return 0;
   }
```

Here we have a base class Base and two derived classes Derv1 and Derv2. There's also a function, isDerv1(), which returns true if the pointer it received as an argument points to an object of class Derv1. This argument is of class Base, so the object passed can be either Derv1 or Derv2. The dynamic_cast operator attempts to convert this unknown pointer pUnknown to type Derv1. If the result is not zero, pUnknown did point to a Derv1 object. If the result is zero, it pointed to something else.

Changing Pointer Types with dynamic_cast

The dynamic_cast operator allows you to cast upward and downward in the inheritance tree. However, it allows such casting only in limited ways. The DYNCAST2 program shows examples of such casts.

```
//dyncast2.cpp
//tests dynamic casts
//RTTI must be enabled in compiler
#include <iostream>
#include <typeinfo>               //for dynamic_cast
using namespace std;
///////////////////////////////////////////////////////////////
class Base
    {
    protected:
        int ba;
    public:
        Base() : ba(0)
            { }
        Base(int b) : ba(b)
            { }
        virtual void vertFunc()   //needed for dynamic_cast
            { }
        void show()
            { cout << "Base: ba=" << ba << endl; }
    };
///////////////////////////////////////////////////////////////
class Derv : public Base
    {
    private:
        int da;
    public:
        Derv(int b, int d) : da(d)
            { ba = b; }
        void show()
            { cout << "Derv: ba=" << ba << ", da=" << da << endl; }
    };
///////////////////////////////////////////////////////////////
int main()
    {
    Base* pBase = new Base(10);           //pointer to Base
    Derv* pDerv = new Derv(21, 22);       //pointer to Derv

    //derived-to-base: upcast -- points to Base subobject of Derv
    pBase = dynamic_cast<Base*>(pDerv);
    pBase->show();                        //"Base: ba=21"

    pBase = new Derv(31, 32);             //normal
    //base-to-derived: downcast -- (pBase must point to a Derv)
    pDerv = dynamic_cast<Derv*>(pBase);
    pDerv->show();                        //"Derv: ba=31, da=32"
    return 0;
    }
```

Here we have a base and a derived class. We've given each of these classes a data item to better demonstrate the effects of dynamic casts.

In an upcast you attempt to change a derived-class object into a base-class object. What you get is the base part of the derived class object. In the example we make an object of class Derv. The base class part of this object holds member data ba, which has a value of 21, and the derived part holds data member da, which has the value 22. After the cast, pBase points to the base-class part of this Derv class object, so when called upon to display itself, it prints Base: ba=21. Upcasts are fine if all you want is the base part of the object.

In a downcast we put a derived class object, which is pointed to by a base-class pointer, into a derived-class pointer.

The typeid Operator

Sometimes you want more information about an object than simple verification that it's of a certain class. You can obtain information about the type of an unknown object, such as its class name, using the typeid operator. The TYPEID program demonstrates how it works.

```
// typeid.cpp
// demonstrates typeid() function
// RTTI must be enabled in compiler
#include <iostream>
#include <typeinfo>              //for typeid()
using namespace std;
/////////////////////////////////////////////////////////////////
class Base
    {
    virtual void virtFunc()      //needed for typeid
        { }
    };
class Derv1 : public Base
    { };
class Derv2 : public Base
    { };
/////////////////////////////////////////////////////////////////
void displayName(Base* pB)
    {
    cout << "pointer to an object of ";  //display name of class
    cout << typeid(*pB).name() << endl;  //pointed to by pB
    }
//-------------------------------------------------------------
int main()
    {
    Base* pBase = new Derv1;
```

```
displayName(pBase);    //"pointer to an object of class Derv1"

pBase = new Derv2;
displayName(pBase);    //"pointer to an object of class Derv2"
return 0;
}
```

In this example the `displayName()` function displays the name of the class of the object passed to it. To do this, it uses the `name` member of the `type_info` class, along with the `typeid` operator. In `main()` we pass this function two objects of class `Derv1` and `Derv2` respectively, and the program's output is

```
pointer to an object of class Derv1
pointer to an object of class Derv2
```

Besides its name, other information about a class is available using `typeid`. For example, you can check for equality of classes using an overloaded `==` operator. We'll show an example of this in the EMPL_IO program in Chapter 12, "Streams and Files." Although the examples in this section have used pointers, `dynamic_cast` and `typeid` work equally well with references.

Summary

Virtual functions provide a way for a program to decide while it is running what function to call. Ordinarily such decisions are made at compile time. Virtual functions make possible greater flexibility in performing the same kind of action on different kinds of objects. In particular, they allow the use of functions called from an array of type pointer-to-base that actually holds pointers (or references) to a variety of derived types. This is an example of *polymorphism*. Typically a function is declared virtual in the base class, and other functions with the same name are declared in derived classes.

The use of one or more pure virtual functions in a class makes the class *abstract*, which means that no objects can be instantiated from it.

A `friend` function can access a class's private data, even though it is not a member function of the class. This is useful when one function must have access to two or more unrelated classes and when an overloaded operator must use, on its left side, a value of a class other than the one of which it is a member. `friend`s are also used to facilitate functional notation.

A `static` function is one that operates on the class in general, rather than on objects of the class. In particular it can operate on static variables. It can be called with the class name and scope-resolution operator.

The assignment operator = can be overloaded. This is necessary when it must do more than merely copy one object's contents into another. The copy constructor, which creates copies during initialization, and also when arguments are passed and returned by value, can also be overloaded. This is necessary when the copy constructor must do more than simply copy an object.

The this pointer is predefined in member functions to point to the object of which the function is a member. The this pointer is useful in returning the object of which the function is a member.

The dynamic_cast operator plays several roles. It can be used to determine what type of object a pointer points to, and, in certain situations, it can change the type of a pointer. The typeid operator can discover certain information about an object's class, such as its name.

The UML object diagram shows the relationship of a group of objects at a specific point in a program's operation.

Questions

Answers to these questions can be found in Appendix G.

1. Virtual functions allow you to

    a. create an array of type pointer-to-base class that can hold pointers to derived classes.

    b. create functions that can never be accessed.

    c. group objects of different classes so they can all be accessed by the same function code.

    d. use the same function call to execute member functions of objects from different classes.

2. True or false: A pointer to a base class can point to objects of a derived class.

3. If there is a pointer p to objects of a base class, and it contains the address of an object of a derived class, and both classes contain a nonvirtual member function, ding(), then the statement p->ding(); will cause the version of ding() in the _____ class to be executed.

4. Write a declarator for a virtual function called dang() that returns type void and takes one argument of type int.

5. Deciding—after a program starts to execute—what function will be executed by a particular function call statement is called _____.

6. If there is a pointer, p, to objects of a base class, and it contains the address of an object of a derived class, and both classes contain a virtual member function, ding(), the statement p->ding(); will cause the version of ding() in the _____ class to be executed.

7. Write the declaration for a pure virtual function called aragorn that returns no value and takes no arguments.

8. A pure virtual function is a virtual function that

    a. causes its class to be abstract.

    b. returns nothing.

    c. is used in a base class.

    d. takes no arguments.

9. Write the definition of an array called parr of 10 pointers to objects of class dong.

10. An abstract class is useful when

    a. no classes should be derived from it.

    b. there are multiple paths from one derived class to another.

    c. no objects should be instantiated from it.

    d. you want to defer the declaration of the class.

11. True or false: A friend function can access a class's private data without being a member of the class.

12. A friend function can be used to

    a. mediate arguments between classes.

    b. allow access to classes whose source code is unavailable.

    c. allow access to an unrelated class.

    d. increase the versatility of an overloaded operator.

13. Write the declaration for a friend function called harry() that returns type void and takes one argument of class george.

14. The keyword friend appears in

    a. the class allowing access to another class.

    b. the class desiring access to another class.

    c. the private section of a class.

    d. the public section of a class.

15. Write a declaration that, in the class in which it appears, will make every member of the class harry a friend function.

16. A static function

    a. should be called when an object is destroyed.

    b. is closely connected to an individual object of a class.

    c. can be called using the class name and function name.

    d. is used when a dummy object must be created.

17. Explain what the default assignment operator does when applied to objects.

18. Write a declaration for an overloaded assignment operator in class zeta.

19. An assignment operator might be overloaded to

    a. help keep track of the number of identical objects.

    b. assign a separate ID number to each object.

    c. ensure that all member data is copied exactly.

    d. signal when assignment takes place.

20. True or false: The user must always define the operation of the copy constructor.

21. The operation of the assignment operator and that of the copy constructor are

    a. similar, except that the copy constructor creates a new object.

    b. similar, except that the assignment operator copies member data.

    c. different, except that they both create a new object.

    d. different, except that they both copy member data.

22. Write the declaration of a copy constructor for a class called Bertha.

23. True or false: A copy constructor could be defined to copy only part of an object's data.

24. The lifetime of a variable that is

    a. local to a member function coincides with the lifetime of the function.

    b. global coincides with the lifetime of a class.

    c. nonstatic member data of an object coincides with the lifetime of the object.

    d. static in a member function coincides with the lifetime of the function.

25. True or false: There is no problem with returning the value of a variable defined as local within a member function so long as it is returned by value.

26. Explain the difference in operation between these two statements.

```
person p1(p0);
person p1 = p0;
```

27. A copy constructor is invoked when

    a. a function returns by value.

    b. an argument is passed by value.

    c. a function returns by reference.

    d. an argument is passed by reference.

28. What does the this pointer point to?

29. If, within a class, da is a member variable, will the statement this.da=37; assign 37 to da?

30. Write a statement that a member function can use to return the entire object of which it is a member, without creating any temporary objects.

31. An object rectangle in an object diagram represents

a. a general group of objects.

b. a class.

c. an instance of a class.

d. all the objects of a class.

32. The lines between objects in a UML object diagram are called _____.

33. True or false: object A may relate to object B at one time but not at another.

34. Object diagrams show

a. which objects exist at a point in time.

b. which objects are communicating at a point in time.

c. which objects participate in a particular behavior of the program.

d. which objects have operations (member functions) that call objects of other classes.

Exercises

Answers to starred exercises can be found in Appendix G.

*1. Imagine the same publishing company described in Exercise 1 in Chapter 9 that markets both book and audiocassette versions of its works. As in that exercise, create a class called publication that stores the title (a string) and price (type float) of a publication. From this class derive two classes: book, which adds a page count (type int); and tape, which adds a playing time in minutes (type float). Each of the three classes should have a getdata() function to get its data from the user at the keyboard, and a putdata() function to display the data.

Write a main() program that creates an array of pointers to publication. This is similar to the VIRTPERS example in this chapter. In a loop, ask the user for data about a particular book or tape, and use new to create an object of type book or tape to hold the data. Put the pointer to the object in the array. When the user has finished entering the data for all books and tapes, display the resulting data for all the books and tapes entered, using a for loop and a single statement such as

```
pubarr[j]->putdata();
```

to display the data from each object in the array.

*2. In the Distance class, as shown in the FRENGL and FRISQ examples in this chapter, create an overloaded * operator so that two distances can be multiplied together. Make it a friend function so that you can use such expressions as

```
Wdist1 = 7.5 * dist2;
```

You'll need a one-argument constructor to convert floating-point values into Distance values. Write a main() program to·test this operator in several ways.

*3. As we saw earlier, it's possible to make a class that acts like an array. The CLARRAY example shown here is a complete program that shows one way to create your own array class:

```cpp
// clarray.cpp
// creates array class
#include <iostream>
using namespace std;
/////////////////////////////////////////////////////////////////
class Array                        //models a normal C++ array
   {
   private:
      int* ptr;                    //pointer to Array contents
      int size;                    //size of Array
   public:
      Array(int s)                 //one-argument constructor
         {
         size = s;                 //argument is size of Array
         ptr = new int[s];         //make space for Array
         }
      ~Array()                     //destructor
         { delete[] ptr; }
      int& operator [] (int j)     //overloaded subscript operator
         { return *(ptr+j); }
   };
/////////////////////////////////////////////////////////////////
int main()
   {
   const int ASIZE = 10;           //size of array
   Array arr(ASIZE);               //make an array

   for(int j=0; j<ASIZE; j++)      //fill it with squares
      arr[j] = j*j;

   for(j=0; j<ASIZE; j++)          //display its contents
      cout << arr[j] << ' ';
   cout << endl;
   return 0;
   }
```

The output of this program is

```
0   1   4   9   16   25   36   49   64   81
```

Starting with CLARRAY, add an overloaded assignment operator and an overloaded copy constructor to the Array class. Then add statements such as

```
Array arr2(arr1);
```

and

```
arr3 = arr1;
```

to the main() program to test whether these overloaded operators work. The copy constructor should create an entirely new Array object with its own memory for storing array elements. Both the copy constructor and the assignment operator should copy the contents of the old Array object to the new one. What happens if you assign an Array of one size to an Array of a different size?

4. Start with the program of Exercise 1 in this chapter, and add a member function of type bool called isOversize() to the book and tape classes. Let's say that a book with more than 800 pages, or a tape with a playing time longer than 90 minutes (which would require two cassettes), is considered oversize. You can access this function from main() and display the string "Oversize" for oversize books and tapes when you display their other data. If book and tape objects are to be accessed using pointers to them that are stored in an array of type publication, what do you need to add to the publication base class? Can you instantiate members of this base class?

5. Start with the program of Exercise 8 in Chapter 8, which overloaded five arithmetic operators for money strings. Add the two operators that couldn't be overloaded in that exercise. These operations

```
long double * bMoney  // number times money
long double / bMoney  // number divided by money
```

require friend functions, since an object appears on the right side of the operator while a numerical constant appears on the left. Make sure that the main() program allows the user to enter two money strings and a floating-point value, and then carries out all seven arithmetic operations on appropriate pairs of these values.

6. As in the previous exercise, start with the program of Exercise 8 in Chapter 9. This time, add a function that rounds a bMoney value to the nearest dollar. It should be used like this:

```
mo2 = round(mo1);
```

As you know, amounts of $0.49 and less are rounded down, while those $0.50 and above are rounded up. A library function called modfl() is useful here. It separates a type long double variable into a fractional part and an integer part. If the fractional part is less than 0.50, return the integer part as is; otherwise add 1.0. In main(), test the function by sending it a sequence of bMoney amounts that go from less than $0.49 to more than $0.50.

7. Remember the PARSE program from Chapter 10? It would be nice to improve this program so it could evaluate expressions with real numbers, say type float, instead of single-digit numbers. For example

```
3.14159 / 2.0 + 75.25 * 3.333 + 6.02
```

As a first step toward this goal, you need to develop a stack that can hold both operators (type char) and numbers (type float). But how can you store two different types on a stack, which is basically an array? After all, type char and type float aren't even the same size. Could you store pointers to different types? They're the same size, but the compiler still won't allow you to store type char* and type float* in the same array. The only way two different types of pointers can be stored in the same array is if they are derived from the same base class. So we can encapsulate a char in one class and a float in another, and arrange for both classes to be derived from a base class. Then we can store both kinds of pointers in an array of pointers to the base class. The base class doesn't need to have any data of its own; it can be an abstract class from which no objects will be instantiated.

Constructors can store the values in the derived classes in the usual way, but you'll need to use pure virtual functions to get the values back out again. Here's a possible scenario:

```cpp
class Token                    // abstract base class
   {
   public:
      virtual float getNumber()=0;    // pure virtual functions
      virtual char getOperator()=0;
   };
class Operator : public Token
   {
   private:
      char oper;              // operators +, -, *, /
   public:
      Operator(char);        // constructor sets value
      char getOperator();    // gets value
      float getNumber();     // dummy function
   };
class Number : public Token
   {
   private:
      float fnum;            // the number
   public:
      Number(float);         // constructor sets value
      float getNumber();     // gets value
      char getOperator();    // dummy function
   };

Token* atoken[100];          // holds types Operator* and Number*
```

Base-class virtual functions need to be instantiated in all derived classes, or the classes themselves become abstract. Thus the Operand class needs a getNumber() function, even though it doesn't store a number, and the Number class needs getOperand(), even though it doesn't store an operand.

Expand this framework into a working program by adding a Stack class that holds Token objects, and a main() that pushes and pops various operators (such as + and *) and floating-point numbers (1.123) on and off the stack.

8. Let's put a little twist into the HORSE example of Chapter 10 by making a class of extra-competitive horses. We'll assume that any horse that's ahead by the halfway point in the race starts to feel its oats and becomes almost unbeatable. From the horse class, derive a class called comhorse (for competitive horse). Overload the horse_tick() function in this class so that each horse can check if it's the front-runner and if there's another horse close behind it (say 0.1 furlong). If there is, it should speed up a bit. Perhaps not enough to win every time, but enough to give it a decided advantage.

How does each horse know where the other horses are? It must access the memory that holds them, which in the HORSE program is hArray. Be careful, however. You want to create comhorses, not horses. So the comhorse class will need to overload hArray. You may need to derive a new track class, comtrack, to create the comhorses.

You can continuously check if your horse is ahead of the (otherwise) leading horse, and if it's by a small margin, accelerate your horse a bit.

9. Exercise 4 in Chapter 10 involved adding an overloaded destructor to the linklist class. Suppose we fill an object of such a destructor-enhanced class with data, and then assign the entire class with a statement such as

```
list2 = list1;
```

using the default assignment operator. Now, suppose we later delete the list1 object. Can we still use list2 to access the same data? No, because when list1 was deleted, its destructor deleted all its links. The only data actually contained in a linklist object is a pointer to the first link. Once the links are gone, the pointer in list2 becomes invalid, and attempts to access the list lead to meaningless values or a program crash.

One way to fix this is to overload the assignment operator so that it copies all the data links, as well as the linklist object itself. You'll need to follow along the chain, copying each link in turn. As we noted earlier, you should overload the copy constructor as well. To make it possible to delete linklist objects in main(), you may want to create them using pointers and new. That makes it easier to test the new routines. Don't worry if the copy process reverses the order of the data.

Notice that copying all the data is not very efficient in terms of memory usage. Contrast this approach with that used in the STRIMEM example in Chapter 10, which used only one set of data for all objects, and kept track of how many objects pointed to this data.

10. Carry out the modification, discussed in Exercise 7, to the PARSE program of Chapter 10. That is, make it possible to parse expressions containing floating-point numbers. Combine the classes from Exercise 7 with the algorithms from PARSE. You'll need to operate on pointers to tokens instead of characters. This involves statements of the kind

```
Number* ptrN = new Number(ans);
s.push(ptrN);
```

and

```
Operator* ptrO = new Operator(ch);
s.push(ptrO);
```

Streams and Files

IN THIS CHAPTER

This chapter focuses on the C++ stream classes. We'll start off with a look at the hierarchy in which these classes are arranged, and we'll summarize their important features. The largest part of this chapter is devoted to showing how to perform file-related activities using C++ streams. We'll show how to read and write data to files in a variety of ways, how to handle errors, and how files and OOP are related. Later in the chapter we'll examine several other features of C++ that are related to files, including in-memory text formatting, command-line arguments, overloading the insertion and extraction operators, and sending data to the printer.

Stream Classes

A *stream* is a general name given to a flow of data. In C++ a stream is represented by an object of a particular class. So far we've used the cin and cout stream objects. Different streams are used to represent different kinds of data flow. For example, the ifstream class represents data flow from input disk files.

Advantages of Streams

C programmers may wonder what advantages there are to using the stream classes for I/O, instead of traditional C functions such as printf() and scanf(), and—for files—fprintf(), fscanf(), and so on.

One reason is simplicity. If you've ever used a %d formatting character when you should have used a %f in printf(), you'll appreciate this. There are no such formatting characters in streams, since each object already knows how to display itself. This removes a major source of errors.

Another reason is that you can overload existing operators and functions, such as the insertion (<<) and extraction (>>) operators, to work with classes that you create. This makes your own classes work in the same way as the built-in types, which again makes programming easier and more error free (not to mention more aesthetically satisfying).

You may wonder whether stream I/O is important if you plan to program in an environment with a graphical user interface such as Windows, where direct text output to the screen is not used. Do you still need to know about C++ streams? Yes, because they are the best way to write data to files, and also to format data in memory for later use in text input/output windows and other GUI elements.

The Stream Class Hierarchy

The stream classes are arranged in a rather complex hierarchy. Figure 12.1 shows the arrangement of the most important of these classes.

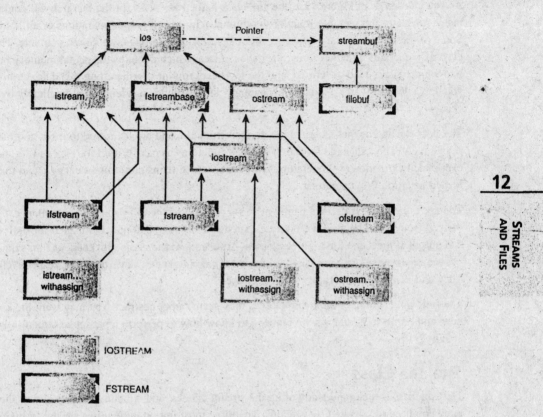

FIGURE 12.1
Stream class hierarchy.

We've already made extensive use of some stream classes. The extraction operator `>>` is a member of the `istream` class, and the insertion operator `<<` is a member of the `ostream` class. Both of these classes are derived from the `ios` class. The `cout` object, representing the standard output stream, which is usually directed to the video display, is a predefined object of the `ostream_withassign` class, which is derived from the `ostream` class. Similarly, `cin` is an object of the `istream_withassign` class, which is derived from `istream`.

The classes used for input and output to the video display and keyboard are declared in the header file IOSTREAM, which we routinely included in our examples in previous chapters. The classes used specifically for disk file I/O are declared in the file FSTREAM. Figure 12.1 shows which classes are in which two header files. (Also, some manipulators are declared in IOMANIP, and in-memory classes are declared in STRSTREAM.) You may find it educational to print out these header files and trace the relationships among the various classes. They're in your compiler's INCLUDE subdirectory. Many questions about streams can be answered by studying their class and constant declarations.

As you can see from Figure 12.1, the `ios` class is the base class for the hierarchy. It contains many constants and member functions common to input and output operations of all kinds. Some of these, such as the `showpoint` and `fixed` formatting flags, we've seen already. The `ios` class also contains a pointer to the `streambuf` class, which contains the actual memory buffer into which data is read or written, and the low-level routines for handling this data. Ordinarily you don't need to worry about the `streambuf` class, which is referenced automatically by other classes.

The `istream` and `ostream` classes are derived from `ios` and are dedicated to input and output, respectively. The `istream` class contains such functions as `get()`, `getline()`, `read()`, and the overloaded extraction (>>) operators, while `ostream` contains `put()` and `write()`, and the overloaded insertion (<<) operators.

The `iostream` class is derived from both `istream` and `ostream` by multiple inheritance. Classes derived from it can be used with devices, such as disk files, that may be opened for both input and output at the same time. Three classes—`istream_withassign`, `ostream_withassign`, and `iostream_withassign`—are inherited from `istream`, `ostream`, and `iostream`, respectively. They add assignment operators to these classes.

The following summary of stream classes may seem rather abstract. You may want to skim it now, and return to it later when you need to know how to perform a particular stream-related activity.

The `ios` Class

The `ios` class is the granddaddy of all the stream classes, and contains the majority of the features you need to operate C++ streams. The three most important features are the formatting flags, the error-status flags, and the file operation mode. We'll look at formatting flags and error-status flags next. We'll save the file operations mode for later, when we talk about disk files.

Formatting Flags

Formatting flags are a set of enum definitions in `ios`. They act as on/off switches that specify choices for various aspects of input and output format and operation. We won't provide a detailed discussion of each flag, since we've already seen some of them in use, and others are more or less self-explanatory. Some we'll discuss later in this chapter. Table 12.1 is a complete list of the formatting flags.

TABLE 12.1 ios Formatting Flags

Flag	Meaning
skipws	Skip (ignore) whitespace on input
left	Left-adjust output [12.34]
right	Right-adjust output [12.34]
internal	Use padding between sign or base indicator and number [+ 12.34]
dec	Convert to decimal
oct	Convert to octal
hex	Convert to hexadecimal
boolalpha	Convert bool to "true" or "false" strings
showbase	Use base indicator on output (0 for octal, 0x for hex)
showpoint	Show decimal point on output
uppercase	Use uppercase X, E, and hex output letters (ABCDEF)—the default is lowercase
showpos	Display + before positive integers
scientific	Use exponential format on floating-point output [9.1234E2]
fixed	Use fixed format on floating-point output [912.34]
unitbuf	Flush all streams after insertion
stdio	Flush stdout, stderror after insertion

There are several ways to set the formatting flags, and different ones can be set in different ways. Since they are members of the ios class, you must usually precede them with the name ios and the scope-resolution operator (for example, ios::skipws). All the flags can be set using the setf() and unsetf() ios member functions. Look at the following example:

```
cout.setf(ios::left);    // left justify output text
cout >> "This text is left-justified";
cout.unsetf(ios::left);  // return to default (right justified)
```

Many formatting flags can be set using manipulators, so let's look at them now.

Manipulators

Manipulators are formatting instructions inserted directly into a stream. We've seen examples before, such as the manipulator endl, which sends a newline to the stream and flushes it:

```
cout << "To each his own." << endl;
```

We've also used the `setiosflags()` manipulator (see the SALEMON program in Chapter 7, "Arrays and Strings"):

```
cout << setiosflags(ios::fixed)        // use fixed decimal point
     << setiosflags(ios::showpoint)    // always show decimal point
     << var;
```

As these examples demonstrate, manipulators come in two flavors: those that take an argument and those that don't. Table 12.2 summarizes the important no-argument manipulators.

TABLE 12.2 No-Argument ios Manipulators

Manipulator	Purpose
ws	Turn on whitespace skipping on input
dec	Convert to decimal
oct	Convert to octal
hex	Convert to hexadecimal
endl	Insert newline and flush the output stream
ends	Insert null character to terminate an output string
flush	Flush the output stream
lock	Lock file handle
unlock	Unlock file handle

You insert these manipulators directly into the stream. For example, to output var in hexadecimal format, you can say

```
cout << hex << var;
```

Note that manipulators affect only the data that follows them in the stream, not the data that precedes them. Table 12.3 summarizes the important manipulators that take arguments. You need the IOMANIP header file for these functions.

TABLE 12.3 ios Manipulators with Arguments

Manipulator	Argument	Purpose
setw()	field width (int)	Set field width for output
setfill()	fill character (int)	Set fill character for output (default is a space)
setprecision()	precision (int)	Set precision (number of digits displayed)
setiosflags()	formatting flags (long)	Set specified flags
resetiosflags()	formatting flags (long)	Clear specified flags

Functions

The ios class contains a number of functions that you can use to set the formatting flags and perform other tasks. Table 12.4 shows most of these functions, except those that deal with errors, which we'll examine separately.

TABLE 12.4 ios Functions

Function	Purpose
ch = fill();	Return the fill character (fills unused part of field; default is space)
fill(ch);	Set the fill character
p = precision();	Get the precision (number of digits displayed for floating-point)
precision(p);	Set the precision
w = width();	Get the current field width (in characters)
width(w);	Set the current field width
setf(flags);	Set specified formatting flags (for example, ios::left)
unsetf(flags);	Unset specified formatting flags
setf(flags, field);	First clear field, then set flags

These functions are called for specific stream objects using the normal dot operator. For example, to set the field width to 12, you can say

```
cout.width(14);
```

The following statement sets the fill character to an asterisk (as for check printing):

```
cout.fill('*');
```

You can use several functions to manipulate the ios formatting flags directly. For example, to set left justification, use

```
cout.setf(ios::left);
```

To restore right justification, use

```
cout.unsetf(ios::left);
```

A two-argument version of setf() uses the second argument to reset all the flags of a particular type or *field*. Then the flag specified in the first argument is set. This makes it easier to reset the relevant flags before setting a new one. Table 12.5 shows the arrangement.

For example

```
cout.setf(ios::left, ios::adjustfield);
```

clears all the flags dealing with text justification and then sets the left flag for left-justified output.

TABLE 12.5 Two-Argument Version of `setf()`

First Argument: Flags to Set	Second Argument: Field to Clear
`dec, oct, hex`	`basefield`
`left, right, internal`	`adjustfield`
`scientific, fixed`	`floatfield`

By using the techniques shown here with the formatting flags, you can usually figure out a way to format I/O not only for the keyboard and display, but, as we'll see later in this chapter, for files as well.

The `istream` Class

The `istream` class, which is derived from `ios`, performs input-specific activities, or extraction. It's easy to confuse extraction and the related output activity, insertion. Figure 12.2 emphasizes the difference.

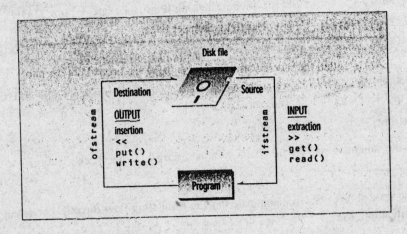

FIGURE 12.2
File input and output.

Table 12.6 lists the functions you'll most commonly use from the `istream` class.

TABLE 12.6 `istream` Functions

Function	Purpose
`>>`	Formatted extraction for all basic (and overloaded) types.
`get(ch);`	Extract one character into `ch`.
`get(str)`	Extract characters into array `str`, until '\n'.

TABLE 12.6 Continued

Function	Purpose
get(str, MAX)	Extract up to MAX characters into array.
get(str, DELIM)	Extract characters into array str until specified delimiter (typically '\n'). Leave delimiting char in stream.
get(str, MAX, DELIM)	Extract characters into array str until MAX characters or the DELIM character. Leave delimiting char in stream.
getline(str, MAX, DELIM)	Extract characters into array str, until MAX characters or the DELIM character. Extract delimiting character.
putback(ch)	Insert last character read back into input stream.
ignore(MAX, DELIM)	Extract and discard up to MAX characters until (and including) the specified delimiter (typically '\n').
peek(ch)	Read one character, leave it in stream.
count = gcount()	Return number of characters read by a (immediately preceding) call to get(), getline(), or read().
read(str, MAX)	For files—extract up to MAX characters into str, until EOF.
seekg()	Set distance (in bytes) of file pointer from start of file.
seekg(pos, seek_dir)	Set distance (in bytes) of file pointer from specified place in file. seek_dir can be ios::beg, ios::cur, ios::end.
pos = tellg(pos)	Return position (in bytes) of file pointer from start of file.

You've seen some of these functions, such as get(), before. Most of them operate on the cin object, which usually represents the data flow from the keyboard. However, the last four deal specifically with disk files.

The ostream Class

The ostream class handles output or insertion activities. Table 12.7 shows the most commonly used member functions of this class. The last four functions in this table deal specifically with disk files.

TABLE 12.7 ostream Functions

Function	Purpose
<<	Formatted insertion for all basic (and overloaded) types.
put(ch)	Insert character ch into stream.
flush()	Flush buffer contents and insert newline.
write(str, SIZE)	Insert SIZE characters from array str into file.

TABLE 12.7 Continued

Function	Purpose
seekp(position)	Set distance in bytes of file pointer from start of file.
seekp(position, seek_dir)	Set distance in bytes of file pointer, from specified place in file. seek_dir can be ios::beg, ios::cur, or ios::end.
pos = tellp()	Return position of file pointer, in bytes.

The iostream and the _withassign Classes

The iostream class, which is derived from both istream and ostream, acts only as a base class from which other classes, specifically iostream_withassign, can be derived. It has no functions of its own (except constructors and destructors). Classes derived from iostream can perform both input and output.

There are three _withassign classes:

- istream_withassign, derived from istream
- ostream_withassign, derived from ostream
- iostream_withassign, derived from iostream

These _withassign classes are much like those they're derived from except that they include overloaded assignment operators so their objects can be copied.

Why do we need separate copyable and uncopyable stream classes? In general, it's not a good idea to copy stream class objects. The reason is that each such object is associated with a particular streambuf object, which includes an area in memory to hold the object's actual data. If you copy the stream object, it causes confusion if you also copy the streambuf object. However, in a few cases it's important to be able to copy a stream.

Accordingly, the istream, ostream, and iostream classes are made uncopyable (by making their overloaded copy constructors and assignment operators private), while the _withassign classes derived from them can be copied.

Predefined Stream Objects

We've already made extensive use of two predefined stream objects that are derived from the _withassign classes: cin and cout. These are normally connected to the keyboard and display, respectively. The two other predefined objects are cerr and clog.

- cin, an object of istream_withassign, normally used for keyboard input
- cout, an object of ostream_withassign, normally used for screen display

- cerr, an object of ostream_withassign, for error messages
- clog, an object of ostream_withassign, for log messages

The cerr object is often used for error messages and program diagnostics. Output sent to cerr is displayed immediately, rather than being buffered, as cout is. Also, it cannot be redirected (more on this later). For these reasons you have a better chance of seeing a final output message from cerr if your program dies prematurely. Another object, clog, is similar to cerr in that it is not redirected, but its output is buffered, while cerr's is not.

Stream Errors

So far in this book we've mostly used a rather straightforward approach to input and output, using statements of the form

```
cout << "Good morning";
```

and

```
cin >> var;
```

However, as you may have discovered, this approach assumes that nothing will go wrong during the I/O process. This isn't always the case, especially with input. What happens if a user enters the string "nine" instead of the integer 9, or pushes the Enter key without entering anything? Or what happens if there's a hardware failure? In this section we'll explore such problems. Many of the techniques we'll see here are applicable to file I/O as well.

Error-Status Bits

The stream error-status flags constitute an ios enum member that reports errors that occurred in an input or output operation. They're summarized in Table 12.8. Figure 12.3 shows how these flags look. Various ios functions can be used to read (and even set) these error flags, as shown in Table 12.9.

TABLE 12.8   Error-Status Flags

Name	Meaning
goodbit	No errors (no flags set, value = 0)
eofbit	Reached end of file
failbit	Operation failed (user error, premature EOF)
badbit	Invalid operation (no associated streambuf)
hardfail	Unrecoverable error

TABLE 12.9   Functions for Error Flags

Function	Purpose
int = eof();	Returns true if EOF flag set
int = fail();	Returns true if failbit or badbit or hardfail flag set
int = bad();	Returns true if badbit or hardfail flag set
int = good();	Returns true if everything OK; no flags set
clear(int=0);	With no argument, clears all error bits; otherwise sets specified flags, as in clear(ios::failbit)

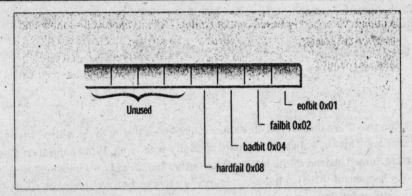

FIGURE 12.3
Stream status flags.

Inputting Numbers

Let's see how to handle errors when inputting numbers. This approach applies to numbers read either from the keyboard or from disk, as we'll see later. The idea is to check the value of goodbit, signal an error if it's not true, and give the user another chance to enter the correct input.

```
while(true)                        // cycle until input OK
   {
   cout << "\nEnter an integer: ";
   cin >> i;
   if( cin.good() )                // if no errors
      {
      cin.ignore(10, '\n');        // remove newline
      break;                       // exit loop
      }
   cin.clear();                    // clear the error bits
   cout << "Incorrect input";
```

```
    cin.ignore(10, '\n');              // remove newline
    }
cout << "integer is " << i;            // error-free integer
```

The most common error this scheme detects when reading keyboard input is the user typing nondigits (for instance, "nine" instead of "9"). This causes the `failbit` to be set. However, it also detects system-related failures that are more common with disk files.

Floating-point numbers (`float`, `double`, and `long double`) can be analyzed for errors in the same way as integers.

Too Many Characters

Too many characters sounds like a difficulty experienced by movie directors, but extra characters can also present a problem when reading from input streams. This is especially true when there are errors. Typically, extra characters are left in the input stream after the input is supposedly completed. They are then passed along to the next input operation, even though they are not intended for it. Often it's a newline character that remains behind, but sometimes other characters are left over as well. To get rid of these extraneous characters the `ignore(MAX, DELIM)` member function of `istream` is used. It reads and throws away up to `MAX` characters, including the specified delimiter character. In our example, the line

```
cin.ignore(10, '\n');
```

causes `cin` to read up to 10 characters, including the `'\n'`, and remove them from the input.

No-Input Input

Whitespace characters, such as tab space and `'\n'`, are normally ignored (skipped) when inputting numbers. This can have some undesirable side effects. For example, users, prompted to enter a number, may simply press the Enter key without typing any digits. (Perhaps they think that this will enter 0, or perhaps they are simply confused.) In the code shown above, as well as the simple statement

```
cin >> i;
```

pressing Enter causes the cursor to drop down to the next line, while the stream continues to wait for the number. What's wrong with the cursor dropping to the next line? First, inexperienced users, seeing no acknowledgment when they press Enter, may assume the computer is broken. Second, pressing Enter repeatedly normally causes the cursor to drop lower and lower until the entire screen begins to scroll upward. This is all right in teletype-style interaction, where the program and the user simply type at each other. However, in text-based graphics programs (such as the ELEV program in Chapter 13, "Multifile Programs"), scrolling the screen disarranges and eventually obliterates the display.

12
STREAMS
AND FILES

Thus it's important to be able to tell the input stream *not* to ignore whitespace. This is handled by clearing the skipws flag:

```
cout << "\nEnter an integer: ";
cin.unsetf(ios::skipws);          // don't ignore whitespace
cin >> i;
if( cin.good() )
   {
   // no error
   }
// error
```

Now if the user types Enter without any digits, the failbit will be set and an error generated. The program can then tell the user what to do, or reposition the cursor so the screen does not scroll.

Inputting Strings and Characters

The user can't really make any serious errors inputting strings and characters, since all input, even numbers, can be interpreted as a string. However, if coming from a disk file, characters and strings should still be checked for errors, in case an EOF or something worse is encountered. Unlike the situation with numbers, you often *do* want to ignore whitespace when inputting strings and characters.

Error-Free Distances

Let's look at a program in which user input to the English Distance class is checked for errors. This program simply accepts Distance values in feet and inches from the user and displays them. However, if the user commits an entry error, the program rejects the input with an appropriate explanation to the user, and prompts for new input.

The program is very simple except that the member function getdist() has been expanded to handle errors. Parts of this new code follow the approach of the fragment shown above. However, we've also added some statements to ensure that the user does not enter a floating-point number for feet. This is important because, while the feet value is an integer, the inches value is floating-point, and the user could easily become confused.

Ordinarily, if it's expecting an integer, the extraction operator simply terminates when it sees a decimal point, without signaling an error. We want to know about such an error, so we read the feet value as a string instead of an int. We then examine the string with a homemade function isFeet(), which returns true if the string proves to be a correct value for feet. To pass the feet test, it must contain only digits, and they must evaluate to a number between –999 and 999. (We assume that the Distance class will never be used for measuring larger feet values.) If the string passes the feet test, we convert it to an actual int with the library function atoi().

The inches value is a floating-point number. We want to check its range, which should be 0 or greater but less than 12.0. We also check it for ios error flags. Most commonly, the `failbit` will be set because the user typed nondigits instead of a number. Here's the listing for ENGLERR:

```cpp
// englerr.cpp
// input checking with English Distance class
#include <iostream>
#include <string>
#include <cstdlib>                    //for atoi(), atof()
using namespace std;
int isFeet(string);                   //declaration
/////////////////////////////////////////////////////////////////////
class Distance                        //English Distance class
   {
   private:
      int feet;
      float inches;
   public:
      Distance()                      //constructor (no args)
         { feet = 0; inches = 0.0; }
      Distance(int ft, float in)      //constructor (two args)
         { feet = ft; inches = in; }
      void showdist()                 //display distance
         { cout << feet << "\'-" << inches << '\"'; }
      void getdist();                 //get length from user
   };
//-----------------------------------------------------------------
void Distance::getdist()              //get length from user
   {
   string instr;                      //for input string

   while(true)                        //cycle until feet are right
      {
      cout << "\n\nEnter feet: ";
      cin.unsetf(ios::skipws);        //do not skip white space
      cin >> instr;                   //get feet as a string
      if( isFeet(instr) )             //is it a correct feet value?
         {                            //yes
         cin.ignore(10, '\n');        //eat chars, including newline
         feet = atoi( instr.c_str() ); //convert to integer
         break;                       //break out of 'while'
         }                            //no, not an integer
      cin.ignore(10, '\n');           //eat chars, including newline
      cout << "Feet must be an integer less than 1000\n";
      }  //end while feet
```

```
    while(true)                        //cycle until inches are right
      {
      cout << "Enter inches: ";
      cin.unsetf(ios::skipws);    //do not skip white space
      cin >> inches;              //get inches (type float)
      if(inches>=12.0 || inches<0.0)
         {
         cout << "Inches must be between 0.0 and 11.99\n";
         cin.clear(ios::failbit); //"artificially" set fail bit
         }
      if( cin.good() )            //check for cin failure
         {                        //(most commonly a non-digit)
         cin.ignore(10, '\n');    //eat the newline
         break;                   //input is OK, exit 'while'
         }
      cin.clear();                //error; clear the error state
      cin.ignore(10, '\n');       //eat chars, including newline
      cout << "Incorrect inches input\n"; //start again
      } //end while inches
   }
//------------------------------------------------------------
int isFeet(string str)             //return true if the string
   {                               //   is a correct feet value
   int slen = str.size();          //get length
   if(slen==0 || slen > 5)         //if no input, or too long
      return 0;                    //not an int
   for(int j=0; j<slen; j++)       //check each character
                                   //if not digit or minus
      if( (str[j] < '0' || str[j] > '9') && str[j] != '-' )
         return 0;                 //string is not correct feet
   double n = atof( str.c_str() ); //convert to double
   if( n<-999.0 || n>999.0 )       //is it out of range?
      return 0;                    //if so, not correct feet
   return 1;                       //it is correct feet
   }
///////////////////////////////////////////////////////////////
int main()
   {
   Distance d;                     //make a Distance object
   char ans;
   do
      {
      d.getdist();                 //get its value from user
      cout << "\nDistance = ";
      d.showdist();                //display it
      cout << "\nDo another (y/n)? ";
      cin >> ans;
```

```
        cin.ignore(10, '\n');        //eat chars, including newline
    } while(ans != 'n');             //cycle until 'n'
    return 0;
}
```

We've used another dodge here: setting an error-state flag manually. We do this because we want to ensure that the inches value is greater than 0 but less than 12.0. If it isn't, we turn on the failbit with the statement

```
cin.clear(ios::failbit);   // set failbit
```

When the program checks for errors with cin.good(), it will find the failbit set and signal that the input is incorrect.

Disk File I/O with Streams

Most programs need to save data to disk files and read it back in. Working with disk files requires another set of classes: ifstream for input, fstream for both input and output, and ofstream for output. Objects of these classes can be associated with disk files, and we can use their member functions to read and write to the files.

Referring back to Figure 12.1, you can see that ifstream is derived from istream, fstream is derived from iostream, and ofstream is derived from ostream. These ancestor classes are in turn derived from ios. Thus the file-oriented classes derive many of their member functions from more general classes. The file-oriented classes are also derived, by multiple inheritance, from the fstreambase class. This class contains an object of class filebuf, which is a file-oriented buffer, and its associated member functions, derived from the more general streambuf class. You don't usually need to worry about these buffer classes.

The ifstream, ofstream, and fstream classes are declared in the FSTREAM file.

C programmers will note that the approach to disk I/O used in C++ is quite different from that in C. The old C functions, such as fread() and fwrite(), will still work in C++, but they are not so well suited to the object-oriented environment. The new C++ approach is considerably cleaner and easier to implement. (Incidentally, be careful about mixing the old C functions with C++ streams. They don't always work together gracefully, although there are ways to make them cooperate.)

Formatted File I/O

In formatted I/O, numbers are stored on disk as a series of characters. Thus 6.02, rather than being stored as a 4-byte type float or an 8-byte type double, is stored as the characters '6', '.', '0', and '2'. This can be inefficient for numbers with many digits, but it's appropriate in many situations and easy to implement. Characters and strings are stored more or less normally.

Writing Data

The following program writes a character, an integer, a type double, and two string objects to a disk file. There is no output to the screen. Here's the listing for FORMATO:

```
// formato.cpp
// writes formatted output to a file, using <<
#include <fstream>                //for file I/O
#include <iostream>
#include <string>
using namespace std;

int main()
   {
   char ch = 'x';
   int j = 77;
   double d = 6.02;
   string str1 = "Kafka";         //strings without
   string str2 = "Proust";        //   embedded spaces

   ofstream outfile("fdata.txt"); //create ofstream object

   outfile << ch                  //insert (write) data
           << j
           << ' '                 //needs space between numbers
           << d
           << str1
           << ' '                 //needs spaces between strings
           << str2;
   cout << "File written\n";
   return 0;
   }
```

Here we define an object called outfile to be a member of the ofstream class. At the same time, we initialize it to the file FDATA.TXT. This initialization sets aside various resources for the file, and accesses or *opens* the file of that name on the disk. If the file doesn't exist, it is created. If it does exist, it is truncated and the new data replaces the old. The outfile object acts much as cout did in previous programs, so we can use the insertion operator (<<) to output variables of any basic type to the file. This works because the insertion operator is appropriately overloaded in ostream, from which ofstream is derived.

When the program terminates, the outfile object goes out of scope. This calls its destructor, which closes the file, so we don't need to close the file explicitly.

There are several potential formatting glitches. First, you must separate numbers (such as 77 and 6.02) with nonnumeric characters. Since numbers are stored as a sequence of characters, rather than as a fixed-length field, this is the only way the extraction operator will know, when the data is read back from the file, where one number stops and the next one begins. Second, strings must be separated with whitespace for the same reason. This implies that strings cannot contain imbedded blanks. In this example we use the space character (' ') for both kinds of delimiters. Characters need no delimiters, since they have a fixed length.

You can verify that FORMATO has indeed written the data by examining the FDATA.TXT file with the Windows WORDPAD accessory or the DOS command TYPE.

Reading Data

We can read the file generated by FORMATO by using an ifstream object, initialized to the name of the file. The file is automatically opened when the object is created. We can then read from it using the extraction (>>) operator.

Here's the listing for the FORMATI program, which reads the data back in from the FDATA.TXT file:

```
// formati.cpp
// reads formatted output from a file, using >>
#include <fstream>                    //for file I/O
#include <iostream>
#include <string>
using namespace std;

int main()
   {
   char ch;
   int j;
   double d;
   string str1;
   string str2;


   ifstream infile("fdata.txt");    //create ifstream object
                                    //extract (read) data from it
   infile >> ch >> j >> d >> str1 >> str2;

   cout << ch << endl               //display the data
        << j << endl
        << d << endl
        << str1 << endl
        << str2 << endl;
   return 0;
   }
```

Here the ifstream object, which we name infile, acts much the way cin did in previous programs. Provided that we have formatted the data correctly when inserting it into the file, there's no trouble extracting it, storing it in the appropriate variables, and displaying its contents. The program's output looks like this:

```
x
77
6.02
Kafka
Proust
```

Of course the numbers are converted back to their binary representations for storage in the program. That is, the 77 is stored in the variable j as a type int, not as two characters, and the 6.02 is stored as a double.

Strings with Embedded Blanks

The technique of our last examples won't work with char* strings containing embedded blanks. To handle such strings, you need to write a specific delimiter character after each string, and use the getline() function, rather than the extraction operator, to read them in. Our next program, OLINE, outputs some strings with blanks embedded in them.

```
// oline.cpp
// file output with strings
#include <fstream>                      //for file I/O
using namespace std;

int main()
    {
    ofstream outfile("TEST.TXT");          //create file for output
                                           //send text to file
    outfile << "I fear thee, ancient Mariner!\n";
    outfile << "I fear thy skinny hand\n";
    outfile << "And thou art long, and lank, and brown,\n";
    outfile << "As is the ribbed sea sand.\n";
    return 0;
    }
```

When you run the program, the lines of text (from Samuel Taylor Coleridge's *The Rime of the Ancient Mariner*) are written to a file. Each one is specifically terminated with a newline ('\n') character. Note that these are char* strings, not objects of the string class. Many stream operations work more easily with char* strings.

To extract the strings from the file, we create an ifstream and read from it one line at a time using the getline() function, which is a member of istream. This function reads characters, including whitespace, until it encounters the '\n' character, and places the resulting string in the buffer supplied as an argument. The maximum size of the buffer is given as the second argument. The contents of the buffer are displayed after each line.

```
// iline.cpp
// file input with strings
#include <fstream>              //for file functions
#include <iostream>
using namespace std;

int main()
   {
   const int MAX = 80;              //size of buffer
   char buffer[MAX];                //character buffer
   ifstream infile("TEST.TXT");     //create file for input
   while( !infile.eof() )           //until end-of-file
      {
      infile.getline(buffer, MAX);  //read a line of text
      cout << buffer << endl;       //display it
      }
   return 0;
   }
```

The output of ILINE to the screen is the same as the data written to the TEST.TXT file by OLINE: the four-line Coleridge stanza. The program has no way of knowing in advance how many strings are in the file, so it continues to read one string at a time until it encounters an end-of-file. Incidentally, don't use this program to read random text files. It requires all the text lines to terminate with the '\n' character, and if you encounter a file in which this is not the case, the program will hang.

Detecting End-of-File

As we have seen, objects derived from ios contain error-status flags that can be checked to determine the results of operations. When we read a file little by little, as we do here, we will eventually encounter an end-of-file (EOF) condition. The EOF is a signal sent to the program from the operating system when there is no more data to read. In ILINE we could have checked for this in the line

```
while( !infile.eof() )    // until eof encountered
```

However, checking specifically for an eofbit means that we won't detect the other error flags, such as the failbit and badbit, which may also occur, although more rarely. To do this, we can change our loop condition:

```
while( infile.good() )    // until any error encountered
```

You can also test the stream directly. Any stream object, such as `infile`, has a value that can be tested for the usual error conditions, including EOF. If any such condition is true, the object returns a zero value. If everything is going well, the object returns a nonzero value. This value is actually a pointer, but the "address" returned has no significance except to be tested for a zero or nonzero value. Thus we can rewrite our `while` loop again:

```
while( infile )          // until any error encountered
```

This is certainly simple, but it may not be quite so clear to the uninitiated what it does.

Character I/O

The `put()` and `get()` functions, which are members of `ostream` and `istream`, respectively, can be used to output and input single characters. Here's a program, OCHAR, that outputs a string, one character at a time:

```
// ochar.cpp
// file output with characters
#include <fstream>                    //for file functions
#include <iostream>
#include <string>
using namespace std;

int main()
   {
   string str = "Time is a great teacher, but unfortunately "
            "it kills all its pupils.  Berlioz";

   ofstream outfile("TEST.TXT");      //create file for output
   for(int j=0; j<str.size(); j++)    //for each character,
      outfile.put( str[j] );          //write it to file
   cout << "File written\n";
   return 0;
   }
```

In this program an `ofstream` object is created as it was in OLINE. The length of the `string` object `str` is found using the `size()` member function, and the characters are output using `put()` in a `for` loop. The aphorism by Hector Berlioz (a 19th-century composer of operas and program music) is written to the file TEST.TXT. We can read this file back in and display it using the ICHAR program.

```
// ichar.cpp
// file input with characters
#include <fstream>                    //for file functions
#include <iostream>
using namespace std;
```

```
int main()
   {
   char ch;                           //character to read
   ifstream infile("TEST.TXT");       //create file for input
   while( infile )                    //read until EOF or error
      {
      infile.get(ch);                 //read character
      cout << ch;                     //display it
      }
   cout << endl;
   return 0;
   }
```

This program uses the get() function and continues reading until the EOF is reached (or an error occurs). Each character read from the file is displayed using cout, so the entire aphorism appears on the screen.

Another approach to reading characters from a file is the rdbuf() function, a member of the ios class. This function returns a pointer to the streambuf (or filebuf) object associated with the stream object. This object contains a buffer that holds the characters read from the stream, so you can use the pointer to it as a data object in its own right. Here's the listing for ICHAR2:

```
// ichar2.cpp
// file input with characters
#include <fstream>              //for file functions
#include <iostream>
using namespace std;

int main()
   {
   ifstream infile("TEST.TXT");     //create file for input

   cout << infile.rdbuf();          //send its buffer to cout
   cout << endl;
   return 0;
   }
```

This program has the same effect as ICHAR. It also takes the prize for the shortest file-oriented program. Note that rdbuf() knows that it should return when it encounters an EOF.

Binary I/O

You can write a few numbers to disk using formatted I/O, but if you're storing a large amount of numerical data it's more efficient to use binary I/O, in which numbers are stored as they are in the computer's RAM memory, rather than as strings of characters. In binary I/O an int is stored in 4 bytes, whereas its next version might be "12345", requiring 5 bytes. Similarly, a float is always stored in 4 bytes, while its formatted version might be "6.02314e13", requiring 10 bytes.

Our next example shows how an array of integers is written to disk and then read back into memory, using binary format. We use two new functions: write(), a member of ofstream; and read(), a member of ifstream. These functions think about data in terms of bytes (type char). They don't care how the data is formatted, they simply transfer a buffer full of bytes from and to a disk file. The parameters to write() and read() are the address of the data buffer and its length. The address must be cast, using reinterpret_cast, to type char*, and the length is the length in bytes (characters), *not* the number of data items in the buffer. Here's the listing for BINIO:

```cpp
// binio.cpp
// binary input and output with integers
#include <fstream>                    //for file streams
#include <iostream>
using namespace std;
const int MAX = 100;                  //size of buffer
int buff[MAX];                        //buffer for integers

int main()
   {
   for(int j=0; j<MAX; j++)           //fill buffer with data
      buff[j] = j;                    //(0, 1, 2, ...)
                                      //create output stream
   ofstream os("edata.dat", ios::binary);
                                      //write to it
   os.write( reinterpret_cast<char*>(buff), MAX*sizeof(int) );
   os.close();                        //must close it

   for(j=0; j<MAX; j++)               //erase buffer
      buff[j] = 0;

                                      //create input stream
   ifstream is("edata.dat", ios::binary);
                                      //read from it
   is.read( reinterpret_cast<char*>(buff), MAX*sizeof(int) );

   for(j=0; j<MAX; j++)               //check data
      if( buff[j] != j )
         { cerr << "Data is incorrect\n"; return 1; }
   cout << "Data is correct\n";
   return 0;
   }
```

You must use the ios::binary argument in the second parameter to write() and read() when working with binary data. This is because the default, text mode, takes some liberties with the data. For example, in text mode the '\n' character is expanded into two bytes—a carriage-return and a linefeed—before being stored to disk. This makes a formatted text file more readable by DOS-based utilities such as TYPE, but it causes confusion when it is applied to binary data, since every byte that happens to have the ASCII value 10 is translated into 2 bytes. The ios::binary argument is an example of a *mode bit*. We'll say more about this when we discuss the open() function later in this chapter.

The reinterpret_cast Operator

In the BINIO program (and many others to follow) we use the reinterpret_cast operator to make it possible for a buffer of type int to look to the read() and write() functions like a buffer of type char.

```
is.read( reinterpret_cast<char*>(buff), MAX*sizeof(int) );
```

The reinterpret_cast operator is how you tell the compiler, "I know you won't like this, but I want to do it anyway." It changes the type of a section of memory without caring whether it makes sense, so it's up to you to use it judiciously.

You can also use reinterpret_cast to change pointer values into integers and vice versa. This is a dangerous practice, but one which is sometimes necessary.

Closing Files

So far in our example programs there has been no need to close streams explicitly because they are closed automatically when they go out of scope; this invokes their destructors and closes the associated file. However, in BINIO, since both the output stream os and the input stream is are associated with the same file, EDATA.DAT, the first stream must be closed before the second is opened. We use the close() member function for this.

You may want to use an explicit close() every time you close a file, without relying on the stream's destructor. This is potentially more reliable, and certainly makes the listing more readable.

Object I/O

Since C++ is an object-oriented language, it's reasonable to wonder how objects can be written to and read from disk. The next examples show the process. The person class, used in several previous examples (for example, the VIRTPERS program in Chapter 11, "Virtual Functions"), supplies the objects.

Writing an Object to Disk

When writing an object, we generally want to use binary mode. This writes the same bit configuration to disk that was stored in memory, and ensures that numerical data contained in objects is handled properly. Here's the listing for OPERS, which asks the user for information about an object of class person, and then writes this object to the disk file PERSON.DAT:

```
// opers.cpp
// saves person object to disk
#include <fstream>                    //for file streams
#include <iostream>
using namespace std;
/////////////////////////////////////////////////////////////////////
class person                         //class of persons
   {
   protected:
      char name[80];                 //person's name
      short age;                     //person's age
   public:
      void getData()                 //get person's data
         {
         cout << "Enter name: "; cin >> name;
         cout << "Enter age: "; cin >> age;
         }
   };
/////////////////////////////////////////////////////////////////////
int main()
   {
   person pers;                      //create a person
   pers.getData();                   //get data for person
                                     //create ofstream object
   ofstream outfile("PERSON.DAT", ios::binary);
                                     //write to it
   outfile.write(reinterpret_cast<char*>(&pers), sizeof(pers));
   return 0;
   }
```

The getData() member function of person is called to prompt the user for information, which it places in the pers object. Here's some sample interaction:

```
Enter name: Coleridge
Enter age: 62
```

The contents of the pers object are then written to disk, using the write() function. We use the sizeof operator to find the length of the pers object.

Reading an Object from Disk

Reading an object back from the PERSON.DAT file requires the read() member function. Here's the listing for IPERS:

```cpp
// ipers.cpp
// reads person object from disk
#include <fstream>              //for file streams
#include <iostream>
using namespace std;
/////////////////////////////////////////////////////////////////
class person                   //class of persons
   {
   protected:
      char name[80];           //person's name
      short age;               //person's age
   public:
      void showData()          //display person's data
         {
         cout << "Name: " << name << endl;
         cout << "Age: " << age << endl;
         }
   };
/////////////////////////////////////////////////////////////////
int main()
   {
   person pers;                    //create person variable
   ifstream infile("PERSON.DAT", ios::binary); //create stream
                                                //read stream
   infile.read( reinterpret_cast<char*>(&pers), sizeof(pers) );
   pers.showData();                             //display person
   return 0;
   }
```

The output from IPERS reflects whatever data the OPERS program placed in the PERSON.DAT file:

```
Name: Coleridge
Age: 62
```

Compatible Data Structures

To work correctly, programs that read and write objects to files, as do OPERS and IPERS, must be talking about the same class of objects. Objects of class person in these programs are exactly 82 bytes long: The first 80 are occupied by a string representing the person's name, and the last 2 contain an integer of type short, representing the person's age. If two programs thought the name field was a different length, for example, neither could accurately read a file generated by the other.

Notice, however, that while the person classes in OPERS and IPERS have the same data, they may have different member functions. The first includes the single function getData(), while the second has only snowData(). It doesn't matter what member functions you use, since they are not written to disk along with the object's data. The data must have the same format, but inconsistencies in the member functions have no effect. However, this is true only in simple classes that don't use virtual functions.

If you read and write objects of derived classes to a file, you must be more careful. Objects of derived classes include a mysterious number placed just before the object's data in memory. This number helps identify the object's class when virtual functions are used. When you write an object to disk, this number is written along with the object's other data. If you change a class's member functions, this number changes as well. If you write an object of one class to a file, and then read it back into an object of a class that has identical data but a different member function, you'll encounter big trouble if you try to use virtual functions on the object. The moral: Make sure a class used to read an object is *identical* to the class used to write it.

You should also not attempt disk I/O with objects that have pointer data members. As you might expect, the pointer values won't be correct when the object is read back into a different place in memory.

I/O with Multiple Objects

The OPERS and IPERS programs wrote and read only one object at a time. Our next example opens a file and writes as many objects as the user wants. Then it reads and displays the entire contents of the file. Here's the listing for DISKFUN:

```
// diskfun.cpp
// reads and writes several objects to disk
#include <fstream>                  //for file streams
#include <iostream>
using namespace std;
/////////////////////////////////////////////////////////////////
class person                        //class of persons
   {
   protected:
      char name[80];                //person's name
      int age;                      //person's age
   public:
      void getData()                //get person's data
         {
         cout << "\n   Enter name: "; cin >> name;
         cout << "   Enter age: "; cin >> age;
```

```
            }
      void showData()                //display person's data
         {
         cout << "\n   Name: " << name;
         cout << "\n   Age: " << age;
         }
   };
//////////////////////////////////////////////////////////////
int main()
   {
   char ch;
   person pers;                    //create person object
   fstream file;                   //create input/output file
                                   //open for append
   file.open("GROUP.DAT", ios::app | ios::out |
                             ios::in | ios::binary );
   do                              //data from user to file
      {
      cout << "\nEnter person's data:";
      pers.getData();             //get one person's data
                                  //write to file
      file.write( reinterpret_cast<char*>(&pers), sizeof(pers) );
      cout << "Enter another person (y/n)? ";
      cin >> ch;
      }
   while(ch=='y');                //quit on 'n'
   file.seekg(0);                 //reset to start of file
                                  //read first person
   file.read( reinterpret_cast<char*>(&pers), sizeof(pers) );
   while( !file.eof() )           //quit on EOF
      {
      cout << "\nPerson:";        //display person
      pers.showData();            //read another person
      file.read( reinterpret_cast<char*>(&pers), sizeof(pers) );
      }
   cout << endl;
   return 0;
   }
```

Here's some sample interaction with DISKFUN. The output shown assumes that the program has been run before and that two person objects have already been written to the file.

```
Enter person's data:
   Enter name: McKinley
   Enter age: 22
```

```
Enter another person (y/n)? n

Person:
   Name: Whitney
   Age: 20
Person:
   Name: Rainier
   Age: 21
Person:
   Name: McKinley
   Age: 22
```

Here one additional object is added to the file, and the entire contents, consisting of three objects, are then displayed.

The fstream Class

So far in this chapter the file objects we have created have been for either input or output. In DISKFUN we want to create a file that can be used for both input and output. This requires an object of the fstream class, which is derived from iostream, which is derived from both istream and ostream so it can handle both input and output.

The open() Function

In previous examples we created a file object and initialized it in the same statement:

```
ofstream outfile("TEST.TXT");
```

In DISKFUN we use a different approach: We create the file in one statement and open it in another, using the open() function, which is a member of the fstream class. This is a useful approach in situations where the open may fail. You can create a stream object once, and then try repeatedly to open it, without the overhead of creating a new stream object each time.

The Mode Bits

We've seen the mode bit ios::binary before. In the open() function we include several new mode bits. The mode bits, defined in ios, specify various aspects of how a stream object will be opened. Table 12.10 shows the possibilities.

TABLE 12.10   Mode Bits for the open() Function

Mode Bit	Result
in	Open for reading (default for ifstream)
out	Open for writing (default for ofstream)
ate	Start reading or writing at end of file (AT End)

TABLE 12.10 Continued

Mode Bit	Result
app	Start writing at end of file (APPend)
trunc	Truncate file to zero length if it exists (TRUNCate)
nocreate	Error when opening if file does not already exist
noreplace	Error when opening for output if file already exists, unless ate or app is set
binary	Open file in binary (not text) mode

In DISKFUN we use ios::app because we want to preserve whatever was in the file before. That is, we can write to the file, terminate the program, and start up the program again, and whatever we write to the file will be added following the existing contents. We use ios:in and ios:out because we want to perform both input and output on the file, and we use ios:binary because we're writing binary objects. The vertical bars between the flags cause the bits representing these flags to be logically combined into a single integer, so that several flags can apply simultaneously.

We write one person object at a time to the file, using the write() function. When we've finished writing, we want to read the entire file. Before doing this we must reset the file's current position. We do this with the seekg() function, which we'll examine in the next section. It ensures we'll start reading at the beginning of the file. Then, in a while loop, we repeatedly read a person object from the file and display it on the screen.

This continues until we've read all the person objects—a state that we discover using the eof() function, which returns the state of the ios::eofbit.

File Pointers

Each file object has associated with it two integer values called the *get pointer* and the *put pointer*. These are also called the *current get position* and the *current put position*, or—if it's clear which one is meant—simply the *current position*. These values specify the byte number in the file where writing or reading will take place. (The term *pointer* in this context should not be confused with normal C++ pointers used as address variables.)

Often you want to start reading an existing file at the beginning and continue until the end. When writing, you may want to start at the beginning, deleting any existing contents, or at the end, in which case you can open the file with the ios::app mode specifier. These are the default actions, so no manipulation of the file pointers is necessary. However, there are times when you must take control of the file pointers yourself so that you can read from and write to an arbitrary location in the file. The seekg() and tellg() functions allow you to set and examine the get pointer, and the seekp() and tellp() functions perform these same actions on the put pointer.

Specifying the Position

We saw an example of positioning the get pointer in the DISKFUN program, where the seekg() function set it to the beginning of the file so that reading would start there. This form of seekg() takes one argument, which represents the absolute position in the file. The start of the file is byte 0, so that's what we used in DISKFUN. Figure 12.4 shows how this looks.

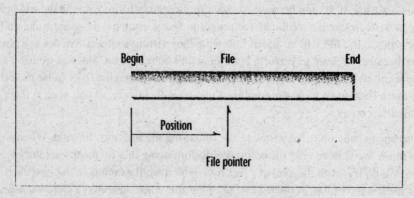

FIGURE 12.4

The seekg() *function with one argument.*

Specifying the Offset

The seekg() function can be used in two ways. We've seen the first, where the single argument represents the position from the start of the file. You can also use it with two arguments, where the first argument represents an offset from a particular location in the file, and the second specifies the location from which the offset is measured. There are three possibilities for the second argument: beg is the beginning of the file, cur is the current pointer position, and end is the end of the file. The statement

```
seekp(-10, ios::end);
```

for example, will set the put pointer to 10 bytes before the end of the file. Figure 12.5 shows how this looks.

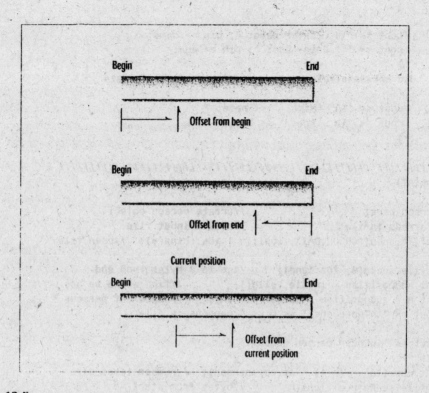

FIGURE 12.5
The seekg() function with two arguments.

Here's an example that uses the two-argument version of seekg() to find a particular person object in the GROUP.DAT file, and to display the data for that particular person. Here's the listing for SEEKG:

```
// seekg.cpp
// seeks particular person in file
#include <fstream>                  //for file streams
#include <iostream>
using namespace std;
//////////////////////////////////////////////////////////////
class person                       //class of persons
   {
   protected:
      char name[80];                //person's name
      int age;                      //person's age
   public:
      void getData()                //get person's data
         {
```

```
            cout << "\n    Enter name: "; cin >> name;
            cout << "    Enter age: "; cin >> age;
            }
        void showData(void)              //display person's data
            {
            cout << "\n    Name: " << name;
            cout << "\n    Age: " << age;
            }
    };
/////////////////////////////////////////////////////////////////
int main()
    {
    person pers;                         //create person object
    ifstream infile;                     //create input file
    infile.open("GROUP.DAT", ios::in | ios::binary);  //open file

    infile.seekg(0, ios::end);           //go to 0 bytes from end
    int endposition = infile.tellg();        //find where we are
    int n = endposition / sizeof(person);    //number of persons
    cout << "\nThere are " << n << " persons in file";

    cout << "\nEnter person number: ";
    cin >> n;
    int position = (n-1) * sizeof(person);  //number times size
    infile.seekg(position);              //bytes from start
                                         //read one person
    infile.read( reinterpret_cast<char*>(&pers), sizeof(pers) );
    pers.showData();                     //display the person
    cout << endl;
    return 0;
    }
```

Here's the output from the program, assuming that the GROUP.DAT file is the same as that just accessed in the DISKFUN example:

```
There are 3 persons in file
Enter person number: 2

    Name: Rainier
    Age: 21
```

For the user, we number the items starting at 1, although the program starts numbering at 0; so person 2 is the second person of the three in the file.

The `tellg()` Function

The first thing the program does is figure out how many persons are in the file. It does this by positioning the get pointer at the end of the file with the statement

```
infile.seekg(0, ios::end);
```

The `tellg()` function returns the current position of the get pointer. The program uses this function to return the pointer position at the end of the file; this is the length of the file in bytes. Next, the program calculates how many `person` objects there are in the file by dividing by the size of a `person`; it then displays the result.

In the output shown, the user specifies the second object in the file, and the program calculates how many bytes into the file this is, using `seekg()`. It then uses `read()` to read one `person`'s worth of data starting from that point. Finally, it displays the data with `showData()`.

Error Handling in File I/O

In the file-related examples so far we have not concerned ourselves with error situations. In particular, we have assumed that the files we opened for reading already existed, and that those opened for writing could be created or appended to. We've also assumed that there were no failures during reading or writing. In a real program it is important to verify such assumptions and take appropriate action if they turn out to be incorrect. A file that you think exists may not, or a filename that you assume you can use for a new file may already apply to an existing file. Or there may be no more room on the disk, or no disk in the drive, and so on.

Reacting to Errors

Our next program shows how such errors are most conveniently handled. All disk operations are checked after they are performed. If an error has occurred, a message is printed and the program terminates. We've used the technique, discussed earlier, of checking the return value from the object itself to determine its error status. The program opens an output stream object, writes an entire array of integers to it with a single call to `write()`, and closes the object. Then it opens an input stream object and reads the array of integers with a call to `read()`.

```cpp
// rewerr.cpp
// handles errors during input and output
#include <fstream>      //for file streams
#include <iostream>
using namespace std;
#include <process.h>    //for exit()

const int MAX = 1000;
int buff[MAX];
```

```
int main()
   {
   for(int j=0; j<MAX; j++)              //fill buffer with data
      buff[j] = j;
   ofstream os;                          //create output stream
                                         //open it
   os.open("a:edata.dat", ios::trunc | ios::binary);
   if(!os)
      { cerr << "Could not open output file\n"; exit(1); }

   cout << "Writing...\n";               //write buffer to it
   os.write( reinterpret_cast<char*>(buff), MAX*sizeof(int) );
   if(!os)
      { cerr << "Could not write to file\n"; exit(1); }
   os.close();                           //must close it

   for(j=0; j<MAX; j++)                  //clear buffer
      buff[j] = 0;

   ifstream is;                          //create input stream
   is.open("a:edata.dat", ios::binary);
   if(!is)
      { cerr << "Could not open input file\n"; exit(1); }

   cout << "Reading...\n";               //read file
   is.read( reinterpret_cast<char*>(buff), MAX*sizeof(int) );
   if(!is)
      { cerr << "Could not read from file\n"; exit(1); }

   for(j=0; j<MAX; j++)                  //check data
      if( buff[j] != j )
         { cerr << "\nData is incorrect\n"; exit(1); }
   cout << "Data is correct\n";
   return 0;
   }
```

Analyzing Errors

In the REWERR example we determined whether an error occurred in an I/O operation by examining the return value of the entire stream object.

```
if(!is)
   // error occurred
```

Here is returns a pointer value if everything went well, but 0 if it didn't. This is the shotgun approach to errors: No matter what the error is, it's detected in the same way and the same action is taken. However, it's also possible, using the ios error-status flags, to find out more specific information about a file I/O error. We've already seen some of these status flags at work in screen and keyboard I/O. Our next example, FERRORS, shows how they can be used in file I/O.

```
// ferrors.cpp
// checks for errors opening file
#include <fstream>              // for file functions
#include <iostream>
using namespace std;

int main()
   {
   ifstream file;
   file.open("a:test.dat");

   if( !file )
       cout << "\nCan't open GROUP.DAT";
   else
       cout << "\nFile opened successfully.";
   cout << "\nfile = " << file;
   cout << "\nError state = " << file.rdstate();
   cout << "\ngood() = " << file.good();
   cout << "\neof() = " << file.eof();
   cout << "\nfail() = " << file.fail();
   cout << "\nbad() = " << file.bad() << endl;
   file.close();
   return 0;
   }
```

This program first checks the value of the object file. If its value is zero, the file probably could not be opened because it didn't exist. Here's the output from FERRORS when that's the case:

```
Can't open GROUP.DAT
file = 0x1c730000
Error state = 4
good() = 0
eof() = 0
fail() = 4
bad() = 4
```

The error state returned by rdstate() is 4. This is the bit that indicates that the file doesn't exist; it's set to 1. The other bits are all set to 0. The good() function returns 1 (true) only when no bits are set, so it returns 0 (false). We're not at EOF, so eof() returns 0. The fail() and bad() functions return nonzero, since an error occurred.

In a serious program, some or all of these functions should be used after every I/O operation to ensure that things went as expected.

File I/O with Member Functions

So far we've let the main() function handle the details of file I/O. When you use more sophisticated classes it's natural to include file I/O operations as member functions of the class. In this section we'll show two programs that do this. The first uses ordinary member functions in which each object is responsible for reading and writing itself to a file. The second shows how static member functions can read and write all the objects of a class at once.

Objects That Read and Write Themselves

Sometimes it makes sense to let each member of a class read and write itself to a file. This is a simple approach, and works well if there aren't many objects to be read or written at once. In this example we add member functions—diskOut() and diskIn()—to the person class. These functions allow a person object to write itself to disk and read itself back in.

We've made some simplifying assumptions. First, all objects of the class will be stored in the same file, called PERSFILE.DAT. Second, new objects are always appended to the end of the file. An argument to the diskIn() function allows us to read the data for any person in the file. To prevent an attempt to read data beyond the end of the file, we include a static member function, diskCount(), that returns the number of persons stored in the file. When inputting data to this program, use only a last name; spaces aren't allowed. Here's the listing for REWOBJ:

```
//   ewobj.cpp
// person objects do disk I/O
#include <fstream>                   //for file streams
#include <iostream>
using namespace std;
//////////////////////////////////////////////////////////////////
class person                         //class of persons
   {
   protected:
      char name[40];                 //person's name
      int age;                       //person's age
   public:
      void getData(void)             //get person's data
         {
         cout << "\n   Enter last name: "; cin >> name;
         cout << "   Enter age: "; cin >> age;
         }
      void showData(void)            //display person's data
         {
         cout << "\n   Name: " << name;
         cout << "\n   Age: " << age;
         }
      void diskIn(int);              //read from file
```

```
        void diskOut();              //write to file
        static int diskCount();      //return number of
                                     //   persons in file
    };
//··············································································
void person::diskIn(int pn)          //read person number pn
    {                                //from file
    ifstream infile;                              //make stream
    infile.open("PERSFILE.DAT", ios::binary);  //open it
    infile.seekg( pn*sizeof(person) );            //move file ptr
    infile.read( (char*)this, sizeof(*this) ); //read one person
    }
//··············································································
void person::diskOut()               //write person to end of file
    {
    ofstream outfile;                  //make stream
                                       //open it
    outfile.open("PERSFILE.DAT", ios::app | ios::binary);
    outfile.write( (char*)this, sizeof(*this) ); //write to it
    }
//··············································································
int person::diskCount()              //return number of persons
    {                                //in file
    ifstream infile;
    infile.open("PERSFILE.DAT", ios::binary);
    infile.seekg(0, ios::end);       //go to 0 bytes from end
                                     //calculate number of persons
    return (int)infile.tellg() / sizeof(person);
    }
//////////////////////////////////////////////////////////////////////////
int main()
    {
    person p;                        //make an empty person
    char ch;

    do {                             //save persons to disk
        cout << "Enter data for person:";
        p.getData();                 //get data
        p.diskOut();                 //write to disk
        cout << "Do another (y/n)? ";
        cin >> ch;
        } while(ch=='y');            //until user enters 'n'

    int n = person::diskCount();     //how many persons in file?
    cout << "There are " << n << " persons in file\n";
    for(int j=0; j<n; j++)           //for each one,
        {
```

```
        cout << "\nPerson " << j;
        p.diskIn(j);               //read person from disk
        p.showData();              //display person
        }
    cout << endl;
    return 0;
    }
```

There shouldn't be too many surprises here; you've seen most of the elements of this program before. It operates in the same way as the DISKFUN program. Notice, however, that all the details of disk operation are invisible to main(), having been hidden away in the person class.

We don't know in advance where the data is that we're going to read and write, since each object is in a different place in memory. However, the this pointer always tells us where we are when we're in a member function. In the read() and write() stream functions, the memory address of the object to be read or written is *this and its size is sizeof(*this).

Here's some output, assuming there were already two persons in the file when the program was started:

```
Enter data for person:
    Enter name: Acheson
    Enter age: 63
Enter another (y/n)? y

Enter data for person:
    Enter name: Dulles
    Enter age: 72
Enter another (y/n)? n

Person #1
    Name: Stimson
    Age: 45
Person #2
    Name: Hull
    Age: 58
Person #3
    Name: Acheson
    Age: 63
Person #4
    Name: Dulles
    Age: 72
```

If you want the user to be able to specify the filename used by the class, instead of hardwiring it into the member functions as we do here, you could create a static member variable (say char fileName[]) and a static function to set it. Or you might want to give each object the name of the file it was associated with, using a nonstatic function.

Classes That Read and Write Themselves

Let's assume you have many objects in memory, and you want to write them all to a file. It's not efficient to have a member function for each object open the file, write one object to it, and then close it, as in the REWOBJ example. It's much faster—and the more objects there are the truer this is—to open the file once, write all the objects to it, and then close it.

Static Functions

One way to write many objects at once is to use a static member function, which applies to the class as a whole rather than to each object. This function can write all the objects at once. How will such a function know where all the objects are? It can access an array of pointers to the objects, which can be stored as static data. As each object is created, a pointer to it is stored in this array. A static data member also keeps track of how many objects have been created. The static write() function can open the file; then in a loop go through the array, writing each object in turn; and finally close the file.

Size of Derived Objects

To make things really interesting, let's make a further assumption: that the objects stored in memory are different sizes. Why would this be true? This situation typically arises when several classes are derived from a base class. For example, consider the EMPLOY program in Chapter 9, "Inheritance." Here we have an employee class that acts as a base class for the manager, scientist, and laborer classes. Objects of these three derived classes are different sizes, since they contain different amounts of data. Specifically, in addition to the name and employee number, which apply to all employees, the manager has a title and golf club dues and the scientist has a number of publications.

We would like to write the data from a list containing all three types of derived objects (manager, scientist, and laborer) using a simple loop and the write() member function of ofstream. But to use this function we need to know how large the object is, since that's its second argument.

Suppose we have an array of pointers (call it arrap[]) to objects of type employee. These pointers can point to objects of the three derived classes. (See the VIRTPERS program in Chapter 11 for an example of an array of pointers to objects of derived classes.) We know that if we're using virtual functions we can make statements like

```
arrap[j]->putdata();
```

The version of the putdata() function that matches the object pointed to by the pointer will be used, rather than the function in the base class. But can we also use the sizeof() function to return the size of a pointer argument? That is, can we say

```
ouf.write( (char*)arrap[j], sizeof(*arrap[j]) );  // no good
```

No, because `sizeof()` isn't a virtual function. It doesn't know that it needs to consider the type of object pointed to, rather than the type of the pointer. It will always return the size of the base class object.

Using the `typeid()` Function

How can we find the size of an object, if all we have is a pointer to it? One answer to this is the `typeid()` function, introduced in Chapter 11. We can use this function to find the class of an object, and use this class name in `sizeof()`. To use `typeid()` you may need to enable a compiler option called *Run-Time Type Information (RTTI)*. (This is the case in the current Microsoft compiler, as described in Appendix C, "Microsoft Visual C++.")

Our next example shows how this works. Once we know the size of the object, we can use it in the `write()` function to write the object to disk.

We've added a simple user interface to the EMPLOY program, and made the member-specific functions virtual so we can use an array of pointers to objects. We've also incorporated some of the error-detection techniques discussed in the last section.

This is a rather ambitious program, but it demonstrates many of the techniques that could be used in a full-scale database application. It also shows the real power of OOP. How else could you use a single statement to write objects of different sizes to a file? Here's the listing for EMPL_IO:

```cpp
// empl_io.cpp
// performs file I/O on employee objects
// handles different sized objects
#include <fstream>              //for file-stream functions
#include <iostream>
#include <typeinfo>             //for typeid()
using namespace std;
#include <process.h>           //for exit()

const int LEN = 32;            //maximum length of last names
const int MAXEM = 100;         //maximum number of employees

enum employee_type {tmanager, tscientist, tlaborer};
//////////////////////////////////////////////////////////////
class employee               //employee class
    {
    private:
        char name[LEN];            //employee name
        unsigned long number;      //employee number
        static int n;              //current number of employees
        static employee* arrap[];  //array of ptrs to emps
    public:
```

```
        virtual void getdata()
           {
           cin.ignore(10, '\n');
           cout << "   Enter last name: "; cin >> name;
           cout << "   Enter number: ";       cin >> number;
           }
        virtual void putdata()
           {
           cout << "\n   Name: " << name;
           cout << "\n   Number: " << number;
           }
        virtual employee_type get_type();  //get type
        static void add();        //add an employee
        static void display();   //display all employees
        static void read();       //read from disk file
        static void write();      //write to disk file
     };
//-------------------------------------------------------------
//static variables
int employee::n;                    //current number of employees
employee* employee::arrap[MAXEM];   //array of ptrs to emps
//////////////////////////////////////////////////////////////
//manager class
class manager : public employee
   {
   private:
      char title[LEN];        //"vice-president" etc.
      double dues;            //golf club dues
   public:
      void getdata()
         {
         employee::getdata();
         cout << "   Enter title: ";          cin >> title;
         cout << "   Enter golf club dues: "; cin >> dues;
         }
      void putdata()
         {
         employee::putdata();
         cout << "\n   Title: " << title;
         cout << "\n   Golf club dues: " << dues;
         }
   };
//////////////////////////////////////////////////////////////
//scientist class
class scientist : public employee
   {
```

```
   private:
      int pubs;                    //number of publications
   public:
      void getdata()
         {
         employee::getdata();
         cout << "   Enter number of pubs: "; cin >> pubs;
         }
      void putdata()
         {
         employee::putdata();
         cout << "\n   Number of publications: " << pubs;
         }
   };
/////////////////////////////////////////////////////////////////
//laborer class
class laborer : public employee
   {
   };
/////////////////////////////////////////////////////////////////
//add employee to list in memory
void employee::add()
   {
   char ch;
   cout << "'m' to add a manager"
           "\n's' to add a scientist"
           "\n'l' to add a laborer"
           "\nEnter selection: ";
   cin >> ch;
   switch(ch)
      {                            //create specified employee type
      case 'm': arrap[n] = new manager;   break;
      case 's': arrap[n] = new scientist; break;
      case 'l': arrap[n] = new laborer;   break;
      default: cout << "\nUnknown employee type\n"; return;
      }
   arrap[n++]->getdata();      //get employee data from user
   }
//..............................................................
//display all employees
void employee::display()
   {
   for(int j=0; j<n; j++)
      {
      cout  << (j+1);            //display number
      switch( arrap[j]->get_type() )   //display type
```

```
      {
      case tmanager:     cout << ". Type: Manager";    break;
      case tscientist:   cout << ". Type: Scientist"; break;
      case tlaborer:     cout << ". Type: Laborer";    break;
      default: cout << ". Unknown type";
      }
   arrap[j]->putdata();      //display employee data
   cout << endl;
   }
}
//·······················································
//return the type of this object
employee_type employee::get_type()
   {
   if( typeid(*this) == typeid(manager) )
      return tmanager;
   else if( typeid(*this)==typeid(scientist) )
      return tscientist;
   else if( typeid(*this)==typeid(laborer) )
      return tlaborer;
   else
      { cerr << "\nBad employee type"; exit(1); }
   return tmanager;
   }
//·······················································
//write all current memory objects to file
void employee::write()
   {
   int size;
   cout << "Writing " << n << " employees.\n";
   ofstream ouf;             //open ofstream in binary
   employee_type etype;      //type of each employee object

   ouf.open("EMPLOY.DAT", ios::trunc | ios::binary);
   if(!ouf)
      { cout << "\nCan't open file\n"; return; }
   for(int j=0; j<n; j++)    //for every employee object
      {                      //get its type
      etype = arrap[j]->get_type();
                             //write type to file
      ouf.write( (char*)&etype, sizeof(etype) );
      switch(etype)          //find its size
         {
         case tmanager:   size=sizeof(manager); break;
         case tscientist: size=sizeof(scientist); break;
         case tlaborer:   size=sizeof(laborer); break;
```

```
            }                       //write employee object to file
      ouf.write( (char*)(arrap[j]), size );
      if(!ouf)
         { cout << "\nCan't write to file\n"; return; }
      }
   }
//- - - - - - - - - - - - - - - - - - - - - - - - - - - - - - - - - - - - - - - - - - - - - - - - - - - - - - - - - - - - - - - - -
//read data for all employees from file into memory
void employee::read()
   {
   int size;                    //size of employee object
   employee_type etype;         //type of employee
   ifstream inf;                //open ifstream in binary
   inf.open("EMPLOY.DAT", ios::binary);
   if(!inf)
      { cout << "\nCan't open file\n"; return; }
   n = 0;                       //no employees in memory yet
   while(true)
      {                         //read type of next employee
      inf.read( (char*)&etype, sizeof(etype) );
      if( inf.eof() )           //quit loop on eof
         break;
      if(!inf)                  //error reading type
         { cout << "\nCan't read type from file\n"; return; }
      switch(etype)
         {                      //make new employee
         case tmanager:         //of correct type
            arrap[n] = new manager;
            size=sizeof(manager);
            break;
         case tscientist:
            arrap[n] = new scientist;
            size=sizeof(scientist);
            break;
         case tlaborer:
            arrap[n] = new laborer;
            size=sizeof(laborer);
            break;
         default: cout << "\nUnknown type in file\n"; return;
         }                      //read data from file into it
      inf.read( (char*)arrap[n], size );
      if(!inf)                  //error but not eof
         { cout << "\nCan't read data from file\n"; return; }
      n++;                      //count employee
      } //end while
   cout << "Reading " << n << " employees\n";
```

```
   }
//////////////////////////////////////////////////////////////
int main()
   {
   char ch;
   while(true)
      {
      cout << "'a' -- add data for an employee"
              "\n'd' -- display data for all employees"
              "\n'w' -- write all employee data to file"
              "\n'r' -- read all employee data from file"
              "\n'x' -- exit"
              "\nEnter selection: ";
      cin >> ch;
      switch(ch)
         {
         case 'a':             //add an employee to list
            employee::add(); break;
         case 'd':             //display all employees
            employee::display(); break;
         case 'w':             //write employees to file
            employee::write(); break;
         case 'r':             //read all employees from file
            employee::read(); break;
         case 'x': exit(0);    //exit program
         default: cout << "\nUnknown command";
         } //end switch
      } //end while
   return 0;
   } //end main()
```

Code Number for Object Type

We know how to find the class of an object that's in memory, but how do we know the class of
the object whose data we're about to read from the disk? There's no magic function to help us
with this one. When we write an object's data to disk, we need to write a code number (the
enum variable employee_type) directly to the disk just before the object's data. Then, when we
are about to read an object back from the file to memory, we read this value and create a new
object of the type indicated. Finally, we copy the data from the file into this new object.

No Homemade Objects, Please

Incidentally, you might be tempted to read an object's data into just anyplace, say into an array
of type char, and then set a pointer-to-object to point to this area, perhaps with a cast to make
it kosher.

```
char someArray[MAX];
aClass* aPtr_to_Obj;
aPtr_to_Obj = reinterpret_cast<aClass*>(someArray);   // don't do this
```

However, this does not create an object, and attempts to use the pointer as if it pointed to an object will lead to trouble. There are only two legitimate ways to create an object. You can define it explicitly at compile time:

```
aClass anObj;
```

Or you can create it with new at runtime, and assign its location to a pointer:

```
aPtr_to_Obj = new aClass;
```

When you create an object properly, its constructor is invoked. This is necessary even if you have not defined a constructor and are using the default constructor. An object is more than an area of memory with data in it; it is also a set of member functions, some of which you don't even see.

Interaction with EMPL_IO

Here's some sample interaction with the program, in which we create a manager, a scientist, and a laborer in memory, write them to disk, read them back in, and display them. (For simplicity, multiword names and titles are not allowed; say VicePresident, not Vice President.)

```
'a' -- add data for an employee
'd' -- display data for all employees
'w' -- write all employee data to file
'r' -- read all employee data from file
'x' -- exit
Type selection: a
'm' to add a manager
's' to add a scientist
'l' to add a laborer
Type selection: m
   Enter last name: Johnson
   Enter number: 1111
   Enter title: President
   Enter golf club dues: 20000

'a' -- add data for an employee
'd' -- display data for all employees
'w' -- write all employee data to file
'r' -- read all employee data from file
'x' -- exit
Type selection: a
'm' to add a manager
's' to add a scientist
```

```
   'l' to add a laborer
Type selection: s
   Enter last name: Faraday
   Enter number: 2222
   Enter number of pubs: 99

'a' -- add data for an employee
'd' -- display data for all employees
'w' -- write all employee data to file
'r' -- read all employee data from file
'x' -- exit
Type selection: a
'm' to add a manager
's' to add a scientist
'l' to add a laborer
Type selection: l
   Enter last name: Smith
   Enter number: 3333

'a' -- add data for an employee
'd' -- display data for all employees
'w' -- write all employee data to file
'r' -- read all employee data from file
'x' -- exit
Type selection: w
Writing 3 employees

'a' -- add data for an employee
'd' -- display data for all employees
'w' -- write all employee data to file
'r' -- read all employee data from file
'x' -- exit
Type selection: r
Reading 3 employees

'a' -- add data for an employee
'd' -- display data for all employees
'w' -- write all employee data to file
'r' -- read all employee data from file
'x' -- exit
Type selection: d
1. Type: Manager
   Name: Johnson
   Title: President
   Golf club dues: 20000
```

```
2. Type: Scientist
   Name: Faraday
   Number: 2222
   Number of publications: 99
3. Type: Laborer
   Name: Smith
   Number: 3333
```

Of course you can also exit the program after writing the data to disk. When you start it up again, you can read the file back in and all the data will reappear.

It would be easy to add functions to this program to delete an employee, retrieve data for a single employee from the file, search the file for employees with particular characteristics, and so forth.

Overloading the Extraction and Insertion Operators

Let's move on to another stream-related topic: overloading the extraction and insertion operators. This is a powerful feature of C++. It lets you treat I/O for user-defined data types in the same way as basic types like int and double. For example, if you have an object of class crawdad called cd1, you can display it with the statement

```
cout << "\ncd1=" << cd1;
```

just as if it were a basic data type.

We can overload the extraction and insertion operators so they work with the display and keyboard (cout and cin) alone. With a little more care, we can also overload them so they work with disk files. We'll look at examples of both of these situations.

Overloading for cout and cin

Here's an example, ENGLIO, that overloads the insertion and extraction operators for the Distance class so they work with cout and cin.

```
// englio.cpp
// overloaded << and >> operators
#include <iostream>
using namespace std;
/////////////////////////////////////////////////////////////////
class Distance                          //English Distance class
   {
   private:
      int feet;
      float inches;
   public:
```

```
        Distance() : feet(0), inches(0.0)  //constructor (no args)
           { }
                                       //constructor (two args)
        Distance(int ft, float in) : feet(ft), inches(in)
           { }
        friend istream& operator >> (istream& s, Distance& d);
        friend ostream& operator << (ostream& s, Distance& d);
     };
//------------------------------------------------------------
istream& operator >> (istream& s, Distance& d)   //get Distance
   {                                              //from user
   cout << "\nEnter feet: ";  s >> d.feet;        //using
   cout << "Enter inches: ";  s >> d.inches;      //overloaded
   return s;                                      //>> operator
   }
//------------------------------------------------------------
ostream& operator << (ostream& s, Distance& d)   //display
   {                                              //Distance
   s << d.feet << "\'-" << d.inches << '\"';      //using
   return s;                                      //overloaded
   }                                              //<< operator
////////////////////////////////////////////////////////////////
int main()
   {
   Distance dist1, dist2;            //define Distances
   Distance dist3(11, 6.25);         //define, initialize dist3

   cout << "\nEnter two Distance values:";
   cin >> dist1 >> dist2;            //get values from user
                                     //display distances
   cout << "\ndist1 = " << dist1 << "\ndist2 = " << dist2;
   cout << "\ndist3 = " << dist3 << endl;
   return 0;
   }
```

This program asks for two Distance values from the user, and then prints out these values and another value that was initialized in the program. Here's a sample interaction:

```
Enter feet: 10
Enter inches: 3.5

Enter feet: 12
Enter inches: 6

dist1 = 10'-3.5"
dist2 = 12'-6"
dist3 = 11'-6.25"
```

Notice how convenient and natural it is to treat `Distance` objects like any other data type, using statements like

```
cin >> dist1 >> dist2;
```

and

```
cout << "\ndist1=" << dist1 << "\ndist2=" << dist2;
```

The `<<` and `>>` operators are overloaded in similar ways. They return, by reference, an object of `istream` (for `>>`) or `ostream` (for `<<`). These return values permit chaining. The operators take two arguments, both passed by reference. The first argument for `>>` is an object of `istream` (such as `cin`). For `<<` it's an object of `ostream` (such as `cout`). The second argument is an object of the class to be displayed, `Distance` in this example. The `>>` operator takes input from the stream specified in the first argument and puts it in the member data of the object specified by the second argument. The `<<` operator removes the data from the object specified by the second argument and sends it into the stream specified by the first argument.

The `operator<<()` and `operator>>()` functions must be friends of the `Distance` class, since the `istream` and `ostream` objects appear on the left side of the operator. (See the discussion of `friend` functions in Chapter 11.)

You can overload the insertion and extraction operators for other classes by following these same steps.

Overloading for Files

Our next example shows how we might overload the `<<` and `>>` operators in the `Distance` class so they work with file I/O as well as with `cout` and `cin`.

```
// englio2.cpp
// overloaded << and >> operators can work with files
#include <fstream>
#include <iostream>
using namespace std;
/////////////////////////////////////////////////////////////////
class Distance                          //English Distance class
   {
   private:
      int feet;
      float inches;
   public:
      Distance() : feet(0), inches(0.0) //constructor (no args)
         { }                            //constructor (two args)
      Distance(int ft, float in) : feet(ft), inches(in)
         { }
```

```
   friend istream& operator >> (istream& s, Distance& d);
   friend ostream& operator << (ostream& s, Distance& d);
   };
//································································
istream& operator >> (istream& s, Distance& d)  //get Distance
   {                                            //from file or
   char dummy;  //for ('), (-), and (")         //keyboard
                                                //with
   s >> d.feet >> dummy >> dummy >> d.inches >> dummy;
   return s;                                    //overloaded
   }                                            //>> operator
//································································
ostream& operator << (ostream& s, Distance& d)  //send Distance
   {                                            //to file or
   s << d.feet << "\'-" << d.inches << '\"';    //screen with
   return s;                                    //overloaded
   }                                            //<< operator
////////////////////////////////////////////////////////////////
int main()
   {
   char ch;
   Distance dist1;
   ofstream ofile;                              //create and open
   ofile.open("DIST.DAT");                      //output stream

   do {
      cout << "\nEnter Distance: ";
      cin >> dist1;                             //get distance from user
      ofile << dist1;                           //write it to output str
      cout << "Do another (y/n)? ";
      cin >> ch;
      } while(ch != 'n');
   ofile.close();                               //close output stream

   ifstream ifile;                              //create and open
   ifile.open("DIST.DAT");                      //input stream

   cout << "\nContents of disk file is:\n";
   while(true)
      {
      ifile >> dist1;                           //read dist from stream
      if( ifile.eof() )                         //quit on EOF
         break;
      cout << "Distance = " << dist1 <<endl;    //display distance
      }
   return 0;
   }
```

We've made minimal changes to the overloaded operators themselves. The >> operator no longer prompts for input, since it doesn't make sense to prompt a file. We assume that the user knows exactly how to enter a feet-and-inches value, including the various punctuation marks. The << operator is unchanged. The program asks for input from the user, writing each Distance value to the file as it's obtained. When the user is finished with input, the program then reads and displays all the values from the file. Here's some sample interaction:

```
Enter Distance: 3'-4.5"
Do another (y/n)? yes

Enter Distance: 7'-11.25"
Do another (y/n)? yes

Enter Distance: 11'-6"
Do another (y/n)? no

Contents of disk file is:
Distance = 3'-4.5"
Distance = 7'-11.25"
Distance = 11'-6"
```

The distances are stored character by character to the file. In this example the contents of the file would be as follows:

```
3'-4.5"7'-11.25"11'-6
```

If the user fails to enter the distances with the correct punctuation, they won't be written to the file correctly and the file won't be readable for the << operator. In a real program it's essential to check the input for errors.

Memory as a Stream Object

You can treat a section of memory as a stream object, inserting data into it just as you would a file. This is useful when you need to format your output in a particular way (such as displaying exactly two digits to the right of the decimal point), but you also need to use a text-output function that requires a string as input. This is common when calling output functions in a GUI environment such as Windows, since these functions often require a string as an argument. (C programmers will remember using the sprintf() function for this purpose.)

A family of stream classes implements such in-memory formatting. For output to memory there is ostrstream, which is derived from (among other classes) ostream. For input from memory there is istrstream, derived from istream; and for memory objects that do both input and output there is strstream, derived from iostream.

Most commonly you will want to use ostrstream. Our next example shows how this works. You start with a data buffer in memory. Then you create an ostrstream object, using the memory buffer and its size as arguments to the stream's constructor. Now you can output formatted text to the memory buffer as if it were a stream object. Here's the listing for OSTRSTR:

```cpp
// ostrstr.cpp
// writes formatted data into memory
#include <strstream>
#include <iostream>
#include <iomanip>                    //for setiosflags()
using namespace std;
const int SIZE = 80;                  //size of memory buffer

int main()
   {
   char ch = 'x';                     //test data
   int j = 77;
   double d = 67890.12345;
   char str1[] = "Kafka";
   char str2[] = "Freud";

   char membuff[SIZE];                //buffer in memory
   ostrstream omem(membuff, SIZE);    //create stream object

   omem << "ch=" << ch << endl        //insert formatted data
        << "j=" << j << endl          //into object
        << setiosflags(ios::fixed)    //format with decimal point
        << setprecision(2)            //two digits to right of dec
        << "d=" << d << endl
        << "str1=" << str1 << endl
        << "str2=" << str2 << endl
        << ends;                      //end the buffer with '\0'
   cout << membuff;                   //display the memory buffer
   return 0;
   }
```

When you run the program, membuff will be filled with the formatted text:

ch=x\nj=77\nd=67890.12\nstr1=Kafka\nstr2=Freud\n\0

We can format floating-point numbers using the usual methods. Here we specify a fixed decimal format (rather than exponential) with ios::fixed, and two digits to the right of the decimal point. The manipulator ends inserts a '\0' character at the end of the string to provide an EOF. Displaying this buffer in the usual way with cout produces the program's output:

ch=x
j=77

```
d=67890.12
str1=Kafka
str2=Freud
```

In this example the program displays the contents of the buffer only to show what it looks like.
Ordinarily you would have a more sophisticated use for this formatted data.

Command-Line Arguments

If you've ever used MS-DOS, you are probably familiar with command-line arguments, used
when invoking a program. They are typically used to pass the name of a data file to an application. For example, you can invoke a word processor application and the document it will work
on at the same time:

```
C>wordproc afile.doc
```

Here afile.doc is a command-line argument. How can we get a C++ program to read the
command-line arguments? Here's an example, COMLINE, that reads and displays as many
command-line arguments as you care to type (they're separated by spaces):

```
// comline.cpp
// demonstrates command-line arguments
#include <iostream>
using namespace std;

int main(int argc, char* argv[] )
   {
   cout << "\nargc = " << argc << endl;  //number of arguments

   for(int j=0; j<argc; j++)                    //display arguments
      cout << "Argument " << j << " = " << argv[j] << endl;
   return 0;
   }
```

And here's a sample interaction with the program:

```
C:\C++BOOK\Chap12>comline uno dos tres

argc = 4
Argument 0 = C:\CPP\CHAP12\COMLINE.EXE
Argument 1 = uno
Argument 2 = dos
Argument 3 = tres
```

To read command-line arguments, the main() function (don't forget it's a function!) must itself
be given two arguments. The first, argc (for *argument count*), represents the total number of

command-line arguments. The first command-line argument is always the pathname of the current program. The remaining command-line arguments are those typed by the user; they are delimited by the space character. In the preceding example they are uno, dos, and tres.

The system stores the command-line arguments as strings in memory, and creates an array of pointers to these strings. In the example, the array is called argv (for *argument values*). Individual strings are accessed through the appropriate pointer, so the first string (the pathname) is argv[0], the second (uno in this example) is argv[1], and so on. COMLINE accesses the arguments in turn and prints them out in a for loop that uses argc, the number of command-line arguments, as its upper limit.

You don't need to use the particular names argc and argv as arguments to main(), but they are so common that any other names would cause consternation to everyone but the compiler.

Here's a program that uses a command-line argument for something useful. It displays the contents of a text file whose name is supplied by the user on the command line. Thus it imitates the DOS command TYPE. Here's the listing for OTYPE:

```cpp
// otype.cpp
// imitates TYPE command
#include <fstream>                    //for file functions
#include <iostream>
using namespace std;
#include <process.h>                  //for exit()

int main(int argc, char* argv[] )
   {
   if( argc != 2 )
      {
      cerr << "\nFormat: otype filename";
      exit(-1);
      }
   char ch;                           //character to read
   ifstream infile;                   //create file for input
   infile.open( argv[1] );            //open file
   if( !infile )                      //check for errors
      {
      cerr << "\nCan't open " << argv[1];
      exit(-1);
      }
   while( infile.get(ch) != 0 )       //read a character
      cout << ch;                     //display the character
   return 0;
   }
```

This program first checks to see whether the user has entered the correct number of command-line arguments. Remember that the pathname of OTYPE.EXE itself is always the first command-line argument. The second argument is the name of the file to be displayed, which the user should have entered when invoking the program:

```
C>otype ichar.cpp
```

Thus the total number of command-line arguments should equal 2. If it doesn't, the user probably doesn't understand how to use the program, and the program sends an error message via cerr to clarify matters.

If the number of arguments is correct, the program tries to open the file whose name is the second command-line argument (argv[1]). Again, if the file can't be opened, the program signals an error. Finally, in a while loop, the program reads the file character by character and writes it to the screen.

A value of 0 for the character signals an EOF. This is another way to check for EOF. You can also use the value of the file object itself, as we've done before:

```
while( infile )
   {
   infile.get(ch);
   cout << ch;
   },
```

You could also replace this entire while loop with the statement

```
cout << infile.rdbuf();
```

as we saw earlier in the ICHAR2 program.

Printer Output

It's fairly easy to use console-mode programs to send data to the printer. A number of special filenames for hardware devices are defined by the operating system. These make it possible to treat the devices as if they were files. Table 12.11 shows these predefined names.

TABLE 12.11   Hardware Device Names

Name	Device
con	Console (keyboard and screen)
aux or com1	First serial port
com2	Second serial port
prn or lpt1	First parallel printer

TABLE 12.11   Continued

Name	Device
lpt2	Second parallel printer
lpt3	Third parallel printer
nul	Dummy (nonexistent) device

In most systems the printer is connected to the first parallel port, so the filename for the printer should be prn or lpt1. (You can substitute the appropriate name if your system is configured differently.)

The following program, EZPRINT, sends a string and a number to the printer, using formatted output with the insertion operator.

```cpp
// ezprint.cpp
// demonstrates simple output to printer
#include <fstream>                    //for file streams
using namespace std;

int main()
    {
    char* s1 = "\nToday's winning number is ";
    int   n1 = 17982;

    ofstream outfile;                 //make a file
    outfile.open("PRN");              //open it for printer
    outfile << s1 << n1 << endl;      //send data to printer
    outfile << '\x0C';                //formfeed to eject page
    return 0;
    }
```

You can send any amount of formatted output to the printer this way. The '\x0C' character causes the page to eject from the printer.

The next example, OPRINT, prints the contents of a disk file, specified on the command line, to the printer. It uses the character-by-character approach to this data transfer.

```cpp
// oprint.cpp
// imitates print command
#include <fstream>                    //for file functions
#include <iostream>
using namespace std;
#include <process.h>                  //for exit()
```

```
int main(int argc, char* argv[] )
   {
   if(argc != 2)
      {
      cerr << "\nFormat: oprint filename";
      exit(-1);
      }
   char ch;                           //character to read
   ifstream infile;                   //create file for input
   infile.open( argv[1] );            //open file
   if( !infile )                      //check for errors
      {
      cerr << "\nCan't open " << argv[1];
      exit(-1);
      }
   ofstream outfile;                   //make file
   outfile.open("PRN");                //open it for printer
   while( infile.get(ch) != 0 )        //read a character
      outfile.put(ch);                 //write character to printer
   outfile.put('\x0C');                //formfeed to eject page
   return 0;
   }
```

You can use this program to print any text file, such as any of your .CPP source files. It acts much the same as the DOS PRINT command. Like the OTYPE example, this program checks for the correct number of command-line arguments, and for a successful opening of the specified file.

Summary

In this chapter we briefly examined the hierarchy of stream classes and showed how to handle various kinds of I/O errors. Then we saw how to perform file I/O in a variety of ways. Files in C++ are associated with objects of various classes, typically ofstream for output, ifstream for input, and fstream for both input and output. Member functions of these or base classes are used to perform I/O operations. Such operators and functions as <<, put(), and write() are used for output, while >>, get(), and read() are used for input.

The read() and write() functions work in binary mode, so entire objects can be saved to disk no matter what sort of data they contain. Single objects can be stored, as can arrays or other data structures of many objects. File I/O can be handled by member functions. This can be the responsibility of individual objects, or the class itself can handle I/O using static member functions.

A check for error conditions should be made after each file operation. The file object itself takes on a value of 0 if an error occurred. Also, several member functions can be used to determine specific kinds of errors. The extraction operator >> and the insertion operator << can be overloaded so that they work with programmer-defined data types. Memory can be considered a stream, and data sent to it as if it were a file.

Questions

Answers to these questions can be found in Appendix G.

1. A C++ stream is
   a. the flow of control through a function.
   b. a flow of data from one place to another.
   c. associated with a particular class.
   d. a file.

2. The base class for most stream classes is the _____ class.

3. Name three stream classes commonly used for disk I/O.

4. Write a statement that will create an object called `salefile` of the `ofstream` class and associate it with a file called SALES.JUN.

5. True or false: Some streams work with input, and some with output.

6. Write an `if` statement that checks whether an `ifstream` object called `foobar` has reached the end of file or has encountered an error.

7. We can output text to an object of class `ofstream` using the insertion operator `<<` because
   a. the `ofstream` class is a stream.
   b. the insertion operator works with all classes.
   c. we are actually outputting to `cout`.
   d. the insertion operator is overloaded in `ofstream`.

8. Write a statement that writes a single character to an object called `fileOut`, which is of class `ofstream`.

9. To write data that contains variables of type `float` to an object of type `ofstream`, you should use
   a. the insertion operator.
   b. `seekg()`.
   c. `write()`.
   d. `put()`.

10. Write a statement that will read the contents of an `ifstream` object called `ifile` into an array called `buff`.

11. Mode bits such as app and ate

    a. are defined in the ios class.

    b. can specify if a file is open for reading or writing.

    c. work with the put() and get() functions.

    d. specify ways of opening a file.

12. Define what *current position* means when applied to files.

13. True or false: A file pointer always contains the address of the file.

14. Write a statement that moves the current position 13 bytes backward in a stream object called f1.

15. The statement

    ```
    f1.write( (char*)&obj1, sizeof(obj1) );
    ```

    a. writes the member functions of obj1 to f1.

    b. writes the data in obj1 to f1.

    c. writes the member functions and the data of obj1 to f1.

    d. writes the address of obj1 to f1.

16. Command-line arguments are

    a. disagreements in the military.

    b. typed following a program name at the command prompt.

    c. accessed through arguments to main().

    d. accessible only from disk files.

17. Used with cin, what does the skipws flag accomplish?

18. Write a declarator for main() that will enable command-line arguments.

19. In console mode programs, the printer can be accessed using the predefined filename _____.

20. Write the declarator for the overloaded >> operator that takes output from an object of class istream and displays it as the contents of an object of class Sample.

Exercises

Answers to starred exercises can be found in Appendix G.

*1. Start with the Distance class from the ENGLCON example in Chapter 6, "Objects and Classes." Using a loop similar to that in the DISKFUN example in this chapter, get a number of Distance values from the user, and write them to a disk file. Append them to existing values in the file, if any. When the user signals that no more values will be input, read the file and display all the values.

*2. Write a program that emulates the DOS COPY command. That is, it should copy the contents of a text file (such as any .CPP file) to another file. Invoke the program with two command-line arguments—the source file and the destination file—like this:

```
C>ocopy srcfile.cpp destfile.cpp
```

In the program, check that the user has typed the correct number of command-line arguments, and that the files specified can be opened.

*3. Write a program that returns the size in bytes of a program entered on the command line:

```
C>filesize program.ext
```

4. In a loop, prompt the user to enter *name data* consisting of a first name, middle initial, last name, and employee number (type unsigned long). Then, using formatted I/O with the insertion (<<) operator, write these four data items to an ofstream object. Don't forget that strings must be terminated with a space or other whitespace character. When the user indicates that no more name data will be entered, close the ofstream object, open an ifstream object, read and display all the data in the file, and terminate the program.

5. Create a time class that includes integer member values for hours, minutes, and seconds. Make a member function get_time() that gets a time value from the user, and a function put_time() that displays a time in 12:59:59 format. Add error checking to the get_time() function to minimize user mistakes. This function should request hours, minutes, and seconds separately, and check each one for ios error status flags and the correct range. Hours should be between 0 and 23, and minutes and seconds between 0 and 59. Don't input these values as strings and then convert them; read them directly as integers. This implies that you won't be able to screen out entries with superfluous decimal points, as does the ENGL_IO program in this chapter, but we'll assume that's not important.

In main(), use a loop to repeatedly get a time value from the user with get_time() and then display it with put_time(), like this:

```
Enter hours: 11
Enter minutes: 59
Enter seconds: 59
time = 11:59:59

Do another (y/n)? y
Enter hours: 25
Hours must be between 0 and 23
Enter hours: 1
Enter minutes: 10
Enter seconds: five
Incorrect seconds input
Enter seconds: 5
time = 1:10:05
```

6. Make a class called name from the data in Exercise 4 (first name, middle initial, last name, employee number). Create member functions for this class that read and write an object's data to a disk file, using ofstream, and read it back using ifstream. Use formatted data with the << and >> operators. The read and write member functions should be self-contained: they should include statements to open the appropriate stream and read or write a record.

The write function can simply append its data to the end of the file. The read function will need a way to select which record it's going to read. One way to do this is to call it with a parameter representing the record number. Once it knows which record it should read, how does the read function find the record? You might think you could use the seekg() function, but that isn't much help because in formatted I/O the records are all different lengths (depending on the number of characters in the strings and the number of digits in the integer). So you'll need to actually read records until you've skipped forward to the one you want.

In main(), call these member functions to allow the user to enter data for a number of objects that are written to a file as they are entered. The program then displays all this data by reading it from the file.

7. Another approach to adding file stream I/O to an object is to make the file stream itself a static member of the object. Why do that? Well, it's often conceptually easier to think of the stream as being related to the class as a whole than to the individual objects of the class. Also, it's more efficient to open a stream only once, then read and write objects to it as needed. For example, once the file is opened, each time the read function is called it can return the data for the next object in the file. The file pointer will progress automatically through the file because the file is not closed between reads.

Rewrite the program in Exercises 4 and 6 to use an fstream object as a static data item of the name class. Keep the same functionality that is in those exercises. Write a static function to open this stream, and another static function to reset the file pointer to the beginning of the file. You can use this reset function when you're done writing and want to read all the records back from the file.

8. Starting with the LINKLIST program in Chapter 10, "Pointers," create a program that gives the user four options, which can be selected by pressing a key.

- Add a link to the list in memory (the user supplies the data, which is one integer)
- Display the data from all the links in memory
- Write the data for all the links to a disk file (creating or truncating the file as necessary)
- Read all the data back from the file, and construct a new linked list in which to store it

The first two options can use the member functions already implemented in LINKLIST. You'll need to write functions to read to, and write from, the disk file. You can use the same file for all reads and writes. The file should store only the data; there's no sense in its storing the contents of pointers, which will probably not be relevant when the list is read back in.

9. Start with Exercise 7 in Chapter 8, "Operator Overloading," and overload the insertion (<<) and extraction (>>) operators for the frac class in the four-function calculator. Note that you can chain the operators, so asking for a fraction, an operator, and a fraction should require only one statement:

```
cin >> frac1 >> op >> frac2;
```

10. Add error checking to the extraction (>>) operator of the frac class in Exercise 9. With error checking it's probably better to prompt for the first fraction, then for the operator, and then for the second fraction, rather than using a single statement as shown in Exercise 9. This makes the format more comprehensible when it is interspersed with error messages.

```
Enter first fraction: 5/0
Denominator cannot be 0
    Enter fraction again: 5/1
Enter operator (+, -, *, /): +
Enter second fraction: one third
Input error
    Enter fraction again: 1/3
Answer is -------------------- 16/3
Do another (y/n)?
```

As implied in this sample interaction, you should check for ios error flags and also for a denominator of 0. If there's an error, prompt the user to enter the fraction again.

11. Start with the bMoney class, last seen in Exercise 5 in Chapter 11. Overload the insertion (<<) and extraction (>>) operators to perform I/O on bMoney quantities. Perform some sample I/O in main().

12. To the EMPL_IO program in this chapter add the ability to search through all the employee objects in a disk file, looking for one with a specified employee number. If it finds a match, it should display the data for the employee. The user can invoke this find() function by typing the 'f' character. The function should then prompt for the employee number. Ask yourself whether the function should be static, virtual, or something else. This search and display operation should not interfere with the data in memory.

> **NOTE**
>
> Note: Don't try to read a file generated with the EMPL_IO program. The classes are not the same because of the find() member function in the new program, and disaster will result if their data is mixed, as discussed in this chapter. You may need to turn on an Enable RTTI option in your compiler. Consult Appendix C, "Microsoft Visual C++," or Appendix D, "Borland C++Builder," as appropriate.

Multifile Programs

IN THIS CHAPTER

In previous chapters we've seen how the various parts of a C++ program—such as class declarations, member functions, and a main() function—are combined. However, the programs in those chapters all consisted of a single file. Now let's look at program organization from a wider perspective, involving multiple files. We'll see how communication is carried out among files, and how header files fit into the picture.

Besides discussing multifile programs in general, this chapter will introduce some longer and more ambitious applications. Our aim in these programs is not that you necessarily understand every detail of their operation, but that you acquire a general understanding of how the elements of larger programs relate to one another. These programs also show how classes can be used in more realistic applications than the short examples we've seen so far. On the other hand, they are not so long that it takes all spring to wade through them.

Reasons for Multifile Programs

There are several reasons for using multifile programs. These include the use of class libraries, the organization of programmers working on a project, and the conceptual design of a program. Let's reflect briefly on these issues.

Class Libraries

In traditional procedure-oriented languages it has long been customary for software vendors to furnish libraries of functions. Other programmers then combine these libraries with their own custom-written routines to create an application for the end user.

Libraries provide ready-made functions for a wide variety of fields. For instance, a vendor might supply a library of functions for handling statistics calculations, or one for advanced memory management.

Since C++ is organized around classes rather than functions, it's not surprising that libraries for C++ programs consist of classes. What may be surprising is how much better a class library is than an old-fashioned function library. Because classes encapsulate both data and functions, and because they more closely model objects in real life, the interface between a class library and the application that makes use of it can be much cleaner than that provided by a function library.

For these reasons class libraries assume a more important role in C++ programming than function libraries do in traditional programming. A class library can take over a greater portion of the programming burden. An applications programmer, if the right class library is available, may find that only a minimal amount of programming is necessary to create a final product. Also, as more and more class libraries are created, the chances of finding one that solves your particular programming problem continues to increase.

We'll see an important example of a class library in Chapter 15, "The Standard Template Library."

A class library usually includes two components: the *interface* and the *implementation*. Let's see what the difference is.

Interface

Let's say that the person who wrote a class library is called the *class developer*, and the person who uses the library is called the *programmer*.

To use a class library, the programmer needs to access various declarations, including class declarations. These declarations can be thought of as the public part of the library and are usually furnished in source-code form as a header file, with the .H extension. This file is typically combined with the client's source code using an #include statement.

The declarations in such a header file need to be public for several reasons. First, it's a convenience to the client to see the actual class definitions rather than to have to read a description of them. More importantly, the programmer will need to declare objects based on these classes and call on member functions from these objects. Only by declaring the classes in the source file is this possible.

These declarations are called the *interface* because that's what a user of the class (the programmer) sees and interacts with. The programmer need not be concerned with the other part of the library, the *implementation*.

Implementation

On the other hand, the inner workings of the member functions of the various classes don't need to be known by the programmer. The class developers, like any other software developers, don't want to release source code if they can help it, since it might be illegally modified or pirated. Member functions—except for short inline functions—are therefore often distributed in object form, as .OBJ files or as library (.LIB) files.

Figure 13.1 shows how the various files are related in a multifile system.

Organization and Conceptualization

Programs may be broken down into multiple files for reasons other than the accommodation of class libraries. As in other programming languages, a common situation involves a project with several programmers (or teams of programmers). Confining each programmer's responsibility to a separate file helps organize the project and define more cleanly the interface among different parts of the program.

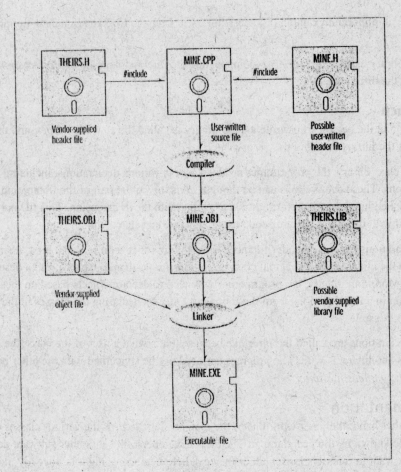

FIGURE 13.1
Files in a multifile application.

It is also often the case that a program is divided into separate files according to functionality: One file can handle the code involved in a graphics display, for example, while another file handles mathematical analysis, and a third handles disk I/O. In large programs, a single file may simply become too large to handle conveniently.

The techniques used for working with multifile programs are similar, whatever the reasons for dividing the program.

Creating a Multifile Program

Suppose that you have purchased a prewritten class file called THEIRS.OBJ. (A library file with the .LIB extension is dealt with in much the same way.) It probably comes with a header file, say THEIRS.H. You have also written your own program to use the classes in the library; your source file is called MINE.CPP. Now you want to combine these component files—THEIRS.OBJ, THEIRS.H, and MINE.CPP—into a single executable program.

Header Files

The header file THEIRS.H is easily incorporated into your own source file, MINE.CPP, with an #include statement:

```
#include "theirs.h"
```

Quotes rather than angle brackets around the filename tell the compiler to look for the file in the current directory, rather than in the default include directory.

Directory

Make sure that all the component files, THEIRS.OBJ, THEIRS.H, and MINE.CPP, are in the same directory. In fact, you will probably want to create a separate directory for each project, to avoid confusion. (This isn't strictly necessary, but it's the simplest approach.)

Each compiler keeps its own library files (such as IOSTREAM and CONIO.H) in a particular directory, often called INCLUDE, and usually buried many levels down in the compiler's directory structure. The compiler already knows where this directory is.

You can also tell the compiler about other include directories that you create yourself. You may want to keep some of your header files in such a directory, where they will be available for several projects. In Appendix C, "Microsoft Visual C++," and Appendix D, "Borland C++Builder," we explain how to tell the compiler where such a directory is located.

Projects

Most compilers manage multiple files using a project metaphor. A project contains all the files necessary for the application. It also contains instructions for combining these files, often in a special file called a *project file*. The extension for this file varies with the compiler vendor. It's .BPR for Borland, and .DSP for Microsoft. Modern compilers construct and maintain this file automatically, so you don't need to worry about it. In general you must tell the compiler about all the source (.CPP) files you plan to use so they can be added to the project. You can add .OBJ and .LIB files in a similar way. Appendixes C and D provide details on creating multifile programs for specific compilers.

Only a single command needs to be given to the compiler to compile all the source (.CPP and .H) files and link the resulting .OBJ files (and any other .OBJ or .LIB files) into a final .EXE file. This is called the *build* process. Often the .EXE file can be executed as well. (In Windows and other advanced programming there are many more types of files.)

One of the nice things about a project is that it keeps track of the dates when you compiled each source file. Only those source files that have been modified since the last build are recompiled; this can save considerable time, especially on large projects. Some compilers distinguish between a Make command and a Build command. Make compiles only those source files that have changed since the last build, whereas Build compiles all files regardless of date.

Inter-File Communication

In a multifile program, program elements in different files need to communicate with each other. In this section we'll discuss how to make this possible. We'll first discuss how communication is handled between separately-compiled source (.CPP) files that are linked together. Then we'll see how header (.H) files that are included in source files fit into the picture.

Communication Among Source Files

This section explores how elements of separate source files communicate. We'll examine three kinds of programming elements: variables, functions, and classes. Each has its own rules for inter-file use.

The idea of scope will be important here, so you may want to refer back to our discussion of scope and storage class in Chapter 5. Scope is the region of a program where a variable or other program element can be accessed. Elements declared within a function have *local* scope; that is, they are visible only within the function body. Similarly, class members are only visible within the class (unless the scope resolution operator is used).

Program elements declared outside any function or class have *global* scope: they can be used throughout an entire file, following the point where they are defined. As we'll see, they are visible in other files as well.

Inter-File Variables

We'll start with simple variables. Recall the distinction between declaration and definition. We *declare* a simple variable by giving it a name and a type. This does not necessarily provide a physical location in memory for the variable; it only tells the compiler that a variable with this name and type may exist somewhere. A variable is *defined* when it is given a place in memory that can hold the variable's value. The definition creates the "real" variable.

Most declarations are also definitions. Actually, the only declaration of a simple variable that is *not* a definition uses the keyword extern (with no initializer).

```
int someVar;           //declaration and also definition
extern int someVar;    //declaration only
```

As you might expect, a global variable can be defined in only one place in a program.

```
//file A
int globalVar;   //definition in file A
```

```
//file B
int globalVar;   //illegal: same definition in file B
```

Of course, this discussion applies only to global variables. You can define as many variables with the same name and type as you like, provided they are all local to different functions or classes.

How do you access a global variable in one file from a different file? The fact that the linker will object to defining the same global variable in more than one file does not mean that a variable in one file is automatically visible to all code in other files. You must declare the variable in every file that uses it. If you say

```
//file A
int globalVar;   //defined
```

```
//file B
globalVar = 3;   //illegal, globalVar is unknown here
```

the compiler will tell you that globalVar is an unidentified identifier.

To allow a variable to be accessed in files other than the one where it's defined, you must declare it in the other files using the keyword extern.

```
//file A
int globalVar;           //definition
```

```
//file B
extern int globalVar;   //declaration
globalVar = 3;          //now this is OK
```

The declaration causes globalVar in file A to be visible in file B. The extern keyword signals that the declaration is *only* a declaration, not a definition. It tells the compiler (which can see only one file at a time) not to worry that the globalVar variable in file B is undefined there. The linker (which sees all the files) will take care of connecting a reference to a variable in one file with its definition in another.

13

MULTIFILE
PROGRAMS

You should note a possibly surprising restriction: you can't initialize a variable in an extern declaration. The statement

```
extern int globalVar = 27;   //not what you might think
```

will cause the compiler to assume that you meant to define globalVar, not just declare it. It will simply ignore the extern keyword and create a definition. If the variable is defined in another file, you'll get the "already defined" error from the linker.

What if you actually want to use global variables with the same name in different files? In that case you can define them using the static keyword. This restricts a variable's visibility to the file where it's defined. Other variables with the same name can be used in other files.

```
//file A
static int globalVar;    //definition; visible only in file A

//file B
static int globalVar;    //definition; visible only in file B
```

Although two variables with the same name are defined here, there is no conflict. Code in file A that refers to globalVar will access the variable in its file, and code in file B behaves likewise. Static variables are said to have *internal linkage*, while non-static global variables have *external linkage*. (As we'll see later in this section, you can also use namespaces to restrict a variable's scope to a single file.)

In a multifile program it's a good idea to make global variables static whenever they are not accessed in other files. This prevents problems when the same name is used by mistake in another file. It also makes it clearer to someone looking at the listing that they don't need to worry about the variable being accessed elsewhere.

Notice that the keyword static has several meanings, depending on whether it's applied to a local or a global variable. We saw in Chapter 5, "Functions," that when static modifies a local variable (one defined inside a function) it changes the variable's lifetime from that of the function to that of the program but keeps its visibility restricted to the function. As we discussed in Chapter 6, "Objects and Classes," a static class data member has the same value for all objects rather than a separate value for each object. However, for a global variable, static simply restricts its visibility to its own file.

A const variable that is defined in one file is normally not visible in other files. In this regard it's like a static variable. However, you can cause a const variable to be visible in another file by using the extern keyword with both the definition and the declaration:

```
//file A
extern const int conVar2 = 99;   //definition

//file B
extern const int conVar2;        //declaration
```

Here, file B has access to the const variable in file A. The compiler can tell the difference between a const definition and a declaration by seeing where the variable is initialized.

Inter-File Functions

Remember that a function declaration specifies the name of the function, its return type, and the type of any arguments. A function definition is a declaration that includes a function body. (The body is the code within braces.)

When the compiler generates a call to a function, it doesn't need to know how the function works. All it needs to know is the function name, its return type, and the types of its arguments. This is exactly what the declaration specifies. It is therefore easy to define a function in one file and make calls to it from a second file. No extra keywords (like extern) are needed. All that's necessary is to declare the function in the second file before making calls to it.

```
//file A
int add(int a, int  b)     //function definition
   { return a+b; }         //(includes function body)


//file B
int add(int, int);         //function declaration (no body)
. . .
int answer = add(3, 2);  //call to function
```

You don't need to use the keyword extern with functions because the compiler can tell the difference between a function's declaration and definition: the declaration has no body.

Incidentally, you can declare (not define) a function or any other program element as many times as you want. The compiler won't object, unless the declarations disagree.

```
//file A
int add(int, int);  //declaration
int add(int, int);  //another declaration is OK
```

Like variables, functions can be made invisible to other files by declaring them static.

```
//file A
static int add(int a, int  b)    //function definition
   { return a+b; }

//file B
static int add(int a, int  b)    //different function
   { return a+b; }
```

This code creates two distinct functions. Neither is visible in the other file.

Inter-File Classes

Classes are unlike simple variables in that the definition of a class does not set aside any memory. It merely informs the compiler what members constitute the class. It's a little like specifying how many bytes will be used for type int, except that the compiler already knows the makeup of type int, but it doesn't know about type someClass until you define it.

A class definition contains declarations or definitions for all its members:

```
class someClass              //class definition
   {
   private:
      int memVar;             //member data definition
   public:
      int memFunc(int, int);  //member function declaration
   };
```

Members must be declared but don't need to be defined in the class definition. As we've seen, member function definitions are routinely placed outside the class and identified with the scope resolution operator.

A class declaration is simply a statement that a certain name applies to a class. It conveys no information to the compiler about the members of the class.

```
class someClass;             //class declaration
```

Don't confuse a class definition with the definition (creation) of an object of that class:

```
someClass anObj;
```

Unlike a class definition, the definition of an object sets aside space in memory for the object.

Classes behave differently from variables and functions in inter-file communication. To access a class across multiple source files it's necessary to define the class (not just declare it) in every file in which its objects will be used. The fact that a class is defined in file A and declared in File B does not mean that the compiler can create objects of that class in file B.

Why does a class need to be defined in every file where it's used? The compiler needs to know the data type of everything it's compiling. A declaration is all it needs for simple variables because the declaration specifies a type already known to the compiler.

```
//declaration
extern int someVar;          //if it sees this, the compiler
someVar = 3;                 //can generate this
```

Similarly, the declaration of a function reveals the data types of everything needed for a function call.

```
//declaration
int someFunc(int, int);        //if it sees this, the compiler
var1 = someFunc(var2, var3);   //can generate this
```

However, for a class, the entire definition is necessary to specify the types of its member data and functions.

```
//definition
class someClass                //if it sees this, the compiler
    {
    private:
        int memVar;
    public:
        int memFunc(int, int);
    };
someClass someObj;             //can generate this
v1 = someObj.memFunc(v2, v3);  //and this
```

A mere declaration is insufficient for the compiler to generate code to deal with class objects (except for pointers and references to objects).

You can't define a class more than once in a source (.CPP) file, but every source file in a program can have its own definition of the same class. Indeed, it must have such a definition if it is to work with objects of that class. In the next section we'll show how to use a header file to supply a class definition to many files.

Header Files

As we noted in Chapter 2, the #include preprocessor directive acts like the paste function in a word processor, causing the text of one file to be inserted in another. We've seen many examples of library files such as IOSTREAM being included in our source files.

We can also write our own header (usually .H) files and include them in our source files.

Common Information

One reason to use a header file is to supply two or more source files with the same information. The header file holds variable or function declarations, and is included in the source files. In this way the variables or functions can be accessed from many files.

Of course, each program element must also be defined somewhere. Here, a variable and a function are declared in FILEH.H and defined in FILEA.CPP. Code in FILEB.CPP can then use these elements without any additional declarations of its own.

```
//fileH.h
extern int gloVar;    //variable declaration
int gloFunc(int);     //function declaration
```

```
//fileA.cpp
int gloVar;                     //variable definition
int GloFunc(int n)              //function definition
   { return n; }

//fileB.cpp
#include "fileH.h"
. . .
gloVar = 5;                     //work with variable
int gloVarB = gloFunc(gloVar);  //work with function
```

Beware: you can put declarations in a header file, but you can't put variable or function definitions in a header file that will be shared by multiple source files (unless they're static or const). If you do, the same definitions will then end up in two different source files and the linker will issue "multiply defined" errors.

A very common and indeed almost essential technique is to put a class definition in a header file that is included in every source file that needs it. This doesn't cause the multiply-defined problem because a class definition does not set aside any memory; it's only a specification.

```
//fileH.h
class someClass                  //class definition
   {
   private:
      int memVar;
   public:
      int memFunc(int, int);
   };

//fileA.cpp
#include "fileH.h"
int main()
   {
   ...
   someClass obj1;                //create an object
   int var1 = obj1.memFunc(2, 3); //work with object
   }

//fileB.cpp
#include "fileH.h"
int func()
   {
   someClass obj2;                //create an object
   int var2 = obj2.memFunc(4, 5); //work with object
   }
```

What if, instead of using a header file, you actually copied the text of the class definition and pasted it manually into each source file? Then any modification to the class would require you to change the definition in each file seperately. This would be time-consuming and prone to errors.

So far we've shown class definitions with no external member-function definitions. Where can external member functions be defined? Like ordinary functions, they can go in any source file, and the linker will connect them as needed. The class definition serves to declare the member functions in each file. As within a single file, the member function definition must include the class name and scope resolution operator.

```
//fileH.h
class someClass                           //class definition
   {
   private:
      int memVar;
   public:
      int memFunc(int, int);              //member-function declaration
   };
;
//fileA.cpp
#include "fileH.h"
int someClass::memFunc(int n1, int n2)   //member function definition
   { return n1 + n2; }

//fileB.cpp
#include "fileH.h"
someClass anObj;                          //create an object
int answer = anObj.memFunc(6,7);          //use the member function
```

The Multiple-Includes Hazard

We've mentioned that you can't define a function or variable in a header file that will be shared by multiple source files. Doing so causes multiple-definition errors. A similar problem arises if you include the same header file twice in a source file. How could such a thing happen? You probably would not make a mistake this obvious:

```
//file app.cpp
#include "headone.h"
#include "headone.h"
```

But suppose you have a source file APP.CPP and two header files, HEADONE.H and HEADTWO.H. Further suppose that HEADONE.H includes HEADTWO.H. Unfortunately you forget this and include them both in APP.CPP:

```
//file headtwo.h
int globalVar;

//file headone.h
#include "headtwo.h"

//file app.cpp
#include "headone.h"
#include "headtwo.h"
```

Now what happens when you compile APP.CPP? Once the #include directives have pasted the text of the header files into APP.CPP, we end up with

```
//file app.cpp
. . .
int globalVar;   //from head2.h via headone.h
. . .
int globalVar;   //from head2.h directly
```

This will cause the compiler to complain that globalVar is defined twice.

Preventing Multiple Includes

Here's how to prevent multiple-definition errors even when a header file is included more than once in your source file. You precede the definitions in the header file with the preprocessor directive

```
#if !defined( HEADCOM )
```

(You can use any identifier, not just HEADCOM.) This statement says that if HEADCOM is *not* defined (the exclamation point is a logical NOT), all the text that follows this directive, up to a closing #endif directive, will be pasted into the source file normally. But if HEADCOM *is* defined, which can be accomplished with the directive

```
#define HEADCOM
```

then the text that follows will not be included in the source file. As they say in the movies, it ends up on the cutting-room floor. Because HEADCOM is not defined when this text is first encountered, but is defined immediately after the #if !defined() directive, the text between there and the closing #endif will be included the first time it's encountered, but never again. Here's the arrangement:

```
#if !defined( HEADCOM )       //if HEADCOM not defined,
#define HEADCOM               //define it

int globalVar;                //define this variable
```

```
int func(int a, int b)          //define this function
    { return a+b; }

#endif                          //end condition
```

You should use this approach whenever there's any possibility a header file will be included in a source file more than once.

An older directive, #ifndef, was used the same way as #if !defined(), and will be seen in many of the header files supplied with your compiler. However, its use is now discouraged.

Note that the #if !defined() approach works in the situation where the definition of globalVar (or some other variable or function) may end up being included multiple times in the same source file. It does not work when globalVar is defined in file H, and file H is included in different source files A and B. The preprocessor is powerless to detect multiple statements in separate files, so the linker will complain that globalVar is multiply defined.

Namespaces

We've seen how to restrict the visibility of program elements by declaring them within a file or class, or by making global elements static or const. Sometimes, however, a more versatile approach is required.

For example, when writing a class library, programmers would prefer to use short and common names for non-member functions and classes, like add() and book. However, short and common names may turn out to be the same names selected by the creators of another library or by an application that uses the library. This can lead to "name clashes" and generate multiple-definition errors from your compiler. Before the advent of namespaces, programmers were forced to use long names to avoid this problem:

```
Henry's_Simplified_Statistics_Library_add();
```

However, long names are difficult to read and write and take up excessive space in a listing. Namespaces can solve this problem. (Note that member functions don't cause name clashes because their scope is limited to the class.)

Defining a Namespace

A namespace is a section of a file that is given a name. The following code defines a namespace geo with some declarations inside it:

```
namespace geo
    {
    const double PI = 3.14159;
    double circumf(double radius)
        { return 2 * PI * radius; }
    }  //end namespace geo
```

Braces delimit the namespace. Variables and other program elements declared within the braces are called namespace *members*. Notice that there is no semicolon following the closing brace, as there is with classes.

Accessing Namespace Members

Code outside a namespace cannot access the elements within it, at least not in the normal way. The namespace makes them invisible:

```
namespace geo
   {
   const double PI = 3.14159;
   double circumf(double radius)
      { return 2 * PI * radius; }
   } //end namespace geo


double c = circumf(10);  //won't work here
```

To make the elements visible outside the namespace you must invoke the namespace name when referring to them. There are two ways to do this. First, you can precede each element's name with the namespace name and the scope resolution operator:

```
double c = geo::circumf(10);  //OK
```

Or you can use the using directive:

```
using namespace geo;
double c = circumf(10);  //OK
```

The using directive ordinarily causes the namespace to be visible from that point onward. However, you can restrict the region where the using directive is in effect to a particular block, such as a function:

```
void seriousCalcs()
   {
   using namespace geo;
   //other code here
   double c = circumf(r);      //OK
   }


double c = circumf(r);           //not OK
```

Here the members of the namespace are visible only within the function body.

Namespaces in Header Files

Namespaces are most commonly used in header files containing library classes or functions. Each such library can have its own namespace. By this time you are familiar with the namespace std, whose members constitute the Standard C++ Library.

Multiple Namespace Definitions

There can be several instances of the same namespace definition:

```
namespace geo
    {
    const double PI = 3.14159;
    }  // end namespace geo

//(some other code here)

namespace geo
    {
    double circumf(double radius)
        { return 2 * PI * radius; }
    }  //end namespace geo
```

This looks like a redefinition, but it's really just a continuation of the same definition. It allows a namespace to be used in several header files, which can then all be included in a source file. In the Standard C++ Library, dozens of header files use the namespace std.

```
//fileA.h
namespace alpha
    {
    void funcA();
    }

//fileB.h
namespace alpha
    {
    void funcB();
    }

fileMain.cpp
#include "fileA.h"
#include "fileB.h"
using namespace alpha;
funcA();
funcB();
```

You can place declarations outside a namespace that behave as if they were inside it. All you need is the scope resolution operator and the namespace name:

```
namespace beta
    {
    int uno;
    }

int beta::dos;
```

Here, both uno and dos are declared in the namespce beta.

Unnamed Namespaces

You can create a namespace without a name. Doing so creates a namespace that is automatically visible throughout the file in which it's defined, but not visible from other files. The compiler gives an unnamed namespace an internal name unique to the file. Elements declared in the unnamed namespace can be accessed from anywhere in the file. In the following listing, funcA() and funcB() can access the gloVar variable in their respective files.

```
//fileA.cpp
namespace      //unnamed namespace unique to fileA.cpp
   {
   int gloVar = 111;
   }
funcA()
   { cout << gloVar; }   //displays 111

//fileB.cpp
namespace      //unnamed namespace unique to fileB.cpp
   {
   int gloVar = 222;
   }
funcB()
   { cout << gloVar; }   //displays 222
```

In this example both files contain a variable named gloVar, but there's no conflict because each variables is declared in an unnamed namespace unique to its file and is invisible everywhere else.

This approach provides an alternative to the use of static for restricting the scope of global variables to their own file. In fact, the namespace approach is now considered preferable to making elements static.

Renaming Types with typedef

You may find the typedef keyword useful in certain situations, and you will certainly run across it in other people's listings. It allows you to create a new name for a data type. For example, the statement

```
typedef unsigned long unlong;
```

makes unlong a synonym for unsigned long. Now you can declare variables using the new name:

```
unlong var1, var2;
```

This may save you a little space or make your listing more readable. More usefully, you can make up new type names that reveal the purpose of any variables declared with that type:

```
typedef int FLAG;        //int variables used to hold flag values
typedef int KILOGRAMS;   //int variables used to hold values in kilograms
```

If you don't like the way pointers are specified in C++, you can change it:

```
int *p1, *p2, *p3;      //normal declaration
typedef int* ptrInt;    //new name for pointer to int
ptrInt p1, p2, p3;      //simplified declaration
```

This avoids all those pesky asterisks.

Because classes are types in C++, you can use typedef to create alternative names for them. Earlier we mentioned that developers sometimes create excessively long names. If you need to use these names, writing them can be an inconvenience and can make the listing hard to read. You can fix the problem, at least for class names, with typedef:

```
class GeorgeSmith_Display_Utility        //class definition
   {
   //members
   };
```

```
typedef GeorgeSmith_Display_Utility GSdu;   //rename the class
```

```
GSdu anObj;                                 //create object using new name
```

Type renaming with typedef is typically handled in header files, so that multiple source files can use the new names. Many software development organizations make extensive use of typedef, resulting in what looks almost like a different language.

Now that we've explored some of the general concepts involved in multifile programs, let's look at some examples. These programs won't demonstrate all the topics we've covered in the previous section, but they will show you some typical situations where an application programmer uses code provided by a library writer.

A Very Long Number Class

Sometimes even the basic data type unsigned long does not provide enough precision for certain integer arithmetic operations. unsigned long is the largest integer type in Standard C++, holding integers up to 4,294,967,295, or about ten digits. This is about the same number of digits a pocket calculator can handle. But if you need to work with integers containing more significant digits than this, you have a problem.

Our next example offers a solution. It provides a class that holds integers up to 1,000 digits long. If you want to make even longer numbers (or shorter ones), you can change a single constant in the program.

Numbers as Strings

The verylong class stores numbers as strings of digits. These are old-fashioned char* C-strings, which are easier to work with in this context than the string class. The use of C-strings explains the large digit capacity: C++ can handle long C-strings, since they are simply arrays. By representing numbers as C-strings we can make them as long as we want. There are two data members in verylong: a char array to hold the string of digits, and an int to tell how long the string is. (This length of data isn't strictly necessary, but it saves us from having to use strlen() repeatedly to find the string length.) The digits in the string are stored in reverse order, with the least significant digit stored first, at vlstr[0]. This simplifies various operations on the string. Figure 13.2 shows a number stored as a string.

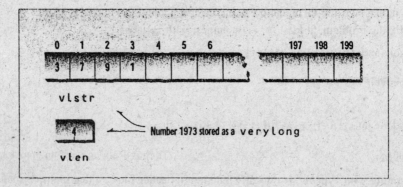

FIGURE 13.2
A verylong number.

We've provided user-accessible routines for addition and multiplication of verylong numbers. (We leave it as an exercise for the reader to write subtraction and division routines.)

The Class Specifier

Here's the header file for VERYLONG. It shows the specifiers for the verylong class.

```
// verylong.h
// class specifier for very long integer type
#include <iostream>
#include <string.h>          //for strlen(), etc.
#include <stdlib.h>          //for ltoa()
using namespace std;

const int SZ = 1000;
        //maximum digits in verylongs
```

```
class verylong
    {
    private:
        char vlstr[SZ];           //verylong number, as a string
        int vlen;                 //length of verylong string
        verylong multdigit(const int) const;   //prototypes for
        verylong mult10(const verylong) const; //private functions
    public:
        verylong() : vlen(0)              //no-arg constructor
            { vlstr[0]='\0'; }
        verylong(const char s[SZ])        //one-arg constructor
            { strcpy(vlstr, s); vlen=strlen(s); }   //for string
        verylong(const unsigned long n)   //one-arg constructor
            {                                   //for long int
            ltoa(n, vlstr, 10);           //convert to string
            strrev(vlstr);                //reverse it
            vlen=strlen(vlstr);           //find length
            }
        void putvl() const;               //display verylong
        void getvl();                     //get verylong from user
        verylong operator + (const verylong); //add verylongs
        verylong operator * (const verylong); //multiply verylongs
    };
```

In addition to the data members, there are two private-member functions in class verylong. One multiplies a verylong number by a single digit, and the other multiplies a verylong number by 10. These routines are used internally by the multiplication routine.

There are three constructors. One sets the verylong to 0 by inserting a terminating null at the beginning of the array and setting the length to 0. The second initializes it to a string (which is in reverse order), and the third initializes it to a long int value.

The putvl() member function displays a verylong, and getvl() gets a verylong value from the user. You can type as many digits as you like, up to 1,000. Note that there is no error checking in this routine; if you type a non-digit the results will be inaccurate.

Two overloaded operators, + and *, perform addition and multiplication. You can use expressions like

```
alpha = beta * gamma + delta;
```

to do verylong arithmetic.

The Member Functions

Here's VERYLONG.CPP, the file that holds the member function definitions:

```
// verylong.cpp
// implements very long integer type
#include "verylong.h"              //header file for verylong
//-------------------------------------------------------------
void verylong::putvl() const          //display verylong
   {
   char temp[SZ];
   strcpy(temp,vlstr);               //make copy
   cout << strrev(temp);             //reverse the copy
   }                                 //and display it
//-------------------------------------------------------------
void verylong::getvl()                //get verylong from user
   {
   cin >> vlstr;                     //get string from user
   vlen = strlen(vlstr);             //find its length
   strrev(vlstr);                    //reverse it
   }
//-------------------------------------------------------------
verylong verylong::operator + (const verylong v) //add verylongs
   {
   char temp[SZ];
   int j;
                     //find longest number
   int maxlen = (vlen > v.vlen) ? vlen : v.vlen;
   int carry = 0;                       //set to 1 if sum >= 10
   for(j = 0; j<maxlen; j++)            //for each position
      {
      int d1 = (j > vlen-1)   ? 0 : vlstr[j]-'0';   //get digit
      int d2 = (j > v.vlen-1) ? 0 : v.vlstr[j]-'0'; //get digit
      int digitsum = d1 + d2 + carry;          //add digits
      if( digitsum >= 10 )              //if there's a carry,
         { digitsum -= 10; carry=1; }   //decrease sum by 10,
      else                              //set carry to 1
         carry = 0;                     //otherwise carry is 0
      temp[j] = digitsum+'0';           //insert char in string
      }
   if(carry==1)                         //if carry at end,
      temp[j++] = '1';                  //last digit is 1
   temp[j] = '\0';                      //terminate string
   return verylong(temp);               //return temp verylong
   }
```

```
//·······················································
verylong verylong::operator * (const verylong v)  //multiply
   {                                               //verylongs
   verylong pprod;                       //product of one digit
   verylong tempsum;                     //running total
   for(int j=0; j<v.vlen; j++)           //for each digit in arg
      {
      int digit = v.vlstr[j]-'0';        //get the digit
      pprod = multdigit(digit);          //multiply this by digit
      for(int k=0; k<j; k++)             //multiply result by
         pprod = mult10(pprod);          //   power of 10
      tempsum = tempsum + pprod;         //add product to total
      }
   return tempsum;                       //return total of prods
   }
//·······················································
verylong verylong::mult10(const verylong v) const //multiply
   {                                               //arg by 10
   char temp[SZ];
   for(int j=v.vlen-1; j>=0; j--)        //move digits one
      temp[j+1] = v.vlstr[j];            //   position higher
   temp[0] = '0';                        //put zero on low end
   temp[v.vlen+1] = '\0';                //terminate string
   return verylong(temp);                //return result
   }
//·······················································
verylong verylong::multdigit(const int d2) const
   {                                     //multiply this verylong
   char temp[SZ];                        //by digit in argument
   int j, carry = 0;
   for(j = 0; j<vlen; j++)               //for each position
      {                                  //   in this verylong
      int d1 = vlstr[j]-'0';             //get digit from this
      int digitprod = d1 * d2;           //multiply by that digit
      digitprod += carry;                //add old carry
      if( digitprod >= 10 )              //if there's a new carry,
         {
         carry = digitprod/10;           //carry is high digit
         digitprod -= carry*10;          //result is low digit
         }
      else
         carry = 0;                      //otherwise carry is 0
      temp[j] = digitprod+'0';           //insert char in string
      }
   if(carry != 0)                        //if carry at end,
      temp[j++] = carry+'0';             //it's last digit
```

```
temp[j] = '\0';                    //terminate string
return verylong(temp);             //return verylong
}
```

The `putvl()` and `getvl()` functions are fairly straightforward. They use the `strrev()` C library function to reverse the C-string, so it is stored in reverse order but input is displayed normally.

The `operator+()` function adds two `verylong`s and leaves the result in a third `verylong`. It does this by considering their digits one at a time. It adds digit 0 from both numbers, storing a carry if necessary. Then it adds the digits in position 1, adding the carry if necessary. It continues until it has added all the digits in the larger of the two numbers. If the numbers are different lengths, the nonexistent digits in the shorter number are set to 0 before being added. Figure 13.3 shows the process.

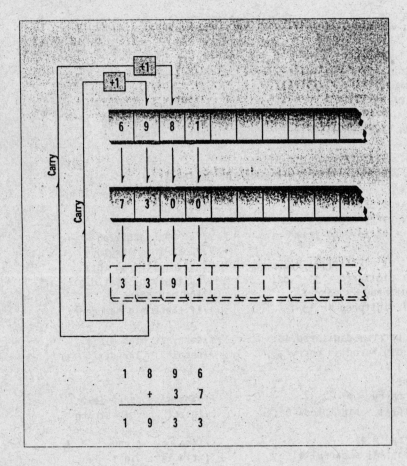

FIGURE 13.3
Adding verylong *numbers.*

Multiplication uses the `operator*()` function. This function multiplies the multiplicand (the top number when you write it by hand) by each separate digit in the multiplier (the bottom number). It calls the `multdigit()` routine to this. The results are then multiplied by 10 an appropriate number of times to shift the result to match the position of the digit, using the `mult10()` function. The results of these separate calculations are then added together using the `operator+()` function.

The Application Program

To test the `verylong` class we use a variation of the FACTOR program from Chapter 3, "Loops and Decisions," to calculate the factorial of a number entered by the user. Here's the listing for VL_APP.CPP:

```
// vl_app.cpp
// calculates factorials of larger numbers using verylong class
#include "verylong.h"                    //verylong header file

int main()
    {
    unsigned long numb, j;
    verylong fact=1;                      //initialize verylong

    cout << "\n\nEnter number: ";
    cin >> numb;                          //input a long int

    for(j=numb; j>0; j--)                 //factorial is numb *
        fact = fact * j;                  //   numb-1 * numb-2 *
    cout << "Factorial is ";              //   numb-3 and so on
    fact.putvl();                         //display factorial
    cout << endl;
    return 0;
    }
```

In this program `fact` is a `verylong` variable. The other variables, `numb` and `j`, don't need to be `verylong`s because they don't get so big. To calculate the factorial of 100, for example, `numb` and `j` require only three digits, while `fact` requires 158.

Notice how, in the expression

```
fact = fact * j;
```

the long variable `j` is automatically converted to `verylong`, using the one-argument constructor, before the multiplication is carried out.

Here's the output when we ask the program to find the factorial of 100:

```
Enter number: 100
Factorial is 9332621544394415268169923885626670049071596826438162
1468592963895217599993229915608941463976156518286253697920827223
758251185210916864000000000000000000000000000
```

Try *that* using type long variables! Surprisingly, the routines are fairly fast; this program executes in a fraction of a second. You can calculate the factorial of numbers up to about 400 before you exceed the 1000 digit capacity of the program.

A High-Rise Elevator Simulation

The next time you're waiting for an elevator in a high-rise office building, ask yourself how the elevators figure out where to go. In the old days, of course, there was a human elevator operator on each car. ("Good morning, Mr. Burberry," "Good morning, Carl.") Riders needed to tell the operator their destination floor when getting on ("Seventeen, please."). A panel of signal lights lit up inside the car to show which floors were requesting service up or down. Operators decided which way to go and where to stop on the basis of these verbal requests and their observation of the signal lights.

Nowadays enough intelligence is built into elevator systems to permit the cars to operate on their own. In our next example we use C++ classes to model an elevator system.

What are the components of such a system? In a typical building there are a number of similar elevators. On each floor there are up and down buttons. Note that there is usually only one such pair of buttons per floor; when you push a button you don't know which elevator will stop for you. Within the elevator there is a larger number of buttons: one for each floor. After entering the elevator, riders push a button to indicate their destination. Our simulation program will model all these components.

Running the ELEV Program

When you start up the ELEV program you'll see four elevators sitting at the bottom of the screen, and a list of numbers on the left, starting at 1 on the bottom of the screen and continuing up to 20 at the top. The elevators are initially on the ground (first) floor. This is shown in Figure 13.4.

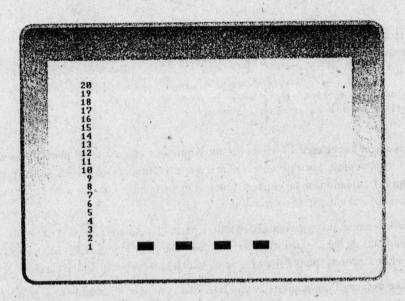

FIGURE 13.4
The ELEV program initial screen.

Making a Floor Request

If you press Enter, text at the bottom of the screen prompts

```
Enter the floor you're on:
```

You can enter any floor number from 1 to 20. If you've just arrived for work on the ground floor, you'll enter 1. If you're leaving a higher floor to go out to lunch, you'll enter your floor's number. The next prompt is

```
Enter direction you want to go (u or d):
```

If you're on the first floor you must go up, and if you're on the 20th floor you must go down. For intermediate floors you can go either way. When you've completed your floor request, a triangle will appear next to the appropriate floor number on the left. It will point either up or down, depending on the direction you requested. As more requests are made, triangles will appear beside additional floor numbers.

If there is an elevator car already at a floor where a request has been made, the door will open immediately. You'll see a happy-face character materialize outside the car, then move into the open door. If there is no car on the floor making the request, one will move up or down toward the floor and open its door once it reaches the floor.

Entering Destinations

Once a car arrives at a floor and the happy-face passenger is inside, a prompt appears on the bottom of the screen:

```
Car 1 has stopped at floor 1
Enter destination floors (0 when finished)
Destination 1: 13
```

Here the passenger has entered 13. However, the happy face can represent more than one passenger getting on at once. Each passenger may request a different destination, so the program allows multiple destinations to be entered. Enter as many numbers as you want (at least 1, but no more than 20) and enter 0 when you're done.

The destinations requested by passengers within a particular car are indicated by small rectangles displayed outside the car, just to its left, opposite the floor number requested. Each car has its own set of destinations (unlike floor requests, which are shared by all the cars).

You can make as many floor requests as you like. The system will remember the requests, along with the destinations selected from within each car, and attempt to service them all. All four cars may be in motion at the same time. Figure 13.5 shows a situation with multiple floor requests and multiple destinations.

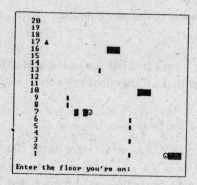

FIGURE 13.5
Elevators in action.

Designing the System

The elevator cars are all roughly the same, so it seems reasonable to make them objects of a single class, called elevator. This class will contain data specific to each car: its present location, the direction it's going, the destination floor numbers requested by its occupants, and so on.

However, there is also data that applies to the building as a whole. This data will be part of the building class. First there is an array of *floor requests*. This is a list of floors where people, waiting for the elevator, have pushed the up or down button to request that an elevator stop at their floor. Any elevator may respond to such a floor request, so each one needs to know about them. We use an N-by-2 array of type bool, where N is the number of floors and the 2 allows separate array elements for up and down for each floor. All the elevators can look at this array when they're trying to figure out where to go next.

Besides knowing about the floor requests, each elevator car must also be aware of where the other elevators are. If we're on the first floor, there's no point in rushing up to the 15th floor to answer a request if there's already another car available on the 10th floor. The closest car should head toward the request. To make it easy for each car to find out about the others, the second data item in building is an array of pointers to elevators. Each elevator car stores its memory address on this list when it's first created, so the other cars can find it.

The third data item in the building class is the number of cars created so far. This allows each car to number itself sequentially when it's created.

Managing Time

The main() program calls a member function of building at fixed intervals to put things into motion. This function is called master_tick(). It in turn calls a function for each elevator car, called car_tick1(). This function, among other things, displays each car on the screen and calls another function to decide what the car should do next. The choices are to go up, to go down, to stop, to load a passenger, or to unload a passenger.

Each car must then be moved to its new position. However, things get slightly complicated here. Because each car must figure out where the other ones are before it can decide what to do, all the cars must go through the decision process before any of them moves. To make sure this happens, we use two time ticks for each car. Thus after car_tick1() has been called to decide where each car will go, another function, car_tick2(), is called to actually move each car. It causes the cars to move by changing the variable current_floor.

The process of loading passengers follows a fixed sequence of steps, during which the car is stopped at the desired floor. The program draws, in order

1. Car with closed door, no happy face.
2. Car with open door, happy face on left.
3. Car with happy face in open door, get destinations from user.
4. Car with closed door, no happy face.

The reverse sequence applies to unloading. These sequences are carried out by starting a timer (an integer variable) and letting it count down from 3 to 0, decrementing it with each time tick. A case statement in the car_display() function then draws the appropriate version of the car for each stage of the process.

Because the ELEV program uses various console graphics functions, it requires a header file available from this book's publisher; either MSOFTCON.H for Microsoft compilers or BORLACON.H for Borland compilers. (See Appendix E, "Console Graphics Lite.")

Listings for ELEV

We've divided the program into four files. Two of these files, ELEV.H and ELEV.CPP, might be created by a vendor supplying elevator-control software. This software would then be purchased by an engineering company interested in designing an elevator system for a particular building. (This program is not certified by the National Elevator Board, so don't try it with real elevators.) The engineering company would then write another pair of files, ELEV_APP.H and ELEV_APP.CPP. The ELEV_APP.H file specifies the characteristics of the high-rise building. It needs to be a separate file because these characteristics must be known by the elevator class member functions, and the easiest way to do this is to include ELEV_APP.H in the ELEV.H file. The ELEV_APP.CPP file initializes the elevators and then calls elevator functions at fixed intervals to simulate the passage of time.

Class Specifier

The ELEV.H file contains the specification for the elevator class. The array of pointers to elevators, car_list[], allows each elevator to query all the others about their location and direction. Here's the listing:

```
// elev.h
// header file for elevators -- contains class declarations

#include "elev_app.h"              //provided by client
#include "msoftcon.h"              //for console graphics
#include <iostream>
#include <iomanip>                 //for setw()
#include <conio.h>                 //for screen output
#include <stdlib.h>                //for itoa()
#include <process.h>               //for exit()
using namespace std;

enum direction { UP, DN, STOP };
const int LOAD_TIME  =   3;    //loading/unloading time (ticks)
const int SPACING    =   7;    //visual spacing between cars
const int BUF_LENGTH =  80;    //length of utility string buffer
```

```
class building;                    //forward declaration
//////////////////////////////////////////////////////////////
class elevator
    {
    private:
    building* ptrBuilding;         //ptr to parent building
    const int car_number;          //our number (0 to nc-1)
    int current_floor;             //where are we? (0 to nf-1)
    int old_floor;                 //where were we? (0 to nf-1)
    direction current_dir;         //which way are we going?
    bool destination[NUM_FLOORS];  //selected by occupants
    int loading_timer;             //non-zero if loading
    int unloading_timer;           //non-zero if unloading

    public:
    elevator(building*, int);      //constructor
    void car_tick1();              //time tick 1 for each car
    void car_tick2();              //time tick 2 for each car
    void car_display();            //display elevator
    void dests_display() const;    //display elevator requests
    void decide();                 //decide what to do
    void move();                   //move the car
    void get_destinations();       //get destinations
    int get_floor() const;         //get current floor
    direction get_direction() const;  //get current direction
    };
//////////////////////////////////////////////////////////////
class building
    {
    private:
    elevator* car_list[NUM_CARS];  //ptrs to cars
    int num_cars;                  //cars created so far
                                   //array of up/down buttons
    bool floor_request[2][NUM_FLOORS]; //false=UP, true=DN

    public:
    building();                    //constructor
    ~building();                   //destructor
    void master_tick();            //send ticks to all cars
    int get_cars_floor(const int) const; //find where a car is
                                   //find which way car is going
    direction get_cars_dir(const int) const;
                                   //check specific floor req
    bool get_floor_req(const int, const int) const;
                                   //set specific floor req
```

```
void set_floor_req(const int, const int, const bool);
void record_floor_reqs();      //get floor requests
void show_floor_reqs() const;  //show floor requests
};
```

Member Functions

The ELEV.CPP file contains the definitions of the elevator class and building class member functions and data. Functions in building initialize the system, provide a master time tick, display the floor requests, and get floor requests from the user. Functions in elevator initialize individual cars (with the constructor), provide two time ticks for each car, display it, display its destinations, decide what to do, move the car to a new floor, and get destinations from the user. Here's the listing:

```
// elev.cpp
// contains class data and member function definitions

#include "elev.h"      //include class declarations
/////////////////////////////////////////////////////////////////
//            function definitions for class building
/////////////////////////////////////////////////////////////////
building::building()                //constructor
   {
   char ustring[BUF_LENGTH];        //string for floor numbers

   init_graphics();                 //initialize graphics
   clear_screen();                  //clear screen
   num_cars = 0;
   for(int k=0; k<NUM_CARS; k++)     //make elevators
      {
      car_list[k] = new elevator(this, num_cars);
      num_cars++;
      }
   for(int j=0; j<NUM_FLOORS; j++)   //for each floor
      {
      set_cursor_pos(3, NUM_FLOORS-j); //put floor number
      itoa(j+1, ustring, 10);          //on screen
      cout << setw(3) << ustring;
      floor_request[UP][j] = false;   //no floor requests yet
      floor_request[DN][j] = false;
      }
   } //end constructor
//-----------------------------------------------------------------
building::~building()               //destructor
   {
   for(int k=0 k<NUM_CARS; k++)
      delete car_list[k];
   }
```

```
//------------------------------------------------------------
void building::master_tick()              //master time tick
   {
   int j;
   show_floor_reqs();                      //display floor requests
   for(j=0; j<NUM_CARS; j++)               //for each elevator
      car_list[j]->car_tick1();            //send it time tick 1
   for(j=0; j<NUM_CARS; j++)               //for each elevator
      car_list[j]->car_tick2();            //send it time tick 2
   } //end master_tick()
//------------------------------------------------------------
void building::show_floor_reqs() const  //display floor requests
   {
   for(int j=0; j<NUM_FLOORS; j++)
      {
      set_cursor_pos(SPACING, NUM_FLOORS-j);
      if(floor_request[UP][j]==true)
         cout << '\x1E';                  //up arrow
      else
         cout << ' ';
      set_cursor_pos(SPACING+3, NUM_FLOORS-j);
      if(floor_request[DN][j]==true)
         cout << '\x1F';                  //down arrow
      else
         cout << ' ';
      }
   } //end show_floor_reqs()
//------------------------------------------------------------
//record_floor_reqs() -- get requests from riders outside car
void building::record_floor_reqs()
   {
   char ch = 'x';               //utility char for input
   char ustring[BUF_LENGTH];    //utility string for input
   int iFloor;                  //floor from which request made
   char chDirection;            //'u' or 'd' for up or down

   set_cursor_pos(1,22);        //bottom of screen
   cout << "Press [Enter] to call an elevator: ";
   if( !kbhit() )               //wait for keypress (must be CR)
      return;
   cin.ignore(10, '\n');
   if(ch=='\x1B')               //if escape key, end program
      exit(0);
   set_cursor_pos(1,22); clear_line();  //clear old text
   set_cursor_pos(1,22);        //bottom of screen
   cout << "Enter the floor you're on: ";
```

```
      cin.get(ustring, BUF_LENGTH);          //get floor
      cin.ignore(10, '\n');        //eat chars, including newline
      iFloor = atoi(ustring);      //convert to integer

      cout << "Enter direction you want to go (u or d): ";
      cin.get(chDirection);        //(avoid multiple linefeeds)
      cin.ignore(10, '\n');        //eat chars, including newline

      if(chDirection=='u' || chDirection=='U')
         floor_request[UP][iFloor-1] = true;  //up floor request
      if(chDirection=='d' || chDirection=='D')
         floor_request[DN][iFloor-1] = true;  //down floor request
      set_cursor_pos(1,22); clear_line();     //clear old text
      set_cursor_pos(1,23); clear_line();
      set_cursor_pos(1,24); clear_line();
      } //end record_floor_reqs()
//·····························································
//get_floor_req() ·· see if there's a specific request
bool building::get_floor_req(const int dir,
                             const int floor) const
   {
   return floor_request[dir][floor];
   }
//··························································
//set_floor_req() -- set specific floor request
void building::set_floor_req(const int dir, const int floor,
                             const bool updown)
   {
   floor_request[dir][floor] = updown;
   }
//··························································
//get_cars_floor() -- find where a car is
int building::get_cars_floor(const int carNo) const
   {
   return car_list[carNo]->get_floor();
   }
//··························································
//get_cars_dir() -- find which way car is going
direction building::get_cars_dir(const int carNo) const
   {
   return car_list[carNo]->get_direction();
   }
//··························································

////////////////////////////////////////////////////////////////
//          function definitions for class elevator
////////////////////////////////////////////////////////////////
```

```
                          //constructor
elevator::elevator(building* ptrB, int nc) :
                        ptrBuilding(ptrB), car_number(nc)
   {
   current_floor = 0;                //start at 0 (user's 1)
   old_floor = 0;                    //remember previous floor
   current_dir = STOP;               //stationary at start
   for(int j=0; j<NUM_FLOORS; j++)   //occupants have not pushed
      destination[j] = false;        //   any buttons yet
   loading_timer = 0;                //not loading yet
   unloading_timer = 0;              //not unloading yet
                             } //end constructor
//............................................................
int elevator::get_floor() const      //get current floor
   {
   return current_floor;
   }
//............................................................
direction elevator::get_direction() const  //get current
   {                                        //   direction
   return current_dir;
   }
//............................................................
void elevator::car_tick1()           //tick 1 for each car
   {
   car_display();                    //display elevator box
   dests_display();                  //display destinations
   if(loading_timer)                 //count down load time
      --loading_timer;
   if(unloading_timer)               //count down unload time
      --unloading_timer;
   decide();                         //decide what to do
   } //end car_tick()
//............................................................
//all cars must decide before any of them move
void elevator::car_tick2()           //tick 2 for each car
   {
   move();                           //move car if appropriate
   }
//............................................................
void elevator::car_display()         //display elevator image
   {
   set_cursor_pos(SPACING+(car_number+1)*SPACING, NUM_FLOORS-old_floor);
   cout << "   ";                    //erase old position
   set_cursor_pos(SPACING-1+(car_number+1)*SPACING,
                              NUM_FLOORS-current_floor);
```

13

MULTIFILE
PROGRAMS

```
      switch(loading_timer)
         {
         case 3:
            cout << "\x01\xDB \xDB ";      //draw car with open door
            break;                          //happy face on left
         case 2:
            cout << " \xDB\x01\xDB ";        //happy face in open door
            get_destinations();             //get destinations
            break;
         case 1:
            cout << " \xDB\xDB\xDB ";         //draw with closed door
            break;                          //no happy face
         case 0:
            cout << " \xDB\xDB\xDB ";         //closed door, no
            break;                          //happy face (default)
         }
      set_cursor_pos(SPACING+(car_number+1)*SPACING,
                                  NUM_FLOORS-current_floor);
      switch(unloading_timer)
         {
         case 3:
            cout << "\xDB\x01\xDB ";         //draw car with open door
            break;                          //happy face in car
         case 2:
            cout << "\xDB \xDB\x01";         //draw car with open door
            break;                          //happy face on right
         case 1:
            cout << "\xDB\xDB\xDB ";          //draw with closed door
            break;                          //no happy face
         case 0:
            cout << "\xDB\xDB\xDB ";          //closed door, no
            break;                          //happy face (default)
         }
      old_floor = current_floor;           //remember old floor
      } //end car_display()
//···············································································
void elevator::dests_display() const //display destinations
      {                               //    selected by buttons
      for(int j=0; j<NUM_FLOORS; j++)  //    inside the car
         {
         set_cursor_pos(SPACING-2+(car_number+1)*SPACING, NUM_FLOORS-j);
         if( destination[j] == true )
            cout << '\xFE';             //small box
         else
            cout << ' ';               //blank
         }
```

```
    } //end dests_display()
//-------------------------------------------------------------
void elevator::decide()                    //decide what to do
    {
    int j;
    //flags indicate if destinations or requests above/below us
    bool destins_above, destins_below;     //destinations
    bool requests_above, requests_below;   //requests
    //floor number of closest request above us and below us
    int nearest_higher_req = 0;
    int nearest_lower_req = 0;
    //flags indicate if there is another car, going in the same
    //direction, between us and the nearest floor request (FR)
    bool car_between_up, car_between_dn;
    //flags indicate if there is another car, going in the
    //opposite direction, on the opposite side of the nearest FR
    bool car_opposite_up, car_opposite_dn;
    //floor and direction of other car (not us)
    int ofloor;                            //floor
    direction odir;                        //direction

    //ensure we don't go too high or too low
    if( (current_floor==NUM_FLOORS-1 && current_dir==UP)
        || (current_floor==0 && current_dir==DN) )
        current_dir = STOP;

    //if there's a destination on this floor, unload passengers
    if( destination[current_floor]==true )
        {
        destination[current_floor] = false;  //erase destination
        if( !unloading_timer)                //unload
            unloading_timer = LOAD_TIME;
        return;
        }
    //if there's an UP floor request on this floor,
    //and if we're going up or stopped, load passengers
    if( (ptrBuilding->get_floor_req(UP, current_floor) &&
         current_dir != DN) )
        {
        current_dir = UP;  //(in case it was STOP)
        //remove floor request for direction we're going
        ptrBuilding->set_floor_req(current_dir,
                            current_floor, false);
        if( !loading_timer)                  //load
            loading_timer = LOAD_TIME;
        return;
```

```
      }
//if there's a down floor request on this floor,
//and if we're going down or stopped, load passengers
if( (ptrBuilding->get_floor_req(DN, current_floor) &&
    current_dir != UP) )
    {
    current_dir = DN;   //(in case it was STOP)
    //remove floor request for direction we're going
    ptrBuilding->set_floor_req(current_dir,
                              current_floor, false);
    if( !loading_timer)                    //load passengers
       loading_timer = LOAD_TIME;
    return;
    }
//check if there are other destinations or requests
//record distance to nearest request
destins_above = destins_below = false;
requests_above = requests_below = false;
for(j=current_floor+1; j<NUM_FLOORS; j++)
    {                                   //check floors above
    if( destination[j] )                //if destinations
       destins_above = true;            //set flag
    if( ptrBuilding->get_floor_req(UP, j) ||
        ptrBuilding->get_floor_req(DN, j) )
        {                               //if requests
        requests_above = true;          //set flag
        if( !nearest_higher_req )       //if not set before
           nearest_higher_req = j;      //   set nearest req
        }
    }
for(j=current_floor-1; j>=0; j--)       //check floors below
    {
    if(destination[j] )                 //if destinations
       destins_below = true;            //set flag
    if( ptrBuilding->get_floor_req(UP, j) ||
        ptrBuilding->get_floor_req(DN, j) )
        {                               //if requests
        requests_below = true;          //set flag
        if( !nearest_lower_req )        //if not set before
           nearest_lower_req = j;       //   set nearest req
        }
    }
//if no requests or destinations above or below, stop
if( !destins_above && !requests_above &&
    !destins_below && !requests_below)
    {
```

```
         current_dir = STOP;
         return;
         }
//if destinations and we're stopped, or already going the
//right way, go toward destinations
if( destins_above && (current_dir==STOP || current_dir==UP) )
      {
      current_dir = UP;
      return;
      }
if( destins_below && (current_dir==STOP || current_dir==DN) )
      {
      current_dir = DN;
      return;
      }
//find out if there are other cars, (a) going in the same
//direction, between us and the nearest floor request;
//or (b) going in the opposite direction, on the other
//side of the floor request
car_between_up = car_between_dn = false;
car_opposite_up = car_opposite_dn = false;

for(j=0; j<NUM_CARS; j++)                //check each car
      {
      if(j != car_number)                      //if it's not us
         {                                      //get its floor
         ofloor = ptrBuilding->get_cars_floor(j);   //and
         odir = ptrBuilding->get_cars_dir(j); //direction

         //if it's going up and there are requests above us
         if( (odir==UP || odir==STOP) && requests_above )
            //if it's above us and below the nearest request
            if( (ofloor > current_floor
               && ofloor <= nearest_higher_req)
            //or on same floor as us but is lower car number
              || (ofloor==current_floor && j < car_number) )
               car_between_up = true;
         //if it's going down and there are requests below us
         if( (odir==DN || odir==STOP) && requests_below )
            //if it's below us and above the nearest request
            if( (ofloor < current_floor
               && ofloor >= nearest_lower_req)
               //or on same floor as us but is lower car number
               || (ofloor==current_floor && j < car_number) )
               car_between_dn = true;
         //if it's going up and there are requests below us
```

```
         if( (odir==UP || odir==STOP) && requests_below )
            //it's below request and closer to it than we are
            if(nearest_lower_req >= ofloor
               && nearest_lower_req - ofloor
                  < current_floor - nearest_lower_req)
               car_opposite_up = true;
         //if it's going down and there are requests above us
         if( (odir==DN || odir==STOP) && requests_above )
            //it's above request and closer to it than we are
            if(ofloor >= nearest_higher_req
               && ofloor - nearest_higher_req
                  < nearest_higher_req - current_floor)
               car_opposite_dn = true;
      }  //end if(not us)
   }  //end for(each car)

   //if we're going up or stopped, and there is an FR above us,
   //and there are no other cars going up between us and the FR,
   //or above the FR going down and closer than we are,
   //then go up
   if( (current_dir==UP || current_dir==STOP)
      && requests_above && !car_between_up && !car_opposite_dn )
      {
      current_dir = UP;
      return;
      }

   //if we're going down or stopped, and there is an FR below
   //us, and there are no other cars going down between us and
   //the FR, or below the FR going up and closer than we are,
   //then go down
   if( (current_dir==DN || current_dir==STOP)
      && requests_below && !car_between_dn && !car_opposite_up )
      {
      current_dir = DN;
      return;
      }
   //if nothing else happening, stop
   current_dir = STOP;
   }  //end decide(), finally
//··················································································
void elevator::move()
   {                             //if loading or unloading,
   if(loading_timer || unloading_timer)  //don't move
      return;
   if(current_dir==UP)           //if going up, go up
```

```
      current_floor++;
   else if(current_dir==DN)     //if going down, go down
      current_floor--;
   } //end move()
//·············································································
void elevator::get_destinations()       //stop, get destinations
   {
   char ustring[BUF_LENGTH];              //utility buffer for input
   int dest_floor;                        //destination floor

   set_cursor_pos(1,22); clear_line();  //clear top line
   set_cursor_pos(1, 22);
   cout << "Car " << (car_number+1)
       << " has stopped at floor " << (current_floor+1)
       << "\nEnter destination floors (0 when finished)";
   for(int j=1; j<NUM_FLOORS; j++)     //get floor requests
      {                                //maximum; usually fewer
      set_cursor_pos(1, 24);
      cout << "Destination " << j << ": ";

      cin.get(ustring, BUF_LENGTH);   //(avoid multiple LFs)
      cin.ignore(10, '\n');          //eat chars, including newline
      dest_floor = atoi(ustring);
      set_cursor_pos(1,24); clear_line(); //clear old input line
      if(dest_floor==0)                //if no more requests,
         {                             //clear bottom three lines
         set_cursor_pos(1,22); clear_line();
         set_cursor_pos(1,23); clear_line();
         set_cursor_pos(1,24); clear_line();
         return;
         }
      --dest_floor;                    //start at 0, not 1
      if(dest_floor==current_floor)    //chose this very floor
         { --j; continue; }            //  so forget it
      //if we're stopped, first choice made sets direction
      if(j==1 && current_dir==STOP)
         current_dir = (dest_floor < current_floor) ? DN : UP;
      destination[dest_floor] = true; //record selection
      dests_display();                //display destinations
      }
   } //end get_destinations()
```

Application

The next two files, ELEV_APP.H and ELEV_APP.CPP, are created by someone with a particular
building in mind. They want to customize the software for their building. ELEV_APP.H does this
by defining two constants that specify the number of floors and the number of elevators the
building will have. Here's its listing:

```
// elev_app.h
// provides constants to specify building characteristics

const int NUM_FLOORS = 20;    //number of floors
const int NUM_CARS = 4;       //number of elevator cars
```

ELEV_APP.CPP initializes the data in the building class and creates a number of elevator objects, using new. (An array could also be used.) Then, in a loop, it calls the building functions master_tick() and get_floor_requests() over and over. The wait() function (declared in MSOFTCON.H or BORLACON.H) slows things down to a human-oriented speed. When the user is answering a prompt, time (the program's time, as opposed to the user's time) stops. Here's the listing for ELEV_APP.CPP:

```
// elev_app.cpp
// client-supplied file

#include "elev.h"              //for class declarations

int main()
   {
   building theBuilding;
   while(true)
     {
     theBuilding.master_tick(); //send time tick to all cars
     wait(1000);                //pause
                                //get floor requests from user
     theBuilding.record_floor_reqs();
     }
   return 0;
   }
```

Elevator Strategy

Building the necessary intelligence into the elevator cars is not a simple task. It's handled in the decide() function, which consists of a series of rules. These rules are arranged in order of priority. If any one applies, the appropriate action is carried out; the following rules are not queried. Here is a slightly simplified version:

1. If the elevator is about to crash into the bottom of the shaft, or through the roof, stop.

2. If this is a destination floor, unload the passengers.

3. If there is an up floor request on this floor, and we are going up, load the passengers.

4. Is there is a down floor request on this floor, and we are going down, load the passengers.

5. If there are no destinations or requests above or below, stop.

6. If there are destinations above us, go up.

7. If there are destinations below us, go down.

8. If we're stopped or going up, and there is a floor request above us, and there are no other cars going up between us and the request, or above it and going down and closer than we are, go up.

9. If we're stopped or going down, and there is a floor request below us, and there are no other cars going down between us and the request, or below it and going up and closer than we are, go down.

10. If no other rules apply, stop.

Rules 8 and 9 are rather complicated. They attempt to keep two or more cars from rushing to answer the same floor request. However, the results are not perfect. In some situations cars are slow to answer requests because they are afraid another car is on its way, when in fact the other car is answering a different floor request. The program's strategy could be improved by allowing the decide() function to distinguish between up and down requests when it checks whether there are requests above or below the current car. However, this would further complicate decide(), which is already long enough. We'll leave such refinements to you.

State Diagram for the ELEV Program

We introduced UML state diagrams in Chapter 10, "Pointers." Now let's look at a state diagram for an elevator object. To simplify things a little, we'll assume that there is only one person in the building and only one elevator in use. Thus there can be only one floor request at a time, and only one destination selected by the rider. The elevator car doesn't need to worry about what the other cars are doing. Figure 13.6 shows how this looks.

In the diagram, "cd" stands for car destination, the button pushed inside the car, roughly corresponding to a value in the destination array in the program. Also, "fr" stands for floor request, the button pushed outside the car, corresponding to the floor_req variable.

The states are derived from the values of the current_dir variable plus the status of the car's loading_timer and unloading_timer. Because all the transitions are the result of time ticks, only the guard conditions are shown. The guards represent what the car finds out about floor requests and car destinations.

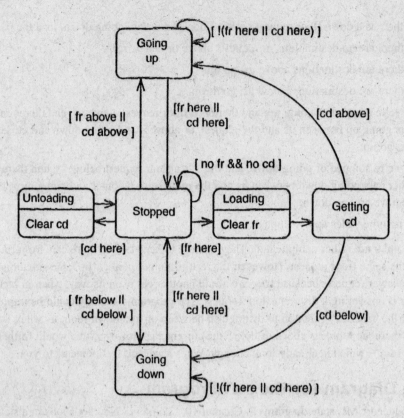

FIGURE 13.6
State diagram of an elevator *object.*

Summary

Vendor-provided object libraries are often distributed as a public component (the interface) containing class declarations in an .H header file, and a private component (the implementation) containing member function definitions in an .OBJ object file or .LIB library file.

C++ compilers allow you to combine several source or object files into a single executable file. This permits files provided by one vendor to be combined with files from another, to create a final application. The project feature simplifies keeping track of what files need to be compiled. It compiles any source file that has been modified since the last linking, and links the resulting object files.

Inter-file communication requires that variables, functions and class objects be defined in one file and declared in any other file where they're used. A class definition must be placed in every file where objects are instantiated. Care must be taken with both source files and header files to ensure that multiple definitions don't occur.

Questions

Answers to these questions can be found in Appendix G.

1. Breaking a program into several files is desirable because

   a. some files don't need to be recompiled each time.

   b. a program can be divided functionally.

   c. files can be marketed in object form.

   d. different programmers can work on a different files.

2. An .H file is associated with a .CPP file using the _____.

3. An .OBJ file is attached to a .CPP file using _____.

4. A *project* file contains

   a. the contents of the files in the project.

   b. the dates of the files in the project.

   c. instructions for compiling and linking.

   d. definitions for C++ variables.

5. A group of related classes, supplied as a separate product, is often called a _____.

6. True or false: A header file may need to be accessed by more than one source file in a project.

7. The so-called private files of a class library

   a. require a password.

   b. can be accessed by friend functions.

   c. help prevent code from being pirated.

   d. may consist only of object code.

8. True or false: Class libraries can be more powerful than function libraries.

9. True or false: the interface is private and the implementation is public.

10. The public part of a class library usually contains

    a. member function declarations.

    b. member function definitions.

    c. class declarations.

    d. definitions of inline functions.

11. Two or more source files can be combined by _____ them.

12. True or false: a variable defined within a function body can be seen thoughout the file in which it's defined.

13. A global variable is defined in file A. To access the variable in file B, you must

    a. define it in file B using the keyword extern.

    b. define it in file B using the keyword static.

    c. no other action is necessary (do nothing).

    d. declare it in file B using the keyword extern.

14. The region in a program where a variable can be accessed by variables in other parts of the program is called its _____.

15. The files that are actually combined by the linker are called _____ files.

16. A function is defined in file A. To call it from file B, the function must first be _____ in _____ .

17. True or false: a function declaration does not require the keyword extern.

18. To define class objects in different files, in each file you must

    a. declare the class.

    b. define the class.

    c. declare the class using extern.

    d. define the class using extern.

19. True or false: a variable defined in a header file can be accessed from two source files if they both include the header file.

20. The #if !defined()...#endif construction can be used to prevent multiple definitions when

    a. Two header files are included in a source file.

    b. A header file is included in two source files.

    c. Two header files are included in two source files.

    d. A header file is included in another header file and both are included in a source file.

21. You use namespaces to

    a. Automate the naming of variables.

    b. Restrict the area where program elements are visible.

    c. Divide a program into separate files.

    d. Prevent the use of long variable names.

22. To define a namespace you use a format similar to a class definition, but substitute the keyword _____ for class.

23. Using typedef allows you to

a. shorten long variable names.

b. substitute one type name for another.

c. shorten long function names.

d. substitute one class name for another.

Projects

Unfortunately, we don't have room in this book for exercises that involve the kind of larger programs discussed in this chapter. However, here are some suggestions for projects you may wish to pursue on your own.

1. Create member functions to perform subtraction and division for the verylong class in the VERYLONG example. These should overload the - and / operators. Warning: There's some work involved here. When you include subtraction, you must assume that any verylong can be negative as well as positive. This complicates the addition and multiplication routines, which must do different things depending on the signs of the numbers.

   To see one way to perform division, do a long-division example by hand and write down every step. Then incorporate these steps into a division member function. You'll find that you need some comparisons, so you'll need to write a comparison routine, among other things.

2. Rewrite the ELEV program so that it handles only one elevator. This will simplify things a great deal. Remove those parts of the program that aren't necessary. Or you can assume there is only one elevator and also only one rider, as is done in the state diagram.

3. Modify the ELEV program to be more efficient in the way it handles requests. As an example of its current non-optimal behavior, start the program and make a down request on floor 20. Then make a down request on floor 10. Car 1 will immediately head up to 20, but car 2, which should head up to 10, waits until car 1 has passed 10 before starting. Modify decide() so this doesn't happen.

4. Create a class library that models something you're interested in. Create a main() or "client" program to test it. Market your class library and become rich and famous.

Templates and Exceptions

IN THIS CHAPTER

This chapter introduces two advanced C++ features: templates and exceptions. Templates make it possible to use one function or class to handle many different data types. Exceptions provide a convenient, uniform way to handle errors that occur within classes. These features are combined in a single chapter largely for historical reasons: they became part of C++ at the same time. They were not part of the original specification for C++, but were introduced as "Experimental" topics in Ellis and Stroustrup (1990, see Appendix H, "Bibliography"). Subsequently they were incorporated into Standard C++.

The template concept can be used in two different ways: with functions and with classes. We'll look at function templates first, then go on to class templates, and finally to exceptions.

Function Templates

Suppose you want to write a function that returns the absolute value of two numbers. As you no doubt remember from high school algebra, the absolute value of a number is its value without regard to its sign: The absolute value of 3 is 3, and the absolute value of −3 is also 3. Ordinarily this function would be written for a particular data type:

```
int abs(int n)              //absolute value of ints
   {
   return (n<0) ? -n : n;  //if n is negative, return -n
   }
```

Here the function is defined to take an argument of type int and to return a value of this same type. But now suppose you want to find the absolute value of a type long. You will need to write a completely new function:

```
long abs(long n)           //absolute value of longs
   {
   return (n<0) ? -n : n;
   }
```

And again, for type float:

```
float abs(float n)         //absolute value of floats
   {
   return (n<0) ? -n : n;
   }
```

The body of the function is written the same way in each case, but they are completely different functions because they handle arguments and return values of different types. It's true that in C++ these functions can all be overloaded to have the same name, but you must nevertheless write a separate definition for each one. (In the C language, which does not support overloading, functions for different types can't even have the same name. In the C function library this leads to families of similarly named functions, such as abs(), fabs(), fabsl(), labs(), and cabs().

Rewriting the same function body over and over for different types is time-consuming and wastes space in the listing. Also, if you find you've made an error in one such function, you'll need to remember to correct it in each function body. Failing to do this correctly is a good way to introduce inconsistencies into your program.

It would be nice if there were a way to write such a function just once, and have it work for many different data types. This is exactly what function templates do for you. The idea is shown schematically in Figure 14.1.

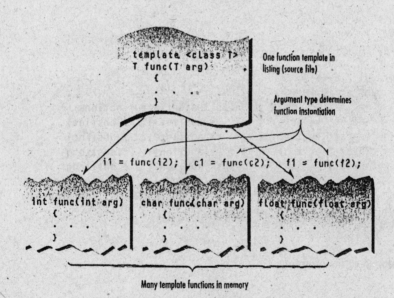

FIGURE 14.1
A function template.

A Simple Function Template

Our first example shows how to write our absolute-value function as a template, so that it will work with any basic numerical type. This program defines a template version of abs() and then, in main(), invokes this function with different data types to prove that it works. Here's the listing for TEMPABS:

```cpp
// tempabs.cpp
// template used for absolute value function
#include <iostream>
using namespace std;
//..........................................................
template <class T>              //function template
T abs(T n)
    {
    return (n < 0) ? -n : n;
    }
//..........................................................
int main()
    {
    int int1 = 5;
    int int2 = -6;
    long lon1 = 70000L;
    long lon2 = -80000L;
    double dub1 = 9.95;
    double dub2 = -10.15;
                                //calls instantiate functions
    cout << "\nabs(" << int1 << ")=" << abs(int1);  //abs(int)
    cout << "\nabs(" << int2 << ")=" << abs(int2);  //abs(int)
    cout << "\nabs(" << lon1 << ")=" << abs(lon1);  //abs(long)
    cout << "\nabs(" << lon2 << ")=" << abs(lon2);  //abs(long)
    cout << "\nabs(" << dub1 << ")=" << abs(dub1);  //abs(double)
    cout << "\nabs(" << dub2 << ")=" << abs(dub2);  //abs(double)
    cout << endl;
    return 0;
    }
```

Here's the output of the program:

```
abs(5)=5
abs(-6)=6
abs(70000)=70000
abs(-80000)=80000
abs(9.95)=9.95
abs(-10.15)=10.15
```

As you can see, the abs() function now works with all three of the data types (int, long, and double) that we use as arguments. It will work on other basic numerical types as well, and it will even work on user-defined data types, provided that the less-than operator (<) and the unary minus operator (-) are appropriately overloaded.

Here's how we specify the abs() function to work with multiple data types:

```
template <class T>              //function template
T abs(T n)
    {
    return (n<0) ? -n : n;
    }
```

This entire syntax, with a first line starting with the keyword template and the function definition following, is called a *function template*. How does this new way of writing abs() give it such amazing flexibility?

Function Template Syntax

The key innovation in function templates is to represent the data type used by the function not as a specific type such as int, but by a name that can stand for *any* type. In the preceding function template, this name is T. (There's nothing magic about this name; it can be anything you want, like Type, or anyType, or FooBar.) The template keyword signals the compiler that we're about to define a function template. The keyword class, within the angle brackets, might just as well be called type. As we've seen, you can define your own data types using classes, so there's really no distinction between types and classes. The variable following the keyword class (T in this example) is called the *template argument*.

Throughout the definition of the template, whenever a specific data type such as int would ordinarily be written, we substitute the template argument, T. In the abs() template this name appears only twice, both in the first line (the function declarator), as the argument type and return type. In more complex functions it may appear numerous times throughout the function body as well.

What the Compiler Does

What does the compiler do when it sees the template keyword and the function definition that follows it? Well, nothing right away. The function template itself doesn't cause the compiler to generate any code. It can't generate code because it doesn't know yet what data type the function will be working with. It simply remembers the template for possible future use.

Code generation doesn't take place until the function is actually called (invoked) by a statement within the program. In TEMPABS this happens in expressions like abs(int1) in the statement

```
cout << "\nabs(" << int << ")=" << abs(int1);
```

When the compiler sees such a function call, it knows that the type to use is int, because that's the type of the argument int1. So it generates a specific version of the abs() function for type int, substituting int wherever it sees the name T in the function template. This is called *instantiating* the function template, and each instantiated version of the function is called a *template function*. (That is, a *template function* is a specific instance of a *function template*. Isn't English fun?)

The compiler also generates a call to the newly instantiated function, and inserts it into the code where abs(int1) is. Similarly, the expression abs(lon1) causes the compiler to generate a version of abs() that operates on type long and a call to this function, while the abs(dub1) call generates a function that works on type double. Of course, the compiler is smart enough to generate only one version of abs() for each data type. Thus, even though there are two calls to the int version of the function, the code for this version appears only once in the executable code.

Simplifying the Listing

Notice that the amount of RAM used by the program is the same whether we use the template approach or actually write three separate functions. The template approaches simply saves us from having to type three separate functions into the source file. This makes the listing shorter and easier to understand. Also, if we want to change the way the function works, we need to make the change in only one place in the listing instead of three places.

The Deciding Argument

The compiler decides how to compile the function based entirely on the data type used in the function call's argument (or arguments). The function's return type doesn't enter into this decision. This is similar to the way the compiler decides which of several overloaded functions to call.

Another Kind of Blueprint

We've seen that a function template isn't really a function, since it does not actually cause program code to be placed in memory. Instead it is a pattern, or blueprint, for making many functions. This fits right into the philosophy of OOP. It's similar to the way a class isn't anything concrete (such as program code in memory), but a blueprint for making many similar objects.

Function Templates with Multiple Arguments

Let's look at another example of a function template. This one takes three arguments: two that are template arguments and one of a basic type. The purpose of this function is to search an array for a specific value. The function returns the array index for that value if it finds it, or −1 if it can't find it. The arguments are a pointer to the array, the value to search for, and the size of the array. In main() we define four different arrays of different types, and four values to search for. We treat type char as a number. Then we call the template function once for each array. Here's the listing for TEMPFIND:

```
// tempfind.cpp
// template used for function that finds number in array
#include <iostream>
using namespace std;
//-----------------------------------------------------------
//function returns index number of item, or -1 if not found
template <class atype>
int find(atype* array, atype value, int size)
   {
   for(int j=0; j<size; j++)
      if(array[j]==value)
         return j;
   return -1;
   }
//-----------------------------------------------------------
char chrArr[] =   {1, 3, 5, 9, 11, 13};  //array
char ch = 5;                             //value to find
int intArr[] =    {1, 3, 5, 9, 11, 13};
int in = 6;
long lonArr[] =   {1L, 3L, 5L, 9L, 11L, 13L};
long lo = 11L;
double dubArr[] = {1.0, 3.0, 5.0, 9.0, 11.0, 13.0};
double db = 4.0;

int main()
   {
   cout << "\n 5 in chrArray: index=" << find(chrArr, ch, 6);
   cout << "\n 6 in intArray: index=" << find(intArr, in, 6);
   cout << "\n11 in lonArray: index=" << find(lonArr, lo, 6);
   cout << "\n 4 in dubArray: index=" << find(dubArr, db, 6);
   cout << endl;
   return 0;
   }
```

Here we name the template argument atype. It appears in two of the function's arguments: as the type of a pointer to the array, and as the type of the item to be matched. The third function argument, the array size, is always type int; it's not a template argument. Here's the output of the program:

```
 5 in chrArray: index=2
 6 in intArray: index=-1
11 in lonArray: index=4
 4 in dubArray: index=-1
```

The compiler generates four different versions of the function, one for each type used to call it. It finds a 5 at index 2 in the character array, does not find a 6 in the integer array, and so on.

Template Arguments Must Match

When a template function is invoked, all instances of the same template argument must be of the same type. For example, in find(), if the array name is of type int, the value to search for must also be of type int. You can't say

```
int intarray[] = {1, 3, 5, 7};        //int array
float f1 = 5.0;                        //float value
int value = find(intarray, f1, 4);    //uh, oh
```

because the compiler expects all instances of atype to be the same type. It can generate a function

```
find(int*, int, int);
```

but it can't generate

```
find(int*, float, int);
```

because the first and second arguments must be the same type.

Syntax Variation

Some programmers put the template keyword and the function declarator on the same line:

```
template<class atype> int find(atype* array, atype value, int size)
    {
    //function body
    }
```

Of course the compiler is happy enough with this format, but we find it more forbidding and less clear than the multiline approach.

More Than One Template Argument

You can use more than one template argument in a function template. For example, suppose you like the idea of the find() function template, but you aren't sure how large an array it might be applied to. If the array is too large then type long would be necessary for the array size, instead of type int. On the other hand, you don't want to use type long if you don't need to. You want to select the type of the array size, as well as the type of data stored, when you call the function. To make this possible, you could make the array size into a template argument as well. We'll call it btype:

```
template <class atype, class btype>
btype find(atype* array, atype value, btype size)
   {
   for(btype j=0; j<size; j++)    //n e use of btype
      if(array[j]==value)
         return j;
   return static_cast<btype>(-1);
   }
```

Now you can use either type int or type long (or even a user-defined type) for the size, whichever is appropriate. The compiler will generate different functions based not only on the type of the array and the value to be searched for, but also on the type of the array size.

Note that multiple template arguments can lead to many functions being instantiated from a single template. Two such arguments, if there were six basic types that could reasonably be used for each one, would allow the creation of 36 functions. This can take up a lot of memory if the functions are large. On the other hand, you don't instantiate a version of the function unless you actually call it.

Why Not Macros?

Old-time C programmers may wonder why we don't use macros to create different versions of a function for different data types. For example, the abs() function could be defined as

```
#define abs(n) ( (n<0) ? (-n) : (n) )
```

This has a similar effect to the class template in TEMPABS, because it performs a simple text substitution and can thus work with any type. However, as we've noted before, macros aren't much used in C++. There are several problems with them. One is that macros don't perform any type checking. There may be several arguments to the macro that should be of the same type, but the compiler won't check whether or not they are. Also, the type of the value returned isn't specified, so the compiler can't tell if you're assigning it to an incompatible variable. In any case, macros are confined to functions that can be expressed in a single statement. There are also other, more subtle, problems with macros. On the whole it's best to avoid them.

What Works?

How do you know whether you can instantiate a template function for a particular data type? For example, could you use the find() function from TEMPFIND to find a C-string (type char*) in an array of C-strings? To see whether this is possible, check the operators used in the function. If they all work on the data type, you can probably use it. In find(), however, we compare two variables using the equal-to (==) operator. You can't use this operator with C-strings; you must use the strcmp() library function. Thus find() won't work on C-strings. However, it does work on the string class because that class overloads the == operator.

Start with a Normal Function

When you write a template function you're probably better off starting with a normal function that works on a fixed type (`int`, for example). You can design and debug it without having to worry about template syntax and multiple types. Then, when everything works properly, you can turn the function definition into a template and check that it works for additional types.

Class Templates

The template concept can be extended to classes. Class templates are generally used for data storage (container) classes. (We'll see a major example of this in the next chapter, "The Standard Template Library.") Stacks and linked lists, which we encountered in previous chapters, are examples of data-storage classes. However, the examples of these classes that we presented could store data of only a single basic type. The `Stack` class in the STAKARAY program in Chapter 7, "Arrays and Strings," for example, could store data only of type `int`. Here's a condensed version of that class.

```
class Stack
   {
   private:
      int st[MAX];        //array of ints
      int top;            //index number of top of stack
   public:
      Stack();            //constructor
      void push(int var); //takes int as argument
      int pop();          //returns int value
   };
```

If we wanted to store data of type `long` in a stack, we would need to define a completely new class:

```
class LongStack
   {
   private:
      long st[MAX];        //array of longs
      int top;             //index number of top of stack
   public:
      LongStack();         //constructor
      void push(long var); //takes long as argument
      long pop();          //returns long value
   };
```

Similarly, we would need to create a new stack class for every data type we wanted to store. It would be nice to be able to write a single class specification that would work for variables of all types, instead of a single basic type. As you may have guessed, class templates allow us to do this. We'll create a variation of STAKARAY that uses a class template. Here's the listing for TEMPSTAK:

```cpp
// tempstak.cpp
// implements stack class as a template
#include <iostream.h>
using namespace std;
const int MAX = 100;            //size of array
/////////////////////////////////////////////////////////////////////
template <class Type>
class Stack
   {
   private:
      Type st[MAX];             //stack: array of any type
      int top;                  //number of top of stack
   public:
      Stack()                   //constructor
         { top = -1; }
      void push(Type var)       //put number on stack
         { st[++top] = var; }
      Type pop()                //take number off stack
         { return st[top--]; }
   };
/////////////////////////////////////////////////////////////////////
int main()
   {
   Stack<float> s1;        //s1 is object of class Stack<float>

   s1.push(1111.1F);       //push 3 floats, pop 3 floats
   s1.push(2222.2F);
   s1.push(3333.3F);
   cout << "1: " << s1.pop() << endl;
   cout << "2: " << s1.pop() << endl;
   cout << "3: " << s1.pop() << endl;

   Stack<long> s2;         //s2 is object of class Stack<long>

   s2.push(123123123L);    //push 3 longs, pop 3 longs
   s2.push(234234234L);
   s2.push(345345345L);
   cout << "1: " << s2.pop() << endl;
   cout << "2: " << s2.pop() << endl;
   cout << "3: " << s2.pop() << endl;
   return 0;
   }
```

Here the class Stack is presented as a template class. The approach is similar to that used in function templates. The template keyword and class Stack signal that the entire class will be a template.

```
template <class Type>
class Stack
    {
    //data and member functions using template argument Type
    };
```

A template argument, named Type in this example, is then used (instead of a fixed data type such as int) everyplace in the class specification where there is a reference to the type of the array st. There are three such places: the definition of st, the argument type of the push() function, and the return type of the pop() function.

Class templates differ from function templates in the way they are instantiated. To create an actual function from a function template, you call it using arguments of a specific type. Classes, however, are instantiated by defining an object using the template argument.

```
Stack<float> s1;
```

This creates an object, s1, a stack that stores numbers of type float. The compiler provides space in memory for this object's data, using type float wherever the template argument Type appears in the class specification. It also provides space for the member functions (if these have not already been placed in memory by another object of type Stack<float>). These member functions also operate exclusively on type float. Figure 14.2 shows how a class template and definitions of specific objects cause these objects to be placed in memory.

Creating a Stack object that stores objects of a different type, as in

```
Stack<long> s2;
```

creates not only a different space for data, but also a new set of member functions that operate on type long.

Note that the name of the type of s1 consists of the class name Stack *plus the template argument*: Stack<float>. This distinguishes it from other classes that might be created from the same template, such as Stack<int> or Stack<long>.

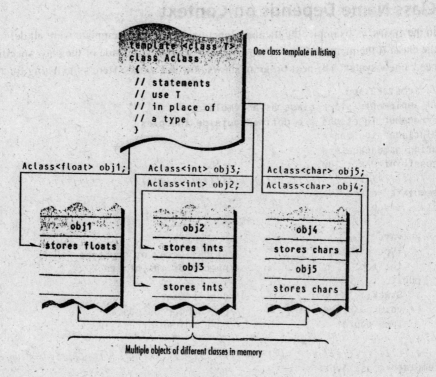

FIGURE 14.2
A class template.

In TEMPSTAK we exercise the s1 and s2 stacks by pushing and popping three values on each one and displaying each popped value. Here's the output:

```
1: 3333.3      //float stack
2: 2222.2
3: 1111.1
1: 345345345    //long stack
2: 234234234
3: 123123123
```

In this example the template approach gives us two classes for the price of one, and we could instantiate class objects for other numerical types with just a single line of code.

Class Name Depends on Context

In the TEMPSTAK example, the member functions of the class template were all defined within the class. If the member functions are defined externally (outside of the class specification), we need a new syntax. The next program shows how this works. Here's the listing for TEMPSTAK2:

```
// temstak2.cpp
// implements stack class as a template
// member functions are defined outside the class
#include <iostream>
using namespace std;
const int MAX = 100;
//////////////////////////////////////////////////////////////////
template <class Type>
class Stack
    {
    private:
        Type st[MAX];              //stack: array of any type
        int top;                   //number of top of stack
    public:
        Stack();                   //constructor
        void push(Type var);       //put number on stack
        Type pop();                //take number off stack
    };
//////////////////////////////////////////////////////////////////
template<class Type>
Stack<Type>::Stack()             //constructor
    {
    top = -1;
    }
//--------------------------------------------------------------
template<class Type>
void Stack<Type>::push(Type var) //put number on stack
    {
    st[++top] = var;
    }
//--------------------------------------------------------------
template<class Type>
Type Stack<Type>::pop()            //take number off stack
    {
    return st[top--];
    }
//--------------------------------------------------------------
int main()
    {
    Stack<float> s1;          //s1 is object of class Stack<float>
```

```
s1.push(1111.1F);        //push 3 floats, pop 3 floats
s1.push(2222.2F);
s1.push(3333.3F);
cout << "1: " << s1.pop() << endl;
cout << "2: " << s1.pop() << endl;
cout << "3: " << s1.pop() << endl;

Stack<long> s2;          //s2 is object of class Stack<long>

s2.push(123123123L);    //push 3 longs, pop 3 longs
s2.push(234234234L);
s2.push(345345345L);
cout << "1: " << s2.pop() << endl;
cout << "2: " << s2.pop() << endl;
cout << "3: " << s2.pop() << endl;
return 0;
}
```

The expression template<class Type> must precede not only the class definition, but each externally defined member function as well. Here's how the push() function looks:

```
template<class Type>
void Stack<Type>::push(Type var)
    {
    st[++top] = var;
    }
```

The name Stack<Type> is used to identify the class of which push() is a member. In a normal non-template member function the name Stack alone would suffice:

```
void Stack::push(int var)  //Stack() as a non-template function
    {
    st[++top] = var;
    }
```

but for a function template we need the template argument as well: Stack<Type>.

Thus we see that the name of the template class is expressed differently in different contexts. Within the class specification, it's simply the name itself: Stack. For externally defined member functions, it's the class name plus the template argument name: Stack<Type>. When you define actual objects for storing a specific data type, it's the class name plus this specific type: Stack<float>, for example.

```
class Stack                         //Stack class specifier
    {  };

void Stack<Type>::push(Type var)    //push() definition
    {  }

Stack<float> s1;                    //object of type Stack<float>
```

You must exercise considerable care to use the correct name in the correct context. It's easy to forget to add the `<Type>` or `<float>` to the `Stack`. The compiler hates it when you get it wrong.

Although it's not demonstrated in this example, you must also be careful of the syntax when a member function returns a value of its own class. Suppose we define a class `Int` that provided safety features for integers, as discussed in Exercise 4 in Chapter 8, "Operator Overloading." If you used an external definition for a member function `xfunc()` of this class that returned type `Int`, you would need to use `Int<Type>` for the return type as well as preceding the scope resolution operator:

```
Int<Type> Int<Type>::xfunc(Int arg)
    {   }
```

The class name used as a type of a function argument, on the other hand, doesn't need to include the `<Type>` designation.

A Linked List Class Using Templates

Let's look at another example where templates are used for a data storage class. This is a modification of our LINKLIST program from Chapter 10, "Pointers," which you are encouraged to reexamine. It requires not only that the `linklist` class itself be made into a template, but that the `link` structure, which actually stores each data item, be made into a template as well. Here's the listing for TEMPLIST:

```cpp
// templist.cpp
// implements linked list as a template
#include <iostream>
using namespace std;
/////////////////////////////////////////////////////////////////////
template<class TYPE>                //struct link<TYPE>
struct link                         //one element of list
//within this struct definition 'link' means link<TYPE>
   {
   TYPE data;                       //data item
   link* next;                      //pointer to next link
   };
/////////////////////////////////////////////////////////////////////
template<class TYPE>                //class linklist<TYPE>
class linklist                      //a list of links
//within this class definition 'linklist' means linklist<TYPE>
   {
   private:
      link<TYPE>* first;            //pointer to first link
   public:
      linklist()                    //no-argument constructor
         { first = NULL; }          //no first link
```

```cpp
                //note: destructor would be nice; not shown for simplicity
      void additem(TYPE d);          //add data item (one link)
      void display();                //display all links
   };
///////////////////////////////////////////////////////////////////
template<class TYPE>
void linklist<TYPE>::additem(TYPE d)  //add data item

   {
   link<TYPE>* newlink = new link<TYPE>;  //make a new link
   newlink->data = d;                //give it data
   newlink->next = first;            //it points to next link
   first = newlink;                  //now first points to this
   }
//-------------------------------------------------------------
template<class TYPE>
void linklist<TYPE>::display()        //display all links
   {
   link<TYPE>* current = first;       //set ptr to first link
   while( current != NULL )           //quit on last link
      {
      cout << endl << current->data;  //print data
      current = current->next;        //move to next link
      }
   }
//-------------------------------------------------------------
int main()
   {
   linklist<double> ld;  //ld is object of class linklist<double>

   ld.additem(151.5);    //add three doubles to list ld
   ld.additem(262.6);
   ld.additem(373.7);
   ld.display();          //display entire list ld

   linklist<char> lch;   //lch is object of class linklist<char>

   lch.additem('a');      //add three chars to list lch
   lch.additem('b');
   lch.additem('c');
   lch.display();         //display entire list lch
   cout << endl;
   return 0;
   }
```

In main() we define two linked lists: one to hold numbers of type double, and one to hold characters of type char. We then exercise the lists by placing three items on each one with the additem() member function, and displaying all the items with the display() member function. Here's the output of TEMPLIST:

```
373.7
262.6
151.5
c
b
a
```

Both the linklist class and the link structure make use of the template argument TYPE to stand for any type. (Well, not really any type; we'll discuss later what types can actually be stored.) Thus not only linklist but also link must be templates, preceded by the line

```
template<class TYPE>
```

Notice that it's not just a class that's turned into a template. Any other programming constructs that use a variable data type must also be turned into templates, as the link structure is here.

As before, we must pay attention to how the class (and in this program, a structure as well) are named in different parts of the program. Within its own specification we can use the name of the class or structure alone: linklist and link. In external member functions, we must use the class or structure name and the template argument: linklist<TYPE>. When we actually define objects of type linklist, we must use the specific data type that the list is to store:

```
linklist<double> ld;   //defines object ld of class linklist<double>
```

Storing User-Defined Data Types

In our programs so far, we've used template classes to store basic data types. For example, in the TEMPLIST program we stored numbers of type double and type char in a linked list. Is it possible to store objects of user-defined types (classes) in these same template classes? The answer is yes, but with a caveat.

Employees in a Linked List

Examine the employee class in the EMPLOY program in Chapter 9, "Inheritance." (Don't worry about the derived classes.) Could we store objects of type employee on the linked list of the TEMPLIST example? As with template functions, we can find out whether a template class can operate on objects of a particular class by checking the operations the template class performs on those objects. The linklist class uses the overloaded insertion (<<) operator to display the objects it stores:

```
void linklist<TYPE>::display()
   {
   ...
   cout << endl << current->data;  //uses insertion operator (<<)
   ...
   };
```

This is not a problem with basic types, for which the insertion operator is already defined. Unfortunately, however, the employee class in the EMPLOY program does not overload this operator. Thus we'll need to modify the employee class to include it. To simplify getting employee data from the user, we overload the extraction (>>) operator as well. Data from this operator is placed in a temporary object emptemp before being added to the linked list. Here's the listing for TEMLIST2:

```
// temlist2.cpp
// implements linked list as a template
// demonstrates list used with employee class

#include <iostream>
using namespace std;
const int LEN = 80;           //maximum length of names
/////////////////////////////////////////////////////////////////
class employee                            //employee class
   {
   private:
      char name[LEN];                      //employee name
      unsigned long number;                //employee number
   public:
      friend istream& operator >> (istream& s, employee& e);
      friend ostream& operator << (ostream& s, employee& e);
   };
//----------------------------------------------------------------
istream& operator >> (istream& s, employee& e)
   {
   cout << "\n   Enter last name: "; cin >> e.name;
   cout << "   Enter number: ";      cin >> e.number;
   return s;
   }
//----------------------------------------------------------------
ostream& operator << (ostream& s, employee& e)
   {
   cout << "\n   Name: " << e.name;
   cout << "\n   Number: " << e.number;
   return s;
   }
```

```
//////////////////////////////////////////////     /////////////////////
template<class TYPE>                    //str     "link<TYPE>"
struct link                             //one         t of list
   {
   TYPE data;                                   /data ite
   link* next;                                  pointer to       nk
   };
//////////////////////////////////////////////////     /////////////
template<class TYPE>                    //cla    "linklist<TYPE
class linklist                          //a list of links
   {
   private:
     link<TYPE>* first;                 //pointer to first link
   public:
     linklist()                         //no-argument constructor
        { first = NULL; }               //no first link
     void additem(TYPE d);              //add data item (one link)
     void display();                    //display all links
   };
//-----------------------------------------------------------------
template<class TYPE>
void linklist<TYPE>::additem(TYPE d)   //add data item
   {
   link<TYPE>* newlink = new link<TYPE>;  //make a new link
   newlink->data = d;                     //give it data
   newlink->next = first;                 //it points to next link
   first = newlink;                       //now first points to this
   }
//-----------------------------------------------------------------
template<class TYPE>
void linklist<TYPE>::display()         //display all links
   {
   link<TYPE>* current = first;        //set ptr to first link
   while( current != NULL )            //quit on last link
      {
      cout << endl << current->data;   //display data
      current = current->next;         //move to next link
      }
   }
/////////////////////////////////////////////////////////////////////
int main()
   {                                   //lemp is object of
   linklist<employee> lemp;            //class "linklist<employee>"
   employee emptemp;                   //temporary employee storage
   char ans;                           //user's response ('y' or 'n')
```

```
do
   {
   cin >> emptemp;        //get employee data from user
   lemp.additem(emptemp); //add it to linked list 'lemp'
   cout << "\nAdd another (y/n)? ";
   cin >> ans;
   } while(ans != 'n');   //when user is done,
lemp.display();          //display entire linked list
cout << endl;
return 0;
}
```

In main() we instantiate a linked list called lemp. Then, in a loop, we ask the user to input data for an employee, and we add that employee object to the list. When the user terminates the loop, we display all the employee data. Here's some sample interaction:

```
Enter last name: Mendez
Enter number: 1233
Add another(y/n)? y

Enter last name: Smith
Enter number: 2344
Add another(y/n)? y

Enter last name: Chang
Enter number: 3455
Add another(y/n)? n

Name: Chang
Number: 3455

Name: Smith
Number: 2344

Name: Mendez
Number: 1233
```

Notice that the linklist class does not need to be modified in any way to store objects of type employee. This is the beauty of template classes: They will work not only with basic types, but with user-defined types as well.

What Can You Store?
We noted that you can tell whether you can store variables of a particular type in a data-storage template class by checking the operators in the member functions of that class. Is it possible to store a string (class string) in the linklist class in the TEMLIST2 program? Member functions in this class use the insertion (<<) and extraction (>>) operators. These operators work perfectly

well with strings, so there's no reason we can't use this class to store strings, as you can verify yourself. But if any operators exist in a storage class's member function that don't operate on a particular data type, you can't use the class to store that type.

The UML and Templates

Templates (also called *parameterized classes* in the UML) are represented in class diagrams by a variation on the UML class symbol. The names of the template arguments are placed in a dotted rectangle that intrudes into the upper right corner of the class rectangle.

Figure 14.3 shows a UML class diagram for the TEMPSTAK program at the beginning of this chapter.

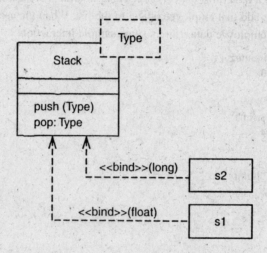

FIGURE 14.3
Template in a UML class diagram.

There's only one template argument here: Type. The operations push() and pop() are shown, with their return types and argument types. (Note that the return type is shown *following* the function name, separated from it by a colon.) The template argument usually shows up in the operation signatures, as Type does in push() and pop().

This diagram also shows the specific classes that are instantiated from the template class: s1 and s2.

Besides the depiction of templates, Figure 14.3 introduces two new UML concepts: *dependencies* and *stereotypes*.

Dependencies in the UML

A UML *dependency* is a relationship between two elements such that a change in the independent one may cause a change in the dependent one. The dependent one depends on, or uses, the independent one, so a dependency is sometimes called a *using* relationship. Here the template class is the independent element, and classes instantiated from it are dependent elements.

A dependency is shown by a dotted line with an arrow pointing to the independent element. In Figure 14.3 the instantiated classes s1 and s2 are dependent on template class Stack, because if Stack were to change, the instantiated classes would probably be affected.

Dependency is a very broad concept and applies to many situations in the UML. In fact, association, generalization, and the other relationships we've already seen are kinds of dependencies. However, they are important enough to be depicted in a specific way in UML diagrams.

One common dependency arises when one class uses another class as an argument in one of its operations.

Stereotypes in the UML

A stereotype is a way of specifying additional detail about a UML element. It's represented by a word in guillemets (double-angle brackets).

For example, the dotted lines in Figure 14.3 represent dependencies, but they don't tell you what kind of dependency it is. The stereotype <<bind>> specifies that the independent element (the template class) instantiates the dependent element (the specific class) using the specified parameters, which are shown in parentheses following the stereotype. That is, it says that Type will be replaced by float or long.

The UML defines many stereotypes as elements of the language. Each one applies to a specific UML element: some to classes, some to dependencies, and so on. You can also add your own.

Exceptions

Exceptions, the second major topic in this chapter, provide a systematic, object-oriented approach to handling errors generated by C++ classes. Exceptions are errors that occur at runtime. They are caused by a wide variety of exceptional circumstance, such as running out of memory, not being able to open a file, trying to initialize an object to an impossible value, or using an out-of-bounds index to a vector.

Why Do We Need Exceptions?

Why do we need a new mechanism to handle errors? Let's look at how the process was handled in the past. C-language programs often signal an error by returning a particular value from the function in which it occurred. For example, disk-file functions often return

NULL or 0 to signal an error. Each time you call one of these functions you check the return value:

```
if( somefunc() == ERROR_RETURN_VALUE )
    //handle the error or call error-handler function
else
    //proceed normally
if( anotherfunc() == NULL )
    //handle the error or call error-handler function
else
    //proceed normally
if( thirdfunc() == 0 )
    //handle the error or call error-handler function
else
    //proceed normally
```

One problem with this approach is that every single call to such a function must be examined by the program. Surrounding each function call with an if...else statement, and adding statements to handle the error (or call an error-handler routine), requires a lot of code and makes the listing convoluted and hard to read.

The problem becomes more complex when classes are used, since errors may take place without a function being explicitly called. For example, suppose an application defines objects of a class:

```
SomeClass obj1, obj2, obj3;
```

How will the application find out if an error occurred in the class constructor? The constructor is called implicitly, so there's no return value to be checked.

Things are complicated even further when an application uses class libraries. A class library and the application that makes use of it are often created by separate people: the class library by a vendor and the application by a programmer who buys the class library. This makes it even harder to arrange for error values to be communicated from a class member function to the program that's calling the function. The problem of communicating errors from deep within class libraries is probably the most important problem solved by exceptions. We'll return to this topic at the end of this section.

Old-time C programmers may remember another approach to catching errors: the setjmp() and longjmp() combination of functions. However, this approach is not appropriate for an object-oriented environment because it does not properly handle the destruction of objects.

Exception Syntax

Imagine an application that creates and interacts with objects of a certain class. Ordinarily the application's calls to the class member functions cause no problems. Sometimes, however, the application makes a mistake, causing an error to be detected in a member function. This member function then informs the application that an error has occurred. When exceptions are used, this is called *throwing* an exception. In the application we install a separate section of code to handle the error. This code is called an *exception handler* or *catch block*; it *catches* the exceptions thrown by the member function. Any code in the application that uses objects of the class is enclosed in a *try block*. Errors generated in the try block will be caught in the catch block. Code that doesn't interact with the class need not be in a try block. Figure 14.4 shows the arrangement.

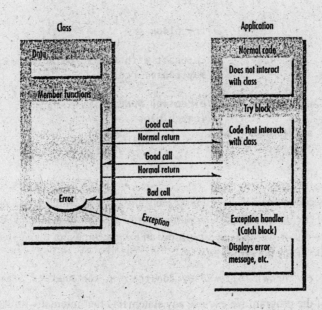

FIGURE 14.4
The exception mechanism.

The exception mechanism uses three new C++ keywords: throw, catch, and try. Also, we need to create a new kind of entity called an exception class. XSYNTAX is not a working program, but a skeleton program to show the syntax.

```
// xsyntax.cpp
// not a working program
/////////////////////////////////////////////////////////////
class AClass                      //a class
   {
```

```
    public:
    class AnError                    //excepti   class
        {
        };
    void Func()                      //a member function
        {
      if( /* error condition */ )
          throw AnError();           //throw exception
        }
    };
/////////////////////////////////////////////////////////////
int main()                          //application
    {
    try                              //try block
        {
        AClass obj1;                 //interact with AClass objects
        obj1.Func();                 //may cause error
        }
    catch(AClass::AnError)           //exception handler
        {                            //(catch block)
        //tell user about error, etc.
        }
    return 0;
    }
```

We start with a class called AClass, which represents any class in which errors might occur. An exception class, AnError, is specified in the public part of AClass. In AClass's member functions we check for errors. If we find one, we throw an exception, using the keyword throw followed by the constructor for the error class:

```
throw AnError();   //'throw' followed by constructor for AnError class
```

In the main() part of the program we enclose any statements that interact with AClass in a try block. If any of these statements causes an error to be detected in an AClass member function, an exception will be thrown and control will go to the catch block that immediately follows the try block.

A Simple Exception Example

Let's look at a working program example that uses exceptions. This example is derived from the STAKARAY program in Chapter 7, which created a stack data structure in which integer data values could be stored. Unfortunately, this earlier example could not detect two common errors. The application program might attempt to push too many objects onto the stack, thus exceeding the capacity of the array, or it might try to pop too many objects off the stack, thus obtaining invalid data. In the XSTAK program we use an exception to handle these two errors.

```
// xstak.cpp
// demonstrates exceptions
#include <iostream>
using namespace std;
const int MAX = 3;                  //stack holds 3 integers
//////////////////////////////////////////////////////////////////
class Stack
    {
    private:
        int st[MAX];                //array of integers
        int top;                    //index of top of stack
    public:
        class Range                 //exception class for Stack
            {                       //note: empty class body
            };

        Stack()                     //constructor
            { top = -1; }

        void push(int var)
            {
            if(top >= MAX-1)        //if stack full,
                throw Range();      //throw exception
            st[++top] = var;        //put number on stack
            }
        int pop()
            {
            if(top < 0)             //if stack empty,
                throw Range();      //throw exception
            return st[top--];       //take number off stack
            }
    };
//////////////////////////////////////////////////////////////////
int main()
    {
    Stack s1;

    try
        {
        s1.push(11);
        s1.push(22);
        s1.push(33);
//      s1.push(44);                            //oops: stack full
        cout << "1: " << s1.pop() << endl;
        cout << "2: " << s1.pop() << endl;
        cout << "3: " << s1.pop() << endl;
        cout << "4: " << s1.pop() << endl; //oops: stack empty
        }
```

```
catch(Stack::Range)                    //exception handler
    {
    cout << "Exception: Stack Full or Empty" << endl;
    }

cout << "Arrive here after catch (or normal exit)" << endl;
return 0;
}
```

Note that we've made the stack small so that it's easier to trigger an exception by pushing too many items.

Let's examine the features of this program that deal with exceptions. There are four of them. In the class specification there is an exception class. There are also statements that throw exceptions. In the main() part of the program there is a block of code that may cause exceptions (the try block), and a block of code that handles the exception (the catch block).

Specifying the Exception Class

The program first specifies an exception class within the Stack class:

```
class Range
    {   //note: empty class body
    };
```

Here the body of the class is empty, so objects of this class have no data and no member functions. All we really need in this simple example is the class name, Range. This name is used to connect a throw statement with a catch block. (The class body need not always be empty, as we'll see later.)

Throwing an Exception

In the Stack class an exception occurs if the application tries to pop a value when the stack is empty or tries to push a value when the stack is full. To let the application know that it has made such a mistake when manipulating a Stack object, the member functions of the Stack class check for these conditions using if statements, and throw an exception if they occur. In XSTAK the exception is thrown in two places, both using the statement

```
throw Range();
```

The Range() part of this statement invokes the implicit constructor for the Range class, which creates an object of this class. The throw part of the statement transfers program control to the exception handler (which we'll examine in a moment).

The try Block

All the statements in main() that might cause this exception—that is, statements that manipulate Stack objects—are enclosed in braces and preceded by the try keyword:

```
try
    {
    //code that operates on objects that might cause an exception
    }
```

This is simply part of the application's normal code; it's what you would need to write even if you weren't using exceptions. Not all the code in the program needs to be in a try block; just the code that interacts with the Stack class. Also, there can be many try blocks in your program, so you can access Stack objects from different places.

The Exception Handler (Catch Block)

The code that handles the exception is enclosed in braces, preceded by the catch keyword, with the exception class name in parentheses. The exception class name must include the class in which it is located. Here it's Stack::Range.

```
catch(Stack::Range)
    {
    //code that handles the exception
    }
```

This construction is called the *exception handler*. It must immediately follow the try block. In XSTAK the exception handler simply prints an error message to let the user know why the program failed.

Control "falls through" the bottom of the exception handler, so you can continue processing at that point. Or the exception handler may transfer control elsewhere, or (often) terminate the program.

Sequence of Events

Let's summarize the sequence of events when an exception occurs:

1. Code is executing normally outside a try block.
2. Control enters the try block.
3. A statement in the try block causes an error in a member function.
4. The member function throws an exception.
5. Control transfers to the exception handler (catch block) following the try block.

That's all there is to it. Notice how clean the resulting code is. Any of the statements in the try block could cause an exception, but we don't need to worry about checking a return value for each one, because the try-throw-catch arrangement handles them all automatically. In this particular example we've deliberately created two statements that cause exceptions. The first

```
s1.push(44);   //pushes too many items
```

causes an exception if you remove the comment symbol preceding it, and the second

```
cout << "4: " << s1.pop() << endl;   //pops item from empty stack
```

causes an exception if the first statement is commented out. Try it each way. In both cases the same error message will be displayed:

```
Stack Full or Empty
```

Multiple Exceptions

You can design a class to throw as many exceptions as you want. To show how this works, we'll modify the XSTAK program to throw separate exceptions for attempting to push data on a full stack and attempting to pop data from an empty stack. Here's the listing for XSTAK2:

```
// xstak2.cpp
// demonstrates two exception handlers
#include <iostream>
using namespace std;
const int MAX = 3;              //stack holds 3 integers
////////////////////////////////////////////////////////////////
class Stack
   {
   private:
      int st[MAX];              //stack: array of integers
      int top;                  //index of top of stack
   public:
      class Full { };           //exception class
      class Empty { };          //exception class
//--------------------------------------------------------------
      Stack()                   //constructor
         { top = -1; }
//--------------------------------------------------------------
      void push(int var)        //put number on stack
         {
         if(top >= MAX-1)       //if stack full,
            throw Full();       //throw Full exception
         st[++top] = var;
         }
```

```
//---------------------------------------------------
     int pop()                    //take number off stack
        {
        if(top < 0)               //if stack empty,
            throw Empty();        //throw Empty exception
        return st[top--];
        }
   };
///////////////////////////////////////////////////////////////
int main()
   {
   Stack s1;

   try
      {
      s1.push(11);
      s1.push(22);
      s1.push(33);
//    s1.push(44);                         //oops: stack full
      cout << "1: " << s1.pop() << endl;
      cout << "2: " << s1.pop() << endl;
      cout << "3: " << s1.pop() << endl;
      cout << "4: " << s1.pop() << endl;   //oops: stack empty
      }
   catch(Stack::Full)
      {
      cout << "Exception: Stack Full" << endl;
      }
   catch(Stack::Empty)
      {
      cout << "Exception: Stack Empty" << endl;
      }
   return 0;
   }
```

In XSTAK2 we specify two exception classes:

```
class Full  {  };
class Empty {  };
```

The statement

```
throw Full();
```

is executed if the application calls push() when the stack is already full, and

```
throw Empty();
```

is executed if pop() is called when the stack is empty.

A separate catch block is used for each exception:

```
try
    {
    //code that operates on Stack objects
    }
catch(Stack::Full)
    {
    //code to handle Full exception
    }
catch(Stack::Empty)
    {
    //code to handle Empty exception
    }
```

All the catch blocks used with a particular try block must immediately follow the try block. In this case each catch block simply prints a message: "Stack Full" or "Stack Empty". Only one catch block is activated for a given exception. A group of catch blocks, or a *catch ladder*, operates a little like a switch statement, with only the appropriate section of code being executed. When an exception has been handled, control passes to the statement following all the catch blocks. (Unlike a switch statement, you don't need to end each catch block with a break. In this way catch blocks act more like functions.)

Exceptions with the Distance Class

Let's look at another example of exceptions, this one applied to the infamous Distance class from previous chapters. A Distance object has an integer value for feet and a floating-point value for inches. The inches value should always be less than 12.0. A problem with this class in previous examples has been that it couldn't protect itself if the user initialized an object with an inches value of 12.0 or greater. This could lead to trouble when the class tried to perform arithmetic, since the arithmetic routines (such as operator +()) assumed inches would be less than 12.0. Such impossible values could also be displayed, thus confounding the user with dimensions like 7' -15".

Let's rewrite the Distance class to use an exception to handle this error, as shown in XDIST:

```
// xdist.cpp
// exceptions with Distance class
#include <iostream>
using namespace std;
//////////////////////////////////////////////////////////////
class Distance                        //English Distance class
    {
```

```
    private:
       int feet;
       float inches;
    public:
       class InchesEx { };           //exception class
//----------------------------------------------------------------
       Distance()                    //constructor (no args)
          { feet = 0; inches = 0.0; }
//----------------------------------------------------------------
       Distance(int ft, float in)    //constructor (two args)
          {
          if(in >= 12.0)             //if inches too big,
             throw InchesEx();       //throw exception
          feet = ft;
          inches = in;
          }
//----------------------------------------------------------------
       void getdist()                //get length from user
          {
          cout << "\nEnter feet: ";  cin >> feet;
          cout << "Enter inches: ";  cin >> inches;
          if(inches >= 12.0)         //if inches too big,
             throw InchesEx();       //throw exception
          }
//----------------------------------------------------------------
       void showdist()               //display distance
          { cout << feet << "\'-" << inches << '\"'; }
    };
///////////////////////////////////////////////////////////////////
int main()
    {
    try
       {
       Distance dist1(17, 3.5);      //2-arg constructor
       Distance dist2;               //no-arg constructor
       dist2.getdist();              //get distance from user
                                     //display distances
       cout << "\ndist1 = ";  dist1.showdist();
       cout << "\ndist2 = ";  dist2.showdist();
       }
    catch(Distance::InchesEx)        //catch exceptions
       {
       cout << "\nInitialization error: "
            "inches value is too large.";
       }
    cout << endl;
    return 0;
    }
```

We install an exception class called InchesEx in the Distance class. Then, whenever the user attempts to initialize the inches data to a value greater than or equal to 12.0, we throw the exception. This happens in two places: in the two-argument constructor, where the programmer may make an error supplying initial values, and in the getdist() function, where the user may enter an incorrect value at the *Enter inches* prompt. We could also check for negative values and other input mistakes.

In main() all interaction with Distance objects is enclosed in a try block, and the catch block displays an error message.

In a more sophisticated program, of course, you might want to handle a user error (as opposed to a programmer error) differently. It would be more user-friendly to go back to the beginning of the try block and give the user a chance to enter a another distance value.

Exceptions with Arguments

What happens if the application needs more information about what caused an exception? For instance, in the XDIST example, it might help the programmer to know what the bad inches value actually was. Also, if the same exception is thrown by different member functions, as it is in XDIST, it would be nice to know which of the functions was the culprit. Is there a way to pass such information from the member function, where the exception is thrown, to the application that catches it?

You can answer this question if you remember that throwing an exception involves not only transferring control to the handler, but also creating an object of the exception class by calling its constructor. In XDIST, for example, we create an object of type InchesEx when we throw the exception with the statement

```
throw InchesEx();
```

If we add data members to the exception class, we can initialize them when we create the object. The exception handler can then retrieve the data from the object when it catches the exception. It's like writing a message on a baseball and throwing it over the fence to your neighbor. We'll modify the XDIST program to do this. Here's the listing for XDIST2:

```
// xdist2.cpp
// exceptions with arguments
#include <iostream>
#include <string>
using namespace std;
////////////////////////////////////////////////////////////////
class Distance                      //English Distance class
   {
```

```
    private:
       int feet;
       float inches;
    public:
//------------------------------------------------------------
       class InchesEx                    //exception class
          {
          public:
            string origin;               //for name of routine
            float iValue;                //for faulty inches value

            InchesEx(string or, float in)  //2-arg constructor
               {
               origin = or;              //store string
               iValue = in;              //store inches
               }
          };                             //end of exception class
//------------------------------------------------------------
       Distance()                        //constructor (no args)
          { feet = 0; inches = 0.0; }
//------------------------------------------------------------
       Distance(int ft, float in)  //constructor (two args)
          {
          if(in >= 12.0)
             throw InchesEx("2-arg constructor", in);
          feet = ft;
          inches = in;
          }
//------------------------------------------------------------
       void getdist()                    //get length from user
          {
          cout << "\nEnter feet: ";  cin >> feet;
          cout << "Enter inches: ";  cin >> inches;
          if(inches >= 12.0)
             throw InchesEx("getdist() function", inches);
          }
//------------------------------------------------------------
       void showdist()                   //display distance
          { cout << feet << "\'-" << inches << '\"'; }
    };
/////////////////////////////////////////////////////////////
int main()
   {
   try
      {
```

```
        Distance dist1(17, 3.5);     //2-arg constructor
        Distance dist2;              //no-arg constructor
        dist2.getdist();             //get value
                                     //display distances
     cout << "\ndist1 = ";  dist1.showdist();
     cout << "\ndist2 = ";  dist2.showdist();
     }
  catch(Distance::InchesEx ix)    //exception handler
     {
     cout << "\nInitialization error in " << ix.origin
          << ".\n   Inches value of " << ix.iValue
          << " is too large.";
     }
  cout << endl;
  return 0;
  }
```

There are three parts to the operation of passing data when throwing an exception: specifying the data members and a constructor for the exception class, initializing this constructor when we throw an exception, and accessing the object's data when we catch the exception. Let's look at these in turn.

Specifying Data in an Exception Class

It's convenient to make the data in an exception class public so it can be accessed directly by the exception-handler. Here's the specification for the new InchesEx exception class in XDIST2:

```
class InchesEx                   //exception class
  {
  public:
     string origin;              //for name of routine
     float iValue;               //for faulty inches value

     InchesEx(string or, float in)  //2-arg constructor
        {
        origin = or;             //put string in object
        iValue = in;             //put inches value in object
        }
  };
```

There are public variables for a string object, which will hold the name of the member function being called, and a type float, for the faulty inches value.

Initializing an Exception Object

How do we initialize the data when we throw an exception? In the two-argument constructor for the Stack class we say

```
throw InchesEx("2-arg constructor", in);
```

and in the getdist() member function for Stack it's

```
throw InchesEx("getdist() function", inches);
```

When the exception is thrown, the handler will display the string and inches values. The string will tell us which member function is throwing the exception, and the value of inches will report the faulty inches value detected by the member function. This additional data will make it easier for the programmer or user to figure out what caused the error.

Extracting Data from the Exception Object

How do we extract this data when we catch the exception? The simplest way is to make the data a public part of the exception class, as we've done here. Then in the catch block we can declare ix as the name of the exception object we're catching. Using this name we can refer to its data in the usual way, using the dot operator:

```
catch(Distance::InchesEx ix)
    {
    //access 'ix.origin' and 'ix.iValue' directly
    }
```

We can then display the value of ix.origin and ix.iValue. Here's some interaction with XDIST2, when the user enters too large a value for inches:

```
Enter feet: 7
Enter inches: 13.5

Initialization error in getdist() function.
    Inches value of 13.5 is too large.
```

Similarly, if the programmer changes the definition of dist1 in main() to

```
Distance dist1(17, 22.25);
```

the resulting exception will cause this error message:

```
Initialization error in 2-arg constructor.
    Inches value of 22.25 is too large.
```

Of course we can make whatever use of the exception arguments we want, but they generally carry information that helps us diagnose the error that triggered the exception.

The bad_alloc Class

Standard C++ contains several built-in exception classes. The most commonly used is probably bad_alloc, which is thrown if an error occurs when attempting to allocate memory with new.

(This exception was called xalloc in earlier versions of C++. At the time of this book's publication, this older approach is still used in Microsoft Visual C++.) If you set up the appropriate try and catch blocks, you can make use of bad_alloc with very little effort. Here's a short example, BADALLOC, that shows how it's used:

```cpp
// badalloc.cpp
// demonstrates bad_alloc exception
#include <iostream>
using namespace std;

int main()
   {
   const unsigned long SIZE = 10000;     //memory size
   char* ptr;                            //pointer to memory

   try
      {
      ptr = new char[SIZE];              //allocate SIZE bytes
      }
   catch(bad_alloc)                      //exception handler
      {
      cout << "\nbad_alloc exception: can't allocate memory.\n";
      return(1);
      }
   delete[] ptr;                         //deallocate memory
   cout << "\nMemory use is successful.\n";
   return 0;
   }
```

Put all the statements that use new in a try block. The catch block that follows handles the exception, often by displaying an error message and terminating the program.

Exception Notes

We've shown only the simplest and most common approach to using exceptions. We won't go into further detail, but we'll conclude with a few thoughts about exception usage.

Function Nesting

The statement that causes an exception need not be located directly in the try block; it can also be in a function that is called by a statement in the try block. (Or in a function called by a function that is called by a statement in the try block, and so on.) So you only need to install a try block on the program's upper level. Lower-level functions need not be so encumbered, provided they are called directly or indirectly by functions in the try block. (However, it is sometimes useful for the intermediate-level functions to add their own identifying data to the exception and rethrow it to the next level.)

Exceptions and Class Libraries

An important problem solved by exceptions is that of errors in class libraries. A library routine may discover an error, but typically it doesn't know what to do about it. After all, the library routine was written by a different person at a different time than was the program that called it. What the library routine needs to do is pass the error along to whatever program called it, saying in effect, "There's been an error. I don't know what you want to do about it, but here it is." The calling program can thus handle the error as it sees fit.

The exception mechanism provides this capability because exceptions are transmitted up through nested functions until a catch block is encountered. The throw statement may be in a library routine, but the catch block can be in the program that knows how to deal with the error.

If you're writing a class library, you should cause it to throw exceptions for anything that could cause problems to the program using it. If you're writing a program that uses a class library, you should provide try and catch blocks for any exceptions that it throws.

Not for Every Situation

Exceptions should not be used for every kind of error. They impose a certain overhead in terms of program size and (when an exception occurs) time. For example, exceptions should probably not be used for user input errors (such as inserting letters into numerical input) that are easily detectable by the program. Instead the program should use normal decisions and loops to check the user's input and ask the user to try again if necessary.

Destructors Called Automatically

The exception mechanism is surprisingly sophisticated. When an exception is thrown, a destructor is called automatically for any object that was created by the code up to that point in the try block. This is necessary because the application won't know which statement caused the exception, and if it wants to recover from the error, it will (at the very least) need to start over at the top of the try block. The exception mechanism guarantees that the code in the try block will have been "reset," at least as far as the existence of objects is concerned.

Handling Exceptions

After you catch an exception, you will sometimes want to terminate your application. The exception mechanism gives you a chance to indicate the source of the error to the user, and to perform any necessary clean-up chores before terminating. It also makes clean-up easier by executing the destructors for objects created in the try block. This allows you to release system resources, such as memory, that such objects may be using.

In other cases you will not want to terminate your program. Perhaps your program can figure out what caused the error and correct it, or the user can be asked to input different data. When this is the case, the try and catch blocks are typically embedded in a loop, so control can be returned to the beginning of the try block (which the exception mechanism has attempted to restore to its initial state).

If there is no exception handler that matches the exception thrown, the program is unceremoniously terminated by the operating system.

Summary

Templates allow you to generate a family of functions, or a family of classes, to handle different data types. Whenever you find yourself writing several identical functions that perform the same operation on different data types, you should consider using a function template instead. Similarly, whenever you find yourself writing several different class specifications that differ only in the type of data acted on, you should consider using a class template. You'll save yourself time and the result will be a more robust and more easily maintained program that is also (once you understand templates) easier to understand.

Exceptions are a mechanism for handling C++ errors in a systematic, OOP-oriented way. An exception is typically caused by a faulty statement in a try block that operates on objects of a class. The class member function discovers the error and throws an exception, which is caught by the program using the class, in exception-handler code following the try block.

Questions

Answers to these questions can be found in Appendix G.

1. A template provides a convenient way to make a family of

    a. variables.

    b. functions.

    c. classes.

    d. programs.

2. A template argument is preceded by the keyword _____.

3. True or false: Templates automatically create different versions of a function, depending on user input.

4. Write a template for a function that always returns its argument times 2.

5. A template class

    a. is designed to be stored in different containers.

    b. works with different data types.

    c. generates objects which must all be identical.

    d. generates classes with different numbers of member functions.

6. True or false: There can be more than one template argument.

7. Creating an actual function from a template is called _____ the function.

8. Actual code for a template function is generated when

    a. the function declaration appears in the source code.

    b. the function definition appears in the source code.

    c. a call to the function appears in the source code.

    d. the function is executed at runtime.

9. The key concept in the template concept is replacing a _____ with a name that stands for _____.

10. Templates are often used for classes that _____ _____.

11. An exception is typically caused by

    a. the programmer who writes an application's code.

    b. the creator of a class who writes the class member functions.

    c. a runtime error.

    d. an operating system malfunction that terminates the program.

12. The C++ keywords used with exceptions are _____, _____, and _____.

13. Write a statement that throws an exception using the class BoundsError, which has an empty body.

14. True or false: Statements that might cause an exception must be part of a catch block.

15. Exceptions are thrown

    a. from the catch block to the try block.

    b. from a throw statement to the try block.

    c. from the point of the error to a catch block.

    d. from a throw statement to a catch block.

16. Write the specification for an exception class that stores an error number and an error name. Include a constructor.

17. True or false: A statement that throws an exception does not need to be located in a try block.

18. The following are errors for which an exception would typically be thrown:

    a. An excessive amount of data threatens to overflow an array.

    b. The user presses the Ctrl+C key combination to terminate the program.

    c. A power failure shuts down the system.

    d. new cannot obtain the requested memory.

19. Additional information sent when an exception is thrown may be placed in

    a. the throw keyword.

    b. the function that caused the error.

    c. the catch block.

    d. an object of the exception class.

20. True or false: A program can continue to operate after an exception has occurred.

21. If we're talking about dependencies, the template class is the _____ element and the instantiated class is the _____ element.

22. A template class is shown in the UML as

    a. an ordinary class with something added.

    b. a dashed line.

    c. a rectangle with a dashed outline.

    d. none of the above.

23. True or false: A dependency is a kind of association.

24. A stereotype gives _____ about a UML element.

Exercises

Answers to starred exercises can be found in Appendix G.

*1. Write a template function that returns the average of all the elements of an array. The arguments to the function should be the array name and the size of the array (type int). In main(), exercise the function with arrays of type int, long, double, and char.

*2. A queue is a data-storage device. It's like a stack, except that, instead of being last-in-first-out, it's first-in-first-out, like the line at a bank teller's window. If you put in 1, 2, 3, you get back 1, 2, 3 in that order.

A stack needs only one index to an array (top in the STAKARAY program in Chapter 7). A queue, on the other hand, must keep track of two indexes to an array: one to the tail, where new items are added, and one to the head, where old items are removed. The tail follows the head through the array as items are added and removed. If either the tail or the head reaches the end of the array, it is reset to the beginning.

Write a class template for a queue class. Assume that the programmer using the queue won't make any mistakes, like exceeding the capacity of the queue or trying to remove an item when the queue is empty. Define several queues of different data types and insert and remove data from them.

*3. Add exceptions to the queue template in Exercise 2. Throw two exceptions: one if the capacity of the queue is exceeded, the other if the program tries to remove an item from an empty queue. One way to handle this is to add a new data member to the queue: a count of the number of items currently in the queue. Increment the count when you insert an item, and decrement it when you remove an item. Throw an exception if this count exceeds the capacity of the queue, or if it becomes less than 0.

You might try making the main() part of this exercise interactive, so the user can put values on a queue and take them off. This makes it easier to exercise the queue. Following an exception, the program should allow the user to recover from a mistake without corrupting the contents of the queue.

4. Create a function called swaps() that interchanges the values of the two arguments sent to it. (You will probably want to pass these arguments by reference.) Make the function into a template, so it can be used with all numerical data types (char, int, float, and so on). Write a main() program to exercise the function with several types.

5. Create a function called amax() that returns the value of the largest element in an array. The arguments to the function should be the address of the array and its size. Make this function into a template so it will work with an array of any numerical type. Write a main() program that applies this function to arrays of various types.

6. Start with the safearay class from the ARROVER3 program in Chapter 8. Make this class into a template, so the safe array can store any kind of data. In main(), create safe arrays of at least two different types, and store some data in them.

7. Start with the frac class and the four-function fraction calculator of Exercise 7 in Chapter 8. Make the frac class into a template so it can be instantiated using different data types for the numerator and denominator. These must be integer types, which pretty much restricts you to char, short, int, and long (unless you develop an integer type of your own). In main(), instantiate a class frac<char> and use it for the four-function calculator. Class frac<char> will take less memory than frac<int>, but won't be able to handle large fractions.

8. Add an exception class to the ARROVER3 program in Chapter 8 so that an out-of-bounds index will trigger the exception. The catch block can print an error message for the user.

9. Modify the exception class in Exercise 8 (adapted from ARROVER3) so that the error message in the catch block reports the value of the index that caused the exception.

10. There are various philosophies about when to use exceptions. Refer to the ENGLERR program from Chapter 12, "Streams and Files." Should user-input errors be exceptions? For this exercise, let's assume so. Add an exception class to the Distance class in that program. (See also the XDIST and XDIST2 examples in this chapter.) Throw an exception in all the places where ENGLERR displayed an error message. Use an argument to the exception constructor to report where the error occurred and the specific cause of the error

14

TEMPLATES
AND EXCEPTIONS

(inches not a number, inches out of range, and so on). Also, throw an exception when an error is found within the isint() function (nothing entered, too many digits, nondigit character, integer out of range). Question: If it throws exceptions, can isint() remain an independent function?

You can insert both the try block and the catch block within the do loop so that after an exception you go back to the top of the loop, ready to ask the user for more input.

You might also want to throw an exception in the two-argument constructor, in case the programmer initializes a Distance value with its inches member out of range.

11. Start with the STRPLUS program in Chapter 8. Add an exception class, and throw an exception in the one-argument constructor if the initialization string is too long. Throw another in the overloaded + operator if the result will be too long when two strings are concatenated. Report which of these errors has occurred.

12. Sometimes the easiest way to use exceptions is to create a new class of which an exception class is a member. Try this with a class that uses exceptions to handle file errors. Make a class dofile that includes an exception class and member functions to read and write files. A constructor to this class can take the filename as an argument and open a file with that name. You may also want a member function to reset the file pointer to the beginning of the file. Use the REWERR program in Chapter 12 as a model, and write a main() program that provides the same functionality, but does so by calling on members of the dofile class.

The Standard Template Library

IN THIS CHAPTER

Most computer programs exist to process data. The data may represent a wide variety of real-world information: personnel records, inventories, text documents, the results of scientific experiments, and so on. Whatever it represents, data is stored in memory and manipulated in similar ways. University computer science programs typically include a course called "Data Structures and Algorithms." The term *data structures* refers to the ways data is stored in memory, and *algorithms* refers to how it is manipulated.

C++ classes provide an excellent mechanism for creating a library of data structures. In the past, compiler vendors and many third-party developers offered libraries of *container classes* to handle the storage and processing of data. Now, however, Standard C++ includes its own built-in container class library. It's called the Standard Template Library (STL), and was developed by Alexander Stepanov and Meng Lee of Hewlett Packard. The STL is part of the Standard C++ class library, and can be used as a standard approach to storing and processing data.

This chapter describes the STL and how to use it. The STL is large and complex, so we won't by any means describe everything about it; that would require a large book. (Many books are available on the STL; see Appendix H, "Bibliography.") We will introduce the STL and give examples of the more common algorithms and containers.

Introduction to the STL

The STL contains several kinds of entities. The three most important are containers, algorithms, and iterators.

A *container* is a way that stored data is organized in memory. In earlier chapters we've explored two kinds of containers: stacks and linked lists. Another container, the array, is so common that it's built into C++ (and most other computer languages). However, there are many other kinds of containers, and the STL includes the most useful. The STL containers are implemented by template classes, so they can be easily customized to hold different kinds of data.

Algorithms in the STL are procedures that are applied to containers to process their data in various ways. For example, there are algorithms to sort, copy, search, and merge data. Algorithms are represented by template functions. These functions are not member functions of the container classes. Rather, they are standalone functions. Indeed, one of the striking characteristics of the STL is that its algorithms are so general. You can use them not only on STL containers, but on ordinary C++ arrays and on containers you create yourself. (Containers also include member functions for more specific tasks.)

Iterators are a generalization of the concept of pointers: they point to elements in a container. You can increment an iterator, as you can a pointer, so it points in turn to each element in a container. Iterators are a key part of the STL because they connect algorithms with containers.

Think of them as a software version of cables (like the cables that connect stereo components, together or a computer to its peripherals).

Figure 15.1 shows these three main components of the STL. In this section we'll discuss containers, algorithms, and iterators in slightly more detail. In subsequent sections we'll explore these concepts further with program examples.

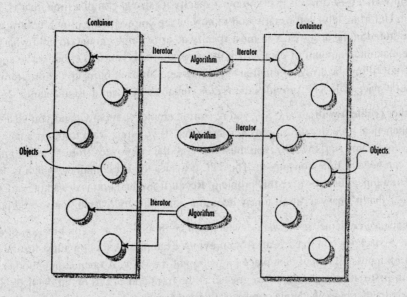

Algorithms use iterators to act on objects in containers

FIGURE 15.1
Containers, algorithms, and iterators.

Containers

A container is a way to store data, whether the data consists of built-in types such as int and float, or of class objects. The STL makes seven basic kinds of containers available, as well as three more that are derived from the basic kinds. In addition, you can create your own containers based on the basic kinds. You may wonder why we need so many kinds of containers. Why not use C++ arrays in all data storage situations? The answer is efficiency. An array is awkward or slow in many situations.

Containers in the STL fall into two main categories: *sequence* and *associative*. The sequence containers are *vector*, *list*, and *deque*. The associative containers are *set*, *multiset*, *map*, and *multimap*. In addition, several specialized containers are derived from the sequence containers. These are *stack*, *queue*, and *priority queue*. We'll look at these categories in turn.

Sequence Containers

A sequence container stores a set of elements in what you can visualize as a line, like houses on a street. Each element is related to the other elements by its position along the line. Each element (except at the ends) is preceded by one specific element and followed by another. An ordinary C++ array is an example of a sequence container.

One problem with a C++ array is that you must specify its size at compile time; that is, in the source code. Unfortunately, you usually don't know, when you write the program, how much data will be stored in the array. So you must specify an array large enough to hold what you guess is the maximum amount of data. When the program runs, you will either waste space in memory by not filling the array, or elicit an error message (or even blow up the program) by running out of space. The STL provides the *vector* container to avoid these difficulties.

Here's another problem with arrays. Say you're storing employee records, and you've arranged them in alphabetical order by the employee's last name. If you now want to insert a new employee whose name starts with L, you must move all the employees from M to Z to make room. This can be very time-consuming. The STL provides the *list* container, which is based on the idea of a linked list, to solve this problem. Recall from the LINKLIST example in Chapter 10, "Pointers," that it's easy to insert a new item in a linked list by rearranging several pointers.

The third sequence container is the *deque*, which can be thought of as a combination of a stack and a queue. A stack, as you may recall from previous examples, works on a last-in-first-out principle. Both input and output take place on the top of the stack. A queue, on the other hand, uses a first-in-first-out arrangement: data goes in at the front and comes out at the back, like a line of customers in a bank. A deque combines these approaches so you can insert or delete data from either end. The word deque is derived from Double-Ended QUEue. It's a versatile mechanism that's not only useful in its own right, but can be used as the basis for stacks and queues, as you'll see later.

Table 15.1 summarizes the characteristics of the STL sequence containers. It includes the ordinary C++ array for comparison.

TABLE 15.1   Basic Sequence Containers

Container	Characteristic	Advantages and Disadvantages
ordinary C++ array	Fixed size	Quick random access (by index number)
		Slow to insert or erase in the middle
		Size cannot be changed at runtime
vector	Relocating, expandable array	Quick random access (by index number)
		Slow to insert or erase in the middle
		Quick to insert or erase at end

TABLE 15.1 Continued

	Characteristic	Advantages and Disadvantages
list	Doubly linked list	Quick to insert or delete at any location
		Quick access to both ends
		Slow random access
deque	Like vector, but can be accessed at either end	Quick random access (using index number)
		Slow to insert or erase in the middle
		Quick insert or erase (push and pop) at either the beginning or the end

Instantiating an STL container object is easy. First you must include an appropriate header file. Then you use the template format with the kind of objects to be stored as the parameter. Examples might be

```
vector<int> aVect;  //create a vector of ints
```

or

```
list<airtime> departure_list;  //create a list of airtimes
```

Notice that there's no need to specify the size of STL containers. The containers themselves take care of all memory allocation.

Associative Containers

An associative container is not sequential; instead it uses *keys* to access data. The keys, typically numbers or stings, are used automatically by the container to arrange the stored elements in a specific order. It's like an ordinary English dictionary, in which you access data by looking up words arranged in alphabetical order. You start with a key value (say the word *aardvark*, to use the dictionary example), and the container converts this key to the element's location in memory. If you know the key, you can access the associated value swiftly.

There are two kinds of associative containers in the STL: *sets* and *maps*. These both store data in a structure called a *tree*, which offers fast searching, insertion, and deletion. Sets and maps are thus very versatile general data structures suitable for a wide variety of applications. However, it is inefficient to sort them and perform other operations that require random access.

Sets are simpler and more commonly used than maps. A set stores a number of items which contain *keys*. The keys are the attributes used to order the items. For example, a set might store objects of the person class, which are ordered alphabetically using their name attributes as keys. In this situation, you can quickly locate a desired person object by searching for the object with a specified name. If a set stores values of a basic type such as int, the key is the entire item stored. Some writers refer to an entire object stored in a set as a *key*, but we'll call it the *key object* to emphasize that the attribute used to order it (the key) isn't necessarily the entire item.

A map stores pairs of objects: a key object and a value object. A map is often used as a container that's somewhat like an array, except that instead of accessing its elements with index numbers, you access them with indices that can be of an arbitrary type. That is, the key object serves as the index, and the value object is the value at that index.

The *map* and *set* containers allow only one key of a given value to be stored. This makes sense in, say, a list of employees arranged by unique employee numbers. On the other hand, the *multimap* and *multiset* containers allow multiple keys. In an English dictionary there might be several entries for the word "set," for example.

Table 15.2 summarizes the associative containers available in the STL.

TABLE 15.2 Basic Associative Containers

Container	Characteristics
set	Stores only the key objects Only one key of each value allowed
multiset	Stores only the key objects Multiple key values allowed
map	Associates key object with value object Only one key of each value allowed
multimap	Associates key object with value object Multiple key values allowed

Creating associative containers is just like creating sequential ones:

```
set<int> intSet;   //create a set of ints
```

or

```
multiset<employee> machinists;   //create a multiset of employees
```

Member Functions

Algorithms are the heavy hitters of the STL, carrying out complex operations like sorting and searching. However, containers also need member functions to perform simpler tasks that are specific to a particular type of container.

Table 15.3 shows some frequently-used member functions whose name and purpose (not the actual implementation) are common to most container classes.

TABLE 15.3 Some Member Functions Common to All Containers

Name	Purpose
size()	Returns the number of items in the container
empty()	Returns true if container is empty
max_size()	Returns size of the largest possible container
begin()	Returns an iterator to the start of the container, for iterating forwards through the container
end()	Returns an iterator to the past-the-end location in the container, used to end forward iteration
rbegin()	Returns a reverse iterator to the end of the container, for iterating backward through the container
rend()	Returns a reverse iterator to the beginning of the container; used to end backward iteration

Many other member functions appear only in certain containers, or certain categories of containers. You'll learn more about these as we go along. Appendix F, "STL Algorithms and Member Functions," includes a table showing the STL member functions and which ones exist for which containers.

Container Adapters

It's possible to create special-purpose containers from the normal containers mentioned previously using a construct called *container adapters*. These special-purpose containers have simpler interfaces than the more general containers. The specialized containers implemented with container adapters in the STL are *stacks*, *queues*, and *priority queues*. As we noted, a stack restricts access to pushing and popping a data item on and off the top of the stack. In a queue, you push items at one end and pop them off the other. In a priority queue, you push data in the front in random order, but when you pop the data off the other end, you always pop the *largest item* stored: the priority queue automatically sorts the data for you.

Stacks, queues, and priority queues can be created from different sequence containers, although the deque is often used. Table 15.4 shows the abstract data types and the sequence containers that can be used in their implementation.

TABLE 15.4   Adapter-Based Containers

Container	Implementation	Characteristics
stack	Can be implemented as vector, list, or deque	Insert (push) and remove (pop) at one end only
queue	Can be implemented as list or deque	Insert (push) at one end, remove (pop) at other
priority queue	Can be implemented as vector or deque	Insert (push) in random order at one end, remove (pop) in sorted order from other end

You use a template within a template to instantiate these classes. For example, here's a stack object that holds type int, instantiated from the deque class:

```
stack< deque<int> > aStak;
```

A detail to note about this format is that you must insert a space between the two closing angle brackets. You can't write

```
stack<deque<int>> astak;   //syntax error
```

because the compiler will interpret the >> as an operator.

Algorithms

An algorithm is a function that does something to the items in a container (or containers). As we noted, algorithms in the STL are not member functions or even friends of container classes, as they are in earlier container libraries, but are standalone template functions. You can use them with built-in C++ arrays, or with container classes you create yourself (provided the class includes certain basic functions).

Table 15.5 shows a few representative algorithms. We'll examine others as we go along. Appendix F contains a table listing most of the STL algorithms.

TABLE 15.5   Some Typical STL Algorithms

Algorithm	Purpose
find	Returns first element equivalent to a specified value
count	Counts the number of elements that have a specified value
equal	Compares the contents of two containers and returns true if all corresponding elements are equal

TABLE 15.5 Continued

Algorithm	Purpose
search	Looks for a sequence of values in one container that corresponds with the same sequence in another container
copy	Copies a sequence of values from one container to another (or to a different location in the same container)
swap	Exchanges a value in one location with a value in another
iter_swap	Exchanges a sequence of values in one location with a sequence of values in another location
fill	Copies a value into a sequence of locations
sort	Sorts the values in a container according to a specified ordering
merge	Combines two sorted ranges of elements to make a larger sorted range
accumulate	Returns the sum of the elements in a given range
for_each	Executes a specified function for each element in the container

Suppose you create an array of type int, with data in it:

```
int arr[8] = {42, 31, 7, 80, 2, 26, 19, 75};
```

You can then use the STL sort() algorithm to sort this array by saying

```
sort(arr, arr+8);
```

where arr is the address of the beginning of the array, and arr+8 is the past-the-end address (one item past the end of the array).

Iterators

Iterators are pointer-like entities that are used to access individual data items (which are usually called *elements*), in a container. Often they are used to move sequentially from element to element, a process called *iterating* through the container. You can increment iterators with the ++ operator so they point to the next element, and dereference them with the * operator to obtain the value of the element they point to. In the STL an iterator is represented by an object of an iterator class.

Different classes of iterators must be used with different types of container. There are three major classes of iterators: forward, bidirectional, and random access. A *forward iterator* can only move forward through the container, one item at a time. Its ++ operator accomplishes this. It can't move backward and it can't be set to an arbitrary location in the middle of the container. A *bidirectional iterator* can move backward as well as forward, so both its ++ and -- operators are defined. A *random access iterator*, in addition to moving backward and forward, can jump to an arbitrary location. You can tell it to access location 27, for example.

There are also two specialized kinds of iterators. An *input iterator* can "point to" an input device (cin or a file) to read sequential data items into a container, and an *output iterator* can "point to" an output device (cout or a file) and write elements from a container to the device.

While the values of forward, bi-directional, and random access iterators can be stored (so they can be used later), the values of input and output iterators cannot be. This makes sense: the first three iterators point to memory locations, while input and output iterators point to I/O devices for which stored "pointer" values have no meaning. Table 15.6 shows the characteristics of these different kinds of iterators.

TABLE 15.6 Iterator Characteristics

Iterator Type	Read/Write	Iterator Can Be Saved	Direction	Access
Random access	Read and write	Yes	Forward and back	Random
Bidirectional	Read and write	Yes	Forward and back	Linear
Forward	Read and write	Yes	Forward only	Linear
Output	Write only	No	Forward only	Linear
Input	Read only	No	Forward only	Linear

Potential Problems with the STL

The sophistication of the STL's template classes places a strain on compilers, and not all of them respond well. Let's look at some potential problems.

First, it's sometimes hard to find errors because the compiler reports them as being deep in a header file when they're really in the class user's code. You may need to resort to brute force methods such as commenting out one line of your code at a time to find the culprit.

Precompilation of header files, which speeds up compilation dramatically on compilers that offer it, may cause problems with the STL. If things don't seem to be working, try turning off precompiled headers.

The STL may generate spurious compiler warnings. "Conversion may lose significant digits" is a favorite. These appear to be harmless, and can be ignored or turned off.

These minor complaints aside, the STL is a surprisingly robust and versatile system. Errors tend to be caught at compile time rather than at runtime. The different algorithms and containers present a very consistent interface; what works with one container or algorithm will usually work with another (assuming it's used appropriately).

This quick overview probably leaves you with more questions than answers. The balance of this chapter should provide enough specific details of STL operation to make things clearer.

Algorithms

The STL algorithms perform operations on collections of data. These algorithms were designed to work with STL containers, but one of the nice things about them is that you can apply them to ordinary C++ arrays. This may save you considerable work when programming arrays. It also offers an easy way to learn about the algorithms, unencumbered with containers. In this section we'll examine how some representative algorithms are used. (Remember that the algorithms are listed in Appendix F.)

The find() Algorithm

The find() algorithm looks for the first element in a container that has a specified value. The FIND example program shows how this looks when we're trying to find a value in an array of ints.

```
// find.cpp
// finds the first object with a specified value
#include <iostream>
#include <algorithm>                    //for find()
using namespace std;

int arr[] = { 11, 22, 33, 44, 55, 66, 77, 88 };

int main()
   {
   int* ptr;
   ptr = find(arr, arr+8, 33);          //find first 33
   cout << "First object with value 33 found at offset "
        << (ptr-arr) << endl;
   return 0;
   }
```

The output from this program is

```
First object with value 33 found at offset 2.
```

As usual, the first element in the array is number 0, so the 33 is at offset 2, not 3.

Header Files

In this program we've included the header file ALGORITHM. Notice that, as with other header files in the Standard C++ Library, there is no file extension (like .H). This file contains the declarations of the STL algorithms. Other header files are used for containers and for other purposes. If you're using an older version of the STL you may need to include a header file with a somewhat different name, like ALGO.H.

Ranges

The first two parameters to find() specify the range of elements to be examined. These values are specified by iterators. In this example we use normal C++ pointer values, which are a special case of iterators.

The first parameter is the iterator of (or in this case the pointer to) the first value to be examined. The second parameter is the iterator of the location one past the last element to be examined. Since there are 8 elements, this value is the first value plus 8. This is called a *past-the-end* value; it points to the element just past the end of the range to be examined.

This syntax is reminiscent of the normal C++ idiom in a for loop:

```
for(int j=0; j<8; j++)    //from 0 to 7
   {
   if(arr[j] == 33)
      {
      cout << "First object with value 33 found at offset "
           << j << endl;
      break;
      }
   }
```

In the FIND example, the find() algorithm saves you the trouble of writing this for loop. In more complicated situations, algorithms may save you from writing far more complicated code.

The count() Algorithm

Let's look at another algorithm, count(), which counts how many elements in a container have a specified value and returns this number. The COUNT example shows how this looks:

```
// count.cpp
// counts the number of objects with a specified value
#include <iostream>
#include <algorithm>                //for count()
using namespace std;

int arr[] = { 33, 22, 33, 44, 33, 55, 66, 77 };

int main()
   {
   int n = count(arr, arr+8, 33);   //count number of 33's
   cout << "There are " << n << " 33's in arr." << endl;
   return 0;
   }
```

The output is

```
There are 3 33's in arr.
```

The `sort()` Algorithm

You can guess what the `sort()` algorithm does. Here's an example, called SORT, of this algorithm applied to an array:

```
// sort.cpp
// sorts an array of integers
#include <iostream>
#include <algorithm>
using namespace std;
                                  //array of numbers
int arr[] = {45, 2, 22, -17, 0, -30, 25, 55};

int main()
   {
   sort(arr, arr+8);             //sort the numbers

   for(int j=0; j<8; j++)        //display sorted array
      cout << arr[j] << ' ';
   cout << endl;
   return 0;
   }
```

The output from the program is

```
-30, -17, 0, 2, 22, 25, 45, 55
```

We'll look at some variations of this algorithm later.

The `search()` Algorithm

Some algorithms operate on two containers at once. For instance, while the `find()` algorithm looks for a specified value in a single container, the `search()` algorithm looks for a sequence of values, specified by one container, within another container. The SEARCH example shows how this looks.

```
// search.cpp
// searches one container for a sequence in another container
#include <iostream>
#include <algorithm>
using namespace std;

int source[] = { 11, 44, 33, 11, 22, 33, 11, 22, 44 };
int pattern[] = { 11, 22, 33 };

int main()
   {
   int* ptr;
   ptr = search(source, source+9, pattern, pattern+3);
```

```
    if(ptr == source+9)                  //if past-the-end
       cout << "No match found\n";
    else
       cout << "Match at " << (ptr - source) << endl;
    return 0;
}
```

The algorithm looks for the sequence 11, 22, 33, specified by the array `pattern`, within the array `source`. As you can see by inspection, this sequence is found in source starting at the fourth element (element 3). The output is

```
Match at 3
```

If the iterator value `ptr` ends up one past the end of the source, no match has been found.

The arguments to algorithms such as `search()` don't need to be the same type of container. The source could be in an STL vector, and the pattern in an array, for example. This kind of generality is a very powerful feature of the STL.

The `merge()` Algorithm

Here's an algorithm that works with three containers, merging the elements from two source containers into a destination container. The MERGE example shows how it works.

```
// merge.cpp
// merges two containers into a third
#include <iostream>
#include <algorithm>            //for merge()
using namespace std;

int src1[] = { 2, 3, 4, 6, 8 };
int src2[] = { 1, 3, 5 };
int dest[8];

int main()
   {                              //merge src1 and src2 into dest
   merge(src1, src1+5, src2, src2+3, dest);
   for(int j=0; j<8; j++)        //display dest
      cout << dest[j] << ' ';
   cout << endl;
   return 0;
   }
}
```

The output, which displays the contents of the destination container, looks like this:

```
1 2 3 3 4 5 6 8
```

As you can see, merging preserves the ordering, interweaving the two sequences of source elements into the destination container.

Function Objects

Some algorithms can take something called a *function object* as an argument. A function object looks, to the user, much like a template function. However, it's actually an object of a template class that has a single member function: the overloaded () operator. This sounds mysterious, but it's easy to use.

Suppose you want to sort an array of numbers into descending instead of ascending order. The SORTEMP program shows how to do it:

```
// sortemp.cpp
// sorts array of doubles in backward order,
// uses greater<>() function object
#include <iostream>
#include <algorithm>               //for sort()
#include <functional>              //for greater<>
using namespace std;
                                   //array of doubles
double fdata[] = { 19.2, 87.4, 33.6, 55.0, 11.5, 42.2 };

int main()
   {                               //sort the doubles
   sort( fdata, fdata+6, greater<double>() );

   for(int j=0; j<6; j++)          //display sorted doubles
      cout << fdata[j] << ' ';
   cout << endl;
   return 0;
}
```

The sort() algorithm usually sorts in ascending order, but the use of the greater<>() function object, the third argument of sort(), reverses the sorting order. Here's the output:

```
87.4 55 42.2 33.6 19.2 11.5
```

Besides comparisons, there are function objects for arithmetical and logical operations. We'll look at function objects more closely in the last section of this chapter.

User-Written Functions in Place of Function Objects

Function objects operate only on basic C++ types and on classes for which the appropriate operators (+, <, ==, and so on) are defined. If you're working with values for which this is not the case, you can substitute a user-written function for a function object. For example, the operator < is not defined for ordinary char* strings, but we can write a function to perform the comparison, and use this function's address (its name) in place of the function object. The SORTCOM example shows how to sort an array of char* strings:

```
// sortcom.cpp
// sorts array of strings with user-written comparison function
#include <iostream>
#include <string>                        //for strcmp()
#include <algorithm>
using namespace std;
                                         //array of strings
char* names[] = { "George", "Penny", "Estelle",
                  "Don", "Mike", "Bob" };

bool alpha_comp(char*, char*);           //declaration

int main()
   {
   sort(names, names+6, alpha_comp);     //sort the strings

   for(int j=0; j<6; j++)                //display sorted strings
      cout << names[j] << endl;
   return 0;
   }

bool alpha_comp(char* s1, char* s2)      //returns true if s1<s2
   {
   return ( strcmp(s1, s2)<0 ) ? true : false;
   }
```

The third argument to the sort() algorithm is the address of the alpha_comp() function, which compares two char* strings and returns true or false, depending on whether the first is lexicographically (that is, alphabetically) less than the second. It uses the C library function strcmp(), which returns a value less than 0 if its first argument is less than its second. The output from this program is what you would expect:

```
Bob
Don
Estelle
George
Mike
Penny
```

Actually you don't need to write your own function objects to handle text. If you use the string class from the standard library, you can use built-in function objects such as less<>() and greater<>().

Adding _if to Algorithms
Some algorithms have versions that end in _if. These algorithms take an extra parameter called a *predicate*, which is a function object or a function. For example, the find() algorithm

finds all elements equal to a specified value. We can also create a function that works with the find_if() algorithm to find elements with any arbitrary characteristic.

Our example uses string objects. The find_if() algorithm is supplied with a user-written isDon() function to find the first string in an array of string objects that has the value "Don". Here's the listing for FIND_IF:

```cpp
// find_if.cpp
// searches array of strings for first name that matches "Don"
#include <iostream>
#include <string>
#include <algorithm>
using namespace std;
//-------------------------------------------------------------
bool isDon(string name)          //returns true if name=="Don"
   {
   return name == "Don";
   }
//-------------------------------------------------------------
string names[] = { "George", "Estelle", "Don", "Mike", "Bob" };

int main()
   {
   string* ptr;
   ptr = find_if( names, names+5, isDon );

   if(ptr==names+5)
      cout << "Don is not on the list.\n";
   else
      cout << "Don is element "
           << (ptr-names)
           << " on the list.\n";
   return 0;
   }
```

Since "Don" is indeed one of the names in the array, the output from the program is

```
Don is element 2 on the list.
```

The address of the function isDon() is the third argument to find_if(), while the first and second arguments are, as usual, the first and the past-the-end addresses of the array.

The find_if() algorithm applies the isDon() function to every element in the range. If isDon() returns true for any element, then find_if() returns the value of that element's pointer (iterator). Otherwise, it returns a pointer to the past-the-end address of the array.

Various other algorithms, such as count(), replace(), and remove(), have _if versions.

The `for_each()` Algorithm

The `for_each()` algorithm allows you to do something to every item in a container. You write your own function to determine what that "something" is. Your function can't change the elements in the container, but it can use or display their values.

Here's an example in which `for_each()` is used to convert all the values of an array from inches to centimeters and display them. We write a function called `in_to_cm()` that multiplies a value by 2.54, and use this function's address as the third argument to `for_each()`. Here's the listing for FOR_EACH:

```cpp
// for_each.cpp
// uses for_each() to output inches array elements as centimeters
#include <iostream>
#include <algorithm>
using namespace std;

void in_to_cm(double);        //declaration

int main()
   {                          //array of inches values
   double inches[] = { 3.5, 6.2, 1.0, 12.75, 4.33 };
                              //output as centimeters
   for_each(inches, inches+5, in_to_cm);
   cout << endl;
   return 0;
   }

void in_to_cm(double in)    //convert and display as centimeters
   {
   cout << (in * 2.54) << ' ';
   }
```

The output looks like this:

```
8.89 15.748 2.54 32.385 10.9982
```

The `transform()` Algorithm

The `transform()` algorithm does something to every item in a container, and places the resulting values in a different container (or the same one). Again, a user-written function determines what will be done to each item. The return type of this function must be the same as that of the destination container. Our example is similar to FOR_EACH, except that instead of displaying the converted values, our `in_to_cm()` function puts the centimeter values into a different array, `centi[]`. The main program then displays the contents of `centi[]`. Here's the listing for TRANSFO:

```cpp
// transfo.cpp
// uses transform() to change array of inches values to cm
```

```cpp
#include <iostream>
#include <algorithm>
using namespace std;

int main()
   {                              //array of inches values
   double inches[] = { 3.5, 6.2, 1.0, 12.75, 4.33 };
   double centi[5];
   double in_to_cm(double);    //prototype
                               //transform into array centi[]
   transform(inches, inches+5, centi, in_to_cm);

   for(int j=0; j<5; j++)       //display array centi[]
      cout << centi[j] << ' ';
   cout << endl;
   return 0;
   }

double in_to_cm(double in)      //convert inches to centimeters
   {
   return (in * 2.54);          //return result
   }
```

The output is the same as that from the FOR_EACH program.

We've looked at just a few of the algorithms in the STL. There are many others, but what we've shown here should give you an idea of the kinds of algorithms that are available, and how to use them.

Sequence Containers

As we noted earlier, there are two major categories of containers in the STL: sequence containers and associative containers. In this section we'll discuss the three sequence containers (vectors, lists, and deques), focusing on how these containers work and on their member functions. We haven't learned about iterators yet, so there will be some operations that we can't perform on these containers. We'll examine iterators in the next section.

Each program example in the following sections will introduce several member functions for the container being described. Remember, however, that different kinds of containers use member functions with the same names and characteristics, so what you learn about, say, push_back() for vectors will also be relevant to lists and queues.

Vectors

You can think of vectors as smart arrays. They manage storage allocation for you, expanding and contracting the size of the vector as you insert or erase data. You can use vectors much like arrays, accessing elements with the [ ] operator. Such random access is very fast with vectors.

It's also fast to add (or *push*) a new data item onto the end (the *back*) of the vector. When this happens, the vector's size is automatically increased to hold the new item.

Member Functions push_back(), size(), and operator[]

Our first example, VECTOR, shows the most common vector operations.

```
// vector.cpp
// demonstrates push_back(), operator[], size()
#include <iostream>
#include <vector>
using namespace std;

int main()
    {
    vector<int> v;                  //create a vector of ints

    v.push_back(10);                //put values at end of array
    v.push_back(11);
    v.push_back(12);
    v.push_back(13);

    v[0] = 20;                      //replace with new values
    v[3] = 23;

    for(int j=0; j<v.size(); j++)   //display vector contents
        cout << v[j] << ' ';        //20 11 12 23
    cout << endl;
    return 0;
    }
```

We use the vector's default (no-argument) constructor to create a vector v. As with all STL containers, the template format is used to specify the type of variable the container will hold (in this case type int). We don't specify the container's size, so it starts off at 0.

The push_back() member function inserts the value of its argument at the back of the vector. (The back is where the element with the highest index number is.) The front of a vector (the element with index 0), unlike that of a list or queue, cannot be used for inserting new elements. Here we push the values 10, 11, 12, and 13, so that v[0] contains 10, v[1] contains 11, v[2] contains 12, and v[3] contains 13.

Once a vector has some data in it, this data can be accessed—both read and written to—using the overloaded [] operator, just as if it were in an array. We use this operator to change the first element from 10 to 20, and the last element from 13 to 23. Here's the output from VECTOR:

20 11 12 23

The size() member function returns the number of elements currently in the container, which in VECTOR is 4. We use this value in the for loop to print out the values of the elements in the container.

Another member function, `max_size()` (which we don't demonstrate here), returns the maximum size to which a container can be expanded. This number depends on the type of data being stored in the container (the bigger the elements, the fewer of them you can store), the type of container, and the operating system. For example, on our system `max_size()` returns 1,073,741,823 for a vector type `int`.

Member Functions `swap()`, `empty()`, `back()`, and `pop_back()`

The next example, VECTCON, shows some additional vector constructors and member functions.

```cpp
// vectcon.cpp
// demonstrates constructors, swap(), empty(), back(), pop_back()
#include <iostream>
#include <vector>
using namespace std;

int main()
   {                                    //an array of doubles
   double arr[] = { 1.1, 2.2, 3.3, 4.4 };

   vector<double> v1(arr, arr+4);  //initialize vector to array
   vector<double> v2(4);           //empty vector of size 4

   v1.swap(v2);                    //swap contents of v1 and v2

   while( !v2.empty() )            //until vector is empty,
      {
      cout << v2.back() << ' ';    //display the last element
      v2.pop_back();               //remove the last element
      }                            //output: 4.4 3.3 2.2 1.1
   cout << endl;
   return 0;
   }
```

We've used two new vector constructors in this program. The first initializes the vector v1 with the values of a normal C++ array passed to it as an argument. The arguments to this constructor are pointers to the start of the array and to the element one past the end. The second constructor sets v2 to an initial size of 4, but does not supply any initial values. Both vectors hold type `double`.

The `swap()` member function exchanges all the data in one vector with all the data in another, keeping the elements in the same order. In this program there is only garbage data in v2, so it's swapped with the data in v1. We display v2 to show that it now contains the data that was in v1. The output is

4.4, 3.3, 2.2, 1.1

The `back()` member function returns the value of the last element in the vector. We display this value with cout. The `pop_back()` member function removes the last element in the vector.

Thus each time through the loop there is a different last element. (It's a little surprising that pop_back() does not simultaneously return the value of the last element and remove it from the vector, as we've seen pop() do in previous examples with stacks, but it doesn't, so back() must be used as well.)

Some member functions, such as swap(), also exist as algorithms. When this is the case, the member function version is usually provided because it's more efficient for that particular container than the algorithm version. Sometimes you can use the algorithm as well. For example, you can use it to swap elements in two different kinds of containers.

Member Functions insert() and erase()

The insert() and erase() member functions insert or remove an element from an arbitrary location in a container. These functions aren't very efficient with vectors, since all the elements above the insertion or erasure must be moved to make space for the new element or close up the space where the erased item was. However, insertion and erasure may nevertheless be useful if speed is not a factor. The next example, VECTINS, shows how these member functions are used:

```
// vectins.cpp
// demonstrates insert(), erase()
#include <iostream>
#include <vector>
using namespace std;

int main()
    {
    int arr[] = { 100, 110, 120, 130 };   //an array of ints

    vector<int> v(arr, arr+4);            //initialize vector to array

    cout << "\nBefore insertion: ";
    for(int j=0; j<v.size(); j++)         //display all elements
        cout << v[j] << ' ';

    v.insert( v.begin()+2, 115);          //insert 115 at element 2

    cout << "\nAfter insertion:  ";
    for(j=0; j<v.size(); j++)             //display all elements
        cout << v[j] << ' ';

    v.erase( v.begin()+2 );               //erase element 2

    cout << "\nAfter erasure:     ";
    for(j=0; j<v.size(); j++)             //display all elements
        cout << v[j] << ' ';
```

```
    cout << endl;
    return 0;
    }
```

The insert() member function (at least this version of it) takes two arguments: the place where an element will be inserted in a container, and the value of the element. We add 2 to the begin() member function to specify element 2 (the third element) in the vector. The elements from the insertion point to the end of the container are moved upward to make room, and the size of the container is increased by 1.

The erase() member function removes the element at the specified location. The elements above the deletion point are moved downward, and the size of the container is decreased by 1. Here's the output from VECTINS:

```
Before insertion: 100 110 120 130
After insertion:  100 110 115 120 130
After erasure:    100 110 120 130
```

Lists

An STL list container is a doubly linked list, in which each element contains a pointer not only to the next element but also to the preceding one. The container stores the address of both the front (first) and the back (last) elements, which makes for fast access to both ends of the list.

Member Functions push_front(), front(), and pop_front

Our first example, LIST, shows how data can be pushed, read, and popped from both the front and the back.

```cpp
//list.cpp
//demonstrates push_front(), front(), pop_front()
#include <iostream>
#include <list>
using namespace std;

int main()
    {
    list<int> ilist;

    ilist.push_back(30);           //push items on back
    ilist.push_back(40);
    ilist.push_front(20);          //push items on front
    ilist.push_front(10);

    int size = ilist.size();       //number of items

    for(int j=0; j<size; j++)
        {
        cout << ilist.front() << ' '; //read item from front
```

```
        ilist.pop_front();                    //pop item off front
        }
    cout << endl;
    return 0;
    }
```

We push data on the back (the end) and front of the list in such a way that when we display and remove the data from the front it's in normal order:

```
10 20 30 40
```

The push_front(), pop_front(), and front() member functions are similar to push_back(), pop_back(), and back(), which we've already seen at work with vectors.

Note that you can't use random access for list elements, because such access is too slow. For this reason the [] operator is not defined for lists. If it were, this operator would need to traverse the list, counting elements as it went, until it reached the correct one, a time-consuming operation. If you need random access, you should use a vector or a deque.

Lists are appropriate when you will make frequent insertions and deletions in the middle of the list. This is not efficient for vectors and deques, because all the elements above the insertion or deletion point must be moved. However, it's quick for lists because only a few pointers need to be changed to insert or delete a new item. (However, it may still be time-consuming to find the correct insertion point.)

The insert() and erase() member functions are used for list insertion and deletion, but they require the use of iterators, so we'll postpone a discussion of these functions.

Member Functions reverse(), merge(), and unique()

Some member functions exist only for lists; no such member functions are defined for other containers, although there are algorithms that do the same things. Our next example, LISTPLUS, shows some of these functions. It begins by filling two list-of-int objects with the contents of two arrays.

```
// listplus.cpp
// demonstrates reverse(), merge(), and unique()
#include <iostream>
#include <list>
using namespace std;

int main()
    {
    int j;
    list<int> list1, list2;

    int arr1[] = { 40, 30, 20, 10 };
    int arr2[] = { 15, 20, 25, 30, 35 };
```

```
    for(j=0; j<4; j++)
        list1.push_back( arr1[j] );      //list1: 40, 30, 20, 10
    for(j=0; j<5; j++)
        list2.push_back( arr2[j] );      //list2: 15, 20, 25, 30, 35

    list1.reverse();                     //reverse list1: 10 20 30 40
    list1.merge(list2);                  //merge list2 into list1
    list1.unique();                      //remove duplicate 20 and 30

    int size = list1.size();
    while( !list1.empty() )
        {
        cout << list1.front() << ' ';    //read item from front
        list1.pop_front();               //pop item off front
        }
    cout << endl;
    return 0;
    }
```

The first list is in backward order, so we return it to normal sorted order using the reverse() member function. (It's quick to reverse a list container because both ends are accessible.) This is necessary because the second member function, merge(), operates on two lists and requires both of them to be in sorted order. Following the reversal, the two lists are

```
10, 20, 30, 40
15, 20, 25, 30, 35
```

Now the merge() function merges list2 into list1, keeping everything sorted and expanding list1 to hold the new items. The resulting content of list1 is

```
10, 15, 20, 20, 25, 30, 30, 35, 40
```

Finally we apply the unique() member function to list1. This function finds adjacent elements with the same value, and removes all but the first. The contents of list1 are then displayed. The output of LISTPLUS is

```
10, 15, 20, 25, 30, 35, 40
```

To display the contents of the list we use the front() and pop_front() member functions in a for loop. Each element, from front to back, is displayed and then popped off the list. The result is that the process of displaying the list destroys it. This may not always be what you want, but for the moment it's the only way we have learned to access successive list elements. Iterators, described in the next section, will solve this problem.

Deques

A deque is like a vector in some ways and like a linked list in others. Like a vector, it supports random access using the [ ] operator. However, like a list, a deque can be accessed at the front as well as the back. It's a sort of double-ended vector, supporting push_front(), pop_front(), and front().

Memory is allocated differently for vectors and queues. A vector always occupies a contiguous region of memory. If a vector grows too large, it may need to be moved to a new location where it will fit. A deque, on the other hand, can be stored in several non-contiguous areas; it is segmented. A member function, capacity(), returns the largest number of elements a vector can store without being moved, but capacity() isn't defined for deques because they don't need to be moved.

```
// deque.cpp
// demonstrates push_back(), push_front(), front()
#include <iostream>
#include <deque>
using namespace std;

int main()
    {
    deque<int> deq;

    deq.push_back(30);                  //push items on back
    deq.push_back(40);
    deq.push_back(50);
    deq.push_front(20);                 //push items on front
    deq.push_front(10);

    deq[2] = 33;                        //change middle item

    for(int j=0; j<deq.size(); j++)
        cout << deq[j] << ' ';          //display items
    cout << endl;
    return 0;
    }
```

We've already seen examples of push_back(), push_front(), and operator [ ]. They work the same for deques as for other containers. The output of this program is

```
10 20 33 40 50
```

Figure 15.2 shows some important member functions for the three sequential containers.

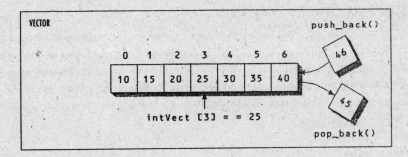

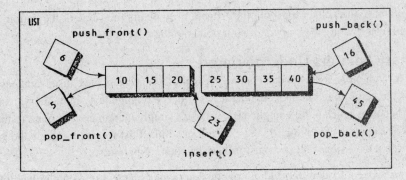

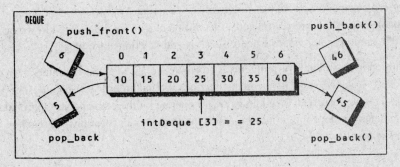

FIGURE 15.2
Sequence containers.

Iterators

Iterators may seem a bit mysterious, yet they are central to the operation of the STL. In this section we'll first discuss the twin roles played by iterators: as smart pointers and as a connection between algorithms and containers. Then we'll show some examples of their use.

Iterators as Smart Pointers

It's often necessary to perform an operation on all the elements in the container (or perhaps a range of elements). Displaying the value of each element in the container or adding its value to a total are examples. In an ordinary C++ array, such operations are carried out using a pointer (or the [ ] operator, which is the same underlying mechanism). For example, the following code iterates through a float array, displaying the value of each element:

```
float* ptr = start_address;
for(int j=0; j<SIZE; j++)
    cout << *ptr++;
```

We dereference the pointer ptr with the * operator to obtain the value of the item it points to, and increment it with the ++ operator so it points to the next item.

Ordinary Pointers Underpowered

However, with more sophisticated containers, plain C++ pointers have disadvantages. For one thing, if the items stored in the container are not placed contiguously in memory, handling the pointer becomes much more complicated; we can't simply increment it to point to the next value. For example, in moving to the next item in a linked list we can't assume the item is adjacent to the previous one; we must follow the chain of pointers.

We may also want to store the address of some container element in a pointer variable so we can access the element at some future time. What happens to this stored pointer value if we insert or erase something from the middle of the container? It may not continue to be valid if the container's contents are rearranged. It would be nice if we didn't need to worry about revising all our stored pointer values when insertions and deletions take place.

One solution to these kinds of problems is to create a class of "smart pointers." An object of such a class basically wraps its member functions around an ordinary pointer. The ++ and * operators are overloaded so they know how to operate on the elements in their container, even if the elements are not contiguous in memory or change their locations. Here's how that might look, in skeleton form:

```
class SmartPointer
    {
    private:
        float* p;    //an ordinary pointer
    public:
        float operator*()
            { }
        float operator++()
            { }
    };
```

```
void main()
   {
   ...
   SmartPointer sptr = start_address;
   for(int j=0; j<SIZE; j++)
      cout << *sptr++;
   }
```

Whose Responsibility?

Should the smart pointer class be embedded in a container, or should it be a separate class? The approach chosen by the STL is to make smart pointers, called *iterators*, into a completely separate class (actually a family of templetized classes). The class user creates iterators by defining them to be objects of such classes.

Iterators as an Interface

Besides acting as smart pointers to items in containers, iterators serve another important purpose in the STL. They determine which algorithms can be used with which containers. Why is this necessary?

In some theoretical sense you should be able to apply every algorithm to every container. And, in fact, many algorithms will work with all the STL containers. However, it turns out that some algorithms are very inefficient (that is, slow) when used with some containers. The sort() algorithm, for example, needs random access to the container it's trying to sort; otherwise, it would need to iterate through the container to find each element before moving it, a time-consuming approach. Similarly, to be efficient, the reverse() algorithm needs to iterate backward as well as forward through a container.

Iterators provide a surprisingly elegant way to match appropriate algorithms with containers. As we noted, you can think of an iterator as a cable, like the cable used to connect a computer and printer. One end of the cable plugs into a container, and the other plugs into an algorithm. However, not all cables plug into all containers, and not all cables plug into all algorithms. If you try to use an algorithm that's too powerful for a given container type, you won't be able to find a cable (an iterator) to connect them. If you try it, you will receive a compiler error alerting you to the problem.

How many kinds of iterators (cables) do you need to make this scheme work? As it turns out, only five types are necessary. Figure 15.3 shows these five categories, arranged from bottom to top in order of increasing sophistication (input and output are equally unsophisticated).

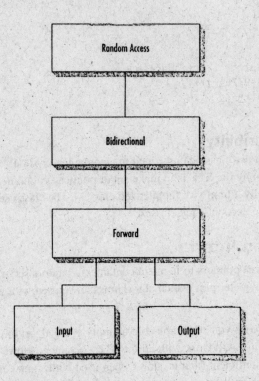

FIGURE 15.3
Iterator categories.

If an algorithm needs only to step forward through a container, reading (but not writing to) one item after another, it can use an *input* iterator to connect itself to the container. Actually, input iterators are typically used, not with containers, but when reading from files or cin.

If an algorithm steps through the container in a forward direction but writes to the container instead of reading from it, it can use an *output* iterator. Output iterators are typically used when writing to files or cout.

If an algorithm steps along forward and may either read from or write to a container, it must use a *forward* iterator.

If an algorithm must be able to step both forward and back through a container, it must use a *bidirectional* iterator.

Finally, if an algorithm must access any item in the container instantly, without stepping along to it, it must use a *random access* iterator. Random access iterators are like arrays, in that you can access any element. They are the only iterators that can be manipulated with arithmetic operations, as in

```
iter2 = iter1 + 7;
```

Table 15.7 shows which operations each iterator supports.

TABLE 15.7 Capabilities of Different Iterator Categories

Iterator Type	Step Forward ++	Read value=*i	Write *i=value	Step Back --	Random Access [n]
Random access iterator	x	x	x	x	x
Bidirectional iterator	x	x	x	x	
Forward iterator	x	x	x		
Output iterator	x		x		
Input iterator	x	x			

As you can see, all the iterators support the ++ operator for stepping forward through the container. The input iterator can use the * operator on the right side of the equal sign (but not on the left):

```
value = *iter;
```

The output iterator can use the * operator only on the right:

```
*iter = value;
```

The forward iterator handles both reading and writing, and the bidirectional iterator can be decremented as well as incremented. The random access iterator can use the [ ] operator (as well as simple arithmetic operators such as + and -) to access any element quickly.

An algorithm can always use an iterator with *more* capability than it needs. If it needs a forward iterator, for example, it's all right to plug it into a bidirectional iterator or a random access iterator.

Matching Algorithms with Containers

We've used a cable as an analogy to an iterator, because an iterator connects an algorithm and a container. Let's focus on the two ends of this imaginary cable: the container end and the algorithm end.

Plugging the Cable into a Container

If you confine yourself to the basic STL containers, you will be using only two kinds of iterators. As shown in Table 15.8, the vector and deque accept any kind of iterator, while the list, set, multiset, map, and multimap accept anything except the random iterator.

TABLE 15.8   Iterator Types Accepted by Containers

	Vector	List	Deque	Set	Multiset	Map	Multimap
Random Access	X		X				
Bidirectional	X	X	X	X	X	X	X
Forward	X	X	X	X	X	X	X
Input	X	X	X	X	X	X	X
Output	X	X	X	X	X	X	X

How does the STL enforce the use of the correct iterator for a given container? When you define an iterator you must specify what kind of container it will be used for. For example, if you've defined a list holding elements of type int

```
list<int> iList;            //list of ints
```

then to define an iterator to this list you say

```
list<int>::iterator iter;  //iterator to list-of-ints
```

When you do this, the STL automatically makes this iterator a bidirectional iterator, because that's what a list requires. An iterator to a vector or a deque is automatically created as a random-access iterator.

This automatic selection process is implemented by causing an iterator class for a specific container to be derived (inherited) from a more general iterator class that's appropriate to a specific container. Thus the iterators to vectors and deques are derived from the random_access_iterator class, while iterators to lists are derived from the bidirectional_iterator class.

We now see how containers are matched to their end of our fanciful iterator cables. A cable doesn't actually plug into a container; it is (figuratively speaking) hardwired to it, like the cord on a toaster. Vectors and deques are always wired to random-access cables, while lists (and all the associative containers, which we'll encounter later in this chapter) are always wired to bidirectional cables.

Plugging the Cable into the Algorithm

Now that we've seen how one end of an iterator cable is "wired" to the container, we're ready to look at the other end of the cable. How do iterators plug into algorithms? Every algorithm, depending on what it will do to the elements in a container, requires a certain kind of iterator. If the algorithm must access elements at arbitrary locations in the container, it requires a random-access iterator. If it will merely step forward through the iterator, it can use the less powerful forward iterator. Table 15.9 shows a sampling of algorithms and the iterators they require. (A complete version of this table is shown in Appendix F.)

TABLE 15.9   Type of Iterator Required by Representative Algorithms

Algorithm	Input	Output	Forward	Bidirec-tional	Random Access
for_each	X				
find	X				
count	X				
copy	X	X			
replace			X		
unique			X		
reverse				X	
sort					X
nth_element					X
merge	X	X			
accumulate	X				

Again, although each algorithm requires an iterator with a certain level of capability, a more powerful iterator will also work. The replace() algorithm requires a forward iterator, but it will work with a bidirectional or a random access iterator as well.

Now, imagine that algorithms have connectors with pins sticking out, like the cable connectors on your computer. This is shown in Figure 15.4. Those requiring random access iterators have 5 pins, those requiring bidirectional iterators have 4 pins, those requiring forward iterators have 3 pins, and so on.

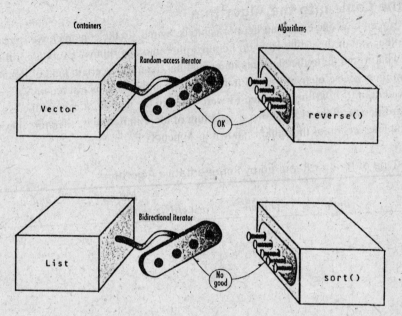

FIGURE 15.4
Iterators connecting containers and algorithms.

The algorithm end of an iterator (a cable) has a connector with a certain number of holes. You can plug a 5-hole iterator into a 5-pin algorithm, and you can also plug it into an algorithm with 4 or fewer pins. However, you can't plug a 4-hole (bidirectional) iterator into a 5-pin (random-access) algorithm. So vectors and deques, with random access iterators, can be plugged into any algorithm, while lists and associative containers, with only a 4-hole bidirectional iterator, can only be plugged into less powerful algorithms.

The Tables Tell the Story

From Tables 15.8 and 15.9 you can figure out whether an algorithm will work with a given container. Table 15.9 shows that the sort() algorithm, for example, requires a random-access iterator. Table 15.8 indicates that the only containers that can handle random-access iterators are vectors and deques. There's no use trying to apply the sort() algorithm to lists, sets, maps, and so on.

Any algorithm that does *not* require a random-access iterator will work with any kind of STL container, because all these containers use bidirectional iterators, which is only one grade below random access. (If there were a singly-linked list in the STL it would use only a forward iterator, so it could not be used with the reverse() algorithm.)

As you can see, comparatively few algorithms require random-access iterators. Therefore most algorithms work with most containers.

Overlapping Member Functions and Algorithms

Sometimes you must choose between using a member function or an algorithm with the same name. The find() algorithm, for example, requires only an input iterator, so it can be used with any container. However, sets and maps have their own find() member function (unlike sequential containers). Which version of find() should you use? Generally, if a member-function version exists, it's because, for that container, the algorithm version is not as efficient as it could be; so in these cases you should probably use the member-function version.

Iterators at Work

Using iterators is considerably simpler than talking about them. We've already seen several examples of one of the more common uses, where iterator values are returned by a container's begin() and end() member functions. We've disguised the fact that these functions return iterator values by treating them as if they were pointers. Now let's see how actual iterators are used with these and other functions.

Data Access

In containers that provide random access iterators (vector and queue) it's easy to iterate through the container using the [] operator. Containers such as lists, which don't support random access, require a different approach. In previous examples we've used a "destructive read-out" to display the contents of a list by popping off the items one by one, as in the LIST and LISTPLUS examples. A more practical approach is to define an iterator for the container. The LISTOUT program shows how that might look:

```
// listout.cpp
// iterator and for loop for output
#include <iostream>
#include <list>
#include <algorithm>
using namespace std;

int main()
   {
   int arr[] = { 2, 4, 6, 8 };
   list<int> theList;

   for(int k=0; k<4; k++)      //fill list with array elements
      theList.push_back( arr[k] );

   list<int>::iterator iter;    //iterator to list-of-ints

   for(iter = theList.begin(); iter != theList.end(); iter++)
      cout << *iter << ' ';      //display the list
```

```
    cout << endl;
    return 0;
    }
```

The program simply displays the contents of the theList container. The output is

```
2 4 6 8
```

We define an iterator of type list<int> to match the container type. As with a pointer variable, we must give an iterator a value before using it. In the for loop we initialize it to iList.begin(), the start of the container. We can increment it with the ++ operator so that it steps through the elements in a container, and we can dereference it with the * operator to obtain the value of each element it points to. We can also compare it for equality using the != operator, so we can exit the loop when it reaches the end of the container at iList.end().

An equivalent approach, using a while loop instead of a for loop, might be

```
iter = iList.begin();
while( iter != iList.end() )
   cout << *iter++ << ' ';
```

The *iter++ syntax is the same as it would be for a pointer.

Data Insertion

We can use similar code to place data into existing elements in a container, as shown in LISTFILL:

```
// listfill.cpp
// uses iterator to fill list with data
#include <iostream>
#include <list>
using namespace std;

int main()
   {
   list<int> iList(5);       //empty list holds 5 ints
   list<int>::iterator it;   //iterator
   int data = 0;
                             //fill list with data
   for(it = iList.begin(); it != iList.end(); it++)
      *it = data += 2;
                             //display list
   for(it = iList.begin(); it != iList.end(); it++)
      cout << *it << ' ';
   cout << endl;
   return 0;
   }
```

The Standard Template Library 761

The first loop fills the container with the int values 2, 4, 6, 8, 10, showing that the overloaded
* operator works on the left side of the equal sign as well as the right. The second loop displays these values.

Algorithms and Iterators

Algorithms, as we've discussed, use iterators as arguments (and sometimes as return values).
The ITERFIND example shows the find() algorithm applied to a list. (We know we can use the
find() algorithm with lists, because it requires only an input iterator.)

```
// iterfind.cpp
// find() returns a list iterator
#include <iostream>
#include <algorithm>
#include <list>
using namespace std;

int main()
   {
   list<int> theList(5);        //empty list holds 5 ints
   list<int>::iterator iter;    //iterator
   int data = 0;
                                //fill list with data
   for(iter = theList.begin(); iter != theList.end(); iter++)
      *iter = data += 2;        //2, 4, 6, 8, 10
                                //look for number 8
   iter = find(theList.begin(), theList.end(), 8);
   if( iter != theList.end() )
      cout << "\nFound 8.\n";
   else
      cout << "\nDid not find 8.\n";
   return 0;
   }
```

As an algorithm, find() takes three arguments. The first two are iterator values specifying the
range to be searched, and the third is the value to be found. Here we fill the container with the
same 2, 4, 6, 8, 10 values as in the last example. Then we use the find() algorithm to look for
the number 8. If find() returns iList.end(), we know it's reached the end of the container
without finding a match. Otherwise, it must have located an item with the value 8. Here the
output is

Found 8.

Can we use the value of the iterator to tell where in the container the 8 is located? You might
think the offset of the matching item from the beginning of the container could be calculated
from (iter - iList.begin()). However, this is not a legal operation on the iterators used for
lists. A list iterator is only a bidirectional iterator, so you can't perform arithmetic with it. You

15
THE STANDARD
TEMPLATE LIBRARY

can do arithmetic with random access iterators, such as those used with vectors and queues. Thus if you were searching a vector v rather than a list iList, you could rewrite the last part of ITERFIND like this:

```
iter = find(v.begin(), v.end(), 8);
if( iter != v.end() )
    cout << "\nFound 8 at location " << (iter-v.begin() );
else
    cout << "\nDid not find 8.";
```

The output would be

```
Found 8 at location 3
```

Here's another example in which an algorithm uses iterators as arguments. This one uses the copy() algorithm with a vector. The user specifies a range of locations to be copied from one vector to another, and the program copies them. Iterators specify this range.

```
// itercopy.cpp
// uses iterators for copy() algorithm
#include <iostream>
#include <vector>
#include <algorithm>
using namespace std;

int main()
    {
    int beginRange, endRange;
    int arr[] = { 11, 13, 15, 17, 19, 21, 23, 25, 27, 29 };
    vector<int> v1(arr, arr+10);   //initialized vector
    vector<int> v2(10);            //uninitialized vector

    cout << "Enter range to be copied (example: 2 5): ";
    cin >> beginRange >> endRange;

    vector<int>::iterator iter1 = v1.begin() + beginRange;
    vector<int>::iterator iter2 = v1.begin() + endRange;
    vector<int>::iterator iter3;
                                //copy range from v1 to v2
    iter3 = copy( iter1, iter2, v2.begin() );
                                //(it3 -> last item copied)
    iter1 = v2.begin();         //iterate through range
    while(iter1 != iter3)       //in v2, displaying values
        cout << *iter1++ << ' ';
    cout << endl;
    return 0;
    }
```

Here's some interaction with this program:

```
Enter range to be copied (example: 2 5): 3 6
17 19 21
```

We don't display the entire contents of v2, only the range of items copied. Fortunately, copy() returns an iterator that points to the last item (actually one past the last item) that was copied to the destination container, v2 in this case. The program uses this value in the while loop to display only the items copied.

Specialized Iterators

In this section we'll examine two specialized forms of iterators: iterator adapters, which can change the behavior of iterators in interesting ways, and stream iterators, which allow input and output streams to behave like iterators.

Iterator Adapters

The STL provides three variations on the normal iterator. These are the *reverse iterator*, the *insert iterator*, and the *raw storage iterator*. The reverse iterator allows you to iterate backward through a container. The insert iterator changes the behavior of various algorithms, such as copy() and merge(), so they insert data into a container rather than overwriting existing data. The raw storage iterator allows output iterators to store data in uninitialized memory, but it's used in specialized situations and we'll ignore it here.

Reverse Iterators

Suppose you want to iterate backward through a container, from the end to the beginning. You might think you could say something like

```
list<int>::iterator iter;          //normal iterator
iter = iList.end();                //start at end
while( iter != iList.begin() )     //go to beginning
   cout << *iter-- << ' ';         //decrement iterator
```

but unfortunately this doesn't work. (For one thing, the range will be wrong (from n to 1, instead of from n−1 to 0).

To iterate backward you can use a *reverse iterator*. The ITEREV program shows an example where a reverse iterator is used to display the contents of a list in reverse order.

```
// iterev.cpp
// demonstrates reverse iterator
#include <iostream>
#include <list>
using namespace std;
```

```
int main()
   {
   int arr[] = { 2, 4, 6, 8, 10 };        //array of ints
   list<int> theList;

   for(int j=0; j<5; j++)                  //transfer array
      theList.push_back( arr[j] );         //to list

   list<int>::reverse_iterator revit;      //reverse iterator

   revit = theList.rbegin();               //iterate backward
   while( revit != theList.rend() )        //through list,
      cout << *revit++ << ' ';             //displaying output
   cout << endl;
   return 0;
   }
```

The output of this program is

10 8 6 4 2

You must use the member functions rbegin() and rend() when you use a reverse iterator.
(Don't try to use them with a normal forward iterator.) Confusingly, you're starting at the end
of the container, but the member function is called rbegin(). Also, you must increment the
iterator. Don't try to decrement a reverse iterator; revit-- doesn't do what you want. With a
reverse_iterator, always go from rbegin() to rend() using the increment operator.

Insert Iterators
Some algorithms, such as copy(), overwrite the existing contents (if any) of the destination
container. The COPYDEQ program, which copies from one deque to another, provides an
example:

```
//. copydeq.cpp
//demonstrates normal copy with queues
#include <iostream>
#include <deque>
#include <algorithm>
using namespace std;

int main()
   {
   int arr1[] = { 1, 3, 5, 7, 9 };
   int arr2[] = { 2, 4, 6, 8, 10 };
   deque<int> d1;
   deque<int> d2;
```

```
for(int j=0; j<5; j++)              //transfer arrays to deques
   {
   d1.push_back( arr1[j] );
   d2.push_back( arr2[j] );
   }                                //copy d1 to d2
copy( d1.begin(), d1.end(), d2.begin() );

for(int k=0; k<d2.size(); k++)  //display d2
   cout << d2[k] << ' ';
cout << endl;
return 0;
}
```

The output of this program is

1 3 5 7 9

The contents of d2 have been written over by the contents of d1, so when we display d2 there's no trace of its former (even-numbered) contents. Usually this behavior is what you want. Sometimes, however, you'd rather that copy() inserted new elements into a container along with the old ones, instead of overwriting the old ones. You can cause this behavior by using an *insert iterator*. There are three flavors of this iterator:

* back_inserter inserts new items at the end
* front_inserter inserts new items at the beginning
* inserter inserts new items at a specified location

The DINSITER program shows how to use a back inserter.

```
//dinsiter.cpp
//demonstrates insert iterators with queues
#include <iostream>
#include <deque>
#include <algorithm>
using namespace std;

int main()
   {
   int arr1[] = { 1, 3, 5, 7, 9 }; //initialize d1
   int arr2[] = {2, 4, 6};         //initialize d2
   deque<int> d1;
   deque<int> d2;

   for(int i=0; i<5; i++)              //transfer arrays to deques
      d1.push_back( arr1[i] );
   for(int j=0; j<3; j++)
      d2.push_back( arr2[j] );
```

```
                                    //copy d1 to back of d2
copy( d1.begin(), d1.end(), back_inserter(d2) );

cout << "\nd2: ";                   //display d2
for(int k=0; k<d2.size(); k++)
   cout << d2[k] << ' ';
cout << endl;
return 0;
}
```

The back inserter uses the container's push_back() member function to insert the new items from source container d1 at the end of the target container d2, following the existing items. Container d1 is unchanged. The output of the program, which displays the new contents of d2, is

d2: 2 4 6 1 3 5 7 9

If we specified a front inserter instead

```
copy( d1.begin(), d1.end(), front_inserter(d2) );
```

then the new items would be inserted into the front of the container. The underlying mechanism of the front inserter is the container's push_front() member function, which pushes the items into the front of the container, effectively reversing their order. The output would be

9 7 5 3 1 2 4 6

You can also insert the new items starting at any arbitrary element by using the *inserter* version of the insert iterator. For example, to insert the new items at the beginning of d2, we would say

```
copy( d1.begin(), d1.end(), inserter(d2, d2.begin()) );
```

The first argument to inserter is the container to be copied into, and the second is an iterator pointing to the location where copying should begin. Because inserter uses the container's insert() member function, the order of the elements is not reversed. The output resulting from this statement would be

1 3 5 7 9 2 4 6

By changing the second argument to inserter we could cause the new data to be inserted anywhere in d2.

Note that a front_inserter can't be used with a vector, because vectors don't have a push_front() member function; they can only be accessed at the end.

Stream Iterators

Stream iterators allow you to treat files and I/O devices (such as cin and cout) as if they were iterators. This makes it easy to use files and I/O devices as arguments to algorithms. (This is another demonstration of the versatility of using iterators to link algorithms and containers.)

The major purpose of the input and output iterator categories is to support these stream iterator classes. Input and output iterators make it possible for appropriate algorithms to be used directly on input and output streams.

Stream iterators are actually objects of classes that are templetized for different types of input or output. There are two stream iterators: ostream_iterator and istream_iterator. Let's look at them in turn.

The ostream_iterator Class

An ostream_iterator object can be used as an argument to any algorithm that specifies an output iterator. In the OUTITER example we'll use it as an argument to copy():

```
//outiter.cpp
//demonstrates ostream_iterator
#include <iostream>
#include <algorithm>
#include <list>
using namespace std;

int main()
   {
   int arr[] = { 10, 20, 30, 40, 50 };
   list<int> theList;

   for(int j=0; j<5; j++)                   //transfer array to list
      theList.push_back( arr[j] );

   ostream_iterator<int> ositer(cout, ", ");  //ostream iterator

   cout << "\nContents of list: ";
   copy(theList.begin(), theList.end(), ositer);  //display list
   cout << endl;
   return 0;
   }
```

We define an ostream iterator for reading type int values. The two arguments to this constructor are the stream to which the int values will be written, and a string value that will be displayed following each value. The stream value is typically a filename or cout; here it's cout. When writing to cout, the delimiting string can consist of any characters you want; here we use a comma and a space.

The copy() algorithm copies the contents of the list to cout. The ostream iterator is used as the third argument to copy(); it's the destination.

The output of OUTITER is

Contents of list: 10, 20, 30, 40, 50,

Our next example, FOUTITER, shows how to use an ostream iterator to write to a file:

```cpp
//foutiter.cpp
//demonstrates ostream_iterator with files
#include <fstream>
#include <algorithm>
#include <list>
using namespace std;

int main()
   {
   int arr[] = { 11, 21, 31, 41, 51 };
   list<int> theList;

   for(int j=0; j<5; j++)              //transfer array
      theList.push_back( arr[j] );     //   to list
   ofstream outfile("ITER.DAT");       //create file object

   ostream_iterator<int> ositer(outfile, " ");  //iterator
                                                 //write list to file
   copy(theList.begin(), theList.end(), ositer);
   return 0;
   }
```

You must define an ofstream file object and associate it with a file, here called ITER.DAT. This object is the first argument to the ostream_iterator. When writing to a file, use a whitespace character in the string argument, not characters like "--". This makes it easier to read the data back from the file. Here we use a space (" ") character.

There's no displayable output from FOUTITER, but you can use a text editor (like the Notepad utility in Windows) to examine the file ITER.DAT, which was created by the ITER program. It should contain the data

11 21 31 41 51

The istream_iterator Class

An istream_iterator object can be used as an argument to any algorithm that specifies an input iterator. Our example, INITER, shows such objects used as the first two arguments to copy(). This program reads floating-point numbers entered into cin (the keyboard) by the user, and stores them in a list.

```
// initer.cpp
// demonstrates istream_iterator
#include <iostream>
#include <list>
#include <algorithm>
using namespace std;

int main()
   {
   list<float> fList(5);                //uninitialized list

   cout << "\nEnter 5 floating-point numbers: ";
                                        //istream iterators
   istream_iterator<float> cin_iter(cin);    //cin
   istream_iterator<float> end_of_stream;    //eos
                                        //copy from cin to fList
   copy( cin_iter, end_of_stream, fList.begin() );

   cout << endl;                        //display fList
   ostream_iterator<float> ositer(cout, "--");
   copy(fList.begin(), fList.end(), ositer);
   cout << endl;
   return 0;
   }
```

Here's some interaction with INITER

```
Enter 5 floating-point numbers: 1.1  2.2  3.3  4.4  5.5
1.1--2.2--3.3--4.4--5.5--
```

Notice that for copy(), because the data coming from cin is the source and not the destination, we must specify both the beginning and the end of the range of data to be copied. The beginning is an istream_iterator connected to cin, which we define as cin_iter using the one-argument constructor. But what about the end of the range? The no-argument (default) constructor to istream_iterator plays a special role here. It always creates an istream_iterator object that represents the end of the stream.

How does the user generate this end-of-stream value when inputting data? By typing the Ctrl+Z key combination, which transmits the end-of-file character normally used for streams. Sometimes several presses of Ctrl+Z are necessary. Pressing Enter won't end the file, although it will delimit the numbers.

We use an ostream_iterator to display the contents of the list, although of course there are many other ways to do this.

770

You must perform any display output, such as the "Enter 5 floating-point numbers" prompt, not only before using the istream iterator, but even before defining it. As soon as this iterator is defined, it locks up the display, waiting for input.

Our next example, FINITER, uses a file instead of cin as input to the copy() algorithm.

```
// finiter.cpp
// demonstrates istream_iterator with files
#include <iostream>
#include <list>
#include <fstream>
#include <algorithm>
using namespace std;

int main()
   {
   list<int> iList;                //empty list
   ifstream infile("ITER.DAT");    //create input file object
                                   //(ITER.DAT must already exist)
                                   //istream iterators
   istream_iterator<int> file_iter(infile);  //file
   istream_iterator<int> end_of_stream;      //eos
                                   //copy from infile to iList
   copy( file_iter, end_of_stream, back_inserter(iList) );

   cout << endl;                   //display iList
   ostream_iterator<int> ositer(cout, "--");
   copy(iList.begin(), iList.end(), ositer);
   cout << endl;
   return 0;
   }
```

The output from FINITER is

11--21--31--31--41--51--

We define an ifstream object to represent the ITER.DAT file, which must already exist and contain data. (The FOUTITER program, if you ran it, will have generated this file.)

Instead of using cout, as in the istream iterator in the INITER example, we use the ifstream object named infile. The end-of-stream object is the same.

We've made another change in this program: it uses a back_inserter to insert data into iList. This makes it possible to define iList as an empty container instead of one with a specified size. This often makes sense when reading input, since you may not know how many items will be entered.

Associative Containers

We've seen that the sequence containers (vector, list, and deque) store data items in a fixed linear sequence. Finding an item in such a container (unless its index number is known or it's located at an end of the container) will involve the slow process of stepping through the items in the container one by one.

In an associative container the items are not arranged in sequence. Instead they are arranged in a more complex way that makes it much faster to find a given item. This arrangement is typically a tree structure, although different approaches (such as hash tables) are possible. The speed of searching is the main advantage of associative containers.

Searching is done using a *key*, which is usually a single value like a number or string. This value is an attribute of the objects in the container, or it may be the entire object.

The two main categories of associative containers in the STL are sets and maps.

A set stores objects containing keys. A map stores pairs, where the first part of the pair is an object containing a key and the second part is an object containing a value.

In both a set and a map, only one example of each key can be stored. It's like a dictionary that forbids more than one entry for each word. However, the STL has alternative versions of set and map that relax this restriction. A *multiset* and a *multimap* are similar to a set and a map, but can include multiple instances of the same key.

Associative containers share many member functions with other containers. However, some algorithms, such as lower_bound() and equal_range(), exist only for associative containers. Also, some member functions that do exist for other containers, such as the push and pop family (push_back() and so on) have no versions for associative containers. It wouldn't make sense to use push and pop with associative containers, because elements must always be inserted in their ordered locations, not at the beginning or end of the container.

Sets and Multisets

Sets are often used to hold objects of user-defined classes such as employees in a database. (You'll see examples of this later in this chapter.) However, sets can also hold simpler elements such as strings. Figure 15.5 shows how this looks. The objects are arranged in order, and the entire object is the key.

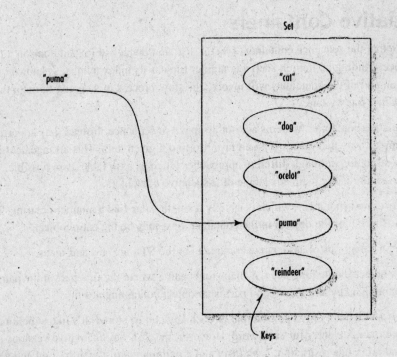

FIGURE 15.5
A set of string objects.

Our first example, SET, shows a set that stores objects of class string.

```cpp
// set.cpp
// set stores string objects
#pragma warning (disable:4786)  //for set (Microsoft only)
#include <iostream>
#include <set>
#include <string>
using namespace std;

int main()
   {                                //array of string objects
   string names[] = {"Juanita", "Robert",
                     "Mary", "Amanda", "Marie"};
                                    //initialize set to array
   set<string, less<string> > nameSet(names, names+5);
                                    //iterator to set
   set<string, less<string> >::iterator iter;

   nameSet.insert("Yvette");  //insert more names
   nameSet.insert("Larry");
```

```
nameSet.insert("Robert");    //no effect; already in set
nameSet.insert("Barry");
nameSet.erase("Mary");       //erase a name
                             //display size of set
cout << "\nSize=" << nameSet.size() << endl;
iter = nameSet.begin();      //display members of set
while( iter != nameSet.end() )
   cout << *iter++ << '\n';

string searchName;           //get name from user
cout << "\nEnter name to search for: ";
cin >> searchName;

                             //find matching name in set
iter = nameSet.find(searchName);
if( iter == nameSet.end() )
   cout << "The name " << searchName << " is NOT in the set.";
else
   cout << "The name " << *iter << " IS in the set.";
cout << endl;
return 0;
}
```

The directive

```
#pragma warning (disable:4786)
```

may be necessary on the Microsoft compiler when you use the SET or MAP files. It disables warning 4786 ("identifier was truncated to 255 characters in the debug information"), whose appearance seems to be a bug. The pragma must preceed the `#includes` for all files, not just for SET and MAP, which cause the problem. A *pragma* is a compiler-specific directive that fine-tunes compiler operations.

To define a set we specify the type of objects to be stored (in this case class `string`) and also the function object that will be used to order the members of the set. Here we use `less<>()` applied to string objects.

As you can see, a set has an interface similar to other STL containers. We can initialize a set to an array, and insert new members into a set with the `insert()` member function. To display the set we can iterate through it.

To find a particular entry in the set we use the `find()` member function. (Sequential containers use `find()` in its algorithm version.) Here's some sample interaction with SET, where the user enters "George" as the name to be searched for:

```
Size = 7
Amanda
Barry
```

```
Juanita
Larry
Marie
Robert
Yvette

Enter name to search for: George
The name George is NOT in the set.
```

Of course the speed advantage of searching an associative container isn't apparent until you have many more entries than in this example.

Let's look at an important pair of member functions available only with associative containers. Our example, SETRANGE, shows the use of lower_bound() and upper_bound():

```cpp
// setrange.cpp
// tests ranges within a set
#pragma warning (disable:4786)  //for set (Microsoft only)
#include <iostream>
#include <set>
#include <string>
using namespace std;

int main()
   {                            //set of string objects
   set<string, less<string> > organic;
                                //iterator to set
   set<string, less<string> >::iterator iter;

   organic.insert("Curine");  //insert organic compounds
   organic.insert("Xanthine");
   organic.insert("Curarine");
   organic.insert("Melamine");
   organic.insert("Cyanimide");
   organic.insert("Phenol");
   organic.insert("Aphrodine");
   organic.insert("Imidazole");
   organic.insert("Cinchonine");
   organic.insert("Palmitamide");
   organic.insert("Cyanimide");

   iter = organic.begin();    //display set
   while( iter != organic.end() )
      cout << *iter++ << '\n';

   string lower, upper;       //display entries in range
   cout << "\nEnter range (example C Czz): ";
```

```
    cin >> lower >> upper;
    iter = organic.lower_bound(lower);
    while( iter != organic.upper_bound(upper) )
        cout << *iter++ << '\n';
    return 0;
    }
```

The program first displays an entire set of organic compounds. The user is then prompted to type in a pair of key values, and the program displays those keys that lie within this range. Here's some sample interaction:

```
Aphrodine
Cinchonine
Curarine
Curine
Cyanimide
Imidazole
Melamine
Palmitamide
Phenol
Xanthine

Enter range (example C Czz): Aaa Curb
Aphrodine
Cinchonine
Curarine
```

The lower_bound() member function takes an argument that is a value of the same type as the key. It returns an iterator to the first entry that is not less than this argument (where the meaning of "less" is determined by the function object used in the set's definition). The upper_bound() function returns an iterator to the first entry that is greater than its argument. Together, these functions allow you to access a specified range of values.

Maps and Multimaps

A *map* stores pairs. A pair consists of a *key object* and a *value object*. The key object contains a key that will be searched for. The value object contains additional data. As in a set, the key objects can be strings, numbers, or objects of more complex classes. The values are often strings or numbers, but they can also be objects or even containers.

For example, the key could be a word, and the value could be a number representing how many times that word appears in a document. Such a map constitutes a *frequency table*. Or the key could be a word and the value could be a list of page numbers. This arrangement could represent an index, like the one at the back of this book. Figure 15.6 shows a situation in which the keys are words and the values are definitions, as in an ordinary dictionary.

15
TEMPLATE LIBRARY

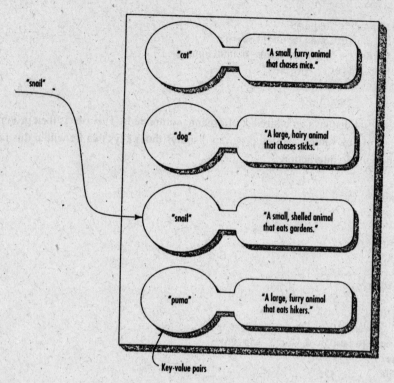

FIGURE 15.6
A map of word-phrase pairs.

One common way to use maps is as associative arrays. In an ordinary C++ array the array index, which is used to access a particular element, is an integer. Thus in the expression anArray[3], the 3 is the array index. An associative array works in a similar way except that you can choose the data type of the array index. If you've defined the index to be a string, for example, you can say anArray["jane"].

An Associative Array

Let's look at a simple example of a map used as an associative array. The keys will be the names of states, and the values will be the populations of the states. Here's the listing for ASSO_ARR:

```cpp
// asso_arr.cpp
// demonstrates map used as associative array
#pragma warning (disable:4786)  //for map (Microsoft only)
#include <iostream>
#include <string>
#include <map>
using namespace std;
```

```
int main()
   {
   string name;
   int pop;

   string states[] = { "Wyoming", "Colorado", "Nevada",
                        "Montana", "Arizona", "Idaho"};
   int pops[] = { 470, 2890, 800, 787, 2718, 944 };

   map<string, int, less<string> > mapStates;        //map
   map<string, int, less<string> >::iterator iter;  //iterator

   for(int j=0; j<6; j++)
      {
      name = states[j];                  //get data from arrays
      pop = pops[j];
      mapStates[name] = pop;             //put it in map
      }
   cout << "Enter state: ";              //get state from user
   cin >> name;
   pop = mapStates[name];                //find population
   cout << "Population: " << pop << ",000\n";

   cout << endl;                         //display entire map
   for(iter = mapStates.begin(); iter != mapStates.end(); iter++)
      cout << (*iter).first << ' ' << (*iter).second << ",000\n";
   return 0;
   }
```

When the program runs, the user is prompted to type the name of a state. The program then looks in the map, using the state name as an index, and returns the population of the state. Finally, it displays all the name-population pairs in the map. Here's some sample output:

```
Enter state: Wyoming
Population: 470,000

Arizona 2718,000
Colorado 2890,000
Idaho 944,000
Montana 787,000
Nevada 800,000
Wyoming 470,000
```

Search speed is where sets and maps excel. Here the program quickly finds the appropriate population when the user enters a state's name. (This would be more meaningful if there were millions of data items.) Iterating through the container, as is shown by the list of states and populations, isn't as fast as in a sequential container, but it's still fairly efficient. Notice that the states are ordered alphabetically, although the original data was not.

The definition of a map takes three template arguments:

```
map<string, int, less<string> > maStates;
```

The first is the type of the key. In this case it's `string`, representing the state name. The second is the type of the value; in this case it's `int`, which represents the population, in 1,000s. The third argument specifies the ordering that will be used for the keys. We choose to have it ordered alphabetically by the names of the states; that's what `less<string>` does. We also define an iterator to this map.

Our input data is in two separate arrays. (In a real program it would probably come from a file.) To put this data into the map we read it into the variables name and pop, and execute the statement

```
mapStates[name] = pop;
```

This is a particularly elegant construction, looking just like an insertion into an ordinary array. However, the array index name is a string, not an integer.

When the user types in a state name, the program finds the appropriate population with the statement

```
pop = mapStates[name];
```

Besides using the array-index syntax, we can also access the two parts of an entry in the map, the key, and the value, using an iterator. The key is obtained from `(*iter).first`, and the value from `(*iter).second`. Otherwise the iterator works as it does in other containers.

Storing User-Defined Objects

Until now our example programs have stored objects of basic types. However, the big payoff with the STL is that you can use it to store and manipulate objects of classes that you write yourself (or that someone else has written). In this section we'll show how this is done.

A Set of person Objects

We'll start with a person class that includes a person's last name, first name, and telephone number. We'll create some members of this class and insert them in a set, thus creating a phone book database. The user interacts with the program by entering a person's name. The program then searches the list and displays the data for that person, if it finds a match. We'll use a multiset so two or more person objects can have the same name. Here's the listing for SETPERS:

```
// setpers.cpp
// uses a multiset to hold person objects
#pragma warning (disable:4786)  //for set (Microsoft only)
#include <iostream>
```

```cpp
#include <set>
#include <string>
using namespace std;

class person
    {
    private:
        string lastName;
        string firstName;
        long phoneNumber;
    public:                         //default constructor
        person() : lastName("blank"),
                   firstName("blank"), phoneNumber(0)
            {  }
                                //3-arg constructor
        person(string lana, string fina, long pho) :
                lastName(lana), firstName(fina), phoneNumber(pho)
            {  }
        friend bool operator<(const person&, const person&);
        friend bool operator==(const person&, const person&);

        void display() const    //display person's data
            {
            cout << endl << lastName << ",\t" << firstName
                 << "\t\tPhone: " << phoneNumber;
            }
    };
                                //operator < for person class
bool operator<(const person& p1, const person& p2)
    {
    if(p1.lastName == p2.lastName)
        return (p1.firstName < p2.firstName) ? true : false;
    return (p1.lastName < p2.lastName) ? true : false;
    }
                                //operator == for person class
bool operator==(const person& p1, const person& p2)
    {
    return (p1.lastName == p2.lastName &&
            p1.firstName == p2.firstName ) ? true : false;
    }
///////////////////////////////////////////////////////////////
int main()
    {                           //create person objects
    person pers1("Deauville", "William", 8435150);
    person pers2("McDonald", "Stacey", 3327563);
    person pers3("Bartoski", "Peter", 6946473);
    person pers4("KuangThu", "Bruce", 4157300);
```

```
        person pers5("Wellington", "John", 9207404);
        person pers6("McDonald", "Amanda", 8435150);
        person pers7("Fredericks", "Roger", 7049982);
        person pers8("McDonald", "Stacey", 7764987);
                            //multiset of persons
     multiset< person, less<person> > persSet;
                            //iterator to a multiset of persons
     multiset<person, less<person> >::iterator iter;

        persSet.insert(pers1);      //put persons in multiset
        persSet.insert(pers2);
        persSet.insert(pers3);
        persSet.insert(pers4);
        persSet.insert(pers5);
        persSet.insert(pers6);
        persSet.insert(pers7);
        persSet.insert(pers8);

        cout << "\nNumber of entries = " << persSet.size();

        iter = persSet.begin();     //display contents of multiset
        while( iter != persSet.end() )
           (*iter++).display();
                            //get last and first name
        string searchLastName, searchFirstName;
        cout << "\n\nEnter last name of person to search for: ";
        cin >> searchLastName;
        cout << "Enter first name: ";
        cin >> searchFirstName;
                            //create person with this name
     person searchPerson(searchLastName, searchFirstName, 0);

                            //get count of such persons
        int cntPersons = persSet.count(searchPerson);
        cout << "Number of persons with this name = " << cntPersons;

                            //display all matches
        iter = persSet.lower_bound(searchPerson);
        while( iter != persSet.upper_bound(searchPerson) )
           (*iter++).display();
        cout << endl;
        return 0;
     }  //end main()
```

Necessary Member Functions

To work with STL containers, the person class needs a few common member functions. These are a default (no-argument) constructor (which is actually not necessary in this example but is usually essential), the overloaded < operator, and the overloaded == operator. These member functions are used by the list class and by various algorithms. You may need other member functions in other specific situations. (As in most classes, you should probably also provide overloaded assignment and copy constructors and a destructor, but we'll ignore these here to avoid complicating the listing.)

The overloaded < and == operators should use const arguments. Generally it's best to make them friends, but you can use member functions as well.

Ordering

The overloaded < operator specifies the way the elements in the set will be ordered. In SETPERS we define this operator to order the last name of the person, and, if the last names are the same, to order the first names.

Here's some interaction with SETPERS. The program first displays the entire list. (Of course this would not be practical on a real database with a large number of elements.) Because they are stored in a multiset, the elements are ordered automatically. Then, at the prompt, the user enters the name "McDonald" followed by "Stacey" (last name first). There are two persons on the list with this particular name, so they are both displayed.

```
Number of entries = 8
Bartoski,       Peter        phone: 6946473
Deauville,      William      phone: 8435150
Fredericks,     Roger        phone: 7049982
KuangThu,       Bruce        phone: 4157300
McDonald,       Amanda       phone: 8435150
McDonald,       Stacey       phone: 3327563
McDonald,       Stacey       phone: 7764987
Wellington,     John         phone: 9207404

Enter last name of person to search for: McDonald
Enter first name: Stacey
Number of persons with this name = 2
McDonald,       Stacey       phone: 3327563
McDonald,       Stacey       phone: 7764987
```

Just Like Basic Types

As you can see, once a class has been defined, objects of that class are handled by the container in the same way as variables of basic types.

We first use the size() member function to display the total number of entries. Then we iterate through the list, displaying all the entries.

Because we're using a multiset, the `lower_bound()` and `upper_bound()` member functions are available to display all elements that fall within a range. In the example output the lower and upper bound are the same, so all persons with the same name are displayed. Notice that we must create a "fictitious" person with the same name as the person (or persons) we want to find. The `lower_bound()` and `upper_bound()` functions then match this person against those on the list.

A List of person Objects

It's very fast to search a set or multiset for a person with a given name, as in the SETPERS example. If, however, we're more concerned with being able to quickly insert or delete a person object, we might decide to use a list instead. The LISTPERS example shows how this looks.

```
// listpers.cpp
// uses a list to hold person objects
#include <iostream>
#include <list>
#include <algorithm>
#include <string>
using namespace std;

class person
   {
   private:
      string lastName;
      string firstName;
      long phoneNumber;
   public:
      person() :                    //no-arg constructor
         lastName("blank"), firstName("blank"), phoneNumber(0L)
         { }
                                   //3-arg constructor
      person(string lana, string fina, long pho) :
         lastName(lana), firstName(fina), phoneNumber(pho)
         { }
      friend bool operator<(const person&, const person&);
      friend bool operator==(const person&, const person&);
      friend bool operator!=(const person&, const person&);
      friend bool operator>(const person&, const person&);

      void display() const    //display all data
         {
         cout << endl << lastName << ",\t" << firstName
              << "\t\tPhone: " << phoneNumber;
         }
```

```cpp
        long get_phone() const //return phone number
            { return phoneNumber; }
    };
                                //overloaded == for person class
bool operator==(const person& p1, const person& p2)
    {
    return (p1.lastName == p2.lastName &&
            p1.firstName == p2.firstName ) ? true : false;
    }
                                //overloaded < for person class
bool operator<(const person& p1, const person& p2)
    {
    if(p1.lastName == p2.lastName)
        return ( .firstName < p2.firstName) ? true : false;
    return (p1.lastName < p2.lastName) ? true : false;
    }
                                //overloaded != for person class
bool operator!=(const person& p1, const person& p2)
    { return !(p1==p2); }
                                //overloaded > for person class
bool operator>(const person& p1, const person& p2)
    { return !(p1<p2) && !(p1==p2); }
////////////////////////////////////////////////////////////
int main()
    {
    list<person> persList;      //list of persons
                                //iterator to a list of persons
    list<person>::iterator iter1;
                                //put persons in list
    persList.push_back( person("Deauville", "William", 8435150) );
    persList.push_back( person("McDonald", "Stacey", 3327563) );
    persList.push_back( person("Bartoski", "Peter", 6946473) );
    persList.push_back( person("KuangThu", "Bruce", 4157300) );
    persList.push_back( person("Wellington", "John", 9207404) );
    persList.push_back( person("McDonald", "Amanda", 8435150) );
    persList.push_back( person("Fredericks", "Roger", 7049982) );
    persList.push_back( person("McDonald", "Stacey", 7764987) );

    cout << "\nNumber of entries = " << persList.size();

    iter1 = persList.begin();  //display contents of list
    while( iter1 != persList.end() )
        (*iter1++).display();

//find person or persons with specified name (last and first)
    string searchLastName, searchFirstName;
```

```
        cout << "\n\nEnter last name of person to search for: ";
        cin >> searchLastName;
        cout << "Enter first name: ";
        cin >> searchFirstName;
                                    //make a person with that name
        person searchPerson(searchLastName, searchFirstName, 0L);
                                    //search for first match of names
        iter1 = find(persList.begin(), persList.end(), searchPerson);
        if( iter1 != persList.end() )  //find additional matches
           {
           cout << "Person(s) with that name is(are)";
           do
              {
              (*iter1).display();  //display match
              ++iter1;             //search again, one past match
              iter1 = find(iter1, persList.end(), searchPerson);
              } while( iter1 != persList.end() );
           }
        else
           cout << "There is no person with that name.";

   //find person or persons with specified phone number
        cout << "\n\nEnter phone number (format 1234567): ";
        long sNumber;                 //get search number
        cin >> sNumber;

                                    //iterate through list
        bool found_one = false;
        for(iter1=persList.begin(); iter1 != persList.end(); ++iter1)
           {
           if( sNumber == (*iter1).get_phone() )  //compare numbers
              {
              if( !found_one )
                 {
                 cout << "Person(s) with that phone number is(are)";
                 found_one = true;
                 }
              (*iter1).display(); //display the match
              }
           } //end for
        if( !found_one )
           cout << "There is no person with that phone number";
        cout << endl;
        return 0;
        } //end main()
```

Finding All Persons with a Specified Name

We can't use the `lower_bound()`/`upper_bound()` member functions because we're dealing with a list, not a set or map. Instead we use the `find()` member function to find all the persons with a given name. If this function reports a hit, we must apply it again, starting one person past the original hit, to see whether there are other persons with the same name. This complicates the programming; we must use a loop and two calls to `find()`.

Finding All Persons with a Specified Phone Number

It's harder to search for a person with a specified phone number than one with a specified name, because the class member functions such as `find()` are intended to be used to find the primary search characteristic. In this example we use the brute force approach to finding the phone number, iterating through the list and making a "manual" comparison of the number we're looking for and each member of the list:

```
if( sNumber == (*iter1).getphone() )
    ...
```

The program first displays all the entries, then asks the user for a name and finds the matching person or persons. It then asks for a phone number and again finds any matching persons. Here's some interaction with LISTPERS:

```
Number of entries = 8
Deauville,     William        phone: 8435150
McDonald,      Stacey         phone: 3327563
Bartoski,      Peter          phone: 6946473
KuangThu,      Bruce          phone: 4157300
Wellington,    John           phone: 9207404
McDonald,      Amanda         phone: 8435150
Fredericks,    Roger          phone: 7049982
McDonald,      Stacey         phone: 7764987

Enter last name of person to search for: Wellington
Enter first name: John
Person(s) with that name is(are)
Wellington,    John           phone: 9207404

Enter phone number (format 1234567): 8435150
Person(s) with that number is(are)
Deauville,     William        phone: 8435150
McDonald,      Amanda         phone: 8435150
```

Here the program has found one person with the specified name and two people with the specified phone number.

When using lists to store class objects we must declare four comparison operators for that class: ==, !=, <, and >. Depending on what algorithms you actually use, you may not need to define (provide function bodies for) all these operators. In this example we only need to define the -= operator, although for completeness we define all four. If we used the sort() algorithm on the list, we would need to define the < operator as well.

Function Objects

Function objects are used extensively in the STL. One important use for them is as arguments to certain algorithms. They allow you to customize the operation of these algorithms. We mentioned function objects earlier in this chapter, and used one in the SORTEMP program. There we showed an example of the predefined function object greater<>() used to sort data in reverse order. In this section we'll examine other predefined function objects, and also see how you can write your own so that you have even greater control over what the STL algorithms do.

Recall that a function object is a function that has been wrapped in a class so that it looks like an object. The class, however, has no data and only one member function, which is the overloaded () operator. The class is often templatized so it can work with different types.

Predefined Function Objects

The predefined STL function objects, located in the FUNCTIONAL header file, are shown in Table 15.10. There are function objects corresponding to all the major C++ operators. In the table, the letter *T* indicates any class, either user-written or a basic type. The variables x and y represent objects of class T passed to the function object as arguments.

TABLE 15.10   Predefined Function Objects

Function Object	Return Value
T = plus(T, T)	x+y
T = minus(T, T)	x-y
T = times(T, T)	x*y
T = divide(T, T)	x/y
T = modulus(T, T)	x%y
T = negate(T)	-x
bool = equal_to(T, T)	x == y
bool = not_equal_to(T, T)	x != y
bool = greater(T, T)	x > y
bool = less(T, T)	x < y
bool = greater_equal(T, T)	x >= y

TABLE 15.10   Continued

Function Object	Return Value
bool = less_equal(T, T)	x <= y
bool = logical_and(T, T)	x && y
bool = logical_or(T, T)	x || y
bool = logical_not(T)	!x

There are function objects for arithmetic operations, comparisons, and logical operations. Let's look at an example where an arithmetic function object might come in handy. Our example uses a class called airtime, which represents time values consisting of hours and minutes, but no seconds. This data type is appropriate for flight arrival and departure times in airports. The example shows how the plus<>() function object can be used to add all the airtime values in a container. Here's the listing for PLUSAIR:

```
//plusair.cpp
//uses accumulate() algorithm and plus() function object
#include <iostream>
#include <list>
#include <numeric>              //for accumulate()
using namespace std;
/////////////////////////////////////////////////////////////////
class airtime
   {
   private:
      int hours;           //0 to 23
      int minutes;         //0 to 59
   public:
                                //default constructor
      airtime() : hours(0), minutes(0)
         { }
                                //2-arg constructor
      airtime(int h, int m) : hours(h), minutes(m)
         { }
      void display() const  //output to screen
         { cout << hours << ':' << minutes; }

      void get()            //input from user
         {
         char dummy;
         cout << "\nEnter airtime (format 12:59): ";
         cin >> hours >> dummy >> minutes;
         }
```

```
                                  //overloaded + operator
        airtime operator + (const airtime right) const
            {                   //add members
            int temph = hours + right.hours;
            int tempm = minutes + right.minutes;
            if(tempm >= 60)     //check for carry
                { temph++; tempm -= 60; }
            return airtime(temph, tempm); //return sum
            }
                                  //overloaded == operator
        bool operator == (const airtime& at2) const
            { return (hours == at2.hours) &&
                     (minutes == at2.minutes); }
                                  //overloaded < operator
        bool operator < (const airtime& at2) const
            { return (hours < at2.hours) ||
                     (hours == at2.hours && minutes < at2.minutes); }
                                  //overloaded != operator
        bool operator != (const airtime& at2) const
            { return !(*this==at2); }
                                  //overloaded > operator
        bool operator > (const airtime& at2) const
            { return !(*this<at2) && !(*this==at2); }
    };  //end class airtime
//////////////////////////////////////////////////////////////////
int main()
    {
    char answer;
    airtime temp, sum;
    list<airtime> airlist;    //list of airtimes

    do {                      //get airtimes from user
        temp.get();
        airlist.push_back(temp);
        cout << "Enter another (y/n)? ";
        cin >> answer;
        } while (answer != 'n');
                              //sum all the airtimes
    sum = accumulate( airlist.begin(), airlist.end(),
                      airtime(0, 0), plus<airtime>() );
    cout << "\nsum = ";
    sum.display();            //display sum
    cout << endl;
    return 0;
    }
```

This program features the `accumulate()` algorithm. There are two versions of this function. The three-argument version always sums (using the + operator) a range of values. In the four-argument version shown here, any of the arithmetic function objects shown in Table 15.10 can be used.

The four arguments to this version of `accumulate()` are the iterators of the first and last elements in the range, the initial value of the sum (often 0), and the operation to be applied to the elements. In this example we add them using `plus<>()`, but we could subtract them, multiply them, or perform other operations using different function objects. Here's some interaction with PLUSAIR:

```
Enter airtime (format 12:59) : 3:45
Enter another (y/n)? y

Enter airtime (format 12:59) : 5:10
Enter another (y/n)? y

Enter airtime (format 12:59) : 2:25
Enter another (y/n)? y

Enter airtime (format 12:59) : 0:55
Enter another (y/n)? n

sum = 12:15
```

The `accumulate()` algorithm is not only easier and clearer than iterating through the container yourself to add the elements, it's also (unless you put a lot of work into your code) more efficient.

The `plus<>()` function object requires that the + operator be overloaded for the `airtime` class. This operator should be a `const` function, since that's what the `plus<>()` function object expects.

The other arithmetic function objects work in a similar way. The logical function objects such as `logical_and<>()` can be used on objects of classes for which these operations make sense (for example, type `bool` variables).

Writing Your Own Function Objects

If one of the standard function objects doesn't do what you want, you can write your own. Our next example shows two situations where this might be desirable, one involving the `sort()` algorithm and one involving `for_each()`.

It's easy to sort a group of elements based on the relationship specified in the class < operator. However, what happens if you want to sort a container that contains pointers to objects, rather than the objects themselves? Storing pointers is a good way to improve efficiency, especially for large objects, because it avoids the copying process that takes place whenever an object is placed in a container. However, if you try to sort the pointers, you'll find that the objects are arranged by pointer address, rather than by some attribute of the object.

To make the sort() algorithm work the way we want in a container of pointers, we must supply it with a function object that defines how we want the data ordered.

Our example program starts with a vector of pointers to person objects. These objects are placed in the vector, then sorted in the usual way, which leads to the pointers, not the persons, being sorted. This isn't what we want, and in this case causes no change in the ordering at all, because the items were inserted in order of increasing addresses. Next, the vector is sorted correctly, using the function object comparePersons(). This orders items using the *contents* of pointers, rather than the pointers themselves. The result is that the person objects are sorted alphabetically by name. Here's the listing for SORTPTRS:

```cpp
// sortptrs.cpp
// sorts person objects stored by pointer
#include <iostream>
#include <vector>
#include <algorithm>
#include <string>
using namespace std;

class person
    {
    private:
        string lastName;
        string firstName;
        long phoneNumber;
    public:
        person() :                  //default constructor
            lastName("blank"), firstName("blank"), phoneNumber(0L)
            { }
                                //3-arg constructor
        person(string lana, string fina, long pho) :
                lastName(lana), firstName(fina), phoneNumber(pho)
            { }
        friend bool operator<(const person&, const person&);
        friend bool operator==(const person&, const person&);

        void display() const    //display person's data
            {
            cout << endl << lastName << ",\t" << firstName
                 << "\t\tPhone: " << phoneNumber;
            }
```

```
        long get_phone() const //return phone number
            { return phoneNumber; }
    }; //end class person
//-------------------------------------------------------------
//overloaded < for person class
bool operator<(const person& p1, const person& p2)
    {
    if(p1.lastName == p2.lastName)
        return (p1.firstName < p2.firstName) ? true : false;
    return (p1.lastName < p2.lastName) ? true : false;
    }
//-------------------------------------------------------------
//overloaded == for person class
bool operator==(const person& p1, const person& p2)
    {
    return (p1.lastName == p2.lastName &&
            p1.firstName == p2.firstName ) ? true : false;
    }
//-------------------------------------------------------------
//function object to compare persons using pointers
class comparePersons
    {
    public:
    bool operator() (const person* ptrP1,
                     const person* ptrP2) const
        { return *ptrP1 < *ptrP2; }
    };
//-------------------------------------------------------------
//function object to display a person, using a pointer
class displayPerson
    {
    public:
    void operator() (const person* ptrP) const
        { ptrP->display(); }
    };
//////////////////////////////////////////////////////////////
int main()
    {                         //a vector of ptrs to persons
    vector<person*> vectPtrsPers;
                              //make persons
    person* ptrP1 = new person("KuangThu", "Bruce", 4157300);
    person* ptrP2 = new person("Deauville", "William", 8435150);
    person* ptrP3 = new person("Wellington", "John", 9207404);
    person* ptrP4 = new person("Bartoski", "Peter", 6946473);
    person* ptrP5 = new person("Fredericks", "Roger", 7049982);
    person* ptrP6 = new person("McDonald", "Stacey", 7764987);
```

```
      vectPtrsPers.push_back(ptrP1);   //put persons in set
      vectPtrsPers.push_back(ptrP2);
      vectPtrsPers.push_back(ptrP3);
      vectPtrsPers.push_back(ptrP4);
      vectPtrsPers.push_back(ptrP5);
      vectPtrsPers.push_back(ptrP6);

      for_each(vectPtrsPers.begin(),              //display vector
               vectPtrsPers.end(), displayPerson() );
                                                  //sort pointers
      sort( vectPtrsPers.begin(), vectPtrsPers.end() );
      cout << "\n\nSorted pointers";
      for_each(vectPtrsPers.begin(),              //display vector
               vectPtrsPers.end(), displayPerson() );

      sort( vectPtrsPers.begin(),                 //sort persons
            vectPtrsPers.end(), comparePersons() );
      cout << "\n\nSorted persons";
      for_each(vectPtrsPers.begin(),              //display vector
               vectPtrsPers.end(), displayPerson() );
      while( !vectPtrsPers.empty() )
         {
         delete vectPtrsPers.back();              //delete person
         vectPtrsPers.pop_back();                 //pop pointer
         }
      cout << endl;
      return 0;
      }  //end main()
```

Here's the output of SORTPTRS:

```
KuangThu,       Bruce           phone: 4157300
Deauville,      William         phone: 8435150
Wellington,     John            phone: 9207404
Bartoski,       Peter           phone: 6946473
Fredericks,     Roger           phone: 7049982
McDonald,       Stacey          phone: 7764987

Sorted pointers
KuangThu,       Bruce           phone: 4157300
Deauville,      William         phone: 8435150
Wellington,     John            phone: 9207404
Bartoski,       Peter           phone: 6946473
Fredericks,     Roger           phone: 7049982
McDonald,       Stacey          phone: 7764987

Sorted persons
Bartoski,       Peter           phone: 6946473
```

```
Deauville,      William       phone: 8435150
Fredericks,     Roger         phone: 7049982
KuangThu,       Bruce         phone: 4157300
McDonald,       Stacey        phone: 7764987
Wellington,     John          phone: 9207404
```

First the original order is shown, then the ordering sorted incorrectly by pointer, and finally the order sorted correctly by name.

The `comparePersons()` Function Object

If we use the two-argument version of the `sort()` algorithm

```
sort( vectPtrsPers.begin(), vectPtrsPers.end() );
```

then only the pointers are sorted, by their addresses in memory. This is not usually what we want. To sort the person objects by name, we use the three-argument version of `sort()`, with the `comparePersons()` function object as the third argument:

```
sort( vectPtrsPers.begin(),
      bectPtrsPers.end(), comparePersons() );
```

The function object `comparePersons()` is defined like this in the SORTPTRS program:

```
//function object to compare persons using pointers
class comparePersons
   {
   public:
   bool operator() (const person* ptrP1,
                    const person* ptrP2) const
      { return *ptrP1 < *ptrP2; }
   };
```

The `operator()` takes two arguments that are pointers to persons and compares their contents, rather than the pointers themselves.

The `displayPerson()` Function Object

We use a different approach to display the contents of a container than we have before. Instead of iterating through the container, we use the `for_each()` function, with a function object as its third argument.

```
for_each(vectPtrsPers.begin(),
         bectPtrsPers.end(), displayPeson() );
```

This causes the `displayPerson()` function object to be called once for each person in the vector. Here's how `displayPerson()` looks:

```
//function object to display a person, using a pointer
class displayPerson
```

```
{
public:
void operator() (const person* ptrP) const
   { ptrP->display(); }
};
```

With this arrangement a single function call displays all the person objects in the vector.

Function Objects Used to Modify Container Behavior

In SORTPTRS we showed function objects used to modify the behavior of algorithms. Function objects can also modify the behavior of containers. For example, if you want a set of pointers to objects to sort itself automatically based on the objects instead of the pointers, you can use an appropriate function object when you define the container. No sort() algorithm need be used. We'll examine this approach in an exercise.

Summary

This chapter has presented a quick and dirty introduction to the STL. However, we've touched on the major topics, and you should have acquired enough information to begin using the STL in a useful way. For a fuller understanding of the STL we recommend that readers avail themselves of a complete text on the topic.

You've learned that the STL consists of three main components: containers, algorithms, and iterators. Containers are divided into two groups: sequential and associative. Sequential containers are the vector, list, and deque. Associative containers are the set and map, and the closely-related multiset and multimap. Algorithms carry out operations on containers, such as sorting, copying, and searching. Iterators act like pointers to container elements and provide connections between algorithms and containers.

Not all algorithms are appropriate for all containers. Iterators are used to ensure that algorithms and containers are appropriately matched. Iterators are defined for specific kinds of containers, and used as arguments to algorithms. If the container's iterators don't match the algorithm, a compiler error results.

Input and output iterators connect directly to I/O streams thus allowing data to be piped directly between I/O devices and containers. Specialized iterators allow backward iteration and can also change the behavior of some algorithms so that they insert data rather than overwriting existing data.

Algorithms are standalone functions that can work on many different containers. In addition, each container has its own specific member functions. In some cases the same function is available as both an algorithm and a member function.

STL containers and algorithms will work with objects of any class, provided certain member functions, such as the < operator, are overloaded for that class.

The behavior of certain algorithms such as find_if() can be customized using function objects. A function object is instantiated from a class containing only an () operator.

Questions

Answers to these questions can be found in Appendix G.

1. An STL container can be used to
    a. hold objects of class employee.
    b. store elements in a way that makes them quickly accessible.
    c. compile C++ programs.
    d. organize the way objects are stored in memory.

2. The STL sequence containers are v_____, l_____, and d_____.

3. Two important STL associative containers are s_____ and ma_____.

4. An STL algorithm is
    a. a standalone function that operates on containers.
    b. a link between member functions and containers.
    c. a friend function of appropriate container classes.
    d. a member function of appropriate container classes.

5. True or false: One purpose of an iterator in the STL is to connect algorithms and containers.

6. The find() algorithm
    a. finds matching sequences of elements in two containers.
    b. finds a container that matches a specified container.
    c. takes iterators as its first two arguments.
    d. takes container elements as its first two arguments.

7. True or false: Algorithms can be used only on STL containers.

8. A range is often supplied to an algorithm by two i_____ values.

9. What entity is often used to customize the behavior of an algorithm?

10. A vector is an appropriate container if you

    a. want to insert lots of new elements at arbitrary locations in the vector.

    b. want to insert new elements, but always at the front of the container.

    c. are given an index number and you want to quickly access the corresponding element.

    d. are given an element's key value and you want to quickly access the corresponding element.

11. True or false: The back() member function removes the element at the back of the container.

12. If you define a vector v with the default constructor, and define another vector w with a one-argument constructor to a size of 11, and insert 3 elements into each of these vectors with push_back(), then the size() member function will return _____ for v and _____ for w.

13. The unique() algorithm removes all _____ element values from a container.

14. In a deque

    a. data can be quickly inserted or deleted at any arbitrary location.

    b. data can be inserted or deleted at any arbitrary location, but the process is relatively slow.

    c. data can be quickly inserted or deleted at either end.

    d. data can be inserted or deleted at either end, but the process is relatively slow.

15. In iterator _____ a specific element in a container.

16. True or false: An iterator can always move forward or backward through a container.

17. You must use at least a _____ iterator for a list.

18. If iter is an iterator to a container, write an expression that will have the value of the object pointed to by iter, and will then cause iter to point to the next element.

19. The copy() algorithm returns an iterator to

    a. the last element copied from.

    b. the last element copied to.

    c. the element one past the last element copied from.

    d. the element one past the last element copied to.

20. To use a reverse_iterator, you should

    a. begin by initializing it to end().

    b. begin by initializing it to rend().

    c. increment it to move backward through the container.

    d. decrement it to move backward through the container.

21. True or false: The back_inserter iterator always causes the new elements to be inserted following the existing ones.

22. Stream iterators allow you to treat the display and keyboard devices, and files, as if they were _____.

23. What does the second argument to an ostream_iterator specify?

24. In an associative container

    a. values are stored in sorted order.

    b. keys are stored in sorted order.

    c. sorting is always in alphabetical or numerical order.

    d. you must use the sort() algorithm to keep the contents sorted.

25. When defining a set, you must specify how _____.

26. True or false: In a set, the insert() member function inserts a key in sorted order.

27. A map stores _____ of objects (or values).

28. True or false: A map can have two or more elements with the same key value.

29. If you store pointers to objects, instead of objects, in a container

    a. the objects won't need to be copied to implement storage in the container.

    b. only associative containers can be used.

    c. you can't sort the objects using object attributes as keys.

    d. the containers will often require less memory.

30. If you want an associative container such as set to order itself automatically, you can define the ordering in a function object and specify that function object in the container's _____.

Exercises

Answers to exercises can be found in Appendix G.

*1. Write a program that applies the sort() algorithm to an array of floating point values entered by the user, and displays the result.

*2. Apply the sort() algorithm to an array of words entered by the user, and display the result. Use push_back() to insert the words, and the [] operator and size() to display them.

*3. Start with a list of int values. Use two normal (not reverse) iterators, one moving forward through the list and one moving backward, in a while loop, to reverse the contents of the list. You can use the swap() algorithm to save a few statements. (Make sure your solution works for both even and odd numbers of items.) To see how the experts do it, look at the reverse() function in your compiler's ALGORITHM header file.

*4. Start with the person class, and create a multiset to hold pointers to person objects. Define the multiset with the comparePersons function object, so it will be sorted automatically by names of persons. Define a half-dozen persons, put them in the multiset, and display its contents. Several of the persons should have the same name, to verify that the multiset stores multiple objects with the same key.

5. Fill an array with even numbers and a set with odd numbers. Use the merge() algorithm to merge these containers into a vector. Display the vector contents to show that all went well.

6. In Exercise 3, two ordinary (non-reverse) iterators were used to reverse the contents of a container. Now use one forward and one reverse iterator to carry out the same task, this time on a vector.

7. We showed the four-argument version of the accumulate() algorithm in the PLUSAIR example. Rewrite this example using the three-argument version.

8. You can use the copy() algorithm to copy sequences within a container. However, you must be careful when the destination sequence overlaps the source sequence. Write a program that lets you copy any sequence to a different location within an array, using copy(). Have the user enter values for first1, last1, and first2. Use the program to verify that you can shift a sequence that overlaps its destination to the left, but not to the right. (For example, you can shift several items from 10 to 9, but not from 10 to 11.) This is because copy() starts with the leftmost element.

9. We listed the function objects corresponding to the C++ operators in Table 15.10, and, in the PLUSAIR program earlier in this chapter, we showed the function object plus<>() used with the accumulate() algorithm. It wasn't necessary to provide arguments to the function objects in that example, but sometimes it is. However, you can't put the argument within the parentheses of the function object, as you might expect. Instead, you use a function adapter called bind1st or bind2nd to bind the argument to the function. For example, suppose you were looking for a particular string (call it searchName) in a container of strings (called names). You can say

```
ptr = find_if(names.begin(), names.end(),
              bind2nd(equal_to<string>(), searchName) );
```

Here equal_to<>() and searchName are arguments to bind2nd(). This statement returns an iterator to the first string in the container equal to searchName. Write a program that incorporates this statement or a similar one to find a string in a container of strings. It should display the position of searchName in the container.

10. You can use the copy_backward() algorithm to overcome the problem described in Exercise 7 (that is, you can't shift a sequence to the left if any of the source overlaps any of the destination). Write a program that uses both copy() and copy_backward() to enable shifting any sequence anywhere within a container, regardless of overlap.

11. Write a program that copies a source file of integers to a destination file, using stream iterators. The user should supply both source and destination filenames to the program. You can use a `while` loop approach. Within the loop, read each integer value from the input iterator and write it immediately to the output iterator, then increment both iterators. The ITER.DAT file created by the FOUTITER program in this chapter makes a suitable source file.

12. A frequency table lists words and the number of times each word appears in a text file. Write a program that creates a frequency table for a file whose name is entered by the user. You can use a map of `string-int` pairs. You may want to use the C library function `ispunct()` (in header file CTYPE.H) to check for punctuation so you can strip it off the end of a word, using the string member function `substr()`. Also, the `tolower()` function may prove handy for uncapitalizing words.

Object-Oriented Software Development

IN THIS CHAPTER

The programs in this book are fairly small and therefore do not require much formality in the way they are developed. This is not the case with full-scale software projects that involve dozens or hundreds of programmers and generate millions of lines of source code. In such projects it's essential to follow a well-defined development process. In this chapter we'll look at one such process (or at least a very condensed version of it). Then we'll show how this process might be applied to an actual program.

We've seen many examples of UML diagrams throughout this book. The UML is not a software development process; it is a visual modeling language. However, the UML can play a key role in the development process, as we'll see.

Evolution of the Software Development Processes

The idea of a process for developing software has evolved slowly over decades of computer use. We'll summarize it very briefly.

The Seat-of-the-Pants Process

In the early days there was hardly any process at all. The programmer would discuss the situation with potential users and then immediately start writing code. This was satisfactory for very small programs.

The Waterfall Process

Later, as programs grew larger, the development process was broken up into several phases, which were carried out in sequence. This approach was derived from the manufacturing industry. The phases were labelled something like analysis, design, coding, and deployment. This was often called the *waterfall* process, because the sequence ran in one direction, from analysis to deployment, as shown in Figure 16.1. Typically, separate teams of workers were used for each phase. After each phase was completed, its results were passed on to a different team.

Experience showed that there were major problems with the waterfall approach. The underlying assumption was that each phase would be completed with no (or at least only minor) errors. This seldom happened in the real world. There were usually serious mistakes or omissions in each phase. These mistakes would snowball from each phase to the next, rendering some or all of the work in succeeding phases either useless or similarly error-ridden.

Also, during the course of development, the needs of the system's users might change, requiring the program to have additional features. However, once the design phase was completed, it was difficult to change the design. This meant that the program was already at least partially obsolete as it was being coded.

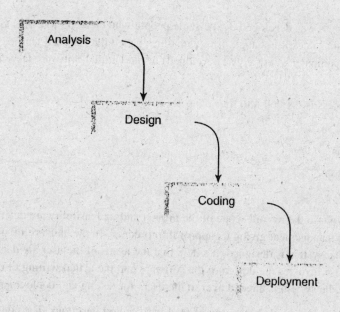

FIGURE 16.1
The waterfall process.

Object-Oriented Programming

As we mentioned in Chapter 1, "The Big Picture," object-oriented programming itself was created to solve some of the problems inherent in the development of large programs. Certainly OOP helps the design process because objects in the program correspond with objects in the user's world.

However, OOP by itself does not tell us what the program should do; it comes into play only after the project's goals have been determined. We need an initial phase that focuses on the program's users and captures their needs. Once this is accomplished we can translate it into an object-oriented program design. But how do we perform the initial step of figuring out what the users really need?

Modern Processes

A large number of software development processes have appeared in recent years. They specify the steps in the process and the way clients, analysts, designers and programmers should work together. To date, no one system has reached the sort of universal acceptance that the UML has in the field of modeling languages. In fact, many experts do not believe that any one development process can be appropriate in every situation. Even when a particular process is chosen, it may need to be modified more or less drastically, depending on the project it is applied to. However, as an example of a modern development process, we will examine some of the highlights of what we'll call the Unified Process.

The Unified Process was developed by the same people who created the UML: Grady Booch, Ivar Jacobson, and James Rumbaugh. It is sometimes called the Rational Unified Process (after the name of the company where it was developed) or the Unified Software Development Process.

The Unified Process is divided into four phases:

- Inception
- Elaboration
- Construction
- Transition

In the inception phase the overall scope of the project and its feasibility are determined. This phase ends with management giving its approval to proceed. In the elaboration phase the basic architecture of the system is designed. It's here that the needs of the user are determined. The construction phase involves the design of the software and the actual writing of code. In the transition phase the system is handed over to the users for testing and deployment.

All four phases may be divided into a number of parts called *iterations*. The construction phase in particular will consist of a number of iterations. Each iteration is a subset of the overall system, and corresponds to a particular task the user wants the program to carry out. (As we'll see, an iteration generally corresponds to a use case.) Figure 16.2 shows the Unified Process.

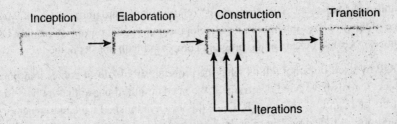

FIGURE 16.2

The Unified Process.

Each iteration involves its own sequence of analysis, design, implementation, and testing. This sequence may be repeated several times. The goal of each iteration is to create a working part of the system.

Unlike the waterfall process, the Unified Process makes it easy to return to earlier phases. For example, discoveries made by users in the transition phase will cause revisions in the construction phase, and perhaps the elaboration phase as well.

We should note that the Unified Process can be applied to any type of software architecture, not just to object-oriented languages. In fact, a potential weakness of this pocess is that it does not actively encourage object-oriented design.

The elaboration phase of the Unified Process usually begins with a technique called *use case modeling*. This is the starting point for developing a detailed design for the system. For this reason the Unified Process is said to be a *use case driven* process. In the next section we'll discuss use case modeling, and in the section after that we'll apply it to a sample software project.

Use Case Modeling

Use case modeling allows future users of a software system as much input as possible into its design. It uses the vocabulary of the users, not programmers. This focus on users means that the initial specification of the program can be understood both by its users and by the software engineers designing it.

There are two main entities in the use case approach: *actors* and *use cases*. Let's see what they are.

Actors

An *actor* is (usually) a person who will use the system we are designing. A bank customer interacting with the software of an ATM machine is an actor. An astronomer inputting the coordinates of a star to a telescope aiming program is an actor. A bookstore clerk checking the computer to see if a particular book is available is an actor. Usually an actor initiates some operation, although sometimes the actor may act in other ways, such as receiving information or assisting in an operation.

Actually, "role" is a probably a better name than "actor." One human playing different roles may be represented by several actors. For example, in a small business, Harry Jones might be represented by an actor called "salesperson" when making a sale, but by an actor called "bookkeeper" when adding up the day's sales. Conversely, a single actor may represent several different individuals. Harry, Jose, and Elma may all be represented by the actor called "salesperson."

Other systems connected to the one we're designing, such as a different computer system or a link to the Web, may also be actors. For example, the computer system in a particular bookstore may be linked to a remote system in the head office. This remote system can be considered an actor in the bookstore's system.

In a large project, just identifying all the actors may be difficult. The designer needs to look for people or other systems that:

- Provide information to the system
- Need information from the system
- Assist other actors

Use Cases

A *use case* is a specific task, usually initiated by an actor. It describes a single goal the actor wants to attain. Examples are the withdrawal of cash by the bank customer, the aiming of the telescope by the astronomer, and the investigation of a book's availability by the bookstore clerk.

In most situations the use case is initiated by the actor, but sometimes it's initiated by the system, as when the electric company's accounting program sends you a reminder that you haven't paid your bill, or your car's computer turns on a warning light when it decides the engine is too hot.

In general, everything you want the system to do should be specified by a use case.

Scenarios

A use case usually consists of a number of *scenarios*. The use case specifies a goal, while a scenario represents a particular outcome when attempting to reach that goal. For example, let's consider a use case consisting of a bookstore clerk querying the store's computer system for the location of a particular book. There are several possible outcomes or scenarios:

- The book is in the store and the computer displays its shelf location.
- The book is out of stock, but the system gives the customer the opportunity to order it from the publisher.
- The book is not only out of stock, it's out of print; so the sytem informs the customer that she or he is out of luck.

In a formal development process, each scenario would have its own documentation, describing in detail all the events in the scenario.

Use Case Diagrams

The UML specifies how to diagram use cases. Actors are represented by stick figures; use cases by ovals. A rectangular frame surrounds the use cases, leaving the actors outside. This rectangle is the *system boundary*. The system inside is what the software developer is trying to design. Figure 16.3 shows a use case diagram for a bookstore computer system.

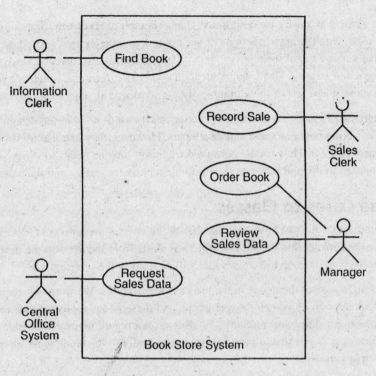

FIGURE 16.3
Use case diagram for a bookstore.

In the use case diagram, lines, called *associations*, connect actors with use cases. Typically the lines don't show any direction, but arrows can be used to show who initiated the use case.

In this diagram we assume that the bookstore is part of a chain, and that accounting and similar functions are handled at a central office. Clerks in the store record the sale of each book and request information about a book's location and availability. The manager can check what books have been sold and order new ones. The actors are Sales Clerk, Information Clerk, Manager, and the Central Office System. The use cases are Record Sale, Find Book, Order Book, Review Sales Data, and Request Sales Data.

Use Case Descriptions

The use case diagram does not have room for detailed descriptions of individual use cases, so these must be supplied separately. Different degrees of formality are used in these use case descriptions, depending on the size of the project and the philosophy of the developers. In most cases there will be a detailed description of each scenario in a use case.

The simplest version of a use case description is a paragraph or so of text. Sometimes two columns are used, with the actor's actions in one column and the system's response in another. A more formal version might include such details as preconditions, postconditions, and a detailed sequence of steps. A UML diagram called an *activity diagram*, which is a form of flowchart, is sometimes used to show graphically the sequence of steps in a use case.

Use case diagrams and use case descriptions are primarily used in the initial design of a system to aid communication between users and developers. However, they are also useful throughout the development process. They can be consulted whenever anyone needs to verify what the system is supposed to do, and they can even provide a basis for testing and documentation.

From Use Cases to Classes

When the actors and use cases have been identified, the development process moves from the elaboration to the construction phase. The emphasis shifts from the users to the developers. Our first concern is to develop the classes that will be used in the program.

One approach is to look at the nouns in the use case descriptions. We want objects in the program to correspond with objects in the real world, and these nouns represent real-world entities specified by the users. They are candidates for classes, but not all nouns make good classes. We need to eliminate nouns that are too general, too trivial, or which are better represented as attributes (simple variables).

Once we have some candidate classes, we can begin to understand how they interact by examining the verbs in the use case descriptions. In many cases a verb translates into a message sent from one object to another, or some other association between classes.

A UML class diagram (described in previous chapters) can be used to show classes and their relationships. A use case is realized by a sequence of messages between objects. We can use another UML diagram, an *interaction diagram*, to detail such a sequence. In fact, we might want to use a separate interaction diagram for each of the scenarios in a use case. We'll see examples of *sequence diagrams*, one kind of interaction diagram, in the next section.

The development process is easier to visualize using an example, so let's walk through the development of a real program. Of necessity this example is so small that it's questionable whether it even requires a formal development process. However, applying the process to even this small project should help to demystify the topics we've mentioned.

The Programming Problem

The program we'll design in this chapter is called LANDLORD. You may or may not like your landlord, but you can understand the sorts of data (such as rents and expenses) that the landlord must deal with. This gets us started with an easily-understood *business domain* (what we're writing the program about).

Let's suppose that you're an independent programmer, and you're approached by a potential customer whose name is Beverly Smith. Beverly is a small-time landlord: She owns an apartment building with 12 units. She wants you to write a program that will make it easier for her to record data and print reports regarding the finances of the apartment building. If you and Beverly can agree on payment, schedule, and the overall purpose of the program, you've completed the inception part of the development process.

Hand-Written Forms

Currently Beverly is recording all the information about her apartment building by hand, in old-fashioned ledger books. She shows you the forms she's currently using. There are four of them:

- The Tenant List
- The Rental Income Record
- The Expense Record
- The Annual Summary

The *Tenant List* shows apartment numbers in one column and the corresponding tenant's names in the adjacent column.

The *Rental Income Record* records incoming rent payments. It contains 12 columns, one for each month and one row for each apartment number. Each time Beverly receives a rent payment from a tenant, she records it in the appropriate row and column of the Rental Income Record, which is shown in Figure 16.4.

The layout of the Rental Income Record makes it easy to see which rents have been paid.

The *Expense Record* records outgoing payments. It's similar to your personal check register. It has columns for the date, the payee (the company or person to whom Beverly writes the check), and the amount being paid. In addition, there's a column where Beverly can specify the budget category to which the payment should be charged. Budget categories include Mortgage, Repairs, Utilities, Taxes, Insurance, and so on. The Expense Record is shown in Figure 16.5.

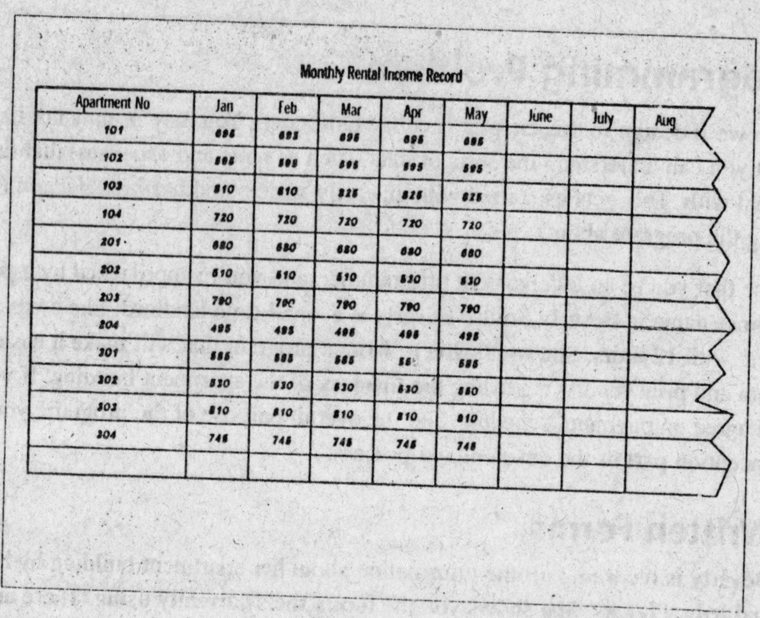

Monthly Rental Income Record

Apartment No	Jan	Feb	Mar	Apr	May	June	July	Aug
101	695	695	695	695	695			
102	595	595	595	595	595			
103	810	810	825	825	825			
104	720	720	720	720	720			
201	680	680	680	680	680			
202	510	510	510	530	530			
203	790	790	790	790	790			
204	495	495	495	495	495			
301	585	585	585	585	585			
302	530	530	530	530	560			
303	810	810	810	810	810			
304	745	745	745	745	745			

FIGURE 16.4

The Rental Income Record.

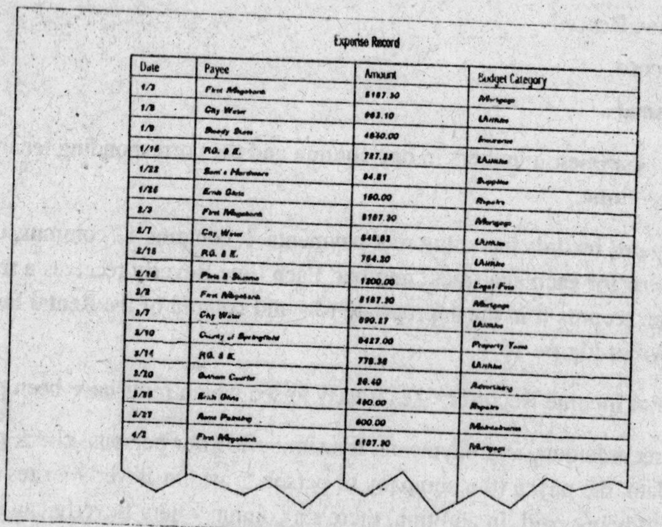

Expense Record

Date	Payee	Amount	Budget Category
1/3	First Maystone	8187.30	Mortgage
1/5	City Water	663.10	Utilities
1/9	Beverly Shore	4630.00	Insurance
1/16	P.G. & E.	727.53	Utilities
1/25	Sam's Hardware	84.81	Supplies
1/26	Erab Glass	160.00	Repairs
2/3	First Maystone	8187.30	Mortgage
2/7	City Water	648.83	Utilities
2/15	P.G. & E.	764.20	Utilities
2/15	Pina & Brunno	1200.00	Legal Fees
3/3	First Maystone	8187.30	Mortgage
3/7	City Water	690.17	Utilities
3/10	County of Springfield	6427.00	Property Taxes
3/14	P.G. & E.	778.38	Utilities
3/20	Daman Courier	56.40	Advertising
3/25	Erab Glass	450.00	Repairs
3/27	Acme Painting	600.00	Maintenance
4/3	First Maystone	8187.30	Mortgage

FIGURE 16.5

The Expense Record.

The *Annual Report* uses data from the Rental Income Record and the Expense Record to summarize how much money came in and how much went out during the year. All the rents are summed and the result is displayed. The expenses are summed and displayed by budget category, which makes it easy to see, for example, how much was spent on repairs during the year. Figure 16.6 shows the Annual Report. Finally, expenses are subtracted from income to show how much money Beverly made (or lost) during the year.

Annual Summary of Business and Statement of Income

#		
1		
2	INCOME	
3	Rent	102,284.00
4	TOTAL INCOME	102,284.00
5		
6	EXPENSES	
7	Mortgage	62,747.60
8	Property taxes	9,427.00
9	Insurance	4,840.00
10	Utilities	18,358.78
11	Supplies	1,189.23
12	Repairs	4,274.60
13	Maintenance	2,609.42
14	Legal fees	1,200.00
15	Landscaping	900.00
16	Advertising	78.64
17		
18	TOTAL EXPENSES	106,054.18
19		
20	NET PROFIT OR (LOSS)	(2,770.18)
21		

FIGURE 16.6
The Annual Report.

In Beverly's existing system, the Annual Report isn't created until the end of the year, when all the rents and expenses for December have been recorded. Our computerized system should be able to show a partial Annual Report at any time in the year.

Beverly tells you she wants the program to pretty much duplicate what she's currently doing on the paper forms. She wants to be able to enter data about tenants, rents, and expenses, and display the various reports.

Assumptions

Of course we've already made some simplifying assumptions. There are other kinds of data associated with running an apartment building, such as damage deposits, depreciation, mortgage interest, and income from late fees and the rental of laundry machines. We won't consider these details.

There are also other kinds of reports Beverly might want, such as a Net Worth statement. It might even be nice to have the program interface with an income tax program and online banking. And from a big-picture perspective, there are commercial landlord programs available, so it might not be smart for Beverly to contract to have one custom-written. We'll ignore all of these distractions to make the problem more tractable.

The Elaboration Phase for the LANDLORD Program

In the elaboration phase of a major software development project, a group of people, which includes the potential users of the program and the software people designing it, meet to discuss what the program should do. In this small example the group is Beverly, who will be using the system, and you, the software expert who will both design and code it.

Actors

The group begins by identifying the actors. Who will be inputting information into the program? Who will be requesting information? Will anyone else interact with the program? Will the program interact with other programs or systems?

In the LANDLORD example, only one person will be using the program: the landlord. The same person inputs information and asks to see it displayed in various ways.

Even in this small project one can imagine other actors. If the landlord's accountant could access the program's data (perhaps via the Internet), the accountant would be an actor, and if the program provided data to an income tax program, that program would also be an actor. For simplicity we'll ignore these possibilities.

Use Cases

Next the group considers what tasks the actor will want to carry out. In a real software project this would be a major effort, with input from many users and much discussion and refining of ideas. Here it's not too complicated to list the tasks the landlord needs. These tasks are recorded on a use case diagram.

In our situation the the landlord actor will need to do the following:

- Start the program
- Add a new tenant to the Tenant List
- Input a rent to the Rent Record
- Input an expense to the Expense Record
- Display the Tenant List
- Display the Rent Record

- Display the Expense Record
- Display the Annual Summary

The resulting use case diagram is shown in Figure 16.7.

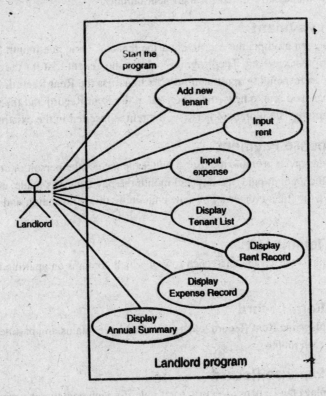

FIGURE 16.7
Use case diagram for the LANDLORD program.

Use Case Descriptions

Now we need to describe each use case in more detail. As noted earlier, use case descriptions can be quite formal and complex. However, our project is so simple that short prose descriptions are all we need.

Start the Program

This may seem too obvious to mention, but when it's first started, the program should display a screen from which the user can choose the task to perform. This can be called the User Interface screen.

Add a New Tenant

The program presents the Tenant Input screen, which prompts the user to enter the new tenant's name and apartment number. It then places this information on a new row in the Tenant List. This list is automatically sorted by apartment number.

Input a Rent Payment

The Rent Input screen prompts the user to enter the tenant's name, the month the rent is for, and the amount of rent received. The program looks in the Tenant List for the name of the tenant, and uses the corresponding apartment number to access the Rent Record. If this is the first time the tenant has paid rent, a new row is created in the Rent Record and the rent amount is inserted for the appropriate month. Otherwise, the rent is inserted in the existing row.

Input an Expense Payment

The Expense Input screen prompts the user to enter the payee (the person or company the landlord is paying), the amount paid, the day and month the payment was made, and the budget category. The program then creates a new row containing this information and inserts it in the Expense Record.

Display the Tenant List

The program displays the Tenant List, each row of which contains an apartment number and the tenant's name.

Display the Rent Record

The program displays the Rent Record, each row of which contains an apartment number and the amount paid each month.

Display the Expense Record

The program displays the Expense Record, each row of which contains the month, day, payee, amount, and budget category.

Display the Annual Summary

The program displays the Annual Summary, which consists of

1. The sum of all rents paid for the year to date
2. A list of the total expenses for each budget category
3. The resulting balance (profit or loss for the year to date)

Scenarios

As we noted, a use case may consist of several scenarios. So far we've described only the main scenario for each use case. This is the scenario where everything works perfectly and the goal is achieved. However, other outcomes are common. As an example of a second scenario in the Add a New Tenant use case, suppose that the user attempts to enter a second tenant into an apartment that is already occupied.

Add a New Tenant, Scenario 2

The program presents the Add Tenant screen, which prompts the user to enter the new tenant's name and apartment number. However, this apartment number has already been entered in the Tenant List, so it's rented to someone else. The Add Tenant screen displays an error message to this effect.

Here's another example of a second scenario, where the user attempts to input a rent payment for a nonexistent tenant.

Input a Rent Payment, Scenario 2

The Rent Input screen prompts the user to enter the name of the tenant, the month the rent is for, and the amount of the rent. The program looks in the Tenant List for the name of the tenant, but does not find it. It displays an error message to the user.

In the interest of simplicity we won't persue such alternative scenarios, although in a real project each scenario should be developed in as much detail as the major scenarios. Only by doing this can all the programming elements be discovered.

UML Activity Diagrams

The UML *activity diagram* can be used to model use cases. This kind of diagram shows the flow of control from one activity to another. It's similar to the flowchart, which has been around since the beginning of programming. However, the activity diagram, like other UML diagrams, is more formally specified and has additional capabilities.

Activities are shown in lozenge-shaped outlines. Lines connecting the activities represent transitions from one activity to another. Branches are shown as diamonds with one incoming and two or more outgoing transitions. As in state diagrams, you can place guards on these transitions to specify which one will be selected. Also as in state diagrams, there is an initial state and an end state, the first represented by a solid circle and the second by a solid circle in a ring.

Figure 16.8 shows the Add a New Tenant use case, including the second scenario just described. The branch depends on whether the apartment number entered by the user is already occupied. If it is, an error message is displayed.

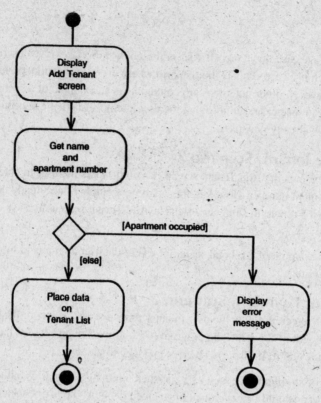

FIGURE 16.8
UML activity diagram.

Activity diagrams can also be used to represent complicated algorithms in program code, just as flowcharts are. They have some capabilities we won't pursue here, such as representing several concurrent activities.

From Use Cases to Classes

The construction phase of our project begins when we begin to design the program. We'll start by examining the nouns in the use case descriptions, as mentioned earlier.

Listing the Nouns

Here's the list of nouns picked out of the use case descriptions:

1. User Interface screen
2. Tenant

3. Tenant Input screen

4. Tenant name

5. Apartment number

6. Tenant row

7. Tenant List

8. Rent payment

9. Rent Input screen

10. Month

11. Rent amount

12. Rent Record

13. Rent row

14. Expense payment

15. Expense Input screen

16. Payee

17. Amount of expense

18. Day

19. Budget category

20. Expense row

21. Expense Record

22. Annual Summary

23. Sum of rents

24. Total expenses by category

25. Balance

Refining the List

For various reasons, many nouns are inappropriate class candidates. Let's see which ones should be rejected.

We've listed the rows in the various records: tenant row, rent row, and expense row. Sometimes these rows make good classes because they are complicated or contain complex data. However, each row in the Tenant Record holds the data for exactly one tenant, and each row in the Expense Record holds the data for exactly one expense. There are already classes for tenant and expense, so we guess that there's no need for two classes with the same data, and discard the tenant row and expense row classes. The rent row, on the other hand, contains an apartment number and an array of 12 rents. A rent row doesn't exist until the first rent of the year has been paid; thereafter, rents are inserted into the existing row. This is a more complicated situation than for tenants and expenses, so we'll leave rent row as a class. This leaves the rent payment class with no data to hold except the rent amount, so we'll eliminate this class.

The program can derive the data in the Annual Summary from the Rent Record and the Expense Record, so we probably won't need to make classes out of the sum of rents, total expenses by category, and balance. These are simply the results of calculations.

This leaves the following classes:

1. User Interface screen
2. Tenant
3. Tenant Input screen
4. Tenant List
5. Rent Input screen
6. Rent Record
7. Rent row
8. Expense payment
9. Expense Input screen
10. Expense Record
11. Annual Summary

Discovering Attributes

Many of the nouns we rejected as classes will be candidates for attributes (member data) in classes. For example, class Tenant will have the attributes Tenant Name and Apartment Number, and class Expense will have the attributes Payee, Month, Day, Amount, and Budget Category. A majority of the attributes can be discovered this way.

From Verbs to Messages

Now let's look at the use cases to see what light they cast on the messages one class will send to another. Because a message is actually a call to a member function in an object, discovering messages is the same as discovering the member functions of the class receiving the message. As with nouns, not every verb is a candidate for a message. Some relate instead to obtaining information from the user, displaying information or doing other things.

As an example, let's look at the Display Tenant List use case, with the verbs underlined:

> The program <u>displays</u> the Tenant List, each row of which <u>contains</u> an apartment number and the tenant's name.

By "the program" we really mean the User Interface screen, so "displays" means that the User Interface screen sends a message to—that is, calls a member function of—the Tenant List, telling it to display itself. You can guess that the member function might be named something like display().

The "contains" verb does not correspond to a message; it merely describes the contents of a row in the Tenant List.

Let's look at a more complicated example: the use case Add a New Tenant:

> The program <u>presents</u> the Tenant Input screen, which <u>prompts</u> the user to <u>enter</u> the new tenant's name and apartment number. It then <u>places</u> this information on a new row in the Tenant List. This list <u>is sorted</u> by apartment number.

The "presents" verb means that the User Interface screen sends a message to the Tenant Input screen telling it to display itself and get data from the user. This message might be a call to a member function in the Tenant Input screen with a name like getTenant().

Both "prompts" and "enter" refer to the Tenant Input screen's communication with the user. They don't represent messages in the object-oriented sense. Rather, getTenant() displays prompts and records the user's responses (the tenant's name and apartment number).

The verb "places" means that that the Tenant Input screen sends a message to the Tenant List class, probably with a new Tenant object as an argument. The Tenant List object can then insert this new object into its list. This function might have a name like insertTenant().

The "is sorted" verb is not a message or indeed any kind of communication, but a description of the Tenant List.

Figure 16.9 shows the Add a New Tenant use case and its connection to these messages.

When we start to write code, we'll find that there are some activities that are not mentioned in the use case but are required by the program. For example, the use case does not say anything about the creation of a Tenant object. However, it's probably clear that the Tenant List holds Tenant objects, and that the Tenant object must be created before being put on the list. The software engineer decides that the getTenant() member function in the Tenant Input screen is an appropriate place to create the Tenant object that will be inserted in the Tenant List.

The other use cases can be similarly analyzed to yield clues to the relationships between classes. Note that at this point we're still using class names as they appeared in the use cases. When we start to write code we will need to rewrite them as single-word C++ class names.

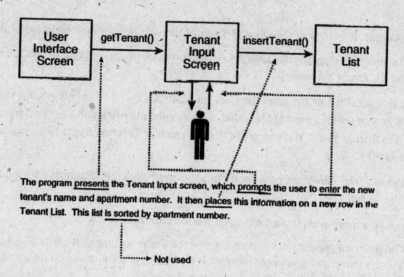

The program presents the Tenant Input screen, which prompts the user to enter the new tenant's name and apartment number. It then places this information on a new row in the Tenant List. This list is sorted by apartment number.

FIGURE 16.9
Verbs in the Add a New Tenant use case.

Class Diagram

Once we have an idea what classes we will need and how they relate to each other, we can create a class diagram. We've seen examples of class diagrams in earlier chapters. Figure 16. 9 is. the class diagram of the LANDLORD program.

Sequence Diagrams

Before starting to code, we might want to understand in more detail the steps involved in each use case. One way to do this is to generate a UML *sequence diagram*. A sequence diagram is one of two kinds of UML interaction diagrams. The other is the *collaboration diagram*. Both show how events unfold over time, but the sequence diagram depicts time in a more graphical way.

In a sequence diagram the vertical axis represents time, starting at the top and flowing downward. Across the top are rectangles containing the names of the objects that will participate in the use case. The action typically starts with the object on the left sending a message to an object on its right. The further to the right they are, the less important (or the more dependent) the objects usually are.

Note that the diagram shows objects, not classes. We're going to be focusing on sequences of messages, and messages are sent from object to object, not class to class. In UML diagrams, object names are underlined to distinquish them from class names.

Extending downward from each object is a dotted line called the *lifeline*. This indicates that the object exists at a particular time. If the object is deleted, its lifeline stops at that point.

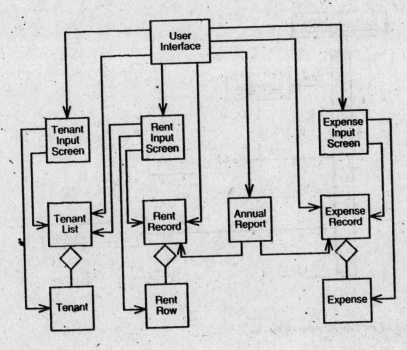

FIGURE 16.10
Class diagram of the LANDLORD program.

Sequence Diagram for "Start the Program"

Let's look at some sequence diagrams for the LANDLORD program. We'll start with an easy one. Figure 16.11 shows the sequence diagram for the Start the Program use case.

When the program first starts, it defines a class called userInterface to handle the User Interface screen discussed in the use cases. Let's assume that the program creates a single object of this class called theUserInterface. It's this object that initiates all the use cases. It will appear on the left in the sequence diagrams. (In these diagrams we condense the use case names into C++ class names.)

When the theUserInterface object starts to run, its first task is to create the three main data structures in the program. These are objects of the classes tenantList, rentRecord, and expenseRecord. As it turns out, the program creates these objects with new, so they are born with no names; only the pointers to them have names. What do we call them? Fortunately, as we saw with object diagrams, the UML allows several ways to write object names. If you don't know the actual name, you can use a colon and the class name: :tenantList. In the diagrams the underlining and the colon remind you that the name applies to an object, not a class.

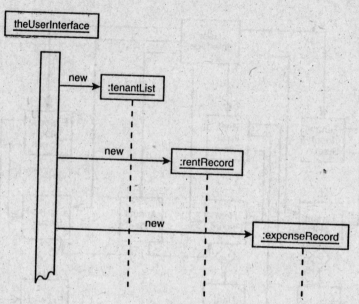

FIGURE 16.11
Sequence diagram for the Start the Program use case.

The vertical position of the object rectangles shows the time they were created, starting with the object of class `tenantList`. All these objects will continue to exist for the life of the program, so their lifelines extend down to the bottom of the diagram. The time dimension is not to scale; it's intended to show only the relationship of various events.

The horizontal lines represent messages (calls to member functions). The solid arrowhead indicates a normal synchronous function call. (An open arrowhead indicates an asynchronous event.)

The rectangle under `theUserInterace` is called the *activation box* (or *focus of control*). It indicates that its object is *active*. In a normal procedural program such as LANDLORD, "active" means that a member function of the object is either executing or has called another function that has not yet returned. The three other objects in this diagram are not active because `theUserInterface` has not yet sent them messages telling them what to do.

Sequence Diagram for "Display Tenant List"

Let's examine another sequence diagram. This one, shown in Figure 16.12, depicts the Display Tenant List use case.

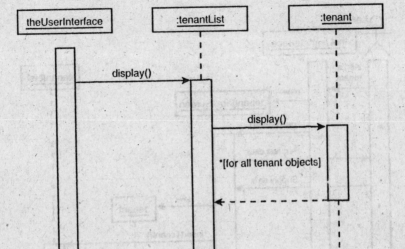

FIGURE 16.12
Sequence diagram for the Display Tenant List use case.

Function returns are represented by dotted lines. Notice how objects are only active (their life-line has an activity box) when one of their member functions has been called by another object. The message lines can show the name of the member function being called.

Here `theUserInterface` tells the `tenantList` object to display itself (by calling its `display()` function), and the `tenantList` object in turn tells all the `tenant` objects it contains to display themselves. The asterisk indicates that this message will be sent repeatedly, and the phrase in brackets, `[for all tenant objects]`, specifies the condition of this repetition. (In the program we'll actually use `cout << ` instead of a `display()` function as shown.)

Sequence Diagram for "Add a New Tenant"

As our last example of a sequence diagram let's look at the Add a New Tenant use case, shown in Figure 16.13. Here we've included the landlord as an object, with its own activity box. This allows us to show the interaction between the program and the user.

The user tells the program to add a new tenant. The `theUserInterface` object creates a new object of class `tenantInputScreen`. This object gets the tenant's data from the user, creates a new tenant object, and calls the object of class `tenantList` to insert the newly created tenant. When it's done, it deletes the `tenantInputScreen` object. The large "X" at the end of the `tenantInputScreen`'s lifeline shows that it is deleted at that point.

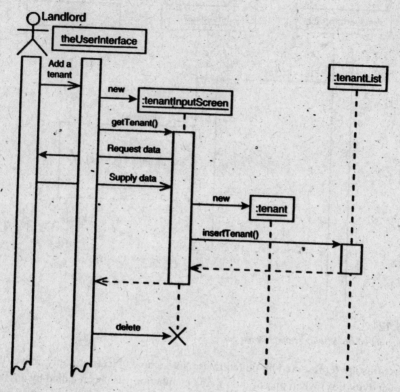

FIGURE 16.13

Sequence diagram for the Add a New Tenant use case.

The sequence diagrams we have shown deal only with the main scenario of each use case. There are ways to show alternate scenarios on sequence diagrams, or you can create a new diagram for each scenario.

Lack of space precludes our illustrating sequence diagrams for all the use cases, but you know enough at this point to create them yourself if you want.

Writing the Code

Finally, armed with the use case diagram, the detailed use cases, the class diagram, and the sequence diagrams, you can crank up your compiler and start writing the actual code. This is the second part of the construction phase.

The use cases determined in the elaboration phase translate into iterations in the construction phase. (See Figure 16.2). In a large project each of these iterations might be handled by a different team of programmers. Each iteration can be developed separately, and sent back to the users to determine changes or refinements. In our small program we don't need this complexity.

The Header File

The best place to start coding is the .H file, where you define class interfaces, rather than the details of their implementations. As we've discussed before, the declarations in the .H file are the public part of the classes, the part that users of these classes see. The function bodies in the .CPP file are the implementations, which should be invisible to class users.

The creation of the .H file is an intermediate step between design and the nitty-gritty of writing method bodies. Here's the LANDLORD.H file:

```
//landlord.h
//header file for landlord.cpp -- contains class declarations, etc.
#pragma warning (disable:4786)  //for set (microsoft only)
#include <iostream>
#include <vector>
#include <set>
#include <string>
#include <algorithm>              //for sort()
#include <numeric>                //for accumulate()
using namespace std;
/////////////////////////////global methods/////////////////////////////
void getaLine(string& inStr);   // get line of text
char getaChar();                // get a character


/////////////////////////////class tenant/////////////////////////////
class tenant
   {
   private:
   string name;    // tenant's name
   int aptNumber;  // tenant's apartment number
   // other tenant information (phone, etc.) could go here

   public:
   tenant(string n, int aNo);
   ~tenant();
   int getAptNumber();
   // needed for use in 'set'
   friend bool operator < (const tenant&, const tenant&);
   friend bool operator == (const tenant&, const tenant&);
   // for I/O
```

```
    friend ostream& operator << (ostream&, const tenant&);
};   // end class tenant
///////////////////////////class compareTenants///////////////////////
class compareTenants   //function object --  compares tenants
    {
    public:
    bool operator () (tenant*, tenant*) const;
    };


//////////////////////////class tenantList////////////////////////////
class tenantList
    {
    private:
    // set of pointers to tenants
    set<tenant*, compareTenants> setPtrsTens;
    set<tenant*, compareTenants>::iterator iter;

    public:
    ~tenantList();                      // destructor (deletes tenants)
    void insertTenant(tenant*);   // put tenant on list
    int getAptNo(string);              // return apartment number
    void display();                    // display tenant list
    };   // end class tenantList


//////////////////////////class tenantInputScreen//////////////////////
class tenantInputScreen
    {
    private:
    tenantList* ptrTenantList;
    string tName;
    int aptNo;

    public:
    tenantInputScreen(tenantList* ptrTL) : ptrTenantList(ptrTL)
        { /* empty */ }
    void getTenant();
    };   //end class tenantInputScreen


//////////////////////////////class rentRow////////////////////////////
// one row of the rent record: an address and 12 rent amounts
class rentRow
    {
    private:
    int aptNo;
    float rent[12];
```

```
public:
rentRow(int);                    // 1-arg ctor
void setRent(int, float);        // record rent for one month
float getSumOfRow();             // return sum of rents in row
// needed to store in 'set'
friend bool operator < (const rentRow&, const rentRow&);
friend bool operator == (const rentRow&, const rentRow&);
// for output
friend ostream& operator << (ostream&, const rentRow&);
};   // end class rentRow

//////////////////////////////////////////////////////////////////
class compareRows  //function object --  compares rentRows
   {
   public:
      bool operator () (rentRow*, rentRow*) const;
   };

/////////////////////////////////class rentRecord//////////////////////////
class rentRecord
   {
   private:
   // set of pointers to rentRow objects (one per tenant)
   set<rentRow*, compareRows> setPtrsRR;
   set<rentRow*, compareRows>::iterator iter;

   public:
   ~rentRecord();
   void insertRent(int, int, float);
   void display();
   float getSumOfRents();          // sum all rents in record
   };   // end class rentRecord

/////////////////////////////class rentInputScreen//////////////////
class rentInputScreen
   {
   private:
   tenantList* ptrTenantList;
   rentRecord* ptrRentRecord;

   string renterName;
   float rentPaid;
   int month;
   int aptNo;
```

```
    public:
    rentInputScreen(tenantList* ptrTL, rentRecord* ptrRR) :
                    ptrTenantList(ptrTL), ptrRentRecord(ptrRR)
       { /*empty*/ }
    void getRent();            //rent for one tenant and one month
    }; // end class rentInputScreen

///////////////////////////////class expense///////////////////////////
class expense
    {
    public:
    int month, day;
    string category, payee;
    float amount;
    expense()
       { }
    expense(int m, int d, string c, string p, float a) :
          month(m), day(d), category(c), payee(p), amount(a)
       { /*empty */ }
    // needed for use in 'set'
    friend bool operator < (const expense&, const expense&);
    friend bool operator == (const expense&, const expense&);
    // needed for output
    friend ostream& operator << (ostream&, const expense&);
    }; // end class expense
//////////////////////////////////////////////////////////////////////
class compareDates  //function object--compares expenses
    {
    public:
       bool operator () (expense*, expense*) const;
    };
//////////////////////////////////////////////////////////////////////
class compareCategories  //function object--compares expenses
    {
    public:
       bool operator () (expense*, expense*) const;
    };

//////////////////////////class expenseRecord///////////////////////////
class expenseRecord
    {
    private:
    // vector of pointers to expenses
    vector<expense*> vectPtrsExpenses;
    vector<expense*>::iterator iter;
```

```
public:
~expenseRecord();
void insertExp(expense*);
void display();
float displaySummary();          // used by annualReport
};   // end class expenseRecord

/////////////////////////class expenseInputScreen///////////////////////
class expenseInputScreen
    {
    private:
    expenseRecord* ptrExpenseRecord;

    public:
    expenseInputScreen(expenseRecord*);
    void getExpense();
    };   // end class expenseInputScreen

/////////////////////////class annualReport///////////////////////////
class annualReport
    {
    private:
    rentRecord* ptrRR;
    expenseRecord* ptrER;
    float expenses, rents;

    public:
    annualReport(rentRecord*, expenseRecord*);
    void display();
    };   // end class annualReport

/////////////////////////class userInterface///////////////////////////
class userInterface
    {
    private:
    tenantList*             ptrTenantList;
    tenantInputScreen*      ptrTenantInputScreen;
    rentRecord*             ptrRentRecord;
    rentInputScreen*        ptrRentInputScreen;
    expenseRecord*          ptrExpenseRecord;
    expenseInputScreen*     ptrExpenseInputScreen;
    annualReport*           ptrAnnualReport;
    char ch;

    public:
    userInterface();
```

```
    ~userInterface();
    void interact();
    };  // end class userInterfac
//////////////////////////////end file landlord.h//////////////////////////
```

Class Declarations

Declaring classes is the easy part. Most class declarations arise directly from the classes discovered by examining the nouns in the use case descriptions and seen on the class diagram. The names are changed from the multi-word English versions to single-word computerese, so that, for example, Tenant List becomes `tenantList`.

A few new classes have been added. We'll find that we're storing pointers to objects in various kinds of STL containers. This means that we must define comparison objects for these containers, as described in Chapter 15, "The Standard Template Library." These comparison objects are actually classes named `compareTenants`, `compareRows`, `compareDates`, and `compareCategories`.

Attribute Declarations

As we noted, many of the attributes (member data) for each class can be determined from nouns that weren't used for classes. For example, `name` and `aptNumber` become attributes of the `tenant` class declaration.

Other attributes can be inferred from the associations in the class diagram. Associations may indicate attributes that are pointers or references to other classes. This is because you can't associate with something if you can't find it. Thus the `rentInputScreen` class has the attributes `ptrTenantList` and `ptrRentRecord`.

Aggregates

Aggregate associations are shown in three places on the class diagram. Often, aggregates indicate containers that are attributes of the containing class (the whole) holding objects (the parts).

Neither the use case descriptions nor the class diagram suggest what sort of container should be used for these aggregates. As a programmer, you'll need to choose an appropriate container for each aggregate, whether it's a simple array, an STL container, or something else. In LANDLORD, we made the following choices:

* The `tenantList` class contains an STL set of pointers to `tenant` objects.
* The `rentRecord` class contains a set of pointers to `rentRow` objects.
* The `expenseRecord` class contains a vector of pointers to `expense` objects.

We used sets for tenantList and rentRecord to provide fast access. We used a vector for expenseRecord because we need to sort the Expense objects both by date and by category, and vectors (unlike sets) can be sorted efficiently.

In all the aggregations, we chose to store pointers, rather than actual objects, to avoid the copying that takes place every time an actual object is stored. Storing objects directly might be appropriate in situations where the objects are small and there aren't many of them. Of course, the performance penalty for storing objects isn't great in a small program like this, but for efficiency you should always consider storing pointers.

The .CPP Files

The .CPP files contain the method bodies whose declarations were given in the .H file. Writing the code for these methods should be fairly straightforward at this point. You know the function name, what it's supposed to do, and probably the arguments passed to it.

We've separated the class method definitions from main(), which is in the short LORDAPP.CPP file. In main() a userInterface object is created and its interact() method is called. Here's the LORDAPP.CPP file:

```
// lordApp.cpp
// client file for apart program
#include "landlord.h"

int main()
    {
    userInterface theUserInterface;

    theUserInterface.interact();
    return 0;
    }
/////////////////////////////end file lordApp.cpp/////////////////////
```

Finally, here's the LANDLORD.CPP file, which contains all the class method definitions.

```
//landlord.cpp
//models the finances for an apartment building
#include "landlord.h" //for class declarations, etc.

//////////////////////////global functions//////////////////////////
void getaLine(string& inStr)     // get line of text
    {
    char temp[21];
    cin.get(temp, 20, '\n');
    cin.ignore(20, '\n');
    inStr = temp;
    }
```

```
//-----------------------------------------------------
char getaChar()                        // get a character
   {
   char ch = cin.get();
   cin.ignore(80, '\n');
   return ch;
   }
//-----------------------------------------------------

/////////////////////////methods for class tenant///////////////////////
tenant::tenant(string n, int aNo) : name(n), aptNumber(aNo)
   { /* empty */ }
//-----------------------------------------------------
tenant::~tenant()
   { /* empty */ }
//-----------------------------------------------------
int tenant::getAptNumber()
   { return aptNumber; }
//-----------------------------------------------------
bool operator < (const tenant& t1, const tenant& t2)
   { return t1.name < t2.name; }
//-----------------------------------------------------
bool operator == (const tenant& t1, const tenant& t2)
   { return t1.name == t2.name; }
//-----------------------------------------------------
ostream& operator << (ostream& s, const tenant& t)
   { s << t.aptNumber << '\t' << t.name << endl;  return s; }
//-----------------------------------------------------

/////////////////////method for class tenantInputScreen//////////////
void tenantInputScreen::getTenant()              //get tenant info
   {
   cout << "Enter tenant's name (George Smith): ";
   getaLine(tName);
   cout << "Enter tenant's apartment number (101): ";
   cin >> aptNo;
   cin.ignore(80, '\n');                         //make tenant
   tenant* ptrTenant = new tenant(tName, aptNo);
   ptrTenantList->insertTenant(ptrTenant); //send to tenant list
   }
//////////////////////////////////////////////////////////////////////
bool compareTenants::operator () (tenant* ptrT1,
                                  tenant* ptrT2) const
   { return *ptrT1 < *ptrT2; }
//-----------------------------------------------------
```

```
/////////////////////methods for class tenantList//////////////////
tenantList::~tenantList()                    //destructor
   {
   while( !setPtrsTens.empty() )             //delete all tenants,
      {                                      //remove ptrs from set
      iter = setPtrsTens.begin();
      delete *iter;
      setPtrsTens.erase(iter);
      }
   }  // end ~tenantList()
//----------------------------------------------------------------
void tenantList::insertTenant(tenant* ptrT)
   {
   setPtrsTens.insert(ptrT);                 //insert
   }
//----------------------------------------------------------------
 int tenantList::getAptNo(string tName) //name on list?
    {
    int aptNo;
    tenant dummy(tName, 0);
    iter = setPtrsTens.begin();
    while( iter != setPtrsTens.end() )
       {
       aptNo = (*iter)->getAptNumber(); //look for tenant
       if(dummy == **iter++)             //on the list?
          return aptNo;                  //yes
       }
    return -1;                           //no
    }
//----------------------------------------------------------------
 void tenantList::display()                   //display tenant list
    {
    cout << "\nApt#\tTenant name\n------------------\n";
    if( setPtrsTens.empty() )
       cout << "***No tenants***\n";
    else
       {
       iter = setPtrsTens.begin();
       while( iter != setPtrsTens.end() )
          cout << **iter++;
       }
    }  // end display()
//----------------------------------------------------------------

/////////////////////methods for class rentRow/////////////////////
rentRow::rentRow(int an) : aptNo(an)          // 1-arg constructor
   { fill( &rent[0], &rent[12], 0); }
```

```
//·······················································
void rentRow::setRent(int m, float am)
   { rent[m] = am; }
//·······················································
float rentRow::getSumOfRow()                    // sum of rents in row
   { return accumulate( &rent[0], &rent[12], 0); }
//·······················································
bool operator < (const rentRow& t1, const rentRow& t2)
   { return t1.aptNo < t2.aptNo; }
//·······················································
bool operator == (const rentRow& t1, const rentRow& t2)
   { return t1.aptNo == t2.aptNo; }
//·······················································
ostream& operator << (ostream& s, const rentRow& an)
   {
   s << an.aptNo << '\t';                       //print apartment n
   for(int j=0; j<12; j++)                      //print 12 rents
      {
      if(an.rent[j] == 0)
         s << "  0  ";
      else
         s << an.rent[j] << "  ";
      }
   s << endl;
   return s;
   }
/////////////////////////////////////////////////////////////////
bool compareRows::operator () (rentRow* ptrR1,
                               rentRow* ptrR2) const
   { return *ptrR1 < *ptrR2; }

///////////////////////methods for class rentRecord/////////////////
rentRecord::~rentRecord()                        //destructor
   {
   while( !setPtrsRR.empty() )                   //delete rent rows,
      {                                          //remove ptrs from set
      iter = setPtrsRR.begin();
      delete *iter;
      setPtrsRR.erase(iter);
      }
   }
//·······················································
void rentRecord::insertRent(int aptNo, int month, float amount)
   {
   rentRow searchRow(aptNo);                     //temp row with same aptNo
   iter = setPtrsRR.begin();                     //search setPtrsRR
```

```
      while( iter != setPtrsRR.end() )
         {
         if(searchRow==**iter)                    //rentRow found?
            {                                      //yes,
            (*iter)->setRent(month, amount);       //put rent in row
            return;
            }
         else
            iter++;
         }                                         //didn't find it
      rentRow* ptrRow = new rentRow(aptNo);        //make new row
      ptrRow->setRent(month, amount);              //put rent in row
      setPtrsRR.insert(ptrRow);                    //put row in vector
      }  // end insertRent()
//----------------------------------------------------------------
void rentRecord::display()
   {
   cout << "\nAptNo\tJan  Feb  Mar  Apr  May  Jun  "
        <<            "Jul  Aug  Sep  Oct  Nov  Dec\n"
        << "....................................."
        << ".....................................\n";
   if( setPtrsRR.empty() )
      cout << "***No rents***\n";
   else
      {
      iter = setPtrsRR.begin();
      while( iter != setPtrsRR.end() )
         cout << **iter++;
      }
   }
//----------------------------------------------------------------
float rentRecord::getSumOfRents()        // return sum of all rents
   {
   float sumRents = 0.0;
   iter = setPtrsRR.begin();
   while( iter != setPtrsRR.end() )
      {
      sumRents += (*iter)->getSumOfRow();
      iter++;
      }
   return sumRents;
   }
//----------------------------------------------------------------

///////////////////////methods for class rentInputScreen///////////////
void rentInputScreen::getRent()
```

```
      {
      cout << "Enter tenant's name: ";
      getaLine(renterName);
      aptNo = ptrTenantList->getAptNo(renterName);
      if(aptNo > 0)                      // if name found,
         {                               // get rent amount
         cout << "Enter amount paid (345.67): ";
         cin >> rentPaid;
         cin.ignore(80, '\n');
         cout << "Enter month rent is for (1-12): ";
         cin >> month;
         cin.ignore(80, '\n');
         month--;                        // (internal is 0-11)
         ptrRentRecord->insertRent(aptNo, month, rentPaid);
         }
      else                               // return
         cout << "No tenant with that name.\n";
      } // end getRent()
//-------------------------------------------------------------

/////////////////////methods for class expense/////////////////////
bool operator < (const expense& e1, const expense& e2)
   {                                     // compares dates
   if(e1.month == e2.month)              // if same month,
      return e1.day < e2.day;            // compare days
   else                                  // otherwise,
      return e1.month < e2.month;        // compare months
   }
//-------------------------------------------------------------
bool operator == (const expense& e1, const expense& e2)
   { return e1.month == e2.month && e1.day == e2.day; }
//-------------------------------------------------------------
ostream& operator << (ostream& s, const expense& exp)
   {
   s << exp.month << '/' << exp.day << '\t' << exp.payee << '\t' ;
   s << exp.amount << '\t' << exp.category << endl;
   return s;
   }
//-------------------------------------------------------------

//////////////////////////////////////////////////////////////
bool compareDates::operator () (expense* ptrE1,
                                expense* ptrE2) const
   { return *ptrE1 < *ptrE2; }
//-------------------------------------------------------------
```

```
/////////////////////////////////////////////////////////////////
bool compareCategories::operator () (expense* ptrE1,
                                     expense* ptrE2) const
   { return ptrE1->category < ptrE2->category; }
//-----------------------------------------------------------

///////////////////////methods for class expenseRecord/////////////////
expenseRecord::~expenseRecord()                //destructor
   {
   while( !vectPtrsExpenses.empty() )      //delete expense objects,
      {                                    //remove ptrs from vector
      iter = vectPtrsExpenses.begin();
      delete *iter;
      vectPtrsExpenses.erase(iter);
      }
   }
//-----------------------------------------------------------
void expenseRecord::insertExp(expense* ptrExp)
   { vectPtrsExpenses.push_back(ptrExp); }
//-----------------------------------------------------------
void expenseRecord::display()
   {
   cout << "\nDate\tPayee\t\tAmount\tCategory\n"
        << "------------------------------------------\n";
   if( vectPtrsExpenses.size() == 0 )
      cout << "***No expenses***\n";
   else
      {
      sort( vectPtrsExpenses.begin(),            // sort by date
            vectPtrsExpenses.end(), compareDates() );
      iter = vectPtrsExpenses.begin();
      while( iter != vectPtrsExpenses.end() )
         cout << **iter++;
      }
   }
//-----------------------------------------------------------
float expenseRecord::displaySummary() // used by annualReport
   {
   float totalExpenses = 0;                 //total, all categories

   if( vectPtrsExpenses.size() == 0 )
      {
      cout << "\tAll categories\t0\n";
      return 0;
      }
   // sort by category
```

```
    sort( vectPtrsExpenses.begin(),
        vectPtrsExpenses.end(), compareCategories() );

 // for each category, sum the entries

   iter = VectPtrsExpenses.begin();
   string tempCat = (*iter)->category;
   float sumCat = 0.0;
   while( iter != vectPtrsExpenses.end() )
      {
      if(tempCat == (*iter)->category)
        sumCat += (*iter)->amount;     // same category
      else
         {                             // different category
         cout << '\t' << tempCat << '\t' << sumCat << endl;
         totalExpenses += sumCat;      // add previous category
         tempCat = (*iter)->category;
         sumCat = (*iter)->amount;     // add final amount
         }
      iter++;
      } // end while
   totalExpenses += sumCat;            // add final category
   cout << '\t' << tempCat << '\t' << sumCat << endl;
   return totalExpenses;
   } // end displaySummary()
   //..............................................................

////////////////methods for class expenseInputScreen//////////////
expenseInputScreen::expenseInputScreen(expenseRecord* per) :
                        ptrExpenseRecord(per)
   { /*empty*/ }
   //..............................................................
void expenseInputScreen::getExpense()
   {
   int month, day;
   string category, payee;
   float amount;

   cout << "Enter month (1-12): ";
   cin >> month;
   cin.ignore(80, '\n');
   cout << "Enter day (1-31): ";
   cin >> day;
   cin.ignore(80, '\n');
   cout << "Enter expense category (Repairing, Utilities): ";
   getaLine(category);
```

```
   cout << "Enter payee "
        << "(Bob's Hardware, Big Electric Co): ";
   getaLine(payee);
   cout << "Enter amount (39.95): ";
   cin >> amount;
   cin.ignore(80, '\n');
   expense* ptrExpense = new
                     expense(month, day, category, payee, amount);
   ptrExpenseRecord->insertExp(ptrExpense);
   }
//-------------------------------------------------------------

/////////////////////methods for class annualReport/////////////
annualReport::annualReport(rentRecord* pRR,
                              expenseRecord* pER) :
                                      ptrRR(pRR), ptrER(pER)
   { /* empty*/ }
//-------------------------------------------------------------
void annualReport::display()
   {
   cout << "Annual Summary\n--------------\n";
   cout << "Income\n";
   cout << "\tRent\t\t";
   rents = ptrRR->getSumOfRents();
   cout << rents << endl;

   cout << "Expenses\n";
   expenses = ptrER->displaySummary();
   cout << "\nBalance\t\t\t" << rents - expenses << endl;
   }
//-------------------------------------------------------------

/////////////////////methods for class userInterface/////////////
userInterface::userInterface()
   {
   //these reports exist for the life of the program
   ptrTenantList    = new tenantList;
   ptrRentRecord    = new rentRecord;
   ptrExpenseRecord = new expenseRecord;
   }
//-------------------------------------------------------------
userInterface::~userInterface()
   {
   delete ptrTenantList;
   delete ptrRentRecord;
   delete ptrExpenseRecord;
   }
```

```
//-------------------------------------------------------------------
void userInterface::interact()
   {
   while(true)
      {
      cout << "Enter 'i' to input data, \n"
           << "        'd' to display a report, \n"
           << "        'q' to quit program: ";
      ch = getaChar();
      if(ch=='i')
         {                                        // enter data
         cout << "Enter 't' to add tenant, \n"
              << "        'r' to record rent payment, \n"
              << "        'e' to record expense: ";
         ch = getaChar();
         switch(ch)
            {
            //input screens exist only while being used
            case 't': ptrTenantInputScreen =
               new tenantInputScreen(ptrTenantList);
               ptrTenantInputScreen->getTenant();
               delete ptrTenantInputScreen;
               break;
            case 'r': ptrRentInputScreen =
               new rentInputScreen(ptrTenantList, ptrRentRecord);
               ptrRentInputScreen->getRent();
               delete ptrRentInputScreen;
               break;
            case 'e': ptrExpenseInputScreen =
               new expenseInputScreen(ptrExpenseRecord);
               ptrExpenseInputScreen->getExpense();
               delete ptrExpenseInputScreen;
               break;
            default: cout << "Unknown input option\n";
               break;
            } // end switch
         } // end if
      else if(ch=='d')
         {                                        // display data
         cout << "Enter 't' to display tenants, \n"
              << "        'r' to display rents\n"
              << "        'e' to display expenses, \n"
              << "        'a' to display annual report: ";
         ch = getaChar();
         switch(ch)
            {
```

```
        case 't': ptrTenantList->display();
            break;
        case 'r': ptrRentRecord->display();
            break;
        case 'e': ptrExpenseRecord->display();
            break;
        case 'a':
            ptrAnnualReport = new annualReport(ptrRentRecord,
                                      ptrExpenseRecord);
            ptrAnnualReport->display();
            delete ptrAnnualReport;
            break;
        default: cout << "Unknown display option\n";
            break;
        } // end switch
    } // end elseif
    else if(ch=='q')
        return;                              // qui.
    else
        cout << "Unknown option. Enter only 'i', 'd' or 'q'\n";
    } // end while
} // end interact()
//////////////////////end of file landlord.cpp///////////////////////
```

More Simplifications

The code we show for LANDLORD, while quite lengthy, still contains many simplifications. It uses a character-mode user interface, not the menus and windows of a modern Graphic User Interface. There's very little error-checking for the user's input. Only one year's worth of data can be handled.

Interacting with the Program

After going to the trouble to design and write the LANDLORD program, you may be interested in seeing some sample interaction with it. Here's how it looks when Beverly uses it to insert a new tenant's name and apartment number. First she enters 'i' followed by 't', for "insert tenant." Then she enters the relevant data at the prompts. (The prompts often show the proper format in parentheses.)

```
Enter 'i' to input data,
      'd' to display a report,
      'q' to quit program: i
Enter 't' to add a tenant,
      'r' to record a rent payment,
      'e' to record an expense: t
```

```
Enter tenant's name (George Smith): Harry Ellis
Enter tenant's apartment number: 101
```

After she's entered all the tenants, she can display the tenant list (for brevity we show only five of the twelve tenants):

```
Enter 'i' to input data,
      'd' to display a report,
      'q' to quit program: d
Enter 't' to display tenants,
      'r' to display rents,
      'e' to display expenses,
      'a' to display annual report: t


Apt#    Tenant name
-------------------------
101     Harry Ellis
102     Wanda Brown
103     Peter Quan
104     Bill  Vasquez
201     Jane  Garth
```

To input a rent paid by a tenant, Beverly enters 'i', then 'r'. (From now on we'll leave out the option lists displayed by the program.) The interaction looks like this:

```
Enter tenant's name: Wanda Brown
Enter amount paid (345.67): 595
Enter month rent is for (1-12): 5
```

Here Wanda Brown has sent a check for the May rent in the amount of $595. (The tenant's name must be typed exactly as it appears in the tenant list. A smarter program would be more flexible.)

To see the entire Rent Record, Beverly types 'd' followed by 'r'. Here's the result after the May rents have been received (for brevity we show the rents for only five of Beverly's 12 units):

AptNo	Jan	Feb	Mar	Apr	May	Jun	Jul	Aug	Sep	Oct	Nov	Dec
101	695	695	695	695	695	0	0	0	0	0	0	0
102	595	595	595	595	595	0	0	0	0	0	0	0
103	810	810	825	825	825	0	0	0	0	0	0	0
104	645	645	645	645	645	0	0	0	0	0	0	0
201	720	720	720	720	720	0	0	0	0	0	0	0

Notice that Beverly raised Peter Quan's rent in March.

To input an expense, Beverly types 'i' followed by 'e'. Here's some sample interaction:

```
Enter month: 1
Enter day: 15
Enter expense category (Repairing, Utilities): Utilities
Enter payee (Bob's Hardware, Big Electric Co): P. G. & E.
Enter amount: 427.23
```

To display the Expense Report, you type 'd' and 'e'. Here we show only the beginning of the report:

```
Date   Payee          Amount  Category
.............................................
1/3    First MegaBank 5187.30 Mortgage
1/8    City Water      963.10 Utilities
1/9    Steady State   4840.00 Insurance
1/15   P. G. & E.      727.23 Utilities
1/22   Sam's Hardware   54.81 Supplies
1/25   Ernie Glotz     150.00 Repairs
2/3    First MegaBank 5187.30 Mortgage
```

To display the Annual Report, Beverly enters 'd' and 'a'. Here's a partial version, covering the first five months of the year:

```
Annual Summary
..............
Income
       Rents          42610.12
Expenses
       Advertising       95.10
       Insurance       4840.00
       Mortgage       25936.57
       Repairs         1554.90
       Supplies         887.22
       Utilities       7636.15
Balance                1660.18
```

The expense categories are sorted in alphabetical order. In a real situation there would be many more budget categories, including legal fees, taxes, travel expenses, landscaping, cleaning and maintenance costs, and so on.

Final Thoughts

In a real project of any size, the development process would probably not go as smoothly as we've portrayed it in this chapter. Several iterations of each of the phases we've shown would be necessary. Programmers may find themselves confused about what the users intended, requiring a return to the elaboration phase while in the midst of the construction phase. Users may change their minds about what they want late in the process, requiring a return to earlier phases.

Summary

Trial and error may be sufficient for simple software development. For complex projects, a more organized approach is usually necessary. In this chapter, we've shown one possible methodology. The Unified Process consists of inception, elaboration, construction, and transition phases. Elaboration corresponds to program analysis, and construction corresponds to design and writing code.

The Unified Process uses the use case approach to capture the program's users (actors) and the tasks (use cases) they want the program to carry out. A UML use case diagram shows the actors and use cases. From the use case descriptions, any noun is a candidate to become a class or a class attribute. Verbs become class member functions (also called operations or methods).

In addition to the use case diagram, other UML diagrams help to facilitate understanding between a program's users and its developers. Relationships among classes can be shown in a class diagram, flow of control from one activity to another can be shown in activity diagrams, and sequence diagrams depict the communication between objects during the course of a use case.

Questions

Answers to these questions can be found in Appendix G.

1. True or false: the use case approach is concerned primarily with which methods a class uses.

2. Use cases are used to (among other things)

   a. summarize problems encountered in program code.

   b. discover what constructors a class may have.

   c. help select appropriate class attributes.

   d. deduce what classes may be necessary in a program.

3. A use case is basically a _____.

4. True or false: After a use case diagram is created, new use cases can be added after coding has begun.

5. A use case description is sometimes written in two _____ .

6. An actor might be

   a. a different system that interacts with the system being developed.

   b. a software entity that helps the developer solve a particular coding problem.

   c. a person who interacts with the system being developed.

   d. the designer of the system.

7. Classes may be related by (among others) g_____, a_____, or a_____.

8. The waterfall process

    a. consists of distinct phases.

    b. was never actually used.

    c. became untenable because of water shortages.

    d. could go in only one direction.

9. True or false: If the UML is used, the Unified Process must also be used.

10. Classes in a program may correspond to

    a. nouns in use case descriptions.

    b. use cases.

    c. associations in a UML diagram.

    d. names of famous programmers.

11. True or false: Vague, general entities (such as "the system") in a use case descriptions are not good candidates for classes in the program.

12. True or false: Entities with a single attribute and no methods are good candidates for classes.

13. In the Unified Process, which of the following may happen from time to time?

    a. A use case diagram will be drawn up before the users have specified all the use cases.

    b. A class diagram will be drawn before some use case descriptions are written.

    c. Some code will be written before the class diagram is complete.

    d. The header file with the class declarations will be changed while methods are still being coded.

14. Actors are _____ or _____ that interact with the _____.

15. For the LANDLORD program, STL container classes

    a. cannot be used because they cannot be represented in use case diagrams.

    b. make a good place to store expenses.

    c. cannot be used because C++ is an object-oriented language.

    d. make a good place to hide method bodies.

16. Class method definitions

    a. should be placed in a header file.

    b. should not be placed in a header file.

    c. should probably not be distributed to customers.

    d. should usually be distributed to customers.

17. True or false: Attribution is one of the major class relationships.

18. Assume there is an association between class A and class B. Also, objA is an object of class A, and objB is an object of class B. Which of the following applies?

    a. objA may send a message to objB.

    b. Class B must be a subclass of class A, or vice versa.

    c. objB must be an attribute of class A, or vice versa.

    d. objB may help objA carry out a task.

19. The LANDLORD program makes use of

    a. generalization.

    b. association.

    c. insubordination.

    d. aggregation.

20. True or false: In a class diagram, an association is shown as a relationship between objects.

21. In a sequence diagram

    a. time goes from left to right.

    b. associations go from right to left.

    c. horizontal arrows represent messages.

    d. vertical dotted lines represent lifetime.

22. A sequence diagram shows messages from one _____ to another.

23. True or false: A sequence diagram often describes a single use case.

24. In a sequence diagram, when a new class instance is created

    a. a rectangle with its name is drawn at the appropriate vertical coordinate.

    b. a large X marks the point in time.

    c. its activity box begins.

    d. its lifeline begins.

Projects

We don't have room in this book for exercises involving the kind of projects involved in this chapter. However, we list some suggestions for projects you may want to pursue on your own.

1. Reread the explanation of the HORSE program from Chapter 10, "Pointers," but do *not* look at the code. Create a use case diagram and a class diagram for this program. Use the results to create a .H file, and compare your results with the program. There are many correct results.

2. Reread the explanation of the ELEV program from Chapter 13, "Multifile Programs," but do *not* look at the code. Create a use case diagram and a class diagram for this program. Use the results to create appropriate .H files. Compare your results with the program.

3. Create a use case diagram and a class diagram for a business situation you're familiar with, whether it's horse trading, software consulting, or dealing in rare comic books.

4. Create a use case diagram and a class diagram for a program you've always wanted to write, but haven't had time for. If you can't think of anything, try a simple word-processing program, a game, or a genealogical program that allows you to enter information about your ancestors and displays a family tree.

ASCII Chart

TABLE A.1 IBM Character Codes

DEC	HEX	Symbol	Key	Use in C
0	00	(NULL)	Ctrl 2	
1	01	☺	Ctr A	
2	02	☻	Ctrl B	
3	03	♥	Ctrl C	
4	04	♦	Ctrl D	
5	05	♣	Ctrl E	
6	06	♠	Ctrl F	
7	07	•	Ctrl G	Beep
8	08	◘	Backspace	Backspace
9	09	○	Tab	Tab
10	0A	◙	Ctrl J	Linefeed (new line)
11	0B	♂	Ctrl K	Vertical Tab
12	0C	♀	Ctrl L	Form Feed
13	0D	♪	Enter	Carriage Return
14	0E	♫	Ctrl N	
15	0F	☼	Ctrl O	
16	10	►	Ctrl P	
17	11	◄	Ctrl Q	
18	12	↕	Ctrl R	
19	13	‼	Ctrl S	
20	14	¶	Ctrl T	
21	15	§	Ctrl U	
22	16	▬	Ctrl V	
23	17	↨	Ctrl W	
24	18	↑	Ctrl X	
25	19	↓	Ctrl Y	
26	1A	→	Ctrl Z	
27	1B	←	Esc	
28	1C	∟	•Ctrl \	
29	1D	↔	Ctrl]	
30	1E	▲	Ctrl 6	
31	1F	▼	Ctrl -	

TABLE A.1 Continued

DEC	HEX	Symbol	Key	Use in C
32	20		spacebar	
33	21	!	!	
34	22	"	"	
35	23	#	#	
36	24	$	$	
37	25	%	%	
38	26	&	&	
39	27	'	'	
40	28	(	(	
41	29	)	)	
42	2A	*	*	
43	2B	+	+	
44	2C	,	,	
45	2D	−	−	
46	2E	.	.	
47	2F	/	/	
48	30	0	0	
49	31	1	1	
50	32	2	2	
51	33	3	3	
52	34	4	4	
53	35	5	5	
54	36	6	6	
55	37	7	7	
56	38	8	8	
57	39	9	9	
58	3A	:	:	
59	3B	;	;	
60	3C	<	<	
61	3D	=	=	
62	3E	>	>	
63	3F	?	?	

TABLE A.1 Continued

DEC	HEX	Symbol	Key	Use in C
64	40	@	@	
65	41	A	A	
66	42	B	B	
67	43	C	C	
68	44	D	D	
69	45	E	E	
70	46	F	F	
71	47	G	G	
72	48	H	H	
73	49	I	I	
74	4A	J	J	
75	4B	K	K	
76	4C	L	L	
77	4D	M	M	
78	4E	N	N	
79	4F	O	O	
80	50	P	P	
81	51	Q	Q	
82	52	R	R	
83	53	S	S	
84	54	T	T	
85	55	U	U	
86	56	V	V	
87	57	W	W	
88	58	X	X	
89	59	Y	Y	
90	5A	Z	Z	
91	5B	[	[	
92	5C	\	\	
93	5D	]	]	
94	5E	^	^	
95	5F	_	_	

TABLE A.1 Continued

DEC	HEX	Symbol	Key	Use in C
96	60	`	`	
97	61	a	a	
98	62	b	b	
99	63	c	c	
100	64	d	d	
101	65	e	e	
102	66	f	f	
103	67	g	g	
104	68	h	h	
105	69	i	i	
106	6A	j	j	
107	6B	k	k	
108	6C	l	l	
109	6D	m	m	
110	6E	n	n	
111	6F	o	o	
112	70	p	p	
113	71	q	q	
114	72	r	r	
115	73	s	s	
116	74	t	t	
117	75	u	u	
118	76	v	v	
119	77	w	w	
120	78	x	x	
121	79	y	y	
122	7A	z	z	
123	7B	{	{	
124	7C	|	|	
125	7D	}	}	
126	7E	~	~	
127	7F	Δ	Ctrl ←	

TABLE A.1 Continued

DEC	HEX	Symbol	Key	Use in C
128	80	Ä	Alt 128	
129	81	ü	Alt 129	
130	82	é	Alt 130	
131	83	É	Alt 131	
132	84	ä	Alt 132	
133	85	à	Alt 133	
134	86	å	Alt 134	
135	87	ç	Alt 135	
136	88	ê	Alt 136	
137	89	ë	Alt 137	
138	8A	è	Alt 138	
139	8B	ï	Alt 139	
140	8C	î	Alt 140	
141	8D	ì	Alt 141	
142	8E	Ä	Alt 142	
143	8F	Å	Alt 143	
144	90	É	Alt 144	
145	91	æ	Alt 145	
146	92	Æ	Alt 146	
147	93	ô	Alt 147	
148	94	ö	Alt 148	
149	95	ò	Alt 149	
150	96	û	Alt 150	
151	97	ù	Alt 151	
152	98	ÿ	Alt 152	
153	99	Ö	Alt 153	
154	9A	Ü	Alt 154	
155	9B	õ	Alt 155	
156	9C	£	Alt 156	
157	9D	¥	Alt 157	
158	9E	û	Alt 158	
159	9F	ü	Alt 159	

TABLE A.1 Continued

DEC	HEX	Symbol	Key	Use in C
160	A0	á	Alt 160	
161	A1	í	Alt 161	
162	A2	ó	Alt 162	
163	A3	ú	Alt 163	
164	A4	ñ	Alt 164	
165	A5	Ñ	Alt 165	
166	A6	ª	Alt 166	
167	A7	º	Alt 167	
168	A8	¿	Alt 168	
169	A9	⌐	Alt 169	
170	AA	¬	Alt 170	
171	AB	½	Alt 171	
172	AC	¼	Alt 172	
173	AD	¡	Alt 173	
174	AE	«	Alt 174	
175	AF	»	Alt 175	
176	B0		Alt 176	
177	B1	▓	Alt 177	
178	B2	▓	Alt 178	
179	B3	│	Alt 179	
180	B4	┤	Alt 180	
181	B5	╡	Alt 181	
182	B6	╢	Alt 182	
183	B7	╖	Alt 183	
184	B8	╕	Alt 184	
185	B9	╣	Alt 185	
186	BA	║	Alt 186	
187	BB	╗	Alt 187	
188	BC	╝	Alt 188	
189	BD	╜	Alt 189	
190	BE	╛	Alt 190	
191	BF	┐	Alt 191	

TABLE A.1 Continued

DEC	HEX	Symbol	Key	Use in C
192	C0	└	Alt 192	
193	C1	┴	Alt 193	
194	C2	┬	Alt 194	
195	C3	├	Alt 195	
196	C4	─	Alt 196	
197	C5	┼	Alt 197	
198	C6	╞	Alt 198	
199	C7	╟	Alt 199	
200	C8	╚	Alt 200	
201	C9	╔	Alt 201	
202	CA	╩	Alt 202	
203	CB	╦	Alt 203	
204	CC	╠	Alt 204	
205	CD	═	Alt 205	
206	CE	╬	Alt 206	
207	CF	╧	Alt 207	
208	D0	╨	Alt 208	
209	D1	╤	Alt 209	
210	D2	╥	Alt 210	
211	D3	╙	Alt 211	
212	D4	╘	Alt 212	
213	D5	╒	Alt 213	
214	D6	╓	Alt 214	
215	D7	╫	Alt 215	
216	D8	╪	Alt 216	
217	D9	┘	Alt 217	
218	DA	┌	Alt 218	
219	DB	█	Alt 219	
220	DC	▄	Alt 220	
221	DD	▌	Alt 221	
222	DE	▐	Alt 222	
223	DF	▀	Alt 223	

TABLE A.1 Continued

DEC	HEX	Symbol	Key	Use in C
224	E0	α	Alt 224	
225	E1	β	Alt 225	
226	E2	Γ	Alt 226	
227	E3	π	Alt 227	
228	E4	Σ	Alt 228	
229	E5	σ	Alt 229	
230	E6	μ	Alt 230	
231	E7	τ	Alt 231	
232	E8	Φ	Alt 232	
233	E9	Θ	Alt 233	
234	EA	Ω	Alt 234	
235	EB	δ	Alt 235	
236	EC	∞	Alt 236	
237	ED	φ	Alt 237	
238	EE	∈	Alt 238	
239	EF	∩	Alt 239	
240	F0	≡	Alt 240	
241	F1	±	Alt 241	
242	F2	≥	Alt 242	
243	F3	≤	Alt 243	
244	F4	⌠	Alt 244	
245	F5	⌡	Alt 245	
246	F6	÷	Alt 246	
247	F7	≈	Alt 247	
248	F8	°	Alt 248	
249	F9	•	Alt 249	
250	FA	·	Alt 250	
251	FB	√	Alt 251	
252	FC	η	Alt 252	
253	FD	²	Alt 253	
254	FE	■	Alt 254	
255	FF	(blank)	Alt 255	

Those key sequences consisting of "Ctrl" are typed by pressing the Ctrl key, and while it is being held down, pressing the key indicated. These sequences are based on those defined for PC Personal Computer series keyboards. The key sequences may be defined differently on other keyboards.

IBM Extended ASCII characters can be displayed by pressing the Alt key and then typing the decimal code of the character on the keypad.

C++ Precedence Table and Keywords

Precedence Table

This precedence table is a more complete version of the one shown in Chapter 3. It includes the bitwise operators, which, although they are not described as such in this book, can be overloaded, as << and >> are for stream input and output.

Operator type	Operators
Scope	::
Various	[], (), . (dot), ->, postfix ++ and --
Unary	prefix ++ and --, &, *, +, -, !
Arithmetic	Multiplicative *, /, %
	Additive +, -
Bitwise shifts	<<, >>
Relational	Inequality <, >, <=, >=
	Equality ==, !=
Bitwise logic	&, ^,	
Logical	&&, ||
Conditional	?:
Assignment	=, *=, /=, %=, +=, -=
	<<=, >>=, &=, ^=, |=
Sequence	, (comma)

Keywords

Keywords implement specific C++ language features. They cannot be used as names for variables or other user-defined program elements. Many of the keywords are common to both C and C++, while others are specific to C++. Some compilers may support additional keywords, which usually begin with one or two underscores, as in _cdecl or __int16.

```
asm
auto

bool
break

case
catch
char
class
const
const_cast
continue
```

default
delete
do
double
dynamic_cast

else
enum
explicit
export
extern

false
float
for
friend

goto

if
inline
int

long

main
mutable

namespace
new

operator

private
protected
public

register
reinterpret_cast
return

short
signed
sizeof
static
static_cast
struct
switch

template
this

```
throw
true
try
typedef
typeid
typename

union
unsigned
using

virtual
void
volatile

wchar_t
while
```

Microsoft Visual C++

IN THIS APPENDIX

This appendix tells you how to use Microsoft Visual C++ (MVC++) to create console-mode applications, which are the kind of applications used in this book. This discussion is based on MVC++ version 6.0.

The present version of MVC++ has good (although not perfect) adherence to Standard C++. It comes in various versions, including a student version for under $100.

We'll assume that MVC++ is installed in your system, and that you know how to start it by using the Windows Start button and navigating to the appropriate menu item.

You'll want to make sure you can see file extensions (like .CPP) when operating MVC++. In Windows Explorer, make sure that the option Hide MS-DOS File Extensions for File Typ That Are Registered is not checked.

Screen Elements

The MVC++ window is initially divided into three parts. On the left is the view pane. This has two tabs, ClassView and FileView. Once you have a project going, the ClassView tab will show you the class hierarchy of your program, and FileView will show you the files used in the project. You can click the plus signs to expand the hierarchies, and double-click a file you want to open.

The largest part of the screen usually holds a document window. It can be used for various purposes, including displaying your source files and the contents of help files. At the bottom of the screen is a long window with more tabs: Build, Debug, and so on. This will display messages when you perform operations such as compiling your program.

Single-File Programs

It's easy to build and execute a single-file console program using Microsoft Visual C++. There are two possibilities: the file already exists or the file needs to be written.

In either case you should begin by making sure that no project is currently open. (We'll discuss projects in a moment.) Click the File menu. If the Close Workspace item is active (not grayed) click it to close the current workspace.

Building an Existing File

If the .CPP source file already exists, as it does for the example programs in this book, select Open from the File menu. (Note that this is not the same as Open Workspace.) Use the Open dialog box to navigate to the appropriate file, select it, and click the Open button. The file will appear in the document window. (If you're compiling an example program that uses Console Graphics Lite, such as the CIRCSTRC program in Chapter 5, "Functions," or the CIRCLES program in Chapter 6, "Objects and Classes," turn to the section "Building Console Graphics Lite Programs.")

To compile and link your source file, select Build from the Build menu. A dialog box will appear asking if you want to create a Default Project Workspace. Click Yes. The file will be compiled and linked with any necessary library files.

To run the program, select Execute from the Build menu. If all goes well, a console window will appear with the program's output displayed in it.

When the program terminates, you'll see the phrase *Press any key to continue*. The compiler arranges for this phrase to be inserted following the termination of any program. It keeps the console display on the screen long enough for you to see the program's output.

When you're done with a program, close its workspace by selecting Close Workspace from the File menu. Answer Yes when asked if you want to close all document windows. You can also run programs directly from MS-DOS. You can start up a box for MS-DOS by clicking the Start button and selecting Programs and then the MS-DOS Prompt item. In the resulting window you'll see what's called the *C-prompt*: the letter C, usually followed by the name of the current directory. You can navigate from one directory to another by typing **cd** (for Change Directory) and the name of the new directory. The .EXE files for programs compiled with MVC++ are placed in a directory called DEBUG, which is a subdirectory of the one holding your project files. To execute a program, including any of the examples from this book, make sure you're in the same directory as this .EXE file, and enter the name of the program (with no extension) at the MS-DOS prompt. You can find out more about MS-DOS using the Windows help system.

Writing a New File

To start writing your own .CPP file in MVC++, close any open workspace, select New from the File menu, and click the Files tab. Select C++ Source File, type the file name, and either type the path into the Location box or navigate to the directory where you want the file. Click OK. A blank document window will appear. Type your program into this window. Save the new file by selecting Save As from the File menu. As before, select Build from the Build menu and click Yes in response to the default workspace question. Your program will be compiled and linked.

Errors

If there are errors, they will appear in the Build window at the bottom of the screen. (You may need to click the Build tab to make this window appear.) If you double-click the error line, an arrow will appear next to the line containing the error in the source file. Also, if you position the cursor on the error number in the Build window (such as C2143) and press the F1 key, an explanation of the error will appear in the document window. You can correct the errors and repeat the build process until the message reads "0 error(s), 0 warning(s)." To execute the program, select Execute from the Build menu.

A common error when writing a new program is forgetting the statement

```
using namespace std;
```

If you leave this out, the compiler will complain that it doesn't recognize cout, <<, endl, and so on.

Before starting work on a new program, don't forget to select Close Workspace from the File menu. This ensures that you begin with a clean workspace. To open a program you've already built, select Open Workspace from the File menu, navigate to its directory, and double-click the file with the appropriate name and the .DSW extension.

Run-Time Type Information (RTTI)

A few programs, such as EMPL_IO.CPP in Chapter 12, "Streams and Files," use RTTI. With MVC++ you need to enable a compiler option to make this feature work. Select Settings from the Project menu and click the C/C++ tab. From the Category list box, select C++ Language. Click the check box named Enable Run-Time Type Information. Then click OK. This will avoid various compiler and linker errors, some of which are misleading.

Multifile Programs

We've shown the quick and dirty approach to building programs. This approach works with one-file programs. When projects have more than one file, things become slightly more complicated. We'll start by reviewing what's meant by the terms *workspace* and *project*.

Projects and Workspaces

MVC++ uses a concept called a *workspace*, which is one level of abstraction higher than a project. A workspace can contain many projects. It consists of a directory and several configuration files. Within it, each project can have its own directory, or the files for all the projects can simply reside in the workspace directory.

Conceptually it's probably easiest, at least for the small programs in this book, to assume that every project has its own separate workspace. That's what we'll assume in this discussion.

A project corresponds to an application (program) that you're developing. It consists of all the files needed to create that application as well as information about how these files are to be combined. The result of building a project is usually a single .EXE file that a user can execute. (Other results are possible, such as .DLL files.)

Developing the Project

Let's assume that the files you want to include in a new project already exist, and that they are in a particular directory. Select New from the File menu, and click the Projects tab in the New dialog box. Select Win32 Console Application from the list. First, in the Location box, type the path to the directory, but do *not* include the directory name itself. Next, type the name of the directory containing the files in the Project Name box. (By clicking the button to the right of the Location field you can navigate to the appropriate directory, but make sure to delete the directory name itself from the location field.) Make sure the Create New Workspace box is checked, and click OK.

For example, if the files are in C:\Book\Ch13\Elev, you would first type C:\Book\Ch13\ in the Location field and then Elev in the Project Name field. When you type the project name, it's automatically added to the location. (If it were there already it would be added again, resulting in a location of C:\Book\Ch13\Elev\Elev, which is not what you want.) Another dialog appears. Make sure the An Empty Project button is selected, and click Finish. Click OK on the next dialog box.

At this point various project-oriented files, with extensions .DSP, .DSW, and so forth, have been added to the directory, along with a DEBUG subdirectory that will hold the final .EXE file.

Adding Source Files

Now you need to add your source files to the project. This includes your .CPP files and any .H files you want to view from the File tab. Select Add To Project from the Project menu, click Files, select the files you want to add, and click OK. You can review the files you've selected by clicking the FileView tab and then the plus sign for the project. You can also see the class structure, complete with member functions and attributes, by clicking the ClassView tab.

To open a file so you can see it and modify it, double-click the file's icon in the FileView window. You can also select Open from the File menu and select the file.

Locating Header Files

Your project may use header files (usually with the .H extension), such as MSOFTCON.H in programs that use Console Graphics Lite. These don't need to be added to the project (unless you want to view them from the File tab), but the compiler must know where to find them. If they're in the same directory as your source files, this isn't a problem. Otherwise, you must tell the compiler where they are.

Select Options from the Tools menu. Click on the Directories tab. Select Include Files from the Show Directories For list. You'll see the directories that hold the compiler's own include files. Double-click the dotted box on the bottom line of this list. Then navigate to the directory containing your header file, using the button that appears on the right. The dotted box will be replaced by the new pathname. Click OK. Alternatively you can type the complete pathname of the directory into the Location box.

Saving, Closing, and Opening Projects

To save the project, select Save Workspace. To close the project, select Close Workspace. (Answer Yes to the Close All Document Windows query.) To open an existing project, select Open Workspace from the File menu, navigate to the proper directory, select the .DSW file, and click (···.

Compiling and Linking

As with one-file programs, the easiest way to compile, link, and run a multifile program is to select Execute from the Build menu. Alternatively, you can compile and link your project without running it by selecting Build from the Build menu.

Building Console Graphics Lite Programs

Building programs that use the Console Graphics Lite functions (described in Appendix E, "Console Graphics Lite") requires some steps in addition to those needed for ordinary example programs. You will need the files MSOFTCON.H and MSOFTCON.CPP. These files, which are specific to this book, can be obtained from the publisher's Web site, mentioned in the Introduction.

- Open the source file for the program as described in the section "Building an Existing File." This file should include the line #include "msoftcon.h".

- Select Build from the Build menu. Answer Yes when asked if you want to create a default project workspace. A project will be created, but the compiler will complain it can't find MSOFTCON.H. This file contains the declarations for the graphics functions.

- An easy solution is to copy MSOFTCON.H into your project's directory. A more elegant approach is to tell the compiler where to find this file. Follow the instructions in the earlier section "Locating Header Files."

- Now try building your file again. This time the compiler can find the header file, but there will be numerous linker errors because the linker doesn't know where to find the definitions for the graphics functions. This code is in MSOFTCON.CPP. Add this file to your project by following the steps in the earlier section "Adding Source Files."

Now your program should compile and link correctly. Select Execute from the Build menu to see it run.

Debugging

In Chapter 3, "Loops and Decisions," we suggest using the debugger to provide an insight into how loops work. Here's how to do that with Microsoft Visual C++. These same steps can help you debug your program if it behaves incorrectly. We'll be discussing one-file programs here, but the same approach applies, with appropriate variations, to larger multifile programs.

Start by building your program as you normally would. Fix any compiler and linker errors. Make sure your program listing is displayed in the Edit window.

Single-Stepping

To start the debugger, simply press the F10 key. You'll see a yellow arrow appear in the margin of the listing, pointing to the opening brace following main.

If you want to start somewhere other than the beginning of the program, position the cursor on the line where you want to start debugging. Then, from the Debug menu (which replaces the Build menu when you're debugging), select Start Debug and then Run to Cursor. The yellow arrow will appear next to the statement selected.

Now press the F10 key. This causes the debugger to step to the next executable statement. The yellow arrow will show where you are. Each press of F10 moves it to the next statement. If you're in a loop, you'll see the yellow arrow move down through the statements in the loop and then jump back to the top of the loop.

Watching Variables

You can watch the values of your program's variables change as you single-step through your program. Click the Locals tab in the window at the bottom left of your screen to see the values of local variables. The Auto tab shows the compiler's selection of variables.

If you want to make your own selection of watch variables, enter them into the Watch window in the bottom right corner of your screen. To do this, right-click a variable name in the source code. A pop-up menu will appear. Select QuickWatch from this menu. In the resulting QuickWatch dialog box, click Add Watch. The variable and its current value will appear in the Watch window. If a variable is out of scope, such as before it's been defined, the Watch window will show an error message instead of a value next to the variable name.

Stepping Into Functions

If your program uses functions, you can *step into* them (single-step through the statements within the function) by using the F11 key. In contrast, the F10 key *steps over* function calls (treats them as a single statement). If you use F11 to trace into library routines like cout <<, you can trace through the source code of the library routine. This can be a lengthy process, so avoid it unless you're really interested. You need to switch judiciously between F11 and F10, depending on whether you want to explore a particular function's inner workings or not.

Breakpoints

Breakpoints allow you to stop the program at any arbitrary location. Why are they useful? We've already shown that you can execute the program up to the cursor location by selecting Run to Cursor. However, there are times when you want to be able to stop the program in multiple locations. For example, you might want to stop it after an `if` and also after the corresponding `else`. Breakpoints solve this problem because you can insert as many as you need. (They also have advanced features we won't describe here.)

Here's how to insert a breakpoint in your listing. First, position the cursor on the line where you want the breakpoint. Then click the right mouse button, and from the resulting menu select Insert/Remove Breakpoint. You'll see a red circle appear in the left margin. Now whenever you run your program at full speed (by selecting Debug/Go, for example) it will stop at the breakpoint. You can then examine variables, single-step through the code, or run to another breakpoint.

To remove a breakpoint, right-click it and select Remove Breakpoint from the menu.

There are many other features of the debugger, but what we've discussed here will get you started.

Borland C++Builder

IN THIS APPENDIX

This appendix tells you how to use Borland C++Builder to create console-mode applications, which are the kind of applications used in this book.

C++Builder is Borland's most advanced development product, and, as of this writing, the C++ product that adheres most closely to Standard C++. It's available in a student version for under $100. (Also, a free compiler-only system is available for download from the Borland Web site. You will need to use Notepad or some similar text editor to write your source files.) This discussion is based on C++Builder 5.0.

We'll assume that C++Builder is installed on your system, and that you can start it by using the Windows Start button and navigating to the appropriate menu item: C++Builder.

You'll want to make sure you can see file extensions (like .CPP) when operating C++Builder. In Windows Explorer, make sure that the option Hide MS-DOS File Extensions for File Types That Are Registered is not checked.

Running the Example Programs in C++Builder

The programs in this book require minor modifications to run under C++Builder. Here's a quick summary.

You can compile most of the example programs and run them without modification in the the Windows MS-DOS window (Start/Programs/MS-DOS Prompt). However, if you want to run them from within C++Builder using the Run command from the Run menu, you'll need to insert a statement at the end of the program to keep the console window on the screen long enough to see. You can do this in two steps:

- Insert the statement getch(); just before the final return statement in main(). This enables you to see the program's output.

- Insert the statement #include <conio.h> at the beginning of main(). This is necessary for getch().

If the program you're building uses Console Graphics Lite functions (described in Appendix E, "Console Graphics Lite"), you'll need to take some additional steps. These are summarized later in this appendix.

In the balance of this appendix we'll cover these points in more detail and describe how to use C++Builder to edit, compile, link, and execute console-mode programs.

Cleaning Up the Screen

When it's first started, C++Builder shows you some screen objects that you won't need for console-mode programs. You'll see a window on the right called Form1. Click on its close button (the X in the upper-right corner) to make it go away. Likewise, you won't need the Object Inspector, so click its close button too. You'll need to get rid of these items every time you start C++Builder.

When you remove the Form1 window you'll find another window under it, with some C++ code in it. This is called the *code editor* window. It's where you'll look at source files and write your own programs. However, it starts with a file called UNIT1, and you don't need this. Click the close button to make this window go away, and answer No if a dialog asks whether you want to save changes.

C++Builder starts with many more toolbars than you need. You probably need the Standard and Debug toolbars. Get rid of the others by selecting Toolbars at the bottom of the View menu and unchecking the toolbars you don't want.

Creating a New Project

C++Builder (like other modern compilers) thinks in terms of *projects* when creating programs. A project consists of one or more source files. It can also contain many other kinds of files that we don't need to be concerned with here, such as resource files and definition files. The result of a project is usually a single .EXE file that a user can execute.

To begin a new project, select New... from the File menu. You'll see a dialog box called New Items. Click the New tab (if necessary). Then double-click the Console Wizard icon. In the resulting dialog box, make sure that the Source Type is C++ and that Console Application is checked. Uncheck Use VCL, Multi Threaded, and Specify Project Source. Click OK. Click No if another dialog asks whether you want to save changes to PROJECT1. You'll see the following source file appear in a new code editor window:

```
//---------------------------------------------------------

#pragma hdrstop

//---------------------------------------------------------

#pragma argsused
int main(int argc, char **argv[])
{
        return 0;
}
//---------------------------------------------------------
```

This is a skeleton version of a console-mode program. You don't need some of the lines in this program, and you will need to add some others. We'll make these changes, and add a statement to print some text so you can see whether the program works. Here's the result:

```
//test1.cpp
#include <iostream>
#include <conio.h>
using namespace std;
//#pragma hdrstop        //not needed
//#pragma argsused       //not needed

int main()                //arguments not needed
   {
   cout << "Happy are they whose programs "
        << "compile the first time.";
   getch();
   return 0;
   }
```

The two #pragmas aren't necessary, and you don't need the arguments to main().

If you run the original skeleton program without these modifications, you'll find that the console window doesn't remain visible long enough to see. As we noted, this is fixed by inserting the statement

```
getch();
```

at the end of the program, just before return. This causes the program to wait for a keystroke, so the console window remains in view until you press any key. The getch() function requires the CONIO.H header file, so you'll need to include it at the beginning of your program.

If you're creating your own program, you can start with the skeleton program and modify it. If you're starting with an existing file, read the section "Starting with Existing Files."

Naming and Saving a Project

You'll need to save and rename both your source file and the project it's in. The compiler automatically names the source file UNIT1.CPP. To save it and rename it, select Save As from the File menu, navigate to the directory for your project, name the file (keeping the .CPP extension) and click Save.

Information about a project is recorded in a file with the extension .BPR. Thus when you save a project, you're actually saving both the .CPP file (or files) and the .BPR file. When you first create a new project, it's called PROJECT1 (or a higher number).

To save the project and change its name, select Save Project As from the File menu, navigate to the directory where you want to store the file, type the name you want to give the project, followed by the .BPR extension, and click Save.

Starting with Existing Files

Here's how to create a project when the source file already exists, as do the examples in this book (assuming you've downloaded them). This discussion applies to programs with a single source file.

Let's assume that your source file is named MYPROG.CPP. Make sure this file is in the directory where you want to build it. Select Open from the File menu, select the file, and press Open. The file appears in the code editor window. A dialog box asks "Would you like to create a project so this file can compile and run?" Answer Yes. A project is created.

Now you need to rename the project, so select Save Project As from the File menu. Replace the PROJECT1.BPR name with your project name, which is usually the name of the program: MYPROG.BPR. Click Save. That's all there is to it.

Compiling, Linking, and Executing

To build an executable program, select Make or Build from the Project menu. This causes your .CPP file to be compiled into an .OBJ file, and the .OBJ file to be linked (with various library files) into an .EXE file. For example, if you're compiling MYPROG.CPP, the result will be MYPROG.EXE. If there are compiler or linker errors, they will be displayed. Edit your program until you've eliminated them.

Executing from C++Builder

If you've modified your program by inserting getch() as described earlier, you can compile, link, and run your program directly in C++Builder by simply selecting Run from the Run menu. If there are no errors, the console window will appear, along with the output of the program.

Executing from MS-DOS

You can also run programs directly from MS-DOS. In Windows you can obtain a box for MS-DOS by clicking the Start button and selecting Programs and then the MS-DOS Prompt item. In the resulting window you'll see what's called the *C-prompt*: the letter C, usually followed by the name of the current directory. You can navigate from one directory to another by typing cd (for Change Directory) and the name of the new directory. To execute a program, including any of the examples from this book, make sure you're in the same directory as the appropriate

.EXE file, and type the name of the program (with no extension). You can find out more about MS-DOS using the Windows help system.

Precompiled Header Files

You can speed up compilation dramatically by selecting Options from the Project menu, selecting the Compiler tab, and clicking on Use Precompiled Headers. In a short program most of the compile time is spent compiling the C++ header files such as iostream. Using the Precompiled Headers option causes these header files to be compiled only once, instead of each time you compile your program.

Closing and Opening Projects

When you're done with a project, you can close it by selecting Close All from the File menu. To open a previously-saved project, select Open Project from the File menu, navigate to the appropriate .BPR file, and double-click it.

Adding a Header File to Your Project

Most serious C++ programs employ one or more user-written header files (in addition to many library header files, such as IOSTREAM and CONIO.H). Here's how to create a header file.

Creating a New Header File

Select New... from the File menu, make sure the New tab is selected, and double-click the Text icon. You'll see a code editor window with a file titled FILE1.TXT. Type in the text of your file and save it using Save As on the File menu, with an appropriate name, followed by the .H file extension. Save it in the same file as your source (.CPP) files. The new filename will appear on a tab next to the other files in the code editor window. You can switch from file to file by clicking the tabs.

Editing an Existing Header File

To open an existing header file, select Open from the File menu, and select Any File (*.*) from the Files of Type list. You can then select the header file from the list.

When you write the #include statement for the header file in your .CPP file, make sure you enclose the filename in quotes:

```
#include "myHeader.h"
```

The quotes tell the compiler to look for the header file in the same directory as your source files.

Telling C++Builder the Header File's Location

If you add a .H file, the compiler must know where to find it. If it's in the same directory as your other files, you don't need to do anything.

However, if your .H file is in a different directory, you'll need to tell C++Builder where to find it. (This is true of the BORLACON.H file necessary for console-mode graphics, unless you copy it to your project file.) Go to Options on the Project menu and select the Directories/Conditionals tab. In the Directories section, click the button with the three dots on the right of the Include Path list. A Directories dialog box will appear.

In the bottom field of the Directories dialog box, type the complete pathname of the directory where the .H file is located. Click the Add button to place the path in the list of include paths. Then click OK twice more to close the dialog boxes.

Don't try to add header files to the project with the Add to Project option in the Project menu.

Projects with Multiple Source Files

Real applications, and some of the example programs in this book, require multiple source (.CPP) files. Incidentally, in C++Builder, source files are often called *units*, a term specific to this product. In most C++ development environments, files are called files or *modules*.

Creating Additional Source Files

You make additional .CPP files the same way you make header files: Select File/New and double-click the Text icon in the New dialog box. Type in the source code, and use Save As to save the file. When using Save As, be sure to select C++Builder Unit (.CPP) from the Save File as Type list. This will automatically supply the .CPP extension, so all you need to type is the name. If you fail to do this, and simply type the .CPP after the name, the file won't be recognized as a C++Builder unit.

Adding Existing Source Files to Your Project

You may have created a new source file as just described, or one may already exist, such as BORLACON.CPP, which is used for Console Graphics Lite programs. To add a source file to the project, select Add to Project from the Project menu, navigate to the appropriate directory (if necessary), and select the filename from the list. Then click Open. That tells C++Builder it's part of the project.

Multiple source files are displayed with tabs in the Edit window (if they're in full-size windows), so you can quickly switch from one file to another. You can open and close these files individually, so they don't all need to be on the screen at the same time.

D

BORLAND
C++BUILDER

The Project Manager

You can see what source files are part of the project by selecting Project Manager from the View menu. You'll see a diagram of file relationships, similar to the one shown in the Windows Explorer. Clicking the plus sign next to the project icon will display all the project's source files. The file you just added to the project should be among them.

If you right-click a file in the Project Manager the context menu will show you choices that include Open, Save, Save As, and Compile. This is a handy way to perform these tasks on individual source files.

In a multifile program you can compile individual files separately by selecting Compile Unit from the Project menu. You can compile and link all the source files by selecting Make from the Project menu. This will cause only those source files that have been changed since the previous compile to be recompiled.

Console Graphics Lite Programs

Here's how to build programs that use the Console Graphics Lite package. This includes such programs as CIRCSTRC from Chapter 5, "Functions," and CIRCLES in Chapter 6, "Objects and Classes."

- Create a new project as described earlier, using the program name as the project name, but with the .BPR extension.
- In the source file, change #include<msoftcon.h> to #include<borlacon.h>.
- Copy (don't just move) BORLACON.H and BORLACON.CPP into your project file. (Or tell the compiler where the header file is located, as described earlier.)
- Add the source file BORLACON.CPP to your project by following the instructions in the section earlier in this Appendix titled "Adding Existing Source Files to your Project."
- To keep the display on the screen, insert the line getch(); just before the return statement at the end of main().
- To support getch(), insert the line #include <conio.h> at the beginning of your program.

Now you can compile, link, and execute Console Graphics Lite programs just like other programs.

Debugging

In Chapter 3, "Loops and Decisions," we suggest using a debugger to provide insight into how loops work. Here's how to do that with C++Builder. These same steps can help you debug your program if it behaves incorrectly. We'll be discussing one-file programs here, but the same approach applies, with appropriate variations, to large multifile programs.

Start by building your program as you normally would. Fix any compiler and linker errors. Make sure your program listing is displayed in the Edit window.

Single-Stepping

To start the debugger, just press the F8 key. The program will be recompiled, and the first line in the program, usually the main() declarator, will be highlighted. Repeated presses of F8 will cause control to move to each statement of the program in turn. When you enter a loop, you'll see the highlighting move down through the loop, then return to the top of the loop for the next cycle.

Watching Variables

To see how the values of variables change as you single-step through the program, select Add Watch from the Run menu. The Watch Properties dialog box will appear. Type the name of the variable you want to watch into the Expression field of this dialog box, then select the appropriate variable type, and click OK. A window called Watch List will appear. By repeatedly using the Add Watch dialog box you can add as many variables as you want to the Watch List.

If you position the Edit Window and the Watch List so you can see them both at the same time, you can watch the value of the variables change as you single step through the program. If a variable is out of scope, such as before it's been defined, the Watch List will show an error message instead of a value next to the variable name.

In the particular case of the CUBELIST program, the watch mechanism doesn't recognize the validity of the cube variable when it's defined within the loop. Rewrite the program so it's defined before the loop; then its value will be displayed properly on the Watch List.

Tracing into Functions

If your program uses functions, you can *trace into* them (single-step through the statements within the function) by using the F7 key. The F8 key *steps over* function calls (treats them as a single statement). If you use F7 to trace into library routines such as cout <<, you can trace through the source code of the library routine. This can be a lengthy process, so avoid it unless you're really interested. You will need to switch judiciously between F7 and F8, depending on whether or not you want to explore a particular function's inner workings.

Breakpoints

Breakpoints allow you to stop the program at any arbitrary location. Why are they useful? We've already shown that you can execute the program up to the cursor location by selecting

Run to Cursor from the Run menu. However, there are times when you want to be able to stop the program in multiple locations. For example, you might want to stop it after an `if` and also after the corresponding `else`. Breakpoints solve this problem because you can insert as many as you need. (They also have advanced features we won't describe here.)

Inserting a breakpoint in your listing is easy. Look at your program listing in the Edit window. You'll see a dot in the left margin opposite each executable program line. Simply left-click the dot where you want to insert the breakpoint. You'll see a red circle appear in the left margin, and the program line will be highlighted. Now whenever you run your program at full speed (by selecting Run from the Run menu, for example) it will stop at the breakpoint. You can then examine variables, single-step through the code, or run to another breakpoint.

To remove the breakpoint, left-click it again. It will vanish.

There are many other features of the debugger, but what we've described here will get you started.

Console Graphics Lite

IN THIS APPENDIX

It's nice to be able to enliven example programs with graphics, so we've included some graphics-based examples in this book. Standard C++ does not include graphics specifications, but it certainly doesn't prohibit graphics, and Windows supports various kinds of graphics.

Microsoft Visual C++ and Borland C++ use different library functions for graphics, and neither does everything we want it to. To avoid having two versions of each graphics example, and to gain extra capability, we use our own set of graphics functions, called Console Graphics Lite. These functions are translated into a Microsoft version or a Borland version, depending on which files you use to build your program: MSOFTCON.H and MSOFTCON.CPP for Microsoft, or BORLACON.H and BORLACON.CPP for Borland. (It's possible that the files used for the Microsoft compiler will work with other compilers as well.)

The files for Console Graphics Lite can be downloaded from the publisher's Web site. If you downloaded the source files for the example programs, you should have these graphics files already. If not, the Introduction has instructions for downloading. Listings for these files appear at the end of this Appendix.

Our graphics routines use console graphics. The console is a character-mode screen, typically arranged with 80 columns and 25 rows. Most of the non-graphics example programs in this book write text to the console window. A console program can run in its own window within Windows, or as a standalone MS-DOS program.

In console graphics, rectangles, circles, and so forth are made up of characters (such as the letter 'X' or a small character-size block) rather than pixels. The results are crude but work fine as demonstration programs.

Using the Console Graphics Lite Routines

To build an example program that uses graphics, you must add several steps to the normal build procedure. These are as follows:

- Include the appropriate header file (MSOFTCON.H or BORLACON.H) in the source (.CPP) file for the example program.
- Add the appropriate source file (MSOFTCON.CPP or BORLACON.CPP) to your project, so it can be linked with the example program.
- Make sure the compiler can find the appropriate header file and source file.

The header files contain declarations for the Console Graphics Lite functions. The source files contain the definitions for these functions. You need to compile the appropriate source file and link the resulting .OBJ file with the rest of your program. This happens automatically during the build process if you add the source file to your project.

To learn how to add a file to your project, read either Appendix C, "Microsoft Visual C++," or Appendix D, "Borland C++Builder." Then apply this process to the source file.

To make sure your compiler can find the header file, you may need to add the pathname where it's located to the Directories option for your compiler. Again, refer to the appropriate appendix to see how this is done.

That's all you need to know if you simply want to run the graphics examples in this book. If you want to use Console Graphics Lite in your own programs, read on.

The Console Graphics Lite Functions

The Console Graphics Lite functions assume a console screen with 80 columns and 25 rows. The upper-left corner is defined as the point (1,1) and the lower-right corner is the point (80,25).

These functions were designed specifically for the example programs in this book and are not particularly robust or sophisticated. If you use them in your own programs you should be careful to draw all shapes entirely within the confines of the 80×25 character screen. If you use invalid coordinates, their behavior is undefined. Table E.1 lists these functions.

TABLE E.1 Functions for Console Graphics Lite

Function Name	Purpose
init_graphics()	Initializes graphics system
set_color()	Sets background and foreground colors
set_cursor_pos()	Puts cursor at specific row and column
clear_screen()	Clears entire console screen
wait(n)	Pauses program for n milliseconds
clear_line()	Clears entire line
draw_rectangle()	Specifies top, left, bottom, right
draw_circle()	Specifies center (x,y) and radius
draw_line()	Specifies end points (x1,y1) and (x2,y2)
draw_pyramid()	Specifies top (x,y) and height
set_fill_style()	Specifies fill character

You must call init_graphics() before you use any other graphics functions. This function sets the fill character, and in the Microsoft version it also initializes other essential parts of the console graphics system.

The set_color() function can use either one or two arguments. The first sets the foreground color of characters displayed subsequently, and the second (if present) sets the background color of the character. Usually you want to keep the background black.

```
set_color(cRED);              //sets foreground to red
set_color(cWHITE, cBLUE);   //foreground white, background blue
```

Here is a list of the color constants that can be used for either foreground or background.

Color Constants for set_color()	
cBLACK	cDARK_GRAY
cDARK_BLUE	cBLUE
cDARK_GREEN	cGREEN
cDARK_CYAN	cCYAN
cDARK_RED	cRED
cDARK_MAGENTA	cMAGENTA
cBROWN	cYELLOW
cLIGHT_GRAY	cWHITE

The functions beginning with draw_ create shapes or lines using a special character called the *fill character*. This character is set to a solid block by default, but can be modified using the set_fill_style() function. Besides the solid block, you can use uppercase 'X' or 'O' characters, or one of three shaded block characters. Here is a list of the fill constants:

Fill Constants for set_fill_style()	
SOLID_FILL	LIGHT_FILL
X_FILL	MEDIUM_FILL
O_FILL	DARK_FILL

The wait() function takes an argument in milliseconds, and pauses for that amount of time.

```
wait(3000);   //pauses for 3 seconds
```

The other functions are largely self-explanatory. Their operation can be seen in those examples that use graphics.

Implementations of the Console Graphics Lite Functions

These routines used for Console Graphics Lite aren't object-oriented, and could have been written in C instead of C++. Thus there's no real reason to study them, unless you're interested in a quick-and-dirty approach to graphics operations such as drawing lines and circles. The idea was to create the minimum routines that would do the job. You can examine the source files at the end of this appendix if you're curious.

Microsoft Compilers

The Microsoft compilers no longer include their own console graphics routines as they did several years ago. However, Windows itself provides a set of routines for simple console graphics operations, such as positioning the cursor and changing the text color. For the Microsoft compilers, the Console Graphics Lite functions access these built-in Windows console functions. (Thanks to André LaMothe for suggesting this solution. His excellent game book is listed in Appendix H, "Bibliography.")

To use the console graphics functions you should use a project of type "Win32 Console Application," as described in Appendix C.

The Windows console functions won't work unless you initialize the console graphics system, so calling the init_graphics() function is essential if you're using the Microsoft compiler.

Borland Compilers

Borland C++ still has built-in graphics functions, both for console-mode graphics and for pixel graphics. If you use the BORLACON.CPP file, the Console Graphics Lite functions are translated into Borland console functions, which they closely resemble.

You might wonder why you can't use the Borland compiler to access the console functions built into Windows. The problem is that to create a console-mode program in Borland C++, you must use either an EasyWin or a DOS target, both of which are 16-bit systems. The Windows console functions are 32-bit functions, and so can't be used in Borland's console mode.

When you use Borland C++, the iostream approach to I/O (cout <<) doesn't produce different colors. Thus some of the example programs, like HORSE.CPP, use console-mode functions such as cputs() and putch(), found in the CONIO.H file.

Source Code Listings

Here are the listings for the four files used in Console Graphics Lite: MSOFTCON.H and MSOFTCON.CPP for Microsoft, and BORLACON.H and BORLACON.CPP for C++Builder. Normally there won't be any reason for you to worry about the internals of these files. They are shown here for reference.

Listing for MSOFTCON.H

```
//msoftcon.h
//declarations for Lafore's console graphics functions
//uses Window's console functions

#ifndef _I C_WCONSOLE    //don't let this file be included
#define _. C_WCONSOLE    //twice in the same source file

#include <windows.h>     //for Windows console functions
#include <conio.h>       //for kbhit(), getche()
#include <math.h>        //for sin, cos

enum fstyle { SOLID_FILL, X_FILL,      O_FILL,
              LIGHT_FILL, MEDIUM_FILL, DARK_FILL };

enum color {
    cBLACK=0,      cDARK_BLUE=1,    cDARK_GREEN=2, cDARK_CYAN=3,
    cDARK_RED=4,   cDARK_MAGENTA=5, cBROWN=6,      cLIGHT_GRAY=7,
    cDARK_GRAY=8,  cBLUE=9,         cGREEN=10,     cCYAN=11,
    cRED=12,       cMAGENTA=13,     cYELLOW=14,    cWHITE=15 };
//------------------------------------------------------------
void init_graphics();
void set_color(color fg, color bg = cBLACK);
void set_cursor_pos(int x, int y);
void clear_screen();
void wait(int milliseconds);
void clear_line();
void draw_rectangle(int left, int top, int right, int bottom);
void draw_circle(int x, int y, int rad);
void draw_line(int x1, int y1, int x2, int y2);
void draw_pyramid(int x1, int y1, int height);
void set_fill_style(fstyle);
#endif /* _INC_WCONSOLE */
```

Listing for MSOFTCON.CPP

```
//msoftcon.cpp
//provides routines to access Windows console functions

//compiler needs to be able to find this file
//in MCV++, /Tools/Options/Directories/Include/type path name

#include "msoftcon.h"
HANDLE hConsole;          //console handle
char fill_char;           //character used for fill
//------------------------------------------------------------
```

```c
void init_graphics()
    {
    COORD console_size = {80, 25};
    //open i/o channel to console screen
    hConsole = CreateFile("CONOUT$", GENERIC_WRITE | GENERIC_READ,
                    FILE_SHARE_READ | FILE_SHARE_WRITE,
                    0L, OPEN_EXISTING, FILE_ATTRIBUTE_NORMAL, 0L);
    //set to 80x25 screen size
    SetConsoleScreenBufferSize(hConsole, console_size);
    //set text to white on black
    SetConsoleTextAttribute( hConsole, (WORD)((0 << 4) | 15) );

    fill_char = '\xDB';  //default fill is solid block
    clear_screen();
    }
//---------------------------------------------------------------
void set_color(color foreground, color background)
    {
    SetConsoleTextAttribute( hConsole,
                        (WORD)((background << 4) | foreground) );
    } //end setcolor()

/* 0  Black           8  Dark gray
   1  Dark blue       9  Blue
   2  Dark green      10 Green
   3  Dark cyan       11 Cyan
   4  Dark red        12 Red
   5  Dark magenta    13 Magenta
   6  Brown           14 Yellow
   7  Light gray      15 White
*/
//---------------------------------------------------------------
void set_cursor_pos(int x, int y)
    {
    COORD cursor_pos;               //origin in upper left corner
    cursor_pos.X = x - 1;           //Windows starts at (0, 0)
    cursor_pos.Y = y - 1;           //we start at (1, 1)
    SetConsoleCursorPosition(hConsole, cursor_pos);
    }
//---------------------------------------------------------------
void clear_screen()
    {
    set_cursor_pos(1, 25);
    for(int j=0; j<25; j++)
        putch('\n');
    set_cursor_pos(1, 1);
    }
```

```
//------------------------------------------------------------
void wait(int milliseconds)
   {
   Sleep(milliseconds);
   }
//------------------------------------------------------------
void clear_line()                        //clear to end of line
   {                                     //80 spaces
   //.....12345678901234567890123456789012345678901234567890
   //.....0........1.........2.........3.........4
   cputs("                                                ");
   cputs("                                                ");
   }
//------------------------------------------------------------
void draw_rectangle(int left, int top, int right, int bottom)
   {
   char temp[80];
   int width = right - left + 1;

   for(int j=0; j<width; j++)          //string of squares
      temp[j] = fill_char;
   temp[j] = 0;                        //null

   for(int y=top; y<=bottom; y++)  //stack of strings
      {
      set_cursor_pos(left, y);
      cputs(temp);
      }
   }
//------------------------------------------------------------
void draw_circle(int xC, int yC, int radius)
   {
   double theta, increment, xF, pi=3.14159;
   int x, xN, yN;

   increment = 0.8 / static_cast<double>(radius);
   for(theta=0; theta<=pi/2; theta+=increment)  //quarter circle
      {
      xF = radius * cos(theta);
      xN = static_cast<int>(xF * 2 / 1); //pixels not square
      yN = static_cast<int>(radius * sin(theta) + 0.5);
      x = xC-xN;
      while(x <= xC+xN)              //fill two horizontal lines
         {                          //one for each half circle
         set_cursor_pos(x,   yC-yN); putch(fill_char);  //top
         set_cursor_pos(x++, yC+yN); putch(fill_char);  //bottom
         }
```

```
        } //end for
    }
//··············································
void draw_line(int x1, int y1, int x2, int y2)
    {

    int w, z, t, w1, w2, z1, z2;
    double xDelta=x1-x2, yDelta=y1-y2, slope;
    bool isMoreHoriz;

    if( fabs(xDelta) > fabs(yDelta) ) //more horizontal
        {
        isMoreHoriz = true;
        slope = yDelta / xDelta;
        w1=x1; z1=y1; w2=x2, z2=y2;    //w=x, z=y
        }
    else                             //more vertical
        {
        isMoreHoriz = false;
        slope = xDelta / yDelta;
        w1=y1; z1=x1; w2=y2, z2=x2;    //w=y, z=x
        }

    if(w1 > w2)                       //if backwards w
        {
        t=w1; w1=w2; w2=t;            //   swap (w1,z1)
        t=z1; z1=z2; z2=t;            //   with (w2,z2)
        }
    for(w=w1; w<=w2; w++)
        {
        z = static_cast<int>(z1 + slope * (w-w1));
        if( !(w==80 && z==25) )       //avoid scroll at 80,25
            {
            if(isMoreHoriz)
                set_cursor_pos(w, z);
            else
                set_cursor_pos(z, w);
            putch(fill_char);
            }
        }
    }
//··············································
void draw_pyramid(int x1, int y1, int height)
    {
    int x, y;
    for(y=y1; y<y1+height; y++)
        {
```

```
        int incr = y - y1;
        for(x=x1-incr; x<=x1+incr; x++)
            {
            set_cursor_pos(x, y);
            putch(fill_char);
            }
        }
    }
//-------------------------------------------------------------------
void set_fill_style(fstyle fs)
    {
    switch(fs)
        {
        case SOLID_FILL:  fill_char = '\xDB'; break;
        case DARK_FILL:   fill_char = '\xB0'; break;
        case MEDIUM_FILL: fill_char = '\xB1'; break;
        case LIGHT_FILL:  fill_char = '\xB2'; break;
        case X_FILL:      fill_char = 'X';    break;
        case O_FILL:      fill_char = 'O';    break;
        }
    }
//-------------------------------------------------------------------
```

Listing for BORLACON.H

```
//borlacon.h
//declarations for Console Graphics Lite functions
//uses Borland's console functions
#ifndef _INC_WCONSOLE  //don't let this file be included
#define _INC_WCONSOLE  //twice in the same source file

#include <windows.h>   //for Sleep()
#include <conio.h>     //for kbhit(), getche()
#include <math.h>      //for sin, cos

enum fstyle { SOLID_FILL, X_FILL, O_FILL,
              LIGHT_FILL, MEDIUM_FILL, DARK_FILL };

enum color {
    cBLACK=0,      cDARK_BLUE=1,    cDARK_GREEN=2, cDARK_CYAN=3,
    cDARK_RED=4,   cDARK_MAGENTA=5, cBROWN=6,      cLIGHT_GRAY=7,
    cDARK_GRAY=8,  cBLUE=9,         cGREEN=10,     cCYAN=11,
    cRED=12,       cMAGENTA=13,     cYELLOW=14,    cWHITE=15 };
//-------------------------------------------------------------------
void init_graphics();
void set_color(color fg, color bg = cBLACK);
void set_cursor_pos(int x, int y);
```

```cpp
void clear_screen();
void wait(int milliseconds);
void clear_line();
void draw_rectangle(int left, int top, int right, int bottom);
void draw_circle(int x, int y, int rad);
void draw_line(int x1, int y1, int x2, int y2);
void draw_pyramid(int x1, int y1, int height);
void set_fill_style(fstyle);
#endif // _INC_WCONSOLE
```

Listing for BORLACON.CPP

```cpp
//borlacon.cpp
//provides drawing routines for Borland console functions
#include "borlaCon.h"

char fill_char;              //character used for fill
//.............................................................
void init_graphics()
    {
    textcolor(WHITE);        //text to white on black
    textbackground(BLACK);
    fill_char = '\xDB';      // default fill is solid block
    clrscr();
    }
//.............................................................
void set_color(color foreground, color background)
    {
    textcolor( static_cast<int>(foreground) );
    textbackground( static_cast<int>(background) );
    }
//.............................................................
void set_cursor_pos(int x, int y)
    {
    gotoxy(x, y);
    }
//.............................................................
void clear_screen()
    {
    clrscr();
    }
//.............................................................
void wait(int milliseconds)
    {
    Sleep(milliseconds);
    }
//.............................................................
```

```
void clear_line()                        // clear to end of line
   {                                     // 80 spaces
   //.....12345678901234567890123456789012345678901234567890
   //.....0........1.........2.........3.........4
   cputs("                                                    ");
   cputs("                                                    ");
   }  //end clreol()
//------------------------------------------------------------
void draw_rectangle(int left, int top, int right, int bottom)
   {
   int j;
   char temp[80];
   int width = right - left + 1;

   for(j=0; j<width; j++)                //string of squares
      temp[j] = fill_char;
   temp[j] = 0;                          //null

   for(int y=top; y<=bottom; y++)  //stack of strings
      {
      set_cursor_pos(left, y);
      cputs(temp);
      }
   }  //end rectangle
//------------------------------------------------------------
void draw_circle(int xC, int yC, int radius)
   {
   double theta, increment, xF, pi=3.14159;
   int x, xN, yN;

   increment = 0.8 / static_cast<double>(radius);
   for(theta=0; theta<=pi/2; theta+=increment)  //quarter circle
      {
      xF = radius * cos(theta);
      xN = static_cast<int>(xF * 2 / 1); // pixels not square
      yN = static_cast<int>(radius * sin(theta) + 0.5);
      x = xC-xN;
      while(x <= xC+xN)                //fill two horizontal lines
         {                            //one for each half circle
         set_cursor_pos(x,   yC-yN); putch(fill_char);  //top
         set_cursor_pos(x++, yC+yN); putch(fill_char);  //bottom
         }
      } //end for
   } //end circle()
//------------------------------------------------------------
void draw_line(int x1, int y1, int x2, int y2)
```

```
   {
   int w, z, t, w1, w2, z1, z2;
   double xDelta=x1-x2, yDelta=y1-y2, slope;
   bool isMoreHoriz;

   if( fabs(xDelta) > fabs(yDelta) ) //more horizontal
      {
      isMoreHoriz = true;
      slope = yDelta / xDelta;
      w1=x1; z1=y1; w2=x2, z2=y2;    //w=x, z=y
      }
   else                              //more vertical
      {
      isMoreHoriz = false;
      slope = xDelta / yDelta;
      w1=y1; z1=x1; w2=y2, z2=x2;    //w=y, z=x
      }

   if(w1 > w2)                       //if backwards w
      {
      t=w1; w1=w2; w2=t;             //    swap (w1,z1)
      t=z1; z1=z2; z2=t;             //    with (w2,z2)
      }
   for(w=w1; w<=w2; w++)
      {
      z = static_cast<int>(z1 + slope * (w-w1));
      if( !(w==80 && z==25) )        //avoid scroll at 80,25
         {
         if(isMoreHoriz)
            set_cursor_pos(w, z);
         else
            set_cursor_pos(z, w);
         putch(fill_char);
         }
      }
   }
//------------------------------------------------------------
void draw_pyramid(int x1, int y1, int height)
   {
   int x, y;
   for(y=y1; y<y1+height; y++)
      {
      int incr = y - y1;
      for(x=x1-incr; x<=x1+incr; x++)
         {
```

```
          set_cursor_pos(x, y);
          putch(fill_char);
          }
      }
   }
//-------------------------------------------------------------
void set_fill_style(fstyle fs)
   {
   switch(fs)
      {
      case SOLID_FILL:  fill_char = '\xDB'; break;
      case DARK_FILL:   fill_char = '\xB0'; break;
      case MEDIUM_FILL: fill_char = '\xB1'; break;
      case LIGHT_FILL:  fill_char = '\xB2'; break;
      case X_FILL:      fill_char = 'X';    break;
      case O_FILL:      fill_char = 'O';    break;
      }
   }
//-------------------------------------------------------------
```

STL Algorithms and Member Functions

IN THIS APPENDIX

This appendix contains charts showing the algorithms and container member functions available in the Standard Template Library (STL). This information is based on *The Standard Template Library* by Alexander Stepanov and Ming Lee (1995), but we have extensively condensed and revised it, taking many liberties with their original formulation in the interest of quick understanding.

Algorithms

Table F.1 shows the algorithms available in the STL. The descriptions in this table offer a quick and condensed explanation of what the algorithms do; they are not intended to be serious mathematical definitions. For more information, including the exact data types to use for arguments and return values, consult one of the books listed in Appendix H, "Bibliography."

The first column gives the function name, the second explains the purpose of the algorithm, and the third specifies the arguments. Return values are not systematically specified. Some are mentioned in the Purpose column and many are either obvious or not vital to using the algorithm.

In the Arguments column, the names first, last, first1, last1, first2, last2, first3, and middle represent iterators to specific places in a container. Names with numbers (like first1) are used to distinguish multiple containers. The name first1, last1 delimits range 1, and first2, last2 delimits range 2. The arguments function, predicate, op, and comp are function objects. The arguments value, old, new, a, b, and init are values of the objects stored in a container. These values are ordered or compared based on the < or == operators or the comp function object. The argument n is an integer.

In the Purpose column, moveable iterators are indicated by iter, iter1, and iter2. When iter1 and iter2 are used together, they are assumed to move together step by step through their respective containers (or possibly two different ranges in the same container).

TABLE F.1   Algorithms

Name	Purpose	Arguments
Non-mutating Sequence Operations		
for_each	Applies function to each object.	first, last, function
find	Returns iterator to first object equal to value.	first, last, value
find_if	Returns iterator to first object for which predicate is true.	first, last, predicate

TABLE F.1   Continued

Name	Purpose	Arguments
adjacent_find	Returns iterator to first adjacent pair of objects that are equal.	first, last
adjacent_find	Returns iterator to first adjacent pair of objects that satisfy predicate.	first, last, predicate
count	Adds to n the number of objects equal to value.	first, last, value, n
count_if	Adds to n the number of objects satisfying predicate.	first, last, predicate, n
mismatch	Returns first non-equal pair of corresponding objects in two ranges.	first1, last1, first2
mismatch	Returns first pair of corresponding objects in two ranges that don't satisfy predicate.	first1, last1, first2, predicate
equal	Returns true if corresponding objects in two ranges are all equal.	first1, last1, first2
equal	Returns true if corresponding objects in two ranges all satisfy predicate.	first1, last1, first2, predicate
search	Checks whether second range is contained within the first. Returns start of match, or last1 if no match.	first1, last1, first2, last2
search	Checks whether second range is contained within the first, where equality is determined by predicate. Returns start of match, or last1 if no match.	first1, last1, first2, last2, predicate

Mutating Sequence Operations

Name	Purpose	Arguments
copy	Copies objects from range 1 to range 2.	first1, last1, first2

TABLE F.1   Continued

Name	Purpose	Arguments
copy_backward	Copies objects from range 1 to range 2, inserting them backwards, from last2 to first2.	first1, last1, first2
swap	Interchanges two objects.	a, b
iter_swap	Interchanges objects pointed to by two iterators.	iter1, iter2
swap_ranges	Interchanges corresponding elements in two ranges.	first1, last1, first2
transform	Transforms objects in range 1 into new objects in range 2 by applying operator.	first1, last1, first2, operator
transform	Combines objects in range 1 and range 2 into new objects in range 3 by applying operator.	first1, last1, first2, first3, operator
replace	Replaces all objects equal to old with objects equal to new.	first, last, old, new
replace_if	Replaces all objects that satisfy predicate with objects equal to new.	first, last, predicate, new
replace_copy	Copies from range 1 to range 2, replacing all objects equal to old with objects equal to new.	first1, last1, first2, old, new
replace_copy_if	Copies from range 1 to range 2, replacing all objects that satisfy predicate with objects equal to new.	first1, last1, first2, predicate, new
fill	Assigns value to all objects in range.	first, last, value
fill_n	Assigns value to all objects from first to first+n.	first, n, value

TABLE F.1 Continued

Name	Purpose	Arguments
generate	Fills range with values generated by successive calls to function gen.	first, last, gen
generate_n	Fills from first to first+n with values generated by successive calls to function gen.	first, n, gen
remove	Removes from range any objects equal to value.	first, last, value
remove_if	Removes from range any objects that satisfy predicate.	first, last, predicate
remove_copy	Copies objects, excepting those equal to value, from range 1 to range 2.	first1, last1, first2, value
remove_copy_if	Copies objects, excepting those satisfying pred, from range 1 to range 2.	first1, last1, first2, pred
unique	Eliminates all but the first object from any consecutive sequence of equal objects.	first, last
unique	Eliminates all but the first object from any consecutive sequence of objects satisfying predicate.	first, last, predicate
unique_copy	Copies objects from range 1 to range 2, except only the first object from any consecutive sequence of equal objects is copied.	first1, last1, first2
unique_copy	Copies objects from range 1 to range 2, except only the first object from any consecutive sequence of objects satisfying predicate is copied.	first1, last1, first2, predicate

TABLE F.1   Continued

Name	Purpose	Arguments
reverse	Reverses the sequence of objects in range.	first, last
reverse_copy	Copies range 1 to range 2, reversing the sequence of objects.	first1, last1, first2
rotate	Rotates sequence of objects around iterator middle.	first, last, middle
rotate_copy	Copies objects from range 1 to range 2, rotating the sequence around iterator middle1.	first1, middle1, last1, first2
random_shuffle	Randomly shuffles objects in range.	first, last
random_shuffle	Randomly shuffles objects in range, using random-number function rand.	first, last, rand
partition	Moves all objects that satisfy predicate so they precede those that do not satisfy it.	first, last, predicate
stable_partition	Moves all objects that satisfy predicate so they precede those that do not, and also preserves relative ordering in the two groups.	first, last, predicate
Sorting and Related Operations		
sort	Sorts objects in range.	first, last
sort	Sorts elements in range, using comp as comparison function.	first, last, comp
stable_sort	Sorts objects in range, maintains order of equal elements.	first, last
stable_sort	Sorts elements in range, using comp as comparison function, maintains order of equal elements.	first, last, comp

TABLE F.1 Continued

Name	Purpose	Arguments
partial_sort	Sorts all objects in range, places as many sorted values as will fit between first and middle. Order of objects between middle and last is undefined.	first, middle, last
partial_sort	Sorts all objects in range, places as many sorted values as will fit between first and middle. Order of objects between middle and last is undefined. Uses predicate to define ordering.	first, middle, last, predicate
partial_sort_copy	Same as partial_sort (first, middle, last), but places resulting sequence in range 2.	first1, last1, first2, last2
partial_sort_copy	Same as partial_sort (first, middle, last, predicate), but places resulting sequence in range 2.	first1, last1, first2, last2, comp
nth_element	Places the nth object in the position it would occupy if the whole range were sorted.	first, nth, last
nth_element	Places the nth object in the position it would occupy if the whole range were sorted using comp for comparisons.	first, nth, last, comp
lower_bound	Returns iterator to first position into which value could be inserted without violating the ordering.	first, last, value
lower_bound	Returns iterator to first position into which value could be inserted without violating an ordering based on comp.	first, last, value, comp

TABLE F.1   Continued

Name	Purpose	Arguments
upper_bound	Returns iterator to last position into which value could be inserted without violating the ordering.	first, last, value
upper_bound	Returns iterator to last position into which value could be inserted without violating an ordering based on comp.	first, last, value, comp
equal_range	Returns a pair containing the lower bound and upper bound between which value could be inserted without violating the ordering.	first, last, value
equal_range	Returns a pair containing the lower bound and upper bound between which value could be inserted without violating an ordering based on comp.	first, last, value, comp
binary_search	Returns true if value is in the range.	first, last, value
binary_search	Returns true if value is in the range, where the ordering is determined by comp.	first, last, value, comp
merge	Merges sorted ranges 1 and 2 into sorted range 3.	first1, last1, first2, last2, first3
merge	Merges sorted ranges 1 and 2 into sorted range 3, where the ordering is determined by comp.	first1, last1, first2, last2, first3, comp
inplace_merge	Merges two consecutive sorted ranges, first, middle and middle, last into first, last.	first, middle, last

TABLE F.1   Continued

Name	Purpose	Arguments
inplace_merge	Merges two consecutive sorted ranges, first, middle and middle, last into first, last, where the ordering is based on comp.	first, middle, last, comp
includes	Returns true if every object in the range first2, last2 is also in the range first1, last1. (Sets and multisets only.)	first1, last1, first2, last2
includes	Returns true if every object in the range first2, last2 is also in the range first1, last1, where ordering is based on comp. (Sets and multisets only.)	first1, last1, first2, last2, comp
set_union	Constructs sorted union of elements of ranges 1 and 2. (Sets and multisets only.)	first1, last1, first2, last2, first3
set_union	Constructs sorted union of elements of ranges 1 and 2, where the ordering is based on comp. (Sets and multisets only.)	first1, last1, first2, last2, first3, comp
set_intersection	Constructs sorted intersection of elements of ranges 1 and 2. (Sets and multisets only.)	first1, last1, first2, last2, first3
set_intersection	Constructs sorted intersection of elements of ranges 1 and 2, where the ordering is based on comp. (Sets and multisets only.)	first1, last1, first2, last2, first3, comp
set_difference	Constructs sorted difference of elements of ranges 1 and 2. (Sets and multisets only.)	first1, last1, first2, last2, first3

TABLE F.1 Continued

Name	Purpose	Arguments
set_difference	Constructs sorted difference of elements of ranges 1 and 2, where the ordering is based on comp. (Sets and multisets only.)	first1, last1, first2, last2, first3, comp
set_symmetric_ difference	Constructs sorted symmetric difference of elements of ranges 1 and 2. (Sets and multisets only.)	first1, last1, first2, last2, first3
set_ symmetric_ difference	Constructs sorted difference of elements of ranges 1 and 2, where the ordering is based on comp. (Sets and multisets only.)	first1, last1, first2, last2, first3, comp
push_heap	Places value from last-1 into resulting heap in range first, last.	first, last
push_heap	Places value from last-1 into resulting heap in range first, last, based on ordering determined by comp.	first, last, comp
pop_heap	Swaps the values in first and last-1; makes range first, last-1 into a heap.	first, last
pop_heap	Swaps the values in first and last-1; makes range first, last-1 into a heap, based on ordering determined by comp.	first, last, comp
make_heap	Constructs a heap out of the range first, last.	first, last
make_heap	Constructs a heap out of the range first, last, based on the ordering determined by comp.	first, last, comp
sort_heap	Sorts the elements in the heap first, last.	first, last

TABLE F.1   Continued

Name	Purpose	Arguments
sort_heap	Sorts the elements in the heap first, last, based on the ordering determined by comp.	first, last, comp
min	Returns the smaller of two objects.	a, b
min	Returns the smaller of two objects, where the ordering is determined by comp.	a, b, comp
max	Returns the larger of two objects.	a, b
max	Returns the larger of two objects, where the ordering is determined by comp.	a, b, comp
max_element	Returns an iterator to the largest object in the range.	first, last
max_element	Returns an iterator to the largest object in the range, with an ordering determined by comp.	first, last, comp
min_element	Returns an iterator to the smallest object in the range.	first, last
min_element	Returns an iterator to the smallest object in the range, with an ordering determined by comp.	first, last, comp
lexicographical_ compare	Returns true if the sequence in range 1 comes before the sequence in range 2 alphabetically.	first1, last1, first2, last2
lexicographical_ compare	Returns true if the sequence in range 1 comes before the sequence in range 2 alphabetically, based on ordering determined by comp.	first1, last1, first2, last2, comp

F

STL ALGORITHMS
AND MEMBER
FUNCTIONS

TABLE F.1 Continued

Name	Purpose	Arguments
next_permutation	Performs one permutation on the sequence in the range.	first, last
next_permutation	Performs one permutation on the sequence in the range, where the ordering is determined by comp.	first, last, comp
prev_permutation	Performs one reverse permutation on the sequence in the range.	first, last
prev_permutation	Performs one reverse permutation on the sequence in the range, where the ordering is determined by comp.	first, last, comp

Generalized Numeric Operations

Name	Purpose	Arguments
accumulate	Sequentially applies init = init + *iter to each object in the range.	first, last, init
accumulate	Sequentially applies init = op(init, *iter) to each object in the range.	first, last, init, op
inner_product	Sequentially applies init=init+(*iter1)*(*iter2) to corresponding values from ranges 1 and 2.	first1, last1, first2, init
inner_product	Sequentially applies init=op1(init,op2(*iter1,*iter2)) to corresponding values from ranges 1 and 2.	first1, last1, first2, init, op1, op2
partial_sum	Adds values from start of range 1 to current iterator, and places the sums in corresponding iterator in range 2. *iter2 = sum(*first1, *(first1+1), *(first1+2), ..*iter1)	first1, last1, first2

TABLE F.1 Continued

Name	Purpose	Arguments
partial_sum	Sequentially applies op to objects between first1 and current iterator in range 1, and places results in corresponding iterator in range 2.	first1, last1, first2, op
	`answer = *first;`	
	`for(iter=first+1; iter != iter1; iter++)` `op(answer, *iter);`	
	`*iter2 = answer;`	
adjacent_ difference	Subtracts adjacent objects in range 1 and places differences in range 2.	first1, last1, first2
	`*iter2 = * (iter1+1) - *iter1;`	
adjacent_ difference	Sequentially applies op to adjacent objects in range 1 and places results in range 2.	first1, last1, first2, op
	`*iter2 = op(*(iter1+1),*iter1);`	

Member Functions

The same names are used for member functions that have similar purposes in the different containers. However, no container class includes all the available member functions. Table F.2 is intended to show which member functions are available for each container. Explanations of the functions are not given, either because they are more or less self-evident, or because they are explained in the text.

TABLE F.2   Member Functions

	Vector	List	Deque	Set	Multi-set	Map	Multi-map	Stack	Queue	Priority Queue
operator==	X	X	X	X	X	X	X	X	X	
operator!=	X	X	X	X	X	X	X	X	X	
operator<	X	X	X	X	X	X	X	X	X	
operator>	X	X	X	X	X	X	X	X	X	
operator<=	X	X	X	X	X	X	X	X	X	
operator>=	X	X	X	X	X	X	X	X	X	
operator =	X	X	X							
operator[]	X		X			X				
operator*		X	X							
operator->		X	X							
operator ()				X	X	X				
operator +			X							
operator -			X							
operator++		X	X							
operator--		X	X							
operator +=			X							
operator -=			X							
begin	X	X	X	X	X	X	X			
end	X	X	X	X	X	X	X			
rbegin	X	X	X	X	X	X	X			
rend	X	X	X	X	X	X	X			
empty	X	X	X	X	X	X	X	X	X	X
size	X	X	X	X	X	X	X	X	X	X
max_size	X	X	X	X	X	X	X			
front	X	X	X						X	
back	X	X	X						X	
push_front		X	X							
push_back	X	X	X							
pop_front		X	X							
pop_back	X	X	X							
swap	X	X	X	X	X	X	X			

TABLE F.2   Continued

	Vector	List	Deque	Set	Multi-set	Map	Multi-map	Stack	Queue	Priority Queue
insert	x	x	x	x	x	x	x			
erase	x	x	x	x	x	x	x			
find				x	x	x	x			
count				x	x	x	x			
lower_bound				x	x	x	x			
upper_bound				x	x	x	x			
equal_range				x	x	x	x			
top								x		x
push								x	x	x
pop								x	x	x
capacity	x									
reserve	x									
splice		x								
remove		x								
unique		x								
merge		x								
reverse		x								
sort		x								

Iterators

Table F.3 lists the type of iterator required by each algorithm.

TABLE F.3   Type of Iterator Required by Algorithm

	Input	Output	Forward	Bidirectional	Random Access
for_each	x				
find	x				
find_if	x				
adjacent_find	x				
count	x				

TABLE F.3   Continued

	Input	Output	Forward	Bidirectional	Random Access
count_if	X				
mismatch	X				
equal	X				
search			X		
copy	X	X			
copy_backward	X	X			
iter_swap			X		
swap_ranges			X		
transform	X	X			
replace			X		
replace_if			X		
replace_copy	X	X			
fill			X		
fill_n		X			
generate			X		
generate_n		X			
remove			X		
remove_if			X		
remove_copy	X	X			
remove_copy_if	X	X			
unique			X		
unique_copy	X	X			
reverse				X	
reverse_copy		X			
rotate			X		
rotate_copy		X	X		
random_shuffle					X
partition				X	
stable_partition				X	
sort					X
stable_sort					X

TABLE F.3 Continued

	Input	Output	Forward	Bidirectional	Random Access
partial_sort					x
partial_sort_copy	x				x
nth_element					x
lower_bound			x		
upper_bound			x		
equal_range			x		
binary_search			x		
merge	x	x			
inplace_merge				x	
includes	x				
set_union	x	x			
set_intersection	x	x			
set_difference	x	x			
set_symmetric_difference	x	x			
push_heap					x
pop_heap					x
make_heap					x
sort_heap					x
max_element	x				
min_element	x				
lexicographical_comparison	x				
next_permutation				x	
prev_permutation				x	
accumulate	x				
inner_product	x				
partial_sum	x	x			
adjacent_difference	x	x			

Answers to Questions and Exercises

IN THIS APPENDIX

Chapter 1

Answers to Questions

1. procedural, object-oriented
2. b
3. data, act on that data
4. a
5. data hiding
6. a, d
7. objects
8. false; the organizational principles are different
9. encapsulation
10. d
11. false; most lines of code are the same in C and C++
12. polymorphism
13. d
14. b
15. b, d

Chapter 2

Answers to Questions

1. b, c
2. parentheses
3. braces { }
4. It's the first function executed when the program starts
5. statement
6.
    ```
    // this is a comment
    /* this is a comment */
    ```
7. a, d

8. a. 4

   b. 10

   c. 4

   d. 4

9. false

10. a. integer constant

    b. character constant

    c. floating-point constant

    d. variable name or identifier

    e. function name

11. a. `cout << 'x';`

    b. `cout << "Jim";`

    c. `cout << 509;`

12. false; they're not equal until the statement is executed

13. `cout << setw(10) << george;`

14. IOSTREAM

15. `cin >> temp;`

16. IOMANIP

17. string constants, preprocessor directives

18. true

19. 2

20. assignment (=) and arithmetic (like + and *)

21.

```
temp += 23;
temp = temp + 23;
```

22. 1

23. 2020

24. to provide declarations and other data for library functions, overloaded operators, and objects

25. library

Solutions to Exercises

1.

```cpp
// ex2_1.cpp
// converts gallons to cubic feet
#include <iostream>
using namespace std;

int main()
    {
    float gallons, cufeet;

    cout << "\nEnter quantity in gallons: ";
    cin >> gallons;
    cufeet = gallons / 7.481;
    cout << "Equivalent in cubic feet is " << cufeet << endl;
    return 0;
    }
```

2.

```cpp
// ex2_2.cpp
// generates table
#include <iostream>
#include <iomanip>
using namespace std;

int main()
    {
    cout << 1990 << setw(8) << 135 << endl
         << 1991 << setw(8) << 7290 << endl
         << 1992 << setw(8) << 11300 << endl
         << 1993 << setw(8) << 16200 << endl;
    return 0;
    }
```

3.

```cpp
// ex2_3.cpp
// exercises arithmetic assignment and decrement
#include <iostream>
using namespace std;

int main()
    {
    int var = 10;
```

```
        cout << var << endl;        // var is 10
        var *= 2;                   // var becomes 20
        cout << var-- << endl;      // displays var, then decrements it
        cout << var << endl;        // var is 19
        return 0;
        }
```

Chapter 3

Answers to Questions

1. b, c

2. george != sally

3. −1 is true; only 0 is false.

4. The initialize expression initializes the loop variable, the test expression tests the loop
   variable, and the increment expression changes the loop variable.

5. c, d

6. true

7.
```
    for(int j=100; j<=110; j++)
        cout << endl << j;
```

8. braces (curly brackets)

9. c

10.
```
    int j = 100;
    while( j <= 110 )
        cout << endl << j++;
```

11. false

12. at least once

13.
```
    int j = 100;
    do
        cout << endl << j++;
    while( j <= 110 );
```

14.
```
    if(age > 21)
        cout << "Yes";
```

15. d

16.
```
if( age > 21 )
   cout << "Yes";
else
   cout << "No";
```

17. a, c

18. '\r'

19. preceding, surrounded by braces

20. reformatting

21.
```
switch(ch)
{
case 'y':
   cout << "Yes";
   break;
case 'n':
   cout << "No";
   break;
default:
   cout << "Unknown response";
}
```

22. `ticket = (speed > 55) ? 1 : 0;`

23. d

24. `limit == 55 && speed > 55`

25. unary, arithmetic, relational, logical, conditional, assignment

26. d

27. the top of the loop

28. b

Solutions to Exercises

1.
```
// ex3_1.cpp
// displays multiples of a number
#include <iostream>
#include <iomanip>                              //for setw()
using namespace std;

int main()
   {
```

```
    unsigned long n;                        //number

    cout << "\nEnter a number: ";
    cin >> n;                               //get number
    for(int j=1; j<=200; j++)               //loop from 1 to 200
       {
       cout << setw(5) << j*n << "  ";  //print multiple of n
       if( j%10 == 0 )                      //every 10 numbers,
          cout << endl;                     //start new line
       }
    return 0;
    }
```

2

```
// ex3_2.cpp
// converts fahrenheit to centigrad, or
// centigrad to fahrenheit
#include <iostream>
using namespace std;

int main()
    {
    int response;
    double temper;

    cout << "\nType 1 to convert fahrenheit to celsius,"
         << "\n     2 to convert celsius to fahrenheit: ";
    cin >> response;
    if( response == 1 )
       {
       cout << "Enter temperature in fahrenheit: ";
       cin >> temper;
       cout << "In celsius that's " << 5.0/9.0*(temper-32.0);
       }
    else
       {
       cout << "Enter temperature in celsius: ";
       cin >> temper;
       cout << "In fahrenheit that's " << 9.0/5.0*temper + 32.0;
       }
    cout << endl;
    return 0;
    }
```

3.

```cpp
// ex3_3.cpp
// makes a number out of digits
#include <iostream>
using namespace std;
#include <conio.h>                        //for getche()

int main()
   {
   char ch;
   unsigned long total = 0;               //this holds the number

   cout << "\nEnter a number: ";
   while( (ch=getche()) != '\r' )         //quit on Enter
      total = total*10 + ch-'0';          //add digit to total*10
   cout << "\nNumber is: " << total << endl;
   return 0;
   }
```

4.

```cpp
// ex3_4.cpp
// models four-function calculator
#include <iostream>
using namespace std;

int main()
   {
   double n1, n2, ans;
   char oper, ch;

   do {
      cout << "\nEnter first number, operator, second number: ";
      cin >> n1 >> oper >> n2;
      switch(oper)
         {
         case '+':  ans = n1 + n2;  break;
         case '-':  ans = n1 - n2;  break;
         case '*':  ans = n1 * n2;  break;
         case '/':  ans = n1 / n2;  break;
         default:   ans = 0;
         }
      cout << "Answer = " << ans;
      cout << "\nDo another (Enter 'y' or 'n')? ";
      cin >> ch;
      } while( ch != 'n' );
   return 0;
   }
```

Chapter 4

Answers to Questions

1. b, d

2. true

3. semicolon

4.
```
struct time
    {
    int hrs;
    int mins;
    int secs;
    };
```

5. false; only a variable definition creates space in memory

6. c

7. `time2.hrs = 11;`

8. 18 in 16-bit systems (3 structures times 3 integers times 2 bytes), or 36 in 32-bit systems

9. `time time1 = { 11, 10, 59 };`

10. true

11. `temp = fido.dogs.paw;`

12. c

13. `enum players { B1, B2, SS, B3, RF, CF, LF, P, C };`

14.
```
players joe, tom;
joe = LF;
tom = P;
```

15. a. no

    b. yes

    c. no

    d. yes

16. 0, 1, 2

17. `enum speeds { obsolete=78, single=45, album=33 };`

18. because false should be represented by 0

Solutions to Exercises

1.

```cpp
// ex4_1.cpp
// uses structure to store phone number
#include <iostream>
using namespace std;
//////////////////////////////////////////////////////////////////
struct phone
    {
    int area;          //area code (3 digits)
    int exchange;      //exchange (3 digits)
    int number;        //number (4 digits)
    };
//////////////////////////////////////////////////////////////////
int main()
    {
    phone ph1 = { 212, 767, 8900 };   //initialize phone number
    phone ph2;                         //define phone number
                                       // get phone no from user
    cout << "\nEnter your area code, exchange, and number";
    cout << "\n(Don't use leading zeros): ";
    cin >> ph2.area >> ph2.exchange >> ph2.number;

    cout << "\nMy number is "          //display numbers
        << '(' << ph1.area << ") "
        << ph1.exchange << '-' << ph1.number;

    cout << "\nYour number is "
        << '(' << ph2.area << ") "
        << ph2.exchange << '-' << ph2.number << endl;
    return 0;
    }
```

2.

```cpp
// ex4_2.cpp
// structure models point on the plane
#include <iostream>
using namespace std;
//////////////////////////////////////////////////////////////////
struct point
    {
    int xCo;        //X coordinate
    int yCo;        //Y coordinate
    };
//////////////////////////////////////////////////////////////////
```

```cpp
int main()
    {
    point p1, p2, p3;                              //define 3 points

    cout << "\nEnter coordinates for p1: "; //get 2 points
    cin >> p1.xCo >> p1.yCo;                       //from user
    cout << "Enter coordinates for p2: ";
    cin >> p2.xCo >> p2.yCo;

    p3.xCo = p1.xCo + p2.xCo;                      //find sum of
    p3.yCo = p1.yCo + p2.yCo;                      //p1 and p2

    cout << "Coordinates of p1+p2 are: "           //display the sum
         << p3.xCo << ", " << p3.yCo << endl;
    return 0;
    }
```

3.

```cpp
// ex4_3.cpp
// uses structure to model volume of room
#include <iostream>
using namespace std;
//////////////////////////////////////////////////////////////////
struct Distance
    {
    int feet;
    float inches;
    };
//////////////////////////////////////////////////////////////////
struct Volume
    {
    Distance length;
    Distance width;
    Distance height;
    };
//////////////////////////////////////////////////////////////////
int main()
    {
    float l, w, h;
    Volume room1 = {  { 16, 3.5 }, { 12, 0.25 }, { 8, 1.75 } };

    l = room1.length.feet + room1.length.inches/12.0;
    w = room1.width.feet  + room1.width.inches /12.0;
    h = room1.height.feet + room1.height.inches/12.0;

    cout << "Volume = " << l*w*h << " cubic feet\n";
    return 0;
    }
```

Chapter 5

Answers to Questions

1. d (half credit for b)
2. definition
3.
   ```
   void foo()
      {
      cout << "foo";
      }
   ```
4. declaration, prototype
5. body
6. call
7. declarator
8. c
9. false
10. To clarify the purpose of the arguments
11. a, b, c
12. Empty parentheses mean the function takes no arguments
13. one
14. Ttrue
15. at the beginning of the declaration and declarator
16. void
17.
   ```
   main()
      {
      int times2(int);         // prototype
      int alpha = times2(37);  // function call
      }
   ```
18. d
19. to modify the original argument (or to avoid copying a large argument)
20. a, c
21.
   ```
   int bar(char);
   int bar(char, char);
   ```

22. faster, more

23. `inline float foobar(float fvar)`

24. a, b

25. `char blyth(int, float=3.14159);`

26. visibility, lifetime

27. those functions defined following the variable definition

28. the function in which it is defined

29. b, d

30. on the left side of the equal sign

Solutions to Exercises

1.

```
// ex5_1.cpp
// function finds area of circle
#include <iostream>
using namespace std;
float circarea(float radius);

int main()
    {
    double rad;
    cout << "\nEnter radius of circle: ";
    cin >> rad;
    cout << "Area is " << circarea(rad) << endl;
    return 0;
    }
//------------------------------------------------------
float circarea(float r)
    {
    const float PI = 3.14159F;
    return r * r * PI;
    }
```

2.

```
// ex5_2.cpp
// function raises number to a power
#include <iostream>
using namespace std;
double power( double n, int p=2);   //p has default value 2
```

```cpp
int main()
    {
    double number, answer;
    int pow;
    char yeserno;

    cout << "\nEnter number: ";        //get number
    cin >> number;
    cout << "Want to enter a power (y/n)? ";
    cin >> yeserno;
    if( yeserno == 'y' )                //user wants a non-2 power?
        {
        cout << "Enter power: ";
        cin >> pow;
        answer = power(number, pow);    //raise number to pow
        }
    else
        answer = power(number);         //square the number
    cout << "Answer is " << answer << endl;
    return 0;
    }
//--------------------------------------------------------------
// power()
// returns number n raised to a power p
double power( double n, int p )
    {
    double result = 1.0;                //start with 1
    for(int j=0; j<p; j++)              //multiply by n
        result *= n;                    //p times
    return result;
    }
```

3.

```cpp
// ex5_3.cpp
// function sets smaller of two numbers to 0
#include <iostream>
using namespace std;

int main()
    {
    void zeroSmaller(int&, int&);
    int a=4, b=7, c=11, d=9;

    zeroSmaller(a, b);
    zeroSmaller(c, d);
```

```
        cout << "\na=" << a << " b=" << b
             << " c=" << c << " d=" << d;
        return 0;
        }
//---------------------------------------------------------------
// zeroSmaller()
// sets the smaller of two numbers to 0
void zeroSmaller(int& first, int& second)
    {
    if( first < second )
        first = 0;
    else
        second = 0;
    }
```

4.

```
// ex5_4.cpp
// function returns larger of two distances
#include <iostream>
using namespace std;
////////////////////////////////////////////////////////////////
struct Distance                    // English distance
    {
    int feet;
    float inches;
    };
////////////////////////////////////////////////////////////////
Distance bigengl(Distance, Distance);   //declarations
void engldisp(Distance);

int main()
    {
    Distance d1, d2, d3;            //define three lengths
                                    //get length d1 from user
    cout << "\nEnter feet: ";  cin >> d1.feet;
    cout << "Enter inches: ";  cin >> d1.inches;
                                    //get length d2 from user
    cout << "\nEnter feet: ";  cin >> d2.feet;
    cout << "Enter inches: ";  cin >> d2.inches;

    d3 = bigengl(d1, d2);           //d3 is larger of d1 and d2
                                    //display all lengths
    cout << "\nd1="; engldisp(d1);
    cout << "\nd2="; engldisp(d2);
    cout << "\nlargest is "; engldisp(d3); cout << endl;
    return 0;
    }
```

```
//--------------------------------------------------------------
// bigeng1()
// compares two structures of type Distance, returns the larger
Distance bigeng1( Distance dd1, Distance dd2 )
   {
   if(dd1.feet > dd2.feet)        //if feet are different, return
      return dd1;                 //the one with the largest feet
   if(dd1.feet < dd2.feet)
      return dd2;
   if(dd1.inches > dd2.inches)    //if inches are different,
      return dd1;                 //return one with largest
   else                           //inches, or dd2 if equal
      return dd2;
   }
//--------------------------------------------------------------
// engldisp()
// display structure of type Distance in feet and inches
void engldisp( Distance dd )
   {
   cout << dd.feet << "\'-" << dd.inches << "\"";
   }
```

Chapter 6

Answers to Questions

1. A class declaration describes how objects of a class will look when they are created.

2. class, object

3. c

4.
```
class leverage
   {
   private:
     int crowbar;
   public:
      void pry();
   };
```

5. false; both data and functions can be private or public

6. leverage lever1;

7. d

8. lever1.pry();

9. inline (also private)

10.
```
int getcrow()
{ return crowbar; }
```

11. created (defined)

12. the class of which it is a member

13.
```
leverage()
    { crowbar = 0; }
```

14. true

15. a

16. `int getcrow();`

17.
```
int leverage::getcrow()
{ return crowbar; }
```

18. member functions and data are, by default, public in structures but private in classes

19. three, one

20. calling one of its member functions

21. b, c, d

22. false; trial and error may be necessary

23. d

24. true

25. `void aFunc(const float jerry) const;`

Solutions to Exercises

1.
```cpp
// ex6_1.cpp
// uses a class to model an integer data type
#include <iostream>
using namespace std;
//////////////////////////////////////////////////////////////////
class Int                          //(not the same as int)
    {
    private:
        int i;
    public:
        Int()                      //create an Int
            { i = 0; }
```

```
        Int(int ii)                 //create and initialize an Int
           { i = ii; }
        void add(Int i2, Int i3)   //add two Ints
           { i = i2.i + i3.i; }
        void display()              //display an Int
           { cout << i; }
   };
/////////////////////////////////////////////////////////////////
int main()
   {
   Int Int1(7);                     //create and initialize an Int
   Int Int2(11);                    //create and initialize an Int
   Int Int3;                        //create an Int

   Int3.add(Int1, Int2);                    //add two Ints
   cout << "\nInt3 = "; Int3.display();  //display result
   cout << endl;
   return 0;
   }
```

2.

```
// ex6_2.cpp
// uses class to model toll booth
#include <iostream>
using namespace std;
#include <conio.h>

const char ESC = 27;          //escape key ASCII code
const double TOLL = 0.5;       //toll is 50 cents
/////////////////////////////////////////////////////////////////
class tollBooth
   {
   private:
      unsigned int totalCars;  //total cars passed today
      double totalCash;        //total money collected today
   public:                     //constructor
      tollBooth() : totalCars(0), totalCash(0.0)
         { }
      void payingCar()                       //a car paid
         { totalCars++; totalCash += TOLL; }
      void nopayCar()                        //a car didn't pay
         { totalCars++; }
      void display() const                   //display totals
         { cout << "\nCars=" << totalCars
                << ", cash=" << totalCash
                << endl; }
   };
```

```
/////////////////////////////////////////////////////////////////
int main()
   {
   tollBooth booth1;              //create a toll booth
   char ch;

   cout << "\nPress 0 for each non-paying car,"
        << "\n        1 for each paying car,"
        << "\n        Esc to exit the program.\n";
   do {
      ch = getche();              //get character
      if( ch == '0' )            //if it's 0, car didn't pay
         booth1.nopayCar();
      if( ch == '1' )            //if it's 1, car paid
         booth1.payingCar();
      } while( ch != ESC );      //exit loop on Esc key
   booth1.display();             //display totals
   return 0;
   }
```

3.

```
// ex6_3.cpp
// uses class to model a time data type
#include <iostream>
using namespace std;
/////////////////////////////////////////////////////////////////
class time
   {
   private:
      int hrs, mins, secs;
   public:
      time() : hrs(0), mins(0), secs(0) //no-arg constructor
         { }
                                        //3-arg constructor
      time(int h, int m, int s) : hrs(h), mins(m), secs(s)
         { }

      void display() const              //format 11:59:59
         { cout << hrs << ":" << mins << ":" << secs; }

      void add_time(time t1, time t2)   //add two times
         {
         secs = t1.secs + t2.secs;      //add seconds
         if( secs > 59 )                //if overflow,
            { secs -= 60; mins++; }     //   carry a minute
         mins += t1.mins + t2.mins;     //add minutes
```

```
        if( mins > 59 )              //if overflow,
           { mins -= 60; hrs++; }    //   carry an hour
        hrs + t1.hrs + t2.hrs;       //add hours
        }
    };
//////////////////////////////////////////////////////////////////
int main()
    {
    const time time1(5, 59, 59);     //creates and initialze
    const time time2(4, 30, 30);     //   two times
    time time3;                      //create another time

    time3.add_time(time1, time2);    //add two times
    cout << "time3 = "; time3.display(); //display result
    cout << endl;
    return 0;
    }
```

Chapter 7

Answers to Questions

1. d

2. same

3. double doubleArray[100];

4. 0, 9

5. cout << doubleArray[j];

6. c

7. int coins[] = { 1, 5, 10, 25, 50, 100 };

8. d

9. twoD[2][4]

10. true

11. float flarr[3][3] = { {52,27,83}, {94,73,49}, {3,6,1} };

12. memory address

13. a, d

14. an array with 1000 elements of structure or class employee

15. emplist[16].salary

16. d

17. `bird manybirds[50];`

18. false

19. `manybirds[26].cheep();`

20. array, char

21. `char city[21]` (An extra byte is needed for the null character.)

22. `char dextrose[] = "C6H1206-H2O";`

23. true

24. d

25. `strcpy(blank, name);`

26.
```
class dog
   {
   private:
      char breed[80];
      int age;
   };
```

27. false

28. b, c

29. `int n = s1.find("cat");`

30. `s1.insert(12, "cat");`

Solutions to Exercises

I.
```
// ex7_1.cpp
// reverses a C-string
#include <iostream>
#include <cstring>                       //for strlen()
using namespace std;

int main()
   {
   void reversit( char[] );              //prototype
   const int MAX = 80;                   //array size
   char str[MAX];                        //string

   cout << "\nEnter a string: ";         //get string from user
   cin.get(str, MAX);
```

```
    reversit(str);                          //reverse the string

    cout << "Reversed string is: ";   //display it
    cout << str << endl;
    return 0;
    }
//........................................................
//reversit()
//function to reverse a string passed to it as an argument
void reversit( char s[] )
    {
    int len = strlen(s);                    //find length of string
    for(int j = 0; j < len/2; j++)          //swap each character
        {                                   //   in first half
        char temp = s[j];                   //   with character
        s[j] = s[len-j-1];                  //   in second half
        s[len-j-1] = temp:
        }
    }
```

```
// reversit()
// function to reverse a string passed to it as an argument
void reversit( char s[] )
    {
    int len = strlen(s);                    // find length of string
    for(int j = 0; j < len/2; j++)          // swap each character
        {                                   //   in first half
        char temp = s[j];                   //   with character
        s[j] = s[len-j-1];                  //   in second half
        s[len-j-1] = temp;
        }
    }
```

2.

```
// ex7_2.cpp
// employee object uses a string as data
#include <iostream>
#include <string>
using namespace std;
/////////////////////////////////////////////////////////////////
class employee
    {
    private:
        string name;
        long number;
```

```
    public:
        void getdata()              //get data from user
            {
            cout << "\nEnter name: ";  cin >> name;
            cout << "Enter number: "; cin >> number;
            }
        void putdata()              //display data
            {
            cout << "\n   Name: " << name;
            cout << "\n   Number: " << number;
            }
    };
////////////////////////////////////////////////////////////////
int main()
    {
    employee emparr[100];        //an array of employees
    int n = 0;                   //how many employees
    char ch;                     //user response

    do {                         //get data from user
        cout << "\nEnter data for employee number " << n+1;
        emparr[n++].getdata();
        cout << "Enter another (y/n)? "; cin >> ch;
        } while( ch != 'n' );

    for(int j=0; j<n; j++)       //display data in array
        {
        cout << "\nEmployee number " << j+1;
        emparr[j].putdata();
        }
    cout << endl;
    return 0;
    }
```

3.

```
// ex7_3.cpp
// averages an array of Distance objects input by user
#include <iostream>
using namespace std;
////////////////////////////////////////////////////////////////
class Distance                     // English Distance class
    {
    private:
        int feet;
        float inches;
```

```
   public:
     Distance()                     //constructor (no args)
        { feet = 0; inches = 0; }
     Distance(int ft, float in)  //constructor (two args)
        { feet = ft; inches = in; }

     void getdist()                 //get length from user
        {
        cout << "\nEnter feet: ";  cin >> feet;
        cout << "Enter inches: ";  cin >> inches;
        }

     void showdist()                //display distance
        { cout << feet << "\'-" << inches << '\"'; }

     void add_dist( Distance, Distance );    //declarations
     void div_dist( Distance, int );
   };
//-------------------------------------------------------------
                                 //add Distances d2 and d3
void Distance::add_dist(Distance d2, Distance d3)
   {
   inches = d2.inches + d3.inches;  //add the inches
   feet = 0;                        //(for possible carry)
   if(inches >= 12.0)               //if total exceeds 12.0,
      {                             //then decrease inches
      inches -= 12.0;              //by 12.0 and
      feet++;                      //increase feet
      }                            //by 1
   feet += d2.feet + d3.feet;      //add the feet
   }
//-------------------------------------------------------------
                                 //divide Distance by int
void Distance::div_dist(Distance d2, int divisor)
   {
   float fltfeet = d2.feet + d2.inches/12.0;  //convert to float
   fltfeet /= divisor;                        //do division
   feet = int(fltfeet);                       //get feet part
   inches = (fltfeet-feet) * 12.0;            //get inches part
   }
/////////////////////////////////////////////////////////////////
int main()
   {
   Distance distarr[100];           //array of 100 Distances
   Distance total(0, 0.0), average; //other Distances
   int count = 0;                   //counts Distances input
```

```
    char ch;                            //user response character

    do {
        cout << "\nEnter a Distance";       //get Distances
        distarr[count++].getdist();         //from user, put
        cout << "\nDo another (y/n)? ";      //in array
        cin >> ch;
        }while( ch != 'n' );

    for(int j=0; j<count; j++)           //add all Distances
        total.add_dist( total, distarr[j] );   //to total
    average.div_dist( total, count );     //divide by number

    cout << "\nThe average is: ";        //display average
    average.showdist();
    cout << endl;
    return 0;
    }
```

Chapter 8

Answers to Questions

1. a, c

2. x3.subtract(x2, x1);

3. x3 = x2 - x1;

4. true

5. void operator -- () { count--; }

6. none

7. b, d

8.
```
void Distance::operator ++ ()
    {
    ++feet;
    }
```

9.
```
Distance Distance::operator ++ ()
    {
    int f = ++feet;
    float i = inches;
    return Distance(f, i);
    }
```

10. It increments the variable prior to use, the same as a non-overloaded ++operator.

11. c, e, b, a, d

12. true

13. b, c

14.

```
String String::operator ++ ()
    {
    int len = strlen(str);
    for(int j=0; j<len; j++)
        str[j] = toupper( str[j] )
    return String(str);
    }
```

15. d

16. false if there is a conversion routine; true otherwise

17. b

18. true

19. constructor

20. true, but it will be hard for humans to understand

21. d

22. attributes, operations

23. false

24. a

Solutions to Exercises

1.

```
// ex8_1.cpp
// overloaded '-' operator subtracts two Distances
#include <iostream>
using namespace std;
//////////////////////////////////////////////////////////////////
class Distance                     //English Distance class
    {
    private:
        int feet;
        float inches;
    public:                        //constructor (no args)
        Distance() : feet(0), inches(0.0)
            { }                    //constructor (two args)
```

```
        Distance(int ft, float in) : feet(ft), inches(in)
           {  }
        void getdist()                    //get length from user
           {
           cout << "\nEnter feet: ";  cin >> feet;
           cout << "Enter inches: ";  cin >> inches;
           }
        void showdist()                   //display distance
           { cout << feet << "\'-" << inches << '\"'; }

     Distance operator + ( Distance );  //add two distances
     Distance operator - ( Distance );  //subtract two distances
   };
//----------------------------------------------------------------
                                //add d2 to this distance
Distance Distance::operator + (Distance d2)    //return the sum
   {
   int f = feet + d2.feet;              //add the feet
   float i = inches + d2.inches;        //add the inches
   if(i >= 12.0)                        //if total exceeds 12.0,
      {                                 //then decrease inches
      i -= 12.0;                        //by 12.0 and
      f++;                              //increase feet by 1
      }                                 //return a temporary Distance
   return Distance(f,i);                //initialized to sum
   }
//----------------------------------------------------------------
                                //subtract d2 from this dist
Distance Distance::operator - (Distance d2)    //return the diff
   {
   int f = feet - d2.feet;              //subtract the feet
   float i = inches - d2.inches;        //subtract the inches
   if(i < 0)                            //if inches less than 0,
      {                                 //then increase inches
      i += 12.0;                        //by 12.0 and
      f--;                              //decrease feet by 1
      }                                 //return a temporary Distance
   return Distance(f,i);                //initialized to difference
   }
///////////////////////////////////////////////////////////////////
int main()
   {
   Distance dist1, dist3;               //define distances
   dist1.getdist();                     //get dist1 from user

   Distance dist2(3, 6.25);             //define, initialize dist2
```

```
         dist3 = dist1 - dist2;                //subtract

                                               //display all lengths
      cout << "\ndist1 = ";  dist1.showdist();
      cout << "\ndist2 = ";  dist2.showdist();
      cout << "\ndist3 = ";  dist3.showdist();
      cout << endl;
      return 0;
      }
```

2.

```
// ex8_2.cpp
// overloaded '+=' operator concatenates strings
#include <iostream>
#include <cstring>          //for strcpy(), strlen()
using namespace std;
#include <process.h>        //for exit()
//////////////////////////////////////////////////////////////////
class String                      //user-defined string type
   {
   private:
      enum { SZ = 80 };                  //size of String objects
      char str[SZ];                      //holds a C-string
   public:
      String()                           //no-arg constructor
         { strcpy(str, ""); }
      String( char s[] )                 //1-arg constructor
         { strcpy(str, s); }
      void display()                     //display the String
         { cout << str; }
      String operator += (String ss)  //add a String to this one
         {                               //result stays in this one
         if( strlen(str) + strlen(ss.str) >= SZ )
            { cout << "\nString overflow"; exit(1); }
         strcat(str, ss.str);            //add the argument string
         return String(str);            //return temp String
         }
   };
//////////////////////////////////////////////////////////////////
int main()
   {
   String s1 = "Merry Christmas!  ";     //uses 1-arg ctor
   String s2 = "Happy new year!";        //uses 1-arg ctor
   String s3;                            //uses no-arg ctor
```

```
    s3 = s1 += s2;              //add s2 to s1, assign to s3

    cout << "\ns1="; s1.display();          //display s1
    cout << "\ns2="; s2.display();          //display s2
    cout << "\ns3="; s3.display();          //display s3
    cout << endl;
    return 0;
    }
```

3.

```
// ex8_3.cpp
// overloaded '+' operator adds two times
#include <iostream>
using namespace std;
//////////////////////////////////////////////////////////////
class time
    {
    private:
        int hrs, mins, secs;
    public:
        time() : hrs(0), mins(0), secs(0) //no-arg constructor
            { }                            //3-arg constructor
        time(int h, int m, int s) : hrs(h), mins(m), secs(s)
            { }
        void display()                    //format 11:59:59
            { cout << hrs << ":" << mins << ":" << secs; }

        time operator + (time t2)         //add two times
            {
            int s = secs + t2.secs;       //add seconds
            int m = mins + t2.mins;       //add minutes
            int h = hrs + t2.hrs;         //add hours
            if( s > 59 )                  //if secs overflow,
                { s -= 60; m++; }         //   carry a minute
            if( m > 59 )                  //if mins overflow,
                { m -= 60; h++; }         //   carry an hour
            return time(h, m, s);         //return temp value
            }
    };
//////////////////////////////////////////////////////////////
int main()
    {
    time time1(5, 59, 59);                //create and initialze
    time time2(4, 30, 30);                //   two times
    time time3;                           //create another time
```

G

ANSWERS TO
QUESTIONS AND
EXERCISES

```
        time3 = time1 + time2;                //add two times
      cout << "\ntime3 = "; time3.display(); //display result
        cout << endl;
        return 0;
        }
```

4.

```
// ex8_4.cpp
// overloaded arithmetic operators work with type Int
#include <iostream>
using namespace std;
#include <process.h>                          //for exit()
/////////////////////////////////////////////////////////////////
class Int
    {
    private:
        int i;
    public:
        Int() : i(0)                          //no-arg constructor
          {  }
        Int(int ii) : i(ii)                   //1-arg constructor
          {  }                                //    (int to Int)
        void putInt()                         //display Int
          { cout << i; }
        void getInt()                         //read Int from kbd
          { cin >> i; }
        operator int()                        //conversion operator
          { return i; }                       //    (Int to int)
        Int operator + (Int i2)               //addition
          { return checkit( long double(i)+long double(i2) ); }
        Int operator - (Int i2)               //subtraction
          { return checkit( long double(i)-long double(i2) ); }
        Int operator * (Int i2)               //multiplication
          { return checkit( long double(i)*long double(i2) ); }
        Int operator / (Int i2)               //division
          { return checkit( long double(i)/long double(i2) ); }

        Int checkit(long double answer)            //check results
          {
          if( answer > 2147483647.0L || answer < -2147483647.0L )
             { cout << "\nOverflow Error\n"; exit(1); }
          return Int( int(answer) );
          }
    };
/////////////////////////////////////////////////////////////////
int main()
    {
```

```
        Int alpha = 20;
        Int beta = 7;
        Int delta, gamma;

        gamma = alpha + beta;              //27
        cout << "\ngamma="; gamma.putInt();
        gamma = alpha - beta;              //13
        cout << "\ngamma="; gamma.putInt();
        gamma = alpha * beta;              //140
        cout << "\ngamma="; gamma.putInt();
        gamma = alpha / beta;              //2
        cout << "\ngamma="; gamma.putInt();

        delta = 2147483647;
        gamma = delta + alpha;             //overflow error
        delta = -2147483647;
        gamma = delta - alpha;             //overflow error

        cout << endl;
        return 0;
        }
```

Chapter 9

Answers to Questions

1. a, c

2. derived

3. b, c, d

4. `class Bosworth : public Alphonso`

5. false

6. `protected`

7. yes (assuming basefunc is not private)

8. `BosworthObj.alfunc();`

9. true

10. the one in the derived class

11. `Bosworth() : Alphonso() { }`

12. c, d

13. true

14. `Derv(int arg) : Base(arg)`

15. a

16. true

17. c

18. `class Tire : public Wheel, public Rubber`

19. `Base::func();`

20. false

21. generalization

22. d

23. false

24. stronger, aggregation

Solutions to Exercises

1.

```
// ex9_1.cpp
// publication class and derived classes
#include <iostream>
#include <string>
using namespace std;
/////////////////////////////////////////////////////////////////
class publication                        // base class
    {
    private:
        string title;
        float price;
    public:
        void getdata()
            {
            cout << "\nEnter title: "; cin >> title;
            cout << "Enter price: "; cin >> price;
            }
        void putdata() const
            {
            cout << "\nTitle: " << title;
            cout << "\nPrice: " << price;
            }
    };
/////////////////////////////////////////////////////////////////
class book : private publication         // derived class
    {
    private:
        int pages;
```

```cpp
public:
    void getdata()
        {
        publication::getdata();
        cout << "Enter number of pages: "; cin >> pages;
        }
    void putdata() const
        {
        publication::putdata();
        cout << "\nPages: " << pages;
        }
    };
//////////////////////////////////////////////////////////////////
class tape : private publication        // derived class
    {
    private:
        float time;
    public:
        void getdata()
            {
            publication::getdata();
            cout << "Enter playing time: "; cin >> time;
            }
        void putdata() const
            {
            publication::putdata();
            cout << "\nPlaying time: " << time;
            }
    };
//////////////////////////////////////////////////////////////////
int main()
    {
    book book1;
    tape tape1;                          // define publications

    book1.getdata();
    tape1.getdata();                     // get data for them

    book1.putdata();
    tape1.putdata();                     // display their data
    cout << endl;
    return 0;
    }
```

2.

```cpp
// ex9_2.cpp
//inheritance from String class
#include <iostream>
```

```cpp
#include <cstring>                    //for strcpy(), etc.
using namespace std;
/////////////////////////////////////////////////////////////////
class String                          //base class
   {
   protected:                         //Note: can't be private
      enum { SZ = 80 };               //size of all String objects
      char str[SZ];                   //holds a C-string
   public:
      String()                        //constructor 0, no args
         { str[0] = '\0'; }
      String( char s[] )              //constructor 1, one arg
         { strcpy(str, s); }          //   convert string to String
      void display() const            //display the String
         { cout << str; }
      operator char*()                //conversion function
         { return str; }              //convert String to C-string
   };
/////////////////////////////////////////////////////////////////
class Pstring : public String         //derived class
   {
   public:
      Pstring( char s[] );            //constructor
   };
//---------------------------------------------------------------
Pstring::Pstring( char s[] )          //constructor for Pstring
   {
   if(strlen(s) > SZ-1)               //if too long,
      {
      for(int j=0; j<SZ-1; j++)       //copy the first SZ-1
         str[j] = s[j];               //characters "by hand"
      str[j] = '\0';                  //add the null character
      }
   else                               //not too long,
      String(s);                      //so construct normally
   }
/////////////////////////////////////////////////////////////////
int main()
   {                                        //define String
   Pstring s1 = "This is a very long string which is probably "
         "no, certainly--going to exceed the limit set by SZ.";
   cout << "\ns1="; s1.display();           //display String

   Pstring s2 = "This is a short string.";  //define String
   cout << "\ns2="; s2.display();           //display String
   cout << endl;
   return 0;
   }
```

3.

```cpp
// ex9_3.cpp
// multiple inheritance with publication class
#include <iostream>
#include <string>
using namespace std;
//////////////////////////////////////////////////////////////////
class publication
   {
   private:
      string title;
      float price;
   public:
      void getdata()
         {
         cout << "\nEnter title: "; cin >> title;
         cout << "   Enter price: "; cin >> price;
         }
      void putdata() const
         {
         cout << "\nTitle: " << title;
         cout << "\n   Price: " << price;
         }
   };
//////////////////////////////////////////////////////////////////
class sales
   {
   private:
      enum { MONTHS = 3 };
      float salesArr[MONTHS];
   public:
      void getdata();
      void putdata() const;
   };
//.................................................................
void sales::getdata()
   {
   cout << "   Enter sales for 3 months\n";
   for(int j=0; j<MONTHS; j++)
      {
      cout << "      Month " << j+1 << ": ";
      cin >> salesArr[j];
      }
   }
```

```
//·····································································
void sales::putdata() const
    {
    for(int j=0; j<MONTHS; j++)
        {
        cout << "\n    Sales for month " << j+1 << ": ";
        cout << salesArr[j];
        }
    }
/////////////////////////////////////////////////////////////////////
class book : private publication, private sales
    {
    private:
        int pages;
    public:
        void getdata()
            {
            publication::getdata();
            cout << "    Enter number of pages: "; cin >> pages;
            sales::getdata();
            }
        void putdata() const
            {
            publication::putdata();
            cout << "\n    Pages: " << pages;
            sales::putdata();
            }
    };
/////////////////////////////////////////////////////////////////////
class tape : private publication, private sales
    {
    private:
        float time;
    public:
        void getdata()
            {
            publication::getdata();
            cout << "    Enter playing time: "; cin >> time;
            sales::getdata();
            }
        void putdata() const
            {
            publication::putdata();
            cout << "\n    Playing time: " << time;
            sales::putdata();
            }
    };
```

```
/////////////////////////////////////////////////////////////////
int main()
   {
   book book1;          // define publications
   tape tape1;

   book1.getdata();     // get data for publications
   tape1.getdata();

   book1.putdata();     // display data for publications
   tape1.putdata();
   cout << endl;
   return 0;
   }
```

Chapter 10

Answers to Questions

1. cout << &testvar;

2. 4 bytes

3. c

4. &var, *var, var&, char*

5. constant; variable

6. float* ptrtofloat;

7. name

8. *testptr

9. pointer to; contents of the variable pointed to by

10. b, c, d

11. No. The address &intvar must be placed in the pointer intptr before it can be accessed.

12. any data type

13. They both do the same thing.

14.

```
for(int j=0; j<77; j++)
   cout << endl << *(intarr+j);
```

15. because array names represent the address of the array, which is a constant and can't be changed

16. reference; pointer

17. a, d

18. `void func(char*);`

19.
```
for(int j=0; j<80; j++)
    *s2++ = *s1++;
```

20. b

21. `char* revstr(char*);`

22. `char* numptrs[] = { "One", "Two", "Three" };`

23. a, c

24. wasted

25. memory that is no longer needed

26. `p->exclu();`

27. `objarr[7].exclu();`

28. a, c

29. `float* arr[8];`

30. b

31. 0..9 at one end; 3..* at the other

32. b

33. false

34. a

Solutions to Exercises

1.
```
// ex10_1.cpp
// finds average of numbers typed by user
#include <iostream>
using namespace std;

int main()
    {
    float flarr[100];                   //array for numbers
    char ch;                            //user decision
    int num = 0;                        //counts numbers input
    do
        {
```

```
            cout << "Enter number: ";              //get numbers from user
            cin >> *(flarr+num++);                 //until user answers 'n'
            cout << "   Enter another (y/n)? ";
            cin >> ch;
            }
      while(ch != 'n');

      float total = 0.0;                            //total starts at 0
      for(int k=0; k<num; k++)                      //add numbers to total
         total += *(flarr+k);
      float average = total / num;                  //find and display average
      cout << "Average is " << average << endl;
      return 0;
      }
```

2.

```
// ex10_2.cpp
// member function converts String objects to upper case
#include <iostream>
#include <cstring>              //for strcpy(), etc
#include <cctype>              //for toupper()
using namespace std;
////////////////////////////////////////////////////////////////////////
class String                    //user-defined string type
   {
   private:
      char* str;                         //pointer to string
   public:
      String(char* s)                    //constructor, one arg
         {
         int length = strlen(s);         //length of string argument
         str = new char[length+1];       //get memory
         strcpy(str, s);                 //copy argument to it
         }
      ~String()                          //destructor
         { delete str; }
      void display()                     //display the String
         { cout << str; }
      void upit();                       //uppercase the String
   };
//--------------------------------------------------------------
void String::upit()                      //uppercase each character
   {
   char* ptrch = str;                    //pointer to this string
   while( *ptrch )                       //until null,
      {
      *ptrch = toupper(*ptrch);          //uppercase each character
```

```
            ptrch++;                        //move to next character
            }
        }
//////////////////////////////////////////////////////////////////////
    int main()
        {
        String s1 = "He who laughs last laughs best.";

        cout << "\ns1=";            //display string
        s1.display();
        s1.upit();                  //uppercase string
        cout << "\ns1=";            //display string
        s1.display();
        cout << endl;
        return 0;
        }
```

3.

```
// ex10_3.cpp
// sort an array of pointers to strings
#include <iostream>
#include <cstring>                   //for strcmp(), etc.
using namespace std;
const int DAYS = 7;                  //number of pointers in array

int main()
    {
    void bsort(char**, int);         //prototype
                                     //array of pointers to char
    char* arrptrs[DAYS] = { "Sunday", "Monday", "Tuesday",
                            "Wednesday", "Thursday",
                            "Friday", "Saturday"  };

    cout << "\nUnsorted:\n";
    for(int j=0; j<DAYS; j++)        //display unsorted strings
        cout << *(arrptrs+j) << endl;

    bsort(arrptrs, DAYS);            //sort the strings

    cout << "\nSorted:\n";
    for(j=0; j<DAYS; j++)            //display sorted strings
        cout << *(arrptrs+j) << endl;
    return 0;
    }
//-----------------------------------------------------------------
void bsort(char** pp, int n)         //sort pointers to strings
    {
```

```
        void order(char**, char**);   //prototype
        int j, k;                     //indexes to array

        for(j=0; j<n-1; j++)          //outer loop
            for(k=j+1; k<n; k++)      //inner loop starts at outer
        order(pp+j, pp+k);            //order the pointer contents
        }
 //- - - - - - - - - - - - - - - - - - - - - - - - - - - - - - - - - - - - - - -
    void order(char** pp1, char** pp2)   //orders two pointers
        {                             //if string in 1st is
        if( strcmp(*pp1, *pp2) > 0)   //larger than in 2nd,
            {
            char* tempptr = *pp1;     //swap the pointers
            *pp1 = *pp2;
            *pp2 = tempptr;
            }
        }
```

4.

```
    // ex10_4.cpp
    // linked list includes destructor
    #include <iostream>
    using namespace std;
    ////////////////////////////////////////////////////////////////
    struct link                       //one element of list
        {
        int data;                     //data item
        link* next;                   //pointer to next link
        };
    ////////////////////////////////////////////////////////////////
    class linklist                    //a list of links
        {
        private:
            link* first;              //pointer to first link
        public:
            linklist()                //no-argument constructor
                { first = NULL; }      //no first link
            ~linklist();              //destructor
            void additem(int d);      //add data item (one link)
            void display();           //display all links
        };
    //- - - - - - - - - - - - - - - - - - - - - - - - - - - - - - - - - - - - - - -
    void linklist::additem(int d)     //add data item
        {
        link* newlink = new link;     //make a new link
        newlink->data = d;            //give it data
```

```
        newlink->next = first;         //it points to next link
        first = newlink;               //now first points to this
        }
//------------------------------------------------------------
void linklist::display()               //display all links
    {
    link* current = first;             //set ptr to first link
    while( current != NULL )           //quit on last link
        {
        cout << endl << current->data; //print data
        current = current->next;       //move to next link
        }
    }
//------------------------------------------------------------
linklist::~linklist()                  //destructor
    {
    link* current = first;             //set ptr to first link
    while( current != NULL )           //quit on last link
        {
        link* temp = current;          //save ptr to this link
        current = current->next;       //get ptr to next link
        delete temp;                   //delete this link
        }
    }
////////////////////////////////////////////////////////////////
int main()
    {
    linklist li;            //make linked list

    li.additem(25);         //add four items to list
    li.additem(36);
    li.additem(49);
    li.additem(64);

    li.display();           //display entire list
    cout << endl;
    return 0;
    }
```

Chapter 11

Answers to Questions

1. d
2. true

3. base

4. `virtual void dang(int);` or `void virtual dang(int);`

5. late binding or dynamic binding

6. derived

7. `virtual void aragorn()=0;` or `void virtual aragorn()=0;`

8. a, c

9. `dong* parr[10];`

10. c

11. true

12. c, d

13. `friend void harry(george);`

14. a, c, d

15. `friend class harry;` or `friend harry;`

16. c

17. It performs a member-by-member copy.

18. `zeta& operator = (zeta&);`

19. a, b, d

20. false; the compiler provides a default copy constructor

21. a, d

22. `Bertha(Bertha&);`

23. true, if there was a reason to do so

24. a, c

25. true; trouble occurs if it's returned by reference

26. They operate identically.

27. a, b

28. the object of which the function using it is a member

29. no; since this is a pointer, use `this->da=37;`

30. `return *this;`

31. c

32. links

33. true

34. a, b, c

Solutions to Exercises

1.

```cpp
// ex11_1.cpp
// publication class and derived classes
#include <iostream>
#include <string>
using namespace std;
/////////////////////////////////////////////////////////////////////
class publication
    {
    private:
        string title;
        float price;
    public:
        virtual void getdata()
            {
            cout << "\nEnter title: "; cin >> title;
            cout << "Enter price: "; cin >> price;
            }
        virtual void putdata()
            {
            cout << "\n\nTitle: " << title;
            cout << "\nPrice: " << price;
            }
    };
/////////////////////////////////////////////////////////////////////
class book : public publication
    {
    private:
        int pages;
    public:
        void getdata()
            {
            publication::getdata();
            cout << "Enter number of pages: "; cin >> pages;
            }
        void putdata()
            {
            publication::putdata();
            cout << "\nPages: " << pages;
            }
    };
/////////////////////////////////////////////////////////////////////
class tape : public publication
    {
```

```
      private:
         float time;
      public:
         void getdata()
            {
            publication::getdata();
            cout << "Enter playing time: "; cin >> time;
            }
         void putdata()
            {
            publication::putdata();
            cout << "\nPlaying time: " << time;
            }
   };
//////////////////////////////////////////////////////////////
int main()
   {
   publication* pubarr[100];          //array of ptrs to pubs
   int n = 0;                         //number of pubs in array
   char choice;                       //user's choice

   do {
      cout << "\nEnter data for book or tape (b/t)? ";
      cin >> choice;
      if( choice=='b' )               //make book object
         pubarr[n] = new book;        //   put in array
      else                            //make tape object
         pubarr[n] = new tape;        //   put in array
      pubarr[n++]->getdata();         //get data for object
      cout << "   Enter another (y/n)? "; //another pub?
      cin >> choice;
      }
   while( choice =='y');              //cycle until not 'y'

   for(int j=0; j<n; j++)             //cycle thru all pubs
      pubarr[j]->putdata();           //print data for pub
   cout << endl;
   return 0;
   }
```

2.

```
// ex11_2.cpp
// friend square() function for Distance
#include <iostream>
using namespace std;
```

```
///////////////////////////////////////////////////////////
class Distance                          //English Distance class
   {
   private:
      int feet;
      float inches;
   public:
      Distance()                        //constructor (no args)
         { feet = 0; inches = 0.0; }
      Distance(float fltfeet)           //constructor (one arg)
         {                              //feet is integer part
         feet = static_cast<int>(fltfeet);
         inches = 12*(fltfeet-feet);  //inches is what's left
         }                              //constructor (two args)
      Distance(int ft, float in) : feet(ft), inches(in)
        { }
      void showdist()                   //display distance
         { cout << feet << "\'-" << inches << '\"'; }
      friend Distance operator * (Distance, Distance); //friend
   };
//.............................................................
                                        //multiply d1 by d2
Distance operator * (Distance d1, Distance d2)
   {
   float fltfeet1 = d1.feet + d1.inches/12;  //convert to float
   float fltfeet2 = d2.feet + d2.inches/12;
   float multfeet = fltfeet1 * fltfeet2;     //find the product
   return Distance(multfeet);        //return temp Distance
   }
///////////////////////////////////////////////////////////
int main()
   {
   Distance dist1(3, 6.0);              //make some distances
   Distance dist2(2, 3.0);
   Distance dist3;

   dist3 = dist1 * dist2;               //multiplication

   dist3 = 10.0 * dist3;                //mult and conversion
                                        //display all distances
   cout << "\ndist1 = "; dist1.showdist();
   cout << "\ndist2 = "; dist2.showdist();
   cout << "\ndist3 = "; dist3.showdist();
   cout << endl;
   return 0;
   }
```

3.

```
// ex11_3.cpp
// creates array class
// overloads assignment operator and copy constructor
#include <iostream>
using namespace std;
//////////////////////////////////////////////////////////////
class Array
    {
    private:
        int* ptr;                    //pointer to "array" contents
        int size;                    //size of array
    public:
        Array() : ptr(0), size(0)    //no-argument constructor
            { }
        Array(int s) : size(s)       //one-argument constructor
            { ptr = new int[s]; }
        Array(Array&);               //copy constructor
        ~Array()                     //destructor
            { delete[] ptr; }
        int& operator [] (int j)     //overloaded subscript op
            { return *(ptr+j); }
        Array& operator = (Array&);  //overloaded = operator
    };
//..................................................................
Array::Array(Array& a)               //copy constructor
    {
    size = a.size;                   //new one is same size
    ptr = new int[size];             //get space for contents
    for(int j=0; j<size; j++)        //copy contents to new one
        *(ptr+j) = *(a.ptr+j);
    }
//..................................................................
Array& Array::operator = (Array& a)  //overloaded = operator
    {
    delete[] ptr;                    //delete old contents (if any)
    size = a.size;                   //make this object same size
    ptr = new int[a.size];           //get space for new contents
    for(int j=0; j<a.size; j++)      //copy contents to this object
        *(ptr+j) = *(a.ptr+j);
    return *this;                    //return this object
    }
//////////////////////////////////////////////////////////////
int main()
    {
    const int ASIZE = 10;            //size of array
```

```
        Array arr1(ASIZE);              //make an array

        for(int j=0; j<ASIZE; j++)      //fill it with squares
            arr1[j] = j*j;

        Array arr2(arr1);               //use the copy constructor
        cout << "\narr2: ";
        for(j=0; j<ASIZE; j++)          //check that it worked
            cout << arr2[j] << "  ";

        Array arr3, arr4;               //make two empty Array objects
        arr4 = arr3 = arr1;             //use the assignment operator
        cout << "\narr3: ";
        for(j=0; j<ASIZE; j++)          //check that it worked on arr3
            cout << arr3[j] << "  ";
        cout << "\narr4: ";
        for(j=0; j<ASIZE; j++)          //check that it worked on arr4
            cout << arr4[j] << "  ";
        cout << endl;
        return 0;
        }
```

Chapter 12

Answers to Questions

1. b, c

2. ios

3. ifstream, ofstream, and fstream

4. ofstream salefile ("SALES.JUN");

5. true

6. if(foobar)

7. d

8. fileOut.put(ch); (where ch is the character)

9. c

10. ifile.read((char*)buff, sizeof(buff));

11. a, b, d

12. the byte location at which the next read or write operation will take place

13. false; file pointer can be a synonym for current position

14. f1.seekg(-13, ios::cur);

15. b

16. b, c

17. skipws causes whitespace characters to be ignored on input so that cin will not assume the input has terminated.

18. int main(int argc, char *argv[])

19. PRN, LPT1

20. istream& operator >> (istream&, Sample&)

Solutions to Exercises

1.

```cpp
// ex12_1.cpp
// write array
#include <iostream>
#include <fstream>                    // for file streams
using namespace std;
///////////////////////////////////////////////////////////////////////
class Distance                         // English Distance class
   {
   private:
      int feet;
      float inches;
   public:
      Distance() : feet(0), inches(0.0) // constructor (no args)
         { }                            // constructor (two args)
      Distance(int ft, float in) : feet(ft), inches(in)
         { }
      void getdist()                    // get length from user
         {
         cout << "\n   Enter feet: ";  cin >> feet;
         cout << ".  Enter inches: ";  cin >> inches;
         }
      void showdist()                   // display distance
         { cout << feet << "\'-" << inches << '\"'; }
   };
///////////////////////////////////////////////////////////////////////
int main()
   {
   char ch;
   Distance dist;                       // create a Distance object
   fstream file;                        // create input/output file
                                        // open it for append
   file.open("DIST.DAT", ios::binary | ios::app |
                   ios::out | ios::in );
```

```
            do                              // data from user to file
                {
            cout << "\nDistance";
            dist.getdist();                 // get a distance
                                            // write to file
            file.write( (char*)&dist, sizeof(dist) );
            cout << "Enter another distance (y/n)? ";
            cin >> ch;
                }
            while(ch=='y');                 // quit on 'n'

            file.seekg(0);                  // reset to start of file
                                            // read first distance
            file.read( (char*)&dist, sizeof(dist) );
            int count = 0;
            while( !file.eof() )            // quit on EOF
                {
            cout << "\nDistance " << ++count << ": "; // display dist
            dist.showdist();
            file.read( (char*)&dist, sizeof(dist) );  // read another
                }                                     // distance
        cout << endl;
        return 0;
        }
```

2.

```
    // ex12_2.cpp
    // imitates COPY command
    #include <fstream>                   //for file functions
    #include <iostream>
    using namespace std;
    #include <process.h>                 //for exit()

    int main(int argc, char* argv[] )
        {
        if( argc != 3 )
            { cerr << "\nFormat: ocopy srcfile destfile"; exit(-1); }
        char ch;                         //character to read

        ifstream infile;                 //create file for input
        infile.open( argv[1] );          //open file
        if( !infile )                    //check for errors
            { cerr << "\nCan't open " << argv[1]; exit(-1); }

        ofstream outfile;                //create file for output
        outfile.open( argv[2] );         //open file
```

```
            if( !outfile )                    //check for errors
               { cerr << "\nCan't open " << argv[2]; exit(-1); }

            while( infile )                    //until EOF
               {
               infile.get(ch);                 //read a character
               outfile.put(ch);                //write the character
               }
            return 0;
            }
```

3.

```
   .// ex12_3.cpp
   // displays size of file
   #include <fstream>                    //for file functions
   #include <iostream>
   using namespace std;
   #include <process.h>                  //for exit()

   int main(int argc, char* argv[] )
      {
      if( argc != 2 )
         { cerr << "\nFormat: filename\n"; exit(-1); }
      ifstream infile;                  //create file for input
      infile.open( argv[1] );           //open file
      if( !infile )                     //check for errors
         { cerr << "\nCan't open " << argv[1]; exit(-1); }
      infile.seekg(0, ios::end);        //go to end of file
                                        // report byte number
      cout << "Size of " << argv[1] << " is " << infile.tellg();
      cout << endl;
      return 0;
      }
```

Chapter 13

Answers to Questions

1. a, b, c, d

2. #include directive

3. the compiler to compile the .CPP file and the linker to link the resulting .OBJ files

4. a, b

5. class library

6. true

7. c, d

8. true

9. false

10. a, c, d

11. linking

12. false

13. d

14. scope

15. object

16. declared, file B

17. true

18. b

19. false

20. d

21. b

22. namespace

22. b, d

Chapter 14

Answers to Questions

1. b and c

2. class

3. false; different functions are created at compile time

4.
```
template<class T>
T times2(T arg)
    {
    return arg*2;
    }
```

5. b

6. true

7. instantiating

8. c

9. fixed data type, any data type

10. store data

11. c

12. try, catch, and throw

13. throw BoundsError();

14. false; they must be part of a try block

15. d

16.
```
class X
    {
    public:
        int xnumber;
        char xname[MAX];
        X(int xd, char* xs)
            {
            xnumber = xd;
            strcpy(xname, xs);
            }
    };
```

17. false

18. a and d

19. d

20. true

21. independent, dependent

22. a

23. false

24. additional information

Solutions to Exercises

1.
```
// ex14_1.cpp
// template used for function that averages array
#include <iostream>
using namespace std;
```

```
//////////////////////////////////////////////////////////////
template <class atype>                  //function template
atype avg(atype* array, int size)
    {
    atype total = 0;
    for(int j=0; j<size; j++)            //average the array
        total += array[j];
    return (atype)total/size;
    }
//////////////////////////////////////////////////////////////
int intArray[] =        {1, 3, 5, 9, 11, 13};
long longArray[] =      {1, 3, 5, 9, 11, 13};
double doubleArray[] = {1.0, 3.0, 5.0, 9.0, 11.0, 13.0};
char charArray[] =      {1, 3, 5, 9, 11, 13};

int main()
    {
    cout << "\navg(intArray)=" << avg(intArray, 6);
    cout << "\navg(longArray)=" << avg(longArray, 6);
    cout << "\navg(doubleArray)=" << avg(doubleArray, 6);
    cout << "\navg(charArray)=" << (int)avg(charArray, 6) << endl;
    return 0;
    }
```

2.

```
// ex14_2.cpp
// implements queue class as a template
#include <iostream>
using namespace std;
const int MAX = 3;
//////////////////////////////////////////////////////////////
template <class Type>
class Queue
    {
    private:
        Type qu[MAX]; //array of any type
        int head;       //index of start of queue (remove item here)
        int tail;       //index of end of queue (insert item here)
    public:
        Queue()                           //constructor
            { head = -1; tail = -1; }
        void put(Type var)                //insert item at queue tail
            {
            qu[++tail] = var;
            if(tail >=MAX-1)              //wrap around if past array end
                tail = -1;
```

```
        }
    Type get()                      //remove item from queue head
      {
      Type temp = qu[++head]; //store item
      if(head >= MAX-1)             //wrap around if past array end
         head = -1;
      return temp;                  //return item
      }
   };
/////////////////////////////////////////////////////////////////
int main()
   {
   Queue<float> q1;      //q1 is object of class Queue<float>

   q1.put(1111.1F);                         //put 3
   q1.put(2222.2F);
   q1.put(3333.3F);
   cout << "1: " << q1.get() << endl;   //get 2
   cout << "2: " << q1.get() << endl;
   q1.put(4444.4F);                         //put 2
   q1.put(5555.5F);
   cout << "3: " << q1.get() << endl;   //get 1
   q1.put(6666.6F);                         //put 1
   cout << "4: " << q1.get() << endl;   //get 3
   cout << "5: " << q1.get() << endl;
   Cout << "6: " << q1.get() << endl;

   Queue<long> q2;       //q2 is object of class Queue<long>

   q2.put(123123123L); //put 3 longs, get 3 longs
   q2.put(234234234L);
   q2.put(345345345L);
   cout << "1: " << q2.get() << endl;
   cout << "2: " << q2.get() << endl;
   cout << "3: " << q2.get() << endl;
   return 0;
   }
```

.3.

```
// ex14_3.cpp
// implements queue class as a template
// uses exceptions to handle errors in queue
#include <iostream>
using namespace std;
const int MAX = 3;
```

```
//////////.          ////////////////////////////////////////////////
template <class Type>
class Queue
    {
    private:
        Type qu[MAX]; //array of any type
        int head;       //index of front of queue (remove old item)
        int tail;       //index of back of queue (insert new item)
        int count;      //number of items in queue
    public:
        class full  { };          //exception classes
        class empty { };
//---------------------------------------------------------------
        Queue()                     //constructor
            { head = -1; tail = -1; count = 0; }

        void put(Type var)          //insert item at queue tail
            {
            if(count >= MAX)        //if queue already full,
                throw full();       //   throw exception
            qu[++tail] = var;       //store item
            ++count;
            if(tail >=MAX-1)        //wrap around if past array end
                tail = -1;
            }
//---------------------------------------------------------------
        Type get()                  //remove item from queue head
            {
            if(count <= 0)          //if queue empty,
                throw empty();      //   throw exception
            Type temp = qu[++head]; //get item
            --count;
            if(head >= MAX-1)       //wrap around if past array end
                head = -1;
            return temp;            //return item
            }
    };
/////////////////////////////////////////////////////////////////////
int main()
    {
    Queue<float> q1;        //q1 is object of class Queue<float>
    float data;             //data item obtained from user
    char choice = 'p';      //'x', 'p' or 'g'

    do                      //do loop (enter 'x' to quit)
        {
```

```
    try                //try block
      {
      cout << "\nEnter 'x' to exit, 'p' for put, 'g' for get: ";
      cin >> choice;
      if(choice=='p')
         {
         cout << "Enter data value: ";
         cin >> data;
         q1.put(data);
         }
      if(choice=='g')
         cout << "Data=" << q1.get() << endl;
      } //end try
    catch(Queue<float>::full)
       {
       cout << "Error: queue is full." << endl;
       }
    catch(Queue<float>::empty)
       {
       cout << "Error: queue is empty." << endl;
       }
    } while(choice != 'x');
  return 0;
  } //end main()
```

Chapter 15

Answers to Questions

1. a, b, d

2. vector, list, deque

3. set, map

4. a

5. true

6. c

7. false

8. iterator

9. a function object

10. c

11. false; it simply returns its value

12. 3, 11

13. duplicate

14. b, c

15. points to

16. false

17. bidirectional

18. *iter++

19. d

20. c

21. true

22. iterators

23. it's a string used to separate the printed values

24. b

25. the elements will be ordered

26. true

27. pairs (or associations)

28. false

29. a, d

30. constructor

Solutions to Exercises

1.

```
// ex15_1.cpp
// type float stored in array, sorted by sort()
#include <iostream>
#include <algorithm>
using namespace std;

int main()
    {
    int j=0, k;
    char ch;
    float fpn, farr[100];

    do {
        cout << "Enter a floating point number: ";
        cin >> fpn;
        farr[j++] = fpn;
```

```
            cout << "Enter another ('y' or 'n'): ";
            cin >> ch;
            } while(ch == 'y');
        sort(farr, farr+j);
        for(k=0; k<j; k++)
            cout << farr[k] << ", ";
        cout << endl;
        return 0;
        }
```

2.

```
// ex15_2.cpp
// vector used with string objects, push_back(), and []
#include <iostream>
#include <string>
#pragma warning (disable:4786)   //Microsoft only
#include <vector>
#include <algorithm>
using namespace std;

int main()
    {
    vector<string> vectStrings;
    string word;
    char ch;

    do {
        cout << "Enter a word: ";
        cin >> word;
        vectStrings.push_back(word);
        cout << "Enter another ('y' or 'n'): ";
        cin >> ch;
        } while(ch == 'y');
    sort( vectStrings.begin(), vectStrings.end() );
    for(int k=0; k<vectStrings.size(); k++)
        cout << vectStrings[k] << endl;
    return 0;
    }
```

3.

```
// ex15_3.cpp
// home-made reverse() algorithm reverses a list
#include <iostream>
#include <list>
using namespace std;
```

```
int main()
    {
    int j;

    list<int> theList;
    list<int>::iterator iter1;
    list<int>::iterator iter2;

    for(j=2; j<16; j+=2)              //fill list with 2, 4, 6, ...
        theList.push_back(j);

    cout << "Before reversal: ";      //display list
    for(iter1=theList.begin(); iter1 != theList.end(); iter1++)
        cout << *iter1 << " ";

    iter1 = theList.begin();          //set to first element
    iter2 = theList.end();            //set to one-past-last
    --iter2;                          //move to last

    while(iter1 != iter2)
        {
        swap(*iter1, *iter2);         //swap front and back
        ++iter1;                      //increment front
        if(iter1==iter2)              //if even number of elements
            break;
        --iter2;                      //decrement back
        }

    cout << "\nAfter reversal: ";     //display list
    for(iter1=theList.begin(); iter1 != theList.end(); iter1++)
        cout << *iter1 << " ";
    cout << endl;
    return 0;
    }
```

4.

```
// ex15_4.cpp
// a multiset automatically sorts person objects stored by pointer
#include <iostream>
#include <set>
#pragma warning (disable:4786)
#include <string>
using namespace std;

class person
    {
```

```
        private:
            string lastName;
            string firstName;
            long phoneNumber;
        public:
            person() :                    // default constructor
                lastName("blank"), firstName("blank"), phoneNumber(0L)
              { }
                                          // 3-arg constructor
            person(string lana, string fina, long pho) :
                   lastName(lana), firstName(fina), phoneNumber(pho)
              { }
            friend bool operator<(const person&, const person&);

            void display() const    // display person's data
              {
                cout << endl << lastName << ",\t" << firstName
                     << "\t\tPhone: " << phoneNumber;
              }
            long get_phone() const // return phone number
              { return phoneNumber; }
        }; //end class person
//----------------------------------------------------------------
// overloaded < for person class
bool operator<(const person& p1, const person& p2)
    {
    if(p1.lastName == p2.lastName)
       return (p1.firstName < p2.firstName) ? true : false;
    return (p1.lastName < p2.lastName) ? true : false;
    }
//----------------------------------------------------------------
// function object to compare persons using pointers
class comparePersons
    {
    public:
    bool operator() (const person* ptrP1,
                     const person* ptrP2) const
      { return *ptrP1 < *ptrP2; }
    };
//////////////////////////////////////////////////////////////////
int main()
    {                                  // a multiset of ptrs to persons
    multiset<person*, comparePersons> setPtrsPers;
    multiset<person*, comparePersons>::iterator iter;
```

```
                              //make persons
person* ptrP1 = new person("KuangThu", "Bruce", 4157300);
person* ptrP2 = new person("McDonald", "Stacey", 3327563);
person* ptrP3 = new person("Deauville", "William", 8435150);
person* ptrP4 = new person("Wellington", "John", 9207404);
person* ptrP5 = new person("Bartoski", "Peter", 6946473);
person* ptrP6 = new person("McDonald", "Amanda", 8435150);
person* ptrP7 = new person("Fredericks", "Roger", 7049982);
person* ptrP8 = new person("McDonald", "Stacey", 7764987);

setPtrsPers.insert(ptrP1);            //put persons in multiset
setPtrsPers.insert(ptrP2);
setPtrsPers.insert(ptrP3);
setPtrsPers.insert(ptrP4);
setPtrsPers.insert(ptrP5);
setPtrsPers.insert(ptrP6);
setPtrsPers.insert(ptrP7);
setPtrsPers.insert(ptrP8);
                                      //display multiset
cout << "\n\nSet sorted when created:";
for(iter=setPtrsPers.begin(); iter != setPtrsPers.end(); iter++ )
   (**iter).display();

iter = setPtrsPers.begin();          //delete all persons
while( iter != setPtrsPers.end() )
   {
   delete *iter;                      //delete person
   setPtrsPers.erase(iter++);         //remove pointer
   }
cout << endl;
return 0;
} // end main()
```

Chapter 16

Answers to Questions

1. false

2. c, d

3. task

4. true

5. columns

6. a, c

7. generalization, association, aggregation

8. a, d

9. false

10. a

11. true

12. false

13. a, b, c, d

14. people (or human beings), other systems, program (or system)

15. b

16. b, c

17. false

18. a, d

19. b, d

20. false

21. c, d

22. object

23. true

24. a, d

Bibliography

IN THIS APPENDIX

This appendix lists some books that might prove useful or interesting to students of C++.

Advanced C++

After you've mastered the fundamentals of C++, the next books you should probably buy are *Effective C++*, by Scott Meyers (Addison Wesley, 1997), and *More Effective C++*, also by Scott Meyers (Addison Wesley, 1996). These books contain, respectively, "50 specific ways to improve your programs and designs" and "35 new ways to improve your programs and designs." Each of the topics in these books is short but clearly presented. These books provide a wealth of important ideas and are widely read by C++ programmers.

Thinking in C++ by Bruce Eckel (Prentice Hall, 1995) is probably a little too fast for beginners, but it covers the fundamentals of the language and is excellent at explaining why things work the way they do.

C++ FAQs (Frequently Asked Questions) by Marshall Cline and Greg Lomow (Addison Wesley, 1995) contains hundreds of topics about C++ in short question-and-answer format. It's easy reading and will contribute to your understanding of C++.

C++ Distilled by Ira Pohl (Addison Wesley, 1997) is a short summary of the important features of C++. It's great if you've forgotten a particular syntax and want to look it up in a hurry.

Defining Documents

Because the author is the language's creator, the most definitive text on C++ is *The C++ Programming Language, Third Edition* by Bjarne Stroustrup (Addison Wesley, 1997). Every serious C++ programmer should have a copy of this book. It assumes a certain level of sophistication, so it's not for beginners. However, it's clearly written, and once you've mastered the fundamentals it's an invaluable aid to the finer points of C++ usage.

You probably won't need the actual defining document for Standard C++ until you've progressed quite far in your study of C++. *The Final Draft Information Standard (FDIS) for the C++ Programming Language*, X3J16/97-14882, is available from the Information Technology Council (NSTIC), Washington, D.C.

The previous defining document on C++ was *The Annotated C++ Reference Manual* by Margaret Ellis and Bjarne Stroustrup (Addison Wesley, 1990). This is fairly heavy going and filled with arcane explanations. It's also out of date.

The Unified Modeling Language

Addison Wesley seems to have cornered the market in UML books: they are the publishers for all the titles we list here. The first two are by Grady Booch, James Rumbaugh, and Ivar

Jacobson, who jointly invented the UML, so we can assume that they know what they're talking about.

The Unified Modeling Language User Guide (1998) is just what the title indicates. It explains the UML in detail, and is usually quite accessible, even for beginners. However, it does cover a great deal of advanced material.

The greater part of *The Unified Modeling Language Reference Manual* (1998) consists of an alphabetical listing of UML terms and constructs. Once you've learned something about the UML, it's a handy reference.

UML Distilled, Second Edition (1999) by Martin Fowler and Kendall Scott is a quick tutorial of the UML. It is somewhat more accessible than the two books just mentioned, and much smaller. A good book for beginners.

Using UML by Perdita Stevens with Rob Pooley (2000) was designed as a textbook for university classes on the UML. However, it is small and easy to read.

Advanced Use Case Modeling (2001) by Frank Armour and Granville Miller tells you everything you might reasonably want to know about using use cases in software development processes.

UML in a Nutshell (1998) by Sinan Si Alhir is a useful reference. It's not primarily a tutorial, so you will need to know something about the UML before you find it useful.

The History of C++

The Design and Evolution of C++ by Bjarne Stroustrup (Addison Wesley, 1994) is a description by its creator of how C++ came to be the way it is. It's interesting in its own right, and knowing the history can even help you understand the language.

Ruminations on C++ by Andrew Koenig (Addison Wesley, 1997) is a rather informal discussion of various topics by one of the pioneers in C and C++. It's easy to read and will give you fresh insights.

Other Topics

C++ IOStreams Handbook by Steve Teale (Addison Wesley, 1993) is a good explanation of the details of streams and files in C++. There's material here you won't find anywhere else.

The Standard Template Library by Alexander Stepanov and Meng Lee (Hewlett-Packard, 1994) is the defining document on the STL. You can learn all about the STL from it, but it doesn't have many examples, and there are books that are easier to read. One is *STL Tutorial and Reference Guide, Second Edition* by David R. Musser, Gillmer J. Derge, and Atul Saini (Addison Wesley, 2001).

H

BIBLIOGRAPHY

Although it's nominally based on Java, *Object-Oriented Design in Java* by Stephen Gilbert and Bill McCarty (Waite Group Press, 1998) is a comprehensive, easy-to-read introduction to OO program design in any language.

Windows Game Programming for Dummies by André LaMothe (IDG Books, 1998) is a fascinating look at the details of game programming. André's book explains (among many other things) how to use the Windows console graphics routines, which form the basis of Console Graphics Lite routines discussed in Appendix E of this book. If you have any interest in writing game programs, buy this book.

The C Programming Language, Second Edition by Brian Kernighan and Dennis Ritchie (Prentice Hall PTR, 1988) is the definitive book about C, the language on which C++ was based. It's not a primer, but once you know some C it's the reference you'll want.

INDEX

SYMBOLS

A